D1085210

The Positive Sum Strategy

Harnessing Technology for Economic Growth

Ralph Landau and Nathan Rosenberg, editors

NATIONAL ACADEMY PRESS
Washington, D.C.   1986

National Academy Press ● **2101 Constitution Avenue, NW** ● **Washington, DC 20418**

This volume is the result of work sponsored by the National Academy of Engineering, the Center for Economic Policy Research at Stanford University, and the Departments of Chemistry and Chemical Engineering at Stanford University.

The National Academy of Engineering is described on the following page.

The Center for Economic Policy Research (CEPR) fosters a more rational and informed approach to economic policy. CEPR pursues four interrelated goals in support of this mission: (1) stimulating research on economic policy; (2) broad dissemination of its research findings; (3) building a community of scholars conducting research on policy issues; and (4) linking the policy community at Stanford with decision makers from business, government, and academia. In addition to a general research seed grant program, CEPR has developed and supports research programs in tax policy, regulation, energy and natural resources, electronics/information industries, and the economics of technological innovation.

The Departments of Chemistry and Chemical Engineering at Stanford, in 1969, organized an Industrial Affiliates Program. The primary purpose of the program, which sponsors conferences and exchanges between industry and the Chemistry and Chemical Engineering faculty, is to serve as a forum for communication between faculty, students, and representatives of industry.

The views expressed in this volume are those of the authors and editors and are not presented as the views of the organizations with which they are affiliated.

Library of Congress Cataloging in Publication Data
The positive sum strategy.
  Bibliography: p.
  Includes index.
  1. Technological innovations—United States—
Congresses. 2. United States—Economic conditions—
Congresses. I. Landau, Ralph. II. Rosenberg,
Nathan, 1927–   III. National Academy of Engineering.
T173.8.P67   1986   338.9'26   85-21713

ISBN 0-309-03630-5

Printed in the United States of America

Introduction

RALPH LANDAU and NATHAN ROSENBERG

Why this volume? We start from the premise that engineers and economists share a common interest in technology and technological change. They do, however, approach the subject from different vantage points, and the very differences in these vantage points have been intensified by the inevitable increase in specialization that has characterized industrial societies.

Specialization has been not only the source of well-known benefits in economic activity but also the source of spectacular advances in the production of knowledge. However, increased specialization of disciplines has fostered compartmentalization and fragmentation of knowledge about particular subjects that can, in some instances, prove to be dysfunctional and therefore costly. This occurs when one group of specialists no longer has even minimal comprehension of bodies of information that are highly relevant to the successful performance of some of its responsibilities.

We have prepared this book because we believe that we are now at such a juncture in our understanding of the determinants of successful technological innovation. We believe that engineers and economists can benefit from a dialogue in which each group of specialists acquires a deeper understanding of the concerns, priorities, insights, and methods of the other.

Thus, this volume presents chapters by engineers who are knowledgeable about technologies and by economists who are knowledgeable about the functioning of markets.* A fruitful exchange of views between these groups

---

*Much of the material contained in this volume was originally presented in somewhat different form at the Symposium on Economics and Technology held at Stanford University on March 17–19, 1985, which we cochaired.

To bring out the various perspectives and to make the most of the opportunity for dialogue among notable thinkers and doers, the design of the symposium called for some authors to address, as discussants, the presentations of other authors. And so, while shorter chapters in this volume could have been expanded by their authors into more lengthy and formal presentations, the symposium discussants graciously accepted their role, as reflected in their briefer comments.

of specialists should lead to a better understanding of the conditions under which technological innovation can be made to function more effectively in the generation of economic growth.

WHY DIALOGUE IS NEEDED

Technology has been *the* critical factor in the long-term economic growth of modern industrial societies. But it functions successfully only within a larger social environment that provides an effective combination of incentives and complementary inputs into the innovation process. Technology may be thought of as an extroverted activity: it involves a search for workable solutions to problems (the practice of technological innovation). When it finds solutions that are workable and effective, it does not pursue the "Why?" question very hard. Moreover, the output of technological activities is a product or a service that must eventually stand the test of the marketplace.

Science, by contrast, is an introverted activity. It studies problems that are usually generated internally—e.g., by logical discrepancies or internal inconsistencies or by anomalous observations that cannot be accounted for within the present intellectual framework. As technologies have become increasingly sophisticated and complex over the past century, the innovation process has become increasingly dependent on the findings and methodology of science, which has been flourishing in the post–World War II era.

Markets are the basic institutional framework within which new technologies are evaluated. Long-term economic growth must, in large measure, be understood in terms of the performance of new technologies within this framework. The functioning of the market has been the specialized concern of the discipline of economics.

Why Should Technologists Be Concerned About Economics?

Just as technological change is related to and operates within the framework of physical science, so the discipline of economics is related to politics. The political sphere establishes the larger societal framework (including the legal structure) within which technological change and economic growth take place. This includes:

1. The macroenvironment flowing from monetary and fiscal policies.

2. The microenvironment resulting from the effects of specific government tax and spending policies, for example.

3. The larger environment established by a changing legal framework; by regulations directed at such problems as health, pollution, and safety; and by foreign trade, antitrust, and other policies.

It is this economic environment, and the political forces that shape it, that in turn determines the effectiveness of the incentives that society provides to the activities of technologists.

The poor performance of the U.S. economy in the past 15 years or so points forcefully to the limitations of economic knowledge, especially as it pertains to the forces that encourage technological innovation and economic growth. As a result, there are sharp differences within the economics profession over how best to provide a stable environment for continued growth within a framework that simultaneously provides for low levels of inflation and unemployment. It is at least arguable that government policies have, in this period of uncertainty and confusion, exacerbated rather than improved matters. The disagreement among economists inevitably has led to improvisation by politicians conscious of the election cycle, with inadequate regard for the economic consequences of political decisions.

It is therefore time for the intellectual stocktaking that this book represents, by which technologists can be offered guidance on what economists know and on the limits of knowledge on how economic forces shape the environment for technological innovation.

It is important, at the same time, to recognize that the intellectual disarray in economics is only partial. There are broad areas of consensus among economists on matters of vital importance to the ongoing activities of technologists. These need to be identified and emphasized. For example, successful technological innovation always involves more than purely technological considerations. Successful innovation involves the fulfillment of needs as they are expressed in the marketplace, where considerations of cost and adaptation to specific needs and determination of appropriate trade-offs between price and performance are likely to be critical. Thus, from a purely technological point of view, the Concorde was a more spectacular innovation than the Boeing 747. From a commercial point of view, however, the Concorde was a failure, whereas the 747 looks quite different. It is itself an interesting commentary on the commercial uncertainties associated with innovation in some industries that, although the 747 has been in service for more than a decade, it is still hard to judge whether it will be a commercial success.

Thus, successful new product design and manufacture are tightly linked to economic variables. Indeed, good engineering design is close, conceptually, to microeconomics. In both cases a central activity consists of optimizing, subject to certain constraints.

Technologists need to participate more in setting the stage for their own specialized efforts, but in order to do so they must understand better the advice that economists are giving to policymakers and the probable economic consequences of political actions.

Why Should Economists Be Concerned About Technology?

Research in the past 30 years has conclusively established the critical role played by technological change in generating long-term economic growth. While considerable differences persist in attempts to quantify the contribution of technological change to such growth with any real precision (partly because there are basic conceptual problems as well as narrow measurement problems), there is broad agreement to its dominating importance.

Despite such agreement, economists have continued to treat the realm of technology as a "black box." While such treatment may have been understandable in an earlier period when the contributions of technological innovation were less appreciated, this neglect is now much more difficult to justify. It seriously limits improved understanding of both the determinants and the consequences of technological innovation. The limited understanding, in turn, is a serious handicap to the formation of more effective government policies. Better understanding may reasonably be expected to improve the prospects for more effective policymaking, with eventual improvements in economic growth rates and in the competitiveness of U.S. products in world markets.

A consequence of these limitations has been the pursuit of a number of different types of microeconomic interventions by governments in the private sector, where most technological innovation takes place. Some of these interventions may well have slowed the pace of technological innovation in many areas, thus reducing economic growth and impairing the competitiveness of U.S. companies in world markets. Likewise, macroeconomic policies have been proposed or adopted that have unexpected, and sometimes unfavorable, impacts on technological innovation.

Before a better understanding of the determinants of technological innovation can be achieved, it will be necessary for economists to come to understand some of the specific characteristics of technologies. These characteristics differ substantially from one industry to another and, as a result, conditions or policies that contribute to successful innovation in one industry may be much less successful in another. Many issues—such as the role of firm size, the highly skewed distribution of R&D expenditures among industrial sectors, the extremely broad range of activities that fall under the rubric of R&D, differences in the organization of R&D activities, the varying gestation periods and uncertainties of the innovation process, the degree of interdependency between scientific research and the development process—pose problems regarding which a willingness on the part of economists to listen carefully to engineers may improve the economic analysis of the innovation process. We anticipate that technological information of the kind readily handled by engineers can explain much about the generation and diffusion of new technologies that will otherwise remain poorly understood by economists. A carefully structured, selective, and discriminating interchange of information between economists and engineers such as takes place in this volume should, we believe, prove beneficial to both groups and therefore also, ultimately, to policymakers.

THEMES OF THIS VOLUME

The overarching themes that the authors were invited to consider in preparing their contributions to this volume were:

1. How technological innovation in the United States actually works in different industries and different forms of organizations and what future trends might be recognized.

2. How the United States' innovative process compares with that of its principal competitors, especially Japan.

3. The comparative role of the educational, financial, and other key infrastructures in United States and competitors' economies as they affect innovation.

4. The impact of government on innovation, particularly from the standpoint of macroeconomic and microeconomic policies of the past and with regard to options for the future.

5. The competitive position of the United States in the light of the preceding analyses, and how economics and technology might work more constructively together to further this position and encourage healthy economic growth.

The first chapter, the "Editors' Overview," presents a selective discussion as we see it of some of the points made in much greater detail by the authors of the individual chapters, who are responsible for their own views. The authors themselves did not participate in the writing of the Overview, so that it represents solely our perceptions of some of the significant themes that were touched on at various times by the different authors and is not to be considered as any kind of consensus reached by the authors. Nor does it reflect any positions or views of the sponsoring organizations; we alone are responsible for this Introduction and for the Overview, which are intended as a preliminary guide to the reader in examining the individual chapters. While the papers can be read individually, we encourage the reader to look at the book as a complex whole, and hope the Overview may be of assistance in this regard.

Although many individuals deserve our sincerest thanks for their assistance throughout the preparations for the symposium and this volume, we wish particularly to express our appreciation here to the heads of the sponsoring organizations:

Dr. Robert M. White, President of the National Academy of Engineering;

Dr. James L. Sweeney, Director of the Center for Economic Policy Research at Stanford University;

Dr. Michel Boudart, Professor of Chemical Engineering at Stanford, who heads the Industrial Affiliates Program at Stanford's Chemistry and Chemical Engineering Departments.

Contents

EDITORS' OVERVIEW   1
  Ralph Landau and Nathan Rosenberg

TECHNOLOGY AND THE DYNAMICS
OF ECONOMIC GROWTH

THE IMPACT OF TECHNOLOGICAL INNOVATION:
  A HISTORICAL VIEW 17
  Nathan Rosenberg

MACROECONOMICS, TECHNOLOGY, AND ECONOMIC GROWTH:
  AN INTRODUCTION TO SOME IMPORTANT ISSUES 33
  Michael J. Boskin

MICROECONOMICS AND PRODUCTIVITY 57
  Dale W. Jorgenson

DYNAMIC COMPETITION AND PRODUCTIVITY ADVANCES 77
  Burton H. Klein

THE EFFECT OF RECENT MACROECONOMIC POLICIES ON
  INNOVATION AND PRODUCTIVITY 89
  Charles B. Reeder

MACROREALITIES OF THE INFORMATION ECONOMY 93
  Stephen S. Roach

xi

HARNESSING TECHNOLOGY FOR GROWTH 105
  Robert Malpas

POLICY, LAW, SCIENCE, AND EDUCATION: THE FRAMEWORK OF TECHNOLOGICAL CHANGE

TECHNOLOGY AND ITS ROLE IN MODERN SOCIETY 115
  Stephen D. Bechtel, Jr.

NATIONAL SCIENCE POLICY AND TECHNOLOGICAL INNOVATION . . 119
  Harvey Brooks

THE ROLE OF THE LEGAL SYSTEM IN TECHNOLOGICAL
  INNOVATION AND ECONOMIC GROWTH 169
  Milton Katz

THE BHOPALIZATION OF AMERICAN TORT LAW 191
  Peter W. Huber

FROM UNDERSTANDING TO MANIPULATING DNA 213
  James D. Watson

THE PHYSICAL SCIENCES AS THE BASIS FOR MODERN
  TECHNOLOGY 227
  William O. Baker

TECHNOLOGICAL EDUCATION 255
  Joseph M. Pettit

BASIC RESEARCH IN THE UNIVERSITIES: HOW MUCH UTILITY? . . . 263
  Donald Kennedy

THE ECONOMICS OF INNOVATION

AN OVERVIEW OF INNOVATION 275
  Stephen J. Kline and Nathan Rosenberg

MICROECONOMICS OF TECHNOLOGICAL INNOVATION 307
  Edwin Mansfield

MACROECONOMICS AND MICROECONOMICS OF INNOVATION:
  THE ROLE OF THE TECHNOLOGICAL ENVIRONMENT 327
  Ann F. Friedlaender

TECHNICAL CHANGE AND INNOVATION IN AGRICULTURE 333
    Vernon W. Ruttan

TECHNOLOGY ADOPTION: THE SERVICES INDUSTRIES 357
    James Brian Quinn

TECHNOLOGY DIFFUSION, PUBLIC POLICY, AND INDUSTRIAL
    COMPETITIVENESS 373
    Paul A. David

DETERMINANTS OF INNOVATIVE ACTIVITY 393
    Keith L. R. Pavitt

THE ORGANIZATION OF TECHNOLOGICAL ADVANCE: ENTREPRENEURSHIP AND THE MANAGEMENT OF INNOVATION

PROGRAMMED INNOVATION—STRATEGY FOR SUCCESS 399
    H. W. Coover

THE CHEMICAL INDUSTRY: CHALLENGES, RISKS, AND
    REWARDS 417
    Edwin C. Holmer

ENTREPRENEURSHIP AND INNOVATION: THE ELECTRONICS
    INDUSTRY 423
    Gordon E. Moore

ENTREPRENEURSHIP AND INNOVATION: BIOTECHNOLOGY 429
    Robert A. Swanson

IMPACT OF ENTREPRENEURSHIP AND INNOVATION ON THE
    DISTRIBUTION OF PERSONAL COMPUTERS 437
    David A. Norman

MAKING THE TRANSITION FROM ENTREPRENEUR TO LARGE
    COMPANY 441
    William R. Hewlett

FINANCING INNOVATION

CULTIVATING TECHNOLOGICAL INNOVATION 443
    William J. Perry

THE ROLE OF LARGE BANKS IN FINANCING INNOVATION 453
  John S. Reed and Glen R. Moreno

A VIEW FROM WALL STREET 467
  Robert H. B. Baldwin

TRENDS IN FINANCING INNOVATION 473
  James D. Marver

TECHNOLOGY AND INTERNATIONAL ECONOMIC COMPETITION

TECHNOLOGY AND TRADE: A STUDY OF U.S. COMPETITIVENESS
  IN SEVEN INDUSTRIES 479
  N. Bruce Hannay

GLOBAL COMPETITION—THE NEW REALITY: RESULTS OF THE
  PRESIDENT'S COMMISSION ON INDUSTRIAL COMPETITIVENESS . . 501
  John A. Young

THE NEED FOR NATIONAL CONSENSUS TO IMPROVE
  COMPETITIVENESS 511
  Albert Bowers

INNOVATION, JOB CREATION, AND COMPETITIVENESS 517
  Ruben F. Mettler

DANGERS IN U.S. EFFORTS TO PROMOTE INTERNATIONAL
  COMPETITIVENESS 527
  George C. Eads

GOVERNMENT POLICIES FOR INNOVATION AND GROWTH 535
  Ed Zschau

THE JAPANESE CHALLENGE IN HIGH TECHNOLOGY 541
  Daniel I. Okimoto

THE MACROECONOMIC BACKGROUND FOR HIGH-TECH
  INDUSTRIALIZATION IN JAPAN 569
  Masahiko Aoki

CAPITAL FORMATION IN THE UNITED STATES AND JAPAN 583
  Ralph Landau and George N. Hatsopoulos

CONTRIBUTORS 607

INDEX 623

The Positive Sum Strategy

Editors' Overview

RALPH LANDAU and NATHAN ROSENBERG

ECONOMIC GROWTH—THE BASIS FOR
ANY SOCIETY'S HOPES FOR THE FUTURE

The idea of progress or economic growth is a concept that arose mainly with the Enlightenment and the Industrial Revolution. Previously, expectations of the general populace about prospects for improvement in the standard of living had risen slowly, at least from one generation to the next. Communications were difficult and time-consuming, and education very limited. Data on actual growth rates were not generally available, and there were few economists to detect trends before Adam Smith's *The Wealth of Nations* was published in 1776.

Consequently, until quite recently relative trends among nations were not soon observed, nor their implications perceived. Boskin, for example, points out that Great Britain's growth rate in the first half of the nineteenth century, when it was the greatest industrial power, was only slightly less than its average from 1850 to the present, and that its growth rate relative to the United States during the latter period averaged about 1 percentage point less than that of the United States. Yet so great is the power of compounding that this growth rate enabled the United States—largely rural in 1850—to become the greatest industrial power in the world by 1985, while the United Kingdom sank to a position of economic inferiority even in Europe

In the late nineteenth century Japan started its rise to industrialization. It achieved a more rapid growth rate than any other major country, and by 1985 had become the second-greatest industrial power. The growth of the United States since World War II, analyzed by Jorgenson, shows a startling

---

Editors' note: Please refer to the explanation at the end of the Introduction regarding the origin and purpose of this Overview. It is solely the work of the editors and does not necessarily reflect the views of the individual authors, who did not participate in its preparation. It does not represent the views of the sponsoring organizations. Those referred to in this Overview exclusively by last name are the authors in this volume.

decline in the late 1960s and 1970s. The revival in 1983 and 1984 may or may not herald a longer-term upward trend. If the recent differences in growth rate between Japan and the United States were to continue for not much more than another generation, Japan would catch up with and surpass the United States in total GNP (Landau and Hatsopoulos). Would history then repeat itself, and the United States lose its industrial leadership?

Expectations of the world's populations are now also clearly rising everywhere, and dissatisfaction with economic conditions affects an increasing number of nations, contributing to world political instability and compounding the problems of operating businesses from a global standpoint, as the current economic trends inexorably dictate. Japanese companies have recognized this dilemma and are following a global strategy of great sophistication, where control is firm and centralized in Japan, and not in various geographic regions as is often the case among United States companies (Landau and Hatsopoulos).

That present and recent U.S. growth rates are unsatisfactory can be seen by:

• Comparing U.S. growth rates not only with those of such countries as Japan, but with those of most of Western Europe prior to 1983–1984, and those of our own past;

• The great need for improving the standard of living of the lower economic levels of the U.S. population, where disparities between earnings and expectations are widening;

• Assessing international requirements for military defense and foreign aid;

• The finding that U.S. growth is too low to avoid increased borrowing (which would imperil the future standard of living and raise the possibility of re-igniting inflation) (Boskin);

• The continuing need for more job formation to provide for a growing population (even though past high rates of population increase are declining).

The reasons for the recent U.S. slowdown are discussed by Boskin, Jorgenson, Katz, and Brooks. In essence, the United States, lulled by special conditions after World War II which engendered a sense of enduring economic superiority, adopted the view that the cornucopia of growth was boundless, and that there was surplus wealth being created in such huge amounts that not only could this country aid the recovery of its friends all over the world, but it could also address many pressing social inequities, reduce the risks of living, and press for greater equity in the distribution of income even at the expense of possible loss of efficiency. That era began to end by the late 1960s, its demise furthered by two oil price shocks in the 1970s and by growing competition from our allies and friends in whose restoration we assisted.

THE BASIC FACTOR IN ECONOMIC GROWTH:
TECHNOLOGY (EMBODIED AND DISEMBODIED)

Classical economics after Adam Smith and throughout most of the nineteenth century focused primarily on long-term growth. In seeking the causes of growth, economists emphasized resources—land, labor, and capital. A very pessimistic view was taken of the prospects for future growth. The growth of the United States in the nineteenth century was seen as arising largely from the exploitation of a continent rich in resources, undertaken by a rapidly rising population of immigrants, and with an influx of essential capital from Europe. Great Britain, a small island, sought its resources abroad, and its great empire served that purpose. Other powers followed the colonization strategy.

Toward the end of the nineteenth century and during the first part of the twentieth, economists shifted their focus to neoclassical economics within a relatively static closed economy, and developed tools for analyzing the optimization of the use of scarce resources by firms. Long-term growth was ignored or taken for granted; more attention was paid to shorter-term cyclical business phenomena in an attempt to smooth out the growth process. This trend was accentuated by the effects of the worldwide depression of the 1930s, and led to J. M. Keynes's aggregate-demand management views on how to reduce cyclical fluctuations and the resulting unemployment.

After World War II Paul Samuelson and Sir John Hicks, among others, combined Keynes's concepts with the neoclassical methods of optimum resource allocation. This synthesis dominated economics until the 1970s, when stagflation and low growth exposed its fundamental weaknesses. The low savings rate of the United States compared with that of Japan and some European countries, and the associated low investment rate, began to show up as important aspects of America's relative economic decline (Boskin, Aoki).

As a result of these unexpected trends new schools of economists arose: monetarists, new classicals, supply-siders. Boskin points out that in reemphasizing longer-term growth—which was the basic (and original) concern of classical economics—economists have found that the truly fundamental factors which can increase the *rate* of growth permanently are the rate of technical change (change resulting primarily from expenditures upon R&D) and the increase in the quality of the labor force. Although increasing the capital:labor ratio can normally increase the rate of growth only temporarily, when improved technologies are available and can be incorporated in new capital, higher investment may also increase the long-run rate of growth. The latest technology is frequently embodied in new investment, and is a spur to it, whereas capital investment that merely exploits old technology does not increase the rate of growth permanently. It is most probable that tax, fiscal, and spending policies by government influence these growth factors more than shorter-term cyclical management practices—points also made by Mansfield and the new classicals.

Throughout much of the period from Adam Smith to the present, economists treated technology as exogenous; Karl Marx, the last of the classical economists, was one of the few who recognized its endogenous nature. However, Marx saw technology as the cause of massive unemployment, which would bring about the destruction of the capitalist system. It was not until the early 1950s that modern economists such as Robert Solow and Moses Abramovitz began to look seriously at the determinants of growth, and at the macroeconomic level encountered a large *residual*—i.e., the huge gap between the growth in GNP and the growth in conventionally measured inputs of labor and capital. The large size of the residual pointed to the importance of a more careful examination of the contribution of technology to economic growth.

This new focus therefore gave rise to the growth-accounting studies of the 1960s and later, primarily by Edward Denison, John Kendrick, and Jorgenson. Quinn observes that, if defined very broadly, technology may create up to 70 or 80 percent of economic growth, and cannot be treated as an unexplained residual. However, such studies at the macroeconomic level failed to explain the slowdown of the 1970s. Some economists even felt the slowdown to be the result of a mysterious disappearance or drastic reduction of technological progress.

Postwar government policy favored a major enlargement of support for R&D by government, especially in universities; a massive increase in support for higher education to improve human capital (via the GI Bill of Rights, for example); and great growth in technological development by private industry (Brooks). The public supported such policies and trends, viewing them as influences for improving the quality of life and standards of living (Bechtel). At the same time, as noted above, economists were recognizing the large role of technological development in economic growth. However, the late 1960s saw public attitudes begin to change as the dark side of technology—toxic wastes, catastrophic accidents, carcinogenicity, and the like—received greater attention (Holmer, Huber). The environmental and antitechnology mood (Brooks) probably contributed to the slowdown in productivity increase, which, as Jorgenson shows, began around 1966.

Some economists saw that this residual of technology in growth accounting needed to be even further examined if we were to learn how to take advantage of technology, and to understand better its function in propelling economic growth. Rosenberg (who insists on the importance of getting inside this "black box" of technology) points out that technology is quite capable of overcoming the so-called limits to growth, limits believed by many to be unavoidable because of a growing scarcity of natural resources. Thus economics has begun to turn from primary concentration on business cycles to a reexamination of the fundamental causes of long-term growth, in which technology plays a major role.

Companies too have been paying much greater attention to harnessing technology for growth. Malpas says:

Harnessing technology for growth, however difficult, is essential for success, of a company and a nation, particularly in a sustained period of low growth. No doubt the world is in such a period now. The 1950s and 1960s were a high-growth era in which prosperity could be achieved by a me-too approach. High growth provided ready-made markets to conquer. A low-growth era requires that products, and processes to make them, have "edge." Both product and process edge flow from technology. . . . This realization of the need for edge to be provided by technology will be the main force that will bring together the money needed to innovate both on a small and on a grand scale.

INSIDE THE BLACK BOX OF TECHNOLOGY

By decomposing the macroeconomic aggregates of the postwar period up to 1979 into 35 industrial sectors, Jorgenson opens the black box somewhat and finds that the energy price increases of the 1970s and the changing net effective tax rates of corporations can be correlated very well with the decline in productivity growth. The tax rates raise the "hurdle" rates for return on investment for private companies (Landau and Hatsopoulos), and investment—especially that embodying new technology—is the key to rising productivity rates.

But this does not answer why some sectors, or even some firms within a given sector, did better than others, as Friedlaender points out. She cites illustrations from automobile manufacture in the United States and Japan and from various transportation systems to show how aggregates conceal real differences, with dissimilar long-term economic results quite possible. Unless one understands why there are differences, and what their magnitude is, good policy judgments are very difficult to make. Thus Boskin's and Friedlaender's questions go to the heart of the economics-and-technology interface. It is essential to disaggregate appropriately and to know why things happen inside the black box. Hannay, in presenting the results of the National Academy of Engineering's (NAE's) work on a group of representative sectors, demonstrates why this disaggregated approach is indeed a fruitful direction for economic research in the future.

Thus, inside the larger black box there are other, smaller black boxes. Through a further decomposition of the aggregates into 387 industrial sectors, Klein shows how competition, by forcing innovation to compensate for falling prices, could explain many of the variations among sectors and companies. A small number of these industries are shown to bear the brunt of the productivity decline. He stresses that dynamic, not static, models must be used in understanding the microeconomy and its link to the macroeconomy, and that increased competition and instability at the microlevel may in fact lead to greater stability in the macroeconomy. In so doing, Klein too concurs with the appropriateness of Friedlaender's questions.

This analysis makes it clear that we must look into the smaller black boxes more closely, and learn to understand the forces that motivate firms and individuals to innovate, to take the risks that bring about technological change, and to compete successfully. Among economists, Mansfield has led the way in such scrutiny, but these studies so far are still very limited and deal with a far-from-representative sample of the huge variety of American industries and companies. It is for these reasons that this volume includes chapters by key figures from the technological, entrepreneurial, financial, and business sectors, who describe from their vantage points inside the black boxes what they perceive as their problems, opportunities, challenges, rewards, and methods. At the same time, the chapters on economics have been prepared by economists in the academic, industrial, and financial worlds, who represent a wide diversity of experience and viewpoints.

THE INNOVATIVE PROCESS AND ITS PROPER CLIMATE

It is evident that government has played an important role in the innovative process by aiding R&D efforts, by its procurement practices in the private sector, by supporting large-scale projects not feasible in the private sector (Brooks, Watson), and by establishing a climate favorable to investment and risk taking. On a macroeconomic level this climate entailed fiscal and monetary policy; on a more microeconomic or second-tier level (Boskin), tax, regulatory, trade, and spending priority policies became important. At various times government policies changed, often abruptly.

Writing from his experiences as an innovator and a congressman, Zschau declares:

It cannot be denied that government plays a role in technological advancement and economic growth, but we must determine government's proper role. It seems to me that rather than targeting specific companies, specific industries, or specific technologies, the proper role of government is to target the process by which those industries, those technologies, and those companies are fostered—the process of innovation. That is, government's proper role is to create in this country an environment in which new ideas and new enterprises are likely to flourish.

Zschau cites four prerequisites for such an environment: a commitment to basic research, encouragement of risk taking, an adequate supply of trained technical people, and ample market opportunities. All policies—research, tax, fiscal, monetary, education, trade, antitrust, and procurement among them—should "be evaluated in terms of whether they strengthen these pre-

requisites for an environment for innovation or whether they are detrimental
to it.''

Following upon the high inflation and poor investment environment of the
1970s, more recent policies seem to have restored some of the conditions
necessary for a favorable economic climate: lower inflation, more rapid
growth rate, diminishing unemployment. But as Zschau, Mettler, Boskin,
Landau and Hatsopoulos, and Jorgenson point out, the outlook for the future
is much less clear: there is a large and growing budget deficit; real interest
rates are still very high; there is a huge and unprecedented deficit in the U.S.
balance of payments; the United States has become a debtor nation for the
first time since 1914; unemployment, especially among minorities, is still
very high; and the dollar is still overvalued, thereby seriously handicapping
the exporting capability of many U.S. firms. Tight monetary and loose fiscal
policies have produced these trends. We may thus be at a point where the
economy can start to deteriorate sharply. Borrowing to cover the federal
deficit threatens new inflation and further erosion of investment incentives
as demands for credit reduce the available pool of domestic capital savings.
For the present, at least, that pool is augmented by the inflow of foreign
capital. The contrasting Japanese macroeconomic policies are described by
Aoki, and to some extent by Okimoto.

These American macroeconomic policies have had varying effects on different sectors of the U.S. economy. Some large companies, facing reality
and the severe competition from abroad, have been cutting costs ruthlessly,
reducing their labor forces and adopting high technology to obtain the ''edge''
Malpas writes of. Mettler puts it this way:

Global competition compels all industries to improve their performance. The margin that
makes for success is very thin. Even a small competitive edge can make a big difference,
but large and aggressive steps may be necessary to achieve even a small competitive
edge. Improvements that only equal those of competitors yield no net gain.

The challenge is to integrate into all of our industries, in innovative ways, the most
advanced technologies in communications, metallurgy and new materials, microelectronics and process control, computer-aided design and manufacturing, expert systems,
and more, in a market-driven and cost-effective way. And of course, that includes using
advanced technology in managing an enterprise—large or small.

The challenge to managers of large and small companies is to learn how to develop
(or buy) technology that is best for their specific purposes, how to control the cost of
using it, and how to finance it, all the while earning enough profit to continue to invest
and compete and grow in world markets on a sustained basis. In short, the challenge is
to be an entrepreneur.

Such efforts by large companies to remain competitive account for much
of the investment boom of 1983–1984, but a substantial proportion of the
equipment for these efforts is coming from abroad (Roach), and, as Moore
and Young indicate, such purchases contribute to a negative balance of

payments in electronics. Roach, illuminating the service sector, points out that this trend has now put as much capital behind the average information worker as there is behind the average manufacturing worker. The service sector actually consists of a number of very different types of service. Financial services clearly fall into one category, being part of a group that also includes insurance, real estate, trade, transportation, communications, and public utilities. These are all part of the new information economy, which now accounts for nearly two-thirds of the total national output. This new process of industrialization has been taking place over the last 20 years, and the potential vitality of the information economy is not in doubt. Roach states that "economic performance over the next several decades now appears to depend critically on the new realities of the information economy." On the other hand, in another category one finds the millions of small service companies that cannot invest so much capital and whose productivity is not increasing (Quinn).

A similar transformation occurred in this century in U.S. agriculture, in which the labor force fell from 25 percent or so to a little more than 3 percent (Ruttan), but agriculture, by adopting new technology and making heavy investments, became very competitive and productive in the process. Ruttan suggests that manufacturing must manage a transition from having about 20 percent of the work force now to having perhaps 10 percent by the year 2000; the transition would be made by adopting new technology and raising productivity and competitiveness. Moore, however, raises the point that if, as a consequence of this change, some manufacturing must move overseas, technological leadership is very likely to follow. Where will the jobs then be, even allowing for a slowing of population increase? One answer lies in the smaller companies—thus the importance of the birth and nurturing of these firms (Quinn, Mettler). Nevertheless, it should not be forgotten that big companies and smaller ones exist in a symbiotic relationship.

If American macroeconomic policy can change in time, therefore, many manufacturing, agricultural, and some service sectors may show very large increases in productivity as their utilization of capacity rises above the current 80 percent to perhaps 86 or 89 percent (Reeder), and their export capability improves. The same would be true for large international banks (Reed and Moreno). On the other hand, Boskin points out if the dollar stays overvalued at around 35 percent, it may drive many firms and even industries out of business permanently, to the detriment of American future competitiveness and jobs.

It is clear that the overvalued dollar has forced many firms to increase innovation and cut costs. The effect has been very uneven across various industrial sectors, as the NAE studies have shown (Hannay). Some firms cannot compete because they are too small, inadequately funded, insufficiently innovative, or too inexperienced in world markets. Others, like many retail and smaller service companies, face no competition from abroad; thus their costs are rising but not their productivity. It follows that the maintenance of a low overall inflation rate depends crucially on the performance of the agricultural and manufacturing sectors, as well as on certain service sectors. How U.S. growth prospects are viewed by any particular firm depends on where it sees itself and its environment—is the situation it faces susceptible to positive actions for competitive success, or is the climate for progress deteriorating? The report of the President's Commission on Industrial Competitiveness (Young) deals with all of these points.

If the U.S. economy's performance is good relative to the United Kingdom (Malpas), it is nevertheless healthy that many Americans are concentrating on the competition from Japan and want to do something about it (Bowers). The United States should examine itself first, and also learn from the experience of others (Pavitt).

The Technological and Entrepreneurial Climate

All the evidence from scientists and technologists shows the potential power of new technology if the economic climate is right (Baker, Watson, Katz). It may even dwarf what has gone before. Thus Perry suggests the possibility of a further 100-fold reduction in the cost of computers and microelectronic equipment, with a concomitant impact on all sectors of our economy. The predictive powers of economists and technologists about technological change have not been good in the past, and the effects of such change have been persistently underestimated (Rosenberg). Yet we detect that there is a common theme among many of the authors in this volume: that new technology is the key to productivity growth, and that capital investment employed by properly trained people is the major expression of such new technology. Technology is what makes the economy a positive sum game (Perry), and this points to a strategy at the national and firm level of harnessing technology for economic growth. Progressive managements of large companies have accordingly been restructuring their thinking to incorporate technology at the highest level of their strategic planning and management (Coover, Mettler). The challenge is to government to view policy in this same broad sense so as to encourage greater economic growth.

The process of innovation involves a somewhat disorderly search between technology and markets (Kline and Rosenberg, Quinn). Probably it is because of this basic characteristic of innovation that small companies and individuals (often from outside the industries they impact) have been so successful at it. Start-up companies are frequently the exploiters of innovation, if not the innovators themselves, because they have "focus" and because small companies are often a more efficient instrument to get things done (Moore). However, we forget the failures that often obliterate many such efforts.

New entrepreneurial companies have traditionally been the source of many breakthrough or revolutionary technologies (Quinn, Rosenberg, Swanson), while bigger companies have followed a more evolutionary path, which is equally important. There is now increasing recognition by large companies that they too must organize themselves in a more entrepreneurial manner (Mettler, Hewlett). Mettler observes, however, that large companies grew precisely because they *were* entrepreneurial.

Summarizing his perceptions of a successful entrepreneurial environment, Moore has this to say:

First, it takes sources of ideas and people, particularly technical people. These sources are typically the large companies with extensive R&D capabilities, and sometimes universities, as in the case of the biotechnologies. Second, it requires a rapidly changing technology, preferably with many varied applications. Third, it requires large and diverse markets to provide many opportunities for market niches to be developed by the companies getting started. Fourth, it requires risk capital—which dried up in the 1970s and seemed overly prevalent in the first few years of the 1980s. Successful examples are valuable in motivating people to overcome the inertia to start a company. And finally, it takes a society that recognizes the entrepreneur when he or she is successful. Certainly these are the things that we have in abundance in Silicon Valley.

The Financial Climate

While there has been a more ample supply of entrepreneurs and venture capital in the United States since the capital gains tax was reduced in 1978 (Swanson, Moore, Quinn), there are now signs of a change: more money is going into second- and third-stage financing, fewer good ideas seem to be arising, and there is less venture capital availability for first-round financing (Perry, Marver). R&D partnerships have also played an important financing role (Swanson, Marver). On the other hand, according to Moore, there is too much venture capital in the United States at present, just as there was too little from 1969 to 1978. He points out that big companies lose valuable personnel as a result. Swanson says venture capital is still a critical need, while Quinn, who discusses the profitability of venture capital, suggests that it is better to have too much than too little, as exact calibration of the market is impossible.

A very different, European experience is illuminated by Malpas:

In Britain . . . Mrs. Thatcher has done a great deal to revive the quest for personal wealth by altering the tax system to reduce the amount government takes away from successful people. Europe in general still has too high a floor of unemployment benefit and too low a ceiling for success. Here again, it is this realization that personal wealth is an essential fuel for entrepreneurial drive, both for individuals and companies, that is causing attitudes to change.

Like large companies, rapidly growing companies, after a successful start-up and after reaching a critical size (about $100 million in revenues), face both a much higher cost for capital than their Japanese competitors (Mettler, Aoki, Young, Hannay, Landau and Hatsopoulos) and serious difficulties in the market for initial public offerings (IPOs) and for technology stocks generally (Marver, Perry). As a consequence of successful growth, they also have management and organizational problems different from those of smaller companies (Hewlett).

Equity issues generally have not been regarded as low-cost capital; instead debt issues are preferred by the larger companies—a preference arising from the fact that interest is tax deductible, whereas dividends are not. Growing companies, however, cannot risk a high debt:equity ratio because of the uncertainties of their prospects; their Japanese competitors, mostly larger companies, have high leverage and a lower cost for capital. American debt:equity ratios even for large companies are generally lower than those of the Japanese (Landau and Hatsopoulos).

Large companies do emphatically play a prominent role in the U.S. economy, despite their handicaps, as Mettler points out. The Japanese indeed have problems with new companies and IPOs (Okimoto), and they also face competitors from other Asian countries and the possibility that conditions may change. Yet even if technology and its applications thrive in the United States, the country still has created for itself a major disadvantage relative to Japan in regard to capital resources. And capital resources are "where economics and technology really merge" (Young). The United Kingdom has found one novel way to improve its competitive situation in this area—the Unlisted Securities Market, described by Malpas. Since such a market is not yet available in the United States, some American firms are utilizing the London securities markets to take advantage of the system.

Large banks, whose main role is with the big companies, deal only peripherally with the more rapidly growing companies, and hardly at all with start-up companies (Reed and Moreno), but as financial innovators and as purchasers of high-tech equipment they still play a major role for many companies. "It is clear," Reed and Moreno state, "that these [large financial] institutions support technological innovation in many ways: as users of technology, venture capitalists, equity underwriters, lenders, advisers and consultants, project financiers, and conduits to the international capital markets." Smaller exporting companies and exports generally are not greatly helped by any of these large banks. The Export-Import Bank's role is very limited in comparison with the resources at the disposition of American competitors abroad, and particularly so in regard to the smaller companies (Hannay). Swanson, describing the situation of rapidly growing companies in biotechnology, notes that the last major U.S. drug company (Syntex) appeared in 1957; Bowers, its present chief executive officer, discusses that industry's present problems, which are not by any means limited to financial concerns.

The larger established high technology companies, even if well managed and financed, are facing stiff competition from the Japanese. Europe has generally fallen behind. But the United States can learn much from the changing Japanese strategies (described by Okimoto and Aoki in detail), even though the great differences in the two cultures obviously preclude simple copying. Major features of the Japanese approach include a high savings rate, low interest rates additionally aided by a stable economic policy (Landau and Hatsopoulos), favorable tax policies (Landau and Hatsopoulos), favorable labor relations, and effective government–industry collaboration. In other words, Japan's is a healthy environment for business in general (Okimoto). There is nothing neutral about Japan's economic policy, which favors high technology, Japan first, and restricted internal markets. Okimoto points out that while targeting was limited in consumer electronics, there has been more intervention in semiconductors in recent times. These factors and strategies, along with certain domestic macroeconomic policies, have presented a major challenge to American high technology companies—even some of the largest of them.

The progressive "smokestack" industries, such as chemicals, which still compete on world markets and generate a favorable balance of payments, are stepping up innovation, R&D, and cost cutting, while seeking their own own special targets or "niches" (Coover). Mettler reminds us, however, that the distinction between high technology and smokestack industries is largely fictitious today, and that manufacturing and services are inextricably intertwined—the "salami economy." As Young and Hannay write, the general feeling is that from now on the United States will be largely dependent on global markets, especially in the manufacturing, agricultural, and certain key service sectors, and must "get its act together" on a permanent basis. With the spread of information technologies, capital markets are also truly global now and exert a discipline on all governments (Reed and Moreno).

OBSTACLES TO U.S. GROWTH: SUMMARY

The first obstacle to U.S. growth is a macroeconomic climate that discourages rather than encourages economic growth and competitiveness. Jorgenson asserts that there are no fewer than three camps in the Republican party arguing about which policy to pursue and that the Democrats have yet to enunciate a clear policy. The argument about policies among economists centers on whether economic growth rates of 3 percent, 4 percent, or 5 percent are sustainable over the longer run; yet the programs being suggested largely fail to take into account the explosive potential of technology waiting to be unleashed by the proper macroeconomic policies (Reeder).

The second obstacle is in the consequences of the proliferation of regulatory policies (Watson), and the growing public sensitivity to potential hazards—such as the nuclear and Bhopal debacles—that threaten agriculture (Ruttan), biotechnology (Watson), chemicals (Holmer), pharmaceuticals (Bowers), and others. Related to the regulatory issue is the liability issue and the associated legal system (described by Katz and by Huber) which introduces broad handicaps to innovation and risk-taking entrepreneurship. Moore asks how, in an industry changing monthly, companies can function effectively under a legal system that is "25 years behind the times." Excessive litigation and a growing tendency to resolve disputes in the courts are further obstacles to growth. Litigiousness has long been a distinctive feature of American society, as Katz and Huber make clear. It was a feature noted by de Tocqueville, who associated it with the absence of a heavy-handed bureaucracy such as existed in Europe. Eads reminds us that our heavy reliance upon the courts throughout our history was one side of a coin, the opposite side of which was a strong determination to avoid the creation of an overreaching government bureaucracy.

A third obstacle is inadequate technical and general education and inadequate retraining at all levels (Pettit, Young, Kennedy). Needed are education and retraining that can inspire a positive outlook toward science and technology, and an urge to maintain the American edge in technological competitiveness and entrepreneurial creativity. In education and training lies an important and enduring long-term American advantage. Kennedy emphasizes the unique American research university structure, where education and research are located in the same place. Nevertheless, there is inadequate government support of basic engineering, manufacturing, and process research in the universities; in this regard the new Engineering Research Centers are potentially a very important innovation (Swanson). The obsolescence of much university equipment and many facilities also represents a serious neglect (Kennedy).

A fourth major obstacle to U.S. growth is the continued belief in an endless cornucopia of production and innovation, a belief that adequate levels of capital formation and technological change will somehow be forthcoming, even in the presence of policies that may adversely affect them. Thus, large deficits are tolerated and a drastic rearrangement of the entire tax structure along untested lines is again proposed, constituting, in effect, an experiment with the entire economy (Landau and Hatsopoulos). Jorgenson has shown how sensitive effective tax rates are for capital investment.

COMPETITIVENESS: THE FIRST PRIORITY FOR FUTURE AMERICAN PROSPERITY

A fundamental challenge is the need to make the American economy more competitive, and firms are responding in numerous ways (Mettler, Young,

Hannay, Pettit, Bechtel, Bowers, Holmer). As various industrial sectors feel the effects of competition differently, generalizations must be very carefully made (Hannay).

Clearly, the role of the large company in the economy is growing, at least in some respects. They have the cash, which smaller companies are finding harder to obtain (Malpas), and are able to take greater risks. With an awareness—honed by intense competition—of the need to innovate, large companies are seeking ways to improve their performance both internally and externally (Coover, Reeder). Perry describes "corporate partnering," an arrangement in which large companies set up associations with small entrepreneurial firms in order to harness the advantages of both. General Motors and IBM are cited as current examples (Marver). Similar practices in Japan are described by Aoki. Mettler urges closer relations between large and small companies, citing as one of the benefits the additional job formation that can result. Emerging marketing and standardization techniques also offer growth opportunities, according to Norman, who illuminates a larger truth: the successful entrepreneur listens to the market and serves it as well as possible. Mettler, in speaking of "market-driven" ways to innovate and meet competitive challenges, arrives at the same fundamental conclusion. If America has a unique entrepreneurial culture that must be nurtured (Quinn, Moore), individuals are still the key to creating value and have many motivations for entrepreneurial risk taking (Quinn).

The diffusion of innovation is another important determinant of the impact of technological change on economic growth (David, Mansfield). At the same time, in an increasingly competitive environment, based ever more solidly in the Information Age, it is important to protect the intellectual property that justifies R&D expenditures and risk taking (Katz, Moore, Swanson). A proper balance between diffusion and protection is not easy to achieve. Diffusion through the movement of people among companies is greater in the United States than in Japan, but in Japan greater cooperation among firms assists diffusion and growth (Okimoto).

It is clear that government does have a key role in economic growth and competitiveness. It is our view that the U.S. economy could be strengthened if we as a nation, with government help, could take these steps:

• Lower real interest rates, which are affected by monetary policy, deficits, and the uncertainty of government policies. This would lead to more favorable incentives for investment activity throughout the economy.

• Adopt a tax structure that really *would* promote saving and investment (Landau and Hatsopoulos). Tax considerations are also of great importance in motivating entrepreneurs (Landau and Hatsopoulos); the R&D tax credit has not been adequately tested, and should be extended (Swanson). Such incentives as the capital gains tax differential have been beneficial for innovation and risk taking and should be retained (Baldwin).

• Adopt sensible regulatory policies and work to ease excessive public fears about poisons, illnesses, and other hazards by increasing the research effort in these areas and by greater openness of communication and preventive actions wherever feasible (Holmer). Wise preservation of the physical environment for future generations is as important as is preservation and promotion of the economic and social environments.

• Reduce the rate of increase in government expenditures, including perhaps even defense (Malpas, Okimoto), but increase R&D expenditures for basic and generic research (Swanson, Watson).

• Avoid excessive government intervention in markets. Quinn and Zschau state that national planning and real innovation are incompatible. Mettler, conscious of the competitiveness problems generated by the low U.S. savings rates, points out that we do have an industrial policy, although it has never been publicly proclaimed, and its name is "consumer spending." Similarly, David emphasizes that the United States has a de facto set of policies, such as in Boskin's second-tier economic policies, which greatly influence innovation and diffusion of technology.

Beyond these steps economic science should look more closely at how the process of innovation translates into economic growth. It should do this by studying the actuality of the process and how it varies across firms and sectors, as well as across national frontiers (Pavitt). From a better understanding of the microeconomics of technical change we should be able to erect a more sensible macroeconomics—the ultimate form of the feedback loops in the innovation process discussed by Kline and Rosenberg.

Further, economists and technologists should work much more closely together to expand our fundamental knowledge as a prerequisite to higher growth. Mettler summarizes the real challenge involved:

American jobs, economic security, and living standards, American social goals and dreams, America's place in the world—all are at stake in the decision we make. If we want to maintain an open, benevolent, and humanely productive society; improve the quality of education; restore our private and public capital resources; pay our debts; defend our national interests; and continue to be a leader in world affairs, then we must also want a competitive economy.

In our culture, economic growth is a prerequisite for a more equitable society. Our own early history—and that of the Japanese—show that we can obtain this objective (Eads, Okimoto). Eads makes the point clearly: failure to progress means decline. But the United States is not a corporation and cannot plan rationally, and it has a constitution and a legal system in the place of the permanent bureaucracies of other nations. The Japanese bureaucracy has been very powerful, and thus Japan has no need for strong intervention by the courts, as Aoki observes. The U.S. legal system is designed to deal fairly with people, but policymakers have overemphasized equity in the recent past. Indeed, policymakers have expanded the concept of equity to include the failures that are the inevitable by-product of the innovation process. A new balance is needed. So far the United States has been unable to reach a national consensus on the importance of restoring our competitiveness and the need to make a commitment to do so (Bowers). Is our form of government really suited for the modern economy?

The Japan that rose from the ashes after its defeat developed a system very different from ours—one that will generate continuous competition from them (Aoki). In addition, unburdened by extensive defense expenditures, the Japanese have demonstrated an amazing ability to manage growth as their principal national goal by linking job security, wages, and sectoral policies (which are coordinated with their macropolicies). Their high savings rate gives them another immense advantage.

Eads is pessimistic about American capabilities for matching the Japanese resolve, and fears that our system excessively favors equity and risk aversion. This situation might lead to greater protection of uncompetitive industries, companies, and jobs through trade and government policies; such protection would further weaken the country instead of strengthening the determination to improve efficiency. For Eads, the NAE studies show the process of declining competitiveness all too clearly. Others—Brooks, Mettler, Malpas, Quinn, Hannay—are more optimistic about the possibility of recovery, particularly when the promising technologies available and foreseeable are taken into account.

So the question becomes: Will a system designed with an increasing concern for equity work as well to promote growth, in the light of the increasingly competitive global market? A provocative question, which this volume poses but does not answer. As Hannay says, in no case is technological leadership by itself sufficient to assure competitive success. But it is evident that many financiers, entrepreneurs, technologists, economists, and business leaders are confident of the U.S. ability to respond to challenge. All need to work together more closely in the future so that policymakers can be shown more clearly what paths the United States must follow, if we are to succeed in developing policies that will be more effective than those of the recent past.

The Impact of Technological Innovation: A Historical View

NATHAN ROSENBERG

Perhaps the reason we do so poorly at predicting the impact of technological change is that we are dealing with an extraordinarily complex and interdependent set of relationships. We should, however, be able to do a somewhat better job of it in the future, if only by developing a better appreciation of some of the reasons why we have done so badly in the past.

It is reasonable to assume that readers of this volume believe, at the very least, that technological change plays a major role in shaping our economy and society generally. I had originally intended to devote this chapter to a historical look at technological change, but the more I thought about it, the more intrigued I became by a different but closely related question, a question that ought to be an urgent and persistent concern to precisely such an audience. The question is, quite simply: Why do we consistently do such a poor job of anticipating the effects of technological change? Why is our intellectual framework for thinking about the way technology transforms our lives so obviously inadequate? This question, which has occurred to me many times over the years, reasserted itself recently when I encountered a piece of futurology given to President McKinley in 1899 by a Mr. Charles H. Duell. Mr. Duell was the commissioner of the Patent and Trademark Office at the time and, rather uncharacteristically for a public officeholder, was encouraging the President to close down his agency. His reason was quite startling in its simplicity: ''Everything that can be invented has been invented.'' I am happy to report, 86 years and approximately 3.8 million patents later, that the President did not heed Mr. Duell's advice.

We are all quite properly disdainful of Mr. Duell's total bankruptcy of

17

imagination. I resurrect him here, for a brief cameo appearance, only because he managed to express in extreme form, but with epigrammatic precision, a widely held view regarding the future impact of technological change, a view that systematically underrates its future contributions. In retrospect, it is apparent that we have persistently underestimated the contribution of technological change to the growth of the economy. As part of the same bias, we have failed to anticipate the contribution that technological change would make to alleviating or eliminating certain future problems that earlier generations regarded as both serious and intractable.

It is time that I did a certain amount of intellectual unpacking. In particular, who is the "we" that I have been invoking so far? That in itself turns out to be an interesting question. Much of what I want to say will focus on the question of who has been responsible for shaping the most influential view of the future and the role played by technological forces in that future.

In examining the views of various professional groups with respect to how accurately they anticipated certain aspects of technological change, it turns out that no group covers itself with glory. What is intriguing is that they all come off badly, although the reasons for the poor performance vary considerably.

For many decades, as far back as the writing of Malthus and Ricardo at the beginning of the nineteenth century, it almost seemed that economists had a stranglehold on the expression of deeply pessimistic views of the future. Malthus, in particular, made clear in the very title of the first edition of his essay, first published in 1798, his intention of rejecting naive Enlightenment views on the future prospects for improvement in the human condition. The full title was *Essay on the Principle of Population as it affects the future improvement of Society, with remarks on the Speculations of Mr. Godwin, M. Condorcet and Others*. More recently, however, there has been an interesting reversal of roles. Very pessimistic forecasts have emanated from other circles, in particular from systems analysts, biologists, ecologists, and other natural scientists who have become concerned with a set of social issues beyond their more narrowly defined professional spheres. Economists, by contrast, have been cast in the role of explaining why these pessimistic forecasts—in some cases, prophecies of doom—were unwarranted.

In fact, I cannot resist the opportunity of pointing out how well economists have come off in the past 15 years or so. I know economists are not accustomed to being praised for the accuracy of their predictions, but that is because the public is so obsessed with predictions about the performance of next year's GNP, or what interest rates will look like in 6 months' time, that it pays little attention to some other, fundamental aspects of economic reasoning and the predictions that they generate.

During the 1970s, public discussion was preoccupied with visions of imminent natural resource exhaustion (as well as pollution-induced ecological disasters) that were bound to bring economic growth to an end. The dominant theme, readers will recall, was *The Limits to Growth*, the title of a well-known book published in 1972. The argument was that there were inexorable natural resource constraints that placed a rigid upper limit on economic growth possibilities. Simple extrapolation of recent rates of utilization of key natural resources was thought sufficient by some futurologists to generate fairly precise predictions of an apocalypse awaiting mankind not too far down the road—perhaps around the middle of the twenty-first century. The whole exercise was remarkably Malthusian. Indeed, it often seemed to me exactly as if Malthus had returned to earth in the 1970s in the guise of a slightly off-the-rails computer programmer.

These purely intellectual preoccupations were powerfully reinforced in late 1973 and 1974 by the Arab oil embargo and by the first of two drastic increases in world petroleum prices orchestrated by the Organization of Petroleum Exporting Countries (OPEC). The sudden sharp rise in energy prices was widely interpreted as powerful confirmation of the "limits to growth" view of the future. But, in this period, economists were no longer the leading spokesmen for an essentially Malthusian view of mankind's dreary future prospects. Rather, economists, far more than other professionals, continually called attention to a number of adjustment mechanisms that market forces could reliably be expected to generate. These mechanisms, they argued, would, at the very least, drastically mitigate the dreariest aspects of the pessimistic predictions that were so rampant at the time. When a specific resource becomes increasingly scarce, they pointed out, one may reasonably expect a number of adjustment mechanisms, generated by its higher price, to come into play—substitution, conservation, and more intensive exploration. Less emphasis was placed on technological change as such an adjustment mechanism, although the historically minded readily pointed to earlier historical experiences as suggesting that new technologies were a highly probable, and highly powerful, response to rising energy prices.

The surprising fact, however, is that the main tradition in economics has never paid extensive attention to technological change. Classical economics, the economics of Malthus and Ricardo, was very much concerned with the long-term prospects for economic growth. Nevertheless, classical economists devoted their main energies to demonstrating the limitations on such growth prospects that were imposed by the niggardliness of nature and the inevitably diminishing returns to capital and labor when the supply of land is fixed. Technological innovation might indeed offset such diminishing returns, but one can only record that classical economists simply did not seem to attach much weight to that possibility. Rather, they placed far greater emphasis on the potential benefits of a policy of free trade between more advanced, densely populated countries and countries where the man:land ratio was more favorable. Although Malthus and Ricardo were writing in the midst of one of

the genuine discontinuities of human history—the Industrial Revolution—
they could only understand progress in the context of painfully slow change
in an agrarian society. It would have taken a major flight of imagination to
escape from the preconceptions imposed on them by their knowledge of past
history.[1]

Although Marx, who may be considered the last of the great classical
economists, did recognize the enormous potential for technological change
under capitalism, that potential was, in his view, increasingly frustrated by
the internal contradictions of capitalism. For Marx, the inherent laws of
motion of capitalism, as he called them, are such that the labor-saving bias
of technological change has the primary effect of generating increasing unemployment. The notion that technological change may generate unemployment of a kind that is not quickly corrected by market forces is traceable
back to Ricardo, but it was Marx who brought the unemployment-creating
aspects to center stage. Thus, ironically, the one major economist of the
nineteenth century who fully foresaw the great productivity-increasing potential of technological change also argued that such change occurred too
rapidly. For, under capitalist institutions, a rapid rate of labor-saving technological change created increases in productivity that capitalism was incapable of absorbing. The eventual result, for Marx, was that rapid technological
change under capitalist institutions would bring about a collapse in the institutional system itself.

The neoclassical tradition in economics, beginning in the late nineteenth
century, turned away from the classical concern with long-term economic
growth prospects and concentrated instead on examining the implications of
maximizing behavior in a static framework. A main concern, which has
dominated this tradition up to the present day, is to analyze how a market
economy generates forces bringing about a return to equilibrium after some
force has disturbed that equilibrium. Considerable attention has been devoted
to analyzing the conditions determining the stability and the efficiency of
the equilibrium state to which the economic system gravitated. However,
neoclassical economics consists largely of a comparison of successive equilibrium states and does not incorporate an analysis of the adjustment process
per se. Technological change, when it is considered at all, is usually treated
as some exogenous, once-and-for-all, cost-reducing process innovation to
which the economy subsequently adjusts. Or, within the firm, the decision
maker might be assumed to be confronted with a range of exogenously
determined technologies among which he has to choose. In fact, the act of
choice itself is a very time-intensive and resource-intensive process of search,
wherein the alternatives being explored are not well defined and have a
number of uncertainties attached to them. Much of what we label ''R&D''
consists of expenditures on precisely this search process.

Thus, the main traditions of classical and neoclassical economics have devoted very little attention to the analysis of technological change. Although classical economists were centrally concerned with the determinants of long-term economic growth and might therefore have been expected to devote considerable attention to technological change, they assumed that the contours of long-term growth would be dominated by natural resource constraints and diminishing returns resulting from the pressures exerted by a growing population against those constraints. Their conclusions were that diminishing returns would swamp the growth in productivity resulting from technological change. Neoclassical economists, on the other hand, focused on short-run problems of optimal resource allocation within a static framework, from which technological change had usually been explicitly excluded. When the question of economic growth was considered by neoclassical economists, it was regarded primarily as involving a rise in the capital:labor ratio.

The great strength of neoclassical reasoning is that it powerfully focuses attention on a wide variety of adjustment mechanisms that permeate all economically motivated behavior. The economic world is indeed full of potential substitution possibilities and, in my view, it is the glory of neoclassical economics that it has provided a profound understanding of such mechanisms and their implications for optimal resource allocation. Thus, shifts in important economic parameters—a sudden rise in petroleum prices— give rise to a range of possible adjustments, and neoclassical economics offers a systematic analysis of the directions in which rational economic agents may be expected to move in response to such shifts.

On the other hand, it is fair to say that economists since the time of Malthus, classical and neoclassical alike, have paid insufficient attention to what has been, in the long run, the most powerful single mechanism of adjustment, technological change. Although in recent years much attention has been devoted to the role of technological change as a determinant of productivity improvement (largely as a result of the work of Abramovitz and Solow in the mid-1950s, which highlighted some of the deficiencies of the neoclassical approach to growth), economists, like virtually everyone else, continue to reason as if the supply of natural resources is permanently fixed. At least, they do not typically address this issue explicitly. Within an analytical framework, technological change is regarded as generating a greater output from a given input of resources. Although this is a perfectly acceptable procedure for many short-run purposes, it is extremely misleading for longer-term issues when it gives rise to the assumptions that natural resource inputs can be unambiguously defined, independently of the state of technical knowledge, and that the quantity of such inputs is fixed in amount.

Although it is obviously true that nature imposes certain constraints on resource supplies, it is also true, and of fundamental importance, that many technological improvements, when they occur, have the effect of vastly enlarging the resource base, that is, they constitute materials-augmenting technological change. By making it possible to exploit resources that could not be exploited before, technological change is making additions to the resource base of the economy, in economic terms if not in geological terms. Thus, it should not be regarded as paradoxical, although many will think it is, to state that the United States has a far larger quantity of iron ore deposits within its borders today than it did 50 years ago. In the past few decades, new processing techniques that prepare the iron ore for the blast furnace—pelletization and beneficiation—have made it possible to exploit the immense deposits of hard, low-grade taconite ores. Such low-grade ores were ignored as long as the high-grade iron ores of the Mesabi Range were still abundant. The development of these new processing techniques has been fully equivalent to a gigantic expansion of resource supplies. In fact, pelletization and beneficiation have brought such great economies in transport costs and blast-furnace efficiency that the energy cost of a finished ton of steel has declined substantially even though the iron content of the taconite ores is very low.[2]

Similar developments had occurred in the nineteenth century. The introduction of the Gilchrist-Thomas basic steel-making process in the late 1870s changed the course of European history by making possible, for the first time, the exploitation of the enormous high-phosphorus iron ore deposits of Western Europe. The "low quality" deposits were simply not usable with the earlier iron-making technology.

The release of energy from the atom during World War II meant a vast expansion of energy supplies, although obviously there had been no changes in the natural environment or in the physical characteristics of uranium. The invention of the internal-combustion engine toward the end of the nineteenth century converted petroleum deposits into an energy source for the first time. Until that engine was developed, it will be recalled, petroleum served primarily as an illuminant.

As recently as the 1930s, natural gas was still regarded as an unavoidable and dangerous nuisance that needed to be safely disposed of. Unless there happened to be some urban markets nearby, it was typically treated as a waste material and flared, as it still is in some parts of the world. Eventually, the perfection of a technique for producing high-pressure pipelines transformed natural gas from a waste product into our most attractive household fuel—a fuel that currently plays a major role in many industrial markets and constitutes a large fraction of total energy supplies.

Thus, the point has been systematically ignored, or systematically underappreciated since the time of Malthus, that natural resources possess economic significance only as a function of technological knowledge, and that increases in such knowledge are fully equivalent to an expansion of the resource base of the economy. The best that can be said for the widespread intellectual parlor game of calculating how long it will take to exhaust the supply of a particular strategic raw material, at recent or current rates of utilization, is that the long division is usually carried out correctly. Such calculations are of very limited relevance to a technologically dynamic economy, however. Technological innovation has been a method for overcoming specific natural resource scarcities by vastly expanding the number and the quality of resources that are capable of being economically exploited. In this sense, technological innovation has been the most efficient of all adjustment mechanisms for dealing with growing natural resource scarcity.

THE LIMITATIONS OF THE EXPERT

I turn now to another category of explanation in accounting for the difficulties in dealing with the future impact of technological change. Much of the difficulty is attributable to the high degree of specialization of technological knowledge that characterizes modern industrial societies. Economists have been at the forefront, at least since the time of Adam Smith, of those who have emphasized the gains resulting from increasing specialization and division of labor. Such gains, from Adam Smith's eighteenth-century pin factory to the research activities of a modern university (Stanford Linear Accelerator Center), have been immense. But there is another side to the specialization coin because, while there are indeed great benefits to specialization, there are also drawbacks. Experts of any kind tend to look at the world in terms of a very limited number of variables—indeed, that is a reasonable definition of what it means to be an expert. The training and experience of experts equip them to deal with movement along some very particular trajectories, but not others. The old aphorism that an expert is a person who knows more and more about less and less conveys an important truth, one that has serious implications for the understanding of technological change ("When all that you have is a hammer, everything looks like a nail.").

A specialist is typically capable of extending and improving the methods of his or her expertness and applying them to new uses. However, the very nature of an expert's education and professional experience is likely to disqualify that person from developing new technologies based on different principles or even from appreciating their potential significance.

The industrial history of the past century is replete with evidence for these assertions. Carriage makers played a negligible role in the development of the automobile (although Fisher Body did make the transition), and the makers of stagecoaches played no role in the development of the steam locomotive. The makers of steam locomotives, in turn, made no contribution to and showed no interest in the new technology that displaced their invention, the diesel locomotive. It is hardly surprising. No amount of expertise in the operation and improvement of steam locomotives would equip an engineer with the capabilities required to develop an engine based on such different principles. Similarly, many of the manufacturers of piston-driven aircraft engines could not negotiate their way into the jet age. The makers of vacuum tubes failed to transfer their dominance to the semiconductor market. Nor were nylon or rayon introduced by experts who knew a great deal about silkworms and mulberry leaves. Western Union showed no initial interest in that newfangled device, the telephone. In fact, Western Union turned down the opportunity to purchase Alexander Graham Bell's telephone patent when it was offered to them for a mere $100,000!

My point is that there are discontinuities as well as continuities in the course of technological change. The failure of industrial firms to make the transition in these episodes of discontinuity is not due to some inherent failing or unavoidable human conservatism. Rather, it reflects the limitations of technical expertise. Whereas experts in an existing field are obviously indispensable for generating improvements that draw on their accumulated technical skills, those very skills may become barriers during periods of discontinuity. At such points those skills are no longer relevant for a technology based on different skills or methodologies.

Although the existing set of technical skills in an industry may be of no use during the transition to a drastically different technological base for that industry, technical skills in other industries may be very useful. For example, although the transition from propeller-driven aircraft engines to jet engines represented a genuine discontinuity for makers of propeller-driven engines, it represented much less of a discontinuity for manufacturers of steam turbines. Manufacturers of steam turbines already possessed designing and manufacturing skills that gave them a great comparative advantage in the exploitation of the new aircraft power plant. Thus, it is not surprising that General Electric, America's largest manufacturer of steam turbines, entered the business of making aircraft engines when jet propulsion was introduced.

When drastically new technologies make their appearance, thinking about their eventual impact is severely handicapped by the tendency to think about them in terms of the old technology. It is difficult even to visualize the complete displacement of an old, long-dominant technology, let alone apprehend a new technology as an entire system. Thus, time and again, new technologies have been thought of as mere supplements to offset certain inherent limitations of the old. In the early years, railroads were thought of merely as feeders into the existing canal system, to be constructed in places where the terrain had rendered canals inherently impractical. In precisely the same fashion, the radio was thought by its originators and proponents to have potential applications mainly where wire communication was impractical, for example, ships at sea and remote mountain locations. (The old term "wireless," still employed in Britain, effectively perpetuates that early perspective.) The extent to which the old continues to dominate thinking about the new is nicely encapsulated in Thomas Edison's practice of regularly referring to his incandescent lamp as "the burner." Rather more seriously, in his work on an electric meter, a biographer reports, Edison for a long time attempted to develop a measure of electricity consumption in units of cubic feet![3] In the case of aircraft engines, the time intervals between overhaul of jet engines were originally based on the earlier practices with piston engines. As a result, a major economic benefit of jet engines—their much greater reliability and durability and, consequently, lower maintenance requirements—was nowhere near fully exploited. It was only after some years that airlines extended the time between overhaul of jet engines to intervals that reflected the performance characteristics of the new power plant. (The time between overhaul of piston engines was 2,000 to 2,500 hours of service. The time interval was extended to as long as 8,000 hours for jet engines.)

But if thinking about the future impact of new technologies is handicapped by the force of conceptualizations based on the old, that form of thinking receives substantial reinforcement from the opposite direction: inventions typically enter the world in very primitive form compared with the shape that they eventually acquire. Thus, a basic reason for underestimating the impact of a new technology is that new technologies often appear distinctly unpromising at the outset. Their dominating characteristics are often high cost and poor performance standards, including an infuriating degree of unreliability ("Get a horse!"). The difficulty here seems to be in predicting the trajectory of improvements that will occur in the course of the life cycle of the new product. A disinterested observer who happened to be passing by at Kitty Hawk on that fateful day in 1903 might surely be excused if he did not walk away with visions of 747s or C-5As in his head.

However, I think there is a deeper issue at stake here. Although, as I argued earlier, existing technical expertise is not very useful in an encounter with genuine technical discontinuities, it is rather different when technical continuities are involved. I believe that technical experts *are* reasonably good at anticipating the kinds of performance improvements that can be teased out of a given technology, once it has been established and its working principles are reasonably well understood. Technical specialists usually have a good appreciation of likely improvement trajectories. Their work is guided by an informed sense of probable directions and rates of future improvement. Why, then, the poor performance in dealing with the future impact of new technologies?

I believe the answer to this question takes us back to the central concern of this volume. The impact of new or improved technologies is not just a matter of improved technical performance. It is, rather, a matter of translating such information into its potential economic and social significance. Doing this requires something much more than purely technical expertise. It is, in fact, an extraordinarily difficult exercise. Understanding the technical basis for wireless communication, which Marconi did, was a very different matter from understanding the possibilities for a vast new entertainment broadcasting industry that would reach into every household (and automobile), which Marconi completely failed to envisage. The point is that social change or economic impact is not something that can be extrapolated out of a piece of hardware.

New technologies are, rather, building blocks. Their eventual impact will depend on what is subsequently designed and constructed with them. New technologies are unrealized potentials that may take a very large number of eventual shapes. What shapes they actually take will depend on a wide range of social priorities and values, on the way the demand for particular goods and services changes in response to rising incomes or declining prices. I will return to this issue shortly.

An additional reason why it is so difficult to anticipate the effects of technological change is that most inventions have their origin in the attempt to solve very specific, even narrowly defined problems. It is very common, however, that a solution, once found, has important applications in totally unintended contexts. In this sense, the eventual impact of new technologies is very difficult to anticipate, because much of the impact is realized through the intersectoral flows of technology that are so characteristic of modern industrial economies. Inventions increasingly have serendipitous life histories.

The steam engine, for example, was invented in the eighteenth century specifically as a device to pump water out of flooded mines. It was, for a long time, regarded exclusively as a pump. A succession of improvements later rendered it a feasible source of power for textile factories, iron mills, and an expanding array of industrial establishments. In the course of the early nineteenth century the steam engine became a generalizable source of power and had major applications in transportation—railroads, steamships, and steamboats. In fact, in the United States before the Civil War, the main use of the steam engine was in transportation. Later in the nineteenth century the steam engine was used to produce a new and even more generalizable source of power—electricity—which, in turn, satisfied innumerable final uses to which steam power itself was not efficiently applicable. Finally, the steam turbine displaced the steam engine in the generation of electric power, and the special features of electricity—its ease of transmission over long distances, the capacity for making power available in ''fractionalized'' units, and the far greater flexibility of electricity-powered equipment—spelled the eventual demise of the steam engine.

Thus, the life history of the steam engine was shaped by forces that could hardly have been foreseen by inventors who were working on ways of removing water from increasingly flooded coal mines. Its subsequent history was shaped by unanticipated applications to industry and transportation and eventually by the systematic exploitation of new technologies that were undreamed of at the time the steam engine itself was invented, such as electricity. Nevertheless, the very existence of the steam engine, once its operating principles had been thoroughly understood, served as a powerful stimulus to other inventions.

Thus, major innovations, such as the steam engine, once they are established, have the effect of inducing further innovation and complementary investments over a wide frontier. Indeed, the ability to induce such further innovations and investments is a reasonably good definition of what constitutes a major innovation. It is a useful way of distinguishing between technological advances that are merely invested with great novelty from advances that have the potential for a major economic impact. But this also highlights the difficulties in foreseeing the eventual impact, since that will depend on the size and the direction of these future complementary innovations and investments.

In the twentieth century there is an additional, increasingly significant relationship that complicates the ability to foresee the eventual impact of technological change. This relationship is partially obscured by the prevailing linear model, which looks on innovation as originating in "blue-sky" basic research, which feeds downstream to applied research and, eventually, to new product development. In fact, to an increasing degree, it is the needs of the technological realm that direct scientific research. Increasingly, the needs of an expanding technological system shape and mobilize scientific research in specific directions. This is what the term "mission-oriented basic research" is all about. More to the point, this is what one of the most important institutional innovations of the twentieth century is all about: the industrial research laboratory. These labs have been specifically established to facilitate the exploitation of scientific knowledge for industrial purposes. But, to an increasing degree, the best of these labs generate much of the scientific knowledge that they exploit. At the same time, the problems encountered by sophisticated industrial technologies, and the anomalous observations or unexpected difficulties they produced, have served as powerful stimuli to scientific research, in the academic community as well as the industrial research lab. In these ways the responsiveness of scientific research to economic needs and opportunities has been powerfully reinforced.

Thus, solid-state physics, presently the largest subdiscipline of physics, attracted only a few physicists before the advent of the transistor. In fact, the subject was not even taught at most universities. The training in solid-state physics that Shockley received at the Massachusetts Institute of Technology in the 1930s was probably unavailable at any other university in America at the time, with the exception of Princeton. The situation was transformed, of course, by the invention of the transistor in 1948. The transistor demonstrated the potentially high payoff of solid-state research and led to a huge concentration of resources in that field. It is important to note that the rapid mobilization of resources in solid-state research after 1948 occurred in the university as well as in private industry. Thus, transistor technology was not building on a vast earlier research commitment. Rather, it was the initial breakthrough of the transistor that gave rise to a subsequent large-scale commitment of scientific resources.

Similarly, the advent of the laser as a potentially important new mode of transmission has served as a powerful focusing device in shaping the direction of scientific research. However, this scientific research has generated a vast array of unanticipated applications, including optic surgery, precision measurement, navigational instruments, military applications in outer space, and the shaping of a wide assortment of materials in manufacturing, ranging from clothing to aircraft composites. At the same time, a high-payoff application of laser technology *was* clearly anticipated and successfully consummated. It was the development of laser technology that suggested the feasibility of using optical fibers for transmission purposes. This possibility, in turn, pointed to the field of optics, where advances in scientific knowledge can now be expected to have high potential payoffs. As a result, optics as a field of scientific research has experienced a great resurgence in recent years. It has been converted by changed expectations, based on past and prospective technological innovations, from a relatively quiet intellectual backwater to a burgeoning field of scientific research. It is likely that this scientific activity, in turn, will yield a new array of unanticipated applications.

The research system within modern industry thus affects technological predictability in two offsetting ways. On the one hand, certain high-payoff applications (as in the case of the laser) can be realized more rapidly and predictably through the application of scientific research to technological breakthroughs. On the other hand, these very same scientific research activities have themselves generated a large number of unanticipated applications. The overall impact of laser and fiber optics technologies is highly uncertain, even as the realization of certain applications appears to have become more predictable.

TECHNOLOGICAL CHANGE AND UNEMPLOYMENT

I turn now to a final category of the dialogue over the impact of technological change. It involves a concern that has been particularly prominent in the past few years, but that has deep intellectual roots going back to Marx and even to Ricardo. That is the concern that the primary impact of technological change will be increased levels of unemployment. There was and there remains a widespread tendency to attribute the higher unemployment levels that emerged during the 1970s to the introduction of new technologies, especially electronic technologies, that purportedly had a strong labor-saving bias. Moreover, there is widespread apprehension that we are now poised at one of those great discontinuities in history and that new technologies are going to have unprecedentedly large effects in generating a permanent pool of unemployed. This is because a number of new technologies—robotics, computer-aided design/computer-aided manufacture (CAD/CAM), the growing capacity of the electronic chip, automation—are expected to have strong labor-saving effects.

It is, of course, always impossible to prove anything about the future by looking at the past. It is impossible to prove that we are *not* poised at some genuine discontinuity in history. Moreover, although there is some evidence of recent improvement, it is painfully clear that the American economy has, in some important respects, been performing poorly for more than a decade. Productivity improvement has been particularly dismal, and the "natural" rate of unemployment seems to have been increasing during the 1970s and 1980s.

It is far from clear, however, that high unemployment has been primarily due to the character of technological change, nor are there compelling reasons to believe that new technologies will have an unusually job-reducing bias in the future. Some categories of employment will, of course, suffer. Technological change has always reduced specific categories of employment— e.g., farm workers, railroad workers, coal miners, lumberjacks. The electric light bulb displaced the candle maker, and the automobile put saddlers and whip makers out of business. The crucial question is whether the thrust of technological change is to reduce total employment, not whether it eliminates specific jobs. Three points are worth making in this regard.

First, a simple empirical observation. Although unemployment levels in the American economy were indeed high, by historical standards, during the 1970s, that decade can hardly provide persuasive evidence that new technologies have been reducing aggregate employment opportunities. In fact, during that decade the number of employed persons rose by a remarkable 20 million—from 80 million in mid-1970 to 100 million in mid-1980. Whatever job-reducing forces may have been at work within the nature of the new technologies were, at the very least, swamped by mechanisms working in the opposite direction.

Second, labor-saving innovations are not the same as job-reducing innovations. The reductions in cost and price associated with labor-saving innovations may bring in their wake vast increases in specific kinds of employment, and in fact have often done so. When Henry Ford introduced the progressive assembly line into the American automobile industry in 1914, the result was a huge reduction in the number of labor hours required to produce a car. But the resulting ability to sell a Model T Ford for only $400 was a revolutionary event that resulted in an immense increase in employment in the automobile industry. The demand for cars turned out to be highly elastic. On the other hand, when demand is inelastic, labor-saving innovations reduce the demand for labor in that sector but shift demand elsewhere. The final employment impact of technological change cannot be confined to the sector (nor to the country) where it occurred—it is a problem in general equilibrium analysis, not partial equilibrium analysis.[4]

Third, as a more general matter, it seems to be much easier to anticipate the employment-displacing effects of technological change than the employment-expanding ones. Partly this is because we do not have a good technique for dealing with the impact of product innovation. The anticipation of the employment-expanding consequences of innovations seems to require a much greater exercise of the social imagination, an ability to foresee uses in entirely new social contexts. As I suggested earlier, no one seems to have correctly anticipated the immense commercial, educational, and entertainment uses to which the radio would be put in the twentieth century. In the 1950s, when the computer was still in its infancy, it was authoritatively predicted that all of America's future needs would be adequately catered to by fewer than a dozen computers. Even earlier, Thomas J. Watson, Sr., president of IBM and perhaps the most experienced person in the business, believed that a single computer (the Selective Sequence Electronic Calculator, built in 1947 and in operation at IBM's New York headquarters) "could solve all the important scientific problems in the world involving scientific calculations." He was reported to believe that computers had no commercial possibilities.[5] Even Thomas Edison, a true inventive genius, is said by one of his biographers to have anticipated that the phonograph would be used primarily to record the deathbed wishes of elderly gentlemen! The point is that it is extremely difficult to anticipate the impact of new innovations, because that impact is not obvious from the hardware itself. It depends, rather, on social uses and cultural contexts, on how society chooses to mobilize and to exploit the potential of a piece of hardware. No one seems to have anticipated the astonishing amount of information processing that would take place in our society when the productivity of the calculating technology was increased by a couple orders of magnitude.

Thus, there appears to be a systematic bias in perceptions about the future. This bias sharpens the awareness of possible job-reducing consequences of technological change but at the same time fails to identify the prospects for enlarged employment opportunities that flow from the ability to produce certain products more cheaply or to invent entirely new products with quite unanticipated uses and applications. A distinctive feature of western capitalism seems to have been the ability to produce very cheap variants of products that, in an earlier age, were consumed only by a small elite—nylon stockings for silk ones, ballpoint pens for Parker 51s, recorded stereophonic music for court musicians. In fact, we are still insufficiently aware of the extent to which sustained high rates of aggregate economic growth have depended on the continual introduction of new products to offset the retardation resulting from the slower rates of growth of older industries.

Equally important, discussions of the future impact of technological change that emphasize its net unemployment-generating effects have systematically ignored what has been perhaps the single most conspicuous feature of structural change in the American economy for several decades: the expansion of the service sector. That sector is now far and away the largest sector of the economy, employing more workers than the entire commodity-producing sector. In 1982, service occupations accounted for 74 percent of all employment. Indeed, the growth in employment in the United States since World War II has been overwhelmingly a growth in the service sector—86 percent of all employment growth has occurred in the service-producing sector. (There are more musicians in the American labor force than coal miners, and several times as many real estate agents.) Although certain aspects of the service sector have received a great deal of attention, e.g., the apparently much slower growth of productivity, far less attention has been given to the connections between technological change and service employment. The story is a complicated one; indeed, a large part of the problem is that it is a great many stories, since the service sector is a huge portmanteau comprising many very different kinds of activities. Moreover, the growth of that sector is not just a matter of technological change. Rather, it is a matter of technological change interacting in subtle ways with changes in the composition of consumers' expenditures as their incomes rise, and with changes associated, not only with the cheapening of certain services, but with highly significant changes of a qualitative nature as well.

There is no quick and easy way to summarize the changes that have occurred in the service sector in the past several decades. However, if we are to come to grips with the impact of technological change, we need to examine the very diverse experiences in the delivery of health care, education, recreation, retailing, insurance, finance, and government, both at federal and state and local levels. I only want to suggest to you, for the moment, the total arbitrariness of assuming that the outcome of these experiences is likely to be declining employment opportunities in the future.

CONCLUSION

Perhaps the end result of my discussion has been simply to persuade you that the reason we do so poorly at predicting the impact of technological change is that we are dealing with an extraordinarily complex and interdependent set of relationships. I would certainly not want to resist that conclusion. I would, however, want to insist that we should be able to do a somewhat better job of it in the future, if only by developing a better appreciation of some of the reasons why we have done so badly in the past. I hope this discussion has pointed in some helpful directions.

NOTES

1. Although Malthus certainly won the debate at the time, some of his opponents took positions that, in retrospect, seem remarkably farsighted. For example, William Godwin, in his book, *Of Population*, made the following fascinating observation in 1820: "Of all the sciences, natural or mechanical, which within the last half century have proceeded with such gigantic strides, chemistry is that which has advanced the most rapidly. All the substances that nature presents, all that proceeds from earth or air, is analyzed by us into its original elements. Thus we have discovered, or may discover, precisely what it is that nourishes the human body. And it is surely no great stretch of the faculty of anticipation, to say, that whatever man can decompose, man will be able to compound. The food that nourishes us, is composed of certain elements; and wherever these elements can be found, human art will hereafter discover the power of reducing them into a state capable of affording corporeal sustenance. No good reason can be assigned, why that which produces animal nourishment, must have previously passed through a process of animal or vegetable life. And, if a certain infusion of attractive exterior qualities is held necessary to allure us to our food, there is no reason to suppose that the most agreeable colours and scents and flavours may not be imparted to it, at a very small expense of vegetable substance. Thus it appears that, wherever earth, and water, and the other original chemical substances may be found, there human art may hereafter produce nourishment: and thus we are presented with a real infinite series of increase of the means of subsistence, to match Mr. Malthus's geometrical ratio for the multiplication of mankind." [William Godwin, *Of Population* (London: Longman, Hurst and Company, 1820), pp. 499–501.]

2. Peter Kakela, Iron ore: Energy, labor and capital changes with technology, *Science*, December 15, 1978.

3. The electric meter, it should be pointed out, was an extremely important complementary invention within the emerging electric power system. Before a satisfactory meter was developed, around 1900, meters were likely to be both very expensive and highly unreliable. As a result, flat-rate contracts were common, and consumers had no incentive to economize on the use of electricity. Moreover, in the absence of a meter, electric utilities had to undertake excessively large investments in generating and transmitting equipment.

4. It may be added that, in the present international context, new steps forward in automation may increase U.S. employment by repatriating activities that have moved offshore. Thus, the automation of a variety of labor-intensive assembly-line work may well bring back to the United States jobs that have recently migrated overseas in search of cheaper labor. Currently, in Silicon Valley, a number of industrial sectors are confronting the choice between robotics or overseas assembly.

5. Barbara G. Katz and Almarin Phillips, The computer industry, in Richard Nelson ed., *Government and Technical Progress* (New York: Pergamon Press, 1982), p. 171. See also William F. Sharpe, *The Economics of Computers* (New York: Columbia University Press, 1969), p. 185.

Macroeconomics, Technology, and Economic Growth: An Introduction to Some Important Issues

MICHAEL J. BOSKIN

It is incumbent on all of us to attempt to understand the relationship of macroeconomic policy, technical change, and economic growth much better than we do today and to make sure that this information, as it is generated, is used in the evaluation of economic policy.

This chapter provides an introduction to some important issues in the interrelationships among macroeconomics, technology, and economic growth. Too often, technology is taken for granted and assumed to be exogenous in the analysis of economists. Similarly, those concerned with technology complain about the macroeconomic environment and macroeconomic policy, but have neither the time nor the resources to analyze how the macroeconomy affects technological advances and subsequent economic growth. And among economists, there is substantial division of labor; macroeconomists have little interaction with those economists generally working on issues of technology, and neither of these groups has much interaction with growth economists.

My purpose in this chapter is to provide a heuristic, and impressionistic, introduction to various issues and events common to macroeconomics, technology, and economic growth. The next section presents a taxonomy of the major economic issues in macroeconomics: fluctuations in output, employment, and price levels; long-run trends in real economic growth; and issues in the composition of output. It suggests that while economic fluctuations may at times be induced by technological occurrences, and certainly the overall relative stability of the macroeconomy may influence investment in new technology and its dissemination, the major issues in economic fluctuations are probably less important for understanding the relationship between technology and economic growth than is an understanding of the details of the underlying long-run growth potential of the economy. It also argues that the relationship of technology and economic growth may be substantially affected by what might be called "second-tier macroeconomic policy": the composition of government spending among R&D and investment, on the one hand, and consumption and transfer payments, on the other; the structure of the tax system used to raise given levels of revenue; and the influence of monetary and fiscal policies on the private economy's decision making.

The discussion then turns to various debates in macroeconomics concerning the structure of the economy and the efficacy of economic policy. It introduces some important but subtle issues to the concerned noneconomist. Included are brief discussions of the economic history of the 1970s; current debates among Keynesians, monetarists, "new classical" macroeconomists, and supply-side economists; and my own tentative conclusions concerning some basic issues of macroeconomic policy.

The final section returns to the discussion of issues relating to technology and long-run economic growth and provides a partial research agenda on the subject of the macroeconomics of technology and economic growth, given the discussion in the preceding sections. It also points out that the microeconomics of technology and economic growth are likely to be at least as important as the macroeconomics thereof.

ISSUES IN MACROECONOMICS RELATED TO TECHNOLOGY

Macroeconomics—a study of the overall economy as opposed to that of a particular firm, market, or industry—primarily deals with three interrelated issues. First, macroeconomics is concerned with fluctuations in the overall economy, particularly fluctuations in output, employment, and the price level. Thus, it is concerned with the causes and consequences of inflation and recession. Analyses of this first issue invariably focus on policies to dampen the amplitude or decrease the frequency of such fluctuations. The primary policies on which such analyses focus are monetary policies (which affect the supply of money and credit to the economy) and fiscal policies (changes in the rate of government spending on goods and services or in taxes and debt). The primary controversies in macroeconomics concern the potential efficacy of monetary and fiscal policies (or a host of other policies) in controlling economic fluctuations. Based on alternative conceptual models, different evaluations of empirical (primarily econometric) analyses, and the study of historical experience, various schools of thought have developed concerning both the efficacy and the propriety of active use of monetary or fiscal policy in attempting to control economic fluctuations. Some of these different opinions are described below.

Second, macroeconomics is concerned with the long-run growth of the economy's potential and actual output. Just as bouts of inflation and persistent unemployment have motivated much of the study of economic fluctuations, so differentials in the growth of various measures of the standard of living motivate much of the analytic and empirical interest in economic growth. Across time in any country and across countries over any span of time, differences in growth rates, as in inflation and unemployment rates, can be substantial. This naturally spurs the scientific curiosity of growth economists. What factors are associated with differences in growth rates in the short or long run? And, as usual, not far behind the "positive" economist seeking to explain the observed economic phenomenon comes (often in the same person) the normative economist: How can we increase the growth rate? What is the optimal rate of economic growth? In my opinion, the study of economic growth is as important, if somewhat less suited to the short-run political time horizon, as that of economic fluctuations. Modest variations in growth rates compounded over, say, a generation or two, can drastically alter the nature of an economy and a society. One need only look at the performance of the United Kingdom relative to that of the United States, Germany, and France to realize how easy it is for a society to transform itself from the wealthiest on earth to a relatively poor member of the advanced economies.

The studies of economic growth usually attempt to decompose the rate of growth of real GNP—or some related measure—into the contributions of various factors thought to explain it. These include such factors as increased labor input, increased capital per worker, improved resource allocation, and a general category labeled "technical change." If we are examining the ability of the economy to improve standards of living per capita, for example, then the growth of real GNP per worker will depend heavily on the capital-labor ratio, the rate of technical change, the rate of improvement in the quality of the labor force, and other factors.

The phrase "economic growth" is often misused in political and media discussions. Often, these discussions are concerned with growth over a few quarters, perhaps from the trough of a recession. An economist focusing on the long-term growth rate has a much longer time horizon and attempts to "net out" cyclical fluctuations. For example, it turns out that increases in real per capita income over the last century in the best-performing advanced economies have averaged a little less than 2 percent per year. While this number is substantially larger in less-developed countries during periods of rapid growth, let us take something like 1.5 to 2 percent as a range of reasonable long-run growth performance. Now, compound real per capita income over two generations in two hypothetical, initially identical economies at 1.5 percent and at 2 percent, respectively. The more rapidly growing economy becomes one-third again as wealthy as the less rapidly growing economy. Thus, we are evaluating differences of fractions of a percentage point in the long-term growth rate in attempting to assess our growth performance. Increasing the growth rate (at minimal opportunity costs) permanently by a few tenths of a percentage point may not sound very exciting, but it is an enormous economic and social achievement.

Policies designed to alter the rate of economic growth directly tend to focus on enhancing technological advances, the quality of the labor force, and the level or rate of growth of capital per worker. It is important to note that the only way to raise the long-run growth rate permanently is to increase the rate of technical change or to increase the rate at which the quality of the labor force is improved. Loosely, the rate of technical change is affected by R&D expenditures, and the rate of improvement of the quality of the labor force is affected by investment in human capital, such as education and training. A policy that can lead to higher levels of income and a temporarily higher growth rate is one that increases the capital-labor ratio (for example, by increasing the rate of investment and net capital formation). But such a policy will lead only temporarily to a higher growth rate, although it will lead permanently to a higher level of income. This is not just semantics. The situation is described in Figure 1, in which we see the economy's original growth path (labeled 1), given its presumed (for the moment exogenous) constant rate of technical change. Real per capita income grows at the rate of technical change and labor-quality improvement, given the capital-labor ratio. Now along comes a policy, perhaps tax policy, that increases the desired capital stock of firms (or perhaps more accurately, the desired wealth of the population, relative to levels of income). This leads to an investment boom for a span of years, which will cause a spurt in the short-run growth rate along the dotted path in Figure 1 until we get to the new long-run growth path (labeled 2). Note that the level of per capita income is permanently higher along (2) than on growth path (1), but that once the transition to the new growth path is complete, the rate of economic growth (given by the slope of the output curve) returns to the original rate given by the underlying factors of the rate of technical change and improvement in labor-force quality.

Anticipating somewhat the discussion below, one is immediately struck by the issue of what caused this rate of technical change. Clearly, it has not been constant; this is just a convenient abstraction. But is it really exogenous? Are there economic policies that can permanently affect it? Are those policies worth the cost of enacting them (for example, foregoing some current consumption in order to finance R&D expenditures)? I shall return to this issue below. But it is already clear that technology lies at the heart of the second great issue in macroeconomics.

Another concern involves the relationship of these two issues of macroeconomics. Is it the case that, in an economy subject to wider swings, to booms and busts, than occur in a more stable economy, the rate of technical change is likely to be systematically different and that, therefore, controlling

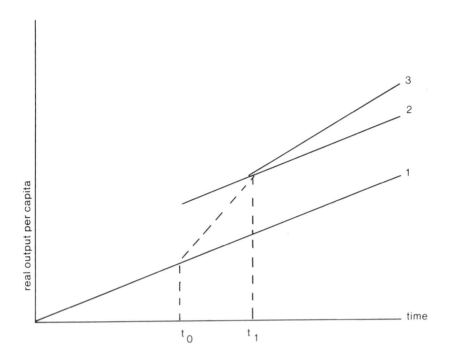

t_0:   proinvestment policy leads to higher capital formation and transition to higher level of income.

t_1:   economy resumes long-run growth rate or, through interaction of investment and technical change, moves to more rapid growth path.

FIGURE 1   Alternative growth paths: technical change and capital formation.

economic fluctuations, if it is possible, might increase or decrease the long-run underlying rate of growth? And is it possible that in an economy with an environment which promotes long-term growth and rapid technological advance, more severe economic fluctuations are more likely? Or less likely? Does the promotion of technological change imply greater flexibility in adapting our institutions to technical change? Or, does it imply greater short-term disruption in the economy?

Finally, a host of policies designed to protect jobs or the capital in particular industries (e.g., tariffs, government loans, and other subsidies) may impede the adoption of new technology in favor of the short-term goal of mitigating the economic distress caused by economic fluctuations or industry- or region-specific foreign competition.

While economic growth is good for the population as a whole, its benefits accrue unevenly. Much of our economic policy is designed to promote equity or spread the cost of economic disruption more evenly. Sometimes, unfortunately, these noble goals result in policies that impede growth.

The third major issue in macroeconomics—closely related to the two above—concerns the composition of the various components of aggregate output, such as consumption, investment, government expenditures, and net exports. Factors primarily affecting (in the first round) any of these major components of GNP obviously also potentially affect the level of aggregate demand and, therefore, the fluctuations in output, employment, and the price level. It is likely that the policies that most directly affect the generation of new technology, and therefore long-term growth, occur here, one layer down from aggregate GNP, at the level of the components of spending in the economy. For example, while some people still focus on the level of real government spending in the control of economic fluctuations, the composition of that spending among research and development expenditures and physical and human investment, versus payments to individuals for income support, net interest, and purchases on noninvestment types of goods and services, obviously can affect the rate of technical change. Probably the most important of these is direct government support of research and development. Table 1 presents data on recent trends in federal government expenditures on R&D, physical investment, and other categories of government spending. As can be seen from the table, current real government spending on R&D and real government physical investment are both substantially lower as a percentage of GNP than in the 1960s, although defense investment and defense R&D have made something of a comeback in the last few years.

Tax policies make up a second set of policies that, by affecting the way in which the private sector utilizes its resources, can affect the generation of new technology. Again, the first major issue, economic fluctuations, tends to focus on the aggregate level of taxes and changes in total tax receipts. But the structure of the tax system can affect substantially the rate of investment in the economy and the rate of R&D spending by changing the costs of such spending relative to other activities a firm might use to produce its current or prospective new product, and the methods by which it does so. Recent examples include a series of changes in depreciation schedules beginning in 1954, the investment tax credit introduced in 1962, the various swings in the differential treatment of long-term capital gains, and the R&D tax credit, to name but a few.

Monetary policy also can affect the composition of output, as well as the level of aggregate demand in the economy. Monetary policy potentially affects the before-tax cost of capital, interest rates and their term structure, and thus, the real cost of embarking on R&D or investment projects.

Finally, it is important to note some potential interactions among major categories of spending and the rate of technical change. Either of two

TABLE 1 Federal Outlays by Category, Selected Years (billions of constant 1972 dollars; percentage of GNP in parentheses)

Fiscal Year	Total Outlays	Physical Investment		Grants-in-Aid	R&D		Payments to Individuals	Net Interest	All Others
		Defense	Nondefense		Defense	Nondefense			
1949	85.3 (17.3)	4.0 (0.8)	1.8 (0.4)	0.9 (0.2)	2.0 (0.4)	0.5 (0.1)	17.6 (3.6)	8.4 (1.7)	50.4 (10.2)
1958	135.3 (19.9)	25.2 (3.7)	1.9 (0.3)	2.8 (0.5)	4.7 (0.7)	1.4 (0.2)	30.1 (4.4)	8.4 (1.2)	60.8 (8.9)
1968	224.6 (21.2)	30.2 (2.9)	3.4 (0.3)	7.6 (0.7)	11.4 (1.1)	10.2 (1.0)	60.1 (5.7)	13.5 (1.3)	88.1 (8.3)
1978	300.4 (20.9)	15.8 (1.1)	4.4 (0.3)	11.0 (0.8)	7.6 (0.5)	7.9 (0.5)	144.7 (10.0)	23.6 (1.6)	85.4 (5.9)
1984	363.5 (22.2)	31.3 (1.9)	3.2 (0.2)	9.0 (0.5)	11.4 (0.7)	5.9 (0.4)	182.0 (11.1)	44.6 (2.7)	76.1 (4.6)

SOURCE: Office of Management and Budget, *Budget of the United States* (Washington, D.C.: U.S. Government Printing Office, selected years).

appealing but difficult-to-document conjectures would imply that a society with a high investment rate would not only have a temporarily high growth rate in its transition to a higher growth path (as in Figure 1) but actually could increase the long-run rate of growth. These are the so-called learning-by-doing and embodiment hypotheses. The former reflects the anecdotal notion that in the process of investment we learn new ways of doing things, such as new production processes, and new potential products become known. Thus, the rate of investment affects the rate of technical change in a positive manner. This process is displayed by growth path number (3) in Figure 1. At the microeconomic level, consider the options opening up in the course of a major project, e.g., oil exploration in the frozen tundra or the ocean depths. Just as new technologies arise—sometimes—to meet such challenges, the rate of technical advance may depend on the level of investment. The embodiment hypothesis entails the notion that it is much too expensive to embody new technology in old capital by converting it and, therefore, that the rate at which new technology really does augment the productivity of labor and machinery will depend on the rate at which new capital is generated, i.e., our investment rate. I shall return to these issues below.

Thus, three very important issues in macroeconomics, which concern the short- and long-run standard of living of our citizens, drive much of our economic policy. They are concerned with economic fluctuations, long-run growth, and a detailed examination of the composition of output. The three issues are interrelated in many ways, only some of which have been hinted at in this discussion. Underlying each issue is the current state of technology and the rate at which new technology enables us to produce more goods and services with the same labor input. Before turning to a more detailed discussion of some of these growth issues and a partial research agenda, I want to develop a framework for analyzing, or at least a perspective on, some of the different schools of thought in macroeconomics that get so much press attention.

CHANGING VIEWS ON A CHANGING ECONOMY: ALLEGED CRISIS IN ECONOMICS

Macroeconomic analysis underwent significant changes in the 1970s as the prevailing Keynesian theories were found wanting in accounting for emerging economic events. Keynesian economics placed great faith in the government's ability to "fine-tune" the economy through aggregate demand management—which means constant adjustments in the level of taxes, government spending, and the money supply. Keynesian analysis stressed the importance of the multiplier effect and the short-run trade-off between inflation and unemployment, popularly known as the Phillips Curve. In the Keynesian perspective, policymakers could simply direct policy to achieve the most desired combination of unemployment and inflation rates, e.g., they could maintain low unemployment by accepting some fixed, stable level of inflation. Unfortunately, events both worldwide and in the United States in the past 15 years have demonstrated the naiveté of these Keynesian models and policy prescriptions.

While there is no single model of the economy around which consensus can be reached, substantial strides have been made in improving our understanding of the operation of the economy, which is much more complex and subtle than had been presumed in earlier models. Since the economic events of the 1970s were so important to the decline in the acceptance of earlier models, there follows a whirlwind tour of the economic history of the 1970s.

Economic Events of the 1970s

The most important economic event from the late 1960s to the early part of this decade was the tremendous slowdown in economic growth. In the decade from 1973 to 1983, the standard of living for most working, taxpaying Americans improved hardly at all. This contrasts with the roughly 2 percent per year growth in real per capita income discussed above and the 2.5 percent per year growth in the period 1948 to 1973 in the United States. While the cause of the slowdown is disputed, its consequences are not: it was without a doubt, for example, a major cause of the tax revolt. Among explanations advanced for the slowdown are reduced sector-specific rates of technical change, a slowing rate of increase in the capital-labor ratio, energy price increases, changes in the legal environment, shifts in the economy toward services, and changes in the age and sex composition of the labor force. One major school of thought, to which I subscribe, is that a major culprit in the slowdown was the decline in the incentives to produce income and wealth. Reasons for these declining incentives include rising marginal tax rates, especially on the return on saving and investment; high and rising inflation, which greatly increased uncertainty about the returns on investment and saving; and the growth of government regulation. Undoubtedly, many other causes of the slowdown in growth and, by implication, potential remedies to restore our long-term growth can be found and defended; an exact allocation of the slowdown by cause is still a subject of some dispute, and additional research on the subject continues to be a high priority.

To place some of these issues in perspective, recall that the 1950s through mid-1960s were years of relatively low inflation, about 2 percent per year, on average. Substantial inflation occurred in the United States primarily with the removal of price controls at the end of wars. We have not experienced anything like the hyperinflation that ravaged Central Europe in the 1920s or the substantial inflation recently experienced in Latin America and Israel. Indeed, by international and historical standards, our inflation was quite modest. But recall that our current 4 percent inflation is down from double-digit rates in 1979–1980. To place this in perspective, President Nixon imposed wage and price controls when inflation was no higher than current levels.

Certainly the energy price shocks in the 1970s caused a substantial disruption in our economy—most importantly, a transfer of wealth from American consumers of energy to producers outside the United States. Although these price shocks and our reaction to them probably contributed to the inflation, increases in energy prices caused no more than 3 percentage points of the double-digit inflation rate in 1979–1980. It was only a few years ago that both economists and politicians understated the cost of high and fluctuating inflation and oversold its benefits in permanently reducing unemployment. It was common to argue that we could learn to live with double-digit inflation merely by indexing various features of our contracts, tax system, and the like. Numerous studies, however, such as those by Martin Feldstein, Stanley Fischer, and Franco Modigliani, illustrated how inflation distorts incentives and increases uncertainty about future returns.

The 1970s destroyed the notion of a stable Phillips Curve relationship between inflation and unemployment. If there ever was a short-run tradeoff, conditions for it have worsened considerably, and it is probably simply a statistical artifact.

Government spending increased substantially in the United States in the 1970s, but more significant was the change in its composition, both by level of government and by type of expenditure. By the late 1970s, exclusive of interest on the national debt, the federal government was spending more on transfer payments to individuals than on purchases of goods and services (see Table 1). By dollar volume, the federal government's major role by 1980 was to redistribute income, not provide goods and services. While the result was a sharp reduction in poverty, the cost was staggering because the benefits were not targeted very effectively toward the poor. Accompanying the growth of spending, was the large increase in effective marginal tax rates—the tax paid on incremental income. The fraction of American taxpayers subject to high marginal tax rates quadrupled between 1966 and 1980. No longer were high marginal tax rates exclusively the right of the rich.

While somewhat controversial with respect to measurement problems, the rates of saving and investment in the United States, I believe, have declined substantially, and, in addition, there has been a bias toward shorter-lived assets. The share of GNP devoted to net nonresidential investment fell from the already dangerously low level of 7 percent in the 1950s and 1960s to only 2 percent in the late 1970s. It fell precisely at a time in which it should have been rising to equip the additional (primarily young and inexperienced) 20 million workers with the capital and technology to make them productive.

While unemployment remains a problem, an amazing achievement of our economy in the 1970s was that we absorbed 20 million additional workers into the labor force. This influx occurred primarily because of the maturing of the baby-boom generation and the substantial increase in the number of second earners in families, primarily working women.

Other major structural changes occurred in the U.S. economy. Besides the demographic bulge described above, the changes included a shift in output away from manufacturing to services, the growth of world trade (sparked by various rounds of tariff reductions), the move from fixed to flexible exchange rates, and the energy price shocks.

Economic policy was also changing. The Kennedy-Johnson tax cut of 1964 was the first major attempt to manage aggregate demand when the economy was not even in a recession. The growth rate was too low, it was argued, and a tax cut could stimulate it. In the early 1960s, inflation in various sectors was dealt with by federal jawboning and threats, such as the proposal to dump excess supplies of government commodities onto the market if prices rose too rapidly. The Federal Reserve Board through 1979 continued activist attempts at managing demand through frequent changes in monetary policy.

The 1970s were also marked by schemes to control wages and prices in an attempt to control modest inflation, such as the administrative bureaucracy spawned by various guidelines under the Carter administration. The notion that you could hold down wages and prices and control inflation through moral suasion and presidential support for cooperation between businessmen and unions was at best naive. Thousands of price decisions are made daily and an attempt to keep a large subset of them under control would have led to a governmental nightmare—so costly as to be beyond any possible gain. Since only about 20 percent of our labor force is unionized, it was strange to believe that hammering the wage demands of the larger unions could be the primary method of controlling inflation.

The 1970s also saw the growth of government regulation of energy matters and new social regulations that attempted to correct perceived market failures in such areas as pollution, safety, and health. Fortunately, a general move to deregulation in traditionally regulated activities began in the late 1970s under President Carter.

Where were we headed with these economic policies? It is useful to recall various proposals made only a few years ago. One example is the proposal for a national reconstruction bank to help revitalize American industry. An appointed group of business and labor leaders would decide where tens of billions of dollars of badly needed capital would be allocated. Fortunately, we were saved from such a policy, perhaps by the results of the election of 1980. One need only look at recent attempts in the United Kingdom, New Zealand, Mexico, and France, among others, to gain some perspective on direct government capital allocation schemes.

Closely connected was the call for industrial policies, that is, that the government should target specific industries with subsidies and tax breaks. We certainly have a de facto industrial policy through the interaction of our monetary, fiscal, regulatory, and trade policies, but this call for industrial policy would have elevated it to a national priority and enormously raised the stakes in the potential government misallocation of resources.

In summary, the 1970s were years of very poor economic growth, rising inflation, and major changes in the role of government in the economy. Attempts at active demand management led to disappointing outcomes, and the desire for incomes policies and controls became stronger as inflation accelerated. Continuation of the policies of the 1970s hardly seemed the best way to deal with our economic dilemma. Our fundamental problem was how to increase long-run growth and, at the same time, improve living standards for the general population, along with general resources for a humane social safety net and a necessary defense buildup. This would require action on a number of levels. On one level were actions to restore incentives to produce income and wealth, which implied reducing inflation substantially (probably through monetary policy); reducing marginal tax rates, especially those on capital income; reducing the relative size of government; and increasing private resources for investment, saving, and research and development. Other necessary measures would remove tax distortions and reform regulation. This, the argument went, would lead to increased saving and investment, generation of new technology, and increased growth in future productivity. But this is a long-run process. No one had a right to believe that this could be accomplished quickly—or that higher productivity growth would come immediately. Nor was it sensible to believe that disinflation could be achieved painlessly.

By any economic standards, the 1970s was the worst decade since the Great Depression. This poor performance led to substantial intellectual ferment in economics and to various new lines of reasoning and schools of thought. Let us explore these briefly, since they form so much of the lexicon of current discussion.

Economic Schools of Thought

The simplest Keynesian analysis postulates that spending decisions are based on short-term economic variables, for example, consumer spending is a function of current disposable income. While this postulation is elaborated in the permanent-income model of Friedman and in the life-cycle hypothesis of Modigliani, most policy analysts working in the Keynesian tradition focus on current disposable income as the variable influencing spending decisions. It is also argued that a reduction in taxes, by increasing disposable income, could lead consumers to spend more and, through the famous multiplier effect, further expand GNP. Similar analyses are made of increases in government spending, or business tax cuts, or monetary policy designed to increase investment spending. In simplest terms, any gap between actual GNP and the economy's potential GNP can be closed by stimulation of demand through fiscal and/or monetary policy.

While Keynesian thought was dominating economic policymaking in the United States and Western Europe during the past several decades, another "school of thought," generally called monetarism, led by Milton Friedman, was emphasizing the role of changes in the rate of growth of the money supply in predicting fluctuations in short-term, real economic activity. The monetarists also tended to be skeptical about active demand management, and they tended to advocate nondiscretionary rules to guide both monetary and fiscal policy, rather than continuously applied discretion aimed at fine-tuning the economy. While the monetarists remained a minority, their critique of the dominant Keynesian analyses did succeed in influencing the Keynesians to expand their attention to the role of money in the economy and to monetary policy.

The most important intellectual development occurred in the late 1960s when Friedman and Edmund Phelps caused a major change in macroeconomic thought by arguing that despite the traditional short-run, Phillips Curve trade-off between inflation and unemployment, a "natural rate" of unemployment made it impossible to have a permanent trade-off between them. The natural rate was the point at which inflation neither accelerated nor decelerated. When unemployment was driven below the natural rate, inflation would accelerate.

Most Keynesians eventually conceded this long-run neutrality of money. They still argued, however, that some gains in employment could be achieved by accepting more inflation and that a primary goal of economic policy should be to improve the inflation-unemployment trade-off. This led to some of the incomes policies and suggestions discussed above.

The Friedman-Phelps hypothesis is extended and elaborated in work by Robert Lucas, Thomas Sargent, Robert Barro, and others. These contributions have come to be called the "new classical" macroeconomics. Lucas emphasized the fact that economic agents (firms, workers, investors, consumers), tend to get confused in the very short-run between changes in relative and absolute prices. For example, a general price rise caused by excessive money growth might be mistaken for higher wage rates, and thus lead to a temporary increase in labor supply and output. The new classical macroeconomists, building on the work of John Muth on rational expectations, were very skeptical about the efficacy of demand management. Eventually, economic agents will include their best guesses about future economic policy—for example, countercyclical action on the part of monetary or fiscal authorities—in their decisions and, thus, these policies will be rendered ineffective as long as they are anticipated. The new classical macroeconomists conflict with Keynesian analysis in their judgment of the fluidity of market adjustments, the extent to which a full set of markets exists, whether markets clear quickly at competitive prices, the length of information and recognition lags, and how expectations are formed.

Clearly, the failure of Keynesian theory to explain the major economic problems of the 1970s was a compelling reason for the emergence and acceptance of at least some components of new classical macroeconomics. Many of the new analyses stress the importance of a longer time horizon, the role of expectations, and the role of incentives in the behavior of firms and households, and therefore, the overall economy.

Focusing on expectations and time horizons has important implications for both monetary and fiscal policies. Consider what happens when an activist (Keynesian) demand-manager uses a particular short-run macroeconometric model (call it Model A) to guide the choice of money growth over, for example, a decade. As Lucas (1981) notes:

If we can see that Model A gives us an inaccurate view of the "long-run," then we have conceded that it leads us to bad short-run decisions because these decisions are sufficient to dictate our long-run situations as well. (This is not a hypothetical story of the 1980s, is it? It is a history of the 1970s.)

A parallel critique of the efficacy of tax cuts to spur spending was elaborated by Barro in the so-called Ricardian equivalence theorem. Briefly, the argument is that for a given level of government spending, a tax cut really does not increase the wealth of consumers, but merely postpones their taxes, because the present value of future taxes to pay the interest on the new debt will equal the size of the tax cut. Under some fairly strong assumptions about the types of taxes available to the economy, bequest behavior, and other things, Barro demonstrates that there will be no changes in spending and, therefore, no stimulative effect through fiscal policy. Note the impact of expected future taxes and the desire to undo a shift of liabilities to future generations by spending less oneself and increasing bequests. Thus, while only illustrative, the work of the new classical macroeconomists casts considerable doubt on the traditional fiscal and monetary remedies for fine-tuning the economy's fluctuations.

While Keynesians, monetarists, and new classical macroeconomists were debating the efficacy of demand management in controlling economic fluctuations, a substantial amount of research has also addressed the effects of economic policies on incentives to work, save, and invest. The work of Feldstein, Jorgenson, Heckman, Hall, Hausman, and Boskin, among many others, has revealed that changes in real after-tax returns to saving, investment, and labor supply have had far greater incentive effect on those factors of production than had previously been thought. These studies and others gradually began to have some influence in macroeconomics, as relative prices, as opposed to just short-run income flows, began to be included in the analyses. The change in emphasis away from short-term cash flows to relative prices and away from aggregate demand management to concern about the economy's potential to produce more output and the increasing concern over the slowdown in productivity growth brought with them the name "supply-side economics." The effects of taxes, inflation, and other government policies on the factors of supply are complex. The studies in the 1970s and early 1980s form the empirical base for supply-side economics and the counter to the Keynesian argument that the level and structure of tax rates, as well as other policy variables, were of only second-order importance relative to the size of the tax take. Supply-side economics was oversold by many in the recent political-economic history of the United States. There never was evidence that the response to a broad across-the-board tax cut, for example, would be large or immediate enough to be self-financing. Debates continue about how large these incentive effects are and how quickly they occur, i.e., what policies will get the biggest bang for the buck. Thus, the growth and productivity slowdown, and new theoretical and empirical research by economists, shifted emphasis in economics toward renewed attention to what was, after all, its original question: the causes and consequences of long-term economic growth.

Before turning to a partial research agenda concerning the macroeconomy, technology, and economic growth, let me just add that in addition to the intramural disputes among Keynesians, monetarists, new classical macroeconomists, and supply-side growth advocates, a very important set of developments occurred that have influenced the thinking of economists about both short-run economic fluctuations and long-run issues. This is the tremendous internationalization of both trade and capital flows.

Until recently, the overwhelming majority of economic analyses, whether Keynesian or monetarist, with or without rational expectations, were done in the context of closed economies. The conclusions of many of the traditional analyses are subject to substantial alteration when one opens up the economy to trade and capital flows. For example, the stimulative impact of fiscal policy, quite aside from any Ricardian equivalence issues, is substantially dampened if there are rapid movements of capital in response to interest differentials and substantial trade responses to changes in relative prices of currencies. For example, consider an economy, such as that of the United States, in which taxes are cut to stimulate aggregate demand. The full impact of the demand stimulus will be offset substantially because the deficit will cause a small increase in interest rates, attract foreign capital, appreciate the dollar, and deteriorate net exports. Indeed, in the 1981–1982 recession, fully 47 percent of the decline in U.S. real GNP was in net exports! Thus, the demand stimulus will be substantially offset.

Also, the substantial flows of capital put a severe brake on the extent to which, at least in the short term, fiscal policies (such as deficit financing of government spending) will drive up interest rates, since as interest rates start to rise, foreign capital will be attracted and domestic capital will remain home, thereby offsetting some of the drag in capital markets caused by the deficit. Currently, for example, fully one-half of the huge federal government deficit is being offset by foreign capital flowing into the United States and less U.S. private capital flowing abroad. How long this will continue no one knows, but it is a stark reminder that, at least in the short run, analyses based on a closed economy can be substantially mistaken.

RECENT ECONOMIC POLICY

While the reduction in inflation and marginal tax rates, the increased investment and saving incentives in the 1981–1982 tax reforms, and reordered budget priorities are substantial achievements, much remains to be done to improve the prospects for long-run growth. Our budget dilemma may ultimately cause severe problems for capital formation, and there is a possibility that the pro-capital-formation tax changes may be repealed. Much controversy surrounds the likely impact of large current and prospective budget deficits on capital formation and growth.

Table 2 shows the base-line budget projections of the Congressional Budget Office, assuming no changes in the laws governing taxes or entitlement spending and including the off-budget spending of $15 billion. (Just to give an idea of the problems in government budgeting, we now have an official category called off-budget spending, though it is only a minute fraction of the total off-budget spending!) But the government does numerous other things that do not get included in the category of off-budget spending. Also shown in Table 2 is the debt held by the public as a percentage of GNP and

TABLE 2 Base-line Budget Projections, Congressional Budget Office (fiscal year)

	1983 Actual	1984 Actual	1985 Base	1986	1987	1988	1989
Total deficit,[a]							
$ billions	208	185	214	215	233	249	272
Deficit as % of GNP	6.4	5.2	5.6	5.2	5.2	5.1	5.2
Debt held by public,							
as % of GNP	35.4	36.7	39.6	41.8	44.0	46.0	47.9

NOTE: Assumes no change in laws governing taxes or entitlement spending.
[a]Includes off-budget deficit of $15 billion or 0.3 percent of GNP per year.
SOURCE: Congressional Budget Office, *The Economic and Budget Outlook, Fiscal Years 1985–1989* (Washington, D.C., Feb. 1984).

TABLE 3 Long-term Social Security and Medicare Deficits (Effect of 1983 Amendments on Actuarial Balance of OASDI and Medicare, Alternative Assumptions, 75-year Period, percent of taxable payroll)

	Pre-1983 Amendments	1983 Amendments, Intermediate Assumptions	Indexing of Taxable Amounts or Dissipation of Surplus	Indexing and Dissipation of Surplus
Social Security	−1.80	0.02	−0.60	−1.20
Medicare	−5.21	−5.21	−5.21	−5.21
Total	−7.01	−5.19	−5.81	−6.41

SOURCE: Author's calculations and 1983 *Annual Report of the Trustees of the Social Security Administration.*

how it is expected to rise under current law. Clearly these are very large deficits. The administration forecasts much lower deficits, partly because it is somewhat more optimistic about what it is going to be able to do on the spending side, and because it assumes that interest rates will fall substantially over the next few years (down to 5 percent). If you take the administration's forecast for the 1989 or 1990 budget and assume that interest rates are going to be what they are today, you would add about $70 billion to that fiscal year's deficit.

Lest anyone think our current fiscal dilemma will be resolved in the course of this decade and that we can then breathe a deep sign of relief, we have impending a major conundrum with respect to the financing of our Social Security and Medicare systems (see Table 3). (Recall that we had a major, bipartisan Social Security reform in 1983.) Table 3 shows the Social Security and Medicare deficits before the 1983 amendments and the Social Security actuaries' intermediate assumptions, and other measures. The Social Security actuaries make assumptions about economic growth, inflation, unemployment, life expectancy, fertility, how many workers there will be relative to the number of retirees, and other such things, and from those they calculate the likely future condition of the retirement fund, disability fund, and the hospital-insurance fund that is part of Social Security (Medicare). Prior to 1983 the Old Age and Survivor Disability Insurance (OASDI) Fund, commonly called Social Security, was running an average 1.8 percent deficit over the 75-year projection period as a fraction of taxable payroll. On average, that 75-year projection includes a deficit in the 1980s, a huge surplus in retirement and disability funds starting in about 1990 that will run for about 25 years and then start to decline, and then an absolutely enormous deficit when the baby-boom generation retires early in the next century. So that 1.8 percent average masks deficits of 5 to 8 percent in the year 2030 and surpluses in the retirement and disability funds that are projected to build up to 5 to 7 times outlays by 2015. Prior to the 1983 amendments, it was not commonly pointed out that the long-term deficit in Medicare was several times that in retirement and disability. That is primarily because the tax rate for Medicare was very low and not scheduled to rise as the tax rate was for retirement and also because of the presumed increase in the cost of medical care.

The 1.8 percent deficit disappears under the intermediate assumptions (col. 2 in Table 3). But the 1983 amendments did two things that are going to be extremely difficult to live by politically. One is that we are now taxing Social Security benefits for well-off retirees. Half of a retiree's Social Security benefits are included in taxable income at an income of above $32,000 a year. But that number is not indexed. So eventually we are going to be taxing middle-class retirees, and it is unclear to me that we will be able to avoid indexing the exempt amounts. If we index the exempt amount we will lose about a third of the financial solvency we gained in the OASDI system.

Second, we should also remember that our Social Security system has never been able to run a surplus. As soon as we start running substantial surpluses we have either raised the benefits or, less commonly, lowered tax rates. The results will be very interesting if we keep the funds separate and do not allow the retirement fund to bail out Medicare when it starts running very large deficits in the next decade. If we do keep the funds separate, as was originally intended, we could use the surplus to try to dissipate the need for a huge Social Security tax increase early in the next century. If we do that, we are going to see, as I mentioned, a surplus in OASDI of 5 to 7 years of Social Security benefits. It will be such a large surplus that it may equal the national debt; indeed, the Social Security Administration may own all the government bonds. If we did still better and ran a higher surplus or we brought some spending under control, we would have to ask ourselves whether we want the Social Security system to start owning other assets, such as corporate shares. But have no fear. Medicare will bail us out of that dilemma. We face enormous long-term deficits in Medicare, deficits that will test not only our political acumen but the moral fiber of our country in the next 20 years.

What are the impacts of budgets and deficits on investment, technical changes, and growth? First, I think all economists would agree that, ultimately, at full employment, large deficits, net of the interest component (the so-called primary deficit), relative to the size of the economy that run for a very long period *must be inflationary*. There is no need for the current budget deficit to be inflationary for the next year or two. But if we run primary deficits of several percent of GNP for a very long period, some strange things are going to happen. To analyze that, examine Table 4. This table indicates where the ratio of privately held federal government national debt (what is called debt held by the public or by the private sector as opposed to the Federal Reserve and government agencies) to GNP is headed if we continue to run deficits as a share of GNP, net of the interest component, of several percent and run the real interest rates and growth rates that are being forecast.

TABLE 4 Some U.S. Fiscal Episodes

	1975–1979[a]	1984–1989	
		CBO Baseline	Administration
D_o	23.4%		37%
d, average	3.7	1.8	1.4
g, average	3.5	3.8	4.0
i (net of monetization)	6.0		
GNP deflator	7.2		
r	−1.2	3.6	2.4
g − r	4.7	0.2	1.6
D_e	79%	900%	88%

NOTE: Let D represent the debt-GNP ratio, d the deficit (net of interest)-GNP ratio, r the real interest rate, and g the growth of real GNP. Then, by definition,

$$D_t = d_t + (r_t - g_t)dt;$$

for a fiscal program with constant d and constant r and g, D will evolve toward an equilibrium D_e (if g > r) of

$$D_e = \frac{d}{g - r}.$$

[a]D_t declined steadily from World War II to 1974.

The ratio of the federal government debt to GNP evolves over time depending on this primary deficit and the relationship of the real rate of interest and the growth rate. For example, if we start out with a positive national debt, and the real interest paid on the national debt exceeds the growth rate, then the interest payments will grow more rapidly than GNP, and if nothing else has changed, eventually the interest payments, in an explosive pattern, will gobble up all of the budget, then all of GNP, then all of national wealth. In the more usual case of the growth rate's exceeding the rate of interest, the debt-GNP ratio will evolve according to the equation

$$D/GNP = d + (r - g)dt.$$

Thus, the equilibrium ratio of the debt to GNP, given constant primary deficit (d), real interest rate (r), and growth rate (g), is simply given by d/(g − r).

Table 4 presents some estimates of two recent major fiscal episodes in the United States. First, we see the substantial increase in the equilibrium debt-GNP ratio toward which we were headed if fiscal policy had not been changed in the 1975–1979 period, a period generally regarded as the beginning of the increase of the ratio of debt to GNP after the substantial postwar decline in this ratio. Second, and more important for this discussion, we see where we are headed starting currently. We can see that under current projections the ratio of debt to GNP is heading toward an equilibrium that is many times, not only current GNP, but the ratio of the entire value of the capital stock of the United States to GNP! This latter number is around three, so it is clear that either the private sector will have to increase its wealth-income ratio by

TABLE 5 Effective Tax Rates for All Assets, 1965–1982, Selected Years

	Auerbach[a]	Hulten-Robertson[b]
1965	35.7	26.3
1970	49.7	52.3
1975	37.0	32.1
1980	31.9	33.1
1981	17.7	4.7
1982	24.6	15.8

[a]Alan Auerbach, Corporate taxation in the United States, *Brookings Papers on Economic Activity*, Vol. 2 (Washington, D.C.: The Brookings Institution, 1983). Auerbach assumes a 4 percent real after-tax rate of return and forecasts inflation based on past values.

[b]C. Hulten and J. Robertson, *Corporate Tax Policy and Economic Growth*, Urban Institute Discussion Paper (Washington, D.C.: The Urban Institute, December 1982). These estimates assume a 4 percent real after-tax rate of return and, for 1981 and 1982, a 6 percent rate of inflation.

an enormous increase in saving, or the rest of the world will have to buy up the T-bills that we float, or if neither of these alternatives is available and we persist in our current fiscal policies for the indefinite future, the Federal Reserve will have to buy up the bonds as the lender of last resort, thereby re-igniting inflation. Can we reasonably expect foreigners to continue to finance our deficits ad infinitum? I believe it would be imprudent of us to operate on the assumption that this is possible, let alone desirable. Eventually, foreign firms and individuals will have a progressively higher fraction of their wealth in dollar-denominated assets, which will mean that further increases in dollar-denominated assets will be even more risky. Thus, we can expect the flow of foreign capital into the United States, *ceteris paribus*, to slow. Nor do I foresee such a huge increase in our saving rate as to increase the capital output ratio by such a large amount. In short, the current fiscal policy, if continued, is either inflationary or unsustainable. This does not mean that we have no time whatsoever to deal with the problem, but the longer we delay in cutting spending or adopting a last-resort tax increase, the worse the problem will become as the interest burden rises still further.

Thus, my conclusion is that while we had an investment boomlet in the United States in 1984, largely as a result of the proinvestment tax policies enacted in the 1981 tax laws, eventually our large deficits will crowd out our own investment. Currently, they are probably playing some role in crowding out our net exports.

Table 5 indicates the decline in effective tax rates on marginal investment due to the Economic Recovery Tax Act (ERTA) of 1981 and the Tax Equity and Fiscal Responsibility Act (TEFRA) of 1982. This decrease was substantial and must be part of the explanation for the resurgence, once out of the recession, of investment. Another reason for the resurgence is that the extended investment tax credit and the accelerated cost recovery system

TABLE 6   Role of Federal Deficit in National Saving and Investment (as percentage of GNP)

	Net Private Saving (1)	State-Local Surplus/ Deficit (2)	Federal Surplus/ Deficit[a] (3)	Net National Saving (4)	Capital Outflow (−) or Foreign Inflow (+) (5)	Net Domestic Investment (4 + 5)
1950–1959	7.2	−0.2	0.0	7.0	−0.2	7.0
1960–1969	7.9	0.0	−0.3	7.6	−0.5	7.1
1970–1979	7.1	1.0	−1.8	6.3	0.0	6.4
1982	5.3	1.0	−4.8	1.5	+0.3	1.8
1983	5.9	1.3	−5.4	1.8	+1.0	2.8
1984	7.4	1.4	−4.8	4.0	+2.6	6.5

[a]National Income and Product Accounts (NIPA) basis.
SOURCE: U.S. Department of Commerce, *National Income and Product Accounts of the United States* (Washington, D.C.: U.S. Government Printing Office, various years).

(ACRS) are available only on domestic investment. This, in turn, has probably also been a cause of the decrease in U.S. capital exports, which again has been part of the reason for relieving some of the potential pressure of deficits on interest rates.

Current net saving and investment figures for the private economy are shown in Table 6. Clearly, while we have had an investment boomlet, our net national saving and net national investment are still quite modest relative to our history and to those of our major trading partners.

Finally, Table 7 reports alternative ways of reviewing the share of society's resources devoted to the present as opposed to the future. It becomes clear that, for a variety of reasons, the U.S. economy has been consuming a huge

TABLE 7   Alternative Measures of National Saving Behavior, Selected Years

Period	National Income Accounts Basis, Net National Saving (1)	Household Consumption Rate (2)	Government Consumption Rate (3)	(2) + (3) (4)	Household Consumption Rate out of NNP-Government Consumption (5)
1951–1960	13.4%	64.3%	22.3%	86.6%	82.7%
1961–1970	13.8	63.7	22.5	86.2	82.2
1971–1980	12.3	65.3	22.4	87.7	84.1
1981–1984	8.6	68.2	23.4	91.6	88.9

NOTE: NIPA data adjusted to treat durable purchases (household and government) as saving and imputed rental flow on household durables, plus government tangible assets on consumption. Net national product (NNP) adjusted to include imputed rent and exclude depreciation on household durables and government tangible assets.

fraction of its net national product in recent years and that our national saving rate has plummeted.

What do I conclude from all of these figures? My tentative conclusion is that we still have an investment problem in the United States, that we will probably have to finance investment by our own domestic saving, and that we have an equally severe savings problem. Economic policies designed to encourage consumption at the expense of saving and investment have marked U.S. fiscal history far too long. It is time we consolidated those policies begun in 1954 (and continued in 1962, 1978, and 1981) to move our tax policy toward neutral consumption taxation and our overall fiscal policy toward achieving appropriately measured budget balance over periods longer than cycles in economic fluctuations. Such policies would renew the prospect of a high-saving and high-investment economy, which in turn could lead to a higher rate of technological change and economic growth.

Let me note that many of the links in this chain of argument are based on less-than-firm footing. Much more research needs to be done, for example, on the determinants of saving and investment in the United States, on the potential links between investment and technical change, and so on. It is my opinion that we badly need to rededicate our economic policies to promoting our long-term growth and international competitiveness and that these, in turn, will ultimately require much higher rates of national saving and investment in plant and equipment as well as research and development in the United States.

CONCLUSION AND PARTIAL RESEARCH AGENDA

While short-term fluctuations in the economy can be quite costly, active demand management may be extremely difficult and counterproductive, and at the very least, fine-tuning is unlikely to be productive. Inflation and high and rising tax rates have eroded incentives to produce income and wealth and are probably part of the explanation for productivity declines. More importantly, however, the sources of long-term growth in the economy have less to do with short-term macroeconomics than with "second-tier macroeconomics." This is certainly only my casual judgment, but the composition of government spending, the structure of taxes, and the effects of monetary and fiscal policies on the composition of output are likely to be more important to the determinants of our long-term growth rate, generation of new technology, and rising standards of living than minor changes in the policies designed to mitigate economic fluctuations. Further, while there probably are links among the overall macroeconomic climate and innovation, technical change, and economic growth, it will not be easy to establish more than anecdotal evidence of a relation. Therefore, it is my conclusion that a much greater emphasis should be placed on the effects of these second-tier policies on physical and human capital formation, research and development expenditures, and therefore, innovation, technical change, and economic growth.

In addition to various and very important microeconomic issues relating to technology and economic growth, a short macroeconomic research agenda would include the following:

1. Analyses of the effects of the composition of government spending, at the federal, state, and local levels;

2. Further analysis of the effects of alternative tax structures on investment, human capital investment, and R&D spending;

3. The relationship of investment and technical change through learning and embodiment, and the diffusion of technology in general;

4. Renewed studies of the sectoral details of technical change and its relationship to aggregate economic growth;

5. Analyses of broad macroeconomic policies to promote innovation and the generation and adoption of new technologies, e.g., comparative international and historical studies;

6. Analyses of the impact of foreign trade and capital flows on investment and technical change both in the United States and abroad and at both the aggregate and industry level.

In conclusion, I hope this discussion proves useful to readers who are not economists. It was designed to introduce a variety of controversies and issues and to provoke discussion and comment. I have deliberately avoided any attempt to be encyclopedic and have stressed my own judgments and impressions, which should be taken for what they are, one economist's opinion. Let me stress, however, the enormous stake that our economy and society have in issues of technology and economic growth. I do not believe that we can continue to go along merrily assuming that the technology will be generated and disseminated, and that our own long-term growth will be assured via some mysterious exogenous process. It is likely that economic policies do affect the generation and dissemination of new technology and our rate of investment in improving the quality of our labor force, both of which have the capacity to affect our long-term growth rate. A difference of even half a percentage point in the long-term growth rate can dramatically transform a society over a generation or two. It is incumbent upon all of us to attempt to understand the relationship of macroeconomic policy, technical change, and economic growth much better than we do today and to make sure that this information, as it is generated, is used in the evaluation of economic policy.

REFERENCES AND BIBLIOGRAPHY

Barro, R. J. 1974. Are government bonds net wealth? *Journal of Political Economy* (November–December): 1095–1117.

Barro, R. J., and C. Sahasakul. 1983. Measuring the average marginal tax rates from the individual income tax, *Journal of Business* (October).

Boskin, M. 1976. Notes on the tax treatment of human capital, U.S. Treasury, Conference on Tax Research.

Boskin, M. 1978. Taxation, saving and the rate of interest, *Journal of Political Economy* 86:S3–S27.

Feldstein, M., and L. Summers. 1979. Inflation and the taxation of capital income in the corporate sector, *National Tax Journal* (December).

Fischer, S., and F. Modigliani. 1977. Aspects of the Costs of Inflation. MIT Working Paper (unpublished).

Friedman, M. 1968. The role of monetary policy, *American Economic Review* 58(March):1–17.

Hall, R., and D. Jorgenson. 1967. Tax policy and investment behavior, *American Economic Review*.

Hausman, J. 1981. Labor supply, in H. Aaron and J. Pechman, eds., *How Taxes Affect Economic Behavior*. Washington, D.C.: Brookings Institution.

Heckman, J. 1974. Shadow prices, market wages and labor supply of married women, *Econometrica*.

Lucas, R. 1981. Tobin and monetarism: A review article, *Journal of Economic Literature* 19(June):558–567.

Phelps, E. 1968. Money-wage dynamics and labor market equilibrium, *Journal of Political Economy* 76(July–August):678–711.

Sargent, T. 1979. *Macroeconomics*. New York: Academic Press.

Sheshinski, E. 1967. Optimal accumulation with learning by doing, in K. Shell, ed., *Essays on the Theory of Optimal Economic Growth*. Cambridge, Mass.: MIT Press.

Microeconomics and Productivity

DALE W. JORGENSON

The explanation for the "Great Growth Slowdown" in the U.S. economy is a decline in the rate of productivity growth. This decline can be traced to the staggering increases in energy prices since 1973. The prospects for increasing productivity growth and capital formation by means of tax policy appear to be very remote. Thus, there seems to be little doubt that one should be pessimistic about future U.S. economic growth.

The purpose of this chapter is to analyze the "Great Growth Slowdown." As will be seen, this is a problem that divides economists in terms of points of view but unites them in terms of interest in the slowdown and its causes. I will begin by discussing the relevance of slower economic growth to current issues in economic policy.

In my view, there are presently three competing schools of thought in the debate over the government's fiscal policy. The moderate school of thought is put forward by the Congressional Budget Office (CBO), the principal analytical arm of the U.S. Congress on budgetary matters. CBO has taken the somewhat pessimistic view that economic growth in the United States will continue at something like 3 percent per year in real terms.

Three percent growth is relatively low by historical standards. Over the three decades from 1948 to 1979, the growth of value added for the U.S. economy was about 3.5 percent. For the two decades between 1929—the beginning of the Great Depression—and 1948, the growth of the U.S. economy was only around 2 percent, according to Christensen and Jorgenson (1970). It is easy to be a pessimist on the basis of historical experience. The implications of 3 percent growth are that radical steps will be required to cut the government deficit. It will be necessary to slow the growth of defense spending and to cut out cost-of-living adjustments in transfer programs. It may also be necessary to increase taxes. Certainly, no halfway measure would be legitimate. That is the moderate point of view.

Proceeding from the moderate to the extreme, we encounter the intermediate point of view of the Office of Management and Budget (OMB), the agency responsible for the administration's proposals on the budget. The OMB view is that U.S. economic growth will continue at 4 percent on an annual basis. Even this view supports the need for fiscal action. According to OMB, the federal deficit will remain very large in the absence of a substantial cut in the government budget. It will be possible to achieve the budget reductions, mainly by cutting nondefense expenditures. It will not be necessary to have a tax increase.

Returning to historical experience, a 4 percent growth rate occurred in two of the seven postwar business cycles. In the immediate postwar period (1948 to 1953) growth averaged almost exactly 4 percent. During the period 1960 to 1966, growth averaged 4.5 percent. Four percent growth is certainly conceivable; however, growth at this rate would represent a substantial improvement over the postwar average and a large increase over the experience of the most recent business cycle (1973 to 1979).

We now come to the extreme view on U.S. economic growth, which is associated with the so-called "supply-siders." The supply-side school projects U.S. economic growth at 5 percent. Obviously, this is completely outside the range of historical experience, at least during the postwar period. If we could conjure up a vision of the U.S. economy's growing at 5 percent, then we would not have to worry about the federal deficit at all. We could continue expanding the defense budget. We would not have to cut back substantially on transfer programs. Economic growth would generate sufficient revenues to pay for the increase in federal spending.

While economic growth is an important political issue, it does not seem to be a partisan issue. In my assessment, the Congressional Budget Office represents moderate opinion and is directed by Rudolph Penner, a well-known Republican. The Office of Management and Budget reflects the Republican mainstream and [as of this writing] is directed by David Stockman, formerly a Republican congressman from Michigan. The supply-side view has come to be the radical opposition on the right. A prominent supply-sider is Paul Craig Roberts, assistant secretary of the Treasury in the first Reagan administration. The debate over economic growth, in other words, is taking place within the Republican party.

My objective here is to sort out the issues that underlie divergent views on future prospects for U.S. economic growth. For this purpose I analyze growth trends in three steps. First, I present a macroscopic view of the economy that begins with the output of the economy as a whole. I then decompose the output of the economy into output levels for individual industrial sectors, which provides a microscopic view of the economy. Finally, I provide an explanation for patterns of economic growth in terms of an econometric model of production at the sectoral level.

The macroscopic view of the economy represents a "top-down" approach. The sources of growth at the aggregate level present something of a mystery to economists. It is very difficult to explain the slowdown in U.S. economic growth at the aggregate level, since the unexplained residual productivity growth turns out to bear the major burden of explaining the growth slowdown.

The second mode of analysis that I present is a "bottom-up" approach. Using this approach I analyze growth at the level of individual industrial sectors, focusing on the causes of the productivity slowdown at the level of specific industries. For this purpose I discuss the implications of a sectoral model of productivity growth. Finally, I conclude with an assessment of growth prospects for the U.S. economy.

GROWTH AND PRODUCTIVITY

Table 1 presents an analysis of U.S. economic growth at the aggregate level.[1] The first row in this table presents growth rates of the economy over the postwar period by business cycle. Beginning with the entire postwar period from 1948 to 1979, we see that growth was about 3.5 percent. As we trace out the business cycles over the postwar period, we see that economic growth was at an all-time low from 1957 to 1960, the last of the Eisenhower years. This was followed by the most rapid growth of the postwar period, under the Kennedy-Johnson administration. Since 1966, growth has been below the average, at 3 percent, and there was a decline of about 1.5 percent between the postwar peak and the period from 1966 to 1979. In other words, the growth slowdown has been with us for a very long time.

To decompose growth into its sources, I use a simple piece of arithmetic to allocate growth among three components. The 3.5 percent growth rate of the U.S. economy is made up of growth in productivity plus the contributions of capital and labor inputs. It is easy to see from the first column of Table 1 that the most important source of economic growth is the contribution of capital input. Capital input accounts for about half of the growth that has taken place. The contribution of labor input is the least important, and the rate of productivity growth comes out in between.

Growth in capital input reflects increased stocks of capital equipment and structures that result from investment. Growth in labor input reflects expansion in employment, hours worked per employee, and the upgrading of the labor force through greater education and experience. Productivity growth is defined as the residual between the growth of output and the contributions of capital and labor inputs. In engineering terms, productivity growth is the increase in the efficiency with which economic resources are utilized.

TABLE 1 Summary of U.S. Economic Growth, 1948–1979

	1948–1979	1948–1953	1953–1957	1957–1960	1960–1966	1966–1969	1969–1973	1973–1979
Growth								
Growth in value added	0.0344	0.0394	0.0305	0.0266	0.0450	0.0323	0.0318	0.0292
Growth in capital input	0.0404	0.0516	0.0389	0.0269	0.0366	0.0487	0.0414	0.0378
Growth in labor input	0.0148	0.0160	0.0023	0.0100	0.0199	0.0185	0.0116	0.0197
Rate of productivity growth	0.0090	0.0092	0.0128	0.0095	0.0180	0.0008	0.0078	0.0019
Contributions								
Contribution of capital input	0.0171	0.0208	0.0165	0.0114	0.0158	0.0210	0.0174	0.0161
Contribution of labor input	0.0084	0.0093	0.0012	0.0056	0.0112	0.0106	0.0066	0.0111

Capital

Growth in capital quality	0.0105	0.0194	0.0107	0.0042	0.0080	0.0128	0.0090	0.0083
Growth in capital stock	0.0299	0.0322	0.0282	0.0227	0.0286	0.0358	0.0324	0.0295
Contribution of capital quality	0.0044	0.0078	0.0045	0.0018	0.0035	0.0055	0.0038	0.0035
Contribution of capital stock	0.0127	0.0130	0.0120	0.0097	0.0124	0.0154	0.0136	0.0126
Reallocations								
Sectoral rates of productivity growth	0.0083	0.0177	0.0147	0.0115	0.0162	0.0013	0.0044	−0.0072
Reallocation of value added	0.0021	−0.0067	−0.0018	0.0002	0.0018	0.0011	0.0048	0.0117
Reallocation of capital input	−0.0005	−0.0015	0.0008	0.0006	0.0004	−0.0007	−0.0009	−0.0019
Reallocation of labor input	−0.0009	−0.0003	−0.0010	−0.0028	−0.0005	−0.0010	−0.0005	−0.0008

SOURCE: Barbara M. Fraumeni and Dale W. Jorgenson, The role of capital in U.S. economic growth, 1948–1979, in A. Dogramaci, ed., *Behavior and Interpretation of Productivity Measures* (Boston: Martinus Nijhoff, 1985), Table 1. Reprinted with permission.

Proceeding to the last period in this analysis, 1973 to 1979, growth has slowed, relative to the postwar average, by about half a percentage point. However, if we view the growth slowdown relative to the 1960–1966 peak, the slowdown is almost 1.5 percentage points. This is the Great Growth Slowdown. The difference in perspective regarding the postwar average and the 1960–1966 peak accounts for much of the divergence in views among economists as to the severity of the growth slowdown.

It is important to emphasize that there has been a growth slowdown and that it began in 1966. However, economists did not begin to focus attention on the growth slowdown until 7 or 8 years later. The slowdown became a major topic for professional discussion during the late 1970s. During the last period in this analysis, 1973 to 1979, consciousness of the growth slowdown became most acute.

In order to obtain additional perspective on the interrelationships between productivity and economic growth, it is useful to look at developments outside the United States. Rapid economic growth in the industrialized countries through 1973 has resulted in unprecedented levels of world economic prosperity. An extreme example is provided by the growth of the Japanese economy. During the period 1960 to 1973, the Japanese economy grew at the astonishing rate of 10.9 percent per year.[2] This growth was sufficient to quadruple the Japanese national product and to move Japan from the ranks of the developing countries to its current status as a major industrial power.

The largest industrialized economies of Europe participated fully in the great economic boom of the 1960s and early 1970s. The economies of France and West Germany expanded at rates of 5.9 and 5.4 percent per year, respectively, during the period 1960 to 1973. Rapid growth in West Germany followed the "economic miracle" of 1952 to 1960, when Germany's economy expanded at 8.2 percent per year, exceeding Japan's growth of 8.1 percent per year during the same period. From 1960 to 1973 Italy's economy grew at 4.8 percent per year, and even the United Kingdom's economy expanded at a respectable 3.8 percent per year. The leading industrialized countries of Europe more than doubled their national products during the postwar period.

In North America, the U.S. economy expanded at the rate of 3.8 percent per year from 1960 to 1973, and Canada's grew at 5.1 percent per year. In Europe rapid economic growth took place with negligible growth in hours worked, while in North America hours worked increased at approximately 1.5 percent per year.

The 1960s and 1970s also witnessed rapid growth among developing countries. Expansion at rates in excess of 5 percent per year were not uncommon. To take another extreme example, South Korea's economy grew at 9.7 percent per year during the period 1960 to 1973, achieving rates of economic expansion almost up to Japanese standards.

The impact of the first oil crisis on economic growth in industrialized countries was disastrous. Growth in the Organization for Economic Cooperation and Development (OECD) countries as a whole plummeted to 2.6 percent per year from 1973 to 1979. Growth in the United States dropped less than in most OECD countries and remained slightly above the OECD average. Growth in Japan fell from the double-digit rates of the 1960s and early 1970s to 3.9 percent per year—almost the same as the expansion in the United Kingdom, the growth laggard among industrialized countries, from 1960 to 1973. The rate of growth in West Germany fell to 2.4 percent for the period 1973 to 1979, and growth in France during this period was only 3.1 percent per year.

What accounts then for the growth slowdown? Relative to the postwar average, the contribution of capital input in the United States has hardly decreased. The contribution of labor input has, if anything, increased. Therefore, the whole of the explanation for the slowdown is in the decline in growth of the efficiency with which resources are used. The Great Growth Slowdown is a slowdown in the rate of productivity growth. Productivity, again, is output per unit of input and, therefore, corresponds to the engineer's concept of efficiency. Of course, this concept of efficiency is being applied to the economy as a whole, what I have referred to as the top-down approach to growth analysis.

The difficulty with this analysis is fairly obvious. The contribution of capital input can be associated with investment, and investment can be attributed to changes in tax policy and changes in government budgetary policy. The contribution of labor input can be associated with basic demographic forces. The rate of productivity growth is what economists refer to as the unexplained residual. It is the part of growth that is not accounted for by the things that we know how to explain. That is an unsatisfactory state of affairs and requires a more careful look at the rate of productivity growth itself.

Returning to Table 1, the last section, which is labeled "reallocations," provides a decomposition of the rate of productivity growth. Previously, I referred to this as the bottom-up approach. Concentrating on the period 1948 to 1979, we can see that the aggregate productivity growth of 0.9 percent per year is made up of four components. First, there is a weighted sum of productivity growth rates at the sectoral level. Second, there is the reallocation of value added among sectors, and, finally, there are the reallocations of capital and labor inputs among industrial sectors.

The first question to ask is: What is the meaning of productivity growth at the sectoral level and how does it compare with productivity growth at the aggregate level? Both concepts of productivity correspond to the engineering notion of efficiency. At the sectoral level economists analyze growth of output in terms of the contributions of capital and labor inputs and the contributions of inputs produced by other sectors. Capital and labor inputs are the so-called primary factors of production that generate the whole of economic activity. Inputs produced by other sectors include the raw materials and the energy that are produced by one set of businesses and supplied to others.

The concept of output at the sectoral level, versus the aggregate level, is much closer to the engineering concept of output. For example, steel is not measured in terms of value added, which is an economist's abstraction, but in terms of tons of steel. The output of the motor vehicle industry is not measured in terms of value added in the motor vehicle industry, again an economist's abstraction, but rather in terms of vehicles produced. The output of the petroleum industry is measured in terms of barrels of petroleum, and so on.

The idea of productivity growth at the sectoral level is much closer to the engineering concept of efficiency and is a much easier concept to appreciate at an intuitive level. In Table 1 we see that the sectoral rates of productivity growth account for almost all of the aggregate productivity growth, at least if we concentrate on the postwar period as a whole. Reallocations reflect the movement of resources either from less productive to more productive uses, or the reverse. In fact, a change in the composition of output in the economy has contributed to the aggregate growth rate of productivity. Regrettably, this has been offset by reallocations of capital and labor to less productive uses, so that reallocations essentially cancel out.

How can resources be allocated to less productive uses? This appears to contradict some fundamental economic law. Consider the following example, however. In the smokestack industry crisis of the 1970s and early 1980s, many highly paid workers, steelworkers for example, have been displaced. They have ended up on the unemployment rolls, or perhaps working at McDonald's. Their wages are, say, one-third the wages they received as steelworkers. This is a reallocation of labor from a highly productive use to a less productive use. If the steel industry is contracting, the reallocation of workers produces a negative contribution to aggregate productivity growth. For the postwar period these reallocations cancel out.

Next, consider the growth slowdown again. Sectoral rates of productivity growth became negative during the period 1973 to 1979. We were losing efficiency in the production of output at the level of individual industrial sectors. How could this happen? Massive efforts to conserve energy resulted from the high energy prices of the early 1970s. In the search for cost reduction, engineers were forced to return to technologies that had not been used for 20 or 30 years. This reduced costs but also produced a decline in sectoral productivity growth.

During the period 1973 to 1979, the reallocation of output away from energy-intensive sectors toward less-energy-intensive sectors produced a tremendous boon for aggregate productivity growth. Offsetting the loss in productivity growth of 1.5 percent was a gain from the reallocation of value added of 1.0 percent. The reallocations of capital and labor input were not very significant. The decline in sectoral productivity growth that actually took place accounts for three times the reduction in aggregate growth and is itself more than sufficient to explain the Great Growth Slowdown.

If we look at sectoral productivity growth rates going back to 1966, which is the high-water mark of growth in the United States, we find that sectoral productivity growth for the average industry has been essentially zero. The positive growth of the 1960s and early 1970s has been completely offset by the decline in productivity growth that occurred during the middle and late 1970s.

The bottom-up approach to growth analysis is as unsatisfying from the intellectual point of view as the top-down approach. Using this approach, one residual, the rate of productivity growth at the aggregate level, is turned into residuals at the level of individual industries, which also require further explanation. If aggregate productivity growth is a mystery, then sectoral productivity growth is a deeper mystery. Resolving this mystery requires an econometric model that explains variations in the rate of productivity growth at the sectoral level.

ENDOGENOUS PRODUCTIVITY GROWTH

The task that remains is to explain productivity growth at the level of individual industries. For that purpose I will employ an econometric model in which the rate of productivity growth is itself a function of the relative prices of all the inputs that are used at the level of individual industrial sectors. The list of those inputs includes capital and labor inputs (the only inputs that appear at the aggregate level), electricity, nonelectrical energy, and the materials that are used in producing output.

For each industry the model of production is based on a sectoral price function that summarizes both possibilities for substitution among inputs and patterns of productivity growth. Each price function gives the price of output of the corresponding industrial sector as a function of the prices of capital, labor, electricity, nonelectrical energy, and materials inputs and time, where time represents the level of productivity in the sector.[3] Obviously, an increase in the price of one of the inputs, holding the prices of the other inputs and the level of productivity constant, necessitates an increase in the price of output. Similarly, if the productivity of a sector improves and the prices of all inputs into the sector remain the same, the price of output must fall. Price functions summarize these and other relationships among the prices of output; capital, labor, electricity, nonelectrical energy, and materials inputs; and the level of productivity.

The sectoral price functions provide a complete model of production patterns for each sector, incorporating both substitution among inputs in response to changes in relative prices and productivity growth in the use of inputs to produce output. To characterize both substitution and productivity growth, it is useful to express the model in an alternative and equivalent form. First, the shares of each of the five inputs—capital, labor, electricity, nonelectrical energy, and materials—in the value of output can be expressed as functions of the prices of those inputs and time, again representing the level of productivity.[4] Second, to these five equations for the value shares can be added an equation that determines productivity growth as a function of the prices of all five inputs and time. The resulting equation is an econometric model of sectoral productivity growth.[5]

Like any econometric model, the relationships determining the value shares of capital, labor, electricity, nonelectrical energy, and materials inputs and the rate of productivity growth involve unknown parameters that must be estimated from data for the individual industries. Included among these unknown parameters are biases of productivity growth that indicate the effect of change in the level of productivity on the value shares of each of the five inputs. For example, the bias of productivity growth for capital gives the change in the share of capital in the value of output in response to changes in the level of productivity, represented by time. Productivity growth is said to be capital using if the bias of productivity growth for capital is positive. Similarly, productivity growth is said to be capital saving if the bias of productivity growth for capital is negative.

The econometric model for each industrial sector of the U.S. economy includes an equation giving the rate of productivity growth as a function of the prices of the five inputs and time. The biases of productivity growth with respect to each of the five inputs appear as the coefficients of time, representing the level of productivity, in the five equations for the value shares of all five inputs. The biases also appear as coefficients of the prices in the equation for the negative of sectoral productivity growth.

The dual role of the bias of productivity growth—expressing the impact of a change in productivity in the value share of an input and the impact of a change in the price of that input on the rate of productivity growth—is the key to an assessment of the determinants of productivity growth. A classification of industries by patterns of the biases of productivity growth is given in Table 2. The pattern that occurs with the greatest frequency is capital-using, labor-using, electricity-using, nonelectrical-energy-using, and materials-saving productivity growth. This pattern occurs for 8 of the 35 industries included in the table. For this pattern the rate of productivity growth decreases with the prices of capital, labor, electricity, and nonelectrical energy inputs and increases with the price of materials input. The pattern that occurs next most frequently is capital-saving, labor-using, electricity-using, nonelectri-

TABLE 2 Classification of Industries by Biases of Productivity Growth

Pattern of Biases	Industries
Capital-using Labor-using Electricity-using Non-electrical-energy-using Materials-saving	Tobacco, textiles, apparel, lumber and wood, printing and publishing, fabricated metal, motor vehicles, transportation
Capital-using Labor-saving Electricity-using Non-electrical-energy-using Materials-using	Electrical machinery
Capital-using Labor-using Electricity-using Non-electrical-energy-saving Materials-saving	Metal mining, services
Capital-using Labor-using Electricity-saving Non-electrical-energy-using Materials-saving	Nonmetallic mining, miscellaneous manufacturing, government enterprises
Capital-using Labor-saving Electricity-using Non-electrical-energy-saving Materials-using	Construction
Capital-using Labor-using Electricity-saving Non-electrical-energy-saving Materials-saving	Coal mining, trade
Capital-using Labor-saving Electricity-saving Non-electrical-energy-using Materials-saving	Agriculture, crude petroleum and natural gas, petroleum refining
Capital-saving Labor-using Electricity-using Non-electrical-energy-using Materials-using	Food, paper
Capital-saving Labor-using Electricity-using Non-electrical-energy-using Materials-saving	Rubber; leather; instruments; gas utilities; finance, insurance, and real estate

Continued on next page

TABLE 2   (Continued)

Pattern of Biases	Industries
Capital-saving Labor-using Electricity-saving Non-electrical-energy-using Materials-using	Chemicals
Capital-saving Labor-saving Electricity-using Non-electrical-energy-using Materials-using	Transportation equipment and ordnance, communications
Capital-saving Labor-using Electricity-saving Non-electrical-energy-using Materials-saving	Stone, clay, and glass; machinery
Capital-saving Labor-using Electricity-using Non-electrical-energy-saving Materials-saving	Primary metals
Capital-saving Labor-saving Electricity-using Non-electrical-energy-using Materials-saving	Electric utilities
Capital-saving Labor-saving Electricity-saving Non-electrical-energy-saving Materials-using	Furniture

SOURCE: Dale W. Jorgenson, The role of energy in productivity growth, in J.W. Kendrick, ed., *International Comparisons of Productivity and Causes of the Slowdown* (Cambridge, Mass.: Ballinger, 1984), Table 7-3, pp. 303–304. Reprinted with permission.

cal-energy-using, and materials-saving productivity growth. This pattern occurs for 5 industries. For this pattern the rate of productivity growth decreases with the prices of labor, electricity, and nonelectrical energy inputs and increases with the prices of capital and materials inputs. These two patterns of productivity growth differ only in the role of the price of capital input.

Productivity growth is capital-using for 20 of the 35 industries included in the table. The first and most important conclusion to be drawn is that the price of capital input plays a very significant role in the determination of productivity growth. A decline in the price of capital input stimulates productivity growth in 20 of the 35 industries and dampens productivity growth in only 15. Alternatively and equivalently, productivity growth results in an increase in the share of capital input in the value of output, holding the relative prices of all inputs constant, in 20 of the 35 industries. Productivity growth results in a decrease in the share of capital input in only 15 of the industries.

Next, we can examine the role of prices of labor, electricity, nonelectrical energy, and materials inputs in the determination of the rate of productivity growth. Productivity growth is labor-using for 26 of the 35 industries included in the table and labor-saving for 9 of the industries. Productivity growth is electricity-using for 23 of the 35 industries and electricity-saving for 12 industries. Similarly, productivity growth is nonelectrical-energy-using for 28 of the 35 industries and nonelectrical-energy-saving for 7 industries. Finally, productivity growth is materials-using in only 8 of the 35 industries and materials-saving for the remaining 27 industries.

To clarify the analysis further, let me analyze the mechanism of productivity growth that underlies this econometric model. The basic idea is very simple; when there are radical changes in the price of an input, the engineers and businessmen who are running the economy have an incentive to economize on the use of that input. Substitution away from an expensive input results in a new path for the development of technology. This path is associated with higher or lower productivity growth rates. It happens that if capital and labor prices increase, then the associated technical developments result in lower productivity growth rates. When taxes on capital go up, the rate of productivity growth in the average industry falls. Similarly, when wage rates rise in the average industry, the rate of productivity growth falls. If energy prices increase, again, the rate of productivity growth declines; only an increase in the price of raw materials stimulates productivity growth. That is characteristic of the wide range of U.S. industries that are included in this microeconomic analysis.

GROWTH PROSPECTS

The sharp decline in economic growth in industrialized countries presents a problem comparable in scientific interest and social importance to the problem of mass unemployment in the Great Depression of the 1930s. Conventional methods of economic analysis have been tried and found to be inadequate. Clearly, a new framework will be required for economic understanding. The analysis in this section contains some of the elements that will be required for an analysis of the prospects for the U.S. economy in the last half of the 1980s.

My analysis of the sources of variations in rates of productivity growth for the U.S. economy begins with the evolution of U.S. tax policy over the period 1948 to 1979. Under current tax law, taxpayers are permitted to deduct depreciation as an expense in arriving at their taxable income. Taxpayers are also allowed to reduce their tax liability by means of an investment tax credit based on purchases of equipment. As tax rates at corporate and personal levels have increased, provisions for capital recovery under the tax code have become increasingly significant for economic policy. These provisions also have an important impact on stimulating or retarding changes in the level of productivity.

The effective tax rates for all corporate investment for each year of the period 1948 to 1979 are listed in Table 3, along with effective tax rates for structures and for equipment separately. If capital-consumption allowances were precisely equal to economic depreciation and the investment tax credit were equal to zero for all assets, the effective tax rate would be the same for all assets and equal to the statutory tax rate. The statutory tax rate is included in Table 3 as a basis for comparison with the effective tax rates under U.S. tax law. As seen in the table, the effective tax rate was below the statutory rate in every year. The ratio of the effective tax rate to the statutory rate is given in the final column of Table 3.

The ratio of the effective tax rate on corporate investment to the statutory rate fluctuated between 70 and 80 percent over the period from 1948 to 1961. When the investment tax credit was first adopted in 1962, the ratio of the effective tax rate to the statutory rate dropped to 55 percent in that year from 76 percent in 1961. When the investment tax credit was repealed in 1969 and 1970, the effective tax rate climbed to 78 percent of the statutory rate in 1969 and to 87 percent of the statutory rate in 1970. Reinstitution of the investment tax credit in 1971 reduced the effective tax rate to 60 percent of the statutory rate in that year and to 48 percent in the following year. Liberalization of the investment tax credit in 1975 reduced the effective tax rate to 43 percent of the statutory rate. The effective tax rate fell to 12.8 percent in 1977 as the rate of inflation decreased, and rose to 19.2 percent in 1979 as the rate of inflation increased.

The main conclusion to be drawn from Table 3 is that the effective tax rate under U.S. tax law has been below the statutory tax rate throughout the period 1948 to 1979. The effect of inflation under any given set of tax provisions for capital recovery is to increase the effective tax rate. This occurs through an increase in the discount rates applied to future capital-consumption allowances. However, tax provisions have been revised at frequent intervals, and major revisions occurred in 1954, 1962, 1970, and 1975. The impact of those revisions has been to reduce effective tax rates very dramatically, especially in 1962 with the adoption of the investment tax credit and more generous capital-consumption allowances and, in 1975, with the liberalization of the investment tax credit.

Since the effective tax rate increases with rate of inflation, a decrease in

TABLE 3   Effective Corporate Tax Rates, 1948–1979

Year	Effective Corporate Tax Rate			Statutory Tax Rate	Ratio (1)/(4)
	Total	Equipment	Structures		
1948	0.264	0.302	0.200	0.380	0.696
1949	0.266	0.307	0.200	0.380	0.699
1950	0.303	0.346	0.226	0.420	0.720
1951	0.389	0.436	0.310	0.510	0.762
1952	0.398	0.445	0.322	0.520	0.766
1953	0.418	0.460	0.348	0.520	0.803
1954	0.366	0.400	0.312	0.520	0.704
1955	0.370	0.405	0.311	0.520	0.712
1956	0.379	0.411	0.325	0.520	0.728
1957	0.394	0.429	0.335	0.520	0.758
1958	0.377	0.408	0.330	0.520	0.725
1959	0.412	0.444	0.355	0.520	0.792
1960	0.411	0.442	0.356	0.520	0.790
1961	0.397	0.428	0.346	0.520	0.764
1962	0.285	0.250	0.345	0.520	0.548
1963	0.265	0.219	0.344	0.520	0.509
1964	0.237	0.189	0.324	0.500	0.474
1965	0.213	0.160	0.309	0.480	0.444
1966	0.274	0.247	0.324	0.480	0.570
1967	0.269	0.240	0.323	0.480	0.560
1968	0.259	0.221	0.330	0.480	0.539
1969	0.372	0.378	0.361	0.480	0.776
1970	0.416	0.429	0.394	0.480	0.867
1971	0.289	0.244	0.367	0.480	0.603
1972	0.229	0.157	0.357	0.480	0.478
1973	0.257	0.188	0.383	0.480	0.536
1974	0.281	0.221	0.394	0.480	0.586
1975	0.206	0.131	0.345	0.480	0.430
1976	0.161	0.081	0.320	0.480	0.336
1977	0.128	0.041	0.308	0.480	0.266
1978	0.180	0.099	0.335	0.480	0.376
1979	0.192	0.121	0.327	0.460	0.418
1980	0.243	0.185	0.352	0.460	0.528

SOURCE: Dale W. Jorgenson and Martin A. Sullivan, Inflation and corporate capital recovery, in C. Hulten, ed., *Depreciation, Inflation and the Taxation of Income from Capital* (Washington, D.C.: The Urban Institute, 1981), Table 11, p. 196. Reprinted with permission.

the rate of inflation to levels below those prevailing since 1973 would reduce the effective tax rate substantially. The decrease in the rates of inflation in the prices of assets from 12.8 percent in 1975 to 5.6 percent in 1976 and 7.7 percent in 1977 brought the effective tax rate down to 16.1 percent in 1976 and 12.8 percent in 1977. These tax rates can be compared with the statutory rate of 48 percent in both years. The increases in the rate of inflation in 1978 and 1979 brought effective tax rates up to 18.0 percent in 1978, and to 19.2 percent in 1979.

The effective tax rates on corporate income are inversely correlated with rates of productivity growth for the U.S. economy as a whole. Effective tax rates declined sharply between 1960 and 1966; the rate of productivity growth attained its postwar peak of 1.80 percent during this period. Effective tax rates rose dramatically from 1966 to 1969; the rate of productivity growth declined to 0.08 percent per year during this period. Effective tax rates declined from 1969 to 1973; the rate of productivity growth revived to 0.78 percent per year.

The most striking change in the relative prices of capital, labor, electricity, nonelectrical energy, and materials inputs that has taken place since 1973 is the staggering increase in the price of energy. At first blush the finding that higher energy prices are an important determinant of the slowdown in economic growth after 1973 seems paradoxical. In studies of sources of aggregate economic growth, energy appears as both an output and an input for individual industries but cancels out for the economy as a whole.[6] It is necessary to disaggregate the sources of economic growth to the sectoral level in order to define an appropriate role for energy.

Within a disaggregated framework for analyzing economic growth, it is not sufficient to decompose the growth of sectoral output among the contributions of inputs and the growth of productivity. It is essential to explain the growth of sectoral productivity. In the absence of such an explanation, the growth of sectoral productivity is simply an unexplained residual between the growth of output and the growth of capital, labor, electricity, nonelectrical energy, and materials inputs.

Finally, the direction and significance of the influence of energy prices on productivity growth at the sectoral level must be determined empirically. From a conceptual point of view, energy prices can have positive, negative, or zero impacts on sectoral productivity growth. From an empirical point of view, the influence of higher energy prices is negative and highly significant. There is no way to substantiate this empirical finding without an econometric model of productivity growth.

The analytic steps outlined here—disaggregation of the sources of economic growth to the sectoral level; decomposition of the rate of growth of sectoral output into productivity growth and the contributions of capital, labor, electricity, nonelectrical energy, and materials inputs; and modeling the growth of productivity—have been taken only recently. Although much additional research will be required to provide an exhaustive explanation of the slowdown of economic growth in industrialized countries within the new framework, it is nonetheless useful to employ this framework in assessing future growth prospects for industrialized countries.

The Arab oil embargo of late 1973 and early 1974 resulted in a dramatic increase in world oil prices. Between 1973 and 1975 crude oil import prices increased by two and a half times in real terms for the seven major OECD countries—Canada, France, West Germany, Italy, Japan, the United Kingdom, and the United States.[7] Japan was the country most affected by the oil price increases and experienced a tripling of crude oil import prices in real terms. Among European countries France was not far behind Japan in the increase in the real price of crude oil imports.

Real energy prices to final users increased considerably less than real oil prices in all major OECD countries. The average increase for the seven countries from 1973 to 1975 was 23.9 percent. Japan and Italy were at the high end of the range with increases in excess of 50 percent. Meanwhile, Canada experienced only a 3.9 percent increase under a regime of price controls on domestic petroleum and natural gas. Similar controls in the United States did not prevent an increase of energy prices to final users of 23 percent in real terms.

In late 1978 the Iranian revolution sent a second wave of oil price increases through world markets. Between 1978 and 1980 crude oil import prices almost doubled in real terms for the seven major OECD countries. Real energy prices to final users climbed by 33.5 percent for those countries. Again, Japan was hard hit with an 80.3 percent increase, and Canada experienced an increase of only 8.7 percent. For the United States the price increase was 34 percent, and major European countries had increases below the average.

Slow growth in productivity at the sectoral level is associated with higher prices of capital input for 20 of the 35 industries that make up the producing sector of the U.S. economy. This helps to account for the high productivity growth of the period 1960 to 1966, the slow growth of the following period, 1966 to 1969, and the revival of productivity growth during the period preceding the first oil crisis, 1969 to 1973. From 1960 to 1966 tax policy stimulated productivity growth; from 1966 to 1969 tax policy retarded productivity growth; and from 1969 to 1973 tax policy again acted as a stimulus to productivity growth.

The slower growth of productivity is also associated with higher prices of electricity for 23 of the 35 industries listed in Table 2; similarly, slower growth of productivity is associated with higher prices of nonelectrical energy for 28 of the 35 industries. Real energy prices began to rise in the early 1970s and increased dramatically after the first oil shock in 1973 and again after the second oil shock in late 1978. These price trends resulted in the substitution of capital, labor, and materials inputs for inputs of electricity and nonelectrical energy, thereby reducing the energy intensity of production. At the same time the energy price trends contributed to a marked slowdown in productivity growth.

CONCLUSION

The overall conclusion of this chapter is that it is no longer necessary for analyses of productivity growth to focus on the "unexplained residual." The econometric model presented here makes the rate of productivity growth itself endogenous. Given that variations in the rate of productivity growth are associated with changes in the growth rate of the aggregate economy, the model provides a full explanation of the slowdown at the aggregate level.

Let us return now to the dispute I perceive among the three contending schools of thought in Washington—the Congressional Budget Office, which is associated with future growth prospects in the range of 3 percent a year; the people at OMB, associated with a 4 percent growth rate; and, finally, the radical supply-side view, associated with a growth rate of approximately 5 percent.

What underlies these different views? Frankly, it is very hard to understand the views of the supply-siders. The OMB view is that changes in tax policy, which began with the incoming Reagan administration in 1981, will stimulate growth by increasing capital formation. However, those tax cuts were followed by the deepest recession in investment that has occurred in the postwar period. In the last two years, the United States has had the strongest recovery in the postwar period.

During the whole of the Reagan administration the United States has had a growth of capital stock that is just about comparable to what prevailed during the period 1973 to 1979, the period during which the growth slowdown was most severe. The OMB view, therefore, does not bear very much weight. We come back to the Congressional Budget Office view, which suggests that real growth in the United States is permanently lodged at a relatively low level, around 3 percent a year. This is a consequence of the permanent increase in energy prices.

The difficulties associated with large deficits and the associated high, real interest rates are still with us. Moreover, the prospects for increasing productivity growth and capital formation by means of tax policy appear to be very remote. I come down on the side of the Congressional Budget Office. There seems to be little doubt that one should be pessimistic about future U.S. economic growth.

NOTES

1. The methodology employed by Fraumeni and Jorgenson (1985) is based on that of Jorgenson (1980). Data sources are described by Fraumeni and Jorgenson (1980, 1985) and by Gollop and Jorgenson (1980, 1983).
2. Comparisons among patterns of economic growth in industrialized countries are given by Christensen et al. (1980, 1981).
3. The price function was introduced by Samuelson (1953).
4. The sectoral price functions are based on the translog price function introduced by Christensen et al. (1971, 1973). The translog price function was first employed at the sectoral level by Berndt and Jorgenson (1973) and by Berndt and Wood (1975). References to sectoral production studies incorporating energy and materials inputs are given by Berndt and Wood (1979).
5. This model of sectoral productivity growth is based on that of Jorgenson (1983). Estimates of the unknown parameters of this model, including biases of technical change, are presented by

Jorgenson (1984). A useful survey of studies of energy prices and productivity growth is given by Berndt (1982).

6. A leading proponent of this view is Denison (1984).

7. Comparisons of energy prices and energy demand patterns in industrialized countries are given by Fujime (1983). Projections of U.S. energy demand are given by Hogan (1984).

REFERENCES

Berndt, Ernst R. 1982. Energy price increases and the productivity slowdown in United States manufacturing. Pp. 60–89 in Federal Reserve Bank of Boston, *The Decline in Productivity Growth*. Boston.

Berndt, Ernst R., and Dale W. Jorgenson. 1973. Production structures. Ch. 3 in Dale W. Jorgenson and Hendrik S. Houthakker, eds., *U.S. Energy Resources and Economic Growth*, Washington, D.C.: Energy Policy Project.

Berndt, Ernst R., and David O. Wood. 1975. Technology, prices, and the derived demand for energy. *Review of Economics and Statistics* 56(3):259–268.

Berndt, Ernst R., and David O. Wood. 1979. Engineering and econometric interpretations of energy-capital complementarity. *American Economic Review* 69(3):342–354.

Christensen, Laurits R., and Dale W. Jorgenson. 1970. U.S. real product and real factor input, 1929–1967. *Review of Income and Wealth* 16(1):19–50.

Christensen, Laurits R., Diane Cummings, and Dale W. Jorgenson. 1980. Economic growth, 1947–1973: An international comparison. Pp. 595–698 in J. W. Kendrick and B. Vaccara, eds., *New Developments in Productivity Measurement and Analysis*. Studies in Income and Wealth, vol. 41. Chicago: University of Chicago Press.

Christensen, Laurits R., Diane Cummings, and Dale W. Jorgenson. 1981. Relative productivity levels, 1947–1973. *European Economic Review* 16(1):61–94.

Christensen, Laurits R., Dale W. Jorgenson, and Lawrence J. Lau. 1971. Conjugate duality and the transcendental logarithmic production function. *Econometrica* 39(3):255–256.

Christensen, Laurits R., Dale W. Jorgenson, and Lawrence J. Lau. 1973. Transcendental logarithmic production frontiers. *Review of Economics and Statistics* 55(1):28–45.

Denison, E. F. 1984. Accounting for slower economic growth: An update. Pp. 1–45 in J. W. Kendrick, ed., *International Comparisons of Productivity and Causes of the Slowdown*. Cambridge, Mass.: Ballinger.

Fraumeni, Barbara M., and Dale W. Jorgenson. 1980. The role of capital in U.S. economic growth, 1948–1976. Pp. 9–250 in G. von Furstenberg, ed., *Capital Efficiency and Growth*. Cambridge, Mass.: Ballinger.

Fraumeni, Barbara M., and Dale W. Jorgenson. 1985. The role of capital in U.S. economic growth, 1948–1979. In A. Dogramaci, ed., *Behavior and Interpretation of Productivity Measures*. Boston: Martinus Nijhoff.

Fujime, Kazuya. 1983. Structural changes in energy demand in the OECD nations, with emphasis on the U.S. and Japan, and a cyclical behavior in oil markets. Energy Laboratory Working Paper No. MIT-EL 83-015WP. Cambridge: Massachusetts Institute of Technology.

Gollop, Frank, and Dale W. Jorgenson. 1980. U.S. productivity growth by industry, 1947–1973. Pp. 17–136 in J. W. Kendrick and B. Vaccara, eds., *New Developments in Productivity Measurement and Analysis*. Studies in Income and Wealth, vol. 41. Chicago: University of Chicago Press.

Gollop, Frank, and Dale W. Jorgenson. 1983. Sectoral measures of labor cost for the United States, 1948–1978. Pp. 185–235, 503–520 in J. E. Triplett, ed., *The Measurement of Labor Cost*. Studies in Income and Wealth, vol. 44. Chicago: University of Chicago Press.

Hogan, William W. 1984. *Patterns of Energy Use*. Harvard University, Energy and Environmental Policy Center, Cambridge, Mass.

Jorgenson, Dale W. 1980. Accounting for capital. Pp. 251–319 in G. von Furstenberg, ed., *Capital Efficiency and Growth*. Cambridge, Mass.: Ballinger.

Jorgenson, Dale W. 1983. Modeling production for general equilibrium analysis. *Scandinavian Journal of Economics* 85(2):101–112.

Jorgenson, Dale W. 1984. The role of energy in productivity growth. Pp. 270–323 in J. W. Kendrick, ed., *International Comparisons of Productivity and Causes of the Slowdown*. Cambridge, Mass.: Ballinger. Earlier, less detailed versions of this material appeared in *American Economic Review* 74(2), May 1978: 26–30; and in *The Energy Journal* 5(3), July 1984: 11–25.

Jorgenson, Dale W., and Martin A. Sullivan. 1981. Inflation and corporate capital recovery. Pp. 171–238, 311–313 in C. Hulten, ed., *Depreciation, Inflation and the Taxation of Income from Capital*. Washington, D.C.: The Urban Institute.

Samuelson, Paul A. 1953. Prices of factors and goods in general equilibrium. *Review of Economic Studies* 21(1):1–20.

Dynamic Competition and Productivity Advances

It seems no accident that the successful industries in the 1970s were either those embodying new technology or those in which plants tended to be relatively small and unspecialized. Moving toward more flexible and less specialized firms will be the principal long-term adjustment required of U.S. industry if it is to thrive in an era of international competition.

During the 1970s a large number of U.S. industries performed splendidly when dealing with a greater degree of foreign competition than they had faced before. Their performance was attributable to an impressive gain in the rate of productivity advance, which made possible the selling of comparable products at lower cost or better products at more or less the same cost. It seems to be no accident that the successful industries were either those embodying new technology, such as semiconductors and computers, in which flexibility was all-important, or those in which plants tended to be relatively small and unspecialized, such as manufacturers of athletic equipment or scientific instruments.

In the first part of this chapter, I discuss the essential features of a dynamic model, particularly the relevance of the model for explaining how productivity gains come about. Next, I present some statistical results of applying the model to groups of U.S. industries. Finally, I argue that moving toward more flexible and less specialized firms is the principal long-term adjustment required if U.S. industry is to thrive in an era of international competition.

MOTIVATED COMPETITION

Dynamic competition consists of developing better or less expensive alternatives, and it requires taking risks to ascertain how particular hypotheses will work out. Not all risk taking will be successful. But if one or another firm is successful, say, every 2 or 3 years, that industry can be described as being "predictably unpredictable." And inasmuch as firms in the industry cannot buy insurance from Lloyds against competitive intrusions, they are motivated to take technological risks to avoid competitive risks. Such competition is measured in terms of the degree of technological risk taken by firms. If, as in a classical economic world, firms took no risks, the menu of alternatives would remain unchanged. If, say, in the mousetrap industry firms were motivated to take risks, such as might be involved in obtaining slightly stronger springs, the menu of alternatives would change, but ever so slowly. On the other hand, if firms in such an industry were more or less simultaneously taking bolder technological risks and imposing larger competitive risks on their rivals, then the menu obviously would change more rapidly. The main purpose of the dynamic model proposed here is to relate the degree of competitive risk taking to the rate of technological progress.

Continuing productivity gains presuppose advances in relevant technologies and a keen desire to make good use of this progress. Indeed, without continuing technological advances, productivity gains would sooner or later die out. Luck is involved in making a technological advance, because the larger the attempted improvement, the more diverse are the hints required to bring it about. Luck is also involved in bringing about productivity gains because, generally speaking, the technological advances (e. g., robots, synthetic fibers) on which productivity gains are premised, whether in the form of reduced labor costs or reduced input costs, come about in industries other than those in which the gains occur. However, productivity performance seldom depends on one critical technological ingredient; ordinarily it depends on several. Hence, just as firms search for ideas with which to bring about technological advances, so must they search for ways to bring about productivity gains. Contrary to neoclassical models of productivity growth, in which firms make instantaneous adjustments to take into account changes in factor prices, there is not, so to speak, a substitute hiding in every bush. Also, contrary to such models, a factor of necessity must be involved. As will be seen, it is simply impossible to make reasonably good predictions without taking the factor of necessity into account. Dynamic economics relates both necessity and luck to the rate of progress.

Three critical assumptions were made in developing the dynamic model. First, differences in "the propensity to engage in risk taking" within an industry are assumed to be smaller than those between industries. I define "the average propensity to engage in risk taking" (PERK) as the degree of risk a firm takes to achieve minor or major gains in productivity. A firm desiring to generate less costly or better-quality alternatives may introduce robots into its production process gradually; or, like Japanese auto firms, it may attempt to develop its own highly specialized robots for the purpose of promoting reliability by substituting robots for workers in the most monotonous tasks. Or, the firm may introduce several new technologies simultaneously, which would imply an even greater degree of risk. Nevertheless, firms are not free to choose which of these risk-taking strategies to adopt. A firm can jeopardize its competitive position by taking either greater or smaller risks than its rivals. Hence, the first assumption—assumption because there is no way to establish its reasonableness definitely—is that firms are in a NASH dynamic equilibrium—an equilibrium wherein if one firm does not change its strategic policies with respect to risk taking other firms will have no incentive to change theirs.

The second critical assumption is that a greater degree of risk taking will lead to a wider distribution of outcomes as measured by the degree of success firms have in bringing about the cost reductions that, in turn, generate productivity gains. A firm that takes only little risk when incorporating a new technology into its production process obviously will be able to obtain only a small reduction in cost. But the larger the attempted cost reduction, the greater will be the variety of technological sources the firm must draw upon and the more the cost reductions will depend on luck. Indeed, if firms' costs were identical, this would indicate that progress had stopped. Even if all productivity gains were embodied in new capital equipment, costs would not be the same for all firms in an industry, because not all would buy new capital equipment simultaneously. Typically, the timing of investment decisions depends on luck in selling new models and on luck in finding machines that will provide significant advantages and fit into an ongoing production process. Moreover, productivity gains, broadly defined, also depend on the outcome of a search to find less expensive inputs.

This is not to say, however, that cost differences are necessarily reflected in price differences: if demand is relatively inelastic—if increases in prices do not result in a commensurate reduction in sales—there will be little incentive to hold costs in check, and little incentive, therefore, to take risks to generate productivity gains. On the other hand, if demand turns out to be elastic—if large output penalties are associated with increases in costs—and if firms cannot find ways to reduce their costs, they risk going out of business.

The third assumption is that progress can be measured in terms of the advantage provided to buyers: namely, the advantage in being able to choose from a wider distribution. As was just indicated, when the elasticity of demand is fairly high, the ability of firms to raise prices is highly constrained. And high-demand elasticities also imply buyers who are both knowledgeable and motivated.

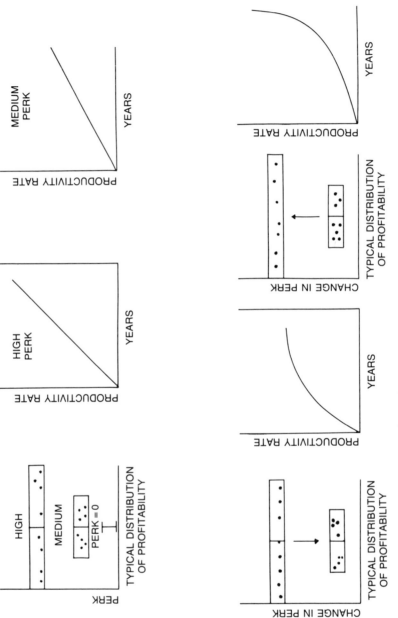

FIGURE 1 Annual average value in PERK versus rate of productivity gain.

A highly oversimplified diagrammatic version of the dynamic model is shown in Figure 1. Note, as shown in the top panels, the greater the degree of risk taking, the more steeply sloping will be the productivity curve. This follows from the fact that the slope of the curve is directly proportional to the width of the distribution. Also note that when PERK is zero, there is no distribution.

When PERK is positive, in some industries engaged in making standardized products, major emphasis is placed on reducing costs. In others, emphasis is on providing more effectiveness per dollar of expenditure, semiconductors, for example. In still others, such as television and, especially, computers, both cost and quality are emphasized. But assuming that the name of the game in those industries is to generate competitive products, they are, in effect, demanding productivity gains from each other. If firms fall behind in such a dynamic game, they will be "taxed" by their competitors. Hence, when firms are in a dynamic equilibrium (a state in which behavior remains predictably unpredictable), it can be predicted that the rate of productivity gain will depend on the value of PERK.

If, as in the bottom panels of Figure 1, PERK declines, then the productivity curve will slope off; that is, if we examine the slope of the curve for a variety of industries in which dynamic competition has declined, we can expect that the average rate of productivity gain will dampen—but not in every industry, because luck is also involved. Conversely, when the value of PERK increases, we can expect the rate of productivity gain to accelerate, but not in all industries, because, again, the factor of luck is involved.

This model was tested against data for all U.S. industries in four-digit SIC manufacturing categories. The data cover the period 1960 to 1980. How the factor of necessity was measured in making the tests is described below, and the results are presented in terms of weighted averages. The statistical test that I employed was Wilcoxson's Signed Rank Test, which takes into account all observations. One group of 11 industries failed to meet the test, but all the others came within the acceptance region, measured at the 5 percent confidence interval.[1]

STATISTICAL RESULTS

All of the industries analyzed (Table 1) were separately classified in terms of their price performance during the periods 1960 to 1970 and 1970 to 1980. The industries were then combined into three groups based on their rank distribution. The best group of industries in each of the periods were those whose prices increased at a rate that was one standard deviation or more *below* the average, and the worst group were those whose prices increased at a rate that was one standard deviation or more *above* the average. The industries whose ranking in the distribution remained the same during both

TABLE 1 Manufacturing Indices Classified in Terms of Price Performance During Each of the Periods 1960–1970 and 1970–1980 (annual average percentage changes)

Industry Group	Price Performance 1960s	Price Performance 1970s	Output Performance 1960s	Output Performance 1970s	Wage Rates 1960s	Wage Rates 1970s	Labor Productivity 1960s	Labor Productivity 1970s	Input Costs[a] 1960s	Input Costs[a] 1970s	Equipment Expenditures[a] 1960s	Equipment Expenditures[a] 1970s
Group I Weight = 28%.[b] 136 industries	2.4%	6.3%	3.9%	3.5%	4.3%	7.7%	2.4%	3.3%	5.8%	10.3%	12.1%	8.1%
Ratio of 1970s to 1960s		2.6		0.9		1.8		1.4		1.8		0.7
Group II Weight = 42%.[b] 145 industries	1.3	6.8	5.6	3.9	4.4	8.5	3.2	3.0	6.6	11.3	12.0	9.6
Ratio of 1970s to 1960s		5.2		0.7		1.9		0.9		1.7		0.8
Group III Weight = 30%.[b] 106 industries	0.4	11.0	5.1	3.0	4.0	11.2	4.0	2.4	5.0	13.7	10.5	7.7
Ratio of 1970s to 1960s		27.5		0.6		2.8		0.6		2.7		0.7

[a]Constant dollars.
[b]Contribution to total sales.
SOURCE: Based on Bureau of Labor Statistics data, 1982.

periods are those shown in Group II; that is, their relative prices remained the same during both periods. On the other hand, prices increased the least in the industries shown in Group I, and, if the calculations had been made in terms of constant prices, the prices for those industries would have actually declined. Conversely, industries shown in Group III are those that exercised less price restraint during the 1970s than they did during the 1960s.

Now, think of competition simply in terms of the elasticity of demand, as nearly all down-to-earth economists do. Though the elasticity of demand relies in part on consumer preferences, it depends mainly on the availability of substitutes. The greater the availability of substitutes, the less freedom of choice firms have with respect to raising prices; the smaller the availability, the more likely it is that prices will rise. As it happens, this concept of competition, in which the availability of substitutes is taken as a given, is a special and limiting case of dynamic competition, because in the short run the availability of substitutes must be taken as a given (i.e., when the value of PERK is, by definition, 0). However, as already shown, in the longer run the rate at which new substitutes are developed depends on the factors of necessity and luck.

The term "unitary elasticity of demand" means that, say, a 10 percent increase in prices will be followed by an equal reduction in output. When this proposition is expressed in terms of rates, it can be seen that the industries in Group II exhibited greater demand inelasticity than those in Group I, and the Group III industries exhibited a far greater degree of demand inelasticity than those in Group II. Thus, while in the last group there was a 40 percent penalty in terms of output performance, this was far outweighed by prices increasing 27 times as rapidly during the 1970s as they did during the 1960s.

Why demand turned out to be so inelastic for the third group of industries is easy to explain: in these industries, substitutes were far from plentiful. The main industries included basic materials of one kind or another—steel, aluminum, copper, cement, and a variety of metal products were the main ones. For the most part, these industries have not featured dynamic competition for some years. Moreover, the increasing degree of protection of the steel industry from foreign imports beginning in the late 1960s protected not only that industry's ability to raise prices, but also that of industries making substitutes. During the 1970s, increases in the costs of steel inputs alone had quite as large an impact on manufacturing prices as did increases in the prices of oil inputs.[2] Indeed, because steel inputs are used in many industries, the impact generated a source of deadweight drag by making American industries less competitive in foreign as well as in domestic markets. Moreover, because the price shocks created by those industries occurred mainly during economic upturns, the generation of deadweight drag not only jeopardized economic growth but made necessary the checking of inflation by very substantial increases in interest rates.

By contrast, the first group of industries exercised a high degree of price restraint not because of their benevolence but, rather, because substitutes were becoming more plentiful. In the 1970s, American firms faced a large increase in foreign competition: well over one-half of the industries in Group I were heavily involved in foreign competition. In other industries, there was an increase in domestic competition. For example, the TV news media became a better and better substitute for newspapers. In the farm machinery industry, there was a substantial increase in dynamic competition due to the efforts of John Deere & Company to become something other than a traditional farm equipment manufacturer. (International Harvester, which remained highly inadaptive, was the main victim of the competition.) Primarily because of the increase in domestic competition, the farm implement industry was able to export almost one-half of its output during the 1970s. Finally, also contributing to higher demand elasticities were some industries in which there were autonomous declines in demand, manufactured milk products and brassieres, for example.

As Table 1 shows, the average movements in wage rates, labor productivity, input costs, and equipment expenditures were more or less as might be predicted, given the decidedly different demand elasticity pressures to which the industries were subjected. Inasmuch as Group I industries suffered a smaller decline in equipment expenditures than either Groups II or III, while experiencing a sharp increase in the average rate of productivity gain and, as a consequence, a relatively small loss in the average output rate, it can be assumed that they were economizing on capital as well as labor inputs.

In his diary, Sadi Carnot, who is now given credit for having discovered the Second Law of Thermodynamics, proposed a tax on the rent of French farms, the purpose of which was to encourage large landholders to sell parcels to individual farmers, who would have an incentive to improve productivity in order, as Carnot wrote, "to excape the tax."[3] Apparently, as of that time productivity on French farms was increasing so slowly that it was almost in a static equilibrium. Note in Table 1 that Group I industries were improving productivity at such a sufficiently rapid rate that they were able to minimize a large positive "tax" imposed on them by their competitors. But, as was also seen, when industries are able to base their expectations on an inelastic demand curve, there is no need to bring about productivity advances to minimize the tax, because it is a negative "tax." Hence, the rate of productivity advance depends on the "tax" difference—and it does because a positive tax encourages a search for a wider diversity of technological inputs. As it happens, this is close to the reasoning contained in the Second Law of Thermodynamics, which is also concerned with explaining movements away from a static equilibrium (i.e., the entropy of the physical world is always increasing).

The same reasoning also provides a good argument for foreign competition.

As was pointed out above, the increasing presence of foreign competition played an important role in increasing the rate of productivity gain, with the consequence that output losses were much smaller than they otherwise would be. And, despite what some labor union leaders and ill-advised politicians have had to say, it was not foreign competition that was robbing Americans of jobs. In the Group I industries, which were the most "taxed" by foreign competition, output during the 1970s declined by about 10 percent compared with the 1960s, but in Group III industries the decline was about 40 percent.

NEED FOR LONGER-RUN ADJUSTMENTS

In the short run, large public deficits may result in serious economic problems because of their well-known effect on keeping interest rates high. But just imagine how much more serious the problems would be in the maintenance of macrostability if the phenomenon of deadweight drag had continued! True, with voluntary quotas some increases in the prices of steel inputs may occur if the current recovery gains further momentum. These increases, however, will be small compared with those involved with the previous method of control (i.e., the target-price mechanism).

Nevertheless, in the longer run some industries face serious adjustment problems. For many years some industries featuring scale economies that were associated with an almost unbelievable degree of specialization—notably, automobiles and steel—were able to escape from foreign competition. But that is no longer the case.

Why, then, have Japanese firms done so well? In particular, why over the past 20 years have productivity gains in the Japanese auto industry averaged about three times those of the U.S. auto industry? Essentially, they have evolved a practice that can be described as "dynamic flexibility." As contrasted with static flexibility, dynamic flexibility is not concerned with producing more than one product (e.g., cars and light trucks) on a single production line—although the Japanese do this, too. Rather, it is concerned with designing production lines in a way that they can quickly evolve in response to changes in either the product or production technology. In other words, the central preoccupation is to get ideas into action quickly. For example, when new Japanese models develop bugs, some companies make changes on the production line before the next model year.

The main purpose of dynamic flexibility, however, is to make rapid changes in production technology for the purpose of lowering costs and thereby improving productivity. Almost every Japanese auto company has a large machine-tool operation in which 200 to 400 people do nothing but create new tools, which are quickly introduced into the production process. In turn, this requires a highly nonspecialized method of operation, which the Japanese often liken to the approach followed in American farming. In particular, workers are rotated from job to job on the production lines every 3 to 6 months, and managers, every 3 to 5 years, often to decidedly different jobs. For example, in one firm I visited, the head of the accounting department was an engineer. Or, when I talked to a Japanese executive in charge of building a new Honda plant to produce Accords in Columbus, Ohio, I found that he was not an engineer—and never before had been concerned with building a plant. "Why did they choose you?" I asked him. He replied that his superiors wanted someone who was good at asking sharp questions—and in the American marketing division of Honda, from which he came, "We Japanese specialize in asking sharp questions!"

Another respect in which Japanese auto plants are like American farms is that there is a high degree of interaction between management and workers. For example, I asked an American worker in charge of the painting line at the Honda motorcycle plant in Columbus, "What is it like to work for a Japanese firm?" He told me in some detail about an experience he had with receiving painting robots from Japan, which, having been designed for painting flat surfaces on automobiles, did a poor job in painting the curved surfaces of motorcycles. He discussed the problem with two managers during lunch in the company cafeteria. Immediately after lunch, the managers went to see

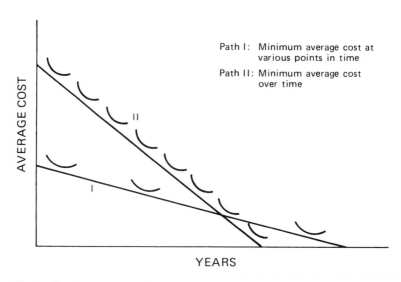

FIGURE 2   Two ways to reduce costs.

for themselves that the robots left bubbles in the paint, and by 4:00 p.m. that day a message was sent to Japan that they were going to revert to the former method of painting until a better-designed painting robot was furnished them. This American worker's reaction? Nothing like that ever before had happened to him!

A diagrammatic representation of the classical American and Japanese approaches is shown in Figure 2. The Japanese long-run cost path is described as a "saturation path," because the Japanese claim that they are introducing innovations about as rapidly as they can. Inasmuch as costs cannot be pinned down for a period longer than 6 months or so, there is a greater multiplicity of long-run cost curves. It also should be noted that Japanese plants for producing cars are only about one-third as large as comparable American plants. Why? The Japanese claim that building larger plants would impede their enjoyment of dynamic flexibility.

Similar practices to those of the Japanese firms are probably not numerous in American industry, but there are some notable exceptions. John Deere & Company operates in much the same way, as does Boeing. As a result of subcontracting with Mitsubishi for parts to be used on the 757 and 767 airplanes, Boeing executives claim that Mitsubishi is a good partner, because they operate in much the same way as Boeing. Moreover, engineers from the Sony television plant located in San Diego claim that they not only make about 90 percent of their components, but by utilizing a highly skilled labor force they are able to operate quite as flexibly as comparable plants in Japan. And engineers from the Honda motorcycle plant in Ohio also make the same claim. Desperately needed, of course, are the data required to substantiate these claims.

CONCLUSIONS

Ending the U.S. quotas on Japanese auto imports was a constructive step. The Japanese did not evolve into their present method of operations overnight; hence, it would be very optimistic to assume that American auto firms will be able to make the adjustment without some serious setbacks.

Is moving toward less specialization contrary to the teachings of Adam Smith? By no means. He understood the secret of the success of the Japanese auto industry as early as 1776:

The man whose whole life is spent in performing a few simple operations, of which the effects are perhaps always the same, or very nearly the same, has no occasion to exert his understanding or to exercise his invention in finding out expedients for removing difficulties which never occur. He naturally loses, therefore, the habit of such exertion, and generally becomes as stupid and ignorant as it is possible for a human creature to become.[4]

NOTES

1. For a more detailed discussion of the statistical results, see Burton H. Klein, *Prices, Wages, and Business Cycles* (New York: Pergamon Press, 1984), pp. 46–127.
2. Ibid., pp. 123–124.
3. N. L. S. Carnot, *Reflections on the Motive Power of Heat*. Translated by R. H. Thurston (New York: Wiley, 1980), pp. 206–208.
4. Adam Smith, *The Wealth of Nations*. London: Everyman's Library, J. M. Dent & Sons Ltd., 1947: vol. II, p. 278.

The Effect of Recent Macroeconomic Policies on Innovation and Productivity

CHARLES B. REEDER

Smaller federal deficits, lower interest rates, and a weaker dollar all are considered necessary and "good" for the economy, but some of the drive to improve efficiency and productivity will be lost without the spur of foreign competition. This is the dilemma that policymakers must contend with as they weigh the pros and cons of various policy choices.

While economic theory has not been able to link macroeconomic policies to the behavior of individual firms in the specific areas of innovation and productivity, there nevertheless are some remarkable developments taking place today in these areas that, I believe, are in response to the *consequences* of recent macroeconomic policies. An examination of these developments will not produce a true theory of innovation based on macroeconomic policy, but it should improve our understanding of the process—particularly the way in which market forces often produce unintended results.

The point at which my analysis begins is the recent changes in government economic policies designed to stimulate saving and investment and simultaneously curb inflation (Reaganomics). These policies included significant reductions in marginal tax rates for individuals, major changes in laws affecting corporate savings through depreciation, and an unrelenting effort on the part of the Federal Reserve Board to limit the growth of the money supply.

There has been, and will continue to be, a debate among economists as to the wisdom of these policies, but few can deny that they produced the intended results at the macro level—albeit with significant time lags and with some undesired side effects. Foremost among these results were the following:

• The gross private saving rate for the nation increased by approximately 2 percentage points between 1982 and 1984, and in 1984 was the highest since the end of World War II.

• Outlays for investment in nonresidential structures and equipment soared 20 percent in 1984 in real terms, the largest 1-year increase since the end of World War II. Business fixed investment was the fastest-growing segment of GNP in 1984 and played a major role in the strong recovery from the 1981–1982 recession.

• The rate of inflation, as measured by the GNP deflator, fell from 9.6 percent in 1981 to 3.8 percent in 1984 even though real economic activity was growing at 6.8 percent.

From an analytical standpoint these results can be regarded as first-order results of the shift in economic policies that occurred in 1981. Second-order results were the sharp increase in the federal deficit, the persistence of high real interest rates, and the spectacular rise in the value of the dollar. The budget deficit increased from $58 billion in 1981 to $195 billion in 1983, real interest rates (the spread between nominal interest rates and the rate of inflation) remained in the 6 to 8 percent range even though nominal rates declined, and the value of the dollar rose over 30 percent from December 1981 to December 1984.

Of these results, the most important in terms of innovation and productivity were the rise in the dollar and the resulting surge in imports to the United States. In 1984 total non-oil imports soared 30 percent and all U.S. manufacturers felt the pressure of this competition from abroad.

Economists tend to focus on the macroeconomic results of macroeconomic policies, i.e., how tax cuts create large deficits, how large deficits cause interest rates to rise, how high interest rates attract foreign capital to finance the deficits, how the inflow of capital raises the value of the dollar, and so on. But businessmen operate in a different world. They see the world at the micro level, where they must compete with foreign-produced goods at prices set by producers whose costs are largely denominated in depreciated currencies relative to the dollar. In this situation they must do whatever they can to survive, and since they cannot control the value of the dollar, they turn to what they can control—their own costs of production. On the labor front they have demanded—and gotten—lower wages as the price of keeping jobs in the United States. On the capital front they have sought whatever new equipment is available to improve productivity and reduce unit costs. Their need for capital has coincided with exciting new developments in the telecommunications field, in computers, robots, lasers, and so on. Most of these products have applications in manufacturing, but the service industries also have been able to take advantage of them.

Without delving into the specific products and their applications, the basic point is that industry has been goaded into a massive cost-reduction and productivity-improvement effort as a response to the results of macroeconomic policies aimed at stimulating saving and investment while controlling inflation. The full consequences of this effort are not yet fully visible because of the continued depressing effect on U.S. production of imports, but the day will come when the dollar declines and growth in other countries accelerates. At that time U.S. manufacturers will see their operating rates rise and their productivity soar because the increased output will be produced with fewer employees and with the most modern plant.

These results were among those desired at the time new macroeconomic policies were undertaken, but the architects of those policies did not expect that the path from cause to effect would be so roundabout—from tax cuts and high interest rates to large deficits, a strong dollar, soaring imports, and the resulting actions of individual firms as they struggled to meet the competition from abroad. These results could not have been achieved without earlier R&D efforts by entrepreneurs and large organizations, but the funding and encouraging of R&D—either by government or private sources—was not the driving force. The marketplace was the force.

These developments have both positive and negative aspects for the nation. The positive aspect is that innovation is being encouraged and that American industry is becoming more efficient. The negative aspect is that our industrial structure is being reshaped drastically, and there is a real risk that costly long-term mistakes will be made. Because there are two sides to this issue there is no simple way to deal with it at the policy level. Smaller federal deficits, lower interest rates, and a weaker dollar all are considered necessary and "good" for the economy, but some of the drive to improve efficiency and productivity will be lost without the spur of foreign competition. This is the dilemma that policymakers must contend with as they weigh the pros and cons of various policy choices.

In summary, these observations do not constitute a new theory in and of themselves, but the linkages described here are not generally recognized by those who are concerned about the theory of innovation and how macroeconomic policy may affect decisions at the level of the firm. Additionally, government policymakers also should recognize that there are secondary and tertiary consequences of their policies, and in some cases the unintended results may be more effective than the direct consequences.

Macrorealities of the Information Economy

STEPHEN S. ROACH

The information economy and the associated surge in high technology spending may well offer promise of renewed productivity growth in the United States, but at current exchange rates the resulting improvements in living standards could well turn out to be built on a foundation of foreign-produced and foreign-owned capital.

Technology has taken on a new role as a conditioner of economic change in the United States. Historically, economists have been preoccupied with technological change in the narrow or microeconomic sense—focusing mainly on the process of innovation, its diffusion, and potential linkages to productivity. A shortcoming of this approach is that it fails to consider the role of technology in the context of dramatic shifts that have occurred in the macrostructure of the economy. Indeed, it can now be demonstrated that high technology holds the key to the evolution of what can be called "the information economy"—a core of activities that increasingly has become a dominant source of economic progress in the United States.

This discussion of the macrodimensions of the information economy draws, in large part, on work we have previously published at Morgan Stanley.[1] The findings of that work can be summarized in a relatively straightforward way. First, the process of structural change in the U.S. economy began in earnest in the 1960s and started with a shift of output and earnings away

---

[1]See The industrialization of the information economy, Morgan Stanley *Economic Perspectives*, June 15, 1984; and S. S. Roach, The information economy comes of age, *Information Management Review*, 1985 (1):9–18.

from traditional manufacturing activities and toward industries engaged predominantly in the creation, manipulation, and distribution of information. An important by-product of such trends was that job growth shifted dramatically away from employment on the factory assembly line and toward the white-collar work force. Such workers had labored for years at a distinct disadvantage because they had relatively limited productive capital at their disposal. With the explosion in high technology spending in the late 1970s, however, that all began to change, and by 1983 U.S. capital endowment per worker had shifted dramatically away from the factory sector and into the information economy. Therein lies the potential for a resumption of improved longer-term performance of the U.S. economy: the industrialization of the information economy.

SHIFTS IN OUTPUT AND EARNINGS

Information has become a reality for most industries—whether they are in the factory or the so-called service sector. The information intensity of a firm's output is highest in such areas as communications, finance, and insurance, as well as in some of the more traditional service areas, such as those provided by business consultants and professionals. In such information-intensive industries, companies usually do not produce physical products, but instead combine the flow of information with their skilled labor force and high technology capital to generate a knowledge-based "commodity." Even in manufacturing the growing use of robotics, computer-aided design/computer-aided manufacturing (CAD/CAM), and management information systems (MIS)-based control underscores the potential applications that information technologies can have on the traditional factory assembly line.

Figure 1 lays out the broad boundaries of the information economy. Shown in the upper panel of the figure is a decomposition of private nonfarm output into two broad groupings of industries. Defined in this context, the "information sector" includes not only traditional services but also finance, insurance, real estate, trade, transportation, communications, and public utilities. The "goods sector" is what is left over: manufacturing, mining, and construction. The share of output going to the goods sector has declined steadily since the mid-1960s from about 45 percent to about 37 percent in 1984. By contrast, the output share of the information sector has risen to over 60 percent, and our Morgan Stanley projections suggest that this group of industries will generate close to two out of every three dollars of national output by the end of 1985.

As the lower panel of Figure 1 indicates, similar shifts can be observed in the composition of corporate profits. In 1984 the information sector accounted for essentially half the volume of total corporate profits in the United

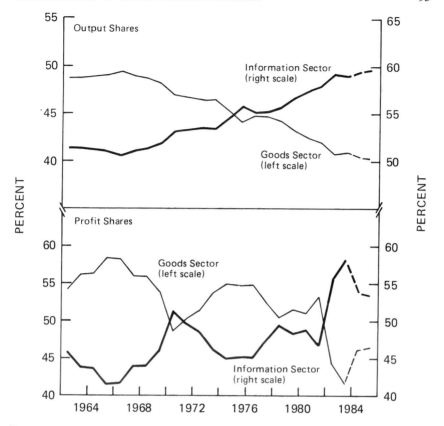

FIGURE 1   The emergence of the information economy.
NOTE: Dashed lines indicate Morgan Stanley economics projections.
SOURCE: Morgan Stanley *Economic Perspectives*, June 15, 1984.

States—increasing its earnings share almost 25 percent over the past decade. Moreover, on a per unit basis, the rise in profitability for information-intensive industries exceeded the growth in output over the past 10 years—a clear sign of an advantageous shift in earnings leverage that is another important by-product of an emerging information economy.

INFORMATION WORKERS AND THE INVESTMENT RESPONSE

Table 1 illustrates one of the most important characteristics of the information sector—the employment of a relatively large share of what traditionally has been referred to as the economy's "white-collar" occupations. These workers, hereafter referred to as the information work force, are

TABLE 1   Growing Information-Intensity of the Work Force
(share of private nonfarm work force)

	Average: 1962 to 1972		1983	
	Information Workers	Production Workers	Information Workers	Production Workers
Private nonfarm work force	49.2%	50.8%	56.2%	43.8%
Information sector	62.3	37.7	65.7	34.3
Finance, insurance, and real estate	92.9	7.1	92.4	7.6
Services	61.9	38.1	66.6	33.4
Trade	62.5	37.5	61.6	38.4
Transportation and public utilities	40.8	59.2	49.7	50.3
Goods sector	28.7	71.3	33.6	66.4
Manufacturing	30.4	69.6	36.8	63.2
Mining	28.8	71.2	44.4	55.6
Construction	21.9	78.1	21.4	78.6

SOURCE: Bureau of Labor Statistics Occupational-Industry Matrix.

defined to include executives, administrators, managers, professional specialists, technicians, salesworkers, and the support staffs of each of these groups. As the table indicates, the concentration of information workers is clearly highest in the information sector of the economy. Indeed, in 1983 information-intensive industries employed, on average, two information workers for every production worker; in contrast, the ratio is reversed in the goods sector. Thus, we can tentatively conclude that the information sector includes not only the fastest-growing and most profitable industries of the economy but, as expected, a highly disproportionate share of the information work force.

If shifts in the mix of output, earnings, and employment persist long enough, it is only natural to expect a complementary response in the composition of the remaining factor of production—the capital stock. It took more than 10 years for such a shift to occur, but when it did it came with a vengeance! Figure 2 overlays compositional shifts in capital spending with the trends in the mix of the work force just described. The upper panel highlights the essence of an emerging information economy: a rising share of the information work force together with an explosion of the high technology portion of business capital spending. From the mid-1960s through 1984, high-tech spending—defined as computers, office machines, communications equipment, instruments, industrial control and measuring devices, and miscellaneous electrical components and machinery—almost tripled as a portion of total business fixed investment, rising from about 12 percent to over 35 percent. Similarly, during the same period, the employment share of information workers climbed an estimated 10 percentage points to about 55 percent of the nonfarm work force.

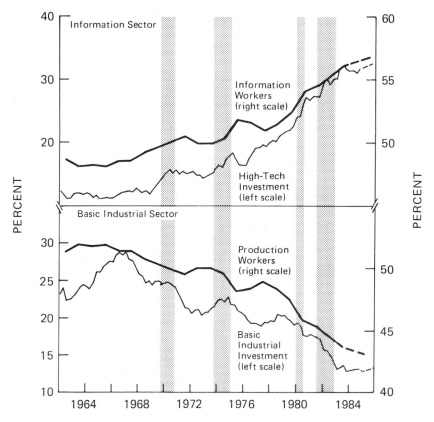

FIGURE 2   Structural change and the information economy (investment and employment shares).

NOTE: Shaded areas indicate recessionary periods as designated by the National Bureau of Economic Research. Dashed lines indicate Morgan Stanley economics projections.

SOURCE: Morgan Stanley *Economic Perspectives*, June 15, 1984.

A COMMON THREAD

The shifts in the composition of employment and capital accumulation turn out to be far more than a mere coincidence. Indeed, it is increasingly important to view the extraordinary acceleration of spending on high technology as the complementary investment response to the rapid expansion of the information work force. This conclusion is based on the fact that high technology capital turns out to be the mainstay of "production" in the information segment of our economy.

This assertion can be verified by examining the interindustry flows of shipments for a large number of high technology items. Figure 3 shows the sectoral allocations of such flows for 1982—the latest year for which there are reliable benchmark statistics. It is no surprise that industries that have been identified as being among the most information-intensive in the economy were also recipients of the bulk of high-tech equipment. Indeed, almost 85 percent of computers, other office machinery, and communications equipment was shipped to the information sector in 1982. To be sure, the share was somewhat lower for instruments and photographic equipment, and clearly, most measuring and control devices are purchased by manufacturing companies. Nonetheless, about 70 percent of all purchases of high-tech equipment were made by information-intensive industries.

Thus, high-tech investment and information-worker employment go hand in hand—more than a decade of parallel trends appears to be far more than just happenstance. Figure 4 brings together these compositional shifts in labor and capital. Shown in the figure are ratios (in real terms) of the stock of basic industrial capital per production worker and high-tech capital per information worker—the most logical way to match the functional categories of productive capital with the workers who actually utilize such facilities in the production process.

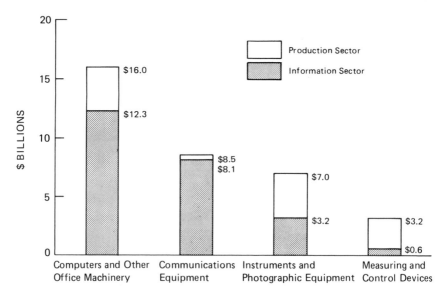

FIGURE 3   Who uses high-tech equipment? (Allocation of private domestic final shipments in 1982.)
SOURCE: Morgan Stanley economics estimates based on input-output industry distribution tables provided by the Interindustry Service of Data Resources, Inc.

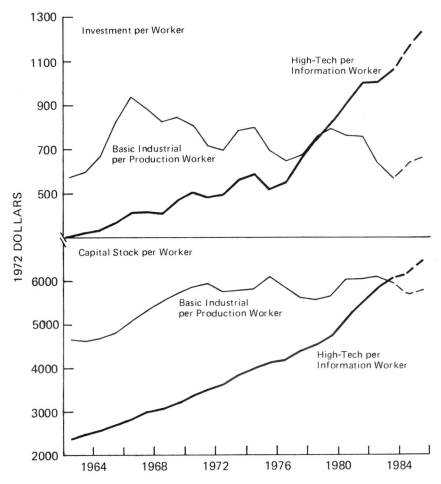

FIGURE 4   Investment and capital stock per worker: high-tech versus basic industrial.
NOTE: Investment and capital stock are expressed in constant 1972 dollars. Dashed lines
indicate Morgan Stanley economics projections.
SOURCE: Morgan Stanley *Economics Projections*, June 15, 1984.

Figure 4 reveals a dramatic convergence between these two components
of the economy's overall capital:labor ratio. Over a span of 20 years, the
stock of high-tech capital per information worker moved from about half the
size of its basic industrial counterpart to a position of relative parity in 1983.
This trend, perhaps more than anything else, brings the information sector
to the forefront of economic change in the United States; its workers are now

as richly endowed with capital as are typical production workers on the factory assembly line. What has occurred is essentially a new process of industrialization—one that should dispel any doubts about the potential vitality of the information economy.

PRODUCTIVITY IMPLICATIONS

During the long sweep of U.S. economic history, trends in capital:labor ratios and productivity change have tended to move together. While many point to the slower growth of the total stock of capital per worker as a key element in this nation's productivity shortfall, what has been overlooked is the dramatic shifts that have been taking place in the mix of capital endowment across sectors. Potentially, these relative movements may have even more to say about this nation's productivity potential than do summary ratios that lump together and weigh the many diverse types of capital against a variety of widely disparate occupational categories of the work force.

A key question, of course, is whether the rapidly rising endowment of high-tech capital embodies efficiencies that ultimately could generate improvements in information-worker productivity. On that count, the verdict is still out. Some believe that there has been unnecessary and indiscriminate spending on new technologies. Others believe that the productivity payback of the information economy cannot be accomplished without major improvements in technology management.

Over time, however, productivity change in the information economy should be less conditioned by managerial behavior and become more a function of the extraordinary revolution in microprocessing. Critical in this regard are the steady miniaturization of the "chip" and increasing economies in the costs of its production. Moreover, the rapidly changing technology of hardware is likely to be increasingly augmented by concomitant breakthroughs in operating systems or software—trends that ultimately hold the potential for the introduction of efficiencies in the workplace that are well beyond the realm of present-day comprehension. Just as economies on the assembly line once were the engine of productivity growth in "smokestack America," high technology also has the potential to spark even greater efficiencies in the information economy.

Of special note in this regard is the "leverage factor"—the fact that information workers currently account for about 60 percent of all hours worked in the economy. That implies, most critically, that improvements in information-worker productivity should add about 50 percent more to overall productivity change than would comparable increments for production workers. Thus, like it or not, productivity change in the aggregate is now increasingly in the hands of improved efficiencies in the information economy.

A DARK SIDE

Despite this constructive turn of events, the emergence of the information economy has a dark side. Unfortunately, it turns out that a strong dollar and an ever-widening foreign trade deficit have taken an unusually heavy toll on U.S. high technology producers. Indeed, in a recent report we at Morgan Stanley estimate that imports of high-tech equipment have risen to over twice the level prevailing in late 1982—producing a 60 percent increase in the market share of foreign-produced technology items (Table 2).[2]

In the context of the steadily growing technological requirements of an expanding information economy, not only does such a development hint at a potentially chronic dimension of the U.S. trade deficit, but it also underscores the risk that American capital-goods producers could be squeezed out of participating in the most dramatic structural transformation of the U.S. economy since the Industrial Revolution. The information economy may well offer a promise of renewed productivity growth, but at current exchange rates, the resulting improvements in living standards could well turn out to be built on a foundation of foreign-produced and foreign-owned capital.

Such a problem underscores the notion that no matter how powerful the forces of transformation are, the dynamics of a technology-based information economy are vulnerable to the same problems that have plagued Washington over the past two decades. Quite simply, an expansive fiscal policy in the context of monetary discipline and flexible exchange rates will continue to cause currency strains and heightened import penetration. And as recent trends strongly hint, the high technology sector in the United States could find itself as the new victim of this untenable imbalance in the mix of public policy.

REALITIES OR VISIONS?

Despite the caution flag raised by import penetration, the U.S. economy is clearly passing through a critical milestone in its postindustrial history. Much has been written about the productivity shortfall of the past decade. Little attention has been given, however, to the possibility that such an occurrence might well be the by-product of an economy making a rather orderly transition from a basic industrial society to one that emphasizes

---

[2]See Trading away the capital spending recovery, Morgan Stanley *Economic Perspectives*, February 6, 1985.

TABLE 2 Functional Breakdown of Capital Goods Imports
(billions of current dollars)

	1982 Quarter 4	1983 Quarter 4	1984 Quarter 1	1984 Quarter 2	1984 Quarter 3	Cumulative Change Over 7 Quarters
Total capital goods imports (excluding motor vehicles)	$34.2	$45.5	$57.5	$55.9	$68.7	$34.5
High technology imports	19.7	29.9	36.8	35.8	42.9	23.2
Computers and office machinery	6.3	10.4	13.8	12.7	15.7	9.4
Communication equipment and electronic components	10.1	15.1	18.1	18.1	21.0	10.9
Instruments	3.3	4.4	4.9	4.9	6.1	2.8
Basic industrial imports	9.8	10.9	14.5	14.9	18.5	8.7
Construction and specialized machinery	3.5	4.2	5.3	5.8	7.0	3.5
Other industrial machinery	6.3	6.8	9.2	9.1	11.4	5.1
Other imports	4.7	4.7	6.3	5.3	7.3	2.6
Memo items:						
Import share of						
High technology	26.6%	33.9%	40.7%	37.8%	43.0%	n.a.
Basic industrial	16.4	16.9	21.2	20.5	24.6	n.a.

SOURCE: Census-based tabulation of U.S. international transactions.

information-intensive activities. The dramatic improvements that have recently occurred in the high-tech capital endowment of the information work force suggest that this transitional interlude may be coming to an end. Instead, around the corner could very well lurk the long-awaited revival of productivity growth in the United States—the seeds of which were sown through the industrialization of the information economy.

There is no assurance, of course, that technology is *the* answer to productivity. One thing is certain, however. The structure of the U.S. economy in the mid-1980s bears little resemblance to that of the past. The eroding market share of manufacturing output and the related loss of assembly-line jobs have forced business managers headlong into the Information Age. For a long time the steps were tentative, but in the last 7 years or so the steps have become more purposeful: a conscious effort has been made to build an infrastructure of productive capital in the information economy. Without that development corporate America would have found itself caught in something of a time warp—outgrowing its industrial heritage but unwilling to look to the future. That hesitation has passed, and economic performance over the next several decades now appears to depend critically on the new realities of the information economy.

Harnessing Technology for Growth

ROBERT MALPAS

Perhaps both Europe and the United States are suffering a little from the "grass is greener" syndrome. From the European perspective, what is happening in America is an enviable and fabulous success story. Ten million jobs have been created in 5 years in the United States—in Europe, none. The United States had phenomenal growth in 1984 and has a strong venture capital market. Some 600,000 companies are created each year in the United States, about a third of them in high technology. Yet Americans, too, are looking over fences, because there is indeed a problem. How do you maintain the tremendous momentum and dynamism generated these last few years to continue to create jobs and to generate wealth?

My particular interest in the interaction between technology and economic growth is that I try to do what H. W. Coover talks about in this volume (chapter on "Programmed Innovation—Strategy for Success"). My responsibilities at British Petroleum include trying to do all those things that Coover discusses, devising and implementing both evolutionary and revolutionary methods to achieve them.

My interest stems also from the fact that I am on a British government committee and the Engineering Council, both of which have the difficult but vitally important task of setting out to reverse Britain's industrial decline. We are trying to counter the erroneous view that Britain is in a postindustrial era, and that our future is to become almost wholly a service society. Until about a year ago the government, heavily committed to the perfection of market forces, was taking a line that gave the impression to some that industry did not matter to Britain.

My discussion is set against a background that is best summarized by the advertisement shown in Figure 1 which was devised by the Engineering Council to shock the nation. It has done so. You don't have to know much about that quaint and very English game cricket to appreciate that what is happening to each of these players is bad. You do have to know that last

106

FIGURE 1 "Once more the world is beating us at our own game. And it's not cricket." Advertisement devised by the Engineering Council (London) shows cricket players in poor form to make some startling points about Britain's industrial decline. Captions below players read as follows:

● After the war Britain was 3rd largest steel producer. Now we are 10th.

● In 1900 Britain made 60% of the world's shipping. Today we make 3%.

● Britain once exported motor bikes to over 100 countries. Now we import almost every machine we buy.

● Before the war almost every car on our roads was British. Now well over half are foreign.

● Britain pioneered the world machine tool industry. Our share is now 3.1%.

● Britain discovered the wireless. We now import 96% of our portable radios.

● Britain made the first practical computer. We now have only 5% of the Information Technology market.

● We once made all the textile machinery in the world. We now make 8%.

● Last year Britain even imported 65% of our sports equipment. How's that!

SOURCE: Reprinted with permission of The Engineering Council, London, England.

year we were beaten by just about every nation that plays this bizarre game. Given that we taught them, "It's not cricket!" that they should beat us, which you know means that we think it is unfair! The caption under each player spells out that for industry after industry others are beating us at our own game. We taught *them*, damn it! So it's not fair! But then, similar complaints seem to be emanating from the United States, concerning your country, and this indeed is a surprise.

Perhaps I am an incurable optimist, but I am confident that we will succeed in my company in harnessing technology for growth to a significantly greater extent than has been the case over the last decade. Similarly, I hold out great hope for Britain despite the national background that I have painted, and despite a Europe where such words as "Eurosclerosis" and "Europessimism" have entered the vocabulary and are fashionable. Daniel I. Okimoto (in this volume), in what is a superb analysis contrasting the situation in the United States and Japan, raises the question: "Is this a two-horse race between the United States and Japan, with Europe straining not to fall too far behind?"

Perhaps we in Europe, and you in the United States, are suffering a little from "the grass is greener" syndrome, for what we in Europe see happening in the United States is an enviable and fabulous success story. You have created 10 million jobs in 5 years—Europe has created none. You had phenomenal growth in 1984. You have a strong venture capital market, which is largely responsible for creating your position in biotechnology, ahead of the rest of the world. You have great mobility in your work force and are not encumbered by such antidynamic forces as rent control acts and old-fashioned institutions. You have been creating 600,000 new companies each year, about a third of them in high technology. You have a very rich society with plenty of aunties and uncles ready to finance fledgling start-up companies either directly or indirectly. You are reviving so-called mature industries by the application of high technology both to the design of the product and to the manufacturing process. Chrysler is a case in point. You have huge defense and space budgets and far better mechanisms than we in Europe to harness the technology these develop for broader commercial use.

Figure 2 shows defense spending as a percentage of gross domestic product (GDP) for selected countries and Figure 3 shows the same in absolute numbers. Compare the United States with Europe, remembering that Europe is still very fragmented and that we have relatively poor mechanisms to harness this effort outside defense. As part of the "grass is greener" syndrome, we in Europe say that obviously the U.S. effort in defense and space is a major reason why you do better, but then we look at Japan, which does not have a similar driving force for technological innovation. So we look around for other reasons and, without decrying the brilliant job the Japanese have done and are doing, we point to their highly protected market. We in Europe are significantly more open and less protected—even more so than the United

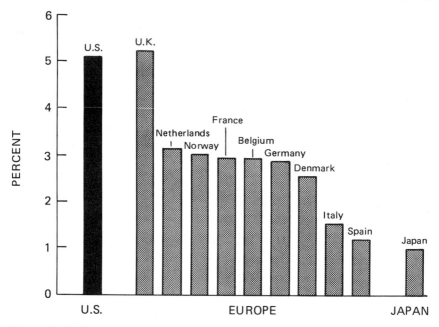

FIGURE 2   Defense expenditures in selected countries as percentage of gross domestic product (GDP), 1980–1984 average.

States. Far be it from me to argue in favor of protectionism, but are we in Europe perhaps too liberal? I think not, and I think that both these reasons reflect a high element of "looking for excuses."

The United States is so attractive to investors that one new investment fund recently was reported to have raised £200 million. They proudly announced that it was all to be invested in high technology in California!

So there is no shortage of money in Britain for investment. The North Sea will call for £60 billion over the next 10 years, much more than the last 10. No one has any doubt that it will be found—and easily. And we have no shortage of ideas in Britain. We have had, and still have, a great capacity for invention. So in the government committee ACARD (Advisory Council for Applied Research and Development), we are addressing the question of why the available money does not meet the abundance of new ideas. It is a difficult and complex question to answer, but in a few words, I would say, "Because there are too many apparently less risky options." You seem to have solved the problem in the United States—but then, perhaps the grass is greener!

You have conferences that set out to develop a proper dialogue between economists and technologists, recognizing that dialogue and mutual understanding are prerequisites of continued success. We are having difficulty in this respect in the United Kingdom. A recent lecture in London brought together financiers, economists, scientists, and industrialists, the aim being to promote dialogue. We failed. The financiers clammed up defensively.

The grass seems unquestionably greener over here, yet you are looking over other fences because there is indeed a problem. How do you maintain the tremendous momentum and dynamism generated these past few years to continue to create jobs as you have done and to generate wealth? You have identified a gap described neatly by Harvey Brooks (in this volume), who said that historically in the United States there has always been a gap between the private enterprise system and government policy, particularly in the development of long-lead-time innovation. The grass certainly does seem greener in Japan in this respect, but harbor no envy for Europe.

And of course everyone is concerned with the gap between invention and commercialization, the process called innovation. On the grand scale, innovation does fall foul of the gap between private enterprise, which is properly preoccupied with the bottom line, and government policy, which should be capable of longer-term, patient money, except that politicians need to be elected too frequently.

There is indeed a problem in financing what I will call "big D." Research (R) and development ("little d") get one to the stage of, say, a prototype and a small-scale manufacturing process. "Big D" involves taking the fruits of R & d to full-scale production and marketing. Innovation is not complete

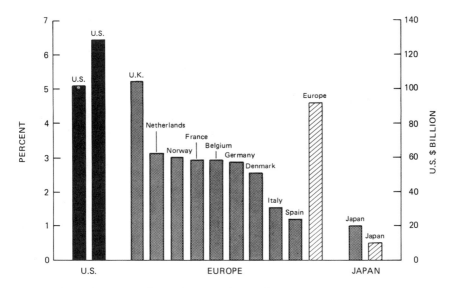

FIGURE 3   Defense expenditures in selected countries as percentage of gross domestic product (GDP), 1980–1984 average; and in U.S. dollars in 1980.

at the prototype stage. Moreover, the marketing element of "big D" and its huge costs are as important as the science and technology. We have all learned that if R costs 1 unit, "little d" costs 10 units, and "big D" costs 100. Herein lies the financing problem, particularly if it takes a long time, which, other than in the field of electronics, is usually the case. It takes heavy front-end money, with a long and risky payback—patient money. If it fails, there is usually a large and visible monument to failure to remind one of the folly. Hence people, whose promotion in a company is based on 3 to 5 years of achievement, are scared of it. Research, on the other hand, is relatively inexpensive. Anywhere from $1 million to $20 million buys considerable effort, and you can stop it without much visibility. Big D, however, involves major investment.

Harnessing technology for growth, however difficult, is essential for success, of a company and a nation, particularly in a sustained period of low growth. No doubt the world is in such a period now. The 1950s and 1960s were a high-growth era in which prosperity could be achieved by a me-too approach. High growth provided ready-made markets to conquer. A low-growth era requires that products, and processes to make them, have "edge." Both product and process edge flow from technology.

This realization is increasingly pervading the boardrooms of all corporations, and this is happening in Britain. For the United States, H. W. Coover described how his company has increased its research effort and has devised new mechanisms to turn it into commercial success. This realization of the need for edge to be provided by technology will be the main force that will bring together the money needed to innovate both on a small and on a grand scale.

In closing, I raise several important issues regarding the commercialization of technology. I suggest eight issues for study.

1. What Is the Role of Government? A number of contributors to this volume discuss the role of government in technology development. Robert Swanson, for example, devotes most of his chapter to it, as does Ed Zschau, who makes several brilliant comments. We must, however, try to be specific about what is needed, particularly in the light of the very large proportion of GDP that is government expenditure, as shown for selected countries in Figure 4. Look at Europe, for instance.

Private enterprise is not quite bridging the financing gap required for expensive, long-lead-time projects, and all governments are trying to reduce expenditure. Swanson has reportedly raised the $56 million he needs; however, he might yet need $300 million or $400 million properly to commercialize his inventions. It is doubtful that venture capital will fill this "big D" need, and indeed we should not expect it to do so. So is he looking to government for help? Perhaps this is where large companies with cash mountains that have resulted from tidying up their operations should step in.

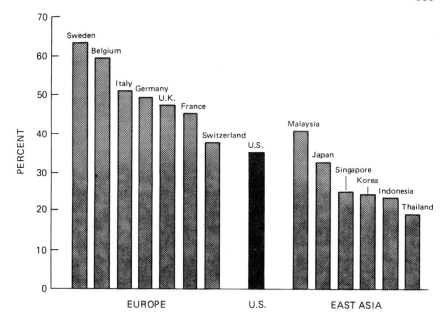

FIGURE 4   General government expenditures in selected countries as percentage of gross domestic product (GDP), 1980–1984 average.

Perhaps they would do better financing innovation on a grand scale than buying each other!

2. Financial Expectations   How often do we hear, "They play it by different rules"? Who plays it by different rules? The Germans? The Japanese? British electronic companies regularly refer to Germany, Japan, and France in these terms. What do we mean by it, that return-on-capital expectations are lower? Well, if they are, certainly the German and Japanese economies as a whole seem to be doing well; the end result is satisfactory. So what formula do they use? We must grapple with this apparent contradiction and not just keep complaining that they play it by different rules.

3. More and Better Mechanisms   We need more mechanisms like R&D partnerships, which have worked, and are working, well. The venture-capital movement has been of major significance in the United States, and we are delighted that it is in full swing in Britain. However, do not expect it to deal with really "big D" expenditure.

The Unlisted Securities Market (USM) was formed in Britain about 3 years ago and is flourishing, providing equity for start-up companies in their second stage of development. The USM market in Britain is now valued at $2.8 billion and is so flexible and effective that U.S. companies are using it to raise equity for investment in the United States!

In Britain, finance has become too centralized in London. It is interesting to reflect that the rapid development of the railway system in England during the last century was financed wholly by provincial banks—London did not want to know! No doubt the U.S. transportation infrastructure was similarly developed by decentralized financial support.

In Britain, we need richer aunties and uncles. Mrs. Thatcher has done a great deal to revive the quest for personal wealth by altering the tax system to reduce the amount government takes away from successful people. Europe in general still has too high a floor of unemployment benefit and too low a ceiling for success. Here again, it is this realization that personal wealth is an essential fuel for entrepreneurial drive, both for individuals and companies, that is causing attitudes to change.

4. The Third Dimension Accounting standards have been built up almost entirely on the concepts of revenue and capital, assets being physical, either products or factories. But increasingly technology is concerned with intellectual property and current accounting practices do not deal with it adequately. Coover (in this volume) touched on this, and in British Petroleum we are looking at the issue fundamentally. Research must have a value greater than zero, yet that is how we treat it. Each year it is written off. Quite apart from anything else, these days when people's performance is increasingly measured by monetary value, it is very demotivating to researchers, and it is a real problem.

5. DCF Is the Enemy of Strategy Discounted Cash Flow (DCF) techniques reduce long-term gain to insignificant value, however brilliant the prospects for the longer term. We need better mechanisms and some are emerging. Professor Hank Jacoby of MIT spent a sabbatical year with British Petroleum and introduced the concept of ''generating options for the future.'' A first project may have a low DCF, but it will open up many options which would not exist if the first investment were not made, for example, a second or third plant, spin-off technology, new markets, a family of products, and so on. We should try to assess these many options, establish their risk value, and add that value to the first project, for they are a consequence of the first low-DCF investment.

6. Excellent Manufacturing Technology Swanson (in this volume) discusses the prime importance of developing innovative, excellent process technology if biotechnology is to realize its full potential. Excellent manufacturing technology is what the Japanese have developed for all their products. Their attention to this, and to excellent product design, is the main reason for their preeminence today.

We in Britain have tended to ignore it. We have a record of producing many firsts—radar, television, jet engines, but we did not devote, for any of these, sufficient attention to how to produce products for world, not just home (which is relatively small in Britain), markets by low-cost manufacturing processes.

In this respect, government intervention can be damaging because of the cost-plus mentality, and government specifications frequently apply only to the needs of the country. Thus, the government as a purchaser is a dangerously soft option that can prejudice world sales.

7. More Engineers Japan produces more engineers than Britain produces total graduates. Engineering in Britain is, as you probably know, regarded as a fairly lowly activity. And a production engineer is near the bottom of the engineers' merit scale. Something of the same attitude is at work here in the United States. Yet we are now realizing that excellent design and manufacturing technology are required to turn invention into world-beating, low-cost products.

I now refer to manufacturing technologists, implying that the activity is broader than being a production, mechanical, electrical, chemical, or any other kind of engineer.

8. The Role of Large Companies Coover has discussed the role of companies, and I have told you what I am trying to do. I have also suggested that companies with cash mountains developing should be a major source of financing for "big D." The problem is that many are apprehensive that the cash mountains will soon vanish if they do not choose the projects well. In other words, it is risky, but then risk taking is the major element necessary to harness technology. Without it, we will be condemned to lower and lower growth.

Technology and Its Role
in Modern Society

STEPHEN D. BECHTEL, JR.

This volume brings together some of the nation's leading thinkers and doers in the fields of economics and technology. Economics and technology are among the most important forces affecting America's industrial leadership. Although it is not always recognized even by people who should *know, these fields are inseparable in the real world, and they must be studied jointly if either is to be fully understood.*

Authors and readers of this volume share much in spirit, if not in circumstance, with our eighteenth-century forefathers. Just as they were, we are presented by circumstances with the opportunity to reexamine our national goals and to reorient our future in the face of adverse economic conditions. And, just as those Revolutionary War patriots were called upon to take a stand 200 years ago, so modern Americans were summoned by President Reagan in his 1985 State of the Union address to what he termed the "Second American Revolution." He spoke optimistically of our opportunities and of our technological prowess. We must, however, be prepared to seize those opportunities if we are to capitalize on them. That can be done only from a position of knowledge and understanding of the interrelationships among all segments of our society.

With the objective of making a contribution to such understanding, this volume brings together some of the nation's leading thinkers and doers in the fields of economics and technology.

I wish to share an observation on the recently published report, *Global Competition: The New Reality*, of the President's Commission on Industrial Competitiveness (see Young, in this volume). Beyond its assemblage of essential data and its perceptive analyses, the report's real importance may lie in the cogency with which it presents ties between technology and our economy, between our economy and the international marketplace, and between the international marketplace and the American work force. We hope that the report, which addresses one of our nation's most critical issues, will be broadly studied and that its recommendations will be implemented. It is a call to action.

REVIEW OF AMERICA'S TECHNOLOGICAL POSITION

We as a nation have not always fully appreciated our technologists and their achievements. There seem to be irregular swings in public favor. At the turn of the century, there was a great outpouring of public interest in and support for the activities of such people as Thomas Edison and the Wright brothers. In the 1930s, some of the civil engineering achievements of our times inspired public interest, awe, and enthusiasm. Hoover Dam, the first American megaproject, attracted a near-continual stream of tourists to the Nevada desert long before construction even started. The Golden Gate Bridge remains one of the best-known symbols of the West, a California Statue of Liberty.

During the initial post–World War II years, the mid-1940s through the 1950s, the public mood continued on the side of technology. Television was new. Automobiles were popular. Jet airplanes were flying higher, farther, and faster. Those years also spawned the computer revolution, which in turn allowed the pace of technological advance to quicken and inspired even greater levels of public interest and support.

But without public support, technology withers. For example, during its infancy and years of coming of age, the nuclear power industry was enthusiastically supported, eagerly awaited by an overwhelming majority of the American public. Yet, with the cooling of public sentiment for technology in the mid-1970s, the nuclear power industry came to a stalemate.

During the decades of the 1960s and 1970s, we saw the rise of an enormous public cynicism toward technologists and technology. Industrialists were characterized as wrong until proven right. Engineers were branded as self-centered, lacking in concern for their environment, or even for their fellow-man. Civil works—dams and bridges and highways—were delayed for years by petitions and lawsuits. America's manned space program, ushered into existence with great fanfare and public interest in the 1960s, almost faded from the skies during the mid-1970s, when the public's fancy turned away.

More recently, however, we have seen signs that the public view has turned around again. Technology seems to be back in favor. Among the indicators is the rise in the amount of money that our society is channeling into research and development—in 1984 this amount was $100 billion; in 1985 it is expected to reach 2.7 percent of the GNP, a level not achieved since 1969. The upswing in the public interest and confidence in technology and engineering is heartening. It is also necessary if our economy is to grow and prosper.

ROLE OF THE NATIONAL ACADEMY OF ENGINEERING

As chairman of the National Academy of Engineering, I have had the opportunity to witness the close interdependency between the public and the technical communities. Our Academy itself was founded in 1964 as a result of the cyclic shift in public attention. For much longer, since 1863, the federal government has had available to it an advisory body, the National Academy of Sciences (NAS), for scientific and technical matters. But by the middle of the twentieth century, with the Russian/American race to space in progress, engineering had achieved a stature of special importance.

The National Academy of Engineering was established under the 1863 congressional charter by which the National Academy of Sciences was created. NAE was created to advise the Congress and the executive branch on matters of engineering. In addition, it was given the following mandate:

1. Further the interests of engineering education.
2. Expand U.S. participation in international technical exchanges.
3. Conduct or encourage engineering research deemed advisable in the national interest.
4. Recognize outstanding individuals for their engineering contributions to the nation.

Today, our Academy is composed of more than 1,300 of the nation's most prominent and eminent engineers. About 55 percent of our membership comes from industry. The remaining 45 percent comes from academia, government, and other organizations. I think it is particularly noteworthy that more than half (7 of the 12) of the National Medal of Technology recipients honored recently by President Reagan are members of our Academy—one of those so honored was Ralph Landau, a guiding spirit behind this volume.

The National Academy of Engineering has been very successful during its first two decades of existence. Yet it, like the rest of the nation, is at a crossroads. Our organization has matured: in our twenties, we have "come of age."

As NAE enters its third decade, we plan to take an aggressive posture in exercising our responsibility to advise the government on matters of engineering and technology. And just as the Young Commission (the President's Commission on Industrial Competitiveness referred to earlier) has identified for the nation and the President specific actions that must be taken if the United States is to prosper into the twenty-first century, so have we at the Academy of Engineering identified some directions that we believe must be pursued.

We share with the Young Commission concern about America's ability to maintain its technological leadership. We, too, see a shifting in the lineup of participants in the international marketplace. We, too, want to help America keep its position of economic and technological leadership as the sands shift around us.

A major such direction was established on March 13, 1985, when the National Academy of Engineering was asked by President Reagan "to take the lead and work with the National Academy of Sciences and other technical organizations, to marshal the nation's technical engineering-based expertise in a campaign that will ensure America's scientific, technological and engineering leadership into the 21st Century." He cited the need to "regain U.S. industrial competitiveness and re-establish our technological leadership."

He noted "two conditions of utmost importance to these efforts:

- "First, we must engage the best minds and experience the country has to offer, and
- "Second, the private sector must take the lead."

He went on to say that the National Academy of Engineering's "Decade III Program will address the broad spectrum of issues essential to industrial competitiveness and technological leadership."

On behalf of the National Academy of Engineering, I wish to state that we are not only honored and pleased with the President's request, but we can hope to meet that challenge only with the help and energetic participation of all the interests represented in the pages of this volume and with the full range of scientific, technological, and engineering interests that are not so represented.

CONCLUSION

The material presented in this volume is intended to elevate public awareness of the mutual needs and contributions binding technology and economic health. Indeed, its importance is exceeded only by the need for continuing dialogue.

The engineering profession is beginning to recognize its responsibility to speak out, to participate in public policy debates. We have learned that we need to communicate the reasoning behind our technological needs if we hope to achieve public understanding of what needs to be done.

I hope the understanding achieved through this volume will take root, flourish, and spread through industry, academia, and government. Of course, it would be unreasonable to hope that we can bridge all the gaps that separate the various interests in various parts of our country. But the key to accommodation of divergent opinions is understanding, and the key to understanding is dialogue.

National Science Policy and Technological Innovation

HARVEY BROOKS

There is little debate about the necessity of a federal role in technological innovation when the government is the ultimate user and the goods or services produced are widely acknowledged to be "public goods." There is general agreement, too, that where the costs of R&D can be entirely recovered from the future revenue streams generated by products, services, or information, there is little justification for a government role. In many cases, however, the proper relative roles of the public and private sector are highly controversial. An important factor in each of these cases is who makes the choices and strategic judgments as the R&D evolves. Here, whether the judgments to be made relate primarily to science or technology considerations or primarily to market considerations is often key.

HISTORIC ROLES OF GOVERNMENT IN SCIENCE AND TECHNOLOGICAL INNOVATION

Although industry is the dominant source of commercially significant technology in the United States, government has been a much more important and direct influence on the direction and rate of technological innovation than much of our national ideology and public rhetoric would lead us to suppose. Government in particular has been a source of much "generic technology," as well as fundamental science, which has then served as a substrate for technological innovation by the private industrial sector.

Government has supported the generation of new knowledge and techniques directly, for example, through sponsoring the exploration of the largely unknown American continent in the early nineteenth century, or through the creation of such government agencies as the Agricultural Research Service, the National Bureau of Standards, the Geological Survey, and the National Advisory Committee for Aeronautics (NACA) in the late nineteenth and early twentieth centuries. It has also subsidized the expansion of certain basic industries: the canal system in the early nineteenth century, the westward extension of the railroads in the mid-nineteenth century, the creation of a national highway system to undergird a growing auto industry, the development of an infrastructure of airports and air traffic control as well as air mail subsidies to sustain the growth of a commercial air transport system, and special tax benefits to stimulate the development of the domestic petroleum industry—to name just a few examples of indirect government involvement. These indirect subsidies had the effect of creating a "demand pull" for new technologies, not only within the industries immediately affected, but also in collateral industries that supplied or serviced the subsidized industries. For example, the demand for durable steel rails for the railroads was a major factor driving technological innovation in the burgeoning steel industry (Morison, 1974:72–86). Tax benefits for the petroleum industry not only resulted in cheaper fuel, which stimulated demand for automobiles, but also fostered innovation in oil exploration and drilling technology, in which the United States still leads the world. The subsidy for highways indirectly stimulated innovation in highway construction and planning techniques, but it also influenced the direction of innovation in the automobile industry toward large and powerful cars with increased driving amenities, a stimulus that was reinforced by tax benefits to the oil industry, which effectively lowered gasoline prices. Thus, in hundreds of ways, government throughout American history has influenced the priorities of entrepreneurs and innovators in the private sector. This influence has been no less when it was inadvertent or incidental to some other government purpose, such as national defense, than when it was explicit and intentional, as in the case of U.S. agricultural programs or water development in the West.

Throughout American history, also, the military has often been a direct or indirect source of technological innovation. Sometimes security considerations have been used as an important justification to command a wider political consensus, as was the case with federal sponsorship of the Interstate Highway System in 1956 (Rose, 1979), the financing of aeronautical research after World War I through the National Advisory Committee for Aeronautics (Mowery and Rosenberg, 1982; Nelson, 1977:111; Nelson, 1984:51–52), and the creation of the U.S. Naval Observatory in the 1840s. A. Hunter Dupree (1957:62) has observed that "the Naval Observatory is the classic example of the surreptitious creation of a scientific institution by underlings in the executive branch of the government in the very shadow of Congressional disapproval." Introduced in the guise of a "Depot of Charts and Instruments," ostensibly to standardize chronometers on naval ships for more accurate navigation, the observatory quickly grew into a major center for studies in hydrography, astronomy, magnetism, and meteorology, so that even today it is the leading world center for astrometric observations and the source of time and star-position standards for practically the entire world.

In the early nineteenth century the military loaned its officers to help survey for the railroads and generally to assist them in solving civil engineering problems. In those days military expeditions and surveys were better staffed and supported, and closer to the best elements of American science, than were any civilian projects (Dupree, 1957:65). Also in the mid-nineteenth century the government arsenals at Harper's Ferry, Virginia, and Springfield, Massachusetts, pioneered in the development and introduction of milling machines and other machine tools, and in proving out the principles of mass production and interchangeable parts (Rosenberg, 1976:20).

Indeed, in the whole evolution of the American scientific establishment to this day one can discern a consistent pattern in which technical sophistication has diffused outward from military science and technology into the civilian economy and eventually into the whole political and social structure. This has even been true for the introduction of new technologies less obviously related to military applications. Medical developments such as antibiotics, techniques of blood preservation, and the use of chemical pesticides to control disease vectors were initially introduced in connection with the military. Much of modern psychology had its origins in techniques of psychological testing first used on a large scale in World War I. Frequently the institutional structures created in wartime to push military applications of science have become permanent in the subsequent period of peace and have been redirected toward the generation of a new level of government support for fundamental science and for advanced scientific and engineering education, as well as new standing and credibility for the scientific community in its influence on national policy (Brooks, 1970).

The Growing Role of Government

The role of government in science and technology has been increasing in all the industrialized countries, but it has probably changed fastest in the United States, especially during and since World War II. Many of the new technologies that have been at the forefront of U.S. economic growth during the postwar period had their origins either in World War II or in the subsequent period of the cold war: commercial transport aircraft; semiconductors, solid-state electronic devices, and integrated circuits; computers; nuclear power; satellite communications; microwave telecommunications and radar applications, such as air traffic control; antibiotics; pesticides; new materials, such as high-strength steel alloys, titanium, high-temperature ceramics, fiber-reinforced plastics, and composites; and new methods of metal fabrication and processing, such as numerical-controlled machine tools or powder metallurgy. Much of this has been derivative from military and space activities, although in many cases, once the basic technology was transferred to the private sector, it tended to take off on its own, with rapid proliferation of incremental improvements, cost reductions, quality enhancements, and ancillary technologies necessary for wide commercial acceptance.

Much commercially significant innovation has also been an indirect derivative of the enormous public investment in biomedical research. Although innovation in pharmaceuticals and medical devices has been largely generated in the private sector by private research and investment, it is doubtful whether much of this would have taken place without the base of knowledge resulting from government-sponsored programs. Much modern medical instrumentation and diagnostics derive from basic advances in the physical sciences, including laboratory instrumentation, which occurred as a result of broad-based government sponsorship of fundamental physics, chemistry, and biology (Handler, 1970:256–257; Grabowski and Vernon, 1982).

It is important to recognize, however, that several other equally innovative industrial areas owe less to government initiative or science sponsorship: industrial chemicals, synthetic fibers, heavy machinery (including construction equipment), electric power generation (other than nuclear steam supply), and telecommunications are specific examples. Moreover, even where government has been an important influence, the civilian applications, market penetration, and broad economic benefits would not have been realized without the strongly complementary initiatives and technical ingenuity of private entrepreneurs. Government-generated science and technology were only the starting point and not the basic driving force. This is nowhere better illustrated than in the semiconductor industry, where government started as almost the sole customer for the early transistors, whereas today military and space end uses account for only about 10 percent of the market for semiconductor devices (Levin, 1982:19, Table 2.1).

Government and Basic Science

The government role in stimulating the broad development of science for it own sake, rather than for well-defined special social purposes, is a relative latecomer to the U.S. science policy scene, especially when compared with many other industrial countries. Although the Founding Fathers showed some concern with the development of a national science policy, and even proposed the creation of a national university (Dupree, 1957:14–15, 40), this interest largely lapsed with the rise of a more pragmatic, populist political orientation following the election of Andrew Jackson in 1828. When the British industrialist Smithson left a bequest to the U.S. government for the founding of a national institution devoted to the cultivation of science in its own terms, Congress debated for 10 years before deciding to accept the bequest, questioning whether the support of science was an appropriate federal function except for specific practical public purposes (Dupree, 1957:76–79). Throughout the nineteenth century American scientists, considering themselves a beleaguered minority, continually bemoaned the country's exclusive concern with applied science and its neglect of pure science. They looked with envy at European governments and their tradition of public patronage of pure science (along with the arts). Well into the twentieth century the support of science was not viewed as a government responsibility, and until World War II, the development of American science depended mainly on private patronage, particularly the great private foundations. A few far-sighted individuals were beginning to point out the dependence of the continued advance of the U.S. economy on a broad-based science, and Herbert Hoover in the 1920s actually proposed a government-industry coalition to provide funds for the support of science in the ultimate interest of industrial innovation (Dupree, 1957:340–343; Layton, 1971:Ch. 8).

The Watershed of World War II

World War II marked a true watershed in the development of American science policy. It was the first war in history in which fundamental scientific or engineering developments originated during wartime came to fruition and were used in battle during the same war; hitherto wars had only stimulated technology which became significant in a subsequent war.

Though the seeds of the wartime science policy had been sown in the activities of private philanthropy, in selected government activities such as NACA and in advocacy by a few leaders of the scientific community (Dupree, 1957:358–361), a new relationship between government and science was triggered by the crisis of the war. In contrast with World War I, when scientists were brought into the service of the war effort primarily as military officers under the direction of military commanders, the scientific war effort in World War II was organized as an independent civilian enterprise under the Office of Scientific Research and Development (OSRD), directed by Vannevar Bush, and managed by industrial and academic scientists in equal partnership with the military rather than subordinate to it. Although the work was fully funded by government, it operated outside the Civil Service with scientists remaining within their familiar institutional settings. Military research and development was conducted under contract to private institutions on an unprecedented scale, with the government bearing all the costs, including those of administration and infrastructure ("overhead"), on a reimbursable basis, generally with no profit, and no financial gain or loss to either individuals or institutions. The research contract with fully reimbursable overhead was a distinctly U.S. invention, which proved to be an extraordinarily flexible instrument in the subsequent partnership between government and private institutions that evolved in basic research, hardware development, and even policy analysis and system management during the postwar period.

It was probably the accident of the cold war and the accelerating military-technological rivalry between the United States and the Soviet Union that prevented the system of research contracting that evolved during the war from being dismantled in the postwar period. The political climate after World War II stood in sharp contrast with that following World War I, when much of the wartime science apparatus was dismantled and military contractors were widely viewed by the public as "merchants of death," the root cause of war itself rather than a source of national security. Instead of government and civilian science turning their backs on each other, the institutional "swords" built to fight the scientific World War II were at least partially forged into the "ploughshares" of a postwar policy for the broad development of science in the interests of society (Bush et al., 1960), even though the military influence on overall scientific priorities remained substantial—e.g., the large emphasis on the physical sciences. The consensus in support of even this much of a civilian science policy was to a considerable extent maintained by the threat of the Soviet Union; the support of even the purest science was justified in terms of its possible ultimate value in the rivalry between the superpowers (England, 1983:212, 219, 280). Nevertheless, it gradually evolved into a full-fledged civilian science policy, increasingly divorced from its national security parentage.

THE POSTWAR ERA AND THE NEW SOCIAL CONTRACT BETWEEN SCIENCE AND SOCIETY

"Science the Endless Frontier"

The public debate on the postwar organization of science was opened in November 1944 by a letter from President Franklin D. Roosevelt to Vannevar Bush (actually drafted by Bush) asking him to set up a committee to study how the lessons learned in OSRD could be applied in peacetime "for the improvement of national health, the creation of new enterprises bringing new jobs, and the betterment of the national standard of living." The resulting report, Science the Endless Frontier (Bush et al., 1960), became the fundamental charter for American postwar science policy, and its general philosophy, though not its specific organizational recommendations, continues to guide government support of science and technology in the United States to this day (Brooks and Schmitt, 1985). It recommended the use of public funds to support basic research in colleges and universities and to "foster the development of scientific talent in our youth." Research was to be supported largely through contracts and grants with universities and research institutes, as well as private firms, leaving "internal control of policy, personnel, and the method and scope of research to the institutions themselves." It also proposed that the governance of the federal agencies sponsoring research in private institutions be left in the hands of "persons of broad interest in and understanding of the peculiarities of scientific research and education." Thus science was to be accorded a high degree of self-governance and intellectual autonomy, in return for which its benefits would be widely diffused through society and the economy. This diffusion was to be further fostered by the extensive use of contracts with private industry in preference to civil service laboratories for developmental activities. As a consequence, industry has accounted for between 70 and 75 percent of total public and private expenditures for R&D and between 50 and 55 percent of all federal R&D expenditures (National Science Foundation, 1984c:3, 11).

In one important respect the postwar scientific system did not follow the pattern envisioned by the Bush committee. The committee had suggested that a single agency be responsible for all extramural research sponsored by the government, to be known as the National Research Foundation. It was to support not only basic research but also long-range applied research that would contribute to various federal missions, including the military and public health. Instead of a single R&D agency with mission-oriented functional divisions, there evolved a pluralistic support system, with several cabinet-level federal agencies having partially sheltered divisions responsible for the support of long-range research related to their missions, e.g., the National Institutes of Health (NIH) in the case of public health; the Office of Naval Research, the corresponding offices for the Army and the Air Force, and the Advanced Research Projects Agency (now the Defense Advanced Research Projects Agency) in the case of the military; and the National Science Foundation (NSF), responsible only for basic research and science education not tied to any particular federal mission (Brooks, 1973a). Both NSF and the newly created Atomic Energy Commission (AEC) were prohibited from setting up their own civil service laboratories, but were encouraged or required to "contract out" the actual conduct of research to private organizations, sometimes created especially for that purpose under independent boards of private citizens. The "contracting out" idea was also adopted by the Air Force, in some measure by the Army, and least by the Navy; it also became the norm when, in the aftermath of sputnik, the largely civil service NACA was converted into the National Aeronautics and Space Administration (NASA) by the Space Act of 1958. Within a few years the transformed agency was converted from one which was 98 percent "in-house" in its conduct of research, to one which contracted more than 80 percent of its R&D, especially the development part, to the private sector (Bok, 1966).

The other major heritage from OSRD was the principle of awarding research and development contracts to the most qualified organization, irrespective of geographical or other nonscientific considerations. This was a sharp break with the tradition that had been established prior to World War II, especially in agricultural research, where the policy had been to distribute federal research facilities and support very widely in each state. This proved to be the most controversial of the Bush committee's recommendations, and one on which the creation of the new science agency, NSF, nearly foundered (England, 1983:5-6).

Today, nearly 40 years after the publication of the Bush report, the "social contract" between science and society that it advocated remains remarkably intact, despite numerous alarums and excursions whose rhetoric has generally outrun their practical effect (Brooks and Schmitt, 1985). In the context of the American political system, this is a rather remarkable political phenomenon, and many would assert it has been responsible for American world leadership in pure science and in most fields of advanced technology (Bush, 1970:65). It may also be said, however, that the Bush social contract is probably under more fundamental challenge today than at any time in its postwar history, largely as a result of the erosion of U.S. international competitiveness in the increasingly interdependent world economy (Brooks and Schmitt, 1985).

Trends in R&D Expenditures

The course of both federally sponsored and privately supported R&D since the end of World War II can be divided into three distinct periods. The first extended from the beginning of the cold war in the late 1940s to about 1967. This period was characterized by more or less steady growth in R&D expenditures, averaging up to 15 percent per year in real terms, with the life sciences considerably exceeding that rate after 1957 following the "take-off" of the budget of the National Institutes of Health at that time. The bulk of federal R&D expenditures was devoted to space, defense, and military-oriented nuclear programs, which reached more than 90 percent of all federal R&D in the early 1960s (Brooks, 1963).

The second period started in about 1967, when an abrupt leveling off in the volume of government-sponsored R&D began. This was associated with a severe budgetary crunch resulting from the attempt of the Johnson administration to maintain a "guns and butter" budget during the Vietnam buildup. However, the period of stagnation was prolonged until about 1977. Military R&D and space expenditures declined and the basic physical sciences also experienced a fall-off in support to about 14 percent below their 1967 peak when measured in constant dollars (using the GNP deflator). The life sciences, riding on the political popularity of biomedical research and backed by an effective political coalition in Congress, maintained continuing, though reduced, growth, considerably assisted by the "War on Cancer" that was

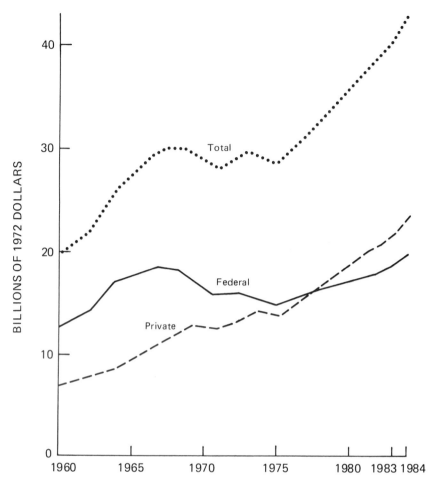

FIGURE 1   Federal, private, and total R&D expenditures, 1960–1984 (billions of constant 1972 dollars).
SOURCE: National Science Foundation, *National Patterns of Science and Technology Resources* (Washington, D.C.: 1984), Table 5.

initiated with bipartisan support in the Nixon administration (U.S. Congress, 1971; Strickland, 1972; Berger, 1980:62–63). During this period privately financed industrial research continued some growth, but with decreased emphasis on fundamental and longer-range research. The general trend is illustrated in Figure 1 (President's Commission, 1985:98). It was during this second period that defense/space R&D dropped nearly to 60 percent of government-sponsored R&D, partly owing to spectacular expansion of energy research, development, and demonstration programs, but also partly due to

TABLE 1   Trends in Federal Funding of Research and
Development (billions of constant FY 1972 dollars)

	FY 1967	FY 1972	FY 1984	FY 1986 (est.)
Defense	$12.4	$9.2	$12.1	$16.1
Space	6.6	2.7	0.8	1.1
Health	1.8	2.0	2.2	2.2
Energy	0.8	0.6	1.2	0.9
General science	0.7	0.7	0.8	0.9
Other	1.7	1.9	1.7	1.6

SOURCE: American Association for the Advancement of Science, *AAAS
Report X: Research and Development, FY 1986*. Intersociety Working
Group (Washington, D.C.: 1985).

research in support of the Great Society programs and of environmental
protection (see Table 2 below for details).

The third period began in 1977 with an acceleration in the growth of self-
financed industrial research, a gradual restoration of government-supported
research in the physical sciences, and a rapid acceleration of defense R&D,
which increased even more rapidly in the 1980s after the advent of the Reagan
administration (American Association for the Advancement of Science,
1985:27). After 1980 civilian R&D shrank, particularly in the Department
of Energy (DOE) and in the social sciences, and the proportion of space/
defense programs in government-sponsored R&D climbed to 72 percent. By
FY 1985 defense R&D had exceeded its FY 1967 peak in real terms and
was scheduled to exceed its FY 1967 peak by 30 percent in the FY 1986
budget. However, space and defense together were still 22 percent below
their FY 1967 level in FY 1984 and would be 9 percent below their FY 1967
level in FY 1986, according to the President's budget. Total federal R&D
was 22 percent lower in FY 1984 and would still be 5 percent lower in FY
1986 compared with its FY 1967 level. These results are summarized in
Table 1.

The changing trends in federal funding of R&D reflect changes in overall
national priorities, which affected science policy. Those changes are analyzed
in greater detail below.

THREE EPOCHS IN POSTWAR SCIENCE POLICY

The postwar period can be divided into three distinct epochs: the cold war
period—1945–1965; the period dominated by social priorities—1965–1978;
and the period dominated by industrial competitiveness—1978 to the present.
In reality these periods overlap, and the onset of each new epoch was foreshadowed by strenuous policy debates in Washington. The three epochs also

coincide fairly closely with the three periods that mark the changes in funding patterns for federal R&D described above.

The Cold War Period: 1945–1965

Until 1965, when the first indications of public revulsion against the Vietnam War began, and when the environmental movement began to be politically effective, the support of even the purest science and of graduate education had been justified to the Congress largely in terms of the military/technological race with the Soviets (England, 1983:154, 218–221). This science race was enormously stimulated by Soviet space achievements, beginning with the launching of the first sputnik in 1957. A simultaneous buildup of military and space investments followed, generating unprecedented new demands for highly trained scientific and engineering manpower. This in turn helped to fuel an expansion of higher education, especially graduate education, which also coincided with the "baby-boom" generation's coming of age. Accommodating the rising public demand for advanced education gradually became a goal in its own right, partially replacing the anticipated manpower demands of federally sponsored programs as a justification for federal support of science and higher education (Brooks, 1965).

Military R&D and procurement undertaken in the 1950s and early 1960s laid the groundwork for American domination of world markets in commercial jet aircraft, semiconductors, and (temporarily) nuclear power (Nelson, 1982). At the same time the so-called GI Bill of Rights introduced at the end of World War II laid the foundation for the U.S. postwar lead in the training of technical manpower, and this helped to staff the explosive growth of government technological programs in the 1960s. In the early 1960s, however, there developed an intense debate among economists and students of science policy as to the net effect of these large government technological programs on the performance of the U.S. civilian economy, a debate that is being revisited today in only slightly revised form. A majority asserted that the civilian "spin-off" from government programs would stimulate technical progress within the civilian economy, but a significant and increasingly vocal minority argued that the insatiable demands of federal programs would drain scarce talent away from the civilian sector by bidding up salaries and by providing more challenging and interesting technical opportunities for scientists and engineers, free of the normal disciplines and economic constraints of the commercial marketplace (Hollomon and Harger, 1971; Brooks, 1972).

The Social Priorities Period: 1965–1978

The growing technical successes of the space program and of some of the military systems programs such as Polaris created heightened public and political expectations about what technology, properly mobilized, could accomplish. If we could organize science and technology to put men on the moon, people said, why could we not organize them to solve problems on earth? If we could accomplish such wonders by pumping money into applied physical science, why could we not do the same by pouring funds into applied biological science or applied social science (Nelson, 1977)? In 1962 President Kennedy expressed a view that later formed one of the underlying assumptions of the Great Society programs. He suggested that "most of the problems, or at least many of them, that we now face are technical problems, are administrative problems" (Schlesinger, 1965:644). The old debates of the New Deal were seen as increasingly irrelevant to the complex technical decisions of modern society. This was the political impetus that first gave rise to the trend toward "civilianization" of federal R&D away from its nearly exclusively military/space emphasis of the early 1960s.

However, the epoch that began with euphoria about the capacity of science to solve social problems soon gave way to disillusionment and ended in what looked almost like a revolt against science, or at least against big science, technology overreaching itself, and excessive claims of rationality. This was in no way better symbolized than by cancellation of funds for the construction of three prototype commercial supersonic transport aircraft by the U.S. Senate late in 1971 (Mowery and Rosenberg, 1982:144–145). The period also saw the meteoric rise of the Great Society, subsequently dissolved in the urban riots of the late 1960s, the civil rights movement, the student revolt, and the fiasco of the Vietnam War. The Great Society idea was predicated in many minds on what was seen as the new capacity of the social sciences to serve as the basis for "engineering" social change. Very soon, however, science and rationality gradually began to be viewed as the source of the problem rather than the basis for its solution, and social problems came increasingly to be talked about as the secondary effects of progress in science and technology (Bauer et al., 1969). Then came the "limits to growth" debate, the environmental movement, the energy crisis, stagflation, and the commodity price explosion, quenching the nation's optimism and its sense of control over its destiny and its environment, which had come to its culmination in about 1963.

Yet in other ways the faith in science persisted beneath the surface. The proliferation of technically oriented regulatory agencies, such as the Environmental Protection Agency (EPA), the conversion of the Atomic Energy Commission first to the Energy Research and Development Administration and then to the Department of Energy (with a greatly expanded role in energy-related R&D beyond nuclear power), the War on Cancer of the early 1970s—all these developments reflected an underlying faith in the capacity of science to cure social ills, including those created by science-based technology itself. In fact, much of the environmental legislation of this period embodied social expectations far exceeding the existing capacity of science to meet them, but

TABLE 2   Percentage Distribution of Federal R&D Expenditures, FY 1969–FY 1984

	1969	1971	1976	1981	1984
Defense	53.4%	52.0%	50.2%	55.3%	70.2%
Health	7.2	8.3	11.3	11.6	9.6
Energy	2.1	3.6	7.9	10.5	4.9
Space	23.9	19.6	15.1	8.1	4.2
General sciences	3.3	3.3	4.1	4.0	3.8
Transport	2.9	4.7	3.0	2.6	2.4
Natural resources and environment	3.3	2.7	3.3	3.2	1.7
Agriculture	1.4	1.7	1.8	2.0	1.6
Education and social services	1.6	1.4	1.2	0.9	0.5
Other	1.5	2.6	2.0	1.8	1.2

SOURCE: National Science Board, *Science Indicators 1982* (Washington, D.C.: National Science Foundation, 1983), Table A2-12.

the feeling persisted that if society could hold the feet of technical people to the fire strongly enough it could force them to fulfill its high expectations (Brooks, 1982a). Thus the metaphor of landing men on the moon drove the regulation of technology as much as its promotion.

Table 2 shows the percentage distribution of federal R&D expenditures among major budgetary functions during the period from FY 1969 to FY 1984. It indicates the shift from military/space orientation to social orientation and back again during this period (National Science Board, 1983:244, Table A2-12).

The socially oriented period also saw the beginnings of concern about U.S. competitiveness in world markets. Following the demise of the U.S. supersonic transport project at the hands of the Senate in 1971, the Nixon administration decided to take an initiative to use government-generated technology to revive the competitiveness of the U.S. economy, whose lagging performance it attributed to a decline in technological innovation. Administration spokesmen testified to Congress on the reverse "technology gap" said to be opening up between the United States and Europe, particularly West Germany (Brooks, 1972). At that time Europe was in the midst of a sharp expansion of its support for research and graduate education, while the United States was in the midst of a "research recession," alleged by some in the scientific community to be the source of its competitive lag (National Science Board, 1983:8). The grandiose federal initiative mostly petered out, leaving only small programs in the National Science Foundation and the National Bureau of Standards (NBS). The NBS Experimental Technology Incentives Program (ETIP) was a rather innovative effort to use government procurement and regulatory programs in a precisely targeted way to induce innovation in the private economy; in its own terms it was rather successful, but on too small a scale to be of any economic significance (Lewis, 1975; 1976; National Research Council, 1976). The ETIP was intended as a pilot program, but was never followed up. Indeed, efforts to use government indirectly to induce innovation for civilian technology had originally been started in the early part of the Kennedy administration, but had run into political roadblocks in the Congress as a result of opposition from some of the potentially affected industries (Nelkin, 1971; Katz, 1982).

The Period of Emphasis on Innovation Policy

During most of the 1970s, concern about the declining competitiveness of the U.S. economy was mounting gradually, but it had to compete for political attention with energy policy and the public anxieties created by the 1973 and 1979 energy crises. The national civilian R&D investment went largely into energy technology, with the Department of Energy being the most rapidly growing of the federal science agencies.

In 1978 the Carter administration took a major initiative to study the impact of federal policies on U.S. competitiveness and to make recommendations for changes in federal policy that would improve private incentives for technological innovation and industrial investment in R&D. The study, carried out jointly by the Office of Science and Technology Policy (OSTP) and the Office of the Assistant Secretary of Commerce for Science and Technology (Jordan J. Baruch), involved wide consultation with industry and with science policy experts in the private sector. In contrast with the abortive initiative of the Nixon administration, it deemphasized direct federal support of industrially oriented R&D and looked to indirect measures, such as changes in patent and antitrust policy, regulatory procedures, and government technical assistance to small business. Many business leaders expressed disappointment in the final recommendations because they tended to steer clear of tampering with tax policies as they affected new investment and R&D by corporations or by would-be high-tech entrepreneurs. Nevertheless, this study, which came to be labeled the White House study on innovation (U.S. Department of Commerce, 1979) served to raise the subject to near the top of the political agenda, and it has since become perhaps the most important topic of national science policy for the 1980s. The recommendations did eventually result in modifications in patent policy (Public Laws, 1980, 1984), a clarification of the Justice Department's interpretation of antitrust legislation to facilitate R&D cooperation among firms (U.S. Department of Justice, 1980; Baxter, 1983), and the setting up of a Regulatory Review group in the Office of Management and Budget (OMB) to evaluate the economic impact of all proposed new federal regulations (Executive Order, 1978).

The incoming Reagan administration picked up on the Carter initiatives and made innovation and new entrepreneurship one of the centerpieces of its economic strategy and science policy, especially after 1982. American competitiveness in the world economy has become the highest-priority item of public discussion, and almost every government policy is being assessed for its impact on the rate and quality of industrial innovation and competitive performance. Except for increased support of basic research, however, the Reagan administration has systematically eschewed direct federal support of R&D whose main purpose is to lead directly to new products that will be sold in private markets. It has repeatedly asserted that the government's role should "be focused on relatively less costly, high risk, longer term high payoff activities that the private sector traditionally has been less willing to undertake" (Office of Management and Budget, 1981). The most dramatic impact of this policy came in the Department of Energy, where the administration rejected "costly near-term activities, such as construction and operation of pilot plants and the operation of demonstration plants using company-specific processes" (Office of Management and Budget, 1981). Research for which a specific commercial product was clearly in view as an outcome should be left to the private sector, whose assessment of the potential market for the product was likely to be more accurate than any judgment by a government official or even an industry committee with no financial stake in the outcome.

The new policy, however, left considerable room for debate on the appropriate dividing line between government and private responsibility. For example, the administration continued to support funding for the Clinch River breeder reactor, which was clearly a demonstration program of the sort it deplored and which the Budget director, David Stockman, had strongly opposed as a congressman, using the same rationale he used later to kill other DOE demonstration programs (Stockman, 1977). On the other hand, it initially proposed to cut back on NASA's financing of aeronautical research, a decision that was later reversed as the result of an evaluation by an OSTP panel (Office of Science and Technology Policy, 1982). It also proposed to "privatize" meteorological and remote sensing satellites, leaving their further development and operation to the private sector (Gregory, W., 1982; Waldrop, 1982).

This most recent epoch has been characterized by strong industrial R&D spending, which continued to grow even through a severe recession, and a shift from previous emphasis on relatively short-term, product-improvement research to longer-term projects (National Science Foundation, 1983a). The pressure of looming competition from the Japanese has forced continuing emphasis on innovation over near-term cost savings from cutting back on R&D expenditures. Much of industry took to heart the lesson learned from the Japanese semiconductor industry, which, unlike its U.S. counterpart, did not cut back on R&D or investment in new plant in 1974 and 1975 and was therefore in a better position to meet resurgent market demand in the 1976–

1979 economic recovery, when its American competitors were unable to meet even domestic demand (Imai and Sakuma, 1983).

The turn around in industrial research has been particularly evident in the automobile industry, which, despite a worsening financial condition in the late 1970s and early 1980s, continued to increase its R&D investments (Eckstein et al., 1984:157). Indeed, one could argue that the U.S. automobile industry has made at least a partial transformation from a typical "mature" industry to a quasi-high-tech industry, with competitive performance much more dependent on technological innovation than in recent history. As a result of the industry's R&D investments in product improvement, prospects for the introduction of new performance features have greatly expanded (Altshuler et al., 1984:Ch. 4). As just one example, as fuel-efficiency performance has improved, the possibility of much greater improvements not hitherto considered likely has become apparent (Altshuler et al., 1984: 91–95).

More broadly, the emphasis on productivity as an element of competitiveness throughout the mass production industries has led to dramatic increases in the use of engineers in manufacturing, and scientific and technological employment growth has outpaced labor force growth by a factor of about three (National Science Foundation, 1983b).

The new emphasis on industrial innovation in the present period has been complicated by the resurgence of defense spending, and particularly defense R&D and procurement. This has helped fuel a dramatic resurgence of demand for technical manpower, particularly that with graduate training, after a long period of slack demand for technical people in the period of social priorities described above. As a result, undergraduate enrollments in engineering schools have doubled since their low point in the mid-1970s, and there has been a strong shift from science to engineering at both the undergraduate and graduate levels, as well as a more modest shift from nontechnical fields into science and engineering (National Science Foundation, 1984b:23). Equally striking is the high percentage of undergraduates in all disciplines who are now declaring an intention to enter business careers. Engineering education has become a priority item of public policy discussion, and more than two-thirds of all the states have developed programs to stimulate technical education, university-industry cooperation, or the establishment of high technology industry within the state (Pear, 1983).

The rise in technically oriented defense spending has also revived the 1960s' debate on the economic impact of defense on the civilian economy. Resurgence of defense spending in the 1980s has occurred in an economy with much lower capacity utilization than existed in the 1960s, so that one might expect less competition for "bottleneck" resources and talents than existed then (Aspin, 1984). As we saw earlier, R&D spending for defense and space is still a considerably smaller fraction of total R&D spending (probably 20–25 percent), especially when industrial spending is also included, than was the case in the 1960s. On the other hand, today's sophisticated weapons systems may have less spin-off benefit for the civilian economy than those of the earlier period. In many component fields, such as semiconductors and computers, as well as many aspects of avionics and aeronautical design, the civilian sector actually leads the military sector in innovative technology, so that there may be much less potential for useful technology transfer from the military to the civilian sector than existed in the late 1950s and early 1960s. In addition, many major items of military hardware, such as ballistic missiles, supersonic aircraft, surface-to-air defense missiles, are much less related to possible civilian applications than jet aircraft, microwave radars, tanks, or fire-control computers. Military systems increasingly have to sustain environments that have no relation to what is necessary for civilian equipment. The specific systems aspects of military hardware are relatively more important and, by the same token, less relevant to civilian applications.

In a recent study of the impact of R&D and basic research on productivity at the firm level, Griliches (1985) found the most comprehensive evidence yet of the strong correlation between R&D investments and the economic health and productivity of firms, including a relatively higher impact for basic research than for R&D overall, but he has also shown that government-funded R&D, though making some contribution, contributes much less to productivity growth in a firm than privately funded R&D—a result which can probably be interpreted as indicating the small civilian impact of defense/space-type R&D, among other factors. On the other hand, a recent study by the Congressional Budget Office provides some indication that government R&D, as well as self-financed R&D spending in an industry, is positively linked to competitive performance in international trade (Congressional Budget Office, 1984). These two results are not necessarily in conflict.

COMPARATIVE INDICATORS OF U.S. PERFORMANCE IN SCIENCE AND TECHNOLOGY

A wealth of literature on science indicators attempts to provide quantitative measures for the comparative performance of the United States and other countries in science and technology. These measures are based both on inputs, such as R&D spending, manpower, and scientific equipment, and on outputs, such as publications, citations, awards, patents, royalty payments, productivity growth, and shares of world markets for high technology products (National Science Board, 1973; Elkana et al., 1978). None of these measures is entirely satisfactory, not only because of the lack of quality factors, but also because of conceptual problems as to what society really ought to expect from its scientific and technological establishment. For example, the more the output measures deal with factors that relate to the interaction between science and society rather than factors entirely internal to the technical establishment, the more uncertain their significance becomes (Brooks, 1982a: 2–5). Even if we focus on purely economic measures without getting into debates about the quality of life or the distribution of the national product among sectors of society, we have a problem in that technology and innovation are only two among many factors that determine economic growth, and the art of differentiating the technical factors from others is an imperfect one. With this caution in mind, let us look at some of the conventional indices (Brooks, 1985b:334–352).

Inputs

R&D Expenditures   A very common input measure is aggregate expenditures on R&D, both private and public, or such expenditures as a fraction of GNP. Even at this level we immediately encounter a conceptual difficulty, for it is quite uncertain whether it is aggregate national R&D expenditures or national R&D expenditures as a proportion of GNP that are of greater economic significance. If there were no barriers to the transfer of information between the R&D performer and the individual or organization that can make economic use of it, then one might say that aggregate R&D should be the more significant indicator. By this measure the United States completely dominates any other plausible grouping of countries, with the exclusion of the Soviet Union, whose statistics are extremely difficult to interpret because of its wholly different economic system. One such comparison (Brooks, 1985a), shown below, compares the United States; West Germany, France, and the United Kingdom as a group; and Japan with respect to total R&D expenditures in 1969 and 1979:

	1969	*1979*
United States	$25.6 billion	$55.0 billion
West Germany, France, United Kingdom	8.3	39.0
Japan	3.0	19.3

Although the R&D investment of other countries has grown relative to that of the United States, this country still dominates, and in fact has probably increased its lead in the past five years. If we restrict our attention to self-financed industrial R&D expenditures, the situation does not change, as shown below (Brooks, 1985a):

	1979
United States	$25.3 billion
West Germany, France, United Kingdom	19.3
Japan	11.4

If we assume that most privately financed R&D is for commercial purposes and that there is no spin-off at all from military R&D, a very conservative assumption, the United States still dominates the civilian R&D picture.

However, using the absolute level of R&D expenditures can be questioned on several grounds. First, the diffusion of the results of R&D is not effortless, so that the institution performing the R&D has an advantage in applying it. This is probably especially true of industrial R&D performed in-house, in close proximity to marketing, production, and general business planning. Second, the diffusion of R&D does not stop at a nation's borders, so that if we assume excellent diffusion within a country we must also assume that the results are nearly equally available to potential industrial innovators outside the country. Thus, the national aggregate of R&D expenditures is misleading whether we assume perfect or imperfect diffusion of R&D results.

If we make the opposite assumption that privately generated research results are entirely proprietary within the organization that generates them, then the average ratio of R&D to sales among all firms becomes the better indicator of innovative effort; each firm is assumed to have to generate most of the knowledge it must use to innovate. With this equally unrealistic assumption, the ratio of industrial R&D to GNP becomes a reasonable proxy for innovative effort. By this measure the United States would be behind both Japan and West Germany, as shown below by the ratios of civilian expenditures to GNP for West Germany, Japan, and the United States in 1981 (National Science Board, 1983:197–198, Appendix Table 1-6):

	1981
United States	1.7%
West Germany	2.5
Japan	2.3

The R&D-GNP ratios above would suggest that Japan and West Germany might be deriving more economic benefit from their R&D expenditures than the United States, but the assumption that aggregate R&D is more significant than the ratio of R&D to GNP seems the better of the two approximations. Consequently, not much should be inferred from the R&D-GNP ratio. Despite its implausibility as an indicator, however, that ratio is frequently quoted in the literature in support of a presumed lag in U.S. innovative effort.

Manpower The United States still leads all major industrial countries, except the Soviet Union, in the number of R&D scientists and engineers per 10,000 civilian workers, but the margin of superiority over Japan and West Germany narrowed greatly in the 1970s (National Science Board, 1983:8, Fig. 1-5). The number of first-degree scientists and engineers produced annually in the United States was still nearly double that in Japan, but 7 percent of the U.S. graduates were engineers compared with 19 percent in Japan, so that Japan was graduating more first-degree engineers than this country

(National Science Board, 1983:6, Fig. 1-3). Considering the large number of U.S. engineers in defense activities compared with the number in Japan and Europe, the slight U.S. advantage in the number of scientists and engineers per 10,000 workers is not much cause for complacency.

Of equal importance to technical graduates may be the general level of "technical literacy" of the labor force, and here there is some reason to believe the United States lags its competitors, particularly West Germany and Japan. These countries have stressed scientific and mathematical proficiency in their secondary educational institutions much more so than the United States, and the achievement of U.S. high school students in mathematics and science proficiency tests is inferior to that of these major competitors (National Science Board, 1983:5; Husen, 1983). In a world in which changing markets and technology require increasing adaptability and the learning of new skills on the job, inferior basic skills necessary for such learning may become a serious competitive disadvantage, which could be compounded when the organization of the workplace discourages the acquisition of broader ranges of skill and the capacity for higher responsibility for those without a college education (Brooks, 1983). There is some indication that outmoded management practices and rigid work rules derived from a tradition of adversarial labor relations place many American workers at a disadvantage in adapting to changing conditions, especially compared with their Japanese counterparts (Skinner, 1983).

The Scientific Infrastructure The stagnation of federal R&D support in the 1967–1977 decade may have had its severest impact in the universities in terms of the declining investment in new instrumentation and renovation of physical facilities. In the last five years several studies of the state of instrumentation in university laboratories have documented the fact that university laboratories have fallen seriously behind government and industrial laboratories in the access they provide to state-of-the-art equipment (National Science Foundation, 1984a; Smith and Karlesky, 1977). Anecdotal evidence indicates that during the 1970s the equipment available to European researchers in leading universities and research institutes became superior to that accessible to their U.S. competitors. The problem first became apparent in relation to advanced research equipment, but more recently it has become equally applicable to teaching laboratories, particularly in engineering and computer science. This has been due both to a lag in investment and to rapid technological change in laboratory instrumentation brought about by the computer revolution.

A part of the instrumentation problem can be ascribed to the impossibility of spreading the most advanced instrumentation in every field among many institutions. Yet there is a tendency for each university department to aspire to comprehensive excellence across a very broad range of fields; the acceptance of specialization and division of labor among institutions and laboratories tends to lag the growth in complexity, cost, and sophistication of modern instrumentation (Brooks, 1971). This is not a new phenomenon. It began early in the postwar period in such fields as high-energy physics and radioastronomy, and it was partially solved for those fields by the creation of national centers, such as the Brookhaven National Laboratory or the National Radioastronomy Observatory (NRAO), in combination with the funding of "user groups" from universities to take advantage of these national facilities (Brooks, 1978). The problem today is that the necessity of concentrating sophisticated resources in a few national centers is extending to more and more fields of research, and now even to several fields of advanced teaching, such as microelectronics and electrooptics. The question is how some measure of cooperative planning can be introduced into this process without eroding the healthy pluralism and competition which have been sources of strength in American science. Indeed, the sharing of expensive equipment and facilities among researchers is already more widespread than is generally realized (National Science Foundation, 1984a:29–33).

Unfortunately, one of the consequences of the drying up of federal funding for research infrastructure in universities has been the politicization of the allocation of resources and the increasing use of backdoor channels through the Congress to secure funding for major new facilities that has not been forthcoming through the normal budgetary processes of executive agencies. The result is the distribution of new facilities and equipment by competitive political influence and lobbying instead of by cooperative planning and peer review (Norman, 1983). The country may have reached the point, however, that *some* new initiatives in research infrastructure, however arbitrary and politicized, may be better than none.

Outputs

Publication Statistics   For research, the main quantitative measure of output is publication, and publication counts have come to be widely accepted as output indicators of scientific activity, generally based on a subset of particularly influential and frequently cited journals. Scientists and engineers in the United States (defined as scientists and engineers working in U.S. institutions, not necessarily American citizens or permanent residents) consistently accounted for about 37 percent of the world's science and engineering literature in the 1970s, considerably higher than the U.S. share of world GNP, and roughly equal to the U.S. share of world R&D expenditures (National Science Board, 1983:11, Table 1-2). There are considerable difference among fields, however, ranging from 43 percent in clinical medicine and 42 percent in earth and space sciences to only 21 percent in chemistry and 30 percent in physics. Only in mathematics did the U.S. share decline significantly between 1973 and 1980, from 48 to 40 percent. In mathematics the absolute U.S. publication count declined by 36 percent in this period compared with only a 23 percent decline for the non-U.S. publication count. For engineering and technology there was a decline of 29 percent in the United States compared with 22 percent outside the United States. Generally speaking, declines in publication counts seem to have followed declines in real research expenditures in various fields (National Science Board, 1983:11).

Citations are often used as a rough indicator of the quality of publications. For this purpose a convenient measure is the citation ratio, that is, the ratio of the total proportion of citations in the world's literature to the publications from a given country to the share of all publications produced by that country. A citation ratio of 1.0 for a given country means that there is no preferential citation of the publications emanating from that country and, hence, that their "quality" is about the world average. The citation ratio for all fields in the United States has remained stable or slightly rising over time: 1.45 in 1978, with a range from 1.88 in chemistry to only 1.09 in general biology. Since the United States accounts for such a large fraction of all publications, there may be a self-citation bias in these measures; the ratio for non-U.S. citations to U.S. papers is in the neighborhood of 1.0 or slightly under 1.0 for most fields, ranging from 0.57 in biology to 1.25 in chemistry. The lower numbers may also reflect a self-citation bias in other countries, so that the true citation ratio would lie somewhere between, thus still indicating some qualitative superiority for U.S. publications (National Science Board, 1983:12).

Recent studies of the comparative performance of research institutions made at the Science Policy Research Unit of the University of Sussex, England, also suggest that U.S. institutions obtain more significant results per dollar of expenditure than do comparable European institutions. Most of these studies, however, have been made for fields of "big science," such as particle physics, fields in which much of the U.S. capability has been in place for longer than the European capability and may therefore have had more opportunity to achieve maximum productivity (*Economist*, 1984).

Other indicators of the comparative scientific performance of the United States come from the award of Nobel and other prizes in science, where the United States enjoys an increasingly predominant position, and from the increasing number of foreign students who come to the United States for advanced training in science and engineering, in the majority of cases with their own sources of funds. However, each of these indicators may also be criticized. Since Nobel prizes are most frequently awarded for work done some time in the past, they may be unreliable indicators of current performance. The big influx of foreign graduate and postdoctoral students has been largely from developing countries; in this case the difference in scientific level between the country of origin and the host country is so great that one suspects that the choice of the United States as host reflects factors other than a judgment on the quality of science and engineering in the United States compared with other developed countries.

Overall, the studies of publication and citation counts can be interpreted as indicating a modest quality advantage for the United States, confirming other, more impressionistic evidence that U.S. science achieves more significant results per unit of expenditure than its main competitors. However, the advantage does not appear to be overwhelming, and its indicators tend to lag considerably in time.

Patents and International Trade in Intellectual Property While there appears to be little doubt about the continuing excellence of the U.S. performance in basic science, despite some closing of the gap, especially by Western Europe, the U.S. performance in applied science and in the commercialization of new knowledge is much more in question. It is frequently pointed out that on a per capita basis Britain has led the world in pure science for several generations, and yet it has experienced a steadily deteriorating economic performance, apparently owing to a poor capacity for reducing knowledge to commercial practice. Because of this general acknowledgment that superior performance in basic science does not guarantee superior economic performance, attention has recently turned to the study of patenting statistics and to international trade in intellectual property. The number of patents is believed to be a better indicator of the state of technology in a country. Moreover, the fact that novelty and originality have to be more formally documented for patents than for scientific publications gives certain advantages to the use of patents as indicators. Pavitt and Soete (1979) have shown that it is possible to compare the technological performance of various non-U.S. countries by studying the share of patents granted to citizens of each country by the U.S. Patent Office. They have also found a remarkably good correlation over time between the relative number of U.S. patents and national R&D expenditures, and, since patent statistics go back much further in time than properly standardized R&D statistics, Pavitt and his colleagues have used patent counts as surrogates for comparative national R&D activity going back much into the nineteenth century. But, by the same token, patent data do not appear to give information which is independent from that provided by comparative R&D statistics.

A much-quoted statistic indicating a U.S. technological lag is the 38 percent drop between 1970 and 1982 in the number of patents granted to U.S. inventors by the U.S. Patent Office, while in the same interval the number of patents granted to foreign inventors nearly doubled, reaching 26 percent of all patents by 1982 (National Science Board, 1983:13). In several product areas foreign patents accounted for 50 percent of all patents, while in other areas, such as petroleum refining and natural gas extraction, foreign patents were only 20 percent of patents (National Science Board, 1983:14, Table 1-4). Overall, over 50 percent of foreign patenting in the United States was accounted for by West Germany and Japan, with Japan showing the most dramatic increase in the 1970s. The U.S. share of foreign patents in other countries declined from 65 percent in 1971 to 59 percent in 1981; the number of patents granted to U.S. inventors in other countries dropped by 44 percent in the 1970s. In the last three or four years, however, there appears to have been a resurgence of patenting by U.S. inventors (National Science Board, 1985). The meaning of such statistics can easily be exaggerated, however, for cross-national patenting may depend as much on judgment of potential markets as on innovation per se. In other words, it is not clear to what extent foreign patenting depends on "market pull" as compared with "technology push" (i.e., level of inventive activity). The work of the University of Sussex group, for example, has shown in a study of 40 product groups that for 23 of them the world export share of Britain correlates very well over time with the rate of patenting by British inventors in the United States (Pavitt and Soete, 1979). On the other hand, some studies by U.S. authors suggest that market pull has little influence on the propensity to patent in foreign countries (National Science Board, 1983:14).

International payments for the use of patents, trademarks, copyrights, and proprietary know-how are also frequently used as an indicator of relative innovative capacity. Since the revenue streams considerably lag the time of innovation, this may be a poor indicator when the distribution of innovative activity is changing rapidly. Nevertheless, by this gross measure the United States is doing well. At the end of the 1970s it was earning nine times as much as it was paying out in royalties and fees, and this ratio had hardly declined since 1967 despite a large growth in the absolute balance. It is important to keep in mind, however, that over 80 percent of such receipts are from foreign affiliates of U.S. companies and thus directly related to foreign direct investment (National Science Board, 1983:24). In a way it is rather surprising that, with the growth of R&D expenditures and patenting rates in other countries relative to the United States, there has not been any decline in the ratio of U.S. receipts to payments. If we had been making as successful use of foreign inventions as our competitors had of ours, one would have expected a decline in the payment ratio as, with increasing R&D levels compared with the United States, foreign nations became a larger potential source of commercializable technology. This may be evidence, pointed out by several observers, that the United States may be lagging its competitors in its ability to scan and adopt foreign technology that could contribute to improving its economic performance (Vernon, 1982). Have we been so accustomed to being the leader in all fields that we simply have not learned how to make optimal use of the technology available worldwide and are thus spending too much of our innovative effort on "reinventing the wheel"?

During the same period the ratio of receipts to payments for Japan was showing a rapid approach to balance in the 1970s, going from 0.2 in 1971 to 0.7 in 1981 (Keizai Koho Center, 1983:18, Fig. 4-7). If one allows for the average age of licenses on which royalties are paid, it seems almost certain that Japan has a positive payments balance on the recent licenses, which suggest that it is already a net exporter of technology and once again confirms that it is becoming a world center for technological innovation (Gregory, G., 1982).

Productivity So much has been said about the lag in U.S. productivity in the 1970s that one is sometimes surprised to note that the GNP per employed civilian worker in the United States, when properly adjusted for relative purchasing power (rather than currency exchange rates), is still the highest in the world (National Science Board, 1983:17, Fig. 1-10). The problem is that from 1960 to 1980 the average annual growth in output per man hour worked in manufacturing has been less in the United States than in any other industrialized country. Moreover, the absolute level of productivity in Japan has overtaken that in the United States in a number of key industries—by 8 percent in steel, by 19 percent in electrical machinery, by 11 percent in general machinery, by 24 percent in motor vehicles, and by 34 percent in precision equipment (Lawrence, 1983). There is a close correlation between these Japanese productivity gains (despite the fact that overall Japan's GNP per employed worker was only 75 percent that of the United States) and Japanese success in penetrating the American domestic market.

The U.S. productivity lag reflects many factors, of which a lag in investment is undoubtedly one of the more important. Recent U.S. emphasis on product as compared with process innovation relative to other countries may also be a factor. The fact that Europe and Japan had been putting much more emphasis than the United States on materials and energy-saving innovations in manufacturing may have strengthened the relative competitive position of those countries when the era of shortages arrived after 1973 (Vernon, 1982:154–156). Changes in the average "quality" of the labor force may also have been significant, since the U.S. labor force grew more rapidly in the 1960s and 1970s and thus encompassed a higher proportion of relatively inexperienced people. However, there is no real consensus among economists as to the relative importance of the various suggested causes of the lower rate of productivity growth in the U.S. economy. While the lower rate may be partly explained by the process of "catch-up" in the 1950s and early 1960s, such an explanation seems less plausible for the 1970s and 1980s.

Table 3 provides an illustration of the likely importance of net investment in determining relative productivity growth among countries over the period 1971–1980. It is doubtful whether these differences in productivity growth can be attributed directly to differences in the level of technology, except to

TABLE 3   Relation Between Net Investment and Productivity Growth

Country	Net Fixed Investment as Percentage of GNP	Growth Rate of Productivity in Manufacturing 1971–1980
Japan	19.5%	7.4%
France	12.2	4.9
West Germany	11.8	4.9
Italy	10.7	4.9
United Kingdom	8.1	2.9
United States	6.6	2.5

SOURCE: Benjamin N. Friedman, Saving, investment, and government deficits in the 1980's, p. 400 in Bruce R. Scott and George C. Lodge, eds., *U.S. Competitiveness in the World Economy* (Boston, Mass.: Harvard Business School Press, 1985), Table 11-2.

the extent that a higher net investment rate means that the capital stock would include a larger fraction of the most recent—and presumably the most advanced and productive—technology. This is especially true at a time when production technology moves as readily as it does among the advanced industrialized countries, especially through internal transfer within multinational companies. In other words, the rate of productivity growth includes a factor reflecting the rate at which the world's state-of-the-art manufacturing technology is being incorporated into a nation's capital stock. In consequence, it is doubtful whether growth in either total factor productivity or labor productivity can be used as an index for the state of a nation's technology except in this indirect sense.

World Market Shares in High Technology Products   The United States has historically had a high concentration of its manufactured exports in products that were R&D-intensive, and also a strong favorable trade balance in such products. However, this position has been slipping, and the balance with Japan has actually turned negative recently (National Science Board, 1983:22, Fig. 1-16). In terms of world exports, the U.S. share of R&D-intensive manufactured good declined from 31 percent in 1962 to 21 percent in 1977, while Japan's share went from 5 percent to 14 percent. World market shares (including domestic market) of the largest U.S. high technology companies declined from 79 percent in 1959 to 47 percent by 1978 (U.S. Department of Commerce, 1983:41). This sounds dramatic, and it is greater than the drop in the U.S. share of world GNP. On the other hand, worldwide economic recovery has been a major goal of U.S. policy since the end of World War II, so that we should not have expected to maintain the kind of overwhelming dominance that existed while Europe and Japan were still recovering from the devastation of the war. In addition, the much greater mobility of information, ideas, and potential inventors across national boundaries, partly through multinational enterprises, has been a powerful force toward equalizing the technological level among the industrial countries (Vernon, 1982:148–154). Nevertheless, the evidence suggests that the erosion of the U.S. position, even in R&D-intensive products, has gone further than might have reasonably been expected from world recovery alone.

In summary, the aggregate data which I have reviewed suggest that, while there has been some erosion in the overall U.S. comparative position, the erosion has so far been rather slight in pure science, somewhat stronger in patenting and the generation of original technological innovations, but by far the greatest in the rate of adoption of innovations from the rest of the world. The biggest lag in innovation has been in manufacturing technology, both in the creation of such technology and, again, even more in its rate of adoption, conditioned primarily but not solely by a low rate of net addition to manufacturing capital stock. At the same time, the United States still invests slightly more than the total of all its major industrial competitors combined in industrial R&D, even after completely excluding defense and space. The U.S. government overall, however, invests a much smaller fraction of its R&D expenditures than other governments in work that is specifically aimed at enhancing the competitive performance of its industries in world markets. However, it is doubtful whether this by itself is an important factor, though it may reflect less political commitment to national competitiveness as a social goal in comparison with other countries.

Other Indices of Competitive Erosion

If the U.S. position on the aggregate indices of comparative performance in science and technology does not indicate a severe problem, how do we account for the widespread perception of a serious competitive problem? Clearly this arises from the dramatic turnarounds that have occurred in the competitive performance of specific industries, particularly the rapid Japanese penetration of American markets in such sectors as consumer electronics, motor vehicles, steel, and machine tools.

Although it has received less public attention the case of machine tools is particularly striking and disturbing. This industry has been one of the key sectors of American export strength since the last quarter of the nineteenth century, and it has especially broad ramifications in contributing to the competitive strength of many other U.S. manufacturing industries. In the early 1970s U.S. machine tool exports exceeded imports by a factor of two, yet in the past five years the U.S. machine tool industry lost half of its traditional market, and over 50 percent of all machine tools purchased in the United States were manufactured abroad, mainly in Japan and to a lesser extent in West Germany. Japan considerably leads the United States in the introduction of robots into manufacturing. More importantly, while the adoption of programmable manufacturing technologies, including robots, has been concentrated in the aerospace industry and the auto industry in the United States, it has been much more widely diffused in Japan. In 1980 sales to auto makers in Japan accounted for only 29 percent of robotics sales, compared with 60 percent in the United States. Moreover, in Japan small and medium-sized firms account for a much higher proportion of programmable automation sales than in the United States, in part because of an explicit government program to encourage adoption of programmable automation widely throughout the economy (Parsons et al., 1984).

Equally disturbing is Japanese world market penetration in fields of materials technology pioneered in the United States. Japan now accounts for half the titanium used in the non-Communist world, mostly exports to the United States, although the basic technology and the industry were first developed here under defense sponsorship. A similar example is that of carbon-fiber reinforced plastics as a substitute for metals. The United States has pioneered in inventing new ways of using such materials, and it has a spectacularly growing market for them, but Japan accounts for about 65 to 80 percent of the world output, most of which is exported to the American market (Ayres, 1984:138).

A typical Japanese competitive strategy is to target a relatively small market niche for an advanced technology just behind the world technological frontier and then to develop a superior manufacturing technology for that product that yields superior quality and delivery reliability, thereby achieving very rapid market penetration accompanied by experience and scale economies, which eventually produce an impregnable market salient on which continuing product and process improvement and an expanding range of product competitiveness can be built (Imai and Sakuma, 1983). Early market success provides the resource base and the infrastructure for an expanding scope of innovation and investment.

RELATIVE ROLES OF PUBLIC AND PRIVATE SECTORS IN GENERATION AND COMMERCIALIZATION OF NEW TECHNOLOGY*

The United States has been slow to accept any notion that government has a responsibility for the generation of innovations that will result in goods and services to be sold in private markets. The only exception to this has been agriculture. The conventional view is that market forces alone will be sufficient to direct innovative resources and investment into the areas of highest potential commercial return, and that government attempts to intervene in or even influence the process are more likely than not to be coun-

---

*Brooks (1982b).

terproductive. This view is reinforced by the notion that industrial innovation is driven primarily by "market pull" rather than "technology push." While government scientists and engineers may be rather good at identifying new technical opportunities, they lack the experience and knowledge to assess market potential and user needs, with the result that the typical government-driven technological development frequently tends to be a technical success but a commercial failure.

The British-French Concorde project is usually cited as the prototypical example of a spectacular technological achievement driven by government initiative which proved to be a commercial disaster (Nelson, 1984:54). In the United States, as noted earlier, such a disaster was probably forestalled by the Senate's killing the prototype supersonic transport program in 1971. However, the United States has seen many other examples of government technical incentives in housing, transportation, and energy that have failed in the market, largely because they were primarily motivated by the recognition of a technological opportunity rather than a clearly demonstrated market need. Of course, market circumstances can change rapidly, and the dimming of commercial prospects of energy technologies such as the breeder reactor and synthetic fuels owes something to this circumstance. Moreover, as we saw above, many revolutionary new technologies of the twentieth century have had their origins in governmental initiatives, usually undertaken originally for noncommercial purposes. Most of the success stories were cases in which the recognition of a technical opportunity was the crucial factor, as opposed to only the fulfillment of a generally recognized societal need.

The preceding generalization, however, is obviously an oversimplification, and does not fit with the generally acknowledged success of federally managed agricultural and biomedical research, to cite two examples. The following sections attempt to assess the federal role in a more discriminating manner, indicating where there is general consensus that government has a role, and where there is disagreement. A crucial issue in this connection is not only the area and character of the candidate technological development but the locus of the decision-making process with respect to the strategy and tactics of the development process.

Areas of Consensus on Federal Responsibility

Government as Customer   There is little debate about the necessity of a federal responsibility when the government, acting as agent for the society as a whole, is the ultimate user and the goods or services produced are widely acknowledged to be "public goods," i.e., goods or services from which everybody benefits whether or not they pay for them. Examples are defense technologies and the generation of the scientific knowledge necessary to underpin the formulation of environmental, health, and safety regulations. This is not to say that there are not strong political controversies as to how much or what kind of defense we need, or as to how much regulation is in the public interest and what should be regulated. But the principle that government should bear the ultimate responsibility for such public goods is not questioned.

Fundamental Research   Although the consensus is more recent and not quite as strong as in the case of public goods like defense, there is wide agreement that the federal government has a responsibility to support the generation of knowledge whose potential benefits are widely diffused among many end uses, so that no one user has sufficient stake in those benefits to sponsor the necessary research. Indeed it can be argued that such general-purpose knowledge is a public good. Moreover, in order to be a public good, such knowledge has to be widely shared and freely and rapidly communicable. Yet the freer and more open the communication the less the chance that the research sponsor can hope to recover his costs from potential beneficiaries. The only hope of recovering the costs of such public knowledge is a compulsory charge to all, namely taxes. The argument for generating this kind of public knowledge in the mostly widely sharable way also involves efficiency: the generation of public knowledge is more rapid and efficient if it can be widely and rapidly shared among all people competent either to build on it for further advances or to use it.

In recent years we have come to accept that responsibility for funding basic research does not necessarily entail a responsibility actually to perform it. Since World War II the belief has been increasing that the separation of funding from performance generally contributes to the cost-effectiveness of R&D because it opens up the possibility of drawing on a broader scientific community. This is not universally acknowledged, but it is recognized de facto, as indicated by the fact that only about 25 percent of government-funded R&D today is performed in civil service laboratories manned by full-time government employees (National Science Foundation, 1984c:3).

Externalities   As mentioned above, where government has a legislated mandate to regulate in matters of environmental protection, health, and safety, it also has an acknowledged responsibility to generate the necessary scientific knowledge base through government-funded R&D. This is not as definitive a criterion as it sounds, however. For example, in the case of the regulation of prescription drugs, the Food and Drug Administration (FDA) relies primarily on the regulated industry itself to generate the scientific data on which both the safety and efficacy of a new drug is to be evaluated before introduction to the market. The FDA has a minimal research program of its own, though it does retain a scientifically competent staff to review and evaluate the data provided by industry. The Environmental Protection Agency and the Nuclear Regulatory Commission (NRC) also depend heavily on the industries they regulate for their data bases, but in addition they have substantial independent research programs, both in-house and under contract. An issue that arises in these agencies is the degree to which they get involved in research to assess equipment designs or to develop pollution-abatement or accident-prevention technologies. At one time, in its early days, the EPA ran a congressionally mandated research program aimed at actually developing alternatives to the internal combustion engine up to the point of demonstration of prototypes (e.g., the "hybrid vehicle" program). The NRC has had large-scale testing programs to evaluate specific engineered safety measures, such as the Emergency Core Cooling System. The line between design research and evaluation research is often a difficult one to draw in practice.

Another issue that arises in connection with government responsibility for externalities is the degree to which government should fund research programs designed to develop a knowledge base for the assessment of technologies that are not yet ripe for regulation, and whether such research would be better left to the industries in which detailed expertise on emerging technologies resides. There are arguments that industry, left to itself, will underinvest in research related to the externalities resulting from its technologies, especially those which are indirect and far in the future—likely to be important only after the technology has been manufactured and marketed on a major scale. The cases of radioactive waste disposal and management of toxic chemical wastes readily come to mind as examples of industry's having probably invested in R&D at less than a socially optimal scale. In the absence of compelling evidence of potential hazard, industry will tend to invest only in that R&D which appears to be necessary to meet existing regulatory requirements and standards, but it will be reluctant to do research intended to anticipate a need for regulation at some time in the future. In this field, in fact, industry has some conflict of interest, in that the discovery of new regulatory needs may appear to increase its costs and reduce its markets. In part the current situation arises from the unusually rapid change in social expectations that has taken place in the last 20 years, particularly as it has been expressed in stricter and stricter interpretations of product liability and managerial negligence. This has led to a considerable change in industry attitudes toward research related to potential but speculative and uncertain negative externalities resulting from its activities (*New York Times*, 1984:16).

Part of industry's attitude arises from the natural human tendency for developers of a new technology to become advocates and to be slow in accepting the possibility of adverse effects until it is forced on their attention by evidence generated outside their industry. A part may also be due to the fact that the expertise required to do research on secondary consequences is likely to be quite different from the expertise required to develop the technology. For example, chemical manufacturers generally lacked expertise in groundwater hydrology and disposed of toxic wastes on their own property in ignorance of the fact that the wastes might eventually migrate into drinking water supplies after a sufficiently long period. One problem is that the time horizon for appearance of externalities tends to be much longer than the time horizon for product or process development. A new development may be completed and the developers dispersed onto new projects before the need to consider waste management becomes apparent.

One might formulate the question here by asking whether the government has a responsibility to support a vigorous research program aimed at searching for trouble arising out of industrial technologies, or whether it should wait for others to identify potential troubles before initiating research. The latter has generally been the practice, and still largely is. Even in the case of nuclear power, for which government was responsible for development of much of the generic technology, the relative investment in R&D on radioactive waste disposal was almost certainly less than socially optimal. Often the government does not support "externality" research unless a regulation is already in place whose implementation or enforcement would require such research. The Office of Technology Assessment (OTA) was created by Congress in 1972 to carry out what might be described as anticipatory studies to identify the secondary and tertiary consequences of emerging technologies or the expansion in the scale of use of existing technologies (Public Law, 1972; National Academy of Sciences, 1969; Brooks, 1985c). However, the OTA of necessity restricts itself to synthesis and interpretation of existing research from all possible sources. It lacks the capacity to initiate original laboratory or theoretical research or to leverage such research on the part of other agencies or of industry, except indirectly through the dissemination of its reports or through its channels of communication to the Congress and other government agencies. There is little to indicate that OTA has much influence on the national research agenda, although this is hard to pin down.

Simon Ramo (1985:26–27), an industrialist, has proposed a novel scheme for dealing with the government's responsibility for research on externalities. "We should start," he says, "by assembling from existing regulatory staffs and outside sources, a competent organization to uncover, study, and assess all hazards to safety, health, and the environment." Ramo goes on to say:

We would relieve this investigatory unit of all responsibility (or even the slightest appearance of it) for considering positives as well as negatives and attempting balanced decisions. . . . This group would be equipped with the required experts, tools, facilities, and budget to enable it to track down hazards and potential hazards in existing or proposed activities with reasonable depth and thoroughness. . . . Efficiency, synergism, and organizational flexibility would all be fostered if the specialists and tools were in one strong unit. It would no longer be necessary for Congress, upon its [usually accidental] discovery of a new danger, to launch still another new agency to investigate it.

Ramo goes on to propose a presidential board to convert all this information into mandatory rules, standards, and enforcement tools, this board to constitute "a pragmatically effective microcosm of the electorate" with the presidential-appointment and Senate-confirmation process guaranteeing that it would be "responsive to citizens' goals and priorities." Although I think this proposal is politically naive in that it assumes a separability between knowledge and its application that is unrealistic in a political context, it does pose the issue of government responsibility for broad-based research on externalities in a more direct way than any other proposal I have seen.

Areas of Consensus on Inappropriateness of Government Role

There is general agreement that where the costs of R&D can be recovered from the future revenue stream generated by sale of the resultant products, services, or information, there is no justification for a government role. However, this prescription is not as simple as it sounds because the appropriability of the benefits of research to its sponsors will depend on the degree to which property rights in the resultant knowledge can actually be secured by law to the sponsor. For this reason leaving the initiative to the private sector implies a positive policy on the part of government to protect and enforce intellectual property rights.

The rapid and efficient generation of new knowledge—the maximum rate of advance of science—demands a wide sharing of knowledge, so that each researcher can build on the advances of others. On the other hand, the assignment of intellectual property rights entails some sacrifice of this public good in order to increase the incentive for private investment in innovation, particularly in the postpatent stage. In other words, the existence of intellectual property rights is necessary to enhance the total investment in innovation and to ensure that its later stages are more responsive to the needs of the market. Where the optimal public benefit lies as between open and proprietary research is a debatable question on which the balance of public policy has shifted back and forth over time.

In general, the national policy has been that discoveries—facts of nature—are in the public domain and cannot be vested with property rights, while artifacts—human constructs—can be so vested. Even here we have invented the patent system, which creates a property right not previously existent in return for public disclosure and open sharing of the underlying knowledge. The actual practice of the knowledge is a commodity, but the use of the knowledge to generate new knowledge is not—an ingenious distinction which has worked quite well in practice. In the absence of the patent, knowledge would be purely proprietary and hence unavailable to be built on by others. Because of the linkage among many different pieces of knowledge, the vesting of property rights may not always be necessary to secure the benefits of innovation to the innovator. The mere fact of being first in the field may itself confer a sufficient monopoly to secure the revenue stream to the innovator for long enough for him to recover his investment before imitators can successfully enter the market and erode his monopoly profits.

In practice, whether an area of R&D is appropriate for government depends on a highly subjective judgment both as to whether the resultant innovation will provide a social benefit commensurate with its cost and whether, if the government does not undertake the effort, the incentives are sufficient for the private sector to undertake it. This is a difficult balancing act. The more attractive the social benefits, the greater the likelihood that the private sector will see a commercial opportunity, but also the more political pressure there will be for the government to ensure the realization of the benefits in the shortest possible time. Hence, while there is widespread agreement on the theoretical criteria for government intervention or participation in the innovation process, it is much harder to get agreement in any concrete case. It is always possible to argue that the social benefits of a prospective innovation exceed the potential private benefits by a sufficient margin to justify public intervention, but because all the benefits are in the future and the costs are uncertain, the possibilities for rationalization of actions desired for nonrational reasons are almost infinite. Efforts to compare the social and private returns for particular innovations indicate wide variation among specific cases even though, on the average, social returns appear to exceed private returns by a factor of about two (Mansfield, 1985b; Griliches, 1985). In practice the benefit of the doubt for private versus public funding tends to shift with the prevailing political climate and ideology. Recently the pendulum has swung heavily in favor of reliance on private incentives and minimizing direct government intervention except in fields directly linked to national security considerations. Even the umbrella of national security, however, can be quite easily stretched, especially in periods of ample resources.

Areas of Controversy

Following are a number of arguments that have frequently been used as justification for direct federal support of R&D when the relative role of the private and public sectors has been controversial and fluctuating. The limitations of each argument are also brought out.

An important factor in each of these cases is who makes the choices and strategic judgments as the R&D evolves. Here the issue of whether the judgments to be made relate primarily to science or technology considerations or primarily to market considerations is often key.

High Risk   At times, the technical or market risks are considered so high that it is improbable any profit-seeking entity will undertake the investment. Clear-cut examples include space technology, nuclear power (in its early, precommercial phase), the breeder reactor, fusion technology, synfuels development, and some types of exploratory assessment of natural resources. Risk in these instances is compounded of three factors: (1) the magnitude of investment required before commercial success can be predicted with sufficiently high confidence, (2) the hazard that government may intervene for public policy reasons to limit the deployment of the resultant technology or the sale of the resultant products or services after a considerable investment has been made (e.g., unforeseeable environmental effects; foreign policy considerations, such as nuclear proliferation; antitrust considerations), and (3) the lack of available expertise to assess the prospects of the technology (e.g., nuclear power and radioisotope applications right after declassification of the Manhattan Project).

Such areas are usually candidates for increased cost sharing by the private sector as they progress from basic and generic research toward commercial application. There is always a tendency, however, for government to hang on too long or to distort the commercial judgment of the private sector by overpromotion based too exclusively on technical considerations (e.g., the case of the light water reactor, discussed below). If the project is large, with long lead times before it can be tested in the marketplace, there is also the danger that the circumstances that made it appear economically attractive in the first place may change without its being recognized (e.g., the fast breeder reactor following the drastic decline in the forecast rate of growth of energy demand after the 1973 embargo and price jump). The cases of the supersonic aircraft, high-speed ground transportation, and prefabricated housing (as in Project Breakthrough) may also be examples of government officials being too much in the position of making market judgments and too much influenced by ''technology push'' considerations, by the existence of challenging technical opportunities without necessary commercial value.

Exceptional Social Returns   There are few R&D projects for which the social returns do not exceed the private returns. Mansfield has shown that, on the average, the social returns to industrial R&D exceed the private returns by a factor of two, despite instances in which social returns are less than private returns (Mansfield, 1985b). Thus it is rather easy to argue for government participation in industrially oriented R&D projects on the grounds of unusually high social, relative to private, returns, leading to underinvestment by private entrepreneurs. This was the argument implicitly or explicitly used to justify the creation and rapid expansion of the Department of Energy after the 1973 oil crisis. The U.S. dependence on imported oil was seen as an ''externality,'' which made benefits to the country as a whole greater than the sum of cost savings to consumers. In fact, using plausible models of the world oil market and the impact of U.S. demand on world oil prices, one could estimate a marginal cost of an imported barrel of oil that ranged anywhere from a 10 percent to a 100 percent premium over the market price to the private consumer (Energy Modeling Forum, 1982). In this way one could justify a federal investment ranging up to anything that might be justified by the excess "social premium" of oil imports. These arguments could be used to justify large public investments in new supply technologies as well as in research and "demonstration" of a variety of energy end-use efficiency improvements as long as the total cost, R&D plus capital investment, was less than the product of the effective price premium and the volume of oil imports. Public subsidies for renewable energy technologies were justified not only by the oil import premium but also by the alleged avoidance of negative environmental externalities that might result from the use of these "benign" technologies.

Fragmented Industries   The principal examples of fragmented industries are medicine and agriculture. In both industries, an important element of the delivery system is individuals or small family enterprises that lack an effective mechanism for joining together for the collective support of research. Such collective support tends to be precluded by the "free rider" problem, the fact that every entity benefits whether or not it contributes to the support of the research. An additional argument is that both food and health care, though sold in part as market goods, are regarded as "merit goods," i.e., private goods to which everybody in society in some sense has an entitlement (Musgrave, 1974:274–275).

In addition, it may be no accident that in both these examples the research supported with public funds is in the life sciences. We rely primarily on complementary activities in the physical sciences and engineering carried out by the private sector to generate the innovations necessary for the system as a whole. Whether this is an accident of history or can be given a more solid rationale is harder to say. It is certainly true that the benefits of life sciences research are less "appropriable" than those of physical science and engineering research in the chemical, pharmaceutical, farm machinery, and medical devices industries.

Nevertheless, there are other fragmented industries, such as housing and construction, in which the public investment in research has been both smaller and less successful. In part this may due to the lack of development of an easily defined natural division of labor between the private and public sectors as there is in biomedicine and food (Brooks, 1982b:337).

Narrow Markets   The classic example of a narrow market is "orphan drugs," drugs to deal with life-threatening diseases that affect only a small fraction of the population. The private market for such drugs is too small for recovery of development costs, including the extensive animal and clinical testing required for FDA approval. Such drugs may not become available at all unless developed at public expense, although a few may be developed for prestige purposes or as a public service by private firms.

Clearly this is a case that falls in the category of a "merit good." In the health area, society does not apply benefit-cost analysis to new techniques in the same way as in other fields. It assumes that if a potential capability exists to cure a life-threatening disease there exists a moral obligation to develop that capability. It is a kind of extension of the philosophy underlying the Hippocratic Oath to the development of new technologies (Brooks, 1973b:21). A society does not necessarily act according to this principle consistently; indeed, if it did, the aggregate cost would be unacceptable. Nevertheless, as a society becomes more affluent, it apparently tends to make larger and larger investments in health care technologies irrespective of the size of benefit-cost ratios at the margin.

Public Policy   Many types of goods and services could be sold either on the private market or as public goods. In most societies they are mixed goods and have a tendency to turn gradually into entitlements or rights of citizenship, rather than private goods, as societies grow in wealth. Examples in this category are health care and education, and even to some extent basic services, such as telephone and electricity.

Other services, such as weather forecasts or monitoring of the environment by remote sensing satellites, in principle could be marketed as private goods, but only at the cost of restricting access to a few users who can pay the price. Many forms of information services are also of this character. As a matter of public policy it is decided that the social benefit of universal access justifies public development and eventually operation. In this view the "positive externality" resulting from universal, or near-universal, access makes private marketing of anything but "value-added" services, specially packaged for users who can justify the premium price, an undesirable policy. It is also often true that the "transaction costs" involved in creating a market or quasi-market, which must include a technique of excluding nonpayers, becomes prohibitive. These are some of the issues bound up with the current administration proposal to "privatize" weather and remote sensing satellite services (Gregory, W., 1982; Waldrop, 1982).

Key Industries   An even more controversial area is that of maintaining industries that have become uneconomic or noncompetitive on the grounds that they are essential for some public purpose, usually national security or, possibly, the maintenance of employment levels. A classic example is shipbuilding and maritime shipping. The United States maintains an uneconomic industry at enormous cost because it might be a vital national resource in wartime. Almost every domestic industry experiencing severe foreign competition uses this argument to obtain government assistance or protection. It is often an argument difficult to prove or disprove, and therefore it tends to be heavily overworked in the political process. It is not always wrong, but it is certainly controversial. Critics often counter that there are more cost-effective ways of maintaining an industrial capability without requiring consumers to foot a large part of the bill (as in the case of import quotas, for example). In general subsidization of R&D or of capital investment embodying the latest production technology in order to restore competitiveness is a more cost-effective strategy than continuing operating or capital subsidies. However, it is often resisted by the industries involved because it requires much more organizational adjustment, almost always including the permanent loss of jobs, since overstaffing and undercapitalization are the most frequent sources of loss of competitiveness.

There is a tendency for many countries to regard the same industries as "key" either for national security reasons or for reasons of linkage to other elements of the national economy. Information technology, for example, is on everybody's list of key industries. This not only gives rise to political frictions between countries, but also generates economic inefficiencies in areas in which world- or continental-scale markets are often required to produce the revenues necessary to underwrite innovation and investment. A striking example is the telecommunications equipment industry within Europe, where each of the national Post Telephone and Telegraph (PTT) agencies procures its equipment from national companies, at least in the larger countries. The key-industry approach is also a prescription for the creation of world overcapacity in certain sectors—overcapacity which eventually requires some form of rationalization and concerted cut-back, and which is also a major source of trade frictions. The petrochemical industry is an especially egregious example, exacerbated, of course, by the dramatic rise of raw material costs and the efforts of OPEC countries with excess natural gas to develop downstream petrochemical industries based on cheap gas (Bower, 1985:267). Steel and shipbuilding are similar examples.

There appears no simple resolution of this problem, which is at root a product of the inherent inconsistency between an increasingly global world economy and the persistence of national sovereignty as a key, and even growing, political force in the world. In general the most successful adjustment strategy appears to be more rapid movement into higher value-added sectors of the world market. To the extent that it supports such a strategy, public investment in R&D is therefore a more acceptable policy than other forms of subsidy or market protection.

Generic Applied Research   There is increasing interest in this country in the possible role of government in the sponsorship of what is called "generic applied research" in areas of industrial interest. This is defined as mission-oriented research that is not aimed at the solution of specific product-related problems or at final design of commercial technology. The classic example is aeronautical research as it was conducted by the National Advisory Committee for Aeronautics after World War I, and as it continued under NASA after its conversion from NACA by the Space Act of 1958. NACA did not design airplanes or even operational aircraft engines. Rather it built wind tunnels in which it tested new airfoil shapes and provided test services to aircraft designers. It also had the most advanced programs in the theory and testing of structures. In its reincarnation as NASA, it pioneered the development of noise-suppression techniques for jet engines and the basic technology of turbofans to improve fuel economy. It worked in close collaboration with designers in both the engine industry and the airframe industry, but left design and testing to the private sector, albeit providing testing services for a fee. NACA is frequently cited by theorists of the division of labor between the private and public sectors in R&D as the ideal model of synergy between the two sectors (Nelson, 1977:11, 121–122, 125, 139; Mowery and Rosenberg, 1982:128–130).

Recently the National Academy of Engineering has put forward proposals for the creation under NSF auspices of industry-university-government cooperative research centers to work on applied problems of industrial interest, and many universities have set up such cooperative arrangements with industry. The "generic" nature of the research is supposed to be guaranteed by the fact that the results are public and open to all; in fact this could be used almost as the definition of "generic" (National Academy of Engineering, 1984).

There has been more experience with this type of generic research abroad than in this country, and the results have been mixed. The most successful country seems to have been Japan, with its well-publicized programs in very large scale integration (VLSI), "fifth generator computers," and robotics. Industries have received public support for such programs in return for agreeing to share the resulting information widely with each other. The ingredients for success seem to be (1) a substantial financial stake by industry, (2) an equal or dominant voice of industry in the planning of the broad strategy of the research, (3) wide sharing of the research results among all the participating organizations, and (4) limitation of development projects to "proof-of-principle" demonstrations or models, leaving final product development to individual firms on the usual proprietary and competitive basis (Bloom, 1984).

International Cooperation   Sometimes the possibility of international cooperation can become the justification for an applied research program supported by governments. The most successful current example is probably the fusion energy program involving the United States, the European Community, the Soviet Union, and Japan, which has aggregate annual expenditures close to $450 million (Thomassen, 1984). In a way the justification for such international programs can be considered as a simple extension of the arguments used for large national government investments in precommercial applied research programs, where commercializable results are in the distant future and the technical risks are high. Such international cooperative programs can be of two kinds. The more usual kind involves an agreed division of labor between national research institutions with wide sharing of results, joint planning of major facilities and experiments, and extensive short-term exchanges of technical personnel (from months up to a year or more). The rarer kind of cooperation involves the setting up of joint laboratories with a more or less permanent multinational staff. An example is the Italian-based laboratory of Euratom at Ispra, generally regarded as less successful than the fusion program. Still another type of international cooperative program is the Super-Phénix fast breeder reactor program, which involves both government and industry, and whose objective is a full-scale commercial prototype (*Nuclear News*, 1985). Although this is a predominantly French project, other European countries have made a significant investment in it in return for sharing in the information and operating experience developed.

From the standpoint of participating researchers, such international programs often have the advantage of being less subject to fluctuations in the budgetary priorities or other policies of individual national governments. Budgetary planning gets locked in by the international nature of the commitment and thus tends to provide an environment of greater policy, as well as financial, stability.

Other Public Policies for Innovation

So far the discussion of government intervention in the innovation process has been concerned with direct government sponsorship of R&D or of prototype construction and testing. Although this is the most visible and widely debated type of intervention, there are many more indirect policies that may be of equal importance. One of the principal advantages of such indirect policies is that they provide a natural means for leaving decisions about viability in the market to industrial managers who are in the best position to judge what the market needs or is likely to accept. Thus, indirect forms of intervention are most appropriate when market judgments are most significant for success.

Tax Benefits to Consumers   One way to stimulate innovation is to provide tax benefits to consumers that lower the effective price of innovative products whose consumption the government decides yields public benefits or "externalities" not offered by alternative products. During the energy crisis many states as well as the federal government provided tax credits for household investments which improved energy efficiency or resulted in the substitution of renewable for nonrenewable energy sources, e.g., solar hot water heating or passive solar house design. The idea was to accelerate the market penetration of new technologies that would result in reduced oil imports, leaving the choice of technologies to the market. One could regard this as compensating the consumer for his contribution to the reduction of a "negative externality," since the alternative would be for him to require more imported oil.

R&D Tax Credits   Almost all the industrialized countries now offer some sort of tax credit or other tax benefit to firms which increase their R&D spending above some base year. This tax benefit could be thought of as compensating the firm for the fact that there will always be some spillover effect from its R&D which will benefit other firms, consumers, or the general public, and which it will not be able to recapture in the price of its products. In addition, since there is an apparent correlation between firm growth and R&D spending, it might be argued that there is a generalized benefit to the economy as a whole from stimulating industries with higher growth potential.

On the other hand, there is considerable debate as to whether the tax credit actually stimulates private R&D spending or merely provides a reward for spending that would have taken place anyway for competitive reasons or an inducement for firms to redefine existing marginal activities as R&D. In a recent study of the impact of R&D tax credits in the United States, Sweden, and Canada, Mansfield (1985a) has concluded that such credits and other allowances "appear to have had only a modest effect on R&D expenditures," and from this he infers that in their present form R&D tax incentives "are unlikely to have a major impact on a nation's rate of innovation" largely because the price elasticity of industrial demand for R&D is quite low.

Technology-Forcing Regulations   One way of stimulating industrial innovation is to use government to set stiff performance standards for industrial products—standards that cannot be met without considerable technological innovation—and then rely on prospective sanctions to induce private R&D to meet the regulations. This was the strategy followed by the U.S. Congress in respect to the auto industry in three areas: exhaust emissions, fuel efficiency, and vehicle safety. It is also implicit in water pollution regulations, notably in the Clean Water Act of 1977 (Public Law, 1977), which originally required zero discharge into waterways by 1985. The advantage of this approach is that it leaves the choice of technology to engineers and managers familiar with the technology of the industry. In the auto industry there is no doubt that the new regulations stimulated the industry to step up its R&D spending rather dramatically from the early 1970s on, and that many technical goals that the industry insisted were unrealistic were eventually achieved—most notably the attainment of lower emissions with virtually no sacrifice in fuel efficiency. On the other hand, many observers have argued that these technology-forcing regulations hurt the industry seriously at a time when it was just beginning to face severe competition in domestic markets from Japanese imports (Abernathy et al., 1982:83–88; Eckstein et al., 1984:50–53). In fact the attainment of the originally specified standards was postponed year after year, and it is at least debatable whether the goals could not have been achieved more efficiently without legislated standards and timetables that had to be continually revised (Goodson, 1977).

Voluntary Standards   Industrywide standards can be an important factor in encouraging the rapid diffusion and adoption of new technology. On the other hand, standards can sometimes be abused to confer unfair advantages on particular firms. This is another example of the fact that arriving at the optimum choice between competition and cooperation (from a societal point of view) is a difficult balancing act. The United States has a unique system of voluntary standard setting through a number of industrywide standard-setting associations, such as the American National Standards Institute (ANSI) or the American Society for Testing Materials (ASTM). Standard setting is carried out and financed by the industry itself under antitrust safeguards that apparently work quite satisfactorily and have been relatively little criticized. It is important that the government maintain a legal regime which is supportive of such voluntary standard setting, which has been an important factor in U.S. competitive success in a number of areas. It is one of the instruments for assuring a continental market for new technologies and thus realizing scale economies at a relatively early stage in an emerging technological area. The lag in standardizing designs, for example, may have been an important factor in the faltering performance of the nuclear power industry in the United States after a promising start.

Intellectual Property   Since the mid-1970s there has been a general trend toward strengthening intellectual property laws so as to improve the appropriability of the benefits of innovation to the innovating organization. The argument for this has been that much of the financial risk involved in introducing a new product or process to the market is incurred after the original invention has been made. Hence, many potentially valuable inventions are not converted into viable innovations because the innovator cannot be confident of a temporary monopoly in the market for long enough to recover his postinvention start-up production and marketing costs. Nevertheless, the benefits to commercial competition of stronger intellectual property rights always have to be balanced against the possibility that too much competition in the earlier ''generic'' phases of new technology development will result in wasteful duplication and slower progress due to a lack of cross-fertilization ideas. In some cases it is possible for too much emphasis on patents or proprietary know-how to result in overinvestment in certain areas, thus reversing the usual argument that the "positive externalities" of R&D result in private underinvestment in R&D. There is now a widespread concern that the pendulum has swung too far in favor of the protection of intellectual property rights, particularly in the relations between industry and universities. Simultaneously, there is concern with government moves to regulate the free flow of scientific information for national security reasons (Corson et al., 1982; Wallerstein, 1984). There is also a question of the degree to which proprietary research, as well as government regulation of the flow of research information, has the effect of shielding emerging technologies from proper public assessment until after irreversible commitments have been made to final design and deployment (National Academy of Sciences, 1969:32–33).

Antitrust Policy   In the recent past there has been much criticism of the overly rigid interpretation of antitrust legislation in relation to cooperation among firms in R&D, particularly in the precommercial phases of innovation before the emergence of specific product designs (U.S. Congress, 1984). One of the sources of Japanese success in technological innovation in recent years is believed to be the Japanese government's policy of encouraging cooperation among firms and even agreed division of markets for products in emerging technology areas. The U.S. Department of Justice has now clarified its interpretation of antitrust legislation to be more positive toward research cooperation among firms, and the Department of Commerce has been actively promoting the idea of R&D limited partnerships (U.S. Department of Justice, 1980; Merrifield, 1982; U.S. Congress, 1984).

Planning vs. the Market   The current debate over industrial policy in the United States has specific implications for R&D and science policy. The question is whether the overall national pattern of R&D—the resultant of government and private R&D decisions—should reflect some kind of consensual national vision of the future of technology. Even granted the desirability of some sort of coherent pattern, there remains a question of the process by which this pattern is arrived at. A decentralized decision-making process does not necessarily imply an incoherent outcome. The pattern does not have to be established deductively from some generalized vision of a future society established by a few "wise men." It can be established inductively through a political and market struggle between competing visions. Essential to the successful outcome from such a struggle, however, is an open process in which ideas and visions can compete "fairly," with widespread public participation.

Even the market and the political process can be considered as competing processes in which the participants have different relative weights. The problem with market-like processes in both the political and economic spheres is that they may tend to give too little weight to "externalities" and systemic effects. Unfortunately, the same tends to be true of the political process, especially in pluralistic societies like the United States. Groups try to use the political process to defend or enhance their interests without reference to the "externalities" of their success. An interesting question is whether the highly communicative and consensual process of Japanese decision making helps to offset this limitation of the decentralized mechanisms preferred in the United States, with the result that more internally consistent systems of action result while still avoiding the large errors that result from patterns imposed by a small group at the top of a hierarchy.

OUTLOOK AND PROSPECT: CAN THE U.S. DECLINE BE REVERSED?

Despite the searching self-criticism that is going on in the United States, in technological innovation we are still perceived by the rest of the world as No. 1. Nevertheless, our relative position has eroded. Some of this erosion was inevitable, especially given the long-term U.S. political interest in equalizing wealth and technical capacity among nations in the interest of greater political stability and the strength of the free world consensus against political and military encroachment by the Communist bloc. The world economic and technical dominance by the United States that existed in the 1950s and early 1960s was not sustainable and was essentially incompatible with the legitimate aspirations of the rest of the world's peoples. Seven percent of the world's population controlling 50 percent of its GNP was probably not a viable situation for any prolonged period of history.

Moreover, the "race for the new frontier" (National Research Council, 1983) does not have to be a zero-sum game internationally any more than it has been nationally among firms or regions of the country. The growing wealth of the rest of the world provides new markets and new opportunities for innovation by U.S. entrepreneurs. In principle I believe the United States still retains the capacity to stay in front of the rest of the industrialized world, but not way in front, if it gives high priority as a society to science, technology, education, and productive investment without sacrificing a reasonable degree of equity among its population. This is not an easy prescription, nor is it an impossible one.

REFERENCES

Abernathy, William J., et al. 1982. *The Competitive Status of the U.S. Auto Industry: A Study of the Influences of Technology in Determining International Industrial Competitive Advantage*, Automobile Panel. Committee on Technology and International Economic and Trade Issues, National Research Council. Washington, D.C.: National Academy Press.

Altshuler, Alan, Martin Anderson, Daniel Jones, Daniel Roos, and James Womack. 1984. *The Future of the Automobile*. Report of MIT's International Automobile Program. Cambridge, Mass.: MIT Press.

American Association for the Advancement of Science. 1985. *AAAS Report X: Research and Development, FY 1986*. Intersociety Working Group. Washington, D.C.

Aspin, Congressman Les. 1984. Defense spending and the economy. News Release, April.

Ayres, Robert U. 1984. *The Next Industrial Revolution: Reviving Industry Through Innovation*. Cambridge, Mass.: Ballinger.

Bauer, Raymond A., with Richard Rosenbloom and Laure Sharp. 1969. *Second Order Consequences, A Methodological Essay on the Impact of Technology*. Cambridge, Mass.: MIT Press.

Baxter, William F. 1983. Transcript of presentation to the National Association of Manufacturers, Prototypists, Inc. Washington, D.C., May 10, 1983.

Berger, Edward J., Jr. 1980. *Science at the White House, A Political Liability*. Baltimore, Md.: Johns Hopkins University Press.

Bloom, Justin L. 1984. *Japan's Ministry of International Trade and Industry (MITI) as a Policy Instrument in the Development of Information Technology*. Program on Information Resources Policy. Harvard University, Cambridge, Mass. October.

Bok, Enid C. 1966. The establishment of NASA. Pp. 161–270 in Sanford A. Lakoff, ed., *Knowledge and Power*. New York: Free Press.

Bower, Joseph L. 1985. Restructuring petrochemicals: A comparative study of business and government strategy to deal with a declining sector. Chapter 7, pp. 263–300, in Bruce R. Scott and George C. Lodge, eds., *U.S. Competitiveness in the World Economy*. Boston, Mass.: Harvard Business School Press.

Brooks, Harvey. 1963. Government support of science. Pp. 11–21 in *McGraw-Hill Yearbook Science and Technology*. New York.

Brooks, Harvey. 1965. Future needs for the support of basic research. Pp. 77–110 in *Basic Research and National Goals*. Report of the Committee on Science and Public Policy, National Academy of Sciences, to the House Science and Astronautics Committee. Washington, D.C.: U.S. Government Printing Office; also reprinted as Chapter 6 in Harvey Brooks. 1968. *The Government of Science*. Cambridge, Mass.: MIT Press.

Brooks, Harvey. 1970. Impact of the defense establishment on science and education. Pp. 931–962 in U.S. Congress, House. *National Science Policy*. House Congressional Resolution 666, Hearings Before the Subcommittee on Science, Research, and Development, Committee on Science and Astronautics, 91st Cong., 2d sess.

Brooks, Harvey. 1971. Thoughts on graduate education. *The Graduate Journal* 8(2):319–336.

Brooks, Harvey. 1972. What's happening to the U.S. lead in technology? *Harvard Business Review*, May/June.

Brooks, Harvey. 1973a. The physical sciences: Bellwether of science policy, in James Shannon, ed., *Science and the Evolution of Public Policy*. New York: The Rockefeller University Press.

Brooks, Harvey. 1973b. Technology and values: New ethical issues raised by technological progress. *ZYGON/Journal of Religion and Science* 8(1).

Brooks, Harvey. 1978. The dynamics of funding, enrollment, curriculum and employment, in Martin L. Perl, ed., *Physics Careers, Employment, and Education*. New York: American Institute of Physics.

Brooks, Harvey. 1982a. Science indicators and science priorities. Chapter 1, pp. 1–32, in Marcel C. La Follette, ed., *Quality in Science*. Cambridge, Mass.: MIT Press.

Brooks, Harvey. 1982b. Towards an efficient public technology policy: Criteria and evidence. Pp. 329–380 in Herbert Giersch, ed., *Emerging Technologies: Consequences for Economic Growth, Structural Change, and Employment*. Symposium 1981, Institut für Weltwirtschaft an der Universität Kiel. (Paul Siebeck). Tübingen: J.C.B. Mohr.

Brooks, Harvey. 1983. Technology, competition and employment. Pp. 115–122 in R.J. Miller, ed.,

Robotics: Future Factories, Future Workers. Special issue of *The Annals of the American Academy of Political and Social Science.* November.

Brooks, Harvey. 1985a. Can science and technology rescue the faltering U.S. economy? *Materials and Society* 9(1):1–12.

Brooks, Harvey. 1985b. Technology as a factor in U.S. competitiveness. Chapter 9 in Bruce R. Scott and George C. Lodge, eds., *U.S. Competitiveness in the World Economy.* Boston, Mass.: Harvard Business School Press.

Brooks, Harvey. 1985c. Technology assessment and environmental impact assessment. Pp. 105–122 in *U.S.-China Conference on Science Policy, January 9–12, 1983.* Washington, D.C.: National Academy Press.

Brooks, Harvey, and Roland W. Schmitt. 1985. *Current Science and Technology Policy Issues: Two Perspectives.* Occasional Paper No. 1, Graduate Program in Science, Technology, and Public Policy. Washington, D.C.: The George Washington University.

Bush, Vannevar. 1970. *Pieces of the Action.* New York: William Morrow.

Bush, Vannevar, et al. 1960. *Science the Endless Frontier: A Report to the President on a Program for Postwar Scientific Research.* Originally issued July 1945; reissued as part of the Tenth Anniversary Observance of the National Science Foundation as NSF 60–40. Washington, D.C.

Corson, Dale R., et al. 1982. *Scientific Communication and National Security.* Report of Panel on Scientific Communication and National Security. Washington, D.C.: National Academy Press.

Dupree, A. Hunter. 1957. *Science in the Federal Government: A History of Policy and Activities to 1940.* Cambridge, Mass.: Harvard University Press.

Eckstein, Otto L., Christopher Caton, Roger Brinner, and Peter Duprey. 1984. *The DRI Report on U.S. Manufacturing Industries.* Lexington, Mass.: Data Resources.

Economist. September 15, 1984. British science policy: Concern over Cern. P. 93.

Elkana, Yehuda, et al. 1978. *Toward a Metric of Science.* New York: John Wiley & Sons.

Energy Modeling Forum. 1982. *World Oil: Summary Report.* EMF Report No. 6, Eric Zausner, Working Group chairman, Stanford University. Especially p. 7, Using the import premium in policymaking, and pp. 67–75, The value of reducing oil imports.

England, J. Merton. 1983. *A Patron of Pure Science.* Washington, D.C.: National Science Foundation.

Executive Order 12044. March 23, 1978. Improving Government Regulations. Washington, D.C.: Executive Office of the President.

Friedman, Benjamin N. 1985. Saving, investment, and government deficits in the 1980's, in Bruce R. Scott and George C. Lodge, eds., *U.S. Competitiveness in the World Economy.* Boston, Mass.: Harvard Business School Press.

Goodson, R. Eugene. 1977. *Federal Regulation of Motor Vehicles: A Summary and Analysis.* Report to the U.S. Department of Transportation. Washington, D.C.: U.S. Department of Transportation.

Grabowski, Henry G., and John M. Vernon. 1982. The pharmaceutical industry. Chapter 6, pp. 283–360, in Richard R. Nelson, ed., *Government and Technical Progress: A Cross-Industry Analysis.* New York: Pergamon Press.

Gregory, Gene. 1982. Japan: New center for innovation, evolving from imitator to inventor. *Speaking of Japan* 3(18):2–9. Tokyo: Keizai Koho Center, Japan Institute of Social and Economic Affairs.

Gregory, William H. 1982. Editorial, Landsat: Public or private? *Aviation Week & Space Technology,* April 5:11.

Griliches, Zvi. 1985. *Productivity, R&D, and Basic Research at the Firm Level in the 1970's.* Harvard Institute of Economic Research. Cambridge, Mass.: Harvard University Press.

Handler, Philip, ed. 1970. *The Life Sciences.* Committee on Research in the Life Sciences of the Committee on Science and Public Policy. Washington, D.C.: National Academy of Sciences.

Hollomon, J. Herbert, and Alan E. Harger. 1971. America's technological dilemma. *Technology Review* 31 (July/August).

Husen, Torsten. 1983. Are standards in U.S. schools really lagging behind those in other countries? *Phi Delta Kappan Journal* 64(7):455–461.

Imai, K., and A. Sakuma. 1983. An analysis of Japan-U.S. semiconductor friction. *Economic Eye, A Quarterly Digest of Views from Japan* 4 (June): pp. 13–18. Tokyo: Keizai Koho Center, Japan Institute for Social and Economic Affairs, June.

Katz, James E. 1982. Planning and legislating technical services: The American experience. *Technology in Society* 4:51–66.

Keizai Koho Center. 1983. *Japan 1983: An International Comparison*. Tokyo: Japan Institute for Social and Economic Affairs.

Lawrence, Robert Z. 1983. Changes in U.S. industrial structure: The role of global forces, secular trends, and transitory cycles. Paper prepared for Symposium on *Industrial Change and Public Policy*, organized by the Federal Reserve Bank of Kansas City, Jackson Hole, Wy. August 25–26, 1983.

Layton, Edwin T., Jr. 1971. *The Revolt of the Engineers: Social Responsibility and the American Engineering Profession*. Cleveland, Ohio: Case Western Reserve University Press.

Lester, Richard K. 1985. National policy options for advanced nuclear power reactor development. Pp. 400–491 in Richard K. Lester et al., eds., *National Strategies for Nuclear Power Reactor Development*. MITNPI-PA-002, Program on Nuclear Power Plant Innovation, Department of Nuclear Engineering. Cambridge, Mass.: Massachusetts Institute of Technology.

Lewis, Jordan D. 1975. *Incentives for Technological Change, A Progress Report, Experimental Technology Incentives Program*. March 26. Memorandum.

Lewis, Jordan D. 1976. Director, Experimental Technology Incentives Program, National Bureau of Standards, Statement Before the Subcommittee on Domestic and International Scientific Planning and Analysis, Committee on Science and Technology, U.S. House of Representatives, May 4.

Mansfield, Edwin. 1985a. Public policy toward industrial innovation: An international study of R&D tax credits, in Robert H. Hayes, Kim B. Clark, and Christopher Lorenz, eds., *The Uneasy Alliance: Managing the Productivity-Technology Dilemma*, Harvard Business School Press, forthcoming.

Mansfield, Edwin. 1985b. Technological change and economic growth. Pp. 1–18 in *U.S.-China Conference on Science Policy, January 9–12, 1983*. Washington, D.C.: National Academy Press.

Merrifield, D. Bruce. 1982. Summary of the use of the R&D limited partnership: A means to enhance our international competitive position. Unpublished draft paper. Washington, D.C.: U.S. Department of Commerce.

Morison, Elting. 1974. *From Know-How to Nowhere: The Development of American Technology*. New York: Basic Books.

Mowery, David C., and Nathan Rosenberg. 1982. The commercial aircraft industry. Chapter 3, pp. 101–161, in Richard R. Nelson, ed., *Government and Technical Progress: A Cross-Industry Analysis*. New York: Pergamon Press.

Musgrave, Richard A. 1974. On social goods and social bads. Pp. 251–293 in Robin Marris, ed., *The Corporate Society*. London: Macmillan.

National Academy of Engineering. 1984. *Guidelines for Engineering Research Centers*. Washington, D.C.: National Academy Press.

National Academy of Sciences. 1969. *Technology: Processes of Assessment and Choice*. Report to the Committee on Science and Astronautics, U.S. House of Representatives. Washington, D.C.: U.S. Government Printing Office.

National Research Council. 1976. *An Evaluative Report on the Experimental Technology Incentives Program*. Evaluative Panel for the National Bureau of Standards, FY 1976. Washington, D.C.: National Academy of Sciences.

National Research Council. 1983, 1984. *The Race for the New Frontier, International Competition in Advanced Technology—Decisions for America*. Panel on Advanced Technology Competition. Washington, D.C.: National Academy Press; New York: Simon & Schuster.

National Science Board. 1983. *Science Indicators 1982*. Washington, D.C.: National Science Foundation.

National Science Board. 1985. *Science Indicators 1984*. Washington, D.C.: National Science Foundation.

National Science Foundation. 1983a. Company and federal support produce 17% industrial R&D spending increase in 1981. *NSF Science Resources Highlights*. NSF 83-313, August 8. Washington, D.C.

National Science Foundation. 1983b. Manufacturing employment becomes increasingly technological. *NSF Science Resources Highlights*. NSF 83-303, March 10. Washington, D.C.

National Science Foundation. 1984a. *Academic Research Equipment in the Physical Sciences and Engineering*. Prepared for Universities and Non-Profit Institute Studies Group, Division of Science Resources Studies, National Science Foundation. Rockville, Md.: Westat.

National Science Foundation. 1984b. *National Patterns of Science and Technology Resources 1984*. NSF 84-311. Washington, D.C.

National Science Foundation. 1984c. *Science and Technology Data Book*. NSF 84-331, October. Washington, D.C.

Nelkin, Dorothy. 1971. *The Politics of Housing Innovation, The Fate of the Civilian Industrial Technology Program*. Ithaca: Cornell University Press.

Nelson, Richard R. 1977. *The Moon and the Ghetto: An Essay on Public Policy Analysis*. New York: W.W. Norton.

Nelson, Richard R. 1982. Government stimulus of technological progress: Lessons from American history. Chapter 9, pp. 451–482, in Richard R. Nelson, ed., *Government and Technical Progress: A Cross-Industry Analysis*. New York: Pergamon Press.

Nelson, Richard R. 1984. *High Technology Policies: A Five-Nation Comparison*. Washington, D.C.: American Enterprise Institute for Public Policy Research.

New York Times. November 21, 1984. The chemical lobby's "Turnaround." Quotation of Louis Fernandez, Monsanto Company. P. 16.

Norman, Colin. 1983. How to win buildings and influence Congress. *News and Comment, Science* 222 (December 16):1211–1213.

Nuclear News. 1984. Report proposes future nuclear strategy for France. 27(9):66–67.

Nuclear News. 1985. Vibration problems at Ánix. 28(5):85–86.

Office of Management and Budget. 1981. *FY 1982 Budget Revisions*. Washington, D.C.

Office of Science and Technology Policy. 1982. *Aeronautical Research and Technology Policy: Volume I, Summary Report*. Washington, D.C.: U.S. Government Printing Office.

Pavitt, Keith, and Luc Soete. 1979. Innovative activities and export shares: Some comparisons between industries and countries. Pp. 38–66 in Keith Pavitt, ed., *Technical Innovation and British Economic Performance*. London: Macmillan.

Parsons, C., R. Scott, P. Crozier, and B. Guile. 1984. *The Development of Programmable Automation Systems in Discrete Parts Manufacturing Industries: Agricultural Machinery; Auto Parts, and Pumps and Compressors*. Draft report to the Office of Technology Assessment by the Berkeley Roundtable on International Economy (BRIE). University of California, Berkeley.

Pear, Robert. 1983. States fostering high technology. *New York Times*, August 16:A1, A21.

President's Commission on Industrial Competitiveness. 1985. *Global Competition: The New Reality*. Vol. 2. John A. Young, chairman. Washington, D.C.: U.S. Government Printing Office.

Public Law 92-484. 1972. Technology Assessment Act of 1972. October.

Public Law 95-217. 1977. Clean Water Act of 1977. December 27.

Public Law 96-515. 1980. Patent and Trademark Laws, Amendment. December 12.

Public Law 98-622. 1984. The Patent Law Improvement Act. November 8.

Ramo, Simon. 1985. The international race for technological superiority. *Bulletin, The American Academy of Arts and Sciences*, 38(4) Stated Meeting report.

Rose, Mark H. 1979. *Interstate: Express Highway Politics, 1941–1956.* Lawrence: Regents Press of Kansas.

Rosenberg, Nathan. 1976. *Perspectives on Technology.* New York: Cambridge University Press.

Schlesinger, Arthur M., Jr. 1965. *A Thousand Days, John F. Kennedy in the White House.* Cambridge, Mass.: Riverside Press.

Skinner, Wickham. 1983. Wanted: Managers for the factory of the future. Pp. 102–114 in R.J. Miller, ed. *Robotics: Future Factories, Future Workers.* Special issue of *The Annals of the American Academy of Political and Social Science.* Beverly Hills, Calif.: Sage Publications.

Smith, Bruce L.R., and Joseph J. Karlesky. 1977. *The State of Academic Science: The Universities in the National Research Effort.* Vol. I. New York: Change Magazine Press.

Stockman, David. 1977. *The Market Case Against the Clinch River Breeder Project.* Washington, D.C. Memorandum, U.S. Congress, September 17.

Strickland, Stephen P. 1972. *Politics, Science, and Dread Disease.* Cambridge, Mass.: Harvard University Press.

Thomassen, K. I. 1984. Progress and directions in magnetic fusion energy. *Annual Review of Energy* 9:281–319. Palo Alto, Calif.: Annual Reviews.

U.S. Congress, House. 1984. *Japanese Technological Advances and Possible United States Responses Using Research Joint Ventures.* Hearings before the Subcommittee on Investigations and Oversight and the Subcommittee on Science, Research and Technology of the Committee on Science and Technology. 98th Cong., 1st sess. [No. 45], June 29–30, 1983. Washington, D.C.: U.S. Government Printing Office.

U.S. Congress, Senate, Committee on Labor and Public Welfare. 1971. *National Program for the Conquest of Cancer.* Report of the National Panel of Consultants on the Conquest of Cancer. Senate Document 92-99. April 14.

U.S. Department of Commerce. International Trade Administration. 1983. *An Assessment of U.S. Competitiveness in High Technology Industries.* Washington, D.C.: U.S. Government Printing Office.

U.S. Department of Commerce, Office of the Assistant Secretary for Science and Technology. 1979. *Domestic Policy Review of Industrial Innovation.* PB-290403, PB-290404, PB-290407, PB-290409, PB-290413, PB-290415, PB-290417. Springfield, Va.: National Technical Information Service. Also, The White House. 1979. White House fact sheet: The President's industrial innovation initiatives. October 31. Reprinted, pp. 155–173 in U.S. Congress, House, Committee on Science and Technology. 1980. *Analyses of President Carter's Initiatives in Industrial Innovation and Economic Revitalization.*

U.S. Department of Justice. 1980. *Antitrust Guide Concerning Research Joint Ventures.* Washington, D.C.

Vernon, Raymond. 1982. Technology's effects on international trade: A look ahead. Pp. 145–170 in Herbert Giersch, ed., *Emerging Technologies: Consequences for Economic Growth, Structural Change, and Employment.* Symposium 1981, Institut für Weltwirtschaft an der Universität Kiel. Tübingen: J.C.B. Mohr (Paul Siebeck).

Waldrop, M. Mitchell. 1982. Imaging the earth (II): The politics of LANDSAT. *Science* 216 (April 2): 40–41.

Wallerstein, Mitchel B. 1984. Scientific communication and national security in 1984. *Science* 224 (May 4): 460–466.

The Role of the Legal System in Technological Innovation and Economic Growth

MILTON KATZ

The current objective of the legal system should be to promote economic growth, technological innovation, productivity, and international competitiveness while protecting consumers, workers, and the environment from the harmful side effects of technology and industrial indifference or mismanagement. The objective should be pursued in the endless variety of particular applications of law, engineering, economic policy, and business management. This would reflect the appropriate interplay between the two central and continuing historic themes of growth and social equity in the contemporary national and international setting.

Businessmen, engineers, and economists typically tend to perceive the legal system as a source of constraints. In this chapter, I shall try to clarify the constraints along three primary lines of inquiry. First, I shall show how the legal system not only constrains but also facilitates and promotes business enterprise, technological innovation, and economic thought. Second, I shall indicate the scope and nature of the burdens placed on the legal system by modern technology and economic organization. In so doing, I shall trace a reciprocal relationship between those burdens and the constraints on technological and business activity prescribed by the legal system. Third, I shall examine the function of law in setting limits and defining channels within which business enterprises and engineers must fit their activities. In so doing, I shall attempt to show how the distribution of emphasis between the facilitating and the constraining functions of law in regard to technology and economic organization has been affected by the interplay between two central and continuing themes of the American experience. I have in mind the theme of growth, expansion, exploratory venture, and innovation that has been endemic in American society from its beginning; and the theme of inalienable personal rights, fair shares, and social equity that has been endemic since its proclamation in the Declaration of Independence and its lusty restatement in the administration of Andrew Jackson.

THE LEGAL SYSTEM AS FACILITATOR

In relation to business enterprise, technological innovation, and economic thought, the legal system not only constrains but also facilitates and promotes. The law not only sets limits and defines channels within which economic activity must take place, but also provides institutions that foster business activity and serve as part of the infrastructure of economic thought. Let me remind businessmen and economists of the role of property and contract in relation to the market; and let me remind them also that property and contract are legal institutions. It is obvious that no market could operate in the absence of property and contract. It may not be obvious but it is nevertheless true that economists could not even have conceived of the market in·the absence of property and contract. Economists and businessmen have taken property and contract for granted in much the way that they have taken the national language for granted as integral to their processes of thought. This is probably why they hardly even think of such institutions when they contemplate the legal system.

There are other legal institutions, not quite as pervasive as property and contract, that work powerfully to promote business enterprise and engineering innovation. There is, for example, the corporation, through which capital from many sources can be accumulated and applied to production and distribution under the protection of limited liability for the participants. The law also makes available other forms of organization for economic activity, such as partnerships and trusts and trusteeship. There are the institutions of patent and copyright to "promote the progress of science and useful arts," in the language of our Constitution. There are various systems of insurance against risk provided by the legal system. Bankruptcy is a dreary prospect for a particular business enterprise, but in the large, this legal institution and its correlative, reorganization, make possible the orderly disposal of economic debris and fresh starts for business enterprises.

The legal system also performs its enabling function in ways that are more technical and less easily recognized than in the prominent legal institutions that I have just mentioned. I offer an illustration from the economic and accounting analysis of costs. In recent years, the extensive public and political debate about environmental protection has semipopularized the concepts of "externalities," "external diseconomies," and "external costs" introduced into economic analysis by Alfred Marshall and refined by his student, A. C. Pigou. The existence and nature of such "external diseconomies" were discerned through fresh and penetrating analysis, but as far as I have been able to ascertain, neither Marshall or Pigou nor modern economists and cost accountants appear to have given much heed to the source of the "externality," i.e., to what makes a particular cost internal or external. The relationship of the legal system to this matter has been overlooked too long and too often. The externality of external costs derives neither from the fundamentals of economics nor from the nature of business nor from technology. It derives from the legal system. If the legal order requires a cost arising from a company's operations to be borne by the company, the cost is internal. If the legal order permits or requires such a cost to be paid or suffered by others, the cost is external. Damage to the environment from pollutants emitted by a petroleum refinery or an electric power company or a steel plant or any other enterprise will be a "social" and "external" cost only if and to the extent that the legal system so decrees.

To a degree deliberately and to a degree as a collateral consequence of doctrinal evolution rooted in other phases of legal experience, it has been the legal system that has determined the allocation of the costs of environmental damage arising as a side effect of human enterprise. If and when the law accepts the initial incidence of such a cost as external to the enterprise, it facilitates the operations of the enterprise by relieving its accounts of a particular cost. If and when the law chooses to alter the initial incidence of such a cost by recognizing a cause of action for a money judgment or an injunction by a victim of environmental damage against an enterprise that is the source of the damage, it constrains the enterprise by adding a particular cost to its accounts. Apart from lawsuits for money damages or injunctions, such a shift from facilitation to constraint may take place through a variety of other legal means. The law may permit the persons involved to modify the incidence of a cost by giving effect to negotiated agreements among them. It make seek to alter the form and to shift the impact of the cost by taxation. In the case of common carriers and public utilities or similarly regulated enterprises, the cost of environmental damage may be reallocated through the orders of regulatory agencies setting rate levels or defining rate bases or methods of accounting.

Whatever the legal means may be for maintaining or altering the incidence of a cost, what determines the choice? What governs the balance of emphasis between facilitation and constraint in the function of law affecting cost allocation? The question is a particular illustrative expression of a general and fundamental inquiry to which I shall return later: What governs the balance between promotion and constraint generally in the functions of law? At this point, let me briefly shift our angle of vision from the effects of law on technology and the economy to the effects of modern technology and economic organization on law and lawyers.

EFFECTS OF TECHNOLOGY AND ECONOMIC
ORGANIZATION ON LAW

In 1967, Congressman Emilio Q. Daddario of Connecticut, then the chairman of the Subcommittee on Science, Research and Development of the House Committee on Science and Astronautics, introduced a bill "to provide a method for identifying, assessing, publicizing, and dealing with the implications and effects of applied research and technology" (H.R. 6698, 90th Cong., 1st sess., March 7, 1967). Recognizing that the implications and effects of technology were beyond measure, Congressman Daddario sought to foster useful discussion by holding hearings on the bill in the form of a "Technology Assessment Seminar" (U.S. Congress, 1967). The witnesses at those hearings, drawn from industry, the professions, universities, and learned societies, stressed the vastness and intricacy of the problems to be investigated, along with the unavoidable need to find a way to come to grips with them. The Subcommittee on Science, Research and Development then turned to the National Academy of Sciences and the National Academy of Engineering for help, requesting that they undertake parallel studies of technology assessment, taking into account the respective roles of business enterprises, the scientific and technical communities, the social sciences, the executive branch of the government, Congress, and the legal system.

In its report, the National Academy of Sciences (1969:8) stressed the scale and complexities of the problems in an observation defining its inquiry:

Conceived most broadly, any inquiry into the interface between technology and the human habitat may become an inquiry into the entire universe of questions that bear upon the most critical problems of contemporary civilization.

The National Academy of Engineering (1969:21) in its report emphasized a balance of functions to be served:

Technology assessment consists of a mixture of warning signals and visions of opportunity. Warning signals arise when the analysis predicts trends leading toward adverse consequences. Similarly, the analysis can point to actions that give promise of substantial improvements in the national quality of life. It is most important that assessment participants pursue with equal fervor the development of both the creative possibilities of technology and the defensive needs of society.

The National Academy of Sciences conducted its investigation through a special panel. The panel's report drew a distinction between technology in the sense of a particular engineering instrument—e.g., an automobile, a pesticide, a drug—and technology in a comprehensive sense encompassing the particular instrument's supporting system, which comprises the organizations for production and distribution together with the economic, social, legal, and governmental matrix. The panel insisted on the need to understand and deal with technology in both senses. In the case of the automobile, the supporting system includes such factors as the highway system, installment credit, traffic regulations, police administration, parking facilities and zoning requirements for off-street parking, automobile purchase taxes, gasoline taxes, insurance, and tort law relating to automobile accidents. This illustrative enumeration of the elements of the supporting system for a single instrument of technology, the automobile, indicates the nature and scope of the tasks cast upon the legal system by modern technology in the widest sense. Apart from the items that are explicitly legal in the automobile's supporting system—e.g., tort law, traffic regulations, and taxes—many of the other items also engage the legal system in a variety of ways. The organizations for production and distribution involve corporation law; installment credit involves the law of contract, sales, and commercial instruments; zoning requirements engage real property, municipal corporations, and constitutional law; and so on throughout the range of these multiple factors. In the operation of so vast a system of interlocking elements, human friction and controversy will be unavoidable. This engages still another of the many functions of law, one that is fundamental and pervasive: to seek to resolve human controversies through orderly processes and on a basis of principle.

The lawyers who, whether as legislators, judges, commissioners, or practitioners, have borne the responsibility for designing, adapting, and applying the legal system to this extensive array of changing factors have had to take their departure from previously evolved bodies of doctrine, institutions, and procedures. They have also had to take their departure from the complaints of public groups or private clients who have turned to them for assistance in seeking relief from injuries.

In the terms of technology assessment, injuries suffered by consumers of a manufactured product, occupational injuries to workers in the workplace, and environmental injuries to a community or a region caused by emissions from an industrial plant are side effects of technology and its applications. In the terms of law, such injuries are either "accidents" or "wrongs." If "accidents," questions arise as to where the costs of such accidents should ultimately fall and how the costs may most appropriately be met. If "wrongs," some appropriate form of redress through a legal proceeding must be sought. To the degree that the injuries, viewed as side effects, can be minimized or eliminated through further technological development or improved applications of existing technology, the remedies can be provided by engineers and business management. To the degree that the injuries, viewed as "accidents" or "wrongs," can be prevented or compensated through action at appropriate points in the legal system, remedies can be provided by law. Such remedial actions through the legal system typically are perceived both by lawyers and by engineers and businessmen as constraints imposed on technology and business enterprise by law. In a larger view appropriate to the needs of the contemporary society, it may be possible to perceive, design, and apply the legal measures, along with technological and managerial improvements, as alternative and mutually supporting ways to optimize the total effects—i.e., the first-order effects and the side effects—of a technology and its supporting system.

CONSTRAINING ASPECT OF LAW

The legal system in its constraining aspect (i.e., in setting and defining channels for economic activity) encompasses the general body of criminal law and tort law; the antitrust laws and other measures to enforce competition or to establish the plane on which competition is conducted; the regulation of banking, the investment process, and the sale of securities; the control of production, distribution, and pricing in such sectors of the economy as transportation, electric power and light, communications, mining, the production of oil and gas, and agriculture; and a variety of other measures. To keep this inquiry in focus, it is necessary to examine the interfaces between technology and economics and law in its constraining aspect through selective illustrations. I believe it will serve our purposes to concentrate on the evolution of substantive doctrine in tort law relating to negligence, nuisance, and strict products liability; and on the procedures of fact-finding in law courts and their implications. This will signify a concentration on judicial behavior and common law development, with only tangential reference to the vast and complicated web of statutes that pervades our national life.

I have chosen this emphasis for several reasons. Statutes are major sources of law, but they are enacted by legislatures and as such fall within the political process; and I have assumed that economists, engineers, and businessmen are more familiar with the political process and hard realities of political lobbying, pressure, and counterpressure than with the judicial process. In their day-to-day impact, statutes are profoundly affected by judicial interpretation and application; and I have assumed that businessmen, engineers, and economists often are as mystified by the interpretive aspect of judicial behavior as by its other manifestations. In exploring negligence, nuisance, strict products liability, and judical fact-finding in relation to economic and technological activity, I shall apply Mr. Justice Holmes's well-known dictum that in regard to such matters, a page of history is worth a volume of logic.

Tort Doctrine of Negligence—Interface With Transportation

In 1871, the Central Iowa Railway was built to bring the power and speed of railroad transportation to the farmlands of Iowa. The railroad crossed a preexisting highway at an acute angle. In consequence, its trains ran very close to the highway for some distance when approaching or leaving the crossing. A local farmer was injured when the horse that he had been riding, frightened by the proximity of a train, shied and went out of control near the intersection. The farmer brought suit against the company, charging it with negligence in the construction of its railroad. Despite a jury finding in a special verdict that the railway company could have built its track so as to avoid the acute angle of intersection, the court decided against the farmer (Beatty v. Central Iowa Railway, 58 Iowa 242, 12 N.W. 332 (1882)). The court's opinion illuminated its conception of the appropriate balance among relevant criteria:

The mere constructing of a railway in close proximity to a highway is not, in itself, an act of negligence. Railways, if constructed at all, must of necessity, cross over highways . . . railways cannot always approach highways at right angles; if they approach at very acute angles, as they sometimes do, it is apparent that they must, of necessity, run for some distance in close proximity to and almost parallel with them. The mere fact that they so run, although it may render the use of the highway less safe, does not of itself constitute negligence upon the part of the railway company. Such increase of danger is necessarily incident to, and attendant upon, this improved mode of transportation. *All persons must accept the advantages of this mode of intercommunication with the danger and inconveniences that necessarily attend it; the price of progress cannot be withheld.* [Emphasis added.]

In economic terms, the court left the cost of the injury to the farmer and his horse where it had initially fallen, external to the railroad's income statement. In legal terms, the court shaped the tort doctrine of negligence to fit its premises derived from the experience, outlook, and priorities of the contemporary society. It assigned priority to "progress," defining "progress" specifically as "improved transportation" and generally as economic growth.

Negligence and Nuisance—Interface With Environmental Protection

In passing from cases arising from traffic accidents to cases arising from pollution and environmental damage, the law typically shifts its frame of reference from the doctrine of negligence to a combination of the doctrine of negligence and a variegated body of doctrine known as "nuisance." A judgment of the Supreme Court of Rhode Island in 1934 exemplifies a judicial doctrine that assigned an explicit priority to industrial production over environmental protection (Rose v. Socony Vacuum Corp., 54 R.I. 411, 173 A. 627 (1934)). The plaintiff was a farmer whose land adjoined the site of a large oil refinery and storage tank owned by the Socony Vacuum Corporation. The farmland and the refinery were separated by a public road. In the course of the company's operations, the soil on which the refinery stood became impregnated with petroleum and waste substances that were carried by subterranean percolation under the road to the plaintiff's farm. The continuous seepage poisoned both the well that supplied drinking water to the farmer and his family and a small stream used by the farmer to water his pigs and chickens. Denied drinking water, and enraged by the death of his livestock, the farmer brought suit against the Socony Vacuum Corporation, grounding his claim for damages on a theory of private nuisance without any allegation of negligence. The Supreme Court of Rhode Island met the issue head on:

> Defendant's refinery is located at the head of Narragansett Bay, a natural waterway for commerce. This plant is situated in the heart of a region highly developed industrially. Here it prepares for use and distributes a product which has become one of the prime necessities of modern life. *It is an unavoidable incident of the growth of population and its segregation in restricted areas that individual rights recognized in a sparsely settled State have to be surrendered for the benefit of the community as it develops and expands.* [Emphasis added.] If, in the process of refining petroleum, injury is occasioned to those in the vicinity, not through negligence or lack of skill or the invasion of a recognized legal right, but by the contamination of percolating waters whose courses are not known, we think that public policy justifies the determination that such injury is *damnum absque injuria* [harm without a legal wrong].

Some 20 years later, in 1953, the Supreme Court of North Carolina adjudicated a conflict reminiscent of the controversy in *Rose* v. *Socony Vacuum Corp.*, weighing similar elements but with a different outcome. In *Morgan* v. *High Penn Oil Company* (238 N.C. 185, 77 S.E.2d 682 (1953)), the alleged culprit was again an oil company, but the victim on this occasion was the proprietor and operator of a restaurant and a trailer camp. The defendant oil company operated a refinery a thousand feet away from the plaintiff's property. Complaining that the refinery emitted nauseating gases that suffused his land as well as other properties up to a distance of two miles from the refinery, the plaintiff brought an action for a private nuisance, seeking both damages and an injunction. At the trial, the High Penn Oil Company introduced evidence to demonstrate that its refinery was highly modern in character and highly efficient, of a type generally used in the industry for renovating used lubricating oils. The plaintiff made no attempt to challenge the defendant's efficiency or the economic usefulness of its operations. There was no intimation that the defendant was in any way negligent. Nevertheless, the North Carolina court decided for the plaintiff, insisting that the High Penn Oil Company ''unreasonably'' caused noxious gases and odors ''to escape onto the nine acres of the plaintiffs to such a degree as to impair in a substantial manner the plaintiffs' use and enjoyment of their land.'' This sufficed to entitle the plaintiffs to recover damages. Since it was evident that the High Penn Oil Company also intended ''to operate the oil refinery in the future in the same manner as in the past,'' it was necessary to supplement the judgment for damages with an appropriate injunction ''to protect the plaintiffs against the threatened irreparable injuries.''

How are the differences in judgment and the apparent differences in outlook between the North Carolina court in *Morgan* v. *High Penn Oil Company* and the Rhode Island court in *Rose* v. *Socony Vacuum Corp.* to be reconciled and explained? In weighing the public interest in the refining of gasoline and in the renovation of used lubricating oils against the public interest in protecting farmland against contaminated waters and protecting restaurants against polluting gases, the two courts plainly struck different final balances. Courts and judges have disagreed before in analogous cases, and the sources of disagreement have been almost as varied as the complexity of the law and the variety of the facts to which the law must be applied. The emergence of a difference may, however, signify a new direction in judicial doctrine, to be subsequently defined in successive decisions that settle into a trend.

I cannot in this chapter attempt to marshal evidence in sufficient volume and detail to demonstrate the existence of such a judicial trend. I can and do avow my opinion that in the balance of considerations that determine the outcome in specific cases, a trend can be discerned in the development of the tort law of negligence and of nuisance in the past half century, and especially in the past three decades, toward an assignment of greater relative weight to such factors as protection of the environment, safety in the workplace, safety on the highways, and protection of the consumer and an assignment of less relative weight to the facilitation of production and technological development.

The trend has been carried to a point where judges have incorporated their own views of technology assessment into their legal opinions. In 1963, in *Renken* v. *Harvey Aluminum, Inc.* (226 F. Supp. 169 (D. Ore. 1963)), the United States District Court for Oregon adjudicated a dispute between farmers in Wasco County, Oregon, and an aluminum reduction plant. Harvey Aluminum had constructed and operated its plant in accordance with the Defense Production Act of 1950, as amended. The plant cost more than $40 million and produced some 80,000 tons of aluminum annually, sold both for general industrial use and national defense purposes. The plaintiff, one of a number of fruit growers in a fertile agricultural valley, complained that his fruit trees and farmland were overlaid with deposits of "particles, particulates, solids and gases," especially fluorides, emitted by the defendant's plant and carried by the wind to his property. Along with others, he sought an injunction. The court's opinion, following the usual pattern of analysis in nuisance cases, was nevertheless distinctive in certain respects. It analyzed the physical structure and chemical operations of the defendant's plant, with emphasis on the apparatus of exhaust and fume control. It took explicit account of the relation between the farmer's difficulties and the general problem of air pollution. I quote:

[The evidence convinced the court] of the feasibility of the introduction of electrostatic precipitators for the removal of the minute or small particulates which are not removed

by the other processes: . . . The great weight of the evidence points to the conclusion
that the installation of the cell hoods and the employment of electrostatic precipitators
would greatly reduce, if not entirely eliminate, the escape of the excessive material now
damaging the orchards of the plaintiffs.

   While the cost of the installations of these additional controls will be a substantial sum,
the fact remains that effective controls must be exercised over the escape of these noxious
fumes. Such expenditures would not be so great as to substantially deprive defendant of
the use of its property. While we are not dealing with the public as such, we must
recognize that air pollution is one of the great problems now facing the American public.
If necessary, the cost of installing adequate controls must be passed on to the ultimate
consumer. The heavy cost of corrective devices is no reason why plaintiff should stand
by and suffer substantial damage. . . .

   The court's statement that, if necessary, "the cost of installing adequate
controls must be passed on to the ultimate consumer," indicates something
more than the incorporation into the opinion of a judicial view of technology
assessment. It illustrates another trend in tort doctrine. In recent decades, an
increasing emphasis on social welfare objectives in tort law has tended to
shift the fulcrum of analysis from a concern with the "fault" of the defendant
to a concern for compensation for the victim and a policy of distributing the
costs of accidents widely. Economists and businessmen may notice that the
court's opinion on its face does not reveal whether and how far the court
may have taken into account such factors as elasticity of demand and other
competitive conditions. Engineers on their part may have doubts concerning
the competence of judges for technology assessment in the endless variety
of industries that are drawn into litigation. If it should be assumed that the
necessary competence for relevant economic and technological judgments
can be supplied in the processes of litigation, questions might nevertheless
be raised concerning the factual basis for such judgments. Engineers, economists, and businessmen may be puzzled as to whether and how the procedures for fact-finding in a court of law can accommodate the kind of data
collection and analysis necessary for technology assessment and economic
judgments. These are questions that I shall examine later in this chapter.

Strict Products Liability

   The trend in the tort doctrines of negligence and nuisance has been matched
by a corresponding trend in the doctrine of strict products liability. In a
seminal decision of the Supreme Court of California in 1963 (Greenman v.
Yuba Power Products, Inc., 59 Cal.2d 57, 377 P.2d 897 (1963)), Justice
Roger Traynor contributed an exemplary definition of the modern concept
of strict products liability:

The purpose of such [strict products] liability is to insure that the costs of injuries resulting
from defective products are borne by the manufacturers that put such products on the

market rather than by the injured persons who are powerless to protect themselves. . . .
To establish the manufacturer's liability it was sufficient that plaintiff [the ultimate consumer] proved that he was injured while using the Shopsmith [a power tool] in a way it was intended to be used as the result of a defect in design and manufacture of which plaintiff was not aware that made the Shopsmith unsafe for its intended use.

The controlling factors are the existence of a "defect" which caused injury to the ultimate consumer. No negligence need be established. In economic terms, strict products liability is intended to "internalize" into the manufacturing process the cost of injuries to the ultimate purchasers by transferring the cost back to the manufacturer.

Justice Traynor's decision was one of several leading cases in a trend vividly described by Judge (formerly Professor) Robert E. Keeton (1969:101):

Decisions advancing this principle [strict products liability] since 1963 have been described as a tidal wave, a flood, and a prairie fire—expressions that disclose . . . perhaps a common ideological perspective of foreboding. Others, whose comments speak of the same development but from a different ideological perspective, hale [*sic*] a breakthrough, a new insight and . . . a new era.

The "defect" to which Justice Traynor's 1963 decision was addressed was a failure of a lathe to hold a piece of wood, which flew out of the machine and struck the plaintiff on the forehead. The defects in other similar cases were a faulty steering apparatus, a bad altimeter in an airplane, the breakdown of a motor in ordinary use. These were manufacturing defects in a familiar sense: the materials or workmanship of particular tools or instruments fell below the level of quality justifiably expected by the purchasers.

The tidal wave described by Judge Keeton also carried along products liability cases of another kind, in which the issues of fact were more subtle, more difficult, and more troublesome in their implications for manufacturing. These are cases involving a so-called "design defect," i.e., a standard feature of an entire line of tools or instruments adopted by the manufacturer as a preferred design which the purchaser seeks to stigmatize as a "defect." In such a case the existence of the condition is conceded. The issue is whether it constitutes a "defect." The Supreme Court of California has been assiduous in protecting consumers from "design defects." Judge Tobriner, of the Supreme Court of California, in a leading case (Barker v. Lull Engineering Co., 20 Cal.3d 413, 573 P.2d 443 (1978)), summed up the determinative criteria:

[A] product is defective in design . . . *if, in light of the relevant factors discussed below, the benefits of the challenged design do not outweigh the risk of danger inherent in such design. . . .*

[I]n evaluating the adequacy of a product's design . . . a jury may consider, among other relevant factors, *the gravity of the danger posed by the challenged design, the likelihood that such danger would occur, the mechanical feasibility of a safer alternative*

design, the financial cost of an improved design, and the adverse consequences to the
product and to the consumer that would result from an alternative design. . . .

[A] manufacturer who seeks to escape liability for an injury . . . caused by its product's design on a risk-benefit theory should bear the burden of persuading the trier of fact that its product should not be judged defective [on the basis of the "relevant factors" described]. [Emphasis added.]

Do these criteria mean that the liability of a manufacturer will be determined by the way in which a jury may second-guess a judgment made by a manufacturer concerning the elements of risk and benefit in the design of his product, the engineering feasibility of a safer alternative design, the cost-benefit calculations relating to a possible improved design, and comparable criteria? Operationally, the doctrine appears to mean just that. Its reach is indicated in a 1978 decision by the Supreme Court of Oregon (Wilson v. Piper Aircraft Corp., 282 Or. 61, 577 P.2d 1322 (1978)).

Two passengers in a light plane manufactured by the Piper Aircraft Corporation were killed when the plane crashed. Their wives brought an action against Piper Aircraft Corporation, contending that the crash was caused by carburetor icing and that a fuel-injection system would have eliminated the danger of icing. This, they alleged, was a design defect. The Oregon court responded to much the same effect as the Supreme Court of California, except that it left the burden of proof upon the plaintiff and acknowledged somewhat greater concern for the possible consequences of its decision:

We are mindful of defendant's argument that a lay jury is not qualified to determine technical questions of aeronautical design, and of the forceful argument by Professor Henderson that problems of conscious product design choices are inherently unsuited to determination by courts. . . . We do not underestimate the difficulties involved in this type of litigation. We are, however, committed to the position that members of the public are entitled to compensation for their injuries if they are damaged because of improper product design. . . . In the absence of an ability to recover through courts, persons injured by such designs would be without a remedy.

Plaintiffs' allegations amount to a contention that an airplane furnished with a standard aircraft engine is defective because an engine of a different type, or with a different carburetor system, would be safer in one particular. . . .

There is not, however, any evidence about what effect the substitution of a fuel injected engine in this airplane design would have had upon the airplane's cost, economy of operation, maintenance, requirements, over-all performance, or safety in respects other than susceptibility to icing. . . .

Taking into account all of the evidence . . . we hold that the plaintiffs did not produce sufficient evidence that a reasonably prudent manufacturer who was aware of the risks of a carburetor icing would not have designed this model of aircraft with a carbureted engine or that substitution of a fuel injected engine was practicable. . . .

Although the manufacturer escaped liability in the immediate case because of the plaintiff's failure of proof, the court's words may well have continued to ring ominously in his ears.

Current litigation arising from injuries caused by asbestos illuminates another phase of strict products liability, referred to by lawyers as the "state-of-the-art" issue. In the courts of some states, the "state-of-the-art defense" is regularly rejected. The meaning of the defense and the consequences of its acceptance or rejection can be traced in a recent decision of the Supreme Court of New Jersey, *Beshada* v. *Johns-Manville Products Corporation* (90 N.J. 191, 447 A.2d 539 (1982)).

In the *Beshada* case, a number of workers and survivors of deceased workers claimed redress for injury or death allegedly caused by exposure to asbestos over varying periods of time in the defendant companies' factories and warehouses. When the companies invoked the state-of-the-art defense, the court disallowed it in a revealing opinion:

. . . the state-of-the-art defense asserts that distributors of products can be held liable only for injuries resulting from dangers that were scientifically discoverable at the time the product was distributed. Defendants argue that the question of whether the product can be made safer must be limited to consideration of the available technology at the time the product was distributed. Liability would be absolute, defendants argue, if it could be imposed on the basis of a subsequently discovered means to make the product safer since technology will always be developing new ways to make products safer. . . .

The most important inquiry, however, is whether imposition of liability for failure to warn of dangers which were undiscoverable at the time of manufacture will advance the goals and policies sought to be achieved by our strict liability rules. We believe that it will.

[Explaining that the goals included risk-spreading and accident avoidance, the court continued:]

Defendants argue that this policy is not forwarded by imposition of liability for unknowable hazards. Since such hazards by definition are not predicted, the price of the hazardous product will not be adjusted to reflect the costs of the injuries it will produce. Rather, defendants state, the cost "will be borne by the public at large and reflected in a general, across-the-board increase in premiums to compensate for unanticipated results." There is some truth in this assertion, but it is not a bad result. . . .

[Since the manufacturer is in the best position to take technological and managerial steps to avoid accidents, the burden should properly be placed on him.] Defendants urge that this argument has no force as to hazards which by definition were undiscoverable. . . . But this view ignores the important role of industry in product safety research. The "state-of-the-art" at a given time is partly determined by how much industry invests in safety research. By imposing on manufacturers the costs of failure to discover hazards, we create an incentive for them to invest more actively in safety research. . . .

. . . We impose strict liability because it is unfair for the distributors of a defective product not to compensate its victims. As between these innocent victims and the distributors, it is the distributors—and the public which consumes their products—which should bear the unforeseen costs of the product.

Here is a judicially developed doctrine directed toward objectives that are in a measure analogous to the purposes of workmen's compensation. Victims of industrial accidents are to be compensated without regard to questions of intention or negligence; and the costs of compensation, imposed initially on the manufacturer, are to be distributed widely through the society by the price mechanism and, if the manufacturer so chooses, through insurance purchased by him. The court also seeks, through the threat of potential tort liability, to stimulate manufacturers toward increased research on product safety in order to avoid or reduce industrial accidents. These are the explicit judicial aims. One can also discern in the doctrine an unspoken but implicit confidence in the capacity of America's industry and technology to promote economic growth, productivity, technological innovation, and international competitiveness with undiminished vigor while carrying the new judicially imposed burdens.[1] Businessmen, engineers, and economists may or may not share this confidence.

Judicial Fact-Finding

The misgivings engendered in engineers and businessmen by recent trends in tort law have been enhanced on occasion by their encounters with the procedures of judicial fact-finding. When a businessman, engineer, or economist experiences these procedures, whether as plaintiff or defendant or expert witness, he is apt to find them a fertile source of misunderstanding and exasperation. The confusion arises from the multiple meanings latent in the concept of a "fact" and a "finding of fact," and from the tensions that can be generated by attempts to mesh one meaning of a finding of fact into another, especially when the participants are unaware of the differences.

Let me suggest that you review in your minds what a fact means to an engineer or economist. I ask you especially to contemplate the processes by which an engineer or economist arrives at a finding of fact and the criteria assumed to be applicable to the processes. To widen our perspective, I ask you now to review in similar terms what a fact means operationally to a physicist or chemist; to a paleontologist or a prehistoric archeologist in the course of research; to a historian in the regular course of work; to a newspaper reporter or to his or her managing editor; and to a businessman facing the need to make a particular decision or to formulate a general policy for the conduct of his enterprise on the basis of the relevant "facts." From such a comparative appraisal, it appears that a fact is the final result of a process of inquiry that varies from profession to profession and occupation to occupation; that the nature of a fact varies correspondingly; and that each

---

[1]Two years later, the Supreme Court of New Jersey sharply qualified this decision, holding that the requirement of a warning by a manufacturer must be measured by whether the manufacturer knew, or should have known, of the danger, given the scientific, technological, and other information available when its product was distributed. Technically, the court refrained from overruling the *Beshada* case, but "restrict[ed] *Beshada* to the circumstances giving rise to its holding" (Feldman v. Lederle Laboratories, 97 N.J. 429, 479 A.2d 374 (1984)).

profession or occupation discusses its facts without explicit recognition of their special meaning derived from the fact-finding processes typical of the particular profession or occupation, because those processes are taken for granted.

In a court of law, facts are found by a jury or a trial judge sitting without a jury. The jury's findings must be based on evidence elicited from witnesses through examination and cross-examination by trial counsel. Some proffered testimony is excluded under rules of evidence derived in part from considerations of logic, in part from technical considerations of judicial organization and practice, and in part from considerations of policy rooted in historical experience. When trial counsel complete their introduction of evidence, that evidence is sifted by a jury in seclusion in accordance with instructions received from the trial judge. The jury's eventual finding of fact is based on a ''preponderance of evidence'' in a civil action or on ''proof beyond a reasonable doubt'' in a criminal proceeding. These processes of fact-finding have evolved to meet conditions, needs, and purposes with a meaning and importance of their own. Apart from encrustations derived from history or accident and maintained through habit, they can be and are accepted and supported by responsible, experienced, and intelligent men and women as essential to the general functions of the legal system. Nevertheless, they cannot always readily be made congruous with fact-finding by engineers, economists, scientists, or business executives. When businessmen, engineers, or economists are involved in litigation, they must try to fit their concepts and methodologies of fact-finding into the concept and method of the courts. They often find the fit to be neither natural nor easy, and tensions arise. The frictions could perhaps be reduced and a better mutual accommodation could perhaps be achieved through a growing reciprocal appreciation of the nature and background of the respective concepts and methods of fact-finding. How might an effort to foster an improved mutual understanding best be undertaken? A possible way to do so has been indicated by the National Conference Group of Lawyers and Scientists, established jointly by the American Association for the Advancement of Science and the American Bar Association in 1975. The National Conference Group has sponsored a general Workshop on Cross-Education of Lawyers and Scientists and workshops on particular aspects of fact-finding, such as the assessment of technological risk. The need for such cross-education has been perceived, and beginnings have been made at several law schools and engineering schools. The need and the possibilities should be called to the attention of the engineering schools, business schools, and law schools of the nation.

CONCLUSIONS

I have tried to show how the legal system not only constrains but also facilitates and fosters business enterprise, technological innovation, and economic thought. I have sought to outline a reciprocal relationship between the constraints on technology and business prescribed by law and the burdens imposed by technology and economic organization on law. I have identified as a core problem the allocation of emphasis between the facilitating and constraining functions of law. I have attempted to trace how the emphasis has shifted from time to time, not only in legislation but also in the continuous and pervasive work of the courts. Cases selected from an earlier period demonstrated a judicial disposition to foster enterprise, technological innovation, and investment even at the expense of acknowledged social costs and risks. Cases selected from the period since the end of World War II, and notably from the 1960s and 1970s, demonstrated a shift in judicial emphasis to a heightened concern for safety in the workplace and marketplace, environmental protection, and general social welfare, with a largely unspoken assumption that technology and business enterprise can be adjusted to these new priorities without a serious burden on technological development, economic growth, or international competitiveness. The constraints imposed on business enterprise and technology by this shift in priorities have been compounded by incongruities between the fact-finding processes of courts and those of technology and business.

To understand the shifting judicial trends, we must project them against the background of national events. The tendency to accord a decisive priority to compensation for victims, widespread diffusion of the costs of compensation through cost internalization, "accident avoidance," and environmental protection emerged after World War II. The tendency became "a tidal wave, a flood, and a prairie fire" or "a breakthrough, a new insight"—to borrow Judge Keeton's vivid terminology—in the 1960s and the 1970s. In the 1960s, President Lyndon Johnson launched his antipoverty program and called on the American people to join him in reshaping America into a "Great Society." Social forces generated in the 1960s by President Johnson's program, together with social forces independently generated to which the Johnson program was in part a political response, gained momentum through the 1970s, producing a striking expansion of federal legislation aimed at environmental protection, occupational safety, consumer protection, and general social welfare. The new statutes applied not only to business enterprises, but also to state and local school systems and other state and local government officials, universities, foundations, the professions, political parties and candidates for elected office, and homeowners and automobile drivers. Whether perceived as a "prairie fire" or a magnificent "breakthrough," the legislation and the social outlook that it reflected became a part of our national life. The effects, pervasive throughout the society, were infused into the thought of lawyers and the judicial process.

I offer a view of certain elements in the changing national outlook which I believe to have been critical for the interaction of law with economic growth and technological innovation. The United States emerged from World War II with an international ascendancy rare in historical experience. The nation's predominance extended through the economic, scientific, technological, military, and diplomatic spheres; and its economic ascendancy extended through the subspheres of industry, agriculture, transportation, communications, and finance. The circumstances produced a correspondingly unprecedented American outlook. Unconsciously or subconsciously, Americans generally came to believe that the nation's strategic security, wealth, production, productivity, technological advancement, and international competitiveness could be taken for granted as virtually beyond challenge or impairment. In consequence, they felt free to turn their primary attention to other historic strands in the fabric of American society. Theodore Roosevelt's Square Deal, Woodrow Wilson's New Freedom, and Franklin Roosevelt's New Deal reemerged as Harry Truman's Fair Deal and Lyndon Johnson's Great Society. Some of the old strands were rewoven with a new twist engendered by the new sense that military security, production, productivity, and international competitiveness could be taken for granted. Social equity, redistribution, and amelioration of the plight of the disadvantaged were pursued with an intensity that, in some quarters of the population, gradually turned into an almost exclusive preoccupation. The post–World War II priorities pervaded the educational system and percolated into the courts.

Concurrently, the very conditions that underlay the American outlook of the 1960s were receding. The passing years restored a wider and less unbalanced distribution of wealth and power to the international scene. The United States retained its primacy in wealth, production, and power, but its extraordinary post–World War II ascendancy declined before the renewed economic vitality of Western Europe and East Asia and the Soviet Union's buildup of its military forces. Rapid developments in the Third World added their own thrust to the processes of change. Although in itself such a redistribution of wealth and economic power might have been acceptable to Americans, the trends and some of the causes were not. Comparative trends in productivity, technological innovation, and competitiveness between the United States and Europe and especially between the United States and East Asia held disquieting portents. In large measure, the causes could be found in postwar recovery in Europe and East Asia, abetted by American programs to help rebuild Europe and Japan and by growing American and European attention to the needs of the developing countries. Realistic analysis, however, exposed critical contributing factors within American society itself. In the 1970s, sophisticated observers began to discern grave internal problems affecting American rates of increase in productivity and the international competitiveness of American industry. In the 1980s, their perceptions were supplemented by a steadily widening general awareness of these problems and their significance. American values and priorities began to shift again toward a restored emphasis on production, productivity, technological innovation, and international competitiveness. If the trend continues, it will make itself felt in the legislatures and the courts. There are indeed signs that it may have already begun to do so.

One such sign is a Model Uniform Product Liability Act[2] proposed by the U.S. Department of Commerce (1977) for consideration and possible voluntary adoption by the several states, and based on extensive preliminary study by a Federal Interagency Task Force on Product Liability and a supplementary Options Paper, organized under the leadership of the Department of Commerce at the request of the Office of Management and Budget and the Domestic Policy staff of the White House. If the proposed Model Act should be enacted by the states, it would introduce uniformity and add clarity to the existing law and narrow the scope of potential liability of manufacturers for design defects by basing liability on criteria essentially equivalent to negligence.

Fifteen years ago, in an effort to assay the functions of tort liability in technology assessment, I recommended (Katz, 1969) that:

> The risk [imposed on manufacturers by tort law] should not be so great as to discourage research, development, or investment in new technology. It should be large enough, however, to impel industrial enterprises to take account of total systems effects in their research and development. They should be stimulated to apply the resources of science and technology to the elimination of harmful side effects as well as the achievement of the desired initial objective.

In what measure is the foregoing paragraph appropriate to the current posture of tort law? In what measure is it appropriate not only to tort law, which we have examined for illustrative purposes, but more generally for the role of the legal system in technological innovation and economic growth? In my judgment, it remains valid in essence but requires an adjustment in emphasis. The adjustment in emphasis would be subtle but critical, reflected in a shift in the order of statement. The current objective should be to promote economic growth, technological innovation, productivity, and international competitiveness while protecting consumers, workers, and the environment from the harmful side effects of technology and industrial indifference or mismanagement. The objective should be pursued in the endless variety of particular applications of law, engineering, economic policy, and business management. This would reflect the appropriate interplay between the two central and continuing historic themes of growth and social equity in the contemporary national and international setting.

---

[2]44 F.R. 62714 (Oct. 31, 1979). See also footnote 1 in this chapter.

RELATED ISSUES

I now turn to three additional law-related questions. Let me comment first on the apparently disproportionate number of lawyers and disproportionate volume and intensity of litigation in the United States as compared with Western Europe and Japan. Comparative statistics on such matters are notoriously difficult to put together on a reliable basis. Nevertheless, I shall proceed on the assumption that the familiar data can be taken as reliable. I suggest several factors that may contribute to a possible explanation. First, there is constitutional review under the U.S. Constitution which opens up a range of litigation that has not been available historically in Western Europe or Japan. Although recent constitutional changes in Japan and West Germany may in time introduce something comparable in those societies, the data on such a possible development are not yet in and the scale in any event would be much more limited than in the United States. Second, the constitutional factor in the United States has increased litigation not only by adding an extra tier of judicial scrutiny, but by a specific mandate. I refer to the Supreme Court's decisions that have compelled the states and the federal government to provide counsel to indigents who might otherwise have been unable to appeal from decisions in lower courts or even to litigate at all. (Gideon v. Wainwright, 372 U.S. 335 (1963); Douglas v. California, 372 U.S. 353 (1963); Argersinger v. Hamlen, 407 U.S. 25 (1972); Scott v. Illinois, 99 S.Ct. 1158 (1979); and Evitts v. Lucey, 105 S.Ct. 830 (1985).) Congress supplemented the thrust of these Supreme Court decisions when it created the Legal Services Corporation to provide general legal assistance to indigents. Third, you will recall that DeTocqueville in his *Democracy in America* not only stressed the role of lawyers in American life but commented also on the absence of what he called an "administration," meaning a bureaucracy or civil service. He pointed out that many matters which in Europe were handled regularly and decisively by the "administration" were handled in America by individuals, groups, or voluntary associations that dealt with such matters on their own independent initiative. When these individuals or groups differed, they turned to the courts for resolution of their controversies. In my judgment, DeTocqueville's observations remain valid today. Much of our litigation is a price we pay for our comparative freedom from a pervasive and authoritative bureaucracy of the kind generally accepted by the peoples of Western Europe and Japan. Fourth, in any national comparison of the numbers of lawyers, account must be taken of the American federal structure, under which the American legal profession consists of 50 separate organized bars, one for each of the 50 states.

Let me turn to the implications for technological innovation and economic growth of current developments in the administration of the antitrust laws.

Many of you are aware of the National Cooperative Research Act of 1984 (P.L. 98-462, 98 Stat. 1815), a statute designed to facilitate joint ventures in research and development by American corporations. In essence, the statute contemplates that no such joint venture should be pronounced illegal by a court without full consideration of the procompetitive benefits of such a venture. In addition, even if such a venture should be found on its facts to be more anticompetitive than procompetitive and therefore illegal, the participants would be exposed only to actual damages and not to triple damages. Perhaps this statute is additional evidence of a current trend in the legal system toward a restored emphasis on productivity, technological innovation, economic growth, and international competitiveness. But beyond this statute, the antitrust prospects are not yet clear.

I turn to the current and prospective interaction between the law of intellectual property and the accelerating expansion and development of information technology and the information industry. For the past two years, Professor Anthony Oettinger at Harvard University has been working on a book which will include, as I understand it, a section devoted to this range of questions. Several law schools have under consideration plans for the development of new institutes of research and advanced training relating to such questions as computer law, trade secrets, and the law relating to genetic engineering and biogenetics, aerospace, and medical technology. At another law school, plans are under way to launch a new journal on information law that will address these and other similar problems. These are signs that the world of scholarship relating to information technology and applicable law has begun to take notice of the changing situation and its possible portents.

In a recent article in the new journal, *Issues in Science and Technology,* published under the auspices of the National Academies of Sciences and Engineering and the Institute of Medicine, a former assistant attorney general in the Justice Department's Antitrust Division deplores the failure of Congress to take action to modify the present state of the law concerning the antitrust implications of patent licensing (Baxter, 1985:80). The author believes that it is in the interest of technological innovation and economic growth to accord to the owners of patents and other forms of intellectual property greater flexibility in licensing in order to put their patents or other forms of intellectual property to productive use. He believes that currently they are unnecessarily inhibited by an unwarranted judicial hostility toward such flexibility. A bill to rectify this situation was introduced but it was not adopted, for reasons which, in the opinion of the author, reflect the unwillingness of congressmen to take political risks in an election year. He concludes his essay by observing that the "relationship between intellectual property rights and antitrust enforcement remains a problem that demands prompt attention" (Ibid., p. 91). In sum, this is another area in which it is currently too early to discern what new developments there may be.

Although we cannot yet discern clear trends, current issues in these sectors of statutory law, as in the common law of torts, reflect the need for an adjustment in emphasis in the contemporary phase of the historic interplay between the theme of growth-innovation-productivity-international competitiveness and the theme of social equity-inalienable rights.

REFERENCES

Baxter, William F. 1985. Antitrust law and technological innovation. *Issues in Science and Technology* 1(2):80.

Katz, Milton. 1969. The function of tort liability in technology assessment. *Cincinnati Law Review* 38:587, 662.

Keeton, Robert E. 1969. *Venturing To Do Justice*. Cambridge, Mass.: Harvard University Press.

National Academy of Engineering. 1969. *A Study of Technology Assessment*. A Report to the Committee on Science and Astronautics, U.S. House of Representatives. Washington, D.C.

National Academy of Sciences. 1969. *Technology: Processes of Assessment and Choice*. A Report to the Committee on Science and Astronautics, U.S. House of Representatives. Washington, D.C.

U.S. Congress. 1967. Technology Assessment Seminar. Proceedings before the Subcommittee on Science, Research and Development of the House Committee on Science and Astronautics, 90th Cong., 1st sess., Sept. 21–22.

U.S. Department of Commerce. 1977. *Interagency Task Force on Product Liability*. Final Report. Report No. 273-220. Springfield, Va.: National Technical Information Service.

The Bhopalization
of American Tort Law

PETER W. HUBER

The new tort law, and the entire vision of "public law" adjudication that animates it, is politically dangerous. It removes the most controversial social issues from the arena in which controversy can be brokered and tensions diffused through the very process of political participation.

Since 1960, American tort law has undergone a revolution that can be accurately (if somewhat disrespectfully) described as a mad scramble by the Trial Lawyers of America to keep pace with the National Academies of Engineering and Sciences. New legal arguments have been prepared, tested, honed, and developed on a wide variety of accidents, nonaccidents, illnesses, and cures. Bendectin, Agent Orange, Love Canal, Three Mile Island, the Dalkon Shield, and the pertussis vaccine have all figured in the training.

The transformation, in a nutshell, has consisted of shifting the focus of American tort law from "private" risks to "public" ones. And the prime mover has been science: the radical changes in tort law are traceable to equally radical improvements in the science of hazard identification and risk assessment. But not science alone, because the courts have often not been successful in recognizing where science ends and other bodies of learning or ignorance begin. Thus, trans-science,[1] nonscience, and a generous dose

This paper was originally presented at a National Academy of Engineering symposium, "Hazards: Technology and Fairness" (Washington, D.C., June 3–4, 1985), and will also appear in the volume based on that symposium (forthcoming from the National Academy Press, 1986).

of sheer nonsense have also figured prominently in the tort law's expansion from the narrow world of private hazards to the universe of public ones.

But though the tort system's reach has been greatly extended, the system has yet to demonstrate that with public risks it offers useful deterrence, fair compensation, or a needed vehicle for resolving festering social disputes. Legislatures are increasingly looking outside the tort system for mechanisms to accomplish these important objectives more effectively.

TORT LAW, OLD AND NEW

"Public" risks are perhaps not self-defining. When I use the term, I mean risks that are centrally produced or mass-produced, broadly distributed, often temporally remote, and largely outside the individual risk bearer's direct understanding and control—the hazards of large-scale electric power plants, air transport in jumbo jets, mass-produced vaccines, chemical additives in food, hazardous wastes, and recombinant DNA technology. These risks generally have a zero-infinity character—either the likelihood of harm to any individual is minuscule but the likelihood of exposure is very large (as with pollution), or the likelihood of exposure is small but the likelihood of widespread harm (should exposure occur) is large (as with a nuclear power plant accident). "Private risks," by contrast, tend to fall in more familiar ranges of the probability-consequence spectrum. They are discretely produced, localized, personally controlled, or of natural origin, and often immediate in their effects—the risks of cottage industries, wood stoves, transportation by car, and the like.

The "old" tort law revolved around private hazards and thus touched a relatively narrow range of human activities. It focused on correcting clear injustices and resolving festering disputes. And it maintained this focus by hewing strictly to two general requirements: a tort dispute had to be bipolar, and it had to be timely. These two overarching principles gave birth to a multitude of subsidiary rules and requirements. In the past 25 years, most of these have been either eroded beyond recognition or entirely discarded.

Bipolarity

Old tort law insisted, first of all, that a dispute be bipolar. Of course, a lawsuit cannot proceed with fewer than two parties. But under the old tort law you generally could not have *more* than two either. There were a few well-established exceptions to cover third-party claimants, joint tortfeasors, and so on. But the general rules strongly disfavored crowded courtrooms.

In addition, under the old tort law the parties had to have character. The plaintiff had to be someone special—someone specially injured. Under the old law of "nuisance," for example, the private individual simply was not permitted to sue for anything in the nature of a "public" nuisance. If the hazard was diffuse, broadly shared by the community, then it was by definition "public," and no private individual could sue. To bring a private lawsuit you had to prove a special injury to you personally—something out of the ordinary, an injury to your land, or to other private interest, an injury *not* largely shared by the community as a whole. If everyone in the community suffered more or less equally, the presumption was that no one suffered at all—unless a government official (typically a public prosecutor) determined otherwise.

Under the old tort law the defendant had to have character, too. His distinction was that he had to be *the* identified, demonstrated source of the plaintiff's injury. The plaintiff was required to show that *this* defendant more likely than not caused *that* particular injury. Just as the plaintiff had to distinguish himself from the grey mass of suffering humanity, so the defendant had to be distinguished from the mass of humanity's oppressors. If there was only a 1 percent chance that I caused your cancer, you could not sue me successfully.

These rules limited the reach of tort law very considerably. They confined tort litigation to the resolution of narrow, bipolar disputes. The old tort system was quite comfortable with car accidents but not with such things as pollution.

Times have changed. The "new" tort law is perfectly happy to take on multiparty disputes of every description. Plaintiffs' class actions, to start with, have become routine. These allow plaintiffs to consolidate numerous small injuries into one large one. It is not uncommon for class actions to embrace tens of thousands, and sometimes millions, of plaintiffs. An asbestos-related insurance dispute in California has been conducted in a large college auditorium—the space is needed simply to provide room for tables for the myriad lawyers involved. The evolution of the enormous lawsuit can be gauged, somewhat indirectly, by the large body of solemn, scholarly, and judicial literature addressing what obligations (if any) a lawyer initiating such litigation may have to notify his "clients" of the very existence of "their" lawsuit. And as the recent Agent Orange settlement is now demonstrating, distributing the damage awards that may be won in such suits can require administrative facilities and technical expertise comparable to those typically available only to a large city or state government.

Things have become equally crowded on the defendants' side of the auditorium. In one recent settlement, more than 150 companies were involved in a tentative agreement to clean up a toxic waste dump. The California litigation involving the drug commonly called DES introduced the radical concept of "market share" liability, which allows plaintiffs to sue undifferentiated *groups* of defendants without ever working out exactly which defendant caused whose injury. Under this rule of law, defendants are simply held liable in proportion to their share of the market in the drug or other product at the time the harm occurred. A similar concept is codified in the Price-Anderson Act (42 U.S.C. § 2210(b)) (and may be significantly expanded when the act comes up for renewal next year)—all nuclear operators will share in the liability if there is an accident at any one of their plants.

The most radical change in the new tort law is one still gleaming in the eyes of various legal commentators—but a moderately serious prospect nonetheless. Powerful forces are pushing, often to receptive audiences in the courts and legislatures, for what has been called a "proportional causation" rule of liability. This would permit me to sue you for my cancer if I could show even 1 percent likelihood that your power plant in fact caused it. Notwithstanding the 99 percent probability in your favor, I would still recover—but only 1 percent of my actual damages. One percent, that is, plus or minus the usual slack allowed by the tort system—which seems to be several hundred percent, at least. Under the old tort law, by contrast, I would not collect at all unless I established a causal link between your conduct and my injury that exceeded 50 percent; once that threshold was exceeded, I would recover my full damages.

Timeliness

The old tort law also had a rigid sense of timeliness. A tort action could not be brought too early. Nor too late. Premature actions were simply dismissed without prejudice to the plaintiff's right to sue again later. Stale actions were dismissed once and for all. Some of the details are worth reviewing.

Tort law entertains—and for a long time has entertained—*prospective* actions for injunctive relief. These are actions designed to cut off a course of dangerous conduct before it culminates in actual harm. Under the old tort law, if you could really show that I was on the brink of doing something terribly, imminently, and irreparably damaging to your interests, you could get an injunction to stop me. But if I was anywhere short of the brink, or if the consequences were anything short of irreparable, no injunction would issue. You (the plaintiff) had to wait for the harm to occur; only then could you sue me for money damages. The rationale was simple enough: what may appear to be a real threat of harm often is not, and litigation postponed will often be litigation avoided altogether.

Thus, for example, in an 1885 English case, *Fletcher* v. *Bealey*,[2] the court rejected an injunction plea from a downriver paper plant whose owner was worried about an upstream chemical manufacturer's wastes being piled at the edge of the river. There was no dispute that the wastes would be injurious; the only question was when, if ever, they would enter the river. The court ruled that the harm was not demonstrably imminent and that, therefore, no injunction should issue. This rule was widely followed in the American courts, and the rationale for embracing the rule on this side of the Atlantic was clear enough. Article III of the Constitution restricts courts to deciding "cases or controversies"—disputes, in other words, that have reached a certain level of ripeness. And American courts of that era were willing to accept the idea that if the wrong lies too far in the future the court's order will necessarily be speculative and prone to error.

Under the old tort law, the would-be plaintiff could not bypass the strict rules against premature injunctions by asking for premature money damages either. Negligence "in the air" was emphatically *not* actionable. Actual loss or damage was an essential element of the cause of action; in all but the most exceptional cases, the threat of future harm, as yet unrealized, was not enough. You could not, in other words, sue for damages alleged to be caused by exposure to risk itself. There were some minor exceptions—to cover cases in which the exposure to the risk caused present damage to land values and so on, or in which the defendant's conduct created such acute and broadly shared fears in the community that the courts felt it appropriate to intervene. But these exceptions were narrow. A tuberculosis hospital, for example, located in a proper place, was not an actionable nuisance.

Finally, under the old tort law a plaintiff was not permitted to sue too late either. Once he had been injured, a plaintiff typically had about one to three years to bring his damage action. This limitation period applied regardless of when he *discovered* that he had been injured. If the discovery came after the expiration of the period, it was simply too bad for the plaintiff.

In short, the old tort law saw timing as a critical factor in litigation. Except in very rare cases, the law embraced two, very limiting presumptions: first, that only time would tell if a risk was real enough to be worth a lawsuit; and, second, that time would heal all wounds without the help of the legal system.

Today, time isn't what it used to be. Through one legal vehicle or another, risks are being litigated earlier and earlier. And also later and later.

We have established, to start with, comprehensive administrative licensing systems for such things as drugs, food additives, nuclear power plants, hazardous waste dumps, aircraft, new chemicals, and the like. In a series of creative interpretations of the law, judges have declared that such statutes as the Administrative Procedure Act and the National Environmental Policy Act grant the courts broad authority to review licensing decisions critically as soon as they are made. For example, a panel of judges decided that they had authority to block research on the fast breeder reactor—not the reactor itself, mind you, but the *research* program going on behind it—because in the very long term such research might shape energy policy and so have a "significant impact" on the environment.[3] Moreover, every time a standard-setting agency such as the Environmental Protection Agency (EPA) or the Occupational Safety and Health Administration (OSHA) sets a new health-based standard, the underlying risk assessment (if any) is immediately subject to challenge in the courts, regardless of how temporally remote the harm at which the standard is directed. There is still a concept of "ripeness" in administrative law litigation of this type, but it has grown pathetically weak.

Similarly, tort plaintiffs seeking injunctions against what they view as unacceptably risky activities are no longer required to establish that harms are imminent. There is not the slightest doubt that an American court would be prepared to issue the *Fletcher* v. *Bealey* injunction today. Judges and lawyers may still pay lip service to "imminent harm" standards of yesteryear, but in fact almost any activity, no matter how remote the harm that it threatens, can qualify.

The "window of opportunity" for bringing *damage* actions has opened even wider. Such actions can now be brought very much later than was formerly allowed, and the evolving trend is to entertain them very much earlier as well.

At the front end, prominent legal commentators and judges are proposing to make the exposure to risk itself a compensable injury. In a nutshell, I could sue you for operating a nuclear power plant or a chemical factory in my neighborhood, and I could recover. How much? Well, as I understand these (in my view ludicrous) proposals, I would recover the present actuarial value of the injury you might some day cause me. We would take the Rasmussen Report on reactor safety,[4] say, multiply the 10^{-7} estimated risk of accident during the plant's life by the 10^{11} dollar value of the consequences and distribute the proceeds among the 10^4 who might collectively suffer those consequences. No, not quite: the recovery would be distributed among 10^4 *plus one* recipients. The lawyer who brought this inspired action would surely get a healthy cut, too.

If this seems utterly fanciful, the same scheme can be dressed up in different clothes, and there are many in my learned profession who are eager to serve as the tailors. Plaintiffs, it is argued, should be allowed to recover for the *anxiety* that exposure to risk can cause. In practical terms, this has much the same effect as suing for the risk itself—the suit can be brought at any convenient time, long before the risk is translated into actual injury, indeed, long before anyone is sure whether the risk is even real. And this highlights the one big advantage of suing for anxiety instead of for the risk itself: anxiety levels—unlike risk levels—are within the exclusive control of the plaintiff. It has not escaped notice in the profession that clever legal work and good (i.e., bad) publicity can create anxiety where none existed previously, and where none could be rationally justified by the hazard at hand.

Damage actions are being brought later and later as well. The other half of the plaintiffs' bar has been arguing (with considerable success) not that the injury occurs earlier than had been previously thought, but that it occurs much later. Thus, an increasing number of jurisdictions have adopted "discovery" statutes of limitation. These start the limitation clock running when the plaintiff discovers his injury, rather than when he was actually injured or exposed to the toxic agent. A variety of other new legal doctrines—based, for example, on the defendant's alleged concealment of information relevant to the hazard—have been successfully developed to extend by decades the period during which damage actions may be filed.

The World in the Oyster

It is these changes that have permitted courts to move from resolving "private" disputes to regulating "public" risks. Tort law's invasion of the enormous "public risk" territory permits almost everyone to sue almost everyone any time and makes the chances of winning something, somewhere, better and better.

The new tort system, to start with, can sweep into any particular risk controversy large fractions of a community, or the population of a state, or even the population of the country. With asbestos, Agent Orange, the Dalkon Shield, the whooping cough vaccine, and so on, tort lawyers can deal directly with hundreds of defendants and millions of plaintiffs; indirectly, they can affect millions more. If, for example, the vaccine industry folds under the current legal onslaught, the largest consequence will be felt by tomorrow's children—individuals who have never been injured by a vaccine and who have never chosen to go to court. The new tort law's reach is greatly extended in time as well. It concerns itself with activities dating back to the 1930s and reaching forward for one or (in controversies involving teratogens and mutagens) even several generations.

The Driving Force

The enormous expansion in the reach of tort law might seem somewhat surprising, considering that the hazards of daily life have been decreasing steadily and significantly for reasons quite independent of the tort system. But the anomaly is easily explained. Tort litigation is definitely a supply-side industry. Its growth has been driven by the availability of *information* about hazards, not by the severity of the hazards themselves. Well-understood though comparatively trivial hazards are much more actionable than poorly understood but graver ones. Tort litigators' practices, in short, have expanded to embrace the science available: science's growing awareness and understanding of diffuse, low-level hazards; its steadily improving ability to quantify very low probability events; its increased capacity to link old causes with new effects many decades later. This means that some excellent scientists have a lot to answer for.

Bruce Ames, for one. Ames, who developed a "quick-and-dirty" lab test for identifying mutagenic chemicals, has had a particularly mischievous impact in the legal world. It is very convenient for a lawyer representing a plaintiff who has (or fears he one day may have) cancer to be able to label a toxin as an Ames-proven mutagen (and thus probably a carcinogen). Then the defendant's lawyer must begin "quibbling" (or so it will seem to the lay jury) about dose-response limits, nonzero thresholds, the ubiquity of all-natural carcinogens, and so on. And of course, Ames is not the only culprit. Many other scientists who have unraveled the etiology of cancer and various chronic illnesses and revealed the long lag times between exposure to a toxin and the onset of disease are responsible, far more than any lawyer, for the law's effective abandonment of statutes of limitation for damage actions and the "imminent harm" prerequisites for injunctions.

Norman Rasmussen has been another major accessory before the fact in the creation of new tort law. Give me a scientist who is willing to put a number—any number—on a risk of dying, and I will give you a plaintiffs' lawyer who is willing to wave that number in court. Then the defendant's lawyer must once again begin "quibbling" (or so it will seem) about the inherently self-negating aspects of risk assessment, the real purpose of conducting probabilistic risk assessment in the first place, the conservatism in the "source term," and so on. And again, Rasmussen alone should not shoulder all the blame. As the Nuclear Regulatory Commission (NRC) has systematically identified, analyzed, and quantified the hazards of nuclear power plants, the plaintiffs' bar has licked its collective chops in anticipation of great meals to come.

CAN THE LEGAL SYSTEM COPE?

Understandably enough, many lawyers recognize the legal flood precipitated by these scientific storms as great progress for the profession. Opening up the tort law hunting grounds (and extending the season to boot) gives lawyers and the courts enormous power to reshape the political and economic landscape.

A separate question, however, is to determine who has benefited by this dramatic expansion in the demographic and temporal reach of tort law. Notwithstanding the most pious and self-serving claims of the plaintiffs' bar, and despite the startling support that tort lawyers have received from various "consumer protection" and "public interest" pressure groups, it increasingly appears that the principal and perhaps exclusive beneficiaries have been lawyers themselves, accompanied by only the tiniest group of self-selected or randomly selected consumers.

Regressive Incentives

The common wisdom among those who would defend the operation of the new tort system is that while the system is a considerable inconvenience to corporate and technological America, it benefits consumers and the public at large. Tort law, it is said, allocates accident costs so as to promote the efficient ordering of the free market and so as to affirm the individual's right in personal security. The traditional judicial assumption is that the tort system protects the public by deterring risky activities.

But science has taught that risk is *everywhere*, in absolutely everything we do or choose not to do. So undiscriminating deterrence of risk is now useless; the tort system regulates progressively only if it picks its targets accurately. The new tort system does not, and this, on reflection, is hardly surprising.

The first and surely the largest problem is that the tort law delegates difficult decisions to simple people. There is something magnificently right in leaving questions of criminal culpability to 12 good persons and true, pulled off the street more or less at random. But there is something profoundly silly in consulting this same group about the safety of drugs or nuclear waste reprocessing plants. To pick one recent and extreme example, the plaintiffs' bar has come close to saving Americans from the "scourge" of vaccination[5] because judges and juries (unlike an almost unanimous American medical community) are still undecided about whether the Sabin polio vaccine is preferable to the Salk vaccine, or whether whole-virus pertussis vaccine is preferable to a vaccine prepared from virus extract. This ambivalence has, of course, proved enormously expensive to manufacturers who followed Food and Drug Administration (FDA) requirements and sold the "wrong" alternative. But the more general lesson is that public-risk analysis is difficult, and lawyers, judges, and lay juries are not well qualified to decide which technologies and activities represent sound, progressive risk investments.

The tort system's risk preferences are further scrambled by the fuel on which it feeds. As we have seen, the system understandably favors as its targets risks that the scientific, parascientific, or plausibly pseudoscientific communities profess to know something about. Pseudoscience does not, of course, provide much rational ordering. And the great paradox when the tort system seeks to rely on real science—a paradox that the system utterly fails to grasp—is that the better the scientific information we have about a risk, the less serious the risk is likely to be. One reason is that new technologies, which are (on average) safer than the old ones they displace, come under much closer scrutiny in the administrative regulatory process. Another is that the more we know, the easier it is to protect against a risk in the first place. Thus, the tort system, driven primarily by the volume of risk information available, has a definite tendency to come down hardest where the deterrence it offers is least needed.

Beyond this, the tort system selects its targets according to criteria that make them attractive to the average, contingency-fee lawyer. It therefore prefers risks that are lurid, that stem from especially new and (to the lay jury) unfamiliar technologies, or that engage socially and politically divisive issues and arouse strong public passions.[6] Criteria such as these provide poor guidance in selecting objectively between good risks and bad ones. As a result, the new tort system brazenly fails to discriminate among the good, the bad, and the ugly in the public-risk world.

The biggest losers in the tort game are those who do not play at all. The traditional judicial assumption—and the only assumption on which the judicial-regulatory machinery can operate—is that in generously compensating the injured consumer the courts also protect the safety interests of other members of the public as well. This may well be true when the court deals with focused, comparatively grave private risks that can readily be identified as antisocial, such as drunk driving or hazardous conditions on land. But with diffuse, low-level, public risks, the balance between risk created and risk averted is much more subtle. Anyone can declare with confidence that drunk driving contributes unfavorably to the state of our risk environment. But it is much less easy to conclude the same of a somewhat risky vaccine, pesticide, or power plant that serves millions and adds both a small (per capita) quantum of risk and a quantum of risk reduction (perhaps smaller, perhaps larger) to our ambient environment.

With public risks there often is, in fact, a sharp division between affirming the security interests of the public as a whole and tending to those who have been injured by the hazard in question. For many somewhat risky—but in the aggregate risk-reducing—products and services that may be deterred by tort law activity, the interests of future consumers are directly opposed to those of unlucky prior consumers who have already been injured by the hazard in question. The injured obviously wish to be compensated, and a compassionate, generous society should surely respond. But compensation at the expense of the creator of the public risk will be against the interests of future consumers whenever the good that the risk attends removes more risk from the environment than it adds. In such cases the public security is best served by absolving the creator of the public risk from responsibility for the private injury, notwithstanding the fact that the private injury is real and its cause is known.

Inefficient Compensation

The new tort law does not serve as an effective tool for compensating public-risk victims, either. One might think that the loss for the large, corporate defendants must be a gain for small, individual plaintiffs, and this is indeed a belief that the Trial Lawyers of America have cultivated with the greatest and most delicate care. But litigation is by no means a zero-sum game—at least not until it is understood that lawyers themselves are always among the players and invariably among the winners.

Study after study has revealed that the tort law is highly capricious, inefficient, unfair, and most of all, terribly costly. For every dollar that finally ends up in the pocket of an injured plaintiff, perhaps three to five are diverted to lawyers—lawyers for the plaintiff and defendant, judges, law clerks, and miscellaneous other camp followers. The tort system is, quite simply, an insurance scheme with astronomically expensive agents and middlemen. If a private insurance company pocketed 80 cents on every dollar collected it would surely be prosecuted for fraud. But the tort system provides insurance at about that price.

On top of this, many injured plaintiffs do not recover at all from Tort Law Insurance, Inc., while a quite unacceptable number of *un*injured plaintiffs recover in large amount. The new tort system has a high degree of randomness to it. This appeals to gamblers, of course, as well as to "house" employees who take their cut in any event. Insurance, however, is supposed to take the gambling *out* of life.

Kindling the Flames

Finally, the new tort law does not offer one useful social function that was certainly provided under the old tort law: resolving fresh, focused, bipolar disputes. Some method must exist for resolving civil controversies, and as a sociological matter it is probably best that ordinary two-person quarrels be resolved by neutral nonexperts and lay juries. Not because these traditional decision makers are more likely than specialists to render verdicts of Solomonic insight and wisdom, but because they are most likely to be perceived by the public at large as accessible, moderate, and experienced with life's more ordinary vicissitudes. As a great judge once pointed out, it is often more important that things be settled than that they be settled right.

The new tort law does not settle, it unsettles. When 3 million plaintiffs sue 60 defendants for something that happened 30 years ago—or that may happen 30 years from now—the courts do not deal with a "dispute." They are engaged, instead, in large-scale social engineering. As such, their activities should be tolerated only if they offer efficient deterrence or fair compensation. As we have seen, the new tort law offers neither.

The Writing on the Wall

Courts, to be sure, have been reluctant to acknowledge their own limitations when it comes to prudent management of broad-ranging "public" risks. Recent judicial trends suggest that the courts generally believe that they are perfectly competent to resolve any public-risk question, no matter how large or complex. Congress and state legislatures, however, appear to be reaching precisely the opposite conclusion with increasing frequency. The list of activities legislatively insulated from the tender mercies of the plaintiffs' bar grows steadily longer.

For years state legislatures have seen fit to place liability limits on employee tort recoveries from employers.[7] The United States, along with 130 other governments, has determined that international civil aviation requires liability limits;[8] likewise, nuclear power has been thought to require liability-limiting legislation.[9] Congress granted tort immunity to pharmaceutical companies in order to assure their participation in the swine flu vaccination program; currently, both Congress and the Reagan administration are looking at a proposal to limit manufacturer liability for all types of vaccination. Other activities that have been granted partial or complete tort immunity include cleaning up a hazardous waste dump,[10] cleaning up accidental discharges of oil and hazardous substances,[11] participating in "unusually hazardous or nuclear" activities on behalf of the Department of Defense,[12] and participating in the Space Shuttle program.[13] Additional statutes that have codified liability limits or immunities include the Outer Continental Shelf Lands Act Amendments of 1978,[14] the Deepwater Port Act,[15] and the Trans-Alaska Pipeline Act.[16] Two recent federal initiatives have advanced comprehensive proposals to curtail and standardize product-liability recoveries through pro-defendant changes in rules of evidence and standards of conduct.[17] And in 1984, Congress passed legislation retroactively barring lawsuits against private contractors who participated in the early atomic weapons testing program.[18] Finally, Congress has recently considered a bill to provide a federal insurance system for "orphan" drugs.[19]

The most striking feature of the long and steadily growing list is that it addresses activities that, in a more rational world, would entail medals of honor, not tort suits. Steady employment in almost any industry is much safer than living in the poverty that attends unemployment; indeed the "healthy worker" effect is such a strong one that epidemiologists attempting to evaluate occupational health risks must expressly make allowance for it in their statistical studies of worker health. Nuclear power is demonstrably much safer than its main alternative—coal-fired power generation. At the time it was enacted, the swine flu vaccination program represented a prudent measure to protect the public health, and vaccination generally has been one of the greatest risk reducers of the century. Consumer products reduce aggregate risk in numerous but modest ways. And it is magnificently ironic to discover that tort immunities are needed for those who *clean up* hazardous waste dumps or oil spills, or who manufacture certain types of valuable drugs.

Lawyers tend to react to liability-limiting initiatives with disgruntlement, recognizing perhaps that liability limits cut off lawyers' livelihoods. It is often suggested, especially in connection with nuclear power, that no industry marketing an "acceptably" safe product or service should require the protection of a liability limit; the very existence of such a limit indicates that the hazards of the activity are unacceptably high. The argument is laughable. Nuclear power, civil aviation, commercial drugs, and the like are creatures of science and engineering, and their risks are therefore both predictable and inherently self-limiting. Yet undertaking a venture that is financially sound considering the physical risk involved is often a pure gamble in light of what may happen in the courts. Immunities and liability limits are the public-risk equivalents of Good Samaritan laws; that they are required at all is a ringing indictment of the level of foolishness to which our contemporary tort system aspires. Something is dangerously wrong when a pharmaceutical company requires legislative protection before it will dare to manufacture a risk-reducing vaccine.

THE AGENCIES AND THE COURTS

The fact remains that the universe of public risk, and compensating victims for their injuries, cannot be left simply to the free market. Public hazards inherently require public control, and despite our unwillingness to socialize many natural risks, our society has been unwilling to leave the victims of many man-made hazards uncompensated. If the courts are not qualified to manage public risks, who is? The answer is painfully obvious to almost everyone outside the legal community—administrative agencies, not the courts.

Institutional Competence

The spheres of competence for the courts and the agencies mirror the division between private and public risks. The courts perform adequately in risk regulation when they deal with private risks—focused, high-probability, bilateral hazards that have ripened (or are about to ripen) into concrete injuries. This class of risks is amenable to rational control through the retail, retrospective regulation that courts have traditionally supplied. The judiciary's competence in dealing with such risks cannot be questioned. The private dispute involving the realized risks of car accidents, slips-and-falls, hazardous conditions on land, and the like can find no better governmental forum for resolution than a court. No doubt the court fulfills some regulatory role in adjudicating tort suits of this nature, but the regulation is of a bilateral controversy for which the antisocial nature of the challenged conduct can be ascertained with relative ease and certainty.

In this private-risk setting, of course, the regulatory agency can be of little help. Constitutional difficulties would attend relegating this type of dispute to an administrative forum, and private-risk controversies are so common and varied that as a practical matter they inevitably will have to be resolved in trial-like proceedings presided over by generalist judges. The administrative agency is not needed here; the judicial arena already provides more or less the right forum for resolving social confrontations of this character.

Precisely the opposite holds true for public-risk choices. The assessment of these diffuse, low-probability, multilateral, and temporally remote hazards requires close attention to both sides of the public-risk picture—risks incurred and risks averted, persons harmed and persons helped by the activity in question. The task, in other words, requires a "public" point of view on the problem.[20] This is a perspective that public agencies can supply, and that courts plainly cannot.

The reasons are not difficult to discern. Beneficiaries of risk-reducing products and services do not litigate, and contingency-fee lawyers rarely seek them out as clients. The courts are thus not likely even to hear from those whose interests are a critical component of public-risk assessment. To be sure, the vaccine manufacturer or the operator of the nuclear power plant will attempt to serve as a surrogate spokesperson. But industry serves very poorly in this representative capacity, because it has every incentive to claim risk-reducing and other social benefits from its activities whether or not they exist.

In contrast, regulatory agencies, such as FDA, EPA, and NRC, can ground their assessment of public risks on a comparison of the hazards of the alternative drug, power plant, or pesticide already on the market. Even in the agencies, comparative-risk regulation is not all that it should be. But there are, at least, some promising signs here. Progressive movement toward more comparative-risk regulation remains possible, perhaps even inevitable in the agencies, because their focus is a relentlessly public one.

"Public law" adjudication in the courts, so eloquently described by Abram Chayes[21] (in general terms) and by Joel Yellin, David Rosenberg, and others[22] (with specific application to risk regulation), simply does not and cannot yield progressive choices among public risks. The public law model of judicial action is a grand design for having lawyers decide everything everywhere. But in risk matters, at least, experience and common sense teach that the only beneficiaries are likely to be lawyers themselves.

Deferring to the Experts

What, then, are the courts to do with individual or class actions that seek redress from risk or injury caused by an intrauterine device (IUD), vaccine, herbicide, morning-sickness drug, nuclear waste reprocessing facility, or the like? My general prescription is less, not more. The courts should defer to the experts. Not experts summoned by the parties for the edification of the judiciary. The scientific community is large and heterogeneous, and a Ph.D. can be found to swear to almost any "expert" proposition, no matter how false or foolish. The expert public-risk choices that should be respected are those made by a risk-regulatory agency concerned with the public risk in question.

This is not the current law. Judges, at present, generally feel quite free, when addressing risk problems, to ignore prior administrative determinations regarding which public risks represent progressive choices. The *Restatement of Torts* flatly declares that "compliance with a legislative enactment or an administrative regulation does not prevent a finding of negligence."[23] Many risk-related administrative statutes, such as the Consumer Products Safety Act, expressly announce that compliance with safety rules is not to serve as a shield from tort liability.[24] When the statute is silent or even the least bit ambiguous on the question of tort-remedy preemption, the courts will always presume that no preemption was intended.[25] The *Karen Silkwood* decision, for example, announced that the operator of a nuclear facility can be assessed punitive damages despite complete compliance with applicable NRC regulations. And in *Chevron* v. *Ferebee*, a recent case from the D.C. Circuit Court of Appeals, a chemical company was held liable for "mislabeling" a can of paraquat, even though the label had been approved by the EPA and even though the manufacturer could not lawfully have used anything else— only EPA had the legal power to change the label.

In short, the settled judicial refusal to defer to agency choices among public risks has spawned a never-ending cycle of truly perverse risk-regulatory decisions.[26] The FDA's experts may conclude after a careful examination of the substitutes that the Sabin polio vaccine is a better bet than the Salk vaccine, or the NRC may conclude that a nuclear power plant is safer than the available alternatives. But a mass-exposure lawyer and an injured or merely frightened client can effectively overturn the expert judgments by finding what is almost too easy to find: a judge who is of the view that the courts have something useful to offer in these matters, and a sympathetic and well-meaning jury. The agency's blessing of the vaccine, or pesticide, or power plant is usually no more than a prelude to a second tier of regulation in the courts.

The resulting you-say-yes-but-I-say-no pattern of public-risk decision making is routinely explained by the courts—and often accepted by the agencies—on the ground that administrative risk regulation is intended to set only a safety "floor"—a threshold of performance, a minimum definition of "acceptable" safety. Agencies will point out that they rely mostly on data furnished by the regulatees themselves and therefore cannot and should not be viewed as the final arbiters of how much safety is enough. It is, of course, politically comfortable for agencies to preserve the tort system as a safety valve. When bodies do fall the agency is grateful to see at least part of the victims' hostility directed at the regulatees.

This rationalization for judicial nondeference may make some sense when the administrative regulatory regime is casual or sporadic, as with consumer products. But it is wholly unpersuasive for comprehensively regulated industries. Vaccines, pesticides, aircraft, electric power plants, and the like all entail potentially enormous mass-exposure hazards. Precisely because they can create public risk of this nature, these products and services are also subject to the most searching and complete state and federal safety regulation. When that regulation reaches a favorable conclusion about a potentially hazardous technology, that conclusion must inevitably be based at some level on a conclusion that the technology represents some measure of progress or, at worst, no measure of regression in the risk market in question.[27]

Once that determination has been made by an expert licensing agency, the courts should respect it. Requiring—or at least strongly encouraging—the courts to respect the comparative-risk choices made by competent, expert agencies would inject a first, small measure of rationality into a judicial regulatory system that currently runs quite wild. The Nuclear Regulatory Commission's licensing of a nuclear power plant or reprocessing facility must be viewed for what it is—considerably more, in other words, than a routine and irrelevant pleasantry, to be forgotten as soon as the first tort plaintiff enters the courthouse. Regulatory agencies are equipped to make the risk comparisons on which all progressive transformation of the risk environment must be based. It has always been true that ignorance of the law is no excuse. At present, knowledge of the law is no excuse either. It should be.

Compensating Victims

The problem remains: How do we attend to the needs of the tragic victims—the unfortunate few who *are* injured by the whooping cough vaccine, or the FDA-approved IUD, or the EPA-approved toxic waste dump? There are some risks that are real, that have tragic consequences, and that *must* be socialized if only because the courts will not allow otherwise. It may seem perverse to insist on a generous social program to deal with the hazards of the whooping cough vaccine when we have only the stingiest social programs to deal with the hazards of whooping cough itself. But the judicial system has left no other choice.

But once again, there are models outside the judicial process to be followed, and once again the lead in adopting these models must come from legislatures and executive branch officials. Two models of administrative compensation systems are already in place to be emulated.

The first is worker's compensation: it addresses public risks falling toward the "infinity-zero" end of the spectrum, in which broad exposure to the hazards is certain but in which the likelihood of consequences to any exposed individual is small. One may start by acknowledging some of the problems that worker's compensation statutes have encountered. Compensation schedules, for example, have not kept pace with inflation. There have been abuses under the worker's compensation statutes, most especially in the areas of causation. Faced with the "deep pocket" of an insurance fund, arbitrators and courts have been inclined to adopt very expansive definitions of what constitutes a "job-related" injury. Finally, worker's compensation schemes have been successfully bypassed, increasingly often, by lawyers and plaintiffs eager to play once again at the judicial gaming tables. Novel theories have been invented, for example, to bootstrap occupational injuries into "product-liability" cases.

Yet despite all the criticisms that have been raised against worker's compensation systems, they have worked tolerably well. It is inconceivable that any jurisdiction in this country will choose to return to the alternative of open-ended tort litigation that preceded the adoption of worker's compensation statutes at the turn of this century. Administrative compensation systems are correctable, and can be corrected across the board, without recourse to expensive legal middlemen, if and when problems develop. Thus the problems relating to "causation" and the definition of "on-the-job" injuries encountered by the present system are not beyond resolution, most especially within an administrative forum that can learn from experience. And the spillover from worker's compensation to product-liability litigation and other areas can be curtailed, most especially if similar administrative compensation schemes are developed around the boundaries of worker's compensation statutes. In the development of administrative compensation schemes for vaccines, drugs, and the like, worker's compensation systems can still serve as a valuable model.

A second compensation model is the one embodied in the much-maligned Price-Anderson Act. This compensation system addresses hazards at the "zero-infinity" end of the public-risk spectrum, in which exposure is very unlikely, but if it occurs it is likely to be in conjunction with a very large and far-reaching accident. Other activities presenting risks of this character (many of them considerably larger than the risks from nuclear power) include the operation of a chemical plant, gas pipeline, liquid natural gas (LNG) tanker, hydroelectric dam, and so on.

If we are to use technologies that present risks of this character at all, we should do so under a regime of definite and predictable disaster insurance. The insurance must establish a fund to be tapped in case of accident, delineate the rights of victims, identify a party with primary financial responsibility, provide for prompt compensation, and establish fixed limits on liability without which none of the other components will be accepted and the enterprises themselves will not be possible. Such schemes need not eliminate the adjudicatory function of the courts altogether, but they must, at a minimum, establish rules to streamline the adjudicatory function and reduce the incentives for tactical maneuvering and delay.

The areas in which streamlined administrative compensation schemes are most suitable share some common features. First, there are areas in which there is a pressing need to provide compensation to the victim (as distinguished from his lawyer) quickly and without a great deal of legal maneuvering. Tragic accidents attributable to vaccines, occupational hazards, nuclear power plants, and the like can be shockingly disruptive and difficult for the injured individual and his or her family. In this context, the ponderous compensation machinery provided by the conventional tort system is unacceptable: it moves too slowly, its outcomes are too unpredictable, and it diverts far too much to lawyers. Almost all nonlawyers who have watched the sordid legal maneuvering over the tragedy at Bhopal, India, have been forced to wonder whether the system that the chemical industry now must use for dealing with the financial aspects of such accidents is as it should be. Most disinterested observers find it clear that compensation in this area could and should have been paid quickly and distributed fairly without the endless legal wrangling already witnessed.

Second, industries that attract legislation often involve novel technologies and rare or unfamiliar hazards. The reason is simple: it is precisely in these areas that insurance is most difficult to obtain, not because the hazards are necessarily large, but because there is no actuarial record of real-world accident experience—or of legal-world tort history—on which the insurance industry can rely. This is most clearly true with the emerging, so-called toxic torts, which usually involve low-level, broadly distributed, long-latency period risks.

It is these two factors—the need to expedite compensation to victims and the need to provide important industries with some measure of protection from the caprices of the tort system—that have applied steady pressure to legislatures across the country. The worker's compensation statutes and the Price-Anderson Act are not anomalies; in an increasing number of areas they are serving as vital models.

Perhaps the major risk in setting up new administrative compensation systems is that they may become the quintessential "deep pocket" targets for nuisance actions and fraudulent claims. One vice in the present tort system is also a virtue—the system is so terribly ponderous, slow, and unpredictable that it filters out some nonmeritorious claims through sheer inertia. But if so-called Orangemail is becoming a real problem even in the tort system, the problem might be magnified under a more streamlined administrative compensation system. Worker's compensation has, for example, been sought by the wife of an executive who suffered a heart attack while engaging in sexual relations with his secretary, and insurance funds set up under the Price-Anderson Act have been occasional targets for nuisance suits.

The only protection against this problem is the old-fashioned one: a claimant for funds must be required to show causation, if not beyond a reasonable doubt, then at least with some serious degree of scientific credibility. In addition, disaster compensation schemes can be insulated from nuisance actions by provisions such as the "Extraordinary Nuclear Occurrence" threshold codified in the Price-Anderson Act: no payouts are permitted until some appropriate, high-level official has found that the alleged disaster *was* a disaster. There has been much criticism from plaintiffs' lawyers of the fact that the accident at Three Mile Island was *not* "extraordinary" enough for Price-Anderson purposes. But then, there has been much criticism in the scientific community of the fact that Bendectin and Agent Orange *were* thought to justify enormous tort settlements, notwithstanding underlying "evidence" of causation that ranged from the tenuous to the entirely fanciful.

PUBLIC RISKS AND POLITICAL LEGITIMACY

The expansion of tort law into public-risk areas provides a poor vehicle for compensating deserving victims of diffuse hazards, even while it provides some compensation to capriciously chosen, nonvictim members of the public, and a great deal of compensation to systematically self-selected members of the legal profession. The expansion serves as a very poor—indeed often counterproductive—regulatory system: tort law provides no vehicle for systematically selecting worse from better performers in the public-risk market. But perhaps most troubling of all, the new tort law undermines the process of democratic self-government.

The Constitution itself embodies a vision of the courts as the retrospective "retailers" of justice and the political branches of government as the prospective "wholesalers." Legislatures and agencies are broadly disqualified from doing the types of things courts traditionally do: singling out individuals for special benefit or burden (barred by the Bill of Attainder Clause) and administering retrospective punishment (barred by the Ex Post Facto Clause). Until recently, activities of the courts were confined by mirror-image restraints found in the constitutional requirement that the courts resolve *only* "cases" or "controversies"—the courts *had* to operate retail, and they *had* to operate more or less retrospectively. These divisions of authority make a good bit of sense: courts do well in administering retail, corrective justice; only the political branches, on the other hand, are qualified to make wholesale public policy.

The new tort law, and the entire vision of "public law" adjudication that animates it, is politically dangerous. It removes the most controversial social issues from the arena in which controversy can be brokered and tensions diffused through the very process of political participation. The legal system is adversarial; the answers it provides are often grudgingly accepted, but rarely leave participants satisfied that the system is reachable and open for change another day. Judges are—by deliberate constitutional design—isolated, remote, not accountable to the electorate. These are valuable assets for decision makers engaged in protecting civil rights and minorities, resolving private disputes, and umpiring the democratic process. But they are grave liabilities for decision makers who would address and determine the broadest terms of the social contract.

Our choices of "acceptable" public risks and the decisions we make to compensate—or not to compensate—for the harms that may attend risks of this character ultimately must be made in the political arenas. Choices of this character that are made anywhere else will not, in the long term, prove acceptable to a people who have grown accustomed to governing themselves.

NOTES

1. See Weinberg, Science and Its Limits: The Regulators' Dilemma, paper presented at the National Academy of Engineering Symposium on Hazards: Technology and Fairness, Washington, D.C., June 3–4, 1985.
2. 28 Ch. 688 (1885).
3. Scientists' Institute for Public Information, Inc. v. Atomic Energy Commission, 481 F.2d 1079 (D.C. Cir. 1973).
4. U.S. Nuclear Regulatory Commission, Reactor Safety Study, Report WASH-1400, NUREG 75/014 (1975).
5. See Kitch, A Shot in the Dark: Product Liability and Vaccination, Regulation, pp. 11–18 (May–June 1985). See also Committee on Public-Private Sector Relations in Vaccine Innovation, Institute of Medicine, National Academy of Sciences, Vaccine Supply and Innovation (Washington, D.C.: National Academy Press, 1985).
6. I discuss these factors at greater length in Huber, Safety and the Second Best: The Hazards of Public Risk Management in the Courts, 85 Colum. L. Rev. 277, 317–320 (1985).
7. Predictably, however, trial lawyers have begun to find their way around these limits by bringing suits against product suppliers and manufacturers rather than against the employers themselves. See, e.g., Kajala v. Johns-Manville Prods. Corp., 523 F.2d 155 (8th Cir. 1975). Courts that believe this is not liability "against" the employer are engaged in self-delusion. Employee awards against manufacturers will be channeled back to employers quickly enough, by means of manufacturer demands to employers for indemnity, insurance, or a risk premium on the products that they sell. See 7 U.S. Dep't of Commerce, Interagency Task Force Report on Product Liability 75-77 (1977). At least one state, Connecticut, has responded by requiring worker's compensation awards to be set off against verdicts or settlements against product manufacturers. 1979 Conn. Pub. Act 79-483, § 11(b).
8. The original agreement is contained in the Warsaw Convention, 137 L.N.T.S. 11 (1929).
9. See 42 U.S.C. § 2210 (1982).
10. See Office of Pesticides and Toxic Substances, U.S. Environmental Protection Agency, Background Report for the Indemnification Report to Congress at A-27 (1983).
11. See 33 U.S.C. § 1321 (1982).
12. See 50 U.S.C. § 1431 (1982); Executive Order 10,789, 23 Fed. Reg. 8897 (1958); see also Stencel Aero Eng'g Corp. v. United States, 431 U.S. 666 (1977) (immunity for suppliers of materials to government where government itself enjoys immunity).
13. See Background Report, supra note 10, at A-26.
14. Pub. L. No. 95-372, 92 Stat. 629 (see § 304(b)(1), liability limit) (codified as amended in scattered sections of 43 U.S.C.).
15. 33 U.S.C. §§ 1501–1524 (1982) (see § 18(d), liability limit).
16. § 204, 43 U.S.C. § 1653(a)(2) (1982).

17. For a summary of recent attempts at federal legislation see Kircher, Federal Product Legislation and Toxic Torts: The Defense Perspective, 28 Vill. L. Rev. 1116 (1983); Phillips, The Proposed Federal Product Liability Statute from the Toxic Tort Plaintiff's Perspective, 28 Vill. L. Rev. 1156 (1983); Schwartz & Means, The Need for Federal Product Liability and Toxic Tort Legislation: A Current Assessment, 28 Vill. L. Rev. 1088 (1983); Twerski, National Product Liability Legislation: In Search For the Best of all Possible Worlds, 18 Idaho L. Rev. 411 (1982). After extensive study, the Commerce Department proposed a Uniform Product Liability Act (UPLA) as a model for state legislation; parallel federal legislation has also been submitted to Congress. See S. 2631, 97th Cong., 2d Sess. (1982). The bill was reported on favorably by the Senate Commerce Committee in October 1982, but was not passed by the Senate. It was reintroduced in the 98th Congress. See S. 44, 98th Cong., 1st Sess. (1983). The springboard for federal action was a study conducted by an interagency task force. The report criticized contemporary tort law for failing to develop a clear standard of responsibility, imposing liability when the product has been misused or altered, failing to apply standards of comparative fault, failing to provide for contribution or indemnity among tortfeasors, imposing liability for design defects beyond the technological state of the art, imposing liability for unknowable risks, and imposing lingering liability beyond the expected useful life of a product. Numerous state legislatures have followed up on the federal initiative. See Ghiardi, Products Liability—Where is the Borderline Now? 13 Forum 206, 212 (1977).

18. See Department of Defense Authorization Act, 1985, § 1631 P.L. 98-525, 98 Stat. 2492, 2646 (1985); see Taylor, New Act Restricts Atomic Test Suits, N.Y. Times, Nov. 4, 1984, § 1 (News), at 26, col. 1. All lawsuits must be brought, instead, against the federal government under the Federal Tort Claims Act. 28 U.S.C. § 2674 (1982). The new legislation eliminates jury trials, punitive damages, and other advantages of state law adjudication that had prompted more than 100 lawsuits by veterans and others against the contractors.

19. See H.R. 7089, 96th Cong., 2d Sess. (1980).

20. It requires, in addition, technical resources that the courts do not possess. See, e.g., Wilkey, Activism by the Branch of Last Resort: Of the Seizure of Abandoned Swords and Purses 10–12 (1984); Muntzing, The Courts and Energy Policy in the Judiciary in a Democratic Society 140 (Theberge, ed., 1977).

21. Chayes, The Role of the Judge in Public Law Litigation, 89 Harv. L. Rev. 1281 (1976).

22. See Yellin, High Technology and the Courts: Nuclear Power and the Need for Institutional Reform, 94 Harv. L. Rev. 489 (1981); Rosenberg, The Causal Connection in Mass Exposure Cases: A "Public Law" Vision of the Tort System, 97 Harv. L. Rev. 851 (1984). Other contributions to the debate include Perrow, Living with High-Risk Technologies (1984); Bazelon, Science and Uncertainty: A Jurist's View, 5 Harv. Envt'l. L. Rev. 209 (1981); Bogen, Public Policy and Technological Risk, 1980 Idea 37; Cohen, Innovation and Atomic Energy: Nuclear Power Regulation, 1966–Present, 43 Law & Contemp. Probs. 67 (1979); Kraus, Environmental Carcinogenesis: Regulation on the Frontiers of Science, 7 Envt'l. L. 83 (1976); Merrill, Risk-Benefit Decisionmaking by the Food and Drug Administration, 45 Geo. Wash. L. Rev. 994 (1977); Pierce, Encouraging Safety: The Limits of Tort Law and Government Regulation, 33 Vand. L. Rev. 1281 (1980).

23. Restatement (Second) of Torts § 288C (1965) .

24. Section 25(a) of the Consumer Products Safety Act provides: "Compliance with consumer product safety rules or other rules or orders under this chapter shall not relieve any person from liability at common law or under State statutory law to any other person." 15 U.S.C. § 2074(a) (1982).

25. The Supreme Court, for example, recently let stand a $4.75-million damage award against a manufacturer of a birth control pill in a suit brought by a woman whose kidneys had failed after several years of using the drug. The manufacturer challenged only the $2.75 million in punitive damages that were awarded notwithstanding its complete compliance with regulatory

requirements imposed by the FDA. Ortho Pharmaceutical Corp. v. Wooderson, 235 Kan. 387, 681 P.2d 1038, cert. denied, 105 S. Ct. 365 (1984).

26. The morning-sickness drug Bendectin, for example, continues to enjoy FDA approval; there is no scientifically credible evidence that Bendectin does anything except what it is supposed to: relieve the misery of morning sickness that can threaten the health of both mother and child. But Bendectin became such a popular target for tort lawsuits that its manufacturer withdrew the drug (the only such drug on the American market) and submitted to a $120-million class-action settlement. This prompted even the *New York Times*, not known for its conservative views on risk-regulatory matters, to editorialize: "With Bendectin . . . the law has made a devastation and called it a settlement." N.Y. Times, July 30, 1984, at A20, col. 2.

27. For further discussion of my view of risk "markets," see Huber, The Market for Risk, Regulation, p. 33 (March–April 1984).

From Understanding to
Manipulating DNA

JAMES D. WATSON

We have every reason to expect that, over the foreseeable future, recombinant DNA-based science will provide masses of new and unanticipated facts that will profoundly transform our knowledge about ourselves and the all-too-many diseases that exist today, as well as generate industrial and agricultural processes that are now unimaginable. But to do so at the rate now potentially possible, using already-worked-out methodologies, will require a massive expansion of our current research budgets. The question now for us to ponder is how to achieve this expansion.

I appear here because my name, together with that of Francis Crick, is associated with the start of what now is properly regarded as the DNA (deoxyribonucleic acid) revolution. But when we found the double helix some 32 years ago, it was not the future that interested me. Instead, I saw our discovery as marking the end of a distinguished 90-year-old intellectual search for the nature of the gene. This climax, as I recalled in my book *The Double Helix*, came suddenly, and it was with elation that we saw that the final answer was indeed a golden one. Viewing the double helix with its self-complementary nature brought joy not only to those of us who had won the race, but to virtually all others, like Sidney Brenner, who quickly came over to the Cavendish Lab from Oxford and heard Francis excitedly run over the implications of our model. The question of how a gene could be replicated was gloriously revealed by mere inspection of the double helix. No longer should there be any further serious debate as to what the gene is. DNA just could not have a self-complementary structure and not be the gene. Any structure that simple had to be right, and almost without exception those rare individuals who later failed to be swayed by its beauty had nowhere to go scientifically. With time they became known only for their iconoclastic views, of interest solely to those journalists who relished controversy more than scientific truth.

Francis Crick, not being a biologist by training, was more interested in the future than the past. He had switched from physics to biology because of what was not known, and he correctly told all who would listen that biology would no longer proceed in its past, frequently desultory, fashion, that at last we had a real starting point for understanding how genes made possible the existence of life. Here, of course, Francis was the optimist, while I then could be perceived as either abnormally cautious in seeing what we had started or as trying to excel many of my newly acquired English friends in their capacity to understate the truly important.

In looking back first to the discovery of the double helix and then to the several key steps that led to the emergence of recombinant DNA as an economic force, I shall repeatedly refer to what I believe are several very essential aspects of these scientific discoveries: (1) the need for sensible dreams (long-term goals), (2) the value of imitating approaches that have worked in the past, (3) the necessity of accepting rapidly unexpected assaults on conventional wisdom, and (4) the virtual necessity for young scientists to receive one or more forms of patronage, be it from former teachers, an institution or foundation, or the government itself.

THE DOUBLE HELIX

Crick and I most certainly did not stumble upon the double helix. It seemed then the most important of all goals, and knowing what we wanted, we felt the most sensible approach was to imitate the best master of the present, who was at that time Linus Pauling. He had found the α-helix conformation of the polypeptide chain by playing with molecular models, always following the laws of chemistry, many of which he himself had discovered. So we thought, Why shouldn't we succeed with these same tricks? Key to this approach was the faith that the answer would not be too complex (life had to arise spontaneously!), and so from the start we limited our search to simple answers. We suspected that we would never be clever enough for success if the answer was abstrusely complex. Thus, we never searched for anything but regular, helical answers. Equally important, we were prepared to change our minds if someone could show us that we had the experimental facts wrong. Essential to our final success was the pronouncement from our across-the-room neighbor, the chemist Jerry Donohue, then fresh from Pauling's lab: he said that we, like the textbooks and virtually all interested chemists, used in our thinking the wrong conformations (tautomeric forms) for several of the DNA building blocks. After a few hours of reluctance we reversed our sights, knowing that our current model had more awkward features than we wanted. Only a week later came the now-famous base pairs and with them the double helix.

But we would never have had the opportunity to find our golden treasure if we had not had the patrons to let us challenge the approaches of the past that were going nowhere. Then, Francis and I were not generally perceived as useful citizens, forever telling others that their problems, not ours, were either unimportant or insoluble given the current state of experimental knowledge. So we required enlightened patronage, which I found in Max Delbruck and Salva Luria, and Francis got from Max Perutz and John Kendrew (but not initially from Sir Lawrence Bragg). Equally important was the necessity of working within a well-equipped laboratory that provided the freedom to work toward long-term important goals, and where we were not put under the pressure of either succeeding fast or being banished to the second rate. Here of prime importance was the Rockefeller Foundation and Warren Weaver. Without the funds Weaver directed to several key university groups in Europe (including the macromolecular structural group at the Cavendish Lab) and in the United States (in particular, to Caltech and Indiana University) after World War II, the dawn of molecular biology would have broken much later. Equally farsighted was the support given to Sir Lawrence Bragg in a then still ration-weary England by the Medical Research Council, then ably run by Harold Himsworth.

THE CENTRAL DOGMA

The first major step forward after the double helix was the elucidation of how DNA provides the information necessary for synthesis of protein. We focused at the start on the structure of RNA (ribonucleic acid) for three reasons: (1) DNA appeared to be absent from the cytoplasm, the most likely site of protein synthesis; (2) it was simple to make a paper scheme for how RNA might be made on a single-stranded DNA template; and (3) until then RNA was a molecule without any known function. So we postulated that DNA provided the information to make RNA, which in turn provided the information to order the amino acids in proteins (DNA → RNA → Protein = The Central Dogma).

Happily, our initial focusing on RNA turned out not only to be simpleminded, but correct. But how RNA could order the amino acids in protein proved much, much trickier to work out. Here the first real breakthrough was a chemical intuition on the part of Francis Crick. He said that RNA had to be a wretched template and that some other intermediate would be found that had recognized amino acids. But from then on, real answers had to come from biochemistry. Here there was growing optimism among the more astute biochemists that macromolecules, as well as small molecules like sugars or amino acids, might be made outside of living cells in extracts containing vital cell components. So I, as well as many others, decided that we would no longer get anywhere trying a Pauling-type approach, but should instead follow in the traditions of the great biochemists of the past, like Warburg and Lippman. Again we chose the right general approach, for within a decade DNA, RNA, and proteins all could be made outside of cells under conditions in which all of the vital molecular ingredients could be identified. In doing so, we had had many initial surprises and in some cases had to accept their reality without yet deeply understanding their significance or evolutionary origin. For example, we started out by assuming that all RNA is template RNA. By 1960, however, we had found three different RNAs, only one of which functioned in the template manner originally postulated.

By this stage, most innovative research on the Central Dogma was being done by medium-sized groups, generally working with bacterial systems, in many leading universities and research institutions. Modest help like that initially provided to Caltech by the Rockefeller Foundation would never have let molecular biology grow into what it already was by 1961. If the National Science Foundation (NSF) and the National Institutes of Health (NIH) had not initially been so freely generous with their monies, we could never have moved so fast, particularly in those days, when each new cell-free synthesis seemed more like good luck than a reflection of the fact that cells exist because they utilize enzymes that have been highly evolved to work well. In those days, we virtually never talked about money. There was enough to support the losers as well as the winners, and so science seemed the best of all occupations to go into starting in the mid-1950s.

THE GENETIC CODE

Solving the genetic code became a commonly accepted goal virtually as soon as the double helix became known. The physicist Gamow first approached it in late 1953 by focusing on how combinations of the four different base pairs (AT, TA, GC, CG) might specify 20 different amino acids. Later a semicollective approach by the 20 members of the RNATIE CLUB,* led to the circulation of a series of papers on research that utilized known amino acid sequences to see if restrictions on amino acid ordering existed. By 1955 it became clear that theory as opposed to experiments had no chance, which led Crick and Brenner to genetic approaches. First they considered a potentially very long term, brute force mutagenesis program, using the viruses (phages) of the then intensively studied bacterium *Escherichia coli*. Within several years, the mutants so obtained were used in a clever series of genetic crosses that resulted in their 1961 proposal that groups of three nucleotides

---

*A loose association of physicists, chemists, mathematicians, and biologists all associated in some way with Gamow.

specified amino acids. It is important to note that initially no elegant approach seemed possible, and it was only through unexpected genetic results, which implied single base-pair deletions and insertions, that Crick and Brenner could really use their heads as well as their hands.

An even more important breakthrough came from the development of systems for in vitro protein synthesis that could be used to test the concept of messenger RNA. Nirenburg and Matthaei's discovery at NIH, also in 1961, that Poly U coded for polyphenylalanine made the genetic code a problem attackable by biochemists and led by early 1966 to the solution of the genetic code. Greatly assisting the biochemists were the techniques of the organic chemists, which permitted the synthesis of short, repetitive RNA chains of known sequences. These were used as mRNA molecules in cell-free syntheses. Here as in the working out of the Central Dogma, well-equipped biochemical laboratories were essential for real steps forward, and most of the funds came from a still very generous NIH.

THE ENZYMOLOGY OF DNA SYNTHESIS

The field of test-tube synthesis of DNA owes its existence almost entirely to one individual, Arthur Kornberg, working first at Washington University in St. Louis and then at Stanford University. Already by the spring of 1956 he had good hints that DNA could be made in a cell-free system made from *E. coli* cells. By 1959 he had shown his synthesis was of double helical DNA and that the templates were always single DNA chains, providing clear proof for our 1953 conjectures about DNA replication arising from the self-complementary double helix. Essential for such work was first-class enzymology. Only later did the value to genetics first emerge through the 1971 discovery of a mutant *E. coli* cell that apparently lacked DNA polymerase. This most unexpected (at first unwanted?) mutant led to the discovery of two other forms of DNA polymerase, one of which is responsible for the majority of DNA synthesis in cells. Subsequently discovered in several places were the very important DNA ligases, which can link DNA chains as well as the enzymes (kinases) that place phosphate groups at the ends of DNA chains that lack them. Equally important has been the discovery and elucidation of the mode of action of a large number of enzymes that degrade DNA chains from their ends (exonucleases). By the mid-1970s this almost entirely enzymological approach was importantly supplemented by genetic approaches in which genes were sought that blocked the various steps in DNA synthesis.

For the most part, DNA replication has been a very American field, totally dominated initially by Kornberg's lab, with the several major DNA synthesis labs coming into existence usually being led by scientists trained by him. In all this basic research, the hands of the intelligent enzymologists, rather than the ideas of the theorists, have been the route to success, and the still freely available federal support was a companion of every major advance. Because of the many enzymes now known to be involved in DNA replication, it has become increasingly difficult for young unknown scientists to make their mark in this field, and an apprenticeship period in a Kornberg-type lab has become a virtual necessity.

RULES FOR GENE EXPRESSION

Gene expression was a problem initially opened up by geneticists who isolated mutants in *E. coli* that led to either increased or decreased expression of given genes. It was first inspired, as well as dominated, by the labs of Jacob and Monod at the Institut Pasteur. With time, however, American labs, led for the most part by Americans once residents in Paris, proved increasingly incisive. Very major breakthroughs achieved by Gilbert and Ptashne, working independently at Harvard in the 1965–1969 period, led to the isolation of the first molecules (repressors) which controlled gene functioning by binding to specific segments of DNA. Through such work the elements (sequences of base pairs) within DNA that control gene functioning (promoters, operators) first became attackable at the molecular level. Such work first demanded the use of genes present on viral chromosomes, since no way then existed, in general, for isolating specifically desired DNA segments. Isolation of these repressors marked the ending of a more-than-10-year interval during which research funds were plentiful for the really top scientists and available in lesser but adequate sums for virtually all competent molecular biologists, biochemists, and geneticists. From then on, the consequences of the Vietnam War became increasingly felt even at the better-funded research-oriented universities.

A PAUSE WITHIN THE GOLDEN AGE

The feeling that we all knew where we were going which marked the 15-year interval of 1953–1968 began to disappear with the finding of the repressors that acted on specific bacterial genes. What future history would regard as equally significant became much less obvious, and several noted molecular biologists (Brenner, Benzer, and Stent) already had moved toward neurobiological objectives that at least for the short term were far from molecular. For most of us, however, seeing whether the genes of higher organisms were regulated like those of bacteria seemed the safest way to proceed. We feared, however, we might not be too excited with our first results. Even given a burning desire to home in on, for example, human genes, how to do incisive experiments was not obvious, since to start with, genetic analysis of the type possible with *E. coli* was impossible. Moreover, there existed no effective way to study the DNA of higher cells. There was even much too much DNA in bacterial cells, which contain only 1/1000 the DNA of mammalian cells. In fact, bacterial genes had only become accessible through the study of their viruses, whose DNA molecules were small enough that we could at last dream of deeply understanding them at the molecular level.

The best way to move on to higher cells, though, seemed to be an initial focusing on their viruses, some of which contained only several thousand base pairs. Luckily the animal viruses whose double helical chromosomes were the smallest also had been recently found to cause tumors when injected into certain animal hosts. So by the 1970s, a steadily increasing group of highly motivated scientists gave up on bacterial cells for research on several groups of DNA tumor viruses. Those viruses that were particularly focused on—SV40, polyoma, and adenoviruses—all could multiply in cells growing in culture as well as cause the transformation of normal-appearing cultured cells into their cancer equivalents.

This intellectual migration into tumor-virus research was strongly encouraged by two additional factors. First, even if higher-cell DNAs followed the same rules as found earlier for bacteria, by emphasizing tumor viruses, important if not incisive facts might be found about putative cancer genes we suspected were present on their chromosomes. Second, any problem that the National Cancer Institute supported strongly invariably received more money than comparably good research aimed at further understanding bacterial DNA. So when many good labs working on bacteria began to feel pinched for money, fiscal worries did not plague those working on cancer viruses. Moreover, when the "War on Cancer" was begun in 1972, there literally were not enough good cancer-oriented labs to consume the funds Congress was more than eager to appropriate.

THE UNANTICIPATED DISCOVERY OF RESTRICTION ENZYMES

Masses of money, however, would not have been enough to ensure the eventual success of one of the several stated goals of the War on Cancer, i.e., to understand the biochemical uniqueness of cancer cells. Even though the DNA (and RNA) chromosomes of several tumor viruses could be isolated in chemically significant amounts, as late as 1969 there was no way for them to be molecularly dissected. Only in 1970 did the first effective enzyme become available (through the work of Hamilton Smith of Johns Hopkins) that cut DNA at well-defined positions into highly reproducible smaller fragments. With this most unexpected discovery the whole nature of DNA research changed. Happily, it soon became apparent that a large number of such specific DNA-cutting (restriction) enzymes existed, each with its own unique specificity. So any given DNA molecule could be routinely cut into large numbers of well-defined fragments. The existence of such fragments immediately provided an incentive for methods to be developed that could sequence fragmented pieces of DNA containing several hundreds of base pairs. By 1977 such methods not only had been developed by Gilbert and Maxam at Harvard and by Sanger of Cambridge, England, but they were highly efficient. Only 2 years later, a small bacterial plasmid chromosome of more than 5,000 base pairs was to have its complete sequence determined in less than a year.

The history of how the DNA-cutting enzymes became found serves as a classic example of the value of so-called pure research. At the same time as the double helix was discovered, a bizarre exception to conventional genetic behavior emerged from studying bacterial viruses that grew in several types of bacteria. Experiments by Bertani and Luria at Indiana University and by the Swiss physicist Jean Weigle, then at Caltech, revealed that growth in new hosts often leads to modification of the respective viral DNAs that make them more capable of multiplying in similar bacteria. Without such modifications these DNA usually were degraded (restricted). Such modification was not the result of classical gene mutation but somehow dependent on some chemical alteration of the viral DNA brought about by the host bacteria. For almost a decade this phenomenon was of limited interest to only several molecular biologists. That its importance eventually became known was the culmination of virtually a decade of patronage given by Weigle to a small incipient molecular biology group that he founded within the physics department of the University of Geneva. Weigle, as one of the initial discoverers of this so-called restriction-modification behavior, wanted someone to understand the phenomenon at the molecular level and provided space in the new physics building for this research. By 1965 it was clear, from Werner Arber's and John Smith's work in Geneva, that DNA became modified by the addition of methyl groups which prevent sequence-specific nucleases from cutting their respective DNAs. The first such enzymes isolated in 1968 proved ineffective for DNA research, and only in 1970, from Hamilton Smith, did a useful enzyme first emerge. In today's climate of chancy grant support, such an apparently off-beat phenomenon most likely would not make it through our peer review procedures, which increasingly favor projects with high probabilities for success.

THE MAKING OF THE FIRST RECOMBINANT DNA MOLECULES

Dreams existed for making recombinant DNA molecules long before it became technically feasible. In fact, one of the potential attractions of the small DNA tumor virus genomes was that they might someday be engineered to carry cellular genes from one cell to another. Paul Berg, one of the first, if not *the* first, scientists to seriously dream thus, was the logical person to encourage the development of procedures for putting back into functional chromosomes the DNA fragments made by specific DNA-cutting (restriction) enzymes. The first such success in Berg's lab at Stanford Medical School came in 1972 using the DNA-joining enzymes DNA ligase to link the appropriate fragments. Greatly aiding such events were the so-called sticky ends created by the action of many restriction enzymes. Such single-stranded tails like to find their complements, and it proved particularly easy to rejoin fragments containing such sticky ends. However, 1973 marked the date when the first universally effective method for making recombinant DNA was announced. Then Boyer and Cohen, working nearby to the Berg lab, inserted DNA fragments into tiny bacterial chromosomes (plasmids), whose small size allowed them to be relatively easily reintroduced back into bacteria. Once so reinserted, such recombinant DNA plasmids multiply autonomously to yield 25 to 50 copies per cell. Subsequently growing cultures of the bacteria-bearing recombinant plasmids effectively "clones" the DNA segments inserted into the respective plasmids. Such recombinant DNA plasmids can be made by virtually any trained scientist, and soon it became clear that with time, virtually any gene could be so cloned in bacteria. The problem then became one of learning how to identify which, say *Drosophila*, gene had actually been inserted into a given recombinant DNA plasmid. Now some 11 years later, a variety of increasingly practical, if not elegant, methods exists to isolate genes of choice.

PRODUCTION OF FOREIGN PROTEINS
BY RECOMBINANT DNA-BEARING PLASMIDS

The isolation of, say, a human DNA molecule into a bacterial cell will not generally lead to the production of the respective human proteins. Several factors underlie such failures. First, the signals (promoters) encoded into DNA which signify the start of RNA synthesis (transcription) are not the same in widely divergent forms of life. To have a reasonable chance for a human gene to be transcribed in the commonly used bacterium *E. coli*, the gene's own promoter should be cut away and replaced by an appropriate high-level bacterial promoter. Second, the study of the genes of higher cells (as opposed to bacteria) has revealed them to have an organization very, if not bizarrely, different from bacterial genes. Higher cells' genes are usually split into DNA segments (exons) that specify amino acids interspersed with segments (introns) that do not code anything but nevertheless are transcribed into RNA. Soon after their synthesis, such noncoding regions (introns) become cut out (spliced away) yielding functional RNA molecules containing only coded segments (exons). Given such structures we must anticipate that most human genes would not function in bacteria. What can function, however, are the so-called cDNA clones made by copying the messages of given mRNA molecules back into DNA chains that subsequently can be inserted into appropriate plasmid DNA.

EXTENSION OF RECOMBINANT DNA METHODS
TO CELLS OTHER THAN BACTERIA

In 1973 we only knew how to clone genes within bacteria. Now, however, there exist plasmids (vectors) that can be used to insert DNA into the cells of many forms of higher organisms, including vertebrates. Already by 1978 DNA could also be reproducibly inserted into yeast cells. By now, very highly sophisticated recombinant DNA procedures exist for putting in and pulling out specific yeast genes from their respective chromosomes. These methods have transformed yeast genetics into a field almost rivaling in its power that of the much more established *E. coli* genetics. Even more unanticipated has been the relatively rapid success in genetically engineering the fruitfly *Drosophila* by injecting DNA into fertilized *Drosophila* eggs. And, at first a highly surprising, but now an almost routine, event is the production of the so-called transgenic mice which have been genetically altered by injecting DNA into fertilized mouse eggs. Already, faster-growing mice (supermice) that resulted from excess production of growth hormones not only exist, but have been shown to be genetically stable for several generations. Genetic engineering of certain plants also is possible working with tobacco; corn is still refractory but hopefully only temporarily.

The first easily reproducible method for introducing DNA into vertebrate cells growing in culture emerged in 1977. Only several years were to pass before elegant procedures were developed for cloning vertebrate DNA within vertebrate cells (as opposed to bacterial cells). Such procedures are now in widespread practice for the important insights that emerge as to the nature of gene regulation in higher cells. They are now also proving in many situations to be indispensable for the large-scale production of commercially desirable human products. Many human proteins (e.g., the blood-clotting factor VIII and the blood-clot destroyer plasminogen activator) are folded up into incorrect three-dimensional forms in bacteria. To make them in functional forms and in the amounts needed for human use, their respective genes must be introduced back into vertebrate cells under conditions which allow their maximum expression. Industrial-scale techniques are thus being developed to enable very large numbers of animal cells to be grown efficiently in large fermentation-type containers. Even though recombinant DNA procedures using higher cells are necessarily more expensive than comparable production using bacteria as factories, they may be the only way to obtain many human proteins. Their development into commercially satisfactory procedures is thus an immediate problem for the recombinant DNA industry.

DECREASING BUT STILL HARMFUL REGULATION
OF RECOMBINANT DNA

It was both the novelty and extraordinarily potential power of recombinant DNA procedures that led in the mid-1970s to the fear that they might generate new forms of life that would pose real dangers to life as it now exists. So initially many leading molecular biologists accepted the need for some form of regulation governing recombinant DNA experimentation. But when it came, it was much more stringent than virtually any practicing scientist wanted or thought necessary. So during the past decade much time and anxiety have gone to chipping away at many of the worst rules that stifled the scientific community. For example, until 1979, the rules prevented effective application of recombinant DNA procedures to understand cancer.

Now *E. coli* is effectively regarded as safe to work with, without the crippling "safe" modifications that make their respective "safe strains" difficult to grow. There now also exist specifically modified vertebrate viruses that can be used to clone desired vertebrate genes within mouse or human cells. Starting to work with new systems (for example, an until now poorly characterized bacteria), however, still requires the approval of the recombinant advisory committee (RAC) of NIH. Thus, younger scientists who often wish to innovate are now temporarily held back when they cannot prove the safety of their proposed research, rather than the burden being on those who wish to assert potential danger.

Given our still very incomplete knowledge of biology, what initially appears to be dangerous may be totally safe (working with laboratory strains of polio virus) and what seems safe could conceivably be risky. So personally, I would abolish all regulation of recombinant DNA. This idea, however, is far from generally accepted, and most molecular biologists, no longer being directly held up by current regulations, see no reason to fight for their total removal. For example, we are still obliged to sterilize all recombinant DNA organisms that we create, so that we cannot be accused of releasing any to the outside world. This can be a nuisance for the individual scientist but is tolerable as long as he or she works with microorganisms or cells in cultures that can be easily killed by autoclaving (steam sterilization). At the industry level, however, real expenses will be incurred in seeing that nothing escapes. Of course, if we thought that there was something essentially dangerous about recombinant DNA-containing organisms, that is the way we should behave. But if we find the whole distinction without merit, then we as scientists, and especially industry, are in the long term harming ourselves as well as our country by going along with false distinctions, merely to seem to be doing good.

Possibly the most ill-conceived regulations now deal with higher plants and animals. Genetically engineered plants, for example, can only be grown in greenhouses that preclude their release to the outside world. Moreover, when we are finished with our experiments, we must autoclave the discarded corn plants! In addition, we must prepare lengthy environmental impact statements for each new genetically engineered plant, to be approved by the Environmental Protection Agency before we can grow such new corn strains in the field. I find it impossible to believe that any genetically engineered corn plant could pose a threat to anything except a corn seed company not possessing the means to genetically engineer a similar plant. Therefore, the sooner we exempt all plant manipulations from regulation, the better.

I sense, however, that there is a passive acceptance in government of the need to administer such unnecessary regulation rather than to find ways to end it. It seems to me that this is due primarily to the historical absence of high-level officials in government with thorough training and experience in molecular biology, at the Ph.D. level as a minimum. Recognizing that so new a major science cannot yet have achieved its full appreciation, nevertheless, on balance, I believe biology has not been a high enough priority concern in the past, but it must become one now. In my opinion, the United States must treat this major new science with the same attention that it has traditionally given other newly emerging fields of science and technology. There is a great need for decisive and informed action on the DNA regulatory issue. A group of high-level DNA experts from both academia and industry should be urgently convened by the White House to discuss these issues, and to prepare a report which can guide policymakers in the future. If followed by appropriate appointments of knowledgeable officials, the present inadequate situation can change, since continued indifference will not help the United States maintain its leading position in biotechnology. I believe the pursuit of its competitive edge in this area is a terribly important matter for the future economic growth of the country and needs urgent attention.

POTENTIAL TO DO SCIENCE FAR EXCEEDS CURRENT FINANCIAL BASE

Virtually every new week brings forth in the scientific journals one or more examples of important research whose accomplishment would have been unthinkable even a decade ago. Then, we knew that recombinant DNA would speed up our science and open new frontiers, but even the most optimistic scientist could not then predict what we now accept as commonplace. Today, we can almost realistically dream that the DNA sequence for a complete human genome will be completely known within this century, and that with two to three more decades we shall be able to identify all the key genes that underlie the functioning of our immunological and nervous systems. By now, we have every reason to expect that, over the foreseeable future, recombinant DNA-based science will provide masses of new and unanticipated facts that will profoundly transform our knowledge about our-selves and the all too many diseases that exist today, as well as generate industrial and agricultural processes that are now unimaginable. But to do so at the rate now potentially possible using already worked out methodol-ogies will require a massive expansion of our current research budgets. Wisely spending twofold more money should be possible within, at most, 10 years.

The question now for us to ponder seriously is how to achieve this ex-pansion. If we can reach this funding level there is no doubt that the United States will maintain its current overwhelming dominance of biological re-search, and this is bound to have powerful positive economic consequences.

By now, however, we have the effective tradition that our federal gov-ernment still favors spending more on research on the physical sciences. The government has indeed appropriated large amounts of funds for National Institutes of Health-sponsored research, and in fact, Congress often insists on greater expenditures than does the administration. But I fear that only with active pressure from the administration will biology's budget become commensurate with its importance to mankind, and to our leading position in this area, and I urge them to do so.

Were support to somehow be mobilized, the next several generations of scientists could continue to dream in the daring ways necessary for further quantum leaps in the human condition.

BIBLIOGRAPHY

For the history of research that led to the double helix, the Central Dogma, and the genetic code, see:
  H. F. Judson. 1979. *The Eighth Day of Creation*. New York: Simon and Schuster.
  J. D. Watson. 1980. *The Double Helix: A Norton Critical Edition*. G. S. Stent, ed. New York: Norton.

For a current understanding of gene structure and function, see:
  J. D. Watson, N. Hopkins, J. Roberts, J. Steitz, and A. Weiner. 1986. *Molecular Biology of the Gene*. 4th ed. Menlo Park, Calif.: Benjamin/Cummings.
  B. M. Lewin. 1985. *Genes*. 2nd ed. New York: Wiley.

For the history of the recombinant DNA controversy, including the Asilomar meetings, see:
  J. D. Watson and J. Tooze. 1981. *The DNA Story*. San Francisco, Calif.: W. H. Freeman.

For the scientific impact generated by the recombinant DNA revolution, see:
  J. D. Watson, J. Tooze, and D. T. Kurtz. 1983. *Recombinant DNA: A Short Course*. New York: W. H. Freeman.

The Physical Sciences As the Basis for Modern Technology

WILLIAM O. BAKER

In some fields of the highest innovation and sophisticated technology, we are now seeing the elegant principles of twentieth-century physical science being combined into operational systems for dramatic advances in economic and social functions. Since this technology involves every aspect of the wide reaches of physical science gained during this century, we have a powerful answer to questions of the practical values of research. Indeed, I submit that the physical sciences have moved to a place where they will increasingly stimulate—not just originate but stimulate—large new frontiers of technology and engineering.

This discussion of the role of the physical sciences is enhanced by the context that the editors of this volume have created. Science is skillfully identified as to its human and institutional settings and its connections with government, academia, and industry in the chapter on science and technology policy by Harvey Brooks. Likewise, Milton Katz's discussion of the legalities of innovation and the economy shows the kind of social system in which science is pursued. And the most challenging and pervasive scientific issues of all, those of bioscience and the genetic process, are treated by one of the primary explorers, James D. Watson. Thus, I have an exceptional and inviting opportunity to report briefly on how the physical sciences (nowadays almost qualifying as the "unnatural sciences") have developed as the intelligence base, perhaps even the mind-set, for invention, discovery, and innovation in world technology.

CHRONOLOGY OF THE PHYSICAL SCIENCES

It is usually assumed that the development of the physical sciences comes from atomic and molecular theory, postulated in Greek civilization and extending into the times of Dalton and other pioneers in Western Europe. Concordantly, notions of waves and energy, of dynamics and mechanics, arose from Newton, Helmholtz, and Maxwell, attended in all cases by the indispensable Newtonian elements of calculus and other mathematics. These matters all have moved along in the last several centuries and form the conventional and highly productive basis for engineering, including modern and sophisticated aerospace designs and vehicles.

But in this century particularly, new and compelling factors in the physical sciences have arisen. These are vastly more subtle than the reasonable and even tactile phenomena of classical mechanics, fluid dynamics, and such phenomenological descriptions of how matter behaves. They were foreshadowed by peculiarities of chemical reactions, whereby atomic and molecular conversions were increasingly shown to be the basis for one category of transformation of matter.

The periodic table of the elements and its rationalization of compound formation, electron exchange, the notion of ions in solution and of "closed shells" all raised compelling questions. They were also implied, but not really foreshadowed, by the other domain, of thermodynamics, with Rumford's demonstration of the interconversion of mechanical work and heat. Especially central is the elegant elaboration of thermodynamics through the Third Law of Nernst, and admirable connections of chemical equilibria and free-energy-driven changes of state, analyzed by Gibbs and demonstrated beautifully at various schools, such as at Berkeley by Gilbert N. Lewis.

What was being foreshadowed, of course, was quantum theory, quantum mechanics, and quantum statistics. Einstein's photoequivalents, Sommerfeld's operators, Heisenberg's uncertainty principle, and Bohr's structure of the atom launched the heroic era of the fine structure of matter. This was not much later than the time that J. J. Thomson, Rutherford, Roentgen, Moseley and the others laid out what was in the nucleus. The electron was the common interconnection (Figure 1). But it is important to remember that these masterworks of physical and chemical meaning came along in pieces, not in unified understandings. Thus, although Rutherford and his school notably extended ideas of the nucleus and electron, when Einstein had thought of relativity and the interconversion of mass and energy ($E = mc^2$), Rutherford was dubious. He is quoted as saying to economist and humorist Stephen Leacock, "Oh, that stuff. We never bother with that in our work."!

Hahn and Strassmann then revealed what other particles could come out of the nucleus in fission, and others showed what could be converted in fusion, bringing us to a world where "unnatural science," and "unnatural technology" combine, even to threaten nature on the planet.

ELECTRON

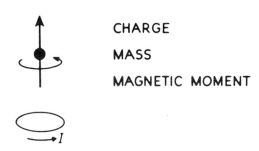

CHARGE

MASS

MAGNETIC MOMENT

FIGURE 1   The electron (represented in this figure by its principal parameters) was recognized as the basic scientific unit for electrical engineering.

I have moved over this chronology of the physical sciences in order to account for what is presented in the remainder of this chapter. I submit that the physical sciences have moved since midcentury beyond their central position in intellectual understanding of the nature of the universe through physics and chemistry to a place where they will increasingly stimulate— not just originate but *stimulate*—large new frontiers of technology and engineering. This relatively recent situation is already having back-reactions of the kind identified by Harvey Brooks. But the complexity of such relations and the implications for research, education, and the acquisition of understanding for its own sake are yet barely grasped.

Let me speculate briefly on how this phase of the physical sciences emerged. It is said that the earlier preoccupation with individual atoms and molecules detached the fundamentals of the then new physics and chemistry from technical applications. The reason was that applications of new knowledge in technology and engineering almost always involved massive assemblies of these new entities recognized as atoms and molecules. Even in the gas phase, which was a less common condition, but always in liquids and solids, there were numerous and complicated collisions and other interactions that were thought to obscure, perhaps hopelessly, the great appeal of being able to deal with individual particle behavior, or at least things beyond three-body interactions.

The great virtue (and indeed charm) of our century, especially of our last half century, has been the casting off of those shackles of thought. More importantly, it has been the inspired realization that the science of masses of matter, namely the thermodynamics noted earlier, and the mechanics of individual molecules, atoms, ions, and particles could be wonderfully and elegantly merged. Thus, the quantum mechanics noted as the portal to the revolution, with its superb principle $H\psi = E\psi$, is joined with the Second

Law of Thermodynamics $\Delta F = \Delta H - T\Delta S$ in concepts and quantitative formulations of matter and energy, of physics and chemistry. Hence, in marvelous ways our description of nature, while incomplete, is now inclusive enough that we are seeing results as technology generated from the understanding of how matter could be adapted to economic and social needs.

One other element ought to be emphasized. It is the work of the Braggs, following Roentgen's discovery of X rays. They found ways to lay out the geometry, or the actual positions, of atoms and molecules in masses, by wave diffraction of X rays. This was reinforced and generalized by Davisson and Germer's discovery in Bell Laboratories of the dualism of waves and electrons and their demonstration of electron diffraction from the interaction of solid surfaces, as well as gases, with electron beams. Important industrial differences between two classes of nylons (a polymer discovered by Carothers at Du Pont) are revealed by X-ray diffraction showing how the molecules associate (Figure 2).

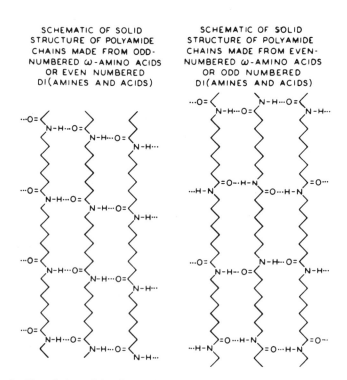

SCHEMATIC OF SOLID STRUCTURE OF POLYAMIDE CHAINS MADE FROM ODD-NUMBERED ω-AMINO ACIDS OR EVEN NUMBERED DI(AMINES AND ACIDS)

SCHEMATIC OF SOLID STRUCTURE OF POLYAMIDE CHAINS MADE FROM EVEN-NUMBERED ω-AMINO ACIDS OR ODD NUMBERED DI(AMINES AND ACIDS)

FIGURE 2   Knowledge of detailed molecular structure and molecular packing in condensed phases—as illustrated in this figure by the varying molecular arrangements in the nylon families originated by Carothers—now underlies the technology of synthetic fibers, plastics, rubbers, and other materials.

APPLIED SCIENCE SUPPORT FOR INNOVATION AND TECHNOLOGY

So now science is prepared to reinforce technology and engineering on the basis of the fundamental units of nature, of particles and energy. And new things are suggested and become technically attractive because of their scientific reality and qualities. This can be illustrated by a few case studies which in fact relate to major innovations and economic forces of these times and the years ahead.

Crystals and Glasses

The first case study is about the solid state and the role of crystals and glasses in modern manufacture and in high-performance systems, such as aerospace, electronics, computers, information handling, and communications.

We see that the scientific concepts described are now permitting statistical descriptions of *real* crystals. These crystals are regular arrangements of atomic units (ions, molecules) in cells. They aggregate in various geometrical forms, often randomly (Figure 3). But there are also vacancies or other imperfections inside the cells as well (Figure 4). We now find that the strength of matter, especially of metals and alloys, is often determined by the quantity and mobility of these dislocations. Science is showing how they can be pinned down, to inhibit the collapse of bridges and supertankers, for example. Computer models of how crystals are formed have been created by Jackson and his contemporaries. The computer models illustrate how modern science is guiding technical improvements in the solidification of matter—where hordes of atoms, not just two or three, are interacting (Figure 5). Yet the composition of the crystals may be pure within parts per billion or better, thanks to the zone refining discovered by W. G. Pfann as a foundation piece for semiconductor electronics and, thus, the modern electronics industries. The scientific knowledge of what must and can be done in terms of the perfection and purity of these systems has supported technical advance, so that electrical conductivity ranging over more than 10 orders of magnitude can be carefully regulated. Further, these solids, as glasses, are forming a new foundation for photonics, again with the requirements of purity from light-absorbing and light-scattering elements of parts per billion (Figure 6). With silica glasses, the light transmission is as much improved in the last decade as it was in 3,000 years of earlier history of making glasses transparent (Figure 7). The latest figures on light beam losses of intensity—less than 0.16 decibel (dB) per kilometer of pathway in the glass—mean a "liquid" so clear that to lose as much light as through an ordinary high-quality windowpane would require that the new glass have a path a mile or so thick! As might be expected, some of this glass is very strong, with filaments

SINGLE CRYSTAL

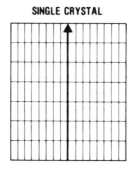

POLYCRYSTAL

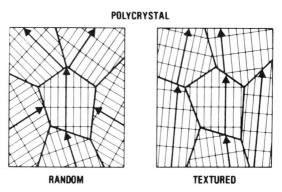

RANDOM   **TEXTURED**

FIGURE 3   The orderly structure of solids creates crystallites, which in turn may them-selves be arranged in various orientations that govern useful properties of the solids.

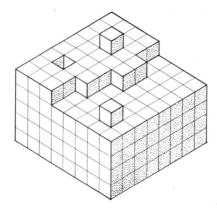

FIGURE 4   Crystallites forming from regular packing of atoms, ions, or molecules are usually not quite perfect. Some missing units or vacancies occur, as shown in the schematic building up of a solid from identical (model) cubes.

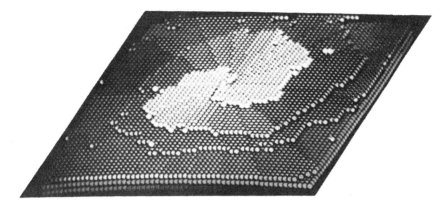

FIGURE 5   Real crystals form by a series of cumulative atom placements, apparently aided by nuclei, or centers, such as in this computer-generated model conceived by Jackson, Gilman, and their co-workers.

MAXIMUM TOLERABLE CONCENTRATIONS FOR VARIOUS IMPURITY IONS

Element	Concentration, parts per billion
Iron	20
Copper	50
Chromium	20
Cobalt	2
Manganese	100
Nickel	20
Vanadium	100

Concentration calculated from published values. Only one element is assumed to be present and in its worst valence state. Maximum tolerable loss is assumed to be 20 dB/km.

FIGURE 6   Technical properties of engineering materials are often influenced by exceedingly small quantities of impurities, through composition, packing, and forces in the solid state. Thus, the clarity of supertransparent light-guide glass is determined by the indicated (tiny) tolerable portions of common metallic elements.

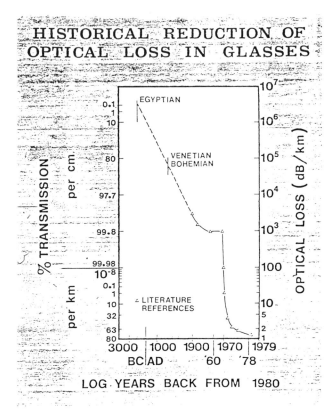

FIGURE 7 Illustration of the application of modern scientific principles to the purification of glass, showing improvement in clarity (reduction in losses). In the past decade photon transmission has been increased almost as much again as the increase achieved through empirical improvements of the preceding 3,000 years.

breaking only rather uniformly in stresses of 800,000 to 1 million pounds per square inch, or much closer to the theoretical strength of SiO_2 than was ever imagined to be possible.

Phase Rule Applications

Another fascinating example of how the bulk science of thermodynamics and the fine structural concepts of crystal structure and atomic interaction have combined is found in the modern applications of the phase rule, enunciated by Gibbs. Namely, Plewes (Figure 8) and his contemporaries have applied the complex distribution of phases in metal alloys, called spinodal decomposition (illustrated by classic gold-platinum liquid-solid curves; (see Figure 9), so precisely for Cu-Ni-Sn systems that defects and dislocations caused by the imperfect nature of crystals have been controlled in bronzes to give 300 percent of more improvement in yield strength (Figures 9 and 10). This has been applied dramatically to bronze springs and relays (Figure 11) and to a host of control systems for machines. But it represents, also, a historic reminder of what the physical sciences lead to. Recall that the destiny of kingdoms, of empires, and indeed of civilization was determined in the Bronze Age by the strength, the hardness, of the weaponry, shields, and spears made of bronze. Certainly much human ingenuity was devoted to the improvement of such metals, yet in the 1970s, the latter part of the twentieth

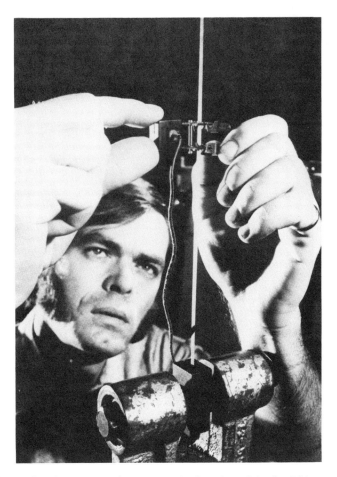

FIGURE 8   Plewes measuring new mechanics of special spinodal bronzes.

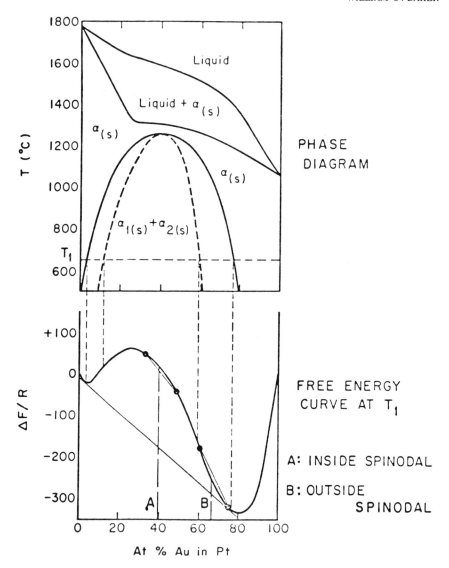

FIGURE 9 Phase diagrams showing the fundamental thermodynamic variations with temperature in the composition of varying amounts of gold in platinum, from which it is possible to select certain processing conditions yielding combinations of crystals of optimal physical properties in the alloy.

MATERIAL	TYPICAL YIELD STRENGTH (10^3psi)	ENHANCED YIELD STRENGTH (10^3psi)
Cu-5Sn (PHOSPHOR BRONZE)	70	110 TEXTURED
Cu-12Ni-28Zn (NICKEL SILVER)	65	125 ”
Cu-9Ni-2Sn (MOD. CUPRONICKEL)	45	105 ”
Cu-1.7Be (COPPER BERYLLIUM)	145	170 ”
Cu-9Ni-6Sn (MOD. CUPRONICKEL)	50	150 SPINODAL

FIGURE 10   Examples of structure enhancement compared to conventional yield strengths of classic bronzes and other copper alloys. Note the twofold improvement of nickel-silver alloy resulting from orientation of crystallites, and the threefold improvement of cupronickel by spinodal control in the processed solid.

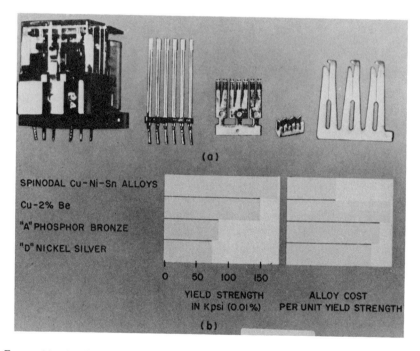

FIGURE 11   Application of scientifically processed alloys in the manufacture of essential commercial control equipment.

century, greater strengths were generated for bronzes (in some cases by controlled texturing from knowing the crystal structure, but in the best cases from the spinodal decomposition) than from the massive empirical efforts of earlier centuries.

These relations of structure within solids to overall properties provide many new ways of improving materials. Purity and heat treatment can modify the content of dislocations, as shown by etch pits in the pioneering work by Pfann and Vogel (Figure 12). These demonstrate that atomic positions indeed affect the total energy balance in the solid. Similarly, the distance between atoms (and ions) is reflected in the mechanical stiffness of the solid (Figure 13). In turn, that stiffness relates to the familiar "hardness" of families of solids, in ways reflecting the valence, or quantum mechanical binding, of the various elements (Figure 14). Thus we can see the reasons for varying the tensile strengths of substances that provide shelter, clothing, machines, and defense (Figure 15).

From gemlike single crystals, at one extreme (Figure 16), to combinations of ordered and amorphous molecules of polymers implied in electron-microscopic images of nylons for textiles (Figure 17), and polyethylene for plastics (Figure 18), scientific principles correlate with engineering uses.

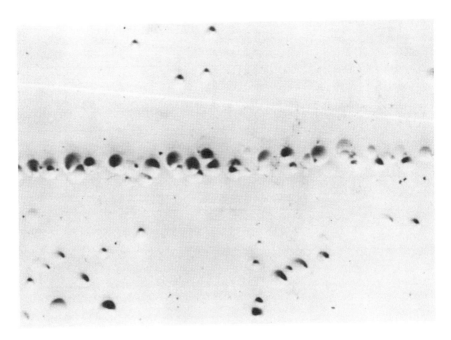

FIGURE 12 Direct evidence of dislocation arrays in crystals, derived from the etching behavior of high-purity germanium.

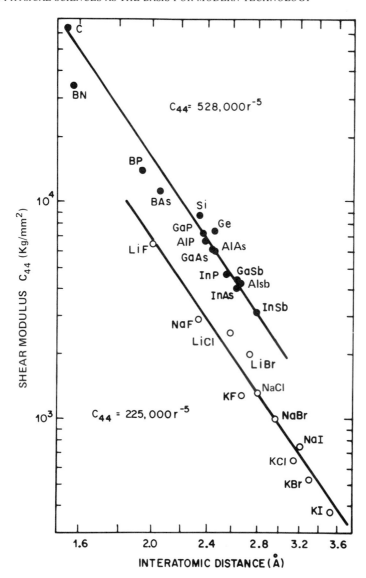

FIGURE 13   Stiffness of a variety of simple solids as a function of the separation of atoms, or ions comprising them, showing that those which are bound tightly at very short distances are 10 to 100 times stiffer than those having longer separation between the units. Again, the fundamental atomic character is directly reflected in gross mechanical behavior.

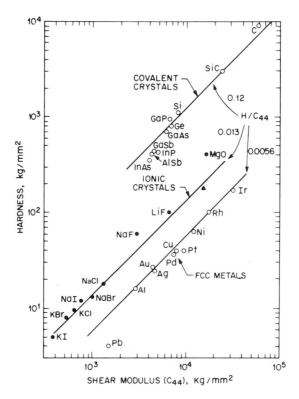

FIGURE 14   The familiar hardness of matter is directly reflected in the shear stiffness (modulus), characterized through the science of atomic composition and spacing.

Material	Tensile Strength (GN/m^2)
Silica	10.5
Boron Filaments Deposited on Tungsten	7.0
Patented Steel (0.9C)	4.2
Tungsten Wire	3.9
Graphite Fiber	3.2
Kevlar 49	2.8
β-Ti (13V-11Cr-3Al)	2.3
Nylon 66 Fiber	1.05
Metallic Glass ($Fe_{.72}Cr_{.08}P_{.13}C_{.07}$)	3.8
Metallic Glass ($Pd_{.775}Cu_{.06}Si_{.165}$)	3.5
Cu-12% Ni-8% Sn	1.6

FIGURE 15   Examples of tensile strength in giganewtons per square meter (gn/m^2) of various atomic and molecular compositions, showing effects of atomic properties on gross mechanical behavior.

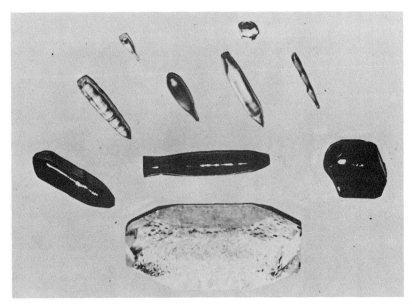

FIGURE 16   Chemically synthesized crystals designed for special electronic and photonic properties, such as the large specimen of quartz (center) and garnets and rubies.

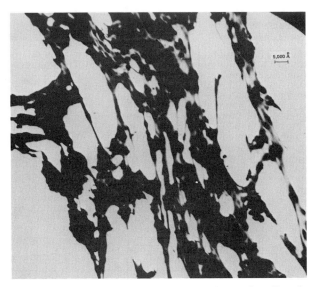

FIGURE 17   Electron micrograph of polymer solids, illustrating fiber formation from orientation of crystallites as a result of extending or drawing the film containing typical spherelike aggregates.

FIGURE 18   Electron microscope picture of complex structure of an important commercial plastic, polyethylene, indicating how long chain molecules form fibrils which then extend between spherulite and semicrystalline aggregates.

Hydrocarbons

The combination of the macroscience of energy and entropy and the microscience of structure and quantum mechanical binding and interactions appears in other domains that are already decisive in twentieth-century civilization and economy, and it is also likely to have continuing profound effects in the developing world for centuries to come. An example is hydrocarbon, among other carbon derivatives. In the case of hydrocarbons, the most prominent application is their use as the energy source for heating and internal-combustion engines, as in automobiles. However, they also play increasingly important roles as hydrocarbon polymers, like polyethylene and polypropylene. Their use as packaging, insulating, and preserving material, even as plumbing and water-distribution ducts, as well as dielectrics for electrical energy and telecommunications systems, may eventually have as profound an impact as in fuels. They constitute, therefore, a rather suitable example of how the vast technologies represented in these uses are directly and effectively supported by physical science. We need to know, for instance, how hydrocarbons oxidize, which is the basis for their use as an energy source. But, on the other hand, for their use for packaging, plastics, ducts, dieletrics, and so on, prevention of oxidation is paramount. It has been admirably established, and is being continually refined, that this is a chain reaction involving radicals whose influence can also be modified (or inhibited) and relatively well controlled (Figures 19 and 20).

We see further that in such crucial uses as cable, piping, plumbing, roofing, and other structures, hydrocarbons like polyethylene and polypropylene can be decisively protected against oxidation by small amounts of carbon black or other chemically and physically elegant reagents (Figure 21).These circumstances are all the result of applying atomic and molecular theory and scientific analysis to these synthetic materials or their natural petroleum precursors.

KINETIC SCHEME FOR HYDROCARBON OXIDATION

(1) RH	$\rightarrow R^{\cdot}$		Initiation
(2) $R^{\cdot} + O_2$	$\rightarrow ROO^{\cdot}$		Propagation
(3) $ROO^{\cdot} + RH$	$\rightarrow ROOH + R^{\cdot}$		
(4) $ROOH$	$\rightarrow RO^{\cdot}$	$+ HO^{\cdot}$	
(5) $RO^{\cdot} + RH$	$\rightarrow ROH$	$+ R^{\cdot}$	Chain Branching
(6) $HO^{\cdot} + RH$	$\rightarrow HOH$	$+ R^{\cdot}$	
(7) $ROO^{\cdot} (RO^{\cdot}$ etc.)	$\rightarrow$ Inert Products		Termination
(8) $ROO^{\cdot} + AH$	$\rightarrow ROOH + A^{\cdot}$		
(9) $RO^{\cdot} + AH$	$\rightarrow ROH$	$+ A^{\cdot}$	Inhibition
(10) $HO^{\cdot} + AH$	$\rightarrow HOH$	$+ A^{\cdot}$	

$$RH = POLYMER \qquad AH = INHIBITOR$$

FIGURE 19 Chemical steps in the major process of burning hydrocarbons, as in automobile engines, and in stabilizing hydrocarbon polymers, as in plastics, against degradation by similar oxidation in the atmosphere.

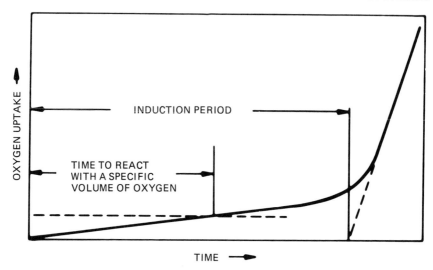

FIGURE 20   Typical example of behavior of an unstabilized hydrocarbon exposed to air, showing gradual early reaction followed by rapid oxidation.

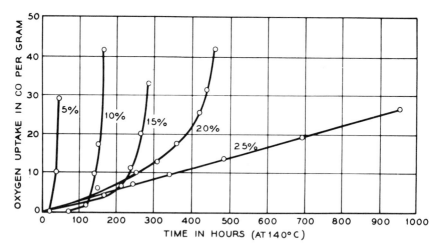

FIGURE 21   Example of important commercial stabilization of plastic against air oxidation, as a function of weight percent of carbon added.

Surface Technology

Beyond the pervasive domains of bulk matter and of media for light guides, cables, and the like lie many other examples of how extensive innovations and engineering are emerging increasingly from applied science. The wide realm of surface technology is a compelling example.

Take first the films on which much of modern society depends, for instance, paper. The control and fabrication of paper depend heavily on gauges and machine responses generated by radioactive isotopes. Indeed, the modern chronicle of surfaces and films, which define so much of our economy and the substance of the information age, now illustrates a fine coalition of atomistic science. In this, quantum mechanical knowledge of particles, fields, charges, and bulk matter behavior developed from work in modern solid-state theory and experiment, reveals the detailed configuration at surfaces. For instance, semiconductors, transistors, and other junction devices are activated electronically by certain additional atoms, called donors or acceptors, which shift the charge populations and field conditions in germanium, silicon, indium phosphide, and so on. These effects are themselves derivatives of the classically recognized electron-holding or electronegativity effects in the elements. For decades, such behavior in ions and homopolar systems, metals, and insulators has been a major topic in physics and chemistry. Classes of matter can be categorized as to electrical conductivity by these electronegativity effects (Figure 22).

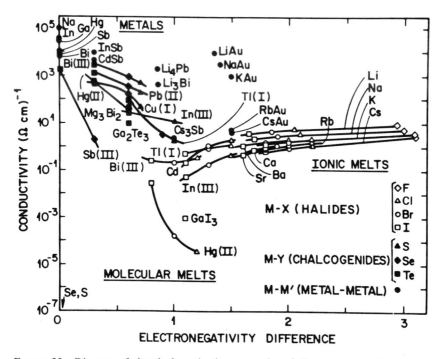

FIGURE 22   Diagram of electrical conducting properties of diverse classes of materials, as determined by the electronegativity differences in their atoms, showing intimate connection of atomic structure with technical electromagnetic behavior.

Inventions for getting these atoms (e.g., arsenic, phosphorus, and others) into the junction devices by diffusion and other clever methods dominated the early periods of integrated circuitry (Frosch and Derick). However, additional ways have especially been applied to thin films and surfaces. One of the best has been to accelerate ions, as Cockcroft and Walton have done in the fundamental study of nuclei and of elementary particles. These ions can then be implanted into the surfaces of the semiconductors and produce, at appropriate depths and concentrations, the desired electronic responses.

The whole system of ion implantation is also interesting for its potential for improving wear on the surface of bearings, for generating new catalysts, and especially for inhibiting corrosion. Every phase of its application in technology, however, is based on the experiences of the original scientists interested in colliding particles and elementary interactions.

A particularly fascinating modern instance of the continuing versatility of this science is how beams of ions can be directed down certain channels or pathways in crystals or films to produce not only importantly modified structures, but also information from scattering and interactions about the nature of their host solid (Figure 23).

Electron beams are among the simplest but most highly useful embodiments of these particles. Here, in the work of J. West and collaborators, the old technology of making electrets has been recast (by charging surfaces of insulators). Now, all advanced telephones depend for their voice transducers not on the century-old (and invaluable) performance of carbon microphones, but on charged films of special polymers like polytetrafluroethylene. These have been treated so that when bombarded with an electron beam (Figure 24) the electrons are trapped quite permanently. The result compares with what we have learned about the trapping of charges in silicon and germanium. This realm of organic-polymer capture of electrons produces the most effective voice transducers so far achieved, and it is opening much more widely the fields of teleconferencing and other special microphonic uses. It is also suggesting new realms of scientific research related to energy processes in living tissue, such as ion transport across membranes.

Particle bombardment can, of course, be extended—in the sense noted earlier about the dualism of waves and particles (Bohr's complementarity principle)—to beams of photons, which are still smaller particles than electrons. In this case laser-pulsed beams on the surfaces of crystals produce valuable and increasingly used effects. A burst of photons lasting a hundred-millionth of a second from a laser of 532-nanometer wavelength causes heating at a depth of a micrometer in a silicon surface. This heating is immediately quenched, at about a billion degrees Kelvin per second transient, by the solid below the surface. Various important metastable conditions can thus be obtained, as the current work of W. Brown and his associates dem-

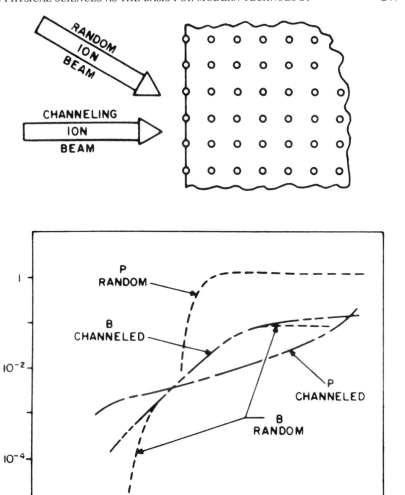

FIGURE 23 Examples of distribution of ions implanted by nuclear accelerators into single crystals of silicon, as determined by the directions in the crystal and subsequent heating to redistribute the acceptor (boron) or donor (phosphorus) units.

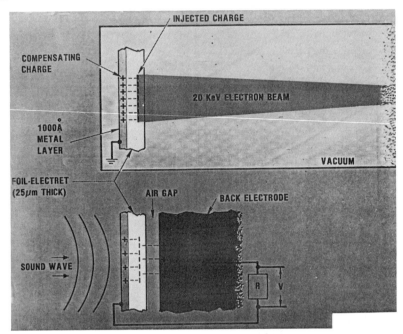

FIGURE 24   Schematic of implantation of electrons in polymer films to form long-lived electrets, which then can act as efficient microphones and other electromechanical transducers.

onstrates, along with that of others working in this field. Indeed, this process can be regulated so that the entire heating effect is due to electron-photon collisions, rather than a conventional phonon excitation by movement of the bulk atoms in the solid.

Nuclear Science and Radioisotopes

Recall, also, the already vast and growing role of the science of charged particles in the characterization of matter and its reactions, far beyond the surface and film phenomena. Namely, the group of more than 1,600 new isotopes created by nuclear reactions (particularly of neutrons), along with 300 naturally occurring stable isotopes, form the corpus of technology for tracing chemical reactions. These methods are especially dominant in research on organic and living matter. Analysis using these schemes commonly involves radioactive counting instruments and mass spectroscopy, in which the isotopic atom becomes a charged particle. Likewise, in reference to the use of unstable nuclei with their useful radiation output, the synthetic technetium-99 derived from neutron bombardment of molybdenum is the most widely used isotope in nuclear medicine nowadays. However, these cases are but symbolic of the immense scope of elementary- and radioactive-particle science in support of a multitude of industrial, governmental, and social initiatives.

This delicacy of identifying atomically the behavior of virtually all technical and engineering systems has, of course, brought along many more conventional analytic and control schemes, themselves derived earlier from the principles of physics and chemistry. Optical spectroscopy is a distinguished example; now with Raman surface-enhanced spectra, the ordinary gas-phase sensitivity may be increased about a million times, to the detection of 10^9 molecules or less. Moreover, using laser activation, studies at Oak Ridge National Laboratory have observed single atoms of cesium in a cloud of 10^{19} other atoms. Similarly, David Joy's ion-impact spectroscopy can determine light elements quantitatively in a sample whose total mass may be only 10^{-18}—a millionth of a millionth of a millionth of a gram. Optical-emission spectroscopy can respond to as few as a million molecules per cubic centimeter, and fluorescence following laser exposure to liquid jets from high-pressure liquid chromatography has permitted the detection of a billion or less aflatoxin molecules per cubic centimeter.

SCIENCE SUPPORTING MEASUREMENT AND SYSTEMS

Physical science thus has not only provided a conceptual and intellectual base for modern technology, but repeatedly has injected quantification. In this way the entire character of technical engineering and economic operation has been enhanced beyond the empirical, often purely descriptive, stages on which manufacture and mining depended for a thousand years.

In some fields of the highest innovation and sophisticated technology, we are now seeing the elegant principles of twentieth-century physical science, along with the experiments and techniques achieved, being combined into operational systems for dramatic advances in economic and social functions. These are seen especially in the new arenas of communications and computers; of information handling; of sensing, command, and control; of industrial automation and national security; and indeed (in the wide range of electonics, photonics, and circuitry) in the new systems of personal action, education, and entertainment. These resources universally involve semiconductor junction devices, which, in turn, have to be assembled with metallic conductors and strong organic or inorganic insulators and with various heat and mechanical qualities. In this systems realm, atoms, molecules, charges, and waves must be made to perform with great precision. This need is being met by synthesizing, preferably in thin film- and surface-controlled forms, new states of matter (Figure 25). This has been done especially by R. Dingle, A. C. Gossard, and W. Wiegmann, based on the liquid-phase epitaxy work of M. Panish, the film studies of J. M. Poate, members of AT&T Bell Laboratories, and now the contributions of a variety of workers in other laboratories around the world.

These schemes of generating beams of atoms or molecules that then form condensed matter of predetermined, and often unprecedented, properties signify a heroic combination of physics and chemistry, of Gibbs's phase principles and Heisenberg, Sommerfeld, and Einstein's quantum mechanics, of the Braggs' and Davisson's structural diffraction waves in crystals, of the Bardeen-Brattain-Shockley discovery of the transistor effect, and, with the solid-state injection laser embodying Schalow and Towne's revelation of new forms of light itself, the laser.

In examining a little further this making in the laboratory, and now in the factory, of unique and productive forms of matter, it should be emphasized that this is only the beginning. For in the times ahead, the exposed surfaces of the manufactures of most industries may involve these same synthetic processes. It is already fair to say, however, that the digital systems (computers, communications, and controls) on which modern industry and government increasingly depend will shortly be using these schemes throughout. Thus, since as noted, this technology does involve nearly every aspect of the wide reaches of physical science gained during this century, we have a powerful answer to questions of the practical values of research. When the press and politicians question its relevance or economic return, it can be

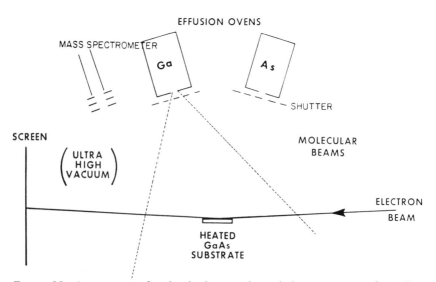

FIGURE 25 Arrangement of molecular beam and atomic beam generators for gallium and arsenic to create new semiconductor films of unique quality for digital circuitry, such as in high-performance computers.

HIGH MOBILITY MODULATION-DOPED SEMICONDUCTORS

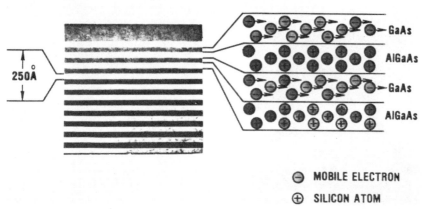

FIGURE 26   Electron micrograph showing the molecularly layered structures deposited by the molecular beam and yielding charge mobilities and other technological advantages previously unknown.

stated that there is simply no evidence that this synthesis of new states of matter by molecular-beam deposition and epitaxy could have happened empirically and without the vast scientific base summarized here.

Indeed, the behavior of the domains produced, for instance, with gallium arsenide and alternating additions of aluminum gallium arsenide in the presence of a silicon substrate, exhibits charge mobilities never before achieved (Figure 26). The resulting transistors are already the essence of supercomputers and superspeed circuitry. However, the theoretical significance of these new structures is also profound. For instance, it happens that quantum mechanics is generally taught, and was early conceived, in terms of the quantized behavior of a particle in a box. The Hamiltonian operator dominant in Schrödinger's equation is illustrated as describing the behavior of such a model. The charges in the layered structures produced by molecular-beam epitaxy (Figure 26) are the best, and in some ways the only, case in which an experimental quantum particle in a box has been achieved. Thus, we are seeing in this, as in so many other cases of the development of solid-state science, and now in photonics, the interaction of technology in stimulating further scientific insight.

Remarkable scientific combinations with technological outputs are also proceeding rapidly in the molecular-beam epitaxy processes themselves (Figure 27). For instance, M. Panish, referred to above with regard to his earlier work in liquid-phase epitaxy, has now introduced gas-phase sources

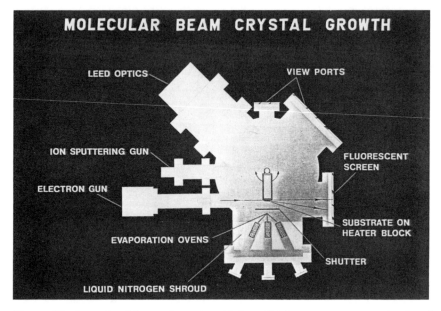

FIGURE 27   Example of the precise and sophisticated high-vacuum apparatus developed by Hagstrom to control and analyze molecular beam epitaxy and the synthesis of new thin crystal forms of matter.

of elements to form the beams. This replaces having to depend on sometimes poorly defined solid reservoirs for atom and molecule emission. This flexibility has moved forward with W. Tsang into "chemical-beam epitaxy," in which all of the component elements come in gas form, such as metallo-organic compounds of gallium and indium. This exceedingly attractive system, which seems certain to have a strong impact on heterogeneous-catalysis creation in the chemical industry, on surface stabilization, and in various other applications mentioned, is termed MOCVD—metallo-organic chemical vapor deposition. It is being controlled by highly sophisticated flow techniques regulated by microprocessors and yielding kinetics of particle synthesis in the high vacuum, which are themselves of deep interest to the chemical and materials industries.

It should be emphasized again at this point that the universe of innovation supported by atomic and molecular surface and film synthesis is a striking derivative of the long-term studies of high vacuum and surface purification, epitomized by the research of Homer Hagstrom. On the one hand, recall that energy states and surface physics were essential in the discovery of the transistor; they were, in fact, the crucial features in Bardeen's pioneering theory. Beyond that, however, the superb experimental extensions of surface physics by Hagstrom and his associates are dependent on the achievement of unprecedented cleanliness and surface characterization involving, among other things, consistent and controllable vacuua of 10^{-11} torr or better. This is an emptiness beyond that of outer space, and yet it has become a factory-controlled process (Figure 27). The intense importance and decisive role of these researchers in the electronic-photonic-materials regime is well symbolized by the diagram of Hagstrom's latest research apparatus (Figure 28), which includes working units of ultraviolet, photoemission, energy-loss, and Auger-electron spectroscopies. These are all notable examples of modern quantum physics, including electron-diffraction and ion-neutralization spectroscopy, which have had their own historic roles in the physical sciences of the twentieth century.

In this context it is also appropriate to denote the rapidly moving frontier use of this science and technology in electronic and photonic systems innovation. Thus, the selectively built heterostructure transistor obtained from molecular-beam epitaxy, including a multilayered sandwich of ultrapure gallium arsenide with aluminum gallium arsenide layers that are heavily doped,

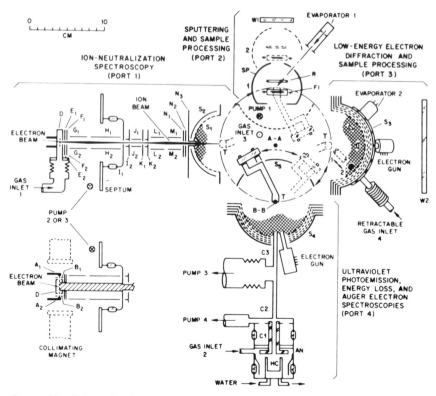

FIGURE 28 Schematic of apparatus for precise surface characterization.

has been shown by J. DiLorenzo to provide a new ring-oscillator circuit. It is effectively operating as a switch at 90 billion operations per second, far beyond anything ever before reached in integrated circuitry. Other embodiments provide such records as frequency dividers working at 10 gigacycles, at low temperatures.

The work of R. Dingle, H. Stürmer, and A. Gossard has indeed already shown the doubling of electron mobility in the gallium arsenide-aluminum gallium arsenide case referred to earlier. Electron motion is 20 times as fast at low temperatures. This will undoubtedly be developed into important structures for photonics, eventually including integrated optoelectronic circuits. In this regard germanium, silicon, and their combinations, which yield strained superlattices, have already been achieved by John Dean of Bell Laboratories. Also, Julia Phillips has grown calcium fluoride on silicon, so that striking new insulator-semiconductor systems are in progress. Likewise, these advanced epitaxial techniques are being used in the production of new magnetic rare-earths systems and in superconductors. Accordingly, our expectations of extensive innovation from this new basic science are appropriate.

Finally, it is appropriate to accent in every connection that physical science, to which I attribute so much of the base for the technology and economy of this age, is, in turn, heavily dependent on mathematics and the conceptions of logic and encoding that are the base for computers, analysis, and the treatment of atomic and molecular events. Newton and Maxwell were referred to at the beginning of this chapter; we should also remember the host of mathematicians who mastered statistical mechanics, group theory, symbolic logic, and an array of other elegant representations of the mind. While our progress in physical science is an adornment of civilization, its modern excellence and extent derive especially from both the content and the modes of thought that mathematics has engendered. Overall, it is gratifying that the science of Aristotle and Plato, of Newton and Einstein, is now so well joined with the technology of humankind, which I have described elsewhere* as "the ways of making things and doing things."

Random House Encyclopedia (New York: Random House, 1977), p. 1578.

Technological Education

JOSEPH M. PETTIT

In industry and government nationally and worldwide, decisions in which technology is a big factor must be made every day. We will make better decisions in the twenty-first century if more of our citizens, managers, school board members, lawmakers—and their economic advisers—have had an analytical, rigorous curriculum—preferably in the application of science to society, which typifies the best of engineering education.

Among the major themes developed in this volume on economics and technology is the role of the key infrastructures, which include education. I was asked originally to discuss engineering education; however, just as the world of economics has more participants than economists, so does technology have more participants than engineers. Hence, this chapter discusses technological education in a broader sense, although it focuses on the education of engineers since theirs is a leadership role. It also addresses the subject of economics in the education of engineers and mentions the need for technology in the education of economists.

Engineers and economists have a common interest in technological change, though they see it from different vantage points. Both engineers and economists become involved in policymaking. There is surely need for improvement in U.S. economic growth and competitiveness in world markets. Better cooperation and mutual understanding between engineers and economists could well lead to better policies. Dialogue between engineers and economists can benefit both as they learn of each other's concerns, priorities, insights, and methods.

TECHNOLOGICAL EDUCATION IN THE UNITED STATES

Let us now turn to the questions of who provides our technology, especially technological innovation, and how they are educated. First, the technology team is like a modern surgical team, which consists not only of the surgeon but also of other competent persons of many specialties and levels of education. In technology, there is not just the engineer, although he or she is a key person, like the surgeon. There are others on the team. Unlike the surgeon, the engineer may have only a bachelor's degree, or a master's or doctor's degree.

Engineering education at the bachelor's level is regulated by a national body, the Accrediting Board for Engineering and Technology (ABET). During the course of ABET's regular 6-year inspection cycle, the visiting teams look for quality and check curriculum content, which is specified as to minimum content in various subjects. An engineering curriculum, to be classed as such, must have at least 2½ years of mathematics, science, and engineering subjects. Included must be at least ½ year of mathematics beyond trigonometry, 1 year of basic sciences (e.g., chemistry and physics), 1 year of engineering sciences (e.g., fluid mechanics—not normally a part of physics courses), and at least ½ year of "engineering design" (synthesis, as opposed to scientific analysis).

These requirements are minimal, and most curricula contain more. To prevent a curriculum's becoming too exclusively technical and theoretical, there are some other important requirements. There must be adequate laboratory experience and competency in oral and written English, and there must be provided "an understanding of the ethical, social, and *economic* [emphasis added] considerations in engineering practice." Finally, there must be at least ½ year in the humanities and social sciences, not counting subjects like ROTC or language-skills courses. Economics is especially mentioned as an appropriate subject in the social sciences.

Engineering is not science, although in modern times it is heavily science-based. The difference is emphasized in the ABET requirement for engineering design. It is this component of the curriculum that is most relevant here, and I shall quote from the ABET criteria:

The requirements . . . have been established in recognition of the need to orient the engineering student toward the solution of important technological problems of society. In this context, engineering design is the process of devising a system, component, or process to meet desired needs. . . . The engineering design component of a curriculum should include some of the following features: development of student creativity, use of open-ended problems, . . . consideration of alternative solutions. . . . It is also desirable to include a variety of realistic constraints such as *economic factors,* safety, reliability, aesthetics, ethics, and social impact. [Emphasis added.]

These nationally accepted criteria for the basic professional education of engineers include two relevant points. First, engineers are expected to become leaders in society and not merely backroom technical workers (some are, of course, but from personal choice). Hence the requirements for humanities, social sciences, communication skills, and an appreciation of the social and economic context of their work. Engineers will also be supported by several classes of technical staff, including craftsmen like machinists and electricians, technicians with 2 years of postsecondary preparation, and persons in a category new since World War II—engineering technologists who are graduates of 4-year curricula accredited by ABET. The engineering technology curriculum is similar to engineering in many respects, but it features more laboratory, hands-on experience, less theory, and more state-of-the-art practical knowledge. Such graduates can design today's equipment, but the engineers are better prepared to design tomorrow's.

Second, engineers are not illiterate in economic factors, in the role of the marketplace, in the trade-offs between price and performance. Nor are they ignorant of the social context of their work, wherein choice between alternative designs may be a political rather than a technical decision.

Engineering work cannot usually be accomplished by individuals. For the most part, an engineer is the leader of a team. Success on small projects leads to responsibility for ever larger activities and a larger management role. Many engineers migrate gradually into general management. They begin to need more management education. If they remain in more technical roles, they gradually need additional education in science and technology, as new developments in their fields make their earlier learning obsolescent. (For example, I was first educated in vacuum-tube electronics and later had to educate myself in solid-state electronics, such as transistors and integrated circuits.) Thus it must be recognized that continuing education has become an important need as the pace of technological innovation has increased.

Much is written about continuing education for engineers—and much of this kind of education is available—but not enough is being utilized. A survey of 3,000 engineers in industry taken in the 1960s revealed that only one-quarter of them were taking continuing education courses, and only one-half had ever done so.*

A brighter picture is to be found in the popularity of graduate, degree-credit courses taken by young engineers at their employment sites. Electronic delivery modes such as microwave transmission in local zones and videotapes delivered by vehicle to more distant sites, overcome distance. Course transmission by satellites at reasonable cost can be anticipated soon.

A brief mention of numbers may be in order. The latest national data, which are for 1983, show that 72,741 bachelor's degrees were awarded by

*R. Perrucci, W. LeBold, W. E. Howland, The engineer in industry and government, *Engineering Education*, March 1966:237–259.

271 institutions.* Of those institutions, 256 have one or more ABET-accredited curricula. At the graduate level, 19,909 master's or graduate professional degrees and 3,023 doctor's degrees were awarded.

Such numbers are not meaningful unless compared with something. Are they large or small compared with figures for other nations? Are they increasing or decreasing? On the latter point, they have been increasing. The nearly 73,000 cited above is the largest bachelor's-degree output ever. But it will decline. The number of engineering freshmen follows the population trend for 18-year-olds, both of which peaked about 1980 and are now declining.

But engineering enrollment is also influenced by a "popularity cycle." Certain fields of engineering are especially popular with students these days, notably electronics and computers. A current force in the popularity cycle is the much-publicized shortage of engineers for our fast-growing microelectronics and computer industry.

I believe that the popularity of engineering is too much influenced by journalists, who tend to treat the output of engineering graduates as a marketplace commodity, to be measured against the number and apparent trends in jobs specifically labeled for engineers. The situation is really quite elastic, and there is probably no definition of shortage or surplus. Even if there are not enough graduates to fill the desired hiring tables, industry does not shut down. If there are more graduates than there are narrowly specified job openings, then we have—or should have—a healthy supply of well-educated young people for industry and government. This is much like the situation for graduates who majored in English, political science, or even economics. Indeed one could argue that in this highly technological age, with so many corporate and political decisions having major technical dimensions, our nation should have more of its decision makers educated in the discipline of engineering.

Coming back to the numbers, it might seem that 73,000 is a large number of bachelor graduates. Yet the United States ranks behind Japan and West Germany in per capita engineers in the population; indeed Japan graduates twice as many engineers per capita as we do—and far fewer lawyers!

TECHNOLOGICAL EDUCATION IN JAPAN

Japan is the formidable competitor of the United States in technological innovation, economic growth, and success with manufactured products in the world marketplace.

The recent success of Japan in world markets for high technology products has been a matter of study and concern in the United States; since the era

---

*Engineering degrees granted, 1983, *Engineering Education* 74 (April 1984):640–645.

following World War II, Japan has become the leader in world markets in autos and electronics. Why? Is Japanese engineering education different from ours? Is it newer and better? My study and visits lead me to believe that it is not. The curriculum is traditional. However, entrance to Japanese universities is highly competitive and requires rigorous preparation for national exams. But an important difference from U.S. engineering occurs after graduation and first employment. At that time there begins a whole new phase of education in industry—utilized to a far greater extent than in U.S. industry. Young Japanese engineers are rotated—over a period of years—through many departments, working closely with all classes of workers. It is not just an orientation tour.

They are also assigned to formal instruction in the special processes and techniques of their employer, in addition to taking further courses outside. The employer can afford to make a large investment in developing engineers because of the long-term employment practice in the leading Japanese companies. The employee is assured of a continuing job and he or she, in turn, does not leave to join a competitor.

There are other important factors in the success of the Japanese, including their highly disciplined study and utilization of technology available from the United States. They use it better than we ourselves have.

The matter of discipline is worth a few more words. It seems to me that the higher the level of technology in a society the higher the degree of discipline required. This discipline must be a characteristic of all persons, not merely of the scientist who finds new knowledge or of the engineer who incorporates that knowledge into the design of a new device or system. It must also include managers and workers who manufacture the device or system, and those who install and maintain it. And, finally, there must be discipline on the part of those who must put this technology to use. Technology cannot be purchased and expected to function well for each new owner. Discipline related to technology is strongly related to cultural factors, which are slow to change and with respect to which certain societies seem to have a time advantage. Japan seems to be doing especially well.

Of course there are other aspects of Japanese competition with the United States that do not derive from engineering education, nor can they be overcome through engineering education alone. For instance, in Japan there has been much better cooperation among labor, industry, and government, evidently built on a national consensus to succeed in the international marketplace. We have no such consensus; instead there seems to be a long-standing distrust between labor and management, between government and business. This can be seen in our antitrust legislation, which was derived, understandably, from conditions during the nineteenth century, but such restrictions are now a serious handicap.

FUTURE DIRECTIONS

Returning now to the U.S. situation in engineering education, we are in a period of tension due to the current imbalance in U.S. engineering manpower. Industry has far more vacant positions designated for engineers than there are graduates emerging from our universities. Those of us in the universities also have a serious imbalance, namely, a large, recent wave of undergraduates wanting to study engineering and a serious shortage of available faculty. Starting salary rates for new engineering faculty have had to be increased sharply, causing us to divert money from laboratory equipment and other needs, with the result that we have a serious deficiency in necessary instructional facilities. At the same time, we should seriously question how much we should expand our engineering colleges, even if we could have the necessary resources. What are the real future needs for engineering graduates in our increasingly high-tech society?

Let us look more closely at our future needs in the educational sector. Engineers and managers are now producing most of our products in established industries. But, in addition, there are newer, high-tech industries. These are the toolmakers of our day—those who provide the means of making high-tech products. Creating, designing, and fabricating the high-tech tools calls for a different mix of engineers and other employees than there would be in general industry. It is not just that more skilled technicians are needed, but more Ph.D.s. There must be more engineers with advanced levels of education and capability, and these must come from our university-level engineering institutions. They must also have participated in research. Not that they will pursue careers in research as such, but they should learn to confront a new field in which not everything is known and to proceed systematically and effectively to accumulate the necessary knowledge. This experience can be provided in a university while the graduate student is taking additional course work, perhaps in mathematics and physics, as well as in engineering itself. We need to attract the very best graduate students, and industry must help them complete their advanced studies. At the present time, too many of our best students are leaving at the bachelor's level to take high-paying jobs in industry.

Then, of course, there is an increasing need for engineers in our basic industries, such as the electric utility industry, as well as in agriculture, transportation, and so on. To this should be added the growing service sector, particularly areas like office automation. Here the objective is clear. We need an ample supply of well-prepared engineering students. Unfortunately, the supply is greatly influenced by the positive or negative impressions gained by young people and their parents from the newspapers as to the apparent future need of society for engineers.

There is a special problem at the present time in the United States. First-year students in engineering curricula are not well prepared when they come to us. Precollege education in mathematics, science, and even English, is so inadequate that many students must spend time doing remedial work, and a large amount of university-level resources must be diverted to this work. The problem has been given much recent attention as a national crisis, but apparently it will be left to state and local corrective action. Yet it seems doubtful that we can adequately meet our problems of international competition in trade or defense if we leave it to the priorities of every local school district.

Furthermore, in the United States the present culture of schools, teachers, and school boards in the precollege educational system is not well suited to facing the economic marketplace and paying what is necessary to get good teachers in mathematics and science. The situation has become more complicated because outstanding young women who in previous years would automatically have gone into teaching are now able to pursue attractive professional careers in engineering or management.

Again, there is the question of the number of engineering graduates that we really need. One measure, of course, is the number of engineering jobs to be filled in industry. Even this is not well defined and is hard to predict very far into the future. As mentioned before, U.S. industry and our total society utilize fewer engineering graduates than does Japan, where there are twice as many engineering graduates per capita, and where the percentage of bachelor's graduates majoring in engineering is several times higher than in the United States.

There is currently a force in the United States opposing any change, a small but strident group in the engineering profession who say that we should not increase the number of engineering graduates, that an increase in supply would merely drive salaries down. This group would rather have us reduce the number of graduates and restrict the immigration of foreign engineering graduates. I think this would not serve our nation well. In fact, I would urge a much greater increase in the number of students studying engineering, regardless of whether or not they later serve in strictly engineering positions.

This brings us to a consideration of our high-tech society of the future. There is a large society of users of technology, as well as the smaller group of decision makers, who should steer us along a course where technology could be a positive factor in the quality of life and in world stability. Not enough of these decision makers in government and industry have had engineering or scientific education. I would urge that we need many more engineering graduates, and in many kinds of positions in society, not merely in jobs labeled "engineering." I would urge a broader view of engineering education. The engineering curriculum is not narrow and only technical, though the content of humanities and social sciences might well be increased even at the expense of providing less of a ready-made engineering specialist at the bachelor's level.

There is the important group of innovators, or the creators of our future technology. These include the engineering specialists in high-tech industry. For them, further advanced study is necessary. We must encourage more of our brightest engineers to go beyond the bachelor's degree, to acquire or sharpen the tools necessary for high-level innovation. Many of them can do this while employed in industry, taking advantage of local universities or video delivery systems. Corporate policy must do better to encourage this activity by young engineers.

I would urge again that we not measure the number of engineers needed for the future by a precise counting of the number of jobs labeled "engineering." This is not done in other fields. Many students take undergraduate majors in subjects like economics or chemistry but do not become career specialists in those fields. Yet somehow we seem to have come to advise young people to go or not to go into engineering based only on predictions of the number of engineering jobs.

I think we need many more people in our society who have had an analytical, rigorous curriculum—preferably in the application of science to society, which typifies the best of engineering education.

In conclusion, I would say that we face a future with more pervasive, more complex technology, with tools quite beyond the capacity of the user to comprehend in detail, let alone to make for himself. Yet, decisions must be made every day in industry and government, nationally and worldwide, in which technology is a big factor. We will make better decisions in the twenty-first century if more of our citizens, managers, school board members, lawmakers—and their economic advisers—have a sound understanding of a technological society and have experienced the rigorous analytical thought processes that it demands.

Only in this way can we hope to achieve what Alfred North Whitehead described as "the art of progress," namely, "to preserve order amid change and to preserve change amid order."

Basic Research in the Universities: How Much Utility?

DONALD KENNEDY

The United States has placed on its universities a responsibility for basic research larger than that imposed in any other society. The result is a unique venture which tightly couples research and research training, improving the quality of both, and is heavily dependent on public funding. Now, because of the drop in government support of the capital infrastructure of university research and because of the need to spread technology transfer, the relationship between quality and utility in basic research is being explored anew, and new relationships between universities and industry are being tested. This renewed emphasis on utility is not without promise, but it should not be permitted to drain off the energies of the best scientists or to sap the vigor of the university laboratories in which journeymen and apprentices work side by side at the bench.

In his splendid chapter on innovation and science policy in this volume, Harvey Brooks has said much of what needs saying. His characterization of the venture of American science spans its entire range, from the publicly funded basic research that begins the trajectory of innovation to the risk capital financing of product development at its end. He makes a point worth amplifying: the dramatic growth of public funding for science after World War II placed most of the responsibility for fundamental research on the nation's universities.

The extent of that responsibility, in fact, exceeds what can be found in any other industrial democracy. (In the United States, less than 15 percent of government research and development expenditures are made in government-run laboratories; the vast majority of the rest, including about two-thirds of the basic research done in the nation, is spent in the research universities.) Things might well have taken a different course; the government could have formed a consortium with leading industries to develop independent, jointly funded research units; or it could have evolved a set of in-house, government-run research institutes. But it did not.

What is the most significant outcome of that self-denying ordinance? Surely it is the collocation of research and research training. Most of the basic science in America today is done by mixed groups of journeymen and apprentices; the result is that the nation's research trainees are being developed alongside the best scientists. That is the singular feature of our pattern of government support for basic science in the universities; to it, our most thoughtful European colleagues usually attribute our special success.

In 1977 Sune Bergström, then president of the Swedish Academy, pondered why Americans had just swept all of the Nobel science awards. He decided that it was because of the "democracy of American science," by which he meant the fellowship of the laboratory bench.

WHY NEW UNIVERSITY–INDUSTRY RELATIONSHIPS ARE DEVELOPING

During the periods of vigorous growth in the 1950s and 1960s, there was an adaptive mixing of objectives in the expenditure of federal funds. The primary objective was the support of research programs, but two important secondary goals were the support of graduate training and the funding of a stable capital infrastructure to underlie the university-based programs. The high-water mark for this consolidated approach was probably reached between 1965 and 1967. After that, the gradual cutting back of the fellowship and training-grant programs began the decline in graduate support, and the end of the Health Research Facilities Act in 1968 signaled the onset of capital wasting. These two events have brought us to a very serious situation.

Of the developments just mentioned, the capital cost disease is surely the more worrisome. Its several ramifications include the following: (1) Graduate students and postdoctoral fellows in many fields of science are working under severe equipment constraints and are emerging from their student days less able than they should be to work at the most creative edge of their disciplines. (2) The vigor of the research effort itself is attenuated, as scientists either make do with what they have or spend more and more time searching for alternative ways to finance and equip their laboratories.

There are collateral problems as well. As deficiencies in the infrastructure for university research worsen, strains emerge in odd and unexpected places. For example, equipment and buildings once paid for by the government are now paid for by private sources instead; this change accounts for the most significant element in the recent rise in the indirect cost rates at major universities. Under the rules by which universities are reimbursed for research costs, depreciation and use charges on such facilities and equipment may be recovered through the indirect cost rate. At universities like Stanford, indirect costs associated with such capital facilities have been by far the fastest-rising component of that rate over the past decade. Because that argument has been set out in greater detail elsewhere,[1] I shall not pursue it here.

There are two major reasons for seeking to enhance and improve the linkages between the research university and industry. The first is the need to fill the void created when the government abandoned its support of capital facilities and major equipment in the research universities. Turning to another source of capital assistance when the one failed, many institutions have been developing new relationships with industry. The second reason is the need—now broadly perceived—to spread the process of technology transfer. While we have built a strong fundamental research base by establishing publicly supported basic science in the universities, many observers believe that our record for transferring discoveries from the laboratory bench into human service has been disappointing. It is hoped that new kinds of institutions built at universities with help from industry will improve technology transfer. At Stanford, we have used that argument in persuading 20 corporations to contribute $750,000 each to fund the Center for Integrated Systems, a research facility for the development of large-scale integrated microelectronic circuits. There are a number of other examples of such centers in biotechnology as well as in microelectronics.

These undertakings, engendered by the capital cost dilemma in the research universities as well as by impatience with the rate of technology transfer, are full of promise. Buy they also resurrect an old debate among those concerned with science policy—a debate concerned with the proper balance between discovery and application, that is, between quality and utility. The rest of this chapter returns to some of those considerations and reexamines them in light of the modern developments in university–industry relations.

THE QUALITY–UTILITY DEBATE

Most of us in the university sector have believed firmly that as long as quality is kept high, as long as principal investigators are decently supported and permitted to follow their own noses, quality will beget discovery, and utility will probably follow. That notion, sometimes called the Columbus theory of research, is actually much older than most people think it is. The eighteenth-century mathematician and physician d'Alembert says in the introduction to Diderot's *Encyclopedia of Science*: "Another motive serves to keep us at such work: utility, which, though it may not be the true aim, can at least serve as a pretext. The mere fact that we have occasionally found concrete advantages in certain fragments of knowledge, when they were hitherto unsuspected, authorizes us to regard all investigations begun out of pure curiosity as being potentially useful to us." He understood grantsmanship before there were grants.

Nowhere is the quality–utility issue more clearly encountered than in health research. In that sector, we have seen a rising political consciousness of the cost of curative medical technology and increasing impatience about the long diffusion time between well-advertised fundamental science breakthroughs and the availability of clinical benefits. Other important elements include a new—and growing—scientific focus on preventive health and the disciplines relevant to its practice, and the recent appearance of strong commercial incentives for the application of new discoveries in molecular genetics.

In 1976 the President's Panel on Biomedical Research, a group of scientists and medical administrators, presented President Ford with a report the Congress had commissioned two years earlier. Among its recommendations, the report strongly urged the continuation of federal funding for basic research in increasing amounts and with greater stability, arguing in a style perhaps best captured by the following example: "The remarkable science base of our nation . . . is an indispensable national resource; this science base provides the only social basis for learning how to prevent and control diseases."[2]

This part of the report was significant not because it was novel, but because the time was ripe for it to usher in a sharp debate over the strategy and social purposes of medical research. At hearings held in 1976 by the Senate Subcommittee on Health and Scientific Research, a parade of distinguished academicians testified on behalf of the report and its conclusions. But other witnesses with equally sound credentials presented a different view. Kerr White, an epidemiologist then at Johns Hopkins University, argued that the emphasis on the "science base" might be too heavy; he pointed to the need to apply existing knowledge more effectively in the health care system, especially in the interest of preventive health:

Are this country's academic medical centers to be concerned only with the provision of "advanced medical care" for the major diseases that are a small segment of the burden of illness? What about the other eighty percent of the ills that beset mankind? Who is to undertake the research, education and services that the public seem to demand or expect for these problems? On whose list of health problems are the behavioral and biomedical scientists of the country to work? Who draws up the list and on what is it to be based— the perceived needs of the public, the curiosity of the investigators, or a sensible balance between the two?[3]

The differences of interpretation that surfaced before the subcommittee presented the first serious challenge to a view of the utility of fundamental science that had dominated research policy in this country for three decades. The dichotomy of these views is captured in a brief passage from the hearing in which Senator Kennedy pressed the panel members on how funds should be allocated between basic and clinical research. He said to panel chairman Murphy:

In your page 3, you say: "The primary mission of the NIH as constituted today is fostering and supporting and conducting laboratory and clinical research to the ultimate end of better understanding of disease.'' The Public Health Service Act seems to describe the ultimate end of the work not to be better understanding of disease, but to be diagnosis, treatment, and control and prevention of disease. The Act, itself, is quite clear in this area.[4]

That fragment of history set the stage for a new political drama, one that could not have played a decade earlier when public faith in the capacity of science was still almost unrestricted. The failure of the War on Cancer began to erode public confidence in biomedical research, making it—for the first time—susceptible to political challenge.

The testimony also illustrates the different views of the state of science that were held by those having different relationships to it. Those who *do* science are, in general, convinced that it is damaged and made less effective by external direction. But, however impressive the accomplishments of unguided basic science, one searches in vain for objective support of the view that it "provides the only . . . basis for learning how to prevent and control diseases.'' In contrast, those who have specific institutional responsibilities to the health care system—especially through political roles—are apt to demand more accountability from research and to be concerned that it be managed to produce specific ends. The difference between these two views is widening and becoming more public.

CONSIDERATIONS IN FORMULATING RESEARCH POLICIES

The issue of the relationship between quality and utility in basic research is a difficult one, chiefly because it involves attempting to define policy for a realm of activity that no one understands. Science has produced enormous gains for this society, but even when we employ so restrictive a definition of scientific progress as to measure *only* intellectual (and not technological) outcomes, we have great difficulty in discovering what makes it work. For example, does progress depend primarily on the contributions of a few extraordinary individuals or is it the cumulative result of smaller efforts by a larger number of workers? Even so basic a question is hard to answer. The formal analysis of research productivity seems to show disproportionate contributions by a relatively small number of scientists, and the histories of disciplines always focus on a few giants.[5] But retrospective examinations of many modern advances reveal a complex web of precursor influences in which dozens of workers have played essential roles. I do not believe that it is possible at this time to generate a hypothesis about the distribution of significant work that would be of much use in formulating research policy.

Nor do we know how the presence of directive forces affects the research enterprise. Does utilitarian influence have a negative impact on quality? It is widely believed among basic researchers today that it does; but in the last century splendid science flourished under industrial sponsorship.

Indeed, we do not even understand much about what motivates scientists to do science. Is it the opportunity to provide some direct benefit to better the human condition? Is it the search for solutions to a major intellectual puzzle that impedes human understanding?

With so little knowledge about why scientists do science and about what kind of guidance for research will therefore work best, what principles can be brought to the design of research policies that optimize quality and utility? Obviously I cannot supply a fully formed strategy, but following are some questions that will be important in developing that strategy.

What Growth and Cost Features Must Be Considered?

Science is an extraordinary growth enterprise, and always has been—even when it was on tight rations. Well before the "golden age" of the 1960s, the rate of increase in the U.S. research and development budget was above 10 percent per year in real terms. For at least two centuries before that, the literature of science had been growing exponentially, at a rate of about 5 percent per year.[6]

Obviously, the commitment of new assets to science cannot indefinitely undergo proportional increases. But there are good reasons for believing that the growth rates we have observed are driven by more than the expansion of resource opportunities. Max Planck observed that "with every advance in science the difficulty of the task is increased"; not only are the easier problems solved first, but new discoveries generate new questions that are inherently more difficult—and more expensive—to answer. For a fixed unit of meaningful output, then, there is a steady increase in cost. This principle has been recognized, implicitly or explicitly, in every modern analysis of the status of the major scientific disciplines. Estimates of the real value of this escalation range from 3.5 to 7.5 percent per year.

Against that background, the "quality structure" of scientific production needs to be considered.[7] A relatively small number of scientists produce a disproportionately large share of the work, and an even smaller number dominate the quality statistics. When the entire enterprise is growing, the highest-quality results will increase at an inherently lower rate than the average for science as a whole.

Developing a national research strategy that took these forces into account would be a complicated business. It would require cognizance of complex interactions among size, cost, and growth rates; and, because the distribution of quality across participants in the enterprise changes with size, any formula developed for blending quality and quantity would have to change with growth.

How Is Quality To Be Recognized and Measured?

In the end, history—with the longest possible view—is the most reliable judge of scientific quality. But the policymaker is seldom in a position to take advantage of that perspective. The time of interest is the present and the future, and the past is useful only for its general lessons about how quality is recognized and about how to determine the level of quality of an individual work. The task of evaluating quality is made more difficult by our failure to agree on what criteria should be used in judging it. It is relatively easy, for example, to establish a consensus that a piece of work is elegant, but much harder to decide whether the problem itself or the avenue of approach is important.

One of the authentic successes of modern science policy is the process of peer review, in which—to employ the term literally—scientists examine and evaluate the research proposed by other scientists in their own quality cohort. Ironically, during the early days of "peer review," when it received the most active and enthusiastic support from the scientific community, the process probably did not fit that definition. Members of the early National Institutes of Health study sections and National Science Foundation panels were, for the most part, extraordinarily accomplished scientists, drawn from the very top of the quality spectrum; their judgments may have been respected in significant part because these scientists were viewed not as peers but as the very best. Now that peer review has become, more literally, review by peers, it is, perhaps not accidentally, being subjected to much sharper challenge from within the scientific community.

The populist criticism of peer review—that it reinforces tradition even when it is maladaptive to do so and leads to growth in elegance at the expense of both importance and utility—contains elements of truth. Nevertheless, some system of peer review is the only means the scientific enterprise has yet found that permits contemporary judgment of the quality of a particular piece of research—as opposed to the quality of the researcher, which can (at least in principle) be judged historically.

How Is Utility To Be Recognized and Measured?

We need to know much more than we do about how the research process works—in particular, about how different kinds of research interact and about what propositions and relations ought to be established between them. It is not easy, however, to distinguish "basic" research from the rest. Basic research is usually described as "seeking an understanding of the laws of nature without initial regard for utilitarian value" or as being undertaken "with no predetermined use in mind." In these and all other definitions of the term that I know, the intentions of the research play a significant role.

It is easy to recognize some important social values in such work. There is a value attached to increasing human understanding and dispelling ignorance. Extraordinary scientific accomplishments, irrespective of application, lift the imagination and provide important points of intellectual contact and consensus for societies that often have too little of both. Because research activity contributes to the intellectual skills of persons who are often doing other things (e.g., teaching) that have social utility of their own, the research may have "overhead" value.

Although all these arguments have been advanced as rationale for the social support of research, never has such an argument played a significant political role in determining this support. Instead, in this society and in all others like it, the allocation of public funds has been based on the prospective social utility of research outcomes. Thus, the accumulated result of research initiated by independent investigators is viewed as a "knowledge bank" against which society may draw for useful applications. It is in these terms that basic research has always had to justify itself—by showing, in effect, how quality begets utility. The traditional keystone of the argument for basic research is a version of the aforementioned Columbus theory: we must proceed on all possible fronts, because (to quote Derek Bok's argument for basic research) "it is so difficult to perceive in advance what particular knowledge will prove important to the solution of a particular practical problem."[8]

The difficulty is that, although the Columbus theory has widespread support, the evidence for it is almost entirely anecdotal—and usually concentrates on a very few historic examples. For a long time, it was accorded almost theological respect by the Congress, especially when offered by distinguished scientists; but, as indicated earlier, that attitude has changed.

Perhaps in response to the political harbingers of that change, there has been a growing tendency to cite more analytical or quantitative approaches. These are very few in number, but—despite conspicuous inadequacies—they have had a striking influence on the politics of research policy. The first was a 1969 study of weapons systems done by the Department of Defense in an effort to satisfy the Congress about the value of research and exploratory development. The study, called Project Hindsight, examined the development of 20 weapons systems and concluded that the critical events identified by the Department of Defense participants were primarily the result of work in applied areas having specific systems requirements as objectives.[9] The systems were not selected using criteria established in advance, nor was the evaluation of critical events done by persons unconcerned with the outcome of the study. The result nevertheless had an important impact on defense research policy in the late 1960s and early 1970s.

Comroe and Dripps, in an effort to improve the objectivity of such historical analyses, studied innovations in medicine that related to diseases accounting for over half the yearly deaths in the United States.[10] Groups of physicians and specialists nominated and then evaluated the top clinical advances in cardiovascular and pulmonary medicine and surgery in the preceding 30 years and selected 10; an independent group of consultants then identified the "bodies of knowledge" essential for their development. Finally, a bibliography of articles contributing to these advances was narrowed to 529 key papers that were then categorized by goal and type of research. About 62 percent of this underlying scientific work was classified as basic research, and in over 40 percent of the work there was no evidence of clinical interest on the part of the investigator at the time the research was done.

The Comroe-Dripps study contains a number of features that should be followed in the design of future evaluations of basic research. The sample of important advances is generated by practitioners, not by the investigators or people concerned with demonstrating a connection to research. An extraordinarily large sample of possible precursor events was examined, again by expert observers disinterested in the outcome. These ought to be the minimal standards for any such design. Further improvements could probably be made, but even without them the Comroe-Dripps design provides a means through which an objective assessment of the contribution of basic research to socially useful application can be judged. It deserves much wider application, but—probably because it is extremely expensive and time-consuming—it has scarcely been applied at all.

Are Commercial Incentives Good Devices for Generating Utility From Quality?

Whatever the status of the "science base" or "knowledge bank," it is clear from studies like the one by Comroe and Dripps that the time delay between laboratory discovery and first practical application is often disturbingly long. Both government agencies and the universities have been urged repeatedly to reduce such applications delays, and much recent legislative attention has been given to incentives of commercialization—including revisions of the tax treatment of industrial contributions to university research.

However laudable these efforts may have been, the emphasis on commercialization incentives is producing some farther-reaching institutional innovations that should be examined carefully for side effects. No more vivid example can be found than in the fevered corporate activity surrounding genetic technology.

To an unexpected degree, the commercial push behind that activity involves the scientists who are themselves responsible for the basic discoveries, and often the academic institutions to which they belong. That has raised problems both for the scientists and for their universities.

Most institutions retain the rights to patents resulting from inventions made by faculty on university-compensated time in university laboratories. A few places give these rights to the faculty member; usually, as at Stanford, incentives are created to encourage the reassignment of these rights to the university through individual patent agreements. The university may then license them, usually nonexclusively if federal funds also contributed to the support of the research. But neither tradition nor rules at most universities prevent the investigators from joining with others in a venture entirely outside the university—or the university from participating in that endeavor at the urging of the investigators. And, of course, individual scientists are also involved in less formal relationships with the commercial sector via consulting and collegial interaction, which may stimulate the movement of ideas from the laboratory toward application.

In the early phases of this new opportunity, most major research universities adopted institutional arrangements to help them support continuing research activity by retrieving some of the rewards generated by the successful efforts of their faculty in the laboratory. The arguments in favor of this position are strong: the financial return is there and someone is going to get it; the universities have sponsored the research and nurtured the climate in which it took place, so a share should go to them in order to replenish their capacity to do more; and donors and trustees, who characteristically press hard for sound and aggressive financial management, insist that legitimate sources of income for these purposes be tapped. The spectrum of possible institutional solutions, beginning with the simplest, could be represented as follows:

1. University as licenser, collecting royalties directly.

2. Separate corporation as licenser, developer, and supporter of research; no relation to university except through agreed sharing of royalty income.

3. Separate corporation as licenser, developer, and supporter of research; university faculty or administrators involved in governance.

4. Separate corporation as licenser, developer, and supporter of research; might also engage in final production. University faculty or administrators involved in governance; university has equity position.

Nearly every major research university has a patent office and is active at level 1. A number have proposed or helped form special institutions, like that at level 2, through which research support could be undertaken on a venture basis and royalty income received by the university. At level 3 a measure of university control is added through participation of university faculty members (the researchers) or administrators in the governance of the corporation. The latter's work would stop at the stage of development; there might be feasibility tests of production at the pilot-plant level, but no income related to product sales. At level 4 there is a full-fledged production company with university participation in equity.

Most universities have decided that levels 3 and 4 present problems of equity and conflict of interest that loom unacceptably large. But, particularly at level 2, there has been some interesting institutional innovation. For example, some nonprofit corporations have been created as independent research organizations with profit-making spin-offs, generating royalties that support basic research programs at one or a group of several universities. The governance of such entities can be clearly separated from that of the university or universities that benefit, so that real or perceived conflict of interest can be avoided.

In addition, consortium efforts by companies have increasingly recognized the desirability of supporting more applied research in on-campus locations. That recognition has given rise to such ventures as the Center for Integrated Systems at Stanford. The support of on-campus university research programs by corporations is also increasing, and research-intensive firms from the energy, chemical, and pharmaceutical industries have all established capital and program support for laboratories at research universities.

The combined impact of these new commercial incentives has been considerable. It has increased, though not by a great proportion, the total participation of private resources in fundamental research. It has provided some possible models for overcoming the impediments to rapid diffusion of basic research advances into human use. Thus, although I continue to worry about the variety of individual commercial arrangements being made by university scientists in biotechnology, I believe that most of the institutional responses to the new commercial incentives have been encouraging steps. Potentially, then, the answer to the question that opened this section—Are commercial incentives good devices for generating utility from quality? is a qualified yes.

CONCLUSION

In concluding, let me return to a point emphasized at the beginning of this chapter. The great strength of American basic science is the tight coupling of research and research training. The main threat posed by overemphasis on utility is to the integrity of that linkage: a set of utilitarian incentives can drain off the energies of the best scientists and sap the vigor of the university laboratories in which journeymen and apprentices work side by side at the bench. The universities should be especially vigilant guardians of the union between research and research training because they are its proprietors. But they are not its ultimate beneficiary; society is.

NOTES

1. Donald Kennedy, Government policies and the cost of doing research, *Science* 227(1985):480–484.
2. U.S. Department of Health, Education and Welfare, *President's Biomedical Research Panel Report*. Pub. No. (OS) 76–500 (Washington, D.C.: U.S. Government Printing Office, 1976).
3. *Basic Issues in Biomedical and Behavioral Research*, Hearings before the Subcommittee on Health and Scientific Research, Committee on Labor and Public Welfare, U.S. Senate, June 16 and 17, 1976. Committee Print, p. 161.

4. Ibid., p. 16.
5. A thorough account of this matter can be found in N. Rescher, *Scientific Progress* (Pittsburgh: University of Pittsburgh Press, 1978). Much of the original analysis is due to Derek J. de Solla Price.
6. Derek J. de Solla Price, *Science Since Babylon* (New Haven: Yale University Press, 1961).
7. Rescher, *Scientific Progress.*
8. Derek Bok, The critical role of basic research, *Advancement of Science and Technology* (Washington, D.C.: May 1976).
9. Office of the Director of Defense Research and Engineering, *Project Hindsight: Final Report* (Washington, D.C.: U.S. Department of Defense, 1969).
10. Julius H. Comroe, Jr., and Robert D. Dripps, Scientific approach to a national biomedical science policy, *Science* 192:(1976)105–111.

An Overview of Innovation

STEPHEN J. KLINE and NATHAN ROSENBERG

Models that depict innovation as a smooth, well-behaved linear process badly misspecify the nature and direction of the causal factors at work. Innovation is complex, uncertain, somewhat disorderly, and subject to changes of many sorts. Innovation is also difficult to measure and demands close coordination of adequate technical knowledge and excellent market judgment in order to satisfy economic, technological, and other types of constraints—all simultaneously. The process of innovation must be viewed as a series of changes in a complete system not only of hardware, but also of market environment, production facilities and knowledge, and the social contexts of the innovation organization.

INTRODUCTION

Commercial innovation* is controlled by two distinct sets of forces that interact with one another in subtle and unpredictable ways. On the one hand are the market forces, that is, such factors as changes in incomes, relative prices, and underlying demographics that combine to produce continual changes in commercial opportunities for specific categories of innovation. On the other hand, the forces of progress at the technological and scientific frontiers often suggest possibilities for fashioning new products, or improving the performance of old ones, or producing those products at lower cost. Successful outcomes in innovation thus require the running of two gauntlets: the commercial and the technological.

Since innovation, by definition, involves the creation and marketing of the new, these gauntlets, singly and in combination, make the outcome of innovation a highly uncertain process. Thus, an important and useful way to consider the process of innovation is as an exercise in the management

---

*We use the modifier "commercial" to indicate that in this chapter we exclude military innovations, which have certain distinctly different characteristics.

and reduction of uncertainty. Generally, the greater the changes introduced, the greater the uncertainty not only about technical performance but also about the market response and the ability of the organization to absorb and utilize the requisite changes effectively. This strong correlation between the amount of change and the degree of uncertainty has important implications for the nature of appropriate innovation under various states of knowledge and at various points in the life cycle of a given product.

The systems used in innovation processes are among the most complex known (both technically and socially), and the requirements for successful innovation vary greatly from case to case. Thus, a general discussion of innovation requires the exploration of a number of dimensions and the use of caution in deciding what can be generalized. Such a discussion must also make sure that the implicit models of the innovation process are adequate, since the use of simplistic models can seriously distort thinking. All of these matters will be dealt with, to some degree, in this chapter.

Within the technological realm it is possible to confine one's thinking exclusively to certain kinds of performance criteria. If one were indifferent to cost considerations, for example, one could devise a large number of technically feasible alternatives for improving the speed of an airplane, or the durability of an automobile, or the purity of a chemical. But technical success (or any purely mechanical measure of performance) is only a necessary and not a sufficient condition in establishing economic usefulness. Indeed, it is obvious from a casual examination of the proceedings in our bankruptcy courts that an excessive or exclusive preoccupation with purely technical measures of performance can be disastrous.

It is worth recalling that the overwhelming majority of the inventions recorded at the U.S. Patent Office were never introduced on a commercial basis. It is also worth recalling that, among more than 1,800 successful innovations tabulated by Marquis (in Tushman and Moore, 1982), almost three-quarters were reported as having been initiated as the result of perceived market needs and only one-quarter from perceived technical opportunity.

At the same time, many characteristics that would have important advantages in the marketplace cannot be realized because they cannot be achieved with current technical infrastructure or are barred by the workings of nature. For example, the laws of thermodynamics place an absolute limit on achievable efficiencies of machinery and on achievable fuel consumption of airplanes and automobiles. The limits of known metallurgical practice place a current feasible upper limit on the temperatures used in numerous machines and processes, and that limit yields only slowly under continuous scientific and developmental efforts. The accuracy of parts is controlled by the available manufacturing processes, and that in turn limits what can be made to work reliably at a given point in time.

As noted, both technical and market needs must be satisfied in a successful innovation. In innovation, one nearly always deals with the optimization of many demands and desiderata simultaneously. Successful innovation requires a design that balances the requirements of the new product and its manufacturing processes, the market needs, and the need to maintain an organization that can continue to support all these activities effectively.

If a technological improvement is to have a significant economic impact, it must combine design characteristics that will match closely with the needs and tastes of eventual users, and it must accomplish these things subject to basic constraints on cost (and frequently other, legally mandated requirements). Commercial success turns on the attainment either of cost levels that are below available substitutes or creation of a superior product at a cost that is at least not prohibitively expensive in comparison with lower-performance substitutes. Higher performance is commonly attainable at a higher price. However, to choose the optimal combination of price and performance at which a firm should aim calls for considerable knowledge of market conditions, as well as a high order of business judgment in making decisions with respect to timing. Success demands not only selecting the right cost and performance combination, but also judging just when the timing is right for the product's introduction.

In the early 1950s, the British introduced a commercial jet (the Comet I) two years or so before the United States did. Yet the American entries quickly won the competition because of substantial performance improvements that became available shortly after Comet I made its commercial appearance. Moreover, of America's two initial entries into the field of commercial jets— Boeing's 707 and Douglas's DC-8—the 707 emerged as the more successful. In part this was due to the fact that Boeing entered the market earlier; but perhaps even more important was the speed with which Boeing corrected some initial misjudgments about the optimal size and range requirements of the new aircraft. Attention to and prompt action on "feedback signals" from users are an important, often critical, part of innovation. This point will be discussed in a more general context below.

More recently, the aircraft industry offers another important example of how excessive preoccupation with purely technical performance characteristics can be a recipe for financial disaster. The Concorde is a brilliant engineering achievement, but also a very costly commercial failure. Although it can indeed cross the Atlantic in about half the time required by a 747, its fuel costs per passenger mile are at least 15 times as great.

Solar energy is another example. It has many attractive characteristics, and at least its share of articulate spokesmen, but it is unlikely to be widely adopted in electric power generation until it at least approaches the cost of other sources. At present that would require an order-of-magnitude reduction in solar costs.

These observations are intended to suggest how closely intertwined the technological and economic realms are in determining the success of a technological innovation. One might therefore expect to find numerous treatments of these technological and economic interrelationships in the economics literature. Unfortunately, such treatments are very rare.

These observations are also intended to suggest the hazards and pitfalls that may be involved in invoking the wrong criteria for success in judging the significance of an innovation. Potential consumers may not attach a sufficiently great value to the superior performance of a highly sophisticated new technology—the number of people prepared to pay a premium of several hundreds of dollars for shortening a transatlantic flight by a few hours turned out to be rather small. Even that innovator par excellence, Thomas Edison, failed this test with his first invention. He created a machine that would tally votes in the Congress, essentially instantaneously, only to be told by several congressmen that it was the last thing they wanted. As a result, Edison wrote in his journal a resolution never again to spend time on an invention until he was sure a sound market was in prospect.

In a different dimension, it is a serious mistake (increasingly common in societies that have a growing preoccupation with high technology industries) to equate economically important innovations with that subset associated with sophisticated technologies. One of the most significant productivity improvements in the transport sector since World War II has derived from an innovation of almost embarrassing technological simplicity—containerization. Although it has brought in its wake very substantial reductions in labor-handling costs, that particular innovation required only easily understood modifications of ship designs and dockside equipment; the primary barrier was resistance from the unions. This particular form of resistance illustrates another point. The operating systems of concern in innovation are not purely technical in nature; they are rather strongly intertwined combinations of the social and the technical—"sociotechnical systems" is a useful descriptor and a useful way to think about such institutions.

Both points are important. Technological sophistication is not something that is intrinsically valued in the marketplace. Major sources of cost reduction are so valued, regardless of their technical source or degree of sophistication. And one ignores the social aspects of the operating systems at no less peril than the technical.

Economists have, by and large, analyzed technological innovation as a "black box"—a system containing unknown components and processes. They have attempted to identify and measure the main inputs that enter that black box, and they have, with much greater difficulty, attempted to identify and measure the output emanating from that box. However, they have devoted very little attention to what actually goes on inside the box; they have largely neglected the highly complex processes through which certain inputs are transformed into certain outputs (in this case, new technologies).

Technologists, on the other hand, have been largely preoccupied with the technical processes that occur inside that box. They have too often neglected, or even ignored, both the market forces within which the product must operate and the institutional effects required to create the requisite adjustments to innovation.

The purpose of this chapter is to peer into that black box and to examine the nature of the technological transformation process, but without losing sight of the external forces of the marketplace or the importance of the internal requirements of the institution making the innovation. There is no need to belabor the point that technological innovation is absolutely central to economic growth and to improvements in efficiency. If there is any residual doubt, one need only think back 100 years to 1885 and ask, "Would any commercial firm operating as it did then survive in today's economy?" The relevant questions are not whether innovation is necessary to increases in efficiency or for survival, but rather: What kind of innovations? At what speed? And, can we understand the nature of innovation more fully in order to employ it more effectively and beneficially?

CHARACTERIZATION OF INNOVATION

Unfortunately, the effects of innovation are hard to measure. There is no single, simple dimensionality to innovation. There are, rather, many sorts of dimensions covering a variety of activities. We might think of innovation as a new product, but it may also be

- a new process of production;
- the substitution of a cheaper material, newly developed for a given task, in an essentially unaltered product;
- the reorganization of production, internal functions, or distribution arrangements leading to increased efficiency, better support for a given product, or lower costs; or
- an improvement in instruments or methods of doing innovation.

A principal point of this chapter is that the transformation process is one that, inescapably, intertwines technological and economic considerations. Another is that the processes and systems used are complex and variable; that there is no single correct formula, but rather a complex of different ideas and solutions that are needed for effective innovation. A third is that these complexities make innovation hard to measure effectively. These themes are addressed below from several different vantage points.

It is product changes that make innovation so difficult to treat in a rigorous way. For it is often extremely difficult to measure the economic significance of product innovations or product modification. In the absence of widely accepted measures, there is no obvious way of metering the output of the technological black box.

A beginning of progress might be the explicit recognition that there are many black boxes rather than just one. This is important in three respects. First, the nature of the market problems and constraints that have to be confronted and, as a result, the manner in which innovations are generated differ significantly from one industry to another. Second, the state of knowledge in the relevant science and technology varies from industry to industry and from firm to firm. Third, the nature and the potential profitability of the output of the black box also differ very much among industries at any given time. As a result, pouring equal incremental inputs into the black boxes of randomly selected industries—A, B, C, and D—may be expected to involve very different kinds of R&D activities and to yield very different rates of return on the resources so invested.

There is evidence that the social and private rates of return on innovations are quite high. Mansfield et al. (1977), in a study of 17 innovations, conservatively estimated the median social rate of return at about 56 percent. The median private rate of return was a good deal lower—about 25 percent before taxes.

There is a further critical aspect of the innovation process that is not illuminated by the black-box approach. That is, innovations will often generate benefits far from the industries in which they originated. It turns out to be extraordinarily difficult to "map" the costs and benefits of many innovations within any single framework of industrial classification. An industry that is thought of as being highly traditional and technologically conservative—the clothing industry—is currently absorbing a number of innovations from electronics, laser technology, and chemistry. Innovations in metallurgy (or other basic materials) will find beneficiaries at many places on the industrial map. The most important advances in machine tools in recent decades have come from joining the tools to digital computers. Indeed, few sectors of the economy have been totally unaffected by the advent of the computer and the associated huge expansion in information-processing capabilities. The computer is a general-purpose, information-processing tool, and thus it provides a service that is required, in varying degrees, in nearly all sectors of the economy. Computers have radically altered both the way this chapter was written and the printing processes used to reproduce it compared with what would have been done only a decade ago. Not the least important of computer-induced changes in the context of this chapter has been in the research process itself. The R&D processes that are a central feature of research have themselves been enormously affected by the advent of the computer, and these changes are not yet nearly completed.

If we focus on a single industry, such as air transport, we can readily identify a diversity of sources of innovation coming into that sector. Many improvements in aircraft design are internally generated by aeronautical engineers, drawing on advances in aeronautical knowledge and more specific design data of the sort made available from component and wind-tunnel testing. It is important to note that neither of these kinds of tests is science in the usual sense of the word, nor would they usually have been done by scientists. Nevertheless, they are often essential parts of the development work in innovations (and hence an integral part of engineering). The point is that innovation often demands the gathering and storing of types of information different from those obtained by scientists, and these different processes very frequently require the development of independent methodologies, theories, test procedures, codes, and the like—all of which become integral parts of engineering and production knowledge. Three excellent examples illustrating types of "engineering knowledge" that are not science, as usually defined, are given by Vincenti (1979, 1982, 1984), one in the realm of performance testing, one in shop processes, and one in analytical methodology.

Both the industrial sectors already cited—metallurgy and computers—have also served as essential sources of technological improvement to air transport. Metallurgical improvements have been a continual source of weight reduction and greater strength, leading directly to improvements in aircraft performance, both airframes and engines. More recently, the advent of new materials, particularly synthetics, offers great promise for further improvements in similar directions. The computer has drastically changed the industry in numerous ways: in cockpit control of the aircraft; in rapid determination of optimal flight paths; and in the instantaneous, worldwide reservation system. The revolutionary changes in electronics in the past generation have been so extensively incorporated into aircraft that "avionics" now constitutes a large fraction of the total manufacturing cost of an airplane.

Another aspect of innovation that makes it hard to measure is the effects of a rapidly expanding industry on its suppliers. A rapidly expanding industry nearly always generates an increased demand on other industries that produce intermediate components and materials for it. This increased demand will often stimulate more rapid rates of technical change in those supplier industries. Thus, the rapid growth of the automobile industry in the early twentieth century served as a powerful stimulant for the development of new methods of petroleum refining. (It is worth remembering that the petroleum industry antedates the automobile by several decades; but, in the late nineteenth century, before the advent of the automobile, petroleum was a source of illumination, not power. Petroleum became an important source of power only with the invention of internal-combustion engines.) In the twentieth century, the voracious demands of the automobile industry have raised the profitability and, presumably, the number of inventions, in several industries producing automobile inputs—not only petroleum but glass, rubber, steel, and plastics as well.

As noted, the impact of a technological innovation is often difficult to trace because those impacts do not always fall neatly within well-defined industry boundary lines. Sometimes, in fact, the effect of technological change may be to bring about a drastic redrawing of the previously existing boundary lines. Twenty years ago it was possible to draw clear boundary lines between the telecommunications industry and the computer industry. These lines, however, have already been blurred, and may well be dissolved, by ongoing technological changes associated with the advent of the microchip. The microchip revolution and the growing information-processing needs of business are converting computers into forms that increasingly resemble telecommunications networks, while the telephone system can already be viewed as a type of gigantic computer. As a simple piece of evidence, consider that a busy signal today may mean something very different from what it would have meant 20 years ago.

As already noted also, innovations have no obvious or uniform dimensionality. There is no generally agreed way of measuring their importance or impact. This affects our perception of the innovation process in two significant ways.

First, there is a tendency to identify technological innovation with major innovations of a highly visible sort—electric power, automobiles, airplanes, television, antibiotics, computers, and so on. There is no reason to complain about an interest in highly visible innovations—unless this leads to a neglect of other important aspects of the innovation process that happen to be less visible. The fact is that much technological change is of a less visible and even, in many cases, an almost invisible sort. A large part of the technological innovation that is carried out in industrial societies takes the form of very small changes, such as minor modifications in the design of a machine that will enable it to serve certain highly specific end-uses better, or that make it easier and therefore cheaper to manufacture; or improving the performance characteristics of a machine by introducing a harder metal, or a new alloy with a higher melting point; or by slight engineering changes that economize on some raw-material requirement, or simply substitute a cheaper material for a more expensive one where possible; or by a design change that reduces friction or vibration and therefore increases the useful life of a machine; or by a mere rearrangement of the sequence of operations, or location of operations, in a plant—such as has occurred in the steel industry—in a way that economizes on fuel inputs by eliminating the need for the frequent reheating of materials—as in the integrated steel mill or continuous casting. A large part of technological innovation is of such kinds, highly inconspicuous to everyone except a technical specialist, and often not even to him or her.

Consider what has happened in electric power generation. Electric power generation has had one of the very highest rates of growth of total factor productivity in the twentieth century. However, no sudden major changes in product or process have occurred in this century. Nevertheless, slow, cumulative improvements in the efficiency of centralized thermal power plants have generated enormous long-term increases in fuel economy. A stream of minor plant improvements have combined to raise energy output sharply per unit of input. These include the steady rise in operating temperatures and pressures made possible by metallurgical improvements, such as new alloy steels; the increasing sophistication of boiler design; the increase in turbine efficiency; and the addition of such components as feedwater heaters and stack economizers. The size of this improvement may be indicated as follows: it required 7 pounds of coal to generate a kilowatt-hour of electricity in 1910; the same amount of electricity could be generated by less than nine-tenths of a pound of coal in the 1960s. Yet, most people would be hard-pressed to identify any of the specific innovations that lay behind this great improvement in productivity.

Second, it is a serious mistake to treat an innovation as if it were a well-defined, homogeneous thing that could be identified as entering the economy at a precise date—or becoming available at a precise point in time. That view is, of course, encouraged by the Patent Office as well as by writers of high school history texts. But inventions as economic entities are very different from inventions as legal entities. The fact is that most important innovations go through rather drastic changes over their lifetimes—changes that may, and often do, totally transform their economic significance. The subsequent improvements in an invention after its first introduction may be vastly more important, economically, than the initial availability of the invention in its original form.

There is quantitative confirmation of this point in a careful study of technical progress in the petroleum-refining industry in the twentieth century. John Enos (1958) examined the introduction of four major new processes in the petroleum-refining industry: thermal cracking, polymerization, catalytic cracking, and catalytic reforming. In measuring the benefits for each new process he distinguished between the "alpha phase" (or the cost reductions that occurred when the new process was first introduced) and the "beta phase" (or cost reductions flowing from the subsequent improvement in the new process). Enos found that the average annual cost reduction generated by the beta phase of each of these innovations considerably exceeded the average annual cost reduction generated by the alpha phase (4.5 percent compared with 1.5 percent). On this basis he concluded: "The evidence from the petroleum-refining industry indicates that improving a process contributes even more to technological progress than does its initial development" (Enos, 1958:180).

A very similar kind of experience could be found in many industries. The fact is that inventions, in their early stages, are typically very crude and primitive and do not even begin to approach the performance characteristics or productivity levels that are attained later on. Consider the performance characteristics of the telephone around 1880; the automobile, vintage 1900; or the airplane when the Wright Brothers achieved their first heavier-than-air flight in 1903—in that form, at best a frail and economically worthless novelty. Or consider the computer around 1950. In innovation after innovation it is the subsequent improvement process, within the framework of an initial innovation, that transforms a mere novelty to a device of great economic significance. There are many instances in which the learning associated with cumulative production of a given item reduced costs by a factor of two or three, including airline costs per passenger-seat mile, automobiles, and industrial chemicals. In the instance of electric light bulbs and semiconductor components, the cost reductions have been more than five to one. There is little doubt that other products and services would show similar trends if data were available in appropriate form.

But whether an innovation will in fact be introduced, and whether it will even be deemed worthwhile to spend money on its improvement, depend not only on its own cost and performance characteristics, but on the range of available alternatives. Once again, the ultimate criterion is economic. For example, synthetic rubber was known to be technically feasible for a long time. The basic scientific research needed to make synthetic rubber had been largely completed before the outbreak of World War I. However, so long as natural rubber was available at low cost, as it was during the interwar years, the commercial prospects for synthetic rubber were extremely dim. Synthetic rubber became economically significant when wartime circumstances sharply reduced the supply of natural rubber, raised natural rubber prices, and created a strategic crisis. These effects drastically improved the prospects for the synthetic product. Until the special conditions generated by World War II, synthetic rubber simply constituted an economically inferior technology, and it deserved to be neglected. It is also worth noting that, once the investment in the development of synthetic rubber had been made, for wartime purposes, and the unit cost reduced along the learning curve of cumulative production, a stable market did develop within the peacetime economy in many applications. This also illustrates the different priorities between the military and commercial sectors. Military developments hinge primarily on performance, including strategic questions of supply. Commercial developments hinge primarily on economic criteria. But the subsidization of development for military reasons can, and has in several very important instances, reduced commercial costs to the point that firms will develop the product. As noted by Nelson (1982), this list includes not only synthetic rubber but also jet aircraft, semiconductor manufacturing processes, and the computer.

Thus, there is no necessary reason why new technologies should replace old ones merely by virtue of their newness. Newness is not, by itself, an economic advantage. Old technologies will often persist, even in the face of new technologies that appear to offer decisive advantages, because the old technologies retain advantages in particular locations, because the old technologies remain competitive due to access to certain low-cost resource inputs, or simply because of persistent performance advantages in certain specific uses. Old technologies are often also spurred into new phases of improved performance through innovations by the arrival of a new competitor. Water power thrived as a source of industrial power in the United States more than a century after James Watt introduced his improved steam engine, and still thrives today, in far more efficient forms, in certain situations. Roughly a third of the electric power supplied in the network at Stanford University is from water power—Pacific Gas and Electric happens to have the highest ratio in the United States currently. Even today vacuum tubes have not been completely displaced by semiconductors. They remain indispensable, for example, for some power transmission purposes. A useful and instructive study of the race between two different products in modern times that covers a number of points we have omitted here for space reasons is the discussion of the origins of the aircraft turbojet engine by Constant (1980).

MODELS OF INNOVATION

There have been a number of attempts in recent years to impose some sort of conceptual order on the innovation process, with the purpose of understanding it better and providing a more secure basis for policy formulation. Unfortunately such attempts, often by scientists and by spokesmen for the scientific community, misrepresent the innovation process by depicting it as a smooth, well-behaved linear process. Such exercises badly misspecify the nature and the direction of the causal factors at work.

We have already seen that innovation is neither smooth nor linear, nor often well-behaved. Rather, it is complex, variegated, and hard to measure. We have also seen that there is a need for an adequate and understandable model on which to base our thinking. Before introducing an improved model that should assist us in thinking more clearly about innovation, this section first describes the model embodied in the conventional wisdom and discusses its shortcomings.

The Linear Model

The generally accepted model of innovation since World War II has been what a few authors have called "the linear model." In this model, one does research, research then leads to development, development to production, and production to marketing. These events are implicitly visualized as flowing smoothly down a one-way street, much as if they were the "begats" of the

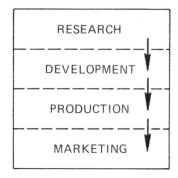

FIGURE 1   The conventional "linear model" of the linkage of research to production.

Bible. A sketch of this model is given in Figure 1. The linear model distorts the reality of innovation in several ways, and most serious students of innovation have now come to recognize those distortions. However, improved models have not yet come into widespread use. Consequently, the linear model is still often invoked in current discussions, particularly in political discussions. This continued use should not surprise us, since, as Thomas Kuhn (1967) has argued, we do not abandon a model for thinking about a complex situation until we have a better model to put in its place.

In the linear model, there are no feedback paths within the ongoing work of development processes. Nor are there feedbacks from sales figures or from individual users. But all these forms of feedback are essential to evaluation of performance, to formulation of the next steps forward, and to assessment of competitive position. Feedbacks are an inherent part of development processes as we have already illustrated above.

In an ideal world of omniscient technical people, one would get the design of the innovation workable and optimized the first time. In the real world of inadequate information, high uncertainty, and fallible people, nothing like this happens. Shortcomings and failures are part of the learning process that creates innovation of every kind. Innovation accordingly demands feedback, and effective innovation demands rapid, accurate feedback with appropriate follow-on actions. Radical, or revolutionary, innovation prospers best when provided with multiple sources of informational input. Ordinary, or evolutionary, innovation requires iterative fitting and trimming of the many necessary criteria and desiderata. In either case, feedbacks and trials are essential.

Another difficulty with the linear model flows from the fact that the central process of innovation is not science but design. A design in some form is essential to initiating technical innovations, and redesigns are essential to ultimate success, for the reasons just stated concerning the need for several types of feedbacks. The problems that are thrown up by the processes of designing and testing new products and new processes often spawn research—true science—and have in some instances even given rise to new branches of mathematics. Moreover, science often is dependent, in an absolute sense, on technological products and processes for its advances. Over the course of history thus far, it is moot whether science has depended more on technological processes and products than innovation has depended on science. Much of the pressure to create new materials is the result of direct feedback on problems encountered in creating such devices as steam turbines, jet engines, combustors, semiconductors, solar energy cells, and numerous other products. In his work on the electric lighting system, Edison was forced by the needs of the system to pay a mathematician to work out the analysis of the parallel circuit—despite Edison's often-expressed contempt for scientists and mathematicians. The parallel circuit is an advance so basic that, without it, electrical engineering as we know it today is unthinkable. In the process of solving problems of the flow over wings, L. Prandtl was forced to invent a mode of analysis that later gave rise to a whole branch of mathematics—today called asymptotic perturbation theory. These examples are not isolated ones; there are many others.

Thus, in a complete picture we must recognize not only that innovation draws on science, but also that the demands of innovation often force the creation of science. As we all know, the interactions of science and technology in the modern world are very strong. But this should not lead us to accept the common wisdom that "technology is merely applied science," for, if we do, our thinking about innovation will forever remain muddled. The illustrations just given, showing that innovation often creates science and the need for feedback, ought to be enough, in themselves, to warn that something is wrong, but they are only some of the reasons for rejecting the simplistic formulation of the linear model.

The idea that innovation is merely applied science is so firmly entrenched and has been so often repeated that it is worth a few sentences to define science, so that we can see its important but limited role more clearly. For our purposes, we can take science to be "the creation, discovery, verification, collation, reorganization, and dissemination of knowledge about physical, biological, and social nature." The two main components of science that affect innovation are (1) the current totality of stored human knowledge about nature and (2) the processes by which we correct and add to that knowledge. The new additions and corrections to science each year that constitute current research are but a small part of the whole. And it is the whole of our knowledge about nature that we bring to bear, insofar as we can, when we confront a problem in innovation. The idea that we could do important innovation with this year's and last year's science as the only input is ludicrous when examined in any depth whatsoever. The design of nearly any new modern system without the accumulated knowledge in mechanics, kinematics and orthographic projection, electromagnetism, or thermodynamics is essentially impossible. And, in many instances, this list must be enlarged to include biology, chemistry, quantum mechanics, optics, biochemistry, and so on. Science is by no means unimportant, but what we need to recognize clearly is that most innovation is done with the available knowledge already in the heads of the people in the organization doing the work, and, to a lesser extent, with other information readily accessible to them. It is only when those sources of information fall short of solving the problem that there is a need for research in order to complete a given innovation.

Thus, the notion that innovation is initiated by research is wrong most of the time. There are a few instances in which research sparks innovation, and these are often important, revolutionary innovations, as in semiconductors, lasers, and current genetic developments; but, even then, the innovation must pass through a design stage and must be coupled to market needs if it is to reach completion. And, as noted above, the invention, or alpha, stage almost always has small economic impact; the innovation must nearly always also pass through a number of "add-on," or beta, phases before it has large economic consequences. Moreover, the beta-stage work may involve little or no science. It will be done utilizing primarily what the people in the innovating organization already know, not only about science, but also about the infrastructure of the technologies of their time, the way their own organization works, and the nature of the ultimate market to the extent it is known.

Even more important, from the viewpoint of understanding innovation, is the recognition that when the science is inadequate, or even totally lacking, we still can, do, and often have created important innovations, and innumerable smaller, but cumulatively important evolutionary changes. Recently, a member of the National Academy of Engineering, highly versed in dynamics and control, attempted to analyze the stability of an ordinary bicycle with a rider—and failed. No acceptable analysis is known. But this lack of theory did not prevent the invention of the bicycle a century ago, nor did it prevent a multitude of beta-phase improvements in bicycle design that have cumulatively created a reliable, relatively inexpensive, and useful machine. Nor does the absence of understanding of the theory of stability prevent a 5-year-old child from mounting a bicycle and with a few tries learning to stabilize the human–machine system. Had the idea been true that science is the initiating step in innovation, we would never have invented the bicycle.

In addition to these shortcomings, the linear model shortchanges the importance of the process innovations that play a crucial role via learning during continued production. Many examples have been cited in this chapter that illustrate the reality of this process of learning through cumulated experience in production of a stable product.

In sum, if we are to think clearly about innovation, we have no choice but to abandon the linear model. What then do we put in its place?

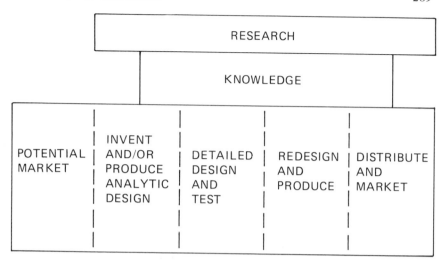

FIGURE 2   Elements of the "chain-linked model" for the relationships among research, invention, innovation, and production.

The Chain-Linked Model

One possible alternative to the linear model, called the "chain-linked model," is shown in Figures 2 and 3. A more detailed discussion of this model is given by Kline (1985). Figure 2 shows the elements in the chain-linked model. In this model of innovation there is not one major path of activity, but five. Some discussion of each of these paths follows.

The first path of innovation processes (see Figure 3) is called the central-chain-of-innovation. It is indicated by the arrows labeled "C." The path begins with a design and continues through development and production to marketing. It is important to note immediately that the second path is a series of feedback links marked "f" and "F" in Figure 3. These feedback paths iterate the steps and also connect back directly from perceived market needs and users to potentials for improvement of product and service performance in the next round of design. In this sense, feedback is part of the cooperation between the product specification, product development, production processes, marketing, and service components of a product line. H. W. Coover (in this volume) makes the same point forcefully in terms of a clear example and its effects in one company. This point will be raised again in the discussion of the implications of the chain-linked model.

A perceived market need will be filled only if the technical problems can be solved, and a perceived performance gain will be put into use only if there is a realizable market use. Arguments about the importance of "market

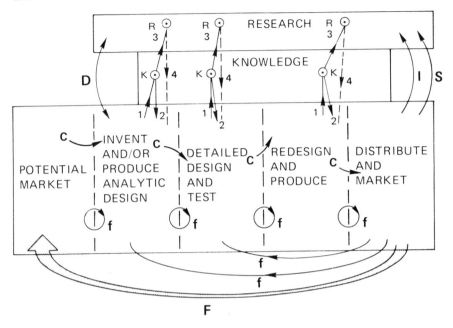

FIGURE 3   Chain-linked model showing flow paths of information and cooperation. Symbols on arrows: **C** = central-chain-of-innovation; **f** = feedback loops; **F** = particularly important feedback.

K–R: Links through knowledge to research and return paths. If problem solved at node K, link 3 to R not activated. Return from research (link 4) is problematic—therefore dashed line.

  D: Direct link to and from research from problems in invention and design.

   I: Support of scientific research by instruments, machines, tools, and procedures of technology.

  S: Support of research in sciences underlying product area to gain information directly and by monitoring outside work. The information obtained may apply anywhere along the chain.

pull'' versus ''technology push'' are in this sense artificial, since each market need entering the innovation cycle leads in time to a new design, and every successful new design, in time, leads to new market conditions.

   We have already seen that modern innovation is often impossible without the accumulated knowledge of science and that explicit development work often points up the need for research, that is, new science. Thus the linkage from science to innovation is not solely or even preponderantly at the beginning of typical innovations, but rather extends all through the process—science can be visualized as lying alongside development processes, to be used when needed. This linkage alongside the central-chain-of-innovation, the third path, is shown in Figure 3 by arrow "D" and links "K–R," and is the reason for the name "chain-linked model."

A much clearer view of innovation is obtained when we understand not only that the linkage to science lies alongside development processes, but also that the use of science occurs in two stages corresponding to the two major parts of science delineated in the definition of science given above. When we confront a problem in technical innovation, we call first on known science, stored knowledge, and we do so in serial stages. Only when all stages fail to supply the needed information, as often happens, is a call for the second part of science, research, needed and justified.

A current, real illustration may help make the processes clear. Suppose you want to innovate an improved carburetion-induction system for a spark-ignition automobile engine—one that will run very lean in order to give improved mileage and reduce pollution. To reach this goal, you must achieve mixing of the fuel and air to the molecule-to-molecule level—something that conventional carburetion systems fail to do by a wide margin. This in turn requires an intimate knowledge of turbulent mixing processes in fluid flow. To do this job, you first ask, "Do I know a current device that will do the job?" The answer initially is, "No!" Next, you ask knowledgeable colleagues. Then you look in the literature and again find no suitable answer. Finally, you go to experts in the field and discuss what is known and what might be done. If the experts also fail to provide an answer, then and only then should you initiate research or development work to solve the problem. In the instance of the carburetion system, the R&D work has recently been done and patented by M. R. Showalter. The underlying science that will provide a firm data base for optimizing the devices does not yet exist, but is in fact suggested in current proposals by one of the authors for government-supported research. Assuming that this research is successful, the results will allow more rapid, accurate, and optimal designs, but only some years hence, since that is the time required for such research.

In sum, the use of the accumulated knowledge called modern science is essential to modern innovation; it is a necessary and often crucial part of technical innovation, but it is not usually the initiating step. It is rather employed at all points along the central-chain-of-innovation, as needed. It is only when this knowledge fails, from all known sources, that we resort to the much more costly and time-consuming process of mission-oriented research to solve the problems of a specific development task.

It is also important to note that the type of science that is typically needed is different at various stages in the central-chain-of-innovation. The science needed at the first stage (design or invention) is often pure, long-range science that is indistinguishable from pure academic science in the relevant discipline. The research generated in the development stage is more often of a systems nature and concerns analysis of how the components of the system interact and of the "holistic" or system properties that are generated when the components of the product envisaged are hooked together to obtain the complete function needed. For example, in a design of a new airplane, steam power plant, or computer, an important consideration will be the stability of the system as a whole when the various new components are put together into a single operating entity—a system. The research that is spawned in the production stage is more often process research: studies of how particular components can be manufactured and how the cost of manufacture can be reduced by improved special machinery or processes or by use of improved or less expensive materials. It is worth noting that, in industries concerned with production of materials for sale to end-producers of goods (for example, steel, rubber, semiconductor silicon), nearly the only technical innovations that bear on profit are process innovations. We do not ordinarily think of process innovations or of system analyses as science, but in many cases they are just as surely research as is the purest of pure science. Moreover, if we are concerned with commercial success, systems and process research not only are necessary ingredients but often play a more important role than science in cost reduction and improved system performance. All these matters are explicit in the chain-linked model, but missing from the linear model.

Adoption of the improved carburetion-induction system recently developed by M. R. Showalter, which offers the potential for major gains in mileage, in pollution control, in the variety of usable fuels, and in reduced cost of production compared with current equivalent systems, is meeting with very great resistance from U.S. auto companies. Such resistance is common and plays an important role in the complete picture of innovation processes. However, analysis of the sources of such resistance would take us too far afield in this chapter.

What is the nature of the designs that initiate innovations? Historically, they have been of two types, "invention" and "analytic design." The notion of invention is generally familiar; an invention is a new means for achieving some function not obvious beforehand to someone skilled in the prior art. It therefore marks a significant departure from past practice. Analytic design, on the other hand, is currently a routine practice on the part of engineers but is little understood by the public at large. It consists of analysis of various arrangements of existing components or of modifications of designs already within the state of the art to accomplish new tasks or to accomplish old tasks more effectively or at lower cost. It is thus not invention in the usual sense. However, analytic design is currently a more common initiator of the central-chain-of-innovation than invention. Given the advent of digital computers, much more can be done via analytic design than in the past, and this form of initiation of the technical parts of innovation will likely play an increasing role in the future. Given current computer capabilities and current trends in computer-aided design/computer-aided manufacturing (CAD/CAM), plus increasing capabilities to model physical processes accurately and to locate optima, it is nearly certain that we will see in the coming decades a merging of analytic design and invention that will constitute a more powerful method for initiating technical innovations than anything we have known in the past. This merging will not happen suddenly, and it is hard at this stage to predict how far and how fast it will go. But it has already commenced, and firms that can utilize it effectively may well be able to create competitive advantages.

The discussion thus far has described three of the five paths in the chain-linked model of innovation. The remaining two need only brief discussion.

First, as already noted, new science does sometimes make possible radical innovations (indicated by arrow "D" in Figure 3). These occurrences are rare, but often mark major changes that create whole new industries, and they should therefore not be left from consideration. Recent examples include semiconductors, lasers, atom bombs, and genetic engineering.

The last path, marked by arrow "I" in Figure 3, is the feedback from innovation, or more precisely from the products of innovations, to science. This pathway has been very important in the past and remains so even today. (For example, see "How Exogeneous Is Science?" in Rosenberg (1982), or Price (1984).) Without the microscope, one does not have the work of Pasteur, and without that work there is no modern medicine. Without the telescope, we would not have the work of Galileo, and without that work we would not have modern astronomy and cosmology, nor would space exploration with its various innovations have been possible. It is probable also that without Galileo's work we would not have had what we now call elementary mechanics until a much later date, and perhaps not at all. Hence the many sciences now built on elementary mechanics would also have been at best delayed. The whole course of what we know about physical nature would have developed differently. Nor has this support of science by technological products ended. Current examples include the CAT (computerized axial tomography) scanner and the BEAM (brain electrical activity mapping) electroencephalogram apparatus, which seem likely to open whole new realms of medicine and psychology. The use of the digital computer in the laboratory and in modeling difficult problems, such as turbulence, is opening new vistas in physical science. And these are only a few examples among many.

In sum, any view of the technical aspects of innovation that suggests a single, central path for innovation, or that science plays the central initiating role, is far too simple and is bound to inhibit and distort our thinking about the nature and use of processes of innovation. The chain-linked model, though a considerable improvement, is only a top-level model and therefore omits many of the details and the rich variety inherent in the totality of innovations processes in current times. The chain-linked model, however, does seem sufficient to help point up a number of conclusions.

UNCERTAINTY IN INNOVATION

In order to see clearly the conclusions that flow from the chain-linked model, it is useful to return to several points made at the beginning of this chapter. First, the central dimension that organizes innovation, if there is one, is uncertainty. By definition, innovation implies creating the new, and the new contains elements that we do not comprehend at the beginning and about which we are uncertain. Moreover, the degree of uncertainty is strongly correlated with the amount of advance that we propose in a given innovation.

It is quite useful to think of the total range of innovations as extending continuously from those that involve almost no uncertainty to those that involve very great uncertainty. At one end we have the small, evolutionary change; we may decide to change the color of paint we use on automobiles. There is virtually no uncertainty in changing the color of paint, but it may nevertheless have important commercial consequences; it was an important ingredient of the competitive advantage in the market that General Motors created to overcome the initial lead of Ford in the 1920s. At the other end of the spectrum, we may need to make a revolutionary change. We may want to do an entirely new job, or use an entirely new product for an old job—we may want to send a man to the moon, or develop a low-cost, solid-state amplifier, to take two examples from modern times. Here the uncertainty will be very high and the initial costs of development so great that no single commercial firm may be willing to bear the costs. In such cases government subsidy, or consortium efforts, may be required to do the necessary tasks, as in the case of synthetic rubber cited above and current work in very large scale integration (VLSI) semiconductor components.

For all these reasons, it is far better to conceptualize this range as a spectrum than to think of two kinds of innovation, revolutionary and evolutionary. Where a given task lies along this spectrum of uncertainty has a major influence on many aspects of what is appropriate innovation.

The chain-linked model of innovation processes shows clearly that there are many points at which the uncertainty of the end product and processes of production and marketing can be reduced. One can do computer studies of a new device to test possibilities and optimize performance. The several uses of testing are obvious. One can pretest production methods for a new product. One can accumulate data that provide bounds on the limits that ensure stability or provide output within given quality ranges for a given process. One can do market sampling with handmade examples of a new product. In short, there is room for reduction of uncertainty at every step and in every feedback link in the chain-linked model. It is also possible to shorten the time for the total development process by using parallel paths for some of the steps of development and production set-up, but this will be risky when the uncertainty about the final design is still high.

Consideration of uncertainty helps understand why different criteria apply and different problems occur in innovation at different times in the production cycle of a product. In the early stages of a product cycle, the uncertainty is very high, and competition is primarily concerned with improvements in the technical performance characteristics of the product as they affect the consumers' needs. As these problems are solved and a dominant design type (or a few types) emerges, the industry matures, and the nature of required innovation shifts to lower-cost production of the dominant designs. At this point, therefore, innovation concerns system and process innovations more than improvement in a product's performance characteristics. Several important and valuable discussions of the impact of these shifts are given in Section I of Tushman and Moore (1982). The task of management in the early stage, while radical change is occurring and is solidifying into a dominant design, is to bring order from chaos and stabilize designs so that reasonable cost levels can be achieved by economies of scale and through the learning processes that only cumulate with reasonably long production experience with stable product designs. In the later stages, long after the product is stable, the task of management is to prevent the loss of ability to create radical innovations either from a lowering of the institutional capability in order to cut overhead costs or from bureaucratization of process and division of functions to the point that R&D, production, and marketing elements can no longer be drawn into effective, agreed goals and cooperative actions. These considerations have important implications for the ways in which institutionalization of R&D is carried out, but there is not sufficient space to explore them here. Coover (in this volume) makes the important points well.

For the technical parts of the innovation process, it is also important to recognize that the state of knowledge in the underlying science and technology strongly affects the cost and time requirements of innovation projects. Knowledge in the physical and biological sciences tends to move through recognizable major stages. In the earliest stage the work in a science is descriptive; in the next stage the work becomes taxonomic; then the work passes to formation of generalizing rules and hypotheses and finally, in some sciences, to the construction of predictive models. A science in the predictive stage, such as mechanics or classical electromagnetism today, is usable immediately by anyone skilled in the art for purposes of analytic design and invention. A science still in a descriptive or taxonomic phase is far less valuable for these purposes; however, it may still be very important in guiding the innovative work. When the state of science is not in a predictive stage with regard to the particular problems in hand, there is no choice but to carry out development of innovations by means of the much longer, and usually much more expensive and uncertain process, of cut and try. In the current era this is seldom a wholly blind process; it is much more often what one could call "guided empiricism." One starts with all available knowledge and makes the first best estimate of a workable design, then proceeds to build it, test it, incorporate learning, redesign, retest, incorporate learning, and so on (sometimes ad nauseam). An important aspect of this set of processes is that the speed of turnaround is a critical factor in the effectiveness of innovation. It follows that the same departmentalization of function that is so desirable for high-volume production may become a major deterrent to successful innovation. When the relevant knowledge is not in a predictive state, the best source for new designs is usually the practice found to be successful in old designs—science may be largely or wholly irrelevant. There is little doubt that the failure to make this distinction about the state of knowledge underlies many fruitless arguments about the value, or lack of value, of science in innovation; in some instances science is essential, a sine qua non, but in other instances it is wholly irrelevant; and there is everything in between. A current example of the lack of sufficient science for design purposes and therefore of the need to rely on prior art is combustion spaces, fireboxes. The results of this lack of predictive science (note that there is no dearth of data and experience) are very high costs in development, long lead times (e.g., for the combustion space in new models of jet engines), and a strong and reasonable conservatism on the part of designers (e.g., of stationary boilers). The development of new proprietary drugs also remains largely in this class currently. There are numerous other examples. It is important that technical experts make clear to managers the state of knowledge in this sense.

For these reasons, there still remain crucial portions of high technology industries in which attempts to advance the state of the art are painstakingly slow and expensive because of the limited guidance available from science. The development of new alloys with specific combinations of properties proceeds very slowly because there is still no good theoretical basis for predicting the behavior of new combinations of materials; the same applies to pharmaceutical drugs. Many problems connected with improved pollution control are severely constrained by the limited scientific understanding of the combustion process, and by the fact that the design of a combustion "firebox" remains in 1985 still an art based primarily on the results of prior designs—not on science. The development of synthetic fuels is at present seriously hampered by scientific ignorance with respect to the details of the oxidation reactions in various forms of coal. The designs of aircraft and steam turbines are both hampered by the lack of a good theory of turbulence.

In the case of aircraft, wind-tunnel tests are still subject to substantial margins of error in terms of predicting actual flight performance. Indeed, in considerable part the high development costs for aircraft are due precisely to the inability to draw more heavily on a predictive science in determining the performance of specific new designs or materials. If science provided a better predictive basis for directly specifying optimal design configurations, development costs (which constitute about two-thirds of total R&D expenditures in the United States) would not be nearly so high. These arguments constitute solid reasons for companies concerned with innovation to maintain scientific work covering the areas underlying their products, not only because the output of the work will itself produce useful long-range results, but even more importantly to be sure that in-house knowledge of scientific advances worldwide are observed, understood, and available to the development projects in the organization.

The degree of uncertainty also affects the appropriate type and amount of planning for an innovation project. Managers of most operations—production, sales, accounting, maintenance—all see planning as a nearly unmitigated benefit. For obvious reasons, they tend to believe that more planning is better planning, and better planning is better business. This is also typically true of the innovation projects that entail virtually no risk. If all we are changing is the color in the paint can at the end of the assembly line, then the change should be, and probably will be, planned in all details.

If, on the other hand, the innovation involves major uncertainties, for example, the creation of some never-before-seen item of hardware, then it is very easy to "overplan" the project and thereby decrease or even destroy the effectiveness of the work. Clear examples of how overplanning markedly decreased effectiveness are given by Marschak et al. (1967), and the idea is understood by nearly all good innovators and researchers. There is no doubt of the effect; it remains only to explain why the effect exists.

In a radical, major innovation, there is by definition the need to learn about various aspects of the work. Like fundamental research, radical innovation is inherently a learning process. The best initial design concepts often turn out to be wrong—dead, hopelessly wrong—simply because not enough is yet known about how the job can (and cannot) be done. There is also what can be called a "false summit" effect. When one climbs a mountain, one sees ahead what appears to be the top of the mountain, but over and over again it is not the summit, but rather a shoulder on the trail that blocks the view of the real summit. When one does innovation, much the same effect often occurs. One starts with problem A. It looks initially as if solving problem A will get the job done. But when one finds a solution for A, it is only to discover that problem B lies hidden behind A. Moreover, behind B lies C, and so on. In many innovation projects, one must solve an unknown number of problems each only a step toward the final workable design—each only a shoulder that blocks the view of further ascent. The true summit, the end of the task, when the device meets all the specified criteria, is seldom visible long in advance. Since good innovators are optimists, virtually by definition, there is a tendency to underestimate the number of tasks that must be solved and hence also the time and costs.

If the project is planned in detail at the beginning, the initial wrong concepts will suggest commitments (of materials, scarce talents, facilities) that are a waste of effort. Even worse, through inertia of ideas, dollars, or people, the force of prior commitments may keep the project from changing paths when it should. Thus, the overall effort may be more costly and slower than if less planning had been done initially, and the end result may be less desirable. In addition, the "false summit" effect makes tight planning of timetables very difficult, and in truly radical innovation probably counterproductive. Experienced personnel usually recognize that the "false summit" effect is a major contributor to conflicts between innovators and management and investors in innovative projects.

Does this mean no planning and no accountability are desirable in radical innovation? The answer is no. Preplanning must be focused on goals, rough overall time schedules, and budgets, and care must be taken not to make decisions that incur large costs or commitments too early in the project. Moreover, information about what is learned and the changes implied by that learning must be communicated regularly and thoroughly between innovators and managers. Finally, managers of innovation must be very clear about the differences in nature between innovation processes and those of production and other business activities.

ECONOMICS OF INNOVATION

The preceding parts of this chapter have mainly characterized the process of technological innovation. Central features of the discussion have been the sheer diversity of activities that make up the innovation process, the variation across industry lines, and innovation's somewhat disorderly character. Any drastically simplified model of the process necessarily misrepresents—or omits—essential aspects of the innovation process. The chain-linked model introduced in this chapter provides a more accurate representation of innovation processes than earlier, simpler models. However, the forces that seem to be shaping the economics of innovation, particularly in high technology industries, must also be addressed.

Rising Development Costs

Perhaps the most important trend is an apparent rise in the development costs of new products, especially new products that genuinely push out the technological frontier by incorporating substantial improvements in product (or process) performance. These rising development costs involve an escalation of the financial risks that are associated with innovation, and they therefore pose a serious threat to an organization's capacity to undertake innovation in the future.

In the case of the commercial aircraft industry, there is currently only one firm—Boeing—that is an active innovator of aircraft of substantially new design. Development costs of a genuinely new generation of aircraft, as opposed to mere modification of an existing aircraft, are accepted as being well over a billion dollars. Boeing has recently resorted to forms of subcontracting that involve at least some degree of risk sharing on the part of the subcontractors. These development costs, and the accompanying large-scale financial risk, also figure prominently in the increasing recourse to international consortiums—as in the case of the European Airbus and the earlier, ill-fated Concorde.

The size of development costs and the associated financial risk in the commercial aircraft industry are, admittedly, at the extreme end of the spectrum. Nevertheless, similar trends are apparent in many high technology sectors. Development costs of nuclear power reactors have skyrocketed because of mounting safety and environmental concerns, as a result of which construction of nuclear power plants has been brought virtually to a halt in the United States. But even more conventional power-generating equipment, which is not plagued by the special problems of nuclear power, also confronts technological and other performance uncertainties of a kind that have resulted in very high development costs. The exploitation of new fossil-fuel energy sources, which involves complex liquefaction and gasification processes, has encountered spectacularly high development costs at the pilot-plant stage. These costs, together with changing expectations about the future pattern of petroleum prices, have led to the termination of numerous projects.

Telecommunications has encountered similar trends in recent years—the cost of the #4 Electronic Switching System is estimated to have been around $400 million. Although the electronics industry has some very different features from the other industries just mentioned, the design and development of reliable, high-capacity memory chips have drastically raised the table stakes for commercial survival. Hundreds of millions of dollars of development costs are being incurred in the international competition for higher circuit densities. In the last several years the relative importance of software development costs has drastically increased. In the computer industry, where IBM is admittedly sui generis, that gigantic, multiproduct firm has recently been supporting an R&D budget of over $2.5 billion. In the fledgling biotechnology industry, a combination of high development costs, the scale requirements to take advantage of bulk manufacture, and uncertainties about future products is already operating as a powerful deterrent to the willingness of venture capital to enter the industry. Finally, development costs and the production facilities needed to introduce a new line of automobiles now make it exceedingly difficult for any but very large, established firms to enter the market. The recent entry of Japanese firms occurred only after some years of protection in the Japanese domestic market. In Fiscal Year 1983–1984, General Motors' R&D spending amounted to $2.6 billion. In the same period, Ford Motor Company spent $1.75 billion on R&D. Although it is not entirely clear in either case what functions are in fact covered within these budgets, it is certainly clear that the table stakes of innovation are very high even in some long-established industries.

Resistance to Radical Innovation

This raising of the table stakes for innovations appears to create significant resistance to radical innovations, as in the case of problems in smog control in automotive engines. For the reasons stated above, organizations that are good at low-cost, very high volume production segregate functions to the point that no single person or small group can make major alterations. They also tend to separate R&D from production, thus decreasing essential feedbacks and forward coupling to real changes in production. For proprietary reasons they also strongly favor in-house expertise, and this often leads to a failure to utilize outside ideas in the conceptual stage. But as the studies of radical innovation have shown, it is nearly always important to maximize the sources of ideas in the early stages of work. These studies also show it is important to isolate new innovative ideas from the fixed ideas and prejudices that nearly always characterize individuals who work for many years on a given dominant design or, worse, a few components of it. For such individuals it is always easy to find many reasons why an innovative idea won't work (as indeed it usually won't in its initial undeveloped stages). At best, they represent important dampers on the enthusiasm that is necessary to carry on the difficult work of innovation. At worst, they may deter or altogether stop promising innovative work that lies beyond their range of experience.

Financial Risks

Many high technology industries appear to be confronting technological trajectories that offer opportunities for rapid improvement, but also high and rapidly rising development costs. Financial risks have thus become exceedingly great. To be financially successful, the products require markets that are, in some cases, substantially larger than can even be provided by a single, moderately sized Western European country of 50 million or so. For technological and other reasons (for example, regulatory constraints in the pharmaceutical industry), very long lead times are often involved that defer the prospect of full recovery of financial commitments, at best, into the far distant future (some new pharmaceutical products, such as contraceptives, must be subject to 15-year tests). In such industries not only are uncertainties over technological factors particularly great, but the large financial commitments are frequently required during precisely that earliest stage when the uncertainties are greatest.

Moreover, the very fact of rapid technological change itself raises the risk of investing in long-lived plant and equipment, since further technological change is likely to render such capital soon obsolete. If product life cycles are themselves becoming shorter, and there is evidence that they are, the agony of the risk-taking process in innovation is even further intensified. For not only has the scale of the financial commitment that is put to risk been drastically increased, the question of the precise timing in the commitment of large amounts of resources to the development process has become even more crucial. Moreover, there is abundant evidence in recent years that new, technologically complex products experience numerous difficulties in their early stages that may take years to iron out. Where this is the case, the earliest Schumpeterian innovators frequently wind up in the bankruptcy courts, whereas the rapid imitator, or "fast second," who stands back and learns from the mistakes of the pioneer, may experience great commercial success.

Coupling the Technical and the Economic

The whole process of technical innovation has to be conceived of as an ongoing search activity—a search for products possessing new or superior combinations of performance characteristics, or for new methods of manufacturing existing products. But this search activity is shaped and structured in fundamental ways not only by economic forces that reflect cost considerations and current supplies of resources, but also by the present state of technological knowledge, and by consumer demand for different categories of products and services. Successful technological innovation is a process of simultaneous coupling at the technological and economic levels—of drawing on the present state of technological knowledge and projecting it in a direction that brings about a coupling with some substantial category of consumer needs and desires. But what constitutes consumers' needs and desires today is sometimes different from what it will be in the future. The truly important innovations have frequently been ahead of their times, and have created a market that did not exist and was not expected by the shortsighted nor the fainthearted.

The process of R&D has often been equated with innovation. If this were true, understanding innovation would be far simpler than it truly is, and the real problems would be far simpler and less interesting than they truly are.

Successful innovation requires the coupling of the technical and the economic in ways that can be accommodated by the organization while also meeting market needs, and this implies close coupling and cooperation among many activities in the marketing, R&D, and production functions.

CONCLUSIONS

A century ago organized innovation was rare, and innovation therefore much slower. The successful innovator could count on gaining significant competitive advantage. Today, innovation is a cost of staying even in the marketplace. Despite this, innovation as a study is quite new and still suffers from an overabundance of specialized comment and a lack of integrated, mature viewpoints in the literature. This chapter attempted to unify the economic and technological views. Since it is an overview, and brief in length, it necessarily omitted many topics and much rich detail. Despite this it seems possible, based on the joint discussion, to reach a number of conclusions.

Illustrations presented throughout this chapter show that innovation is inherently uncertain, somewhat disorderly, made up of some of the most complex systems known, and subject to changes of many sorts at many different places within the innovating organization. Innovation is also difficult to measure and demands close coordination of adequate technical knowledge and excellent market judgment in order to satisfy economic, technological, and often other types of constraints—all simultaneously. Any model that describes innovation as a single process, or attributes its sources to a single cause, or gives a truly simple picture will therefore distort the reality and thereby impair our thinking and decision making.

Contrary to much common wisdom, the initiating step in most innovations is not research, but rather a design. Such initiating designs are usually either inventions or analytic design. The term "analytic design" is used to denote a study of new combinations of existing products and components, rearrangements of processes, and designs of new equipment within the existing state of the art. Emergent computer applications, for example, appear to be merging these functions into more powerful and faster tools than have been available in the past.

Science has two major parts that directly affect innovation but have different roles. One part, stored knowledge about physical, biological, and social nature, is an essential ingredient in the bulk of current innovations. It is unthinkable for successful technical innovations to be created today without utilizing significant inputs from the stored technical knowledge in science and other forms of thought. Even inventors who decry science will have absorbed some of the modern views toward mechanics and other subjects that permeate modern thinking. But this knowledge enters primarily through knowledge already in the heads of the people in the innovative organization, and to a lesser degree through information quickly accessible to them. Research is needed only when all these sources of stored knowledge are inadequate for the task at hand.

While current research sometimes does potentiate major innovations, more frequently research is used in innovation to solve problems all along the chain-of-innovation from the initial design to the finished production processes. In the early stages of this chain, the research is often indistinguishable from the pure research in the relevant field. Later in the development, research shifts toward system and then to process questions; these forms of research are not usually considered as science, but they are nevertheless usually essential to completion of a successful product innovation. The importance of these types of research has been underestimated in the recent past, probably in part because of the use of an oversimplified "linear" model of innovation that entirely omits them as categories of research. An improved model of innovation, summarized in this chapter, indicates not one, but rather five major pathways that are all important in innovation processes. These paths include not only the central-chain-of-innovation, but also the following:

- numerous feedbacks that link and coordinate R&D with production and marketing;
- side-links to research all along the central-chain-of-innovation;
- long-range generic research for backup of innovations;
- potentiation of wholly new devices or processes from research; and
- much essential support of science itself from the products of innovative activities, i.e., through the tools and instruments made available by technology.

Two variables that provide major assistance in thinking about the nature of appropriate innovations are the degree of uncertainty in achieving success and the life-cycle stage of the product concerned. Larger uncertainty is strongly correlated with the degree of change. In the early stages of a product's life cycle, major changes in product design are occurring rapidly, and the key problem of management is to find dominant successful designs and to organize stable production and marketing around them. In the later stages of the product's life cycle, innovations typically are more concerned with process changes that reduce production costs. It is likely that a variety of changes, many of them seemingly small, will cumulate along a learning curve from very high volume production of a relatively stable product to reduce costs by a factor of at least two (and in some instances much more). After this learning stage is well advanced, the central problem in the management of innovation will usually be to avoid so much personnel reduction, specialization of tasks, and routinization of procedures that truly revolutionary advances become essentially impossible.

The degree of uncertainty in innovation also depends strongly on the state of underlying science and relevant engineering knowledge. When the underlying knowledge allows accurate predictions, far more rapid and reliable innovations are possible. When predictive knowledge is lacking, a resort to the far slower, less predictable, and more costly cut and try of "guided empiricism" is required. We tend to think of technical problems as predictive in the current high-tech area, but in reality many important areas still remain in a stage where adequate predictions are not possible, and "design-build-test: redesign . . ." remains the essential methodology for innovations.

Some organizations are very effective in high-risk, radical innovation, others in the small, cumulative, evolutionary changes that reduce costs and bring better fit of the product to various market niches. Both types of innovation are important. The control of costs is important to remain competitive in the short run, and the movement to radically improved product designs is often necessary to survival over the long haul.

In this connection, the very high costs for development of new products, the shortening product life-cycle times, and the forces tending to squeeze out independent entrepreneurs in some heavy industrial sectors all suggest that the United States may need to rethink the way it has financed and managed innovations in some types of cases.

If there is a single lesson this review of innovation emphasizes, it is the need to view the process of innovation as changes in a complete system of not only hardware, but also market environment, production facilities and knowledge, and the social contexts of the innovating organization.

REFERENCES AND BIBLIOGRAPHY

Constant, Edward W., II. 1980. *The Origins of the Turbojet Revolution*. Baltimore, Md.: Johns Hopkins University Press.

Enos, John. 1958. A measure of the rate of technological progress in the petroleum refining industry. *Journal of Industrial Economics*, June.

Hill, C. T., and James T. Utterback. 1979. *Technological Innovation for a Dynamic Economy*. London (Elmsford, N.Y.): Pergamon Press.

Kelly, Patrick, and Melvin Kranzberg, eds. 1978. *Technological Innovation: A Critical Review of the Literature*. Calif.: The San Francisco Press.

Klein, Burton. 1977. *Dynamic Economics*. Cambridge, Mass.: Harvard University Press.

Kline, Stephen J. 1985. Research, Invention, Innovation and Production: Models and Reality, Rept. INN-1, Department of Mechanical Engineering, Stanford University (to be published).

Kuhn, Thomas. 1967. *The Structure of Scientific Revolutions*. Ill.: University of Chicago Press.

Mansfield, Edwin, John Rapoport, Anthony Romeo, Samuel Wagner, and George Beardsley. 1977. Social and private rates of return from industrial innovations. *Quarterly Journal of Economics*, May.

Mansfield, Edwin, John Rapoport, Jerome Schnee, Samuel Wagner, and Michael Hamburger. 1971. *Research and Innovation in the Modern Corporation*. New York: W. W. Norton.

Marschak, Thomas, Thomas G. Glennan, Jr., and Robert Summers. 1967. *Strategies for R&D: Studies in the Microeconomics of Development*. Rand Corporation Research Study. New York: Springer-Verlag.

Nelson, Richard R., ed. 1982. *Government and Technical Progress: A Cross-Industry Analysis.* London (Elmsford, N.Y.): Pergamon Press.

Price, Derek de Solla. 1984. The unsung genius of sealing wax and string. *Natural History* (Jan.): 49–56.

Rogers, Everett M. 1983. *Diffusion of Innovations.* 3rd ed. New York: Free Press of Macmillan.

Rosenberg, Nathan. 1982. *Inside the Black Box: Technology and Economics.* New York: Cambridge University Press.

Tushman, Michael L., and William M. Moore. 1982. *Readings in the Management of Innovation.* Marshfield, Mass.: Pitman.

Vincenti, Walter G. 1979. The air propeller tests of W. F. Durand and E. P. Leslie: A case study in technological methodology. *Technology and Culture* 20(October):712–751.

Vincenti, Walter G. 1982. Control volume analysis: A difference in thinking between engineering and physics. *Technology and Culture* 23(April):145–174.

Vincenti, Walter G. 1984. Technological knowledge without science: The innovation of flush riveting in American airplanes, ca. 1930–ca. 1950. *Technology and Culture* 25(July):540–576.

Microeconomics
of Technological Innovation

EDWIN MANSFIELD

We are still very far from having a satisfactory understanding of the innovation process, the determinants of the rate of innovation, the measurement of the rate and direction of technological change, and the effects of changes in technology. In view of the enormous difficulties that studies in these areas face, it is not surprising that existing knowledge remains limited. Nonetheless, steady progress has been made in this area.

Until the 1950s, the economics profession generally was woefully deficient in its treatment of technological change. With few exceptions, like Joseph Schumpeter (1934), economists failed to recognize the central importance of industrial innovation. In the past 30 years, however, a great deal of research, much of it financed by the National Science Foundation, has been carried out by economists to extend their limited understanding of the nature, determinants, and effects of technological change. Without question, significant progress has been made. New models have been constructed and new kinds of data have been assembled. Yet we are far from a satisfactory understanding of this very difficult topic.

This chapter describes briefly some of the principal work that has been done to help answer the following questions: (1) What has been the effect of research and development (R&D) on the rate of productivity growth? (2) What has been the rate of return from investments in industrial innovation? (3) What have been the size, determinants, and effects of imitation costs? (4) How much effect have patents had on imitation costs and the rate of innovation? (5) How great has been the rate of inflation in R&D? (6) What factors determine the rate of diffusion of an innovation? (7) To what extent has the rate of international technology transfer increased?

While these are not the only questions that microeconomists have dealt with, they clearly are among the most important. Since there is a considerable literature on each of these questions, my treatment is selective, and it will tend to focus on the kinds of work that my students and I have been doing in recent years.

RELATIONSHIP BETWEEN R&D AND PRODUCTIVITY GROWTH

For both analytical and policy purposes, it is important to investigate the relationship between the amount spent by an industry or firm on R&D and its rate of productivity increase. During the past 30 years a number of studies of this kind have been carried out. They are by no means free of problems, however, as I have indicated in detail elsewhere (Mansfield et al., 1982). Perhaps the most important of their findings is that R&D has a very significant effect on the rate of productivity increase in the industries and the time periods that have been studied. In one of the earliest studies of this topic, Minasian (1969) found that the rate of productivity increase in chemical firms was directly related to their expenditures on R&D. His results indicated that, during the period to which his data pertained, the marginal rate of return—that is, the rate of return from an additional dollar spent—was about 50 percent for R&D in chemicals. A study of my own indicated that the marginal rate of return from R&D was about 40 percent or more in the petroleum industry and about 30 percent in the chemical industry (Mansfield, 1965). In agriculture, Griliches (1964) found that output was related in a statistically significant way to the amount spent on research and extension. Assuming a 6-year lag between research input and its returns, his results indicated a marginal rate of return from agricultural R&D of 53 percent. Another study, by Evenson (1968), used time-series data to estimate the marginal rate of return from agricultural R&D, which it found to be about 57 percent. Peterson's study (1971) of R&D in poultry indicated a marginal rate of return of about 50 percent.

Throughout the 1970s these studies were extended. Griliches (1980) used data for almost 900 manufacturing firms to examine the relationship between R&D and the rate of productivity growth. The results indicated that the amount spent by a firm on R&D was directly related to its rate of productivity growth. Also, he found that the private rate of return from R&D was about 17 percent. It seemed much higher than this in chemicals and petroleum and lower in aircraft and electrical equipment.[1]

Terleckyj (1974) studied the effects of R&D expenditures on productivity change in 33 manufacturing and nonmanufacturing industries during the years 1948 to 1966. In manufacturing, the results suggested about a 30 percent rate of return from an industry's R&D on its own productivity. In addition, his findings showed a very substantial effect of an industry's R&D on productivity growth in other industries, resulting in a social rate of return greatly exceeding that of 30 percent. Nadiri and Bitros (1980) constructed an econometric model in which output was treated as an exogenous variable and R&D, labor, and capital inputs were regarded as functions of input prices, sales, the rate of capacity utilization, and the lagged dependent variables. They found that labor productivity is significantly affected in both the short run and the long run by the level of a firm's R&D expenditures.

During the 1980s, studies by Griliches, Link, Nadiri, Scherer, Terleckyj, and myself, among others, provided still further evidence concerning the rates of return from R&D.[2] In interpreting the rates of return obtained, both in these studies and in those done before, it is important to distinguish between private rates of return and social rates of return. The private rate of return is the rate of return to the firm carrying out the R&D; the social rate of return is the rate of return to society as a whole. Since the firm that carries out the R&D frequently cannot appropriate many of the benefits of doing so, the social rate of return may be considerably in excess of the private rate of return. Thus, many of the rates of return cited above, because they are social rates of return, are likely to be higher than the private rate of return to the firm carrying out the R&D.

How do the results of the studies of the 1980s compare with those of the studies of the 1970s and 1960s? In general, they are quite consistent, in the sense that they continue to indicate that the level of R&D seems to be closely related to the rate of productivity growth, and that the marginal rate of return from investment in R&D is high, although perhaps not as high as in earlier years. The high marginal social rate of return from R&D is important because it suggests that there may be an underinvestment in R&D, a phenomenon that many economists attribute partly to the differences between private and social rates of return from innovative activities.

SOCIAL AND PRIVATE RETURNS FROM SPECIFIC INNOVATIONS

The types of econometric studies just described have been employed by economists to estimate the social rates of return from investments in new technology. But they are by no means the only type of study carried out by economists for this purpose. A number of microeconomic studies of the returns from specific innovations have been carried out as well. To estimate the social benefits from an innovation, economists have often used a model of the following sort. If the innovation results in a shift downward in the supply curve for a product, they have used the area under the product's demand curve between the preinnovation and postinnovation supply curves as a measure of the social benefit from the innovation during the relevant time period. If all other prices remain constant, this area equals the social value of the additional quantity of the product plus the social value of the resources saved as a consequence of the innovation. Consequently, if one compares the stream of R&D (and other) inputs relating to the innovation with the stream of social benefits measured in this way, it is possible to estimate the social rate of return from the investment in the new technology.

The first such studies concerned only agricultural R&D. Although only a few studies of this sort were conducted, notably by Griliches (1958), Peterson (1971), and Schmitz and Seckler (1970), the results were quite consistent in the sense that they all indicated that the rate of return from agricultural R&D in the United States has tended to be high. Until the 1970s, no such estimates were made for industries other than agriculture. In an attempt to help fill this gap, my co-workers and I estimated the rate of return from the investment in 17 industrial innovations, which occurred in a variety of industries and which stemmed from firms of quite different sizes (Mansfield et al., 1977b). Most of these innovations were of average or routine importance, not major breakthroughs. Although this sample cannot be regarded as randomly chosen, there is no obvious indication that it was biased toward very profitable innovations—socially or privately—or relatively unprofitable ones.

To estimate the social rate of return from the investment in each of these innovations, we extended the model described above to include the pricing behavior of the innovator, the effects on displaced products, and the costs of uncommercialized R&D and of R&D done outside the innovating organization. The results indicate that the median social rate of return from the investment in the innovations studied was 56 percent, a very high figure. On the other hand, the median private rate of return was 25 percent. (In interpreting the latter figure, it is important to note that innovation is a risky activity; see Mansfield et al., 1971.)

Information also was obtained concerning the returns from the innovative activities of one of America's largest firms, from 1960 to 1972. For each year this firm had made an inventory of the technological innovations resulting from its R&D and estimated its effects on its profit stream in detail. When the average rate of return from this firm's total investment in innovative activities was computed, the result was 19 percent, which is not too different from the median private rate of return (25 percent) noted above. Also, lower bounds were computed for the social rate of return from this firm's investment, which was about double that for its private rate of return (see Mansfield et al., 1977a).

To extend our sample and replicate our analysis, the National Science Foundation commissioned two studies, one by Robert R. Nathan Associates and one by Foster Associates. Their results, like ours, indicated that the median social rate of return tends to be very high and much higher than the median private rate of return. Based on its sample of 20 innovations, Nathan Associates (1978) found the median social rate of return to be 70 percent and the median private rate of return to be 36 percent. Foster Associates

(1978), based on its sample of 20 innovations, found the median social rate of return to be 99 percent and the median private rate of return to be 24 percent.

These findings pertain to the average rate of return. As pointed out in the previous section, econometric investigations indicate that the marginal rate of return has also tended to be high. In sum, practically all of the studies carried out to date indicate that the average social rate of return from investments in new technology in both agriculture and industry has tended to be very high. Moreover, the marginal social rate of return also seems high, generally at least 30 percent. As I have stressed repeatedly elsewhere, there are very important problems and limitations inherent in each of these studies. Certainly, they are frail needs on which to base policy conclusions. But recognizing this fact, it nonetheless is remarkable that so many independent studies based on so many types of data result in so consistent a set of conclusions. As noted above, many economists view these conclusions as evidence of an underinvestment in civilian technology.

BASIC RESEARCH AND PRODUCTIVITY

While the foregoing studies provide valuable information concerning the relationship between total R&D input and productivity change, they tell us nothing about the effect of the composition of an industry's or firm's R&D on its rate of productivity change. In particular, they tell us nothing about the role of basic research in promoting productivity increase. Basic research is defined by the National Science Foundation as "original investigation for the advancement of scientific knowledge . . . which [does] not have immediate commercial objectives." Does basic research, as contrasted with applied research and development, make a significant contribution to an industry's or firm's rate of technological innovation and productivity change? Although the studies cited above indicated that an industry's or firm's R&D expenditures have been directly related to its rate of productivity change, they were unable to shed light on this question because no attempt was made to separate basic research from applied research and development.

About 5 years ago, an econometric study was carried out to determine whether an industry's or firm's rate of productivity change in recent years had been related to the amount of basic research it performed, when other relevant variables (such as its rate of expenditure on applied R&D) were held constant. This study (Mansfield, 1980, 1981) has various limitations, but its results are of interest, particularly since so little research has been done on this subject. The findings indicate that there was a statistically significant and direct relationship between the amount of basic research carried out by an industry or firm and its rate of increase of total factor productivity, when its expenditures on applied R&D were held constant. To some extent, this may reflect a tendency for basic research findings to be exploited more fully by the industries and firms that were responsible for them. Or it may reflect a tendency for applied R&D to be more effective when carried out in conjunction with some basic research.

Whether the relevant distinction is between basic and applied research is by no means clear: there is some evidence that basic research may be acting to some extent as a proxy for long-term R&D. Holding constant the amount spent on both applied R&D and basic research, an industry's rate of productivity increase seems to be directly and significantly related to the extent to which its R&D is long term. This constituted the first systematic evidence that the composition, as well as the size, of an industry's or firm's R&D expenditures affect its rate of productivity increase. However, the study was really just a beginning. Much more work is required in this area, since the composition of R&D is for many purposes as important as its total amount.

CENTRAL ROLE OF IMITATION COSTS AND TIMES

Economists have long recognized that the costs of imitating new products have an important effect on the incentives for innovation in a market economy. As Arrow (1962) and others have pointed out, if firms can imitate an innovation at a cost that is substantially below the cost to the innovator of developing the innovation, there may be little or no incentive for the innovator to carry out the innovation. In their discussions of the innovation process, economists frequently have called attention to the major role played by the costs of imitation, but there has been little or no attempt to measure those costs, to test various hypotheses concerning the factors influencing them, or to estimate their effects.

In the first empirical study of this topic (Mansfield et al., 1981) data were obtained from firms in the chemical, drug, electronics, and machinery industries concerning the cost and time of imitating (legally) 48 product innovations.[3] By imitation cost is meant all costs of developing and introducing the imitative product, including applied research, product specification, pilot plant or prototype construction, investment in plant and equipment, and manufacturing and marketing start-up. (If there was a patent on the innovation, the cost of inventing around it is included.) By imitation time is meant the length of time that elapses from the beginning of the imitator's applied research (if there was any) on the imitative product to the date of its commercial introduction.

The sample of firms for this study was chosen more or less at random from among the major firms in these four industries in the Northeast, and the new products were chosen more or less at random from among those introduced recently by these firms. For 34 of the products, the data are based on actual experience, because the new product had already been imitated.

For the remaining 14 products, no imitator had appeared as yet, but the innovating firm provided detailed estimates that we regarded as reliable. Also, for all 48 products, data were obtained from the innovating firm concerning the costs of the innovation, as well as the time it took to bring the innovation to market (from the beginning of applied research to the date of its commercial introduction).

The ratio of the imitation cost to the innovation cost averaged about 0.65, and the ratio of the imitation time to the innovation time averaged about 0.70. There was considerable variation about these averages, however. For about half of the products, the ratio of imitation cost to innovation cost was either less than 0.40 or more than 0.90. For about half of the products, the ratio of imitation time to innovation time was either less than 0.40 or more than 1.00. Products with a relatively high (low) ratio of imitation cost to innovation cost tended to have a relatively high (low) ratio of imitation time to innovation time.

It is worth noting that the imitation cost was no smaller than the innovation cost for about one-seventh of the products. This was not due to any superiority of the imitative product over the innovation. Instead, in a substantial percentage of the cases, it was due to the innovator's having a technological edge over its rivals in the relevant field. Often this edge was due to superior "know-how"—that is, better and more extensive technical information based on highly specialized experience with the development and production of related products and processes. Such know-how is not divulged in patents and is relatively inaccessible (at least for a period of time) to potential imitators.

Thus, these data indicate that innovators routinely introduce new products despite the fact that other firms can imitate those products for about two-thirds (often less) of the cost and time expended by the innovator. In some cases, this is because, although other firms could imitate these products in this way, there are other barriers to entry (for example, lack of a well-known brand name) that discourage potential imitators. But to a greater extent (at least in this sample), it seems to be due to a feeling on the part of the innovators that, even if imitators do begin to appear in a relatively few years, the innovation will still be profitable.

Patents and Imitation Costs

In recent years, economists have also begun to study more systematically the effects of patents. Of particular interest is the question: To what extent is the ratio of imitation cost to innovation cost affected by whether the innovator has patents on the new product? Contrary to popular opinion, patent protection does not make entry impossible, or even unlikely. Within 4 years of their introduction, 60 percent of the patented successful innovations in the above sample were imitated. Nonetheless, patent protection generally increased imitation costs. To obtain information concerning the size of this increase, my co-workers and I asked the firms in the sample described above to estimate how much the imitation cost for each patented product increased because it was patented. The median estimated increase was 11 percent.[4] We also asked the firms to estimate how much the imitation cost for each unpatented product would have increased if it had been patented. The median estimated increase was only about 6 percent. (Indeed, for two of these products, patent protection would have reduced the money and time required for imitation because without patent protection the innovator was able to keep secret the essential information underlying the product, whereas if the product had been patented, some of the information would have had to be disclosed.) The fact that a patent resulted in a larger increase in the imitation costs of the patented products than of the unpatented products was, of course, a major reason why some products were patented and others were not.

Patents had a larger impact on imitation costs in ethical drugs than in the other industries sampled, which helps to account for survey results indicating that patents are regarded as more important in ethical drugs than elsewhere. The median estimated increase in imitation cost due to patent protection was about 30 percent in ethical drugs, in contrast to about 10 percent in chemicals and about 7 percent in electronics and machinery. Without patent protection, it frequently would have been relatively inexpensive (and quick) for an imitator to determine the composition of a new drug and to begin producing it. These results are in accord with the conclusion of Taylor and Silberston (1973) that the lack of patent protection would reduce the rate of expenditure on innovative activity to a greater extent in drugs than in other industries.

Imitation Costs, Entry, and Concentration

Let us turn now from the determinants of imitation costs to their effects on market entry and industry concentration. Holding constant the discounted profit (gross of the imitation cost) that the imitator expects to earn by imitating a new product, the new product is more likely to be imitated if the imitation cost is small. To discourage market entry, the innovator may adopt pricing (and other) policies to reduce the imitator's expected discounted gross profit if the imitation cost is low. Taking this into account, is it still true that the probability of entry is inversely related to the size of the imitation cost? To find out, my co-workers and I determined whether each product innovation in the sample described above was imitated within 4 years of its introduction. (Innovations that had been on the market fewer than 4 years and unsuccessful innovations clearly had to be omitted.) We then carried out a logit analysis[5] to determine whether the ratio of imitation cost to innovation cost influenced the probability that entry of this sort occurred within 4 years. Based on the results, imitation cost seemed to be related in the expected way to whether entry occurs.

Imitation cost may also affect an industry's level of concentration. One would expect an industry's concentration level to be relatively low if its members' products and processes can be imitated easily and cheaply. Existing econometric findings, which are based on limited data, have been entirely consistent with this hypothesis. Given the large number of factors influencing an industry's concentration level, it is interesting that this relationship is relatively close. Differences among industries in the technology transfer process (including transfers that are both voluntary and involuntary from the point of view of the innovator) may be able to explain much more of the interindustry variation in concentration levels than is generally recognized.

PATENTS AND THE RATE OF INNOVATION

One of the most important and controversial questions concerning the patent system is: What proportion of innovations would be delayed or not introduced at all if they could not be patented? To shed light on this question, economists have carried out carefully designed surveys to determine the proportion of their patented innovations that firms report they would have introduced (with no appreciable delay) if patent protection had not been available. Although answers to such questions have obvious limitations and must be treated with caution, they should shed some light on this topic, about which so little is known. According to the firms in one such study (Mansfield et al., 1981), about one-half of the patented innovations would not have been introduced without patent protection. The bulk of these innovations occurred in the drug industry. Excluding drug innovations, the lack of patent protection would have affected less than one-fourth of the patented innovations in the sample.

One important reason why patents frequently are not regarded as crucial is that they often have only a limited effect on the rate at which imitators enter the market. For about half of the innovations, the firms in this study believed that patents had delayed the entry of imitators by less than a few months. Although patents generally increased the imitation costs, they did not increase the costs enough in these cases to have an appreciable effect on the rate of entry. But although patent protection seems to have only a limited effect on entry in about half of the cases, it seems to have a very important effect in a minority of them. For about 15 percent of the innovations, patent protection was estimated to have delayed the time when the first imitator entered the market by 4 years or more.

In another study (Mansfield, 1985) based on a random sample of 100 firms from 12 industries (excluding very small firms) in the United States, the results indicate that patent protection was judged by the firms to have been essential for the development or introduction of 30 percent or more of the inventions commercialized in 2 industries—pharmaceuticals and chemicals. In another 3 industries (petroleum, machinery, and fabricated metal products), patent protection was estimated to be essential for the development and introduction of about 10 to 20 percent of their inventions. In the remaining 7 industries (electrical equipment, office equipment, motor vehicles, instruments, primary metals, rubber, and textiles), patent protection was estimated to be of much more limited importance in this regard. Indeed, in office equipment, motor vehicles, rubber, and textiles, the firms were unanimous in reporting that patent protection was not essential for the development or introduction of any of their inventions during the years 1981 to 1983.

This does not mean, however, that firms make little use of the patent system. On the contrary, even in those industries in which practically all inventions would be introduced without patent protection, the bulk of the patentable inventions seem to be patented. And in such industries as pharmaceuticals and chemicals, in which patents are important, over 80 percent of the patentable inventions are reported to have been patented. Clearly, firms generally prefer not to rely on trade secret protection when patent protection is possible. Even in industries, like motor vehicles, in which patents are frequently said to be relatively unimportant, about 60 percent of the patentable inventions seem to be patented.

Despite the frequent assertions that firms are making less use of the patent system than in the past, the evidence does not seem to bear this out. Even in electronics, where "potting" (that is, black boxing, such as the encapsulation of products in epoxy resin to deter imitation) is said to have come into prominence, and patents are claimed to be less important, the firms in our sample reported no such trend. This is important because it is the first systematic evidence concerning the extent to which the reduction in the patent rate during the 1970s was due to a shift away from patents and toward trade secrets and other forms of protection. If, as some responsible observers have claimed, "the so-called patent decline may be merely a patent bypass" (Shapley, 1978:848–849), it is important that policymakers be aware that this is the case. Based on these results, there is no indication that this is true.

PRICE INDEXES FOR R&D INPUTS

Economists, policymakers, and analysts are interested in the changes over time in real R&D expenditure—that is, the changes in the amount of real resources devoted to R&D. To estimate such changes, it is necessary to have price indexes for R&D inputs. Unfortunately, until very recently no such price indexes existed. Official government statistics in the United States use the GNP deflator to deflate R&D expenditures. The relevant government agencies are well aware that the GNP deflator is only a rough approximation, but little has been known about the extent to which the results would change if price indexes for R&D inputs were constructed and used instead of the GNP deflator.

In the late 1970s, Goldberg (1978) and Schankerman (1979) constructed price indexes for R&D inputs. These price indexes were based on the use of proxies (that is, series that were thought to be highly correlated with the relevant input prices). For example, Goldberg used data from the National Survey of Professional, Technical, and Clerical Pay to represent the changes over time in the level of wages for R&D engineers and scientists, and Schankerman used the Index of Cost of Materials of the Bureau of Economic Analysis as a proxy for R&D materials prices.

Although indexes based on proxies are interesting and useful, there are obvious advantages in constructing price indexes for R&D inputs based on data obtained from firms regarding actual prices and expenditures. Many observers have urged that such indexes be constructed. Recently, a study financed by the National Science Foundation was carried out along these lines, based on detailed data obtained from about 100 firms in 12 industries (Mansfield et al., 1983; Mansfield, 1985). The study results indicate that, if one is interested in making short-term comparisons of total real R&D expenditure in the nation as a whole, the GNP deflator is reasonably adequate. For example, in comparisons of successive years, the percentage change in real R&D expenditure based on the GNP deflator is generally within a percentage point of that based on the R&D price index produced by the study. However, for long-term comparisons of national R&D expenditure, the use of the GNP deflator can result in substantial errors. Thus, whereas real R&D expenditure went up by 26 percent in the years 1969 to 1981, based on the GNP deflator, it really went up by only 15 percent, according to the R&D price index.

The reason why the GNP deflator performs worse in the long run than in the short run is that, for the vast majority of years for which we have data, it has tended to underestimate the rate of inflation in R&D. This problem is especially severe in particular industries. For example, based on the GNP deflator, real R&D expenditure in the chemical industry grew by about 42 percent during 1969–1981, but based on the R&D price index, it grew by only about 22 percent during this period. Similar errors occur in the oil, primary metals, fabricated metal products, rubber, automobile, instruments, and "other" industries. In all of these industries, the GNP deflator results in an overestimation of the 1969–1981 growth of real R&D expenditure of 15 percentage points or more.

Given the obvious importance of the R&D figures to economic analysis in this area, the availability of these improved R&D price indexes should be a significant step forward. This is the sort of data improvement that tends to be invisible to people who are not involved closely with empirical work. But such improvements can be important.

THE DIFFUSION OF INNOVATIONS

Whereas R&D price indexes have attracted the attention of relatively few economists, the diffusion of innovations has been the focus of a considerable amount of work. Although we are far from having completely satisfactory models of the diffusion process, substantial progress has been made in this area.

In general, the diffusion of a major new technique tends to be a slow process. For example, measuring from the date of first commercial application, it generally took more than 10 years for all of the major American firms in the bituminous coal, steel, railroad, and brewing industries to begin using a sample of important new techniques. (Among the innovations included in this sample were the shuttle car, trackless mobile loader, and continuous mining machine in the bituminous coal industry, and the by-product coke oven, continuous annealing, and continuous wide strip mill in the steel industry.) More recently, similar findings have been reported for the chemical and other industries. Also, the rate of diffusion varies widely. Sometimes it took decades for firms to install a new technique, but in other cases they imitate the innovator very quickly. To some extent, these differences may reflect a tendency for the diffusion process to go on more rapidly in more recent times than in the past (Mansfield, 1961, 1968).

Based on the available evidence, the rate of diffusion of an innovation depends on the average profitability of the innovation; the variation among firms in the profitability of the innovation; the size of the investment required to introduce the innovation; and the number of firms in the industry, their average size, the inequality in their sizes, and the amount that they spend on research and development. Using these variables, one can explain a large proportion of the variation among innovations in the rate of diffusion. Moreover, this seems to be the case in a wide variety of industries and in other countries as well as in the United States. Econometric models using these variables seem to be useful devices for technological forecasting (Mansfield, 1977[6]).

According to studies of a number of industries, firms in which the expected returns from the innovation are highest tend to be quickest to introduce an innovation. Also, holding constant the profitability of the innovation, large firms tend to introduce an innovation more quickly than do small firms. In some industries, this may be due to the fact that larger firms—although not necessarily the largest ones—are more progressive than small firms. But even if the larger firms were not more progressive, one would expect them to be quicker, on the average, to begin using a new technique, for reasons discussed elsewhere (Mansfield, 1968b). Also, holding other factors constant, firms with younger and better-educated managers tend to be quicker to introduce new techniques—or at least, this seems to be the case in industries in which the relevant data have been collected.

Companies also differ greatly with regard to the intrafirm rate of diffusion—the rate at which, once it has begun to use the new technique, a firm substitutes it for older methods. A considerable amount of this variation can be explained by differences among firms in the profitability of the innovation, the size of the firm, and the firm's liquidity. Also, there is a tendency for late starters to catch up. That is, firms that are slow to begin using an innovation tend to substitute it for older techniques more rapidly than those that are quick to begin using it. It is also relevant to note that the same sort of process occurs on the international scene: countries that are slow to begin using an innovation tend to substitute it for older techniques more rapidly than countries that are quick to begin using it. The reasons for this tendency, both at the company and national levels, seem clear enough (Mansfield, 1968a; Nasbeth and Ray, 1974).

Sociologists have studied the nature and sources of information obtained by managers concerning new techniques. The sources of information sometimes vary depending on how close the manager is to adopting the innovation. For example, in agriculture, mass media are most important sources at the very early stages of a manager's awareness of the innovation, but friends and neighbors are most important sources when a manager is ready to try the innovation. Also, there is evidence of a "two-step flow of communication." The early users of an innovation tend to rely on sources of information beyond their peer group's experience; after they have begun using the innovation, they become a model for their less expert peers, who can imitate their performance (Rogers, 1962, and subsequent publications).

Turning to other factors that also influence the rate of diffusion of an innovation, the diffusion process may be slowed by bottlenecks in the production of the innovation—as in the case of the Boeing 707. Also, the extent of advertising and other promotional activities used by producers of the new product or equipment will have an effect. So, too, will the innovation's requirements with respect to knowledge and coordination. The diffusion process will be impeded if the innovation requires new kinds of knowledge on the part of the user, new types of behavior, and the coordinated efforts of a number of organizations. If an innovation requires few changes in sociocultural values and behavior patterns, it is likely to spread more rapidly. Also, the policies adopted by relevant labor unions influence the rate of diffusion. For example, some locals of the painters' union have refused to use the spray gun. In addition, the users' willingness to take risks can have an important influence on an innovation's rate of diffusion. Nonetheless, while the diffusion process is probably better understood than many other aspects of technological change, much more research is needed.[7]

INTERNATIONAL TECHNOLOGY TRANSFER

One aspect of the diffusion process that has received considerable attention in recent years is international technology transfer. Economists have long recognized that the transfer of technology is at the heart of the process of economic growth, and that the progress of both developed and developing countries depends on the extent and efficiency of such transfer. In recent years, economists also have come to realize (or rediscover) the impact of international technology transfer on the size and patterns of world trade.

The work of Hufbauer (1966), Tilton (1971), Schwartz, myself, and others indicates that technology is being transferred across national boundaries more rapidly than in the past. Based on a sample of chemical, semiconductor, and pharmaceutical innovations, this was found to be true even when a variety of other relevant factors were held constant. In considerable part, this is due to the growing influence of multinational firms, many of which are heavily involved in transferring technology. U.S.-based multinational firms are transferring their technology to their foreign subsidiaries much more quickly than in the past. One study of technology diffusion found that in 1969 to 1978 about 75 percent of the technologies that were transferred to subsidiaries in developed countries were less than 5 years old; in 1960 to 1968, the proportion was about 27 percent (Mansfield and Romeo, 1980).

Nations that spend relatively large amounts on R&D (in the relevant industry) tend to be relatively quick to begin producing a new product, even if they are not the innovator. This finding is analogous to the finding (cited above) that firms that spend relatively large amounts on R&D tend to be quick adopters of new technology developed by others. Both for entire nations and individual firms, R&D provides a window on various parts of the environment, and it enables the nation or firm to evaluate external developments and react more quickly to them. In some economic models, R&D is viewed as an invention-producing or innovation-producing activity. While correct as far as it goes, this view misses much of the point of R&D, which is that it is also aimed at a quick response to rivals and at clever modification, adaptation, and improvement of their results.

In many important industries, like pharmaceuticals, international technology transfer is being promoted by the fact that companies have been carrying on increasing shares of their R&D overseas. About 10 percent of the R&D carried out by U.S. firms is performed outside the United States. In some industries, again like pharmaceuticals, this percentage is much larger. When compared with the total R&D expenditures in various host countries, the size of overseas R&D is perhaps even more striking. In the early 1970s, about one-half of the industrial R&D performed in Canada and about one-seventh of the industrial R&D performed in the United Kingdom and West Germany was done by U.S.-based firms (Mansfield, 1984).

International technology transfer has also been promoted by the fact that, in many areas, the process of innovation has been internationalized. For example, in the pharmaceutical industry, a new drug is no longer discovered, tested, and commercialized, all within a single country. Instead, the discovery phase often involves collaboration among laboratories and researchers located in several different countries, even when they are within the same firm. And clinical testing generally becomes a multicountry project. Even in the later phases of drug development, such as dosage formulation, work often is done in more than one country. In contrast, older economic models of the process of international technology transfer often tended to assume that innovations were carried out in a single country, generally the United States, and that the technology resided exclusively within that country for a considerable period after the innovation's initial commercial introduction. Economists are in the process of replacing these models with others that conform more closely to current conditions.

EFFECTS ON OTHER COUNTRIES OF THE
OUTFLOW OF U.S. TECHNOLOGY

As pointed out earlier, technology transfer lies at the heart of the process of economic development. Innovations are primarily responsible for many increases in output per capita. How rapidly innovations spread—and thus raise per capita output in countries other than the innovating nation—depends on the process of technology transfer. The multinational firm is, of course, a major agent in the process of international technology transfer, but its role is highly controversial. Many host countries, although eager for modern technology, are suspicious of the activities of multinational firms.

One of the most important unanswered questions concerning the transfer of technology via the multinational firm is: How big have the economic benefits to countries outside the United States been from technology transfer of this sort? Put somewhat more precisely, how much lower would total output outside the United States have been if technology transfer of this sort had not occurred, but if the relevant technology and goods were perhaps available from the United States or elsewhere? Economists have begun to assemble some quantitative evidence bearing on this question. Based on the limited data available, it has been suggested that total annual output of countries outside the United States would have been at least $35 billion, or at least 1 percent, less if technology transfer of this sort had not occurred (Mansfield and Romeo, 1980). (Note that this estimate is a lower bound.) However, much more work is required in this area. International technology transfer, like so many other aspects of technological change, is very imperfectly understood.

CONCLUSIONS

Microeconomists have been making steady progress in the 30 years that have elapsed since the economics profession began to direct a substantial proportion of its energies and resources to the study of technological change. About 15 years ago, I was asked by the National Science Foundation to write a report (which subsequently appeared in *Science*) describing what we thought we knew in this area and what types of research needed to be done (Mansfield, 1972). It is gratifying to say that significant progress has been made on practically all of the topics identified there as being in great need of further work.

In a chapter of this length, it is impossible to do more than sample some of the many kinds of research that microeconomists have carried out in the past 30 years. A wide variety of econometric models, empirical investigations, computer simulations, and other kinds of output has resulted from the extensive work (largely financed by the National Science Foundation) that has been done. I have made no attempt to cover all, or even most, of the relevant results. Among the interesting contributions in recent years have been Paul David's (1975) diffusion studies, George Eads's (e.g., 1980) policy research, Zvi Griliches's (1958, 1964, 1980, 1984) and Dale Jorgenson's econometric investigations (e.g., Gollop and Jorgenson, 1980), the theoretical work of Kamien and Schwartz (1982), the dynamic models of Burton Klein (1977), the computer simulation models of Nelson and Winter (1982), the empirical studies of Pavitt and his associates at Sussex University's Science Policy Research Unit (e.g., 1974), Nathan Rosenberg's historical investigations (1982), Richard Levin's (1984) and F. M. Scherer's statistical studies (e.g., 1982), and Vernon Ruttan's innovation models (e.g., Evenson et al., 1979). Many of these investigators are contributors to this volume, so I have not attempted to summarize their results, since they obviously have both an absolute and comparative advantage in this regard.[8]

Finally, although we clearly know a great deal more about the economics of technological change than we did 30 years ago, it is evident that we are still very far from a satisfactory understanding of the innovation process, the determinants of the rate of innovation, the measurement of the rate and direction of technological change, and the effects of changes in technology. In view of the enormous difficulties that studies in these areas face, it is not surprising that existing knowledge remains limited.

The extent to which economists are able and willing to work with, and learn from, technologists and scientists may play a significant role in determining how successful we are in chipping away at the many perplexing problems that remain. To my mind, economists frequently have been far too insular and divorced from technological realities. This volume is a very welcome step in the right direction. I hope that it will set the stage for more extensive and effective collaboration between economists and technologists in attempts to deal with the many fundamental problems in this area that concern us all.

NOTES

1. Also, he found that the returns from R&D seemed to be lower in industries in which much R&D is federally funded.
2. Many of these studies are contained in or referred to in Griliches (1984).
3. Much of this section and the next two sections draw heavily on Mansfield et al. (1981).
4. The empirical results presented in this section are largely from Mansfield et al. (1981).
5. A logit analysis is a statistical technique used to estimate the effects of independent variables on a dependent variable that assumes values of zero or one.
6. Blackman (1971) and others have found this model useful in their forecasting studies, and Hsia (1973) and others have found it useful in studies of countries other than the United States.
7. Models devised by economists to represent the diffusion process have been used (with some success) by a variety of firms and government agencies. Although the applicability and power of such models should not be exaggerated, they have proved to be reasonably helpful, if crude, devices, when used with proper caution.
8. This list does not include many of the major figures in this field, let alone the promising younger economists on which the future development of the field will largely depend. Several dozen economists are currently doing interesting work in this field; I have named primarily those who participated in the Symposium on Economics and Technology held at Stanford University, March 17–19, 1985.

REFERENCES

Arrow, K. 1962. Economic welfare and the allocation of resources for invention. In National Bureau of Economic Research, *The Rate and Direction of Inventive Activity*. New York.

Blackman, A. 1971. The rate of innovation in the commercial aircraft jet engine market. *Technological Forecasting and Social Change*.

David, P. 1975. *Technical Choice, Innovation, and Economic Growth*. New York: Cambridge University Press.

Eads, G. 1980. Regulation and technical change: Some unexplored issues. *American Economic Review*.

Evenson, R. 1968. The Contribution of Agricultural Research and Extension to Agricultural Production. Ph.D. dissertation, University of Chicago.

Evenson, R., P. Waggoner, and V. Ruttan. 1979. Economic benefits from research: An example from agriculture. *Science*, September 14, 1979.

Foster Associates. 1978. *A Survey on Net Rates of Return on Innovations*. Washington, D.C.: National Science Foundation.

Goldberg, L. 1978. Federal policies affecting industrial research and development. Presented at the meetings of the Southern Economic Association, November 9, 1978.

Gollop, F., and D. Jorgenson, 1980. U.S. productivity growth by industry, 1947–73. In J. Kendrick and B. Vaccara, eds., *New Developments in Productivity Measurement and Analysis*. Chicago: University of Chicago Press.

Griliches, Z. 1958. Research costs and social returns: Hybrid corn and related innovations. *Journal of Political Economy.*

Griliches, Z. 1964. Research expenditures, education, and the aggregate agricultural production function. *American Economic Review.*

Griliches, Z. 1980. Returns to research and development expenditures in the private sector. In J. Kendrick and B. Vaccara, eds., *New Developments in Productivity Measurement and Analysis.* Chicago: University of Chicago Press.

Griliches, Z., ed. 1984. *R&D, Patents, and Productivity.* Chicago: University of Chicago Press.

Hsia, R. 1973. Technological change in the industrial growth of Hong Kong. In B. Williams, ed., *Science and Technology in Economic Growth.* New York: Macmillan.

Hufbauer, G. 1966. *Synthetic Materials and the Theory of International Trade.* Cambridge, Mass.: Harvard University.

Kamien, M., and N. Schwartz. 1982. *Market Structure and Innovation.* New York: Cambridge University Press.

Klein, B. 1977. *Dynamic Economics.* Cambridge, Mass.: Harvard University Press.

Levin, R., and P. Reiss. 1984. Tests of a Schumpeterean model of R&D and market structure. In Z. Griliches, ed., *R&D, Patents, and Productivity.* Chicago: University of Chicago Press.

Mansfield, E. 1961. Technical change and the rate of innovation. *Econometrica.*

Mansfield, E. 1965. Rates of return from industrial research and development. *American Economic Review.*

Mansfield, E. 1968a. *The Economics of Technological Change.* New York: W. W. Norton.

Mansfield, E. 1968b. *Industrial Research and Technological Innovation.* New York: W. W. Norton for the Cowles Foundation for Research in Economics at Yale University.

Mansfield, E. 1972. Contribution of R&D to economic growth in the United States. *Science*, February 4, 1972.

Mansfield, E. 1980. Basic research and productivity increase in manufacturing. *American Economic Review.*

Mansfield, E. 1981. Composition of R&D expenditures: Relationship to size of firm, concentration, and innovative output. *Review of Economics and Statistics.*

Mansfield, E. 1984. Technological change and the international diffusion of technology. To be published by the Royal Commission on the Economic Union and Development Prospects for Canada.

Mansfield, E. 1985a. *Patents and Innovation: An Empirical Study.* Philadelphia: University of Pennsylvania.

Mansfield, E. 1985b. *Price Indexes for R&D Inputs, 1969–83.* Philadelphia: University of Pennsylvania.

Mansfield, E., and A. Romeo. 1980. Technology transfer to overseas subsidiaries by U.S.-based firms. *Quarterly Journal of Economics*, December.

Mansfield, E., et al. 1971. *Research and Innovation in the Modern Corporation.* New York: W. W. Norton.

Mansfield, E., et al. 1977a. *The Production and Application of New Industrial Technology.* New York: W. W. Norton.

Mansfield, E., et al. 1977b. Social and private rates of return from industrial innovations. *Quarterly Journal of Economics.*

Mansfield, E., M. Schwartz, and S. Wagner. 1981. Imitation costs and patents: An empirical study. *Economic Journal.*

Mansfield, E., et al. 1982. *Technology Transfer, Productivity, and Economic Policy.* New York: W. W. Norton.

Mansfield, E., A. Romeo, and L. Switzer. 1983. R&D price indexes and real R&D expenditures in the United States. *Research Policy.*

Minasian, J. 1969. Research and development, production functions, and rates of return. *American Economic Review*.

Nabseth, L., and G. Ray. 1974. *The Diffusion of New Industrial Processes*. London: Cambridge University Press.

Nadiri, M., and G. Bitros. 1980. Research and development expenditures and labor productivity at the firm level. In J. Kendrick and B. Vaccara, eds., *New Developments in Productivity Measurement and Analysis*. Chicago: University of Chicago Press.

Robert R. Nathan Associates. 1978. *Net Rates of Return on Innovations*. Washington, D.C.: National Science Foundation.

Nelson, R., and S. Winter. 1982. *An Evolutionary Theory of Economic Change*. Cambridge, Mass.: Belknap.

Pavitt, K. 1974. In National Science Foundation, *The Effects of International Technology Transfers on U.S. Economy*, Washington, D.C.: Government Printing Office.

Peterson, W. 1971. The returns to investment in agricultural research in the United States. In *Resource Allocation in Agricultural Research*. Minneapolis: University of Minnesota.

Rogers, E. 1962. *Diffusion of Innovations*. New York: The Free Press.

Rosenberg, N. 1982. *Inside the Black Box: Technology and Economics*. New York: Cambridge University Press.

Schankerman, M. 1979. Essays in the Economics of Technical Change. Ph.D. dissertation, Harvard University.

Scherer, F. M. 1982. Inter-industry technology flows and productivity growth. *Review of Economics and Statistics*.

Schmitz, A., and D. Seckler. 1980. Mechanized agriculture and social welfare: The case of the tomato harvester. *American Journal of Agricultural Economics*.

Schumpeter, J. 1934. *The Theory of Economic Development*. Cambridge, Mass.: Harvard University Press.

Shapley, D. 1978. Electronics industry takes to potting the products for market. *Science*, November 24: 848–849.

Taylor, C., and Z. Silberston. 1973. *The Economic Impact of the Patent System*. New York: Cambridge University Press.

Terleckyj, N. 1974. *Effects of R&D on the Productivity Growth of Industries*. Washington, D.C.: National Planning Association.

Tilton, J. 1971. *International Diffusion of Technology: The Case of Semiconductors*. Washington, D.C.: The Brookings Institution.

Macroeconomics and Microeconomics of Innovation: The Role of the Technological Environment

ANN F. FRIEDLAENDER

If America is to continue to grow and thrive, the answer to the question of how productivity growth and technical change take place is crucial. The answer can perhaps only be obtained by using analytic frameworks that combine and synthesize the insights of technologists, engineers, and economists.

As an economist who has worked with engineers and technologists for many years, I am struck by the fundamental lack of communication that exists between them in discussing the sources and nature of innovation and productivity growth. This arises, I believe, because of basic differences in the way each group visualizes the production process and the nature of innovation. Since each group brings a very different perspective to the problem, increased communication should lead to a richer analytic framework and a deeper understanding of the sources and nature of technological change.

OVERVIEW

A brief description of the approach of each group will indicate some of the ways in which a greater synthesis of the two approaches could increase our understanding of technical change and productivity growth.

While something of a caricature, it is probably fair to state that economists view the production function as an abstraction, a "black box" if you will, that permits the transformation of certain inputs (labor, capital, materials, and so forth) into different outputs; they have little, if any, interest in the inner workings of that black box. Thus, to economists, the production function is merely that—a general functional expression relating outputs to inputs; they have little regard for the specific functional form or how the specific technology employed may affect either the functional form or the parameters of the production function. Indeed, it is only within the past decade that economists have generally realized that the specific functional form used to describe technology may impose severe restrictions on its assumed nature (e.g., the unitary elasticity of substitution associated with the Cobb-Douglas production function) and have adopted so-called flexible functional forms in analyzing production relationships and productivity growth.

In contrast, engineers and technologists have little interest in the abstract "production function" as such; instead, they are interested in describing the actual technical relationships that permit the translation of specific amounts of labor, machines, and materials into widgets or other commodities. Thus, engineering production functions tend to be very detailed and to focus on the technical environment in which production takes place. Consequently, although relative input prices drive the allocation of inputs within the context of the economists' production or cost functions, they tend to be ignored in engineering production functions. Conversely, while the technological environment tends to drive engineering production functions, it is often ignored in economic production functions. Thus, by focusing on the technological environment, engineers and technologists can provide economists with important insights that could enrich the economists' framework and analytic models.

IMPORTANCE OF THE TECHNOLOGICAL ENVIRONMENT

A few examples will illustrate the kinds of things that I am referring to. Consider the question of productivity growth in the automobile industry. In recent years, there has been considerable concern about the level of productivity in the American automobile industry relative to that in Japan. In particular, the concern has focused on two organizational differences between the two countries: the use of "quality-control circles" in the organization of Japanese labor and the use of "just-in-time" inventories in the Japanese production process. The use of the former presumably makes labor more productive, and the use of the latter permits considerable savings on capital that is tied up in inventories.

Suppose American producers adopted both of these innovations tomorrow and that 5 years hence an econometrician attempted to measure productivity growth in the U.S. automobile industry. What would be the likely outcome of this econometric investigation? To see this, consider how each innovation would appear within the context of the abstract production function. Since the introduction of the quality-control circles would presumably permit more output for given amounts of labor and increase the marginal product of labor relative to that of capital, it would show up as a labor-saving innovation. In contrast, since the introduction of just-in-time inventories would lead to lower capital requirements, it would show up as a capital-saving innovation. On balance, depending on the relative magnitude of these effects, one would observe increased productivity growth and technical change that could be described as labor saving, neutral, or capital saving. Clearly, however, the ex post aggregate characterization of technological change in any of these terms is not particularly enlightening, since it does not indicate how this technical change came about and what specific innovations contributed to it. What is useful is the knowledge of the specific innovations that led to the change, or, how the workings inside the "black box" were altered. While this is something that a few economists attempt to unravel, in general too much attention is paid to the aggregate concepts rather than to the technological environment that created the changes.

As another example, consider industries such as transportation or communications, in which the configuration and utilization of the network can have a significant impact on productive relationships and technical change. To point out the implications of this, let me discuss the way in which the introduction of network variables can enhance our understanding of productive relationships and technical change. First, consider a "typical" economic production function that relates output (ton-miles, passenger-miles, message units, or some disaggregated version thereof) to generalized inputs (labor, capital, materials, and so forth). It should be clear that both the configuration and utilization of the network will have a significant impact on the way in which inputs are transformed into outputs. Suppose, for example, that firm A utilizes a network composed of a limited number of corridors, each of which is between major urban centers and thus has high density of usage. In contrast, firm B utilizes a "hub-and-spoke" network, with a central core that services a hinterland. Finally, firm C utilizes a network composed of a large number of corridors linking small urban areas without a hub-and-spoke network. One can readily imagine a situation in which each firm utilizes the same amount of each input, but produces very different levels of output and, thus, has very different implied levels of productivity. Although the economist may simply retort that this is a problem of aggregation, the problem is really deeper than that, because the configuration and utilization of the network add a dimension that make the three production processes fundamentally different, regardless of the specification of output. Thus again, what is going on inside the "black box" adds fundamental insights to our understanding of the production process. (For a full discussion of these and related points, see Chiang et al., 1984.)

As a final example, let me describe a recent study I have undertaken on the trucking industry (Friedlaender and Bruce, 1985) to try to explain its productivity growth in the period prior to deregulation (1975 to 1979). In this particular study, costs were estimated as a function of input prices (capital, labor, fuel, and so forth), output levels (ton-miles), shipment characteristics (average load, average length of haul, shipment size, and so forth), and a time trend. Thus, in addition to the usual arguments in the cost function (output, input prices, and a time trend to capture productivity growth), the study included variables to reflect the technological environment or the way in which inputs were transformed into outputs. In this connection, it was interesting to note that virtually all of the productivity growth and technical change could be attributed to the technological factors considered rather than to the various inputs or to the scale of output. While the measures of the technological environment used in this study were admittedly crude, their statistical significance clearly indicates that what often drives productivity is the way in which inputs are utilized and the way in which output is configured. Although changes in the technological environment could have been labeled capital- or labor-saving innovations, we are surely better off knowing that what was really driving productivity growth was the way in which shipments were distributed over the network. Ideally, both for purposes of policy and for purposes of understanding technical change, we would like to know the specific organizational or logistical changes that were made and how they could be expected to affect productivity so that all firms could be encouraged to undertake them.

To summarize my basic point, I believe that a much richer analytic framework is possible if economists would attempt to incorporate the fundamental insight of engineers and technologists—that the organizational and technological environment can have a major impact on productivity and technical change. While abstractions relating to the elasticities of substitution, returns to scale, and neutral or nonneutral technical change are useful, they are that much more meaningful if the interactions between input utilization and the technological environment are recognized and taken into account.

COMMENTS ON CHAPTERS BY JORGENSON AND MANSFIELD

I am disappointed to note that in their discussions in this volume, which deal with microeconomic issues related to technical change and productivity growth, Dale W. Jorgenson and Edwin Mansfield largely ignore the potential insights of technologists and engineers with respect to innovation and productivity growth.

Let me begin with Jorgenson's chapter, which analyzes the sources of productivity growth in the American economy in the postwar period. As is true in most analyses of this type, Jorgenson employs a neoclassical framework, which assumes that firms operate in perfectly competitive input and output markets and that they utilize an aggregate production function that transforms aggregate inputs (capital, labor, electrical energy, and nonelectrical energy) into an aggregate output. Recognizing the importance of sectoral differences, Jorgenson utilizes a disaggregated sectoral analysis and estimates a price frontier, adjusted for productivity growth, for 35 industries. Not surprisingly, he finds that patterns of productivity growth are not uniform, but vary widely among industries; no more than 8 of the industries exhibited common patterns of productivity growth.

It is admittedly useful to know that 8 of the 35 industries exhibited a pattern of productivity growth in which increases in the prices of capital, labor, electrical energy, and nonelectrical energy retard productivity growth and in which a rise in the price of materials stimulates productivity growth. Moreover, it is also useful to know that 20 of the 35 industries exhibited a pattern of capital-using productivity growth. Nevertheless, it would be even more useful to know why those industries exhibited different patterns of growth and what determined the magnitude of the stimulating or inhibiting effects of input price changes on productivity growth. Without such knowledge, neither businessmen nor policymakers have any real guides concerning appropriate actions they could take to increase productivity growth in particular industries and in the nation as a whole; nor do they know whether past relationships between input prices and productivity growth can be expected to continue in the future.

To continue with this theme, the following 8 industries exhibited a common pattern in which price increases in all inputs (with the exception of materials) inhibited productivity growth: tobacco, textiles, apparel, lumber and wood, printing and publishing, fabricated metals, motor vehicles, and transportation. In contrast, the following 5 industries exhibited the same pattern of productivity growth, with the exception that increases in the cost of capital stimulated rather than retarded productivity growth: rubber; leather; instruments; gas utilities; and finance, insurance, and real estate. These lists of industries immediately bring the following questions to mind: (1) What was there in the technological environment in the 8 industries that led them to exhibit a common pattern of productivity growth? (2) What was there in the technological environment of the 5 industries that led them to exhibit a common pattern of productivity growth? (3) What was there in the technological environment of the 13 industries that led them to exhibit common patterns of productivity growth, with the exception of capital? (4) And finally, to what extent were these similarities and differences due to the nature of the output, the nature of the inputs, or the technological environment in which production took place? Thus, Jorgenson seems to skirt the basic question of why productivity growth is stimulated in some industries by rises in certain input prices and why it is inhibited by similar price increases in other industries. Whether the answers to these questions can be found in the analyses of engineers and technologists is unclear, but it would be interesting to get their insights into this problem.

My comments on Mansfield's discussion echo this theme, although perhaps in a somewhat gentler voice, since Mansfield does attempt to focus on the following specific factors that affect innovation and productivity growth: (1) the level and nature of expenditures on R&D and basic research; (2) the role of imitation costs, imitation times, patents, barriers to entry, and industrial concentration; and (3) the diffusion of innovation and technology transfer. Thus, instead of focusing on the aggregate production function, Mansfield focuses on issues that relate to the productive and technological environment.

Nevertheless, one wishes that Mansfield and his fellow economists had gone further. If, for example, labor and capital productivity are positively affected by the level of R&D expenditures, one would like to know how this process takes place. Is it the existence of R&D expenditures, per se, that stimulates labor and capital productivity, or are R&D expenditures transformed into specific innovations that make labor or capital more productive? Similarly, why does basic research stimulate total factor productivity independent of the level of R&D expenditures? As Mansfield points out, the question is whether this reflects a tendency for basic research findings to be exploited more fully by firms and industries that were responsible for it; whether it reflects a tendency for applied R&D expenditures to be more effective when carried out in conjunction with some basic research; or whether basic research is merely serving as a proxy for long-term R&D.

Again, we are left with many tantalizing questions, but little analysis to answer them. Thus, I would like to close by encouraging economists to think more seriously about and confront the issues posed by the disassembly of the black-box production function. While such a disassembly would certainly reduce the elegance of economic analysis and limit the generality of the models employed, it should also provide greater insights into the question of how productivity growth and technical change take place. If America is to continue to grow and thrive, the answer to this question is crucial. In this regard, I suspect it can only be obtained by using analytic frameworks that combine and synthesize the insights of technologists, engineers, and economists.

REFERENCES

Chiang, Wang, Judy S. Friedlaender, and Ann F. Friedlaender. 1984. Output aggregation, network effects, and the measurement of trucking technology. *Review of Economics and Statistics* 66(May):267–277.

Friedlaender, Ann F., and Sharon Schur Bruce. 1985. Augmentation effects and technical change in the regulated trucking industry, 1974–1979. In *Studies in Transportation Economics*, Andrew Daughety, ed. New York: Cambridge University Press (Forthcoming).

Technical Change and
Innovation in Agriculture

VERNON W. RUTTAN

Over the past 50 years, U.S. agriculture has been transformed from a resource-based industry to a science-based industry. It has been transformed from a traditional to a high technology sector. Agriculture is one of the relatively few sectors in the U.S. economy that have been able to maintain their technological leadership—to achieve or maintain world class. A number of lessons can be drawn from the agricultural research system that may be relevant for research policy in other sectors of the economy.

During the past half century U.S. agriculture has retained and enhanced its status as a world-class industry. This has occurred at a time when a number of other U.S. basic industries, most notably automobiles and steel, were experiencing substantial erosion in their capacity to compete in world markets.

The focus of this chapter is primarily on innovation on the part of the suppliers of technology rather than on innovation in the farm production sector itself. The new technologies employed in agricultural production are, by and large, not a product of research and development by the firms that engage in the production of agricultural commodities. Even the largest farm firms are too small to capture more than a small share of the gains that might be realized by research and development efforts. New technologies in agriculture are, with the exception of some mechanical technologies, largely the product of research and development by public sector research institutions and private sector suppliers of technical inputs to agriculture. These new technologies reach the farmer embodied in inputs that are purchased from the farm-supply industries and in the form of disembodied knowledge provided by the private suppliers of technology, private consultants, and public sector educational institutions. No attempt is made in this chapter to discuss the diffusion of technology—the sequence of innovation—within the farm production sector. There is a large literature that suggests that profitable new technologies are adopted very rapidly by farmers in both developed and underdeveloped countries.[1]

This chapter (a) discusses the evidence on productivity growth and on the returns to agricultural research, (b) reviews the changing role of the public and private sector in agricultural research, (c) discusses the dominant role of factor prices in directing productivity growth, and (d) suggests some of the implications of the agricultural experience.

THE CONTRIBUTION OF RESEARCH TO PRODUCTIVITY GROWTH

The beginning of modernization in agriculture is signaled by sustained growth in productivity.[2] During the initial stages of development, productivity growth is usually accounted for by improvement in a single, partial productivity ratio, such as output per unit of labor or output per unit of land. As modernization progresses there is a tendency for growth in total productivity—output per unit of total input—to be sustained by a more balanced combination of improvement in partial productivity ratios. This was clearly the case in the United States. Prior to the mid-1920s productivity growth in U.S. agriculture was driven almost entirely by growth in labor productivity—output per worker (Table 1). Since the mid-1920s growth in labor productivity has been complemented by growth in land productivity. The contrast with the Japanese experience is quite striking. Prior to the mid-1950s productivity growth in Japanese agriculture was driven almost entirely by growth in land productivity (Table 2). Since the mid-1950s growth in land productivity has been complemented by growth in labor productivity.

TABLE 1   Average Annual Rates of Change (percentage per year) in Output, Inputs, and Productivity in U.S. Agriculture, 1870–1982

Item	1870–1900	1900–1925	1925–1950	1950–1965	1965–1982
Farm output	2.9	0.9	1.6	1.7	2.1
Total inputs	1.9	1.1	0.2	−0.4	0.2
Total productivity	1.0	−0.2	1.3	2.2	1.8
Labor inputs[a]	1.6	0.5	−1.7	−4.8	−3.4
Labor productivity	1.3	0.4	3.3	6.6	5.8
Land inputs[b]	3.1	0.8	0.1	−0.9	0.0
Land productivity	−0.2	0.0	1.4	2.6	1.8

[a]Number of workers, 1870–1910; worker-hour basis, 1910–1982.
[b]Cropland used for crops, including crop failures and cultivated summer fallow.
SOURCES: Data from U.S. Department of Agriculture, *Changes in Farm Production and Efficiency* (Washington, D.C.: 1984); and D. D. Durost and G. T. Barton, *Changing Sources of Farm Output*, Production Research Report No. 36 (Washington, D.C.: U.S. Department of Agriculture, Feb. 1960). Data are 3-year averages centered on the dates shown.

TABLE 2   Average Annual Change in Total Output, Inputs, and Productivity in Japanese Agriculture, 1880–1980

Item	1880–1920	1920–1935	1935–1955	1955–1965	1965–1980
Farm output	1.8	0.9	0.6	3.5	1.2
Total inputs	0.5	0.5	1.2	1.3	0.7
Total productivity	1.3	0.4	−0.6	2.2	0.5
Labor inputs	−0.3	−0.2	0.6	−2.5	−3.7
Labor productivity	2.1	1.1	0.0	6.0	4.9
Land inputs	0.6	0.1	−0.1	0.1	−0.6
Land productivity	1.2	0.8	0.7	3.4	1.8

SOURCES: Data from Saburo Yamada and Yujiro Hayami, Agricultural growth in Japan, 1880–1970, pp. 33–58 in *Agricultural Growth in Japan, Taiwan, Korea and the Philippines*, Yujiro Hayami, Vernon W. Ruttan, and Herman Southworth, eds. (Honolulu: University Press of Hawaii, 1979); Saburo Yamada, The secular trends in input-output relations of agricultural production in Japan, 1878–1978, paper presented at the Conference of Agricultural Development in China, Japan, and Korea, Academica Sinica, Taipei, December 17–20, 1980; and Saburo Yamada, Country Study on Agricultural Productivity Measurement and Analysis—Japan. Mimeograph (University of Tokyo Institute of Oriental Culture, October 1984). Data are 3-year averages centered on the dates shown.

The transition from one growth path to another has not been easy for either the United States or Japan. The United States experienced a dramatic slowing of productivity growth following the closing of the land frontier in the 1890s. Japan experienced a slowing of total productivity growth as it made the transition from a land-saving to a more balanced path of technical change between 1935 and 1955. And Japan has again experienced a reduction in the rate of productivity growth beginning in the late 1960s. Adjustments in farm size in response to rising wage rates have been inhibited by institutional constraints.

In the United States the transition from resource-based to science-based agriculture was made possible by the institutionalization of public sector research capacity designed to speed the advance of land-saving biological, chemical, and managerial capacity. Public sector agricultural research institutions were established during the nineteenth century. But financial support was niggardly and research capacity remained rudimentary until the closing of the frontier induced a demand for land-saving or yield-increasing technical change. Productivity growth in U.S. agriculture slowed moderately from the 1950–1965 rate during 1965–1982. I anticipate a further slowing until at least the mid-1990s, when less-energy-intensive biological technologies will begin to exert a measurable impact on agricultural productivity growth.

Estimates of rates of return suggest that public agricultural research has clearly been among the most productive investments available to the American economy (Table 3). There remain a number of serious gaps in our knowledge about sources of productivity growth, however. Public sector agricultural research appears to have accounted for about one-fourth of the

TABLE 3   Estimated Impacts of Research and Extension Investments in U.S. Agriculture

Period and Subject	Annual Rate of Return (%)	Percentage of Productivity Change Realized in the State Undertaking the Research
1868–1926		
All agricultural research	65	not estimated
1927–1950		
Technology-oriented agricultural research	95	55
Science-oriented agricultural research	110	33
1948–1971		
Technology-oriented agricultural research		
South	130	67
North	93	43
West	95	67
Science-oriented agricultural research	45	32
Farm management and agricultural extension	110	100

SOURCE: Adapted from Robert E. Evenson, Paul E. Waggoner, and Vernon W. Ruttan, Economic benefits from research: An example from agriculture. *Science* 205 (Sept. 14, 1979): 1101–1107.

growth in total productivity in the agricultural sector. Increases in the educational level of farm people have accounted for somewhat more than one-fourth of productivity growth.

But why has investment in agricultural research not had more growth leverage? The answer must be found in very substantial underinvestment. The total investment in agricultural research is so small relative to agricultural production that even investments that generate very high rates of return exert only a modest impact on the rate of growth of agricultural output and productivity. Among the factors that have not been adequately studied in recent research is the impact on productivity growth of private sector research, technology development, and technology-transfer activities.

PUBLIC AND PRIVATE SECTOR GENERATION OF AGRICULTURAL TECHNOLOGY

Innovative behavior in the public sector has been largely ignored in the literature on innovation. Indeed, it would not be too inaccurate to argue that we have no agreed theory of public sector innovation. This is a particularly critical limitation in attempting to understand the process of scientific and technical innovation in agricultural development.[3] In all of the countries that have been successful in achieving rapid rates of technical progress in agriculture, the "socialization" of agricultural research has been deliberately employed as an instrument of modernization in agriculture. The appropriate role of the public and private sectors in agricultural research will depend, however, on the state of a nation's technical and institutional development.

In this section[4] I discuss recent trends in agricultural research and development in the public and private sectors in the United States and present two case studies that illustrate the complex and changing relationships that have emerged between public and private sector research and development.

Three criteria have been used to gauge the appropriate role of the public and private sectors in agricultural research. The primary rationale for public sector investment has been that in many areas incentives for private sector research have been inadequate to induce an optimum level of research investment—that is, the social rate of return exceeds the private rate of return because a large share of the gains from research accrue to other firms, to producers, and to consumers rather than to the innovating firm.

A second criterion for public sector investment in agricultural research is its complementarity with education. There is a strong synergistic interaction between research and education in the agricultural sciences and technology. This relationship is so strong that in many fields research productivity carries a strong penalty when research is conducted apart from graduate education. And graduate education can hardly be effective when both students and teachers are not engaged in research.

A third argument for public sector research is that it contributes to the maintenance or enhancement of a competitive structure in the agricultural input, production, and marketing sectors. There is, for example, considerable evidence that the flow of new technology from public sector research and development has contributed to competitive behavior in the seed and fertilizer industries.

There is, however, no reason to believe that the optimum level of public sector investment in research implied by the several criteria would be identical. Where incentives for private research investment are particularly strong, for example, the level of public sector research implied by the training criterion could exceed the level implied by the criterion of social rate of return.

Recent Trends in Public and Private Sector Research

The extent of research and development expenditures by the private sector in support of the U.S. food system is poorly documented. The best single set of data available are the 1965 estimates developed by the Agricultural Research Institute.[5] The 1978 and 1979 estimates assembled by Malstead (1980) suggest that private research expenditures by firms in the agricultural-

TABLE 4   Estimates of Industry R&D Expenditures for Farming and
Postfarming Efficiency ($ millions)

	1978	1979
Farm input industries	751–846	814–909
Plants	348–443	402–497
Plant breeding	55–150	60–155
Pesticides	290	339
Plant nutrients	3	3
Animals	178	187
Animal breeding	49	55
Animal health (mostly veterinary drugs)	99	99
Animal feed and feed ingredients	30	33
Farm equipment and machinery	225	225
Processing and Distribution	641–651	734–744
Farm produce transport equipment	40	45
Food processing machinery	85	100
Food processing	350	400
Tobacco manufacturing	40–50	40–50
Natural fiber processing	10	20
Packaging materials	116	129

SOURCE: From Illona Malstead, Agriculture: The relationship of R&D to federal goals. Photocopy (Washington, D.C.: 1980). Sources consulted in constructing the estimates included the Agricultural Research Institute, the National Agricultural Chemical Association, the Animal Health Institute, the American Feed Manufacturers' Association, the Farm and Industrial Equipment Institute, the Southeastern Poultry Association, and the National Association for Animal Breeders, and individual company representatives.

input industries and in the processing and distribution industries were about $1.6 billion in 1979 (Table 4). The R&D data presented in Table 4 include expenditures in the area of processing and distribution that do not contribute directly to agricultural production or even very significantly to consumer satisfaction. Yet there are also important research expenditures that are not reflected in the data in Table 4. During 1969–1977 less than 10 percent of the patents for processes and products for the food industry originated in the U.S. food industry (Mueller, et al., 1980). A relatively high percentage of inventions leading to patents in the farm-machinery industry emerge outside formal R&D laboratories and shops.

A complete accounting of private sector R&D in support of the agricultural-input industries and the food processing and distribution industries for 1979 would, in my judgment, show total expenditures in excess of $2.0 billion. In comparison, public sector agricultural research, performed by the U.S. Department of Agriculture (USDA) and the state agricultural experiment stations, amounted to approximately $1.2 billion in 1979. Since the late 1970s private sector research in the service-based biological and chemical technologies in support of animal health, plant protection, and plant breeding has expanded rapidly. This expansion may have been partially offset by some reductions in research by the farm equipment and machinery industry. It would not be too surprising, when the results of the 1984 Agricultural Research Institute survey become available, to find that private sector agricultural research had risen to between $2.5 billion and $3.0 billion by 1984 (in 1979 dollars). It also seems likely that a larger share of the total will be accounted for by the input industries than in 1978 and 1979.

Despite the tentative data available, a number of relatively clear-cut generalizations can be made. First, private sector R&D has grown more rapidly than public sector agricultural research since 1965. In 1965 private sector R&D probably accounted for about 55 percent of total public and private sector research in support of the food system. By 1979 the private sector share was probably about 65 percent. In both 1965 and 1979 the private sector research effort was apparently divided about equally between agricultural inputs and food marketing and distribution.

Second, the animal drug industry, which allocates over 12 percent of its sales dollar to research, and the pesticide industry, which allocates about 10 percent of its sales dollar to research, are the most research intensive of the agricultural-input industries. The farm machinery industry, which allocates about 3 percent of sales to research, is apparently slightly above the average for all U.S. industry in R&D intensity. The fertilizer industry, on the other hand, spends well below 1 percent of its sales dollar on R&D. The food and kindred products industry apparently allocates less than 0.05 percent of its sales dollar to R&D. (See Ruttan, 1982b:24.)

Third, R&D activity in the agricultural-input and food industries is focused primarily on product development. The food industry, for example, focuses its effort on new product development but buys its process technology from suppliers. Similarly, the agricultural chemicals industry focuses its efforts on new products but not on the processes used to produce the products. The definition of what is a product or a process innovation is, however, quite arbitrary. A product innovation in the farm machinery industry becomes a process innovation when adopted by agricultural producers.

Fourth, there are quite striking differences in the relative emphasis given to the several fields of science and technology between the public and private sectors and, within the public sector, between the U.S. Department of Agriculture and the state agricultural experiment stations. Close to two-thirds of private sector R&D is concentrated in the physical sciences and engineering. Public sector research is much more heavily concentrated in the biological sciences and technology. At the state agricultural experiment stations, approximately three-quarters of the research is in the biological science and technology area. The share of the research dollar allocated to social science research related to agriculture is less than 5 percent in the private sector and less than 10 percent in the public sector.

Finally, it seems likely that the relative emphasis among research performers will undergo substantial change over the next decade. Within the private sector the balance appears to be shifting from the physical sciences and engineering toward the biological sciences and biotechnology. Institutional innovations—including plant variety registration, legal interpretation favorable to the patenting of new life forms, and the design of regulatory regimes that more effectively differentiate between chemical and biological technologies—are providing additional incentives for private sector investment in the development of science-based biological technologies (Office of Technology Assessment, 1984:383–410). As this trend continues public sector research institutions will need to reexamine the allocation of their research resources. This will involve a shift in the distribution of research resources from applied toward more basic research. But it does not imply that a withdrawal from applied research by the public sector is appropriate. There continue to be important areas of agricultural technology development that do not lend themselves to packaging in the form of proprietary products and hence offer little incentive for private sector research investment. If the public sector were to confine itself to basic research and abandon technology development, the result would be a slowing of the rate of productivity growth in agriculture.

Mechanization Research   The appropriate boundary between private and public sector research on mechanization has been a continuing area of concern. Two issues have been prominent. One is whether public sector research duplicates or displaces private sector research. A second is who gains and who loses as a result of the introduction of new technology. The critics of public sector research on mechanization have emphasized its effect on labor displacement. However, the best empirical evidence suggests that in the United States the development of mechanical equipment and motive power has been induced by long-term increases in the price of labor. Mechanization in agriculture has been primarily a response to a declining agricultural labor force rather than a major cause of agricultural labor-force displacement (Hayami and Ruttan, 1985; Peterson and Kislev, in press).

Recent concern about the public funding of mechanization research has been focused by the controversy about the role of the University of California in the development of integrated mechanical and biological technology for production and harvesting of tomatoes and a number of specialty crops. The rationale for public support for research and development of machinery in California has relied on two arguments. One is that many of the specialty crops grown are unique to California. Because of limited acreage and the small market potential, the argument has been made that there was little incentive for private research and development. A second rationale has been made in terms of improving the ability of California farmers to compete with producers in other areas in the United States, as in the case of tomatoes, or with imports from other countries, as in the case of strawberries. Both arguments are, in principle, consistent with the traditional use of the social rate of return as a criterion for public support for agricultural research.

The history of the development of the tomato harvester extended over a period of about three decades (de Janvry et al., 1980:97–99). Its development was speeded by the ending of the *bracero* program, which permitted Mexican citizens to enter the United States to harvest crops and do other field work. A combination of yield-increasing biological technology and labor-displacing harvest technology enabled California producers to capture a large share of the processed tomato market from the older producing areas in the Midwest and the East. Initially, this led to an increase in demand for labor in tomato production. Later, however, it led to the displacement of harvest labor. The implications for state economic development were ambiguous. The gains to producers exceeded the losses to workers by a substantial margin. But since the losers were typically poor and the gainers relatively well off, a major issue of equity was involved. And the equity issue was exacerbated by the fact that, while the gains were sufficient to compensate for the losses, compensation was not made (Schmitz and Seckler, 1970; Brandt and French, 1983).

The implication of the mechanization debate for research policy seems reasonably clear. The private sector has been an effective source of new mechanical technology. Lack of knowledge has seldom been a serious constraint on advances in mechanical technology for agriculture. Some observers believe that the Blackwelder Company would have developed a fully effective tomato harvester by the early 1970s, even without the participation of the University of California. The development of the mechanical cucumber harvester in Michigan points to a similar conclusion. For both the tomato and the cucumber harvester, the demand-side impetus for commercial development associated with the ending of the *bracero* program appeared to be more important than the supply-side public sector research effort.

The social rate of return provides a weak rationale for substantial federal support for research and development of mechanical equipment for agriculture. The rationale for support by state agricultural experiment stations must be primarily in terms of local rather than national benefits. Any rationale for public sector mechanization research must draw more heavily on the educational, than on the social rate of return, criterion.

Development of Plant Varieties In the United States the seed industry evolved along two relatively distinct lines. The private sector tended to be the predominant source of new varieties for the home gardener and for horticultural crops. The public sector tended to be the dominant supplier of new varieties for field crops. This pattern began to change with the advent of hybrid corn. Control of inbred lines capable of serving as the parents for superior hybrids enabled the private sector to establish proprietary control over new hybrid corn varieties. In the mid-1970s, over 80 percent of the corn and sorghum varieties used in commercial production and approximately 70 percent of the sugarbeet and cotton varieties were private varieties. Over 80 percent of the rye, wheat, oats, soybeans, rice, barley, peanuts, dry edible beans, and forage grasses were public varieties.

The rather complex public sector involvement in varietal crop development, seed certification, and varietal recommendations that prevails in the United States can be illustrated using the State of Minnesota as an example. Individual variations exist from state to state but the general features are similar. When the performance of a new public variety of soybeans developed by the Minnesota Agricultural Experiment Station warrants seed multiplication, breeder seed is released by the station to the Minnesota Crop Improvement Association for multiplication. The association, a nonprofit corporation whose owners are mostly farmers and seed companies, has also been designated by the state legislature as the official seed-certifying agency in Minnesota. To assure the quality of the seed grown by seed growers, the association carries out field inspection of the seed crops and conducts laboratory tests for purity and viability on samples taken from the growers' processed seed before issuing certification certificates and labels.

Minnesota's system has been remarkably effective in the generation and distribution of new seed varieties. It has also been an important factor in maintaining a competitive structure in the seed industry. However, it is highly dependent on the level of public support for plant breeding and varietal development.

In the United States, the first legislation protecting plant varieties was passed in 1930. The Plant Patent Act of 1930 extended patenting rights to breeders of a number of asexually reproduced plants. In 1970 the U.S. Congress passed a Plant Variety Protection Act, which was developed by a committee of the American Seed Trade Association. The 1970 act covered seeds, transplants, and plants of about 350 species. Several "soup vegetable" species (tomatoes, carrots, cucumbers, okra, celery, and peppers) were omitted because of objections by canners and freezers. There was also substantial opposition to the act from scientists and breeders in the state agricultural experiment stations and from the U.S. Department of Agriculture. It was argued that adequate consideration had not been given to such factors as (a) variability in crop performance and genetic drift under different environmental conditions and (b) the exchange of information and germ plasm among public and private breeders.

Experience with the 1970 act resulted in a number of changes in perception regarding the effect of variety protection. Most participants in the debate have concluded that the act has encouraged expansion of plant breeding in the private sector. Fears that the act would lead to excessive litigation have not been realized. A good deal of the opposition to variety protection by public sector breeders has disappeared. And the canning and freezing industry did not register opposition to inclusion of the "soup vegetables" when the act was amended in 1980. (The 1980 amendments also extended the period of protection from 17 to 18 years in conformity with the provisions of the International Convention for the Protection of New Varieties of Plants.)

The concern about the free flow of scientific information among public and private breeders has not been fully resolved. At present much germ plasm that does not have variety status is being released by the USDA and the state agricultural experiment stations. It is elite germ plasm or parental lines useful for breeding but not for immediate cultivation. It has no legal status under the Plant Variety Protection Act. A partial response to this concern is that the U.S. legislation does not restrict the use of a variety registered under the Plant Variety Protection Act in the breeding program of either a public or private breeder.

A definitive evaluation of the effects of protecting plant varieties on the performance of private sector varietal-improvement efforts is still premature. Experience with hybrid maize, for which proprietary inbred lines have provided even more secure protection than the provisions of legislation, is not entirely reassuring with respect to the efficiency of private sector breeding programs. Inbred lines developed by public sector breeders continue to account for well over 50 percent of hybrid maize seed production in the United States. The private seed companies continue to make only limited investments in the supporting sciences, such as genetics, plant pathology, and plant physiology.

Perspective

In the two areas examined in this chapter—R&D on mechanization and plant varieties—the appropriate balance between public and private sector research and development is being subjected to intensive scrutiny. Yet the broad implications of the case studies seem clear.

Research directed to advancing mechanical technology should remain a low priority in the allocation of public sector research resources. Market incentives have been adequate to induce substantial private sector innovative effort and a rapid rate of improvement in mechanical technology. The level of public sector research on mechanization is more appropriately guided by the demands arising out of educational needs rather than the demand for new technology.

Continuation of strong public sector involvement in research and development directed to improving plant varieties is clearly warranted. The social rate of return to public sector research remains high. Advances in technology remain closely linked to advances in basic knowledge. Market incentives do not yet appear adequate to generate an efficient level of private sector research and development. As institutional innovations provide more secure property rights and private sector varietal-development efforts continue to evolve, there will be a need to reevaluate the appropriate division of labor between public and private sector breeding programs.

INDUCED TECHNICAL CHANGE IN AGRICULTURE

The previous section presented cases that illustrate the complex interaction between public and private sector research that has led to advances in mechanical and biological technology in U.S. agriculture. In this section we turn to a discussion of the role of changes or differences in the economic environment that influence the direction of technical change. In this discussion it is useful, at the risk of some oversimplification, to use the term *mechanical technology* to refer to those technologies that substitute for labor and the term *biological technology* to refer to those technologies that generate increases in output per hectare.

Mechanical Processes

The mechanization of agricultural production operations cannot be treated as simply an adaptation of industrial methods of production to agriculture. The spatial nature of agricultural production results in significant differences between agriculture and industry in patterns of machine use (Brewster, 1950). It imposes severe limits on the efficiency of large-scale production in agriculture.

The spatial dimension of crop production requires that the machines used for agricultural production be mobile—they must move across or through materials that are immobile, in contrast to moving material through stationary machines as in most industrial processes. Moreover, the seasonal and spatial characteristics of agricultural production require a series of specialized machines—for land preparation, planting, weed control, and harvesting—specifically designed for sequential operations, each of which is carried out for only a few days or weeks in each season. This means that it is no more feasible for workers to specialize in one operation in mechanized agriculture than in premechanized agriculture. It also means that in a "fully mechanized" agricultural system the capital:labor ratio tends to be much higher than in the industrial sector in the same country.

Biological and Chemical Processes

In agriculture biological and chemical processes are more fundamental than mechanization or machine processes. This generalization was as true during the last century as it will be during the era of the "new biotechnology." Advances in biological and chemical technology in crop production have typically involved one or more of the following four elements: (1) land and water resource development to provide a more satisfactory environment for plant growth; (2) modification of the environment by the addition of organic and inorganic sources of plant nutrients to the soil to stimulate plant growth; (3) use of biological and chemical means to protect plants from pests and disease; and (4) selection and design of new biologically efficient crop varieties specifically adapted to respond to those elements in the environment that are subject to human control. Similar processes can be observed in advances in animal agriculture.

INDUCED TECHNICAL CHANGE: THE UNITED STATES AND JAPAN

One implication of the discussion of mechanical and biological processes is that there are multiple paths of technical change in agriculture available to a society. The constraints imposed by an inelastic supply of land, for example, may be offset by advances in biological technology. The constraints imposed by an inelastic supply of labor may be offset by advances in mechanical technology. These alternatives are illustrated in Figure 1. The 1880–1980 land and labor productivity growth paths for Japan, Denmark, France, Germany, the United Kingdom, and the United States are plotted along with the 1980 partial productivity ratios for a number of developing countries. The impression given by the several growth paths is that nature is relatively "plastic."

In economics it had generally been accepted, at least since the publication of *Theory of Wages* by Hicks (1932:124–125), that changes or differences in the relative prices of factors of production could influence the direction of invention or innovation. There has also been a second tradition that traces to the work of Griliches (1957) and Schmookler (1962, 1966) that has focused attention on the influence of growth in product demand on the rate of technical change.[6]

Let us turn now to an illustration of the role of relative factor endowments and prices in the evolution of alternative paths of technical change in agriculture in the United States and Japan.

Japan and the United States are characterized by extreme differences in relative endowments of land and labor (Table 5). In 1880, total agricultural land area per male worker was more than 60 times as large in the United States as in Japan, and arable land area per worker was about 20 times as large in the United States as in Japan. The differences have widened over time. By 1980 total agricultural land area per male worker was more than 100 times as large and arable land area per male worker about 50 times as large in the United States as in Japan.

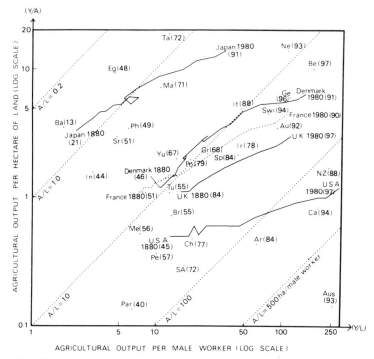

FIGURE 1   Historical growth paths of agricultural productivity of Denmark, France, Japan, the United Kingdom, and the United States for 1880–1980, compared with intercountry cross-section observations of selected countries in 1980. Values in parentheses are percentage of male workers employed in nonagriculture.

SOURCE: Data from Yujiro Hayami and Vernon W. Ruttan, *Agricultural Development: An International Perspective*, 2d ed. (Baltimore, Md: Johns Hopkins University Press: 1985, Appendixes.

SYMBOL KEY

Argentina: Ar	Greece: Gr	Portugal: Po
Australia: Aus	India: In	South Africa: SA
Austria: Au	Ireland: Ir	Spain: Sp
Bangladesh: Ba	Israel: Is	Sri Lanka: Sr
Belgium (and	Italy: It	Surinam: Su
Luxembourg): Be	Japan: Ja	Sweden: Swe
Brazil: Br	Libya: Li	Switzerland: Swi
Canada: Ca	Mauritius: Ma	Syria: Sy
Chile: Ch	Mexico: Me	Taiwan: Ta
Colombia: Co	Netherlands: Ne	Turkey: Tu
Denmark: De	New Zealand: NZ	United Kingdom: UK
Egypt: Eg	Norway: No	United States of America: USA
Finland: Fi	Pakistan: Pak	Venezuela: Ve
France: Fr	Paraguay: Par	Yugoslavia: Yu
Germany, Federal	Peru: Pe	
Republic of: Ge	Philippines: Ph	

TABLE 5   Land-Labor Endowments and Relative Prices in Agriculture: United States and Japan, Selected Years

Country	1880	1900	1920	1940	1960	1980
UNITED STATES						
(1) Agricultural land area (million ha)	327	465	458	452	440	427
(2) Arable land area (million ha)	93	157	194	189	185	191
(3) Number of male farm workers (thousand)	7,959	9,880	10,221	8,487	3,973	1,792
(4) (1)/(3) (ha/worker)	41	47	45	50	111	238
(5) (2)/(3) (ha/worker)	12	16	19	22	47	107
(6) Value of arable land ($/ha)	109	106	341	178	696	3,393
(7) Farm wage rate ($/day)	0.90	1.00	3.30	1.60	6.60	25.31
(8) (6)/(7) (days/ha)	188	106	103	111	105	134
JAPAN						
(9) Agricultural land area (thousand ha)[a]	5,509	6,032	6,958	7,102	7,042	5,729
(10) Arable land area (thousand ha)	4,749	5,200	5,998	6,122	6,071	5,461
(11) Number of male farm workers (thousand)	8,336	8,483	7,577	6,362	6,230	2,674
(12) (9)/(11) (ha/worker)	0.66	0.71	0.92	1.12	1.13	2.14
(13) (10)/(11) (ha/worker)	0.57	0.61	0.79	0.96	0.97	2.04
(14) Value of arable land (yen/ha)	343	917	3,882	4,709	1,415,000	7,642,000
(15) Farm wage rate (yen/day)	0.22	0.31	1.39	1.90	440	5,054
(16) (14)/(15) (days/ha)	1,559	2,958	2,793	2,478	3,216	1,512

[a]Agricultural land areas in Japan for 1880 to 1960 are estimated by multiplying arable land areas by 1.16, the ratio of agricultural land area to arable land area in the 1960 Census of Agriculture; this conversion factor changed to 1.05 for 1980 based on the 1980 Census of Agriculture.

SOURCE: Data from Yujiro Hayami and Vernon W. Ruttan, *Agricultural Development: An International Perspective*, 2d ed. (Baltimore, Md.: Johns Hopkins University Press; 1985), Tables C2–C3.

The relative prices of land and labor also differed sharply in the two countries. In 1880 in order to buy a hectare of arable land (compare row 8 and row 16 in Table 5), it would have been necessary for a Japanese hired farm worker to work 8 times as many days as a U.S. farm worker. In the United States the price of labor rose relative to the price of land, particularly between 1880 and 1920. In Japan the price of land rose sharply relative to the price of labor, particularly between 1880 and 1900. By 1960 a Japanese farm worker would have had to work 30 times as many days as a U.S. farm worker in order to buy 1 hectare of arable land. This gap was reduced after 1960, partly due to extremely rapid increases in wage rates in Japan during the two decades of "miraculous" economic growth. In the United States land prices rose sharply in the postwar period, primarily because of the rising demand for land for nonagricultural use and the anticipation of continued inflation. Yet, in 1980 a Japanese farm worker still would have had to work 11 times as many days as a U.S. worker to buy 1 hectare of land.

Despite these substantial differences in land area per worker and in the relative prices of land and labor, both the United States and Japan experienced relatively rapid rates of growth in production and productivity in agriculture. Overall agricultural growth performance for the 100 years covered in Table 1 was very similar in the two countries. In both countries total agricultural output increased at an annual compound rate of 1.6 percent while total inputs (aggregate of conventional inputs) increased at a rate of 0.7 percent. Total factor productivity (total output divided by total input) increased at an annual rate of 0.9 percent in both countries. Meanwhile, labor productivity, as measured by agricultural output per male worker, increased at rates of 3.1 percent per year in the United States and 2.7 percent in Japan. It is remarkable that the overall growth rates in output and productivity were so similar despite the extremely different factor proportions and absolute productivity levels that characterize the two countries.[7]

Although there is a resemblance in the overall rates of growth in production and productivity, the timing of the relatively fast-growing phases and the relatively stagnant phases differs between the two countries. In the United States agricultural output grew rapidly up to 1900; then the growth rate decelerated (Table 1). From the 1900s to the 1930s, there was little gain in total productivity. This stagnation phase was succeeded by a dramatic rise in production and productivity in the 1940s and 1950s. Japan experienced rapid increases in agricultural production and productivity from 1880 to the 1910s, then entered into a stagnation phase, which lasted until the mid-1930s (Table 2). Another rapid expansion phase commenced during the period of recovery from the devastation of World War II. Roughly speaking, the United States experienced a stagnation phase two decades earlier than Japan and also shifted to the second development phase two decades earlier.

The effect of relative prices on the development and choice of technology

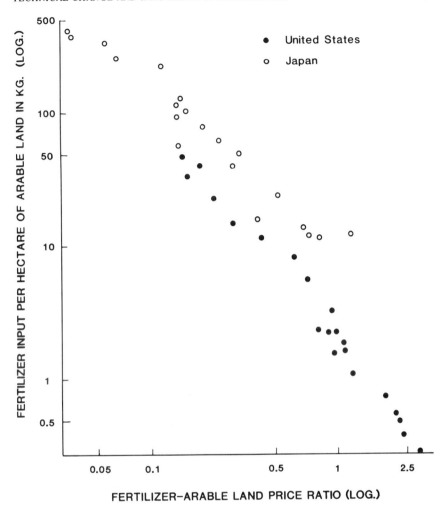

FIGURE 2 Relation between fertilizer input per hectare of arable land and fertilizer:arable land price ratio (= hectares of arable land that can be purchased by 1 ton of N + P_2O_5 + K_2O contained in commerical fertilizers), the United States and Japan, quinquennial observations for 1880–1980.

SOURCE: Data from Yujiro Hayami and Vernon W. Ruttan, *Agricultural Development: An International Perspective*, 2d ed. (Baltimore, Md. Johns Hopkins University Press, 1985), Appendix C.

is illustrated for biological technology in Figure 2: U.S. and Japanese data on the relationship between fertilizer input per hectare of arable land and the fertilizer:land price ratio are plotted for the period 1880 to 1980. In both

1880 and 1980 U.S. farmers were using less fertilizer than Japanese farmers. However, despite enormous differences in both physical and institutional resources, the relationship between these variables has been almost identical in the two countries. As the price of fertilizer declined relative to other factors, scientists in both countries responded by inventing crop varieties that were more responsive to fertilizer. American scientists, however, always lagged behind the Japanese by several decades because the lower prices of land relative to the price of fertilizer in the United States resulted in a lower priority being placed on yield-increasing technology.

The effect of changes in the relative prices of mechanical power and labor in the United States and Japan for 1880–1980 is illustrated in Figure 3. In both 1880 and 1980 U.S. farmers were using more mechanical power than Japanese farmers. But the relationship between the power:labor price ratio and the use of power per worker is, again, almost identical in the two countries. But because labor was always less expensive in Japan, the Japanese suppliers of mechanical technology always lagged behind U.S. suppliers by several decades.

The same relationships that hold for Japan and the United States have now been demonstrated for the period 1880–1960 for a number of European countries. The relationship has also been tested and confirmed in using contemporary cross sectional data.[8]

The effect of a rise in the price of fertilizer relative to the price of land or of the price of labor relative to the price of machinery has been to induce advances in biological and mechanical technology. The effect of the introduction of lower cost and more productive biological and mechanical technology has been to induce farmers to substitute fertilizer for land and mechanical power for labor. These responses to differences in resource endowments among countries and to changes in resource endowments over time by agricultural research institutions, by the farm supply industries, and by farmers, have been remarkably similar despite differences in cultures and traditions.

The results of these comparative analyses can be summarized as follows: Agricultural growth in the United States and Japan during the period 1880–1980 can best be understood when viewed as a dynamic factor-substitution process. Factors have been substituted for each other along a metaproduction function in response to long-run trends in relative factor prices. Each point on the metaproduction surface is characterized by a technology that can be described in terms of specific sources of power, types of machinery, crop varieties, and animal breeds. Movements along this metaproduction surface involve technical changes. These technical changes have been induced to a significant extent by the long-term trends in relative factor prices.

Technical change in agriculture has, of course, not been wholly induced by economic forces. In addition to the effects of change (or differences) in resource endowments and growth in demand, technical change may occur

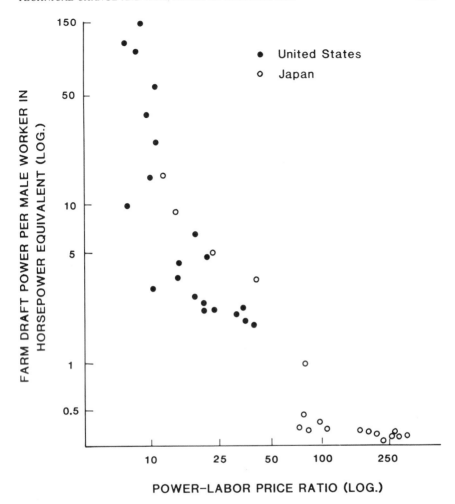

FIGURE 3 Relation between farm draft power per male worker and power:labor price ratio (= hectares of work days that can be purchased by 1 horsepower of tractor or draft animal), the United States and Japan, quinquennial observations for 1880–1980.

NOTE: Number of male workers = U3 and J3; power = U7 + U8 and J7 + J8; land price = U19 and J19; power price = average retail price of tractor per horsepower extrapolated by U21 from the 1976–1980 average of $216 for the United States, and extrapolated by J21 from the average of 65,170 yen for Japan.

SOURCE: Data from Yujiro Hayami and Vernon W. Ruttan, *Agricultural Development: An International Perspective*, 2d ed. (Baltimore, Md.: Johns Hopkins University Press: 1985), Appendix C.

in response to autonomous advances in scientific knowledge. Progress in general services that lowers the "cost" of technical and institutional innovations generates technical changes that are unrelated to changes in factor endowments or product demand. Even in these cases, however, the rate of adoption and the impact on productivity of autonomous or exogenous changes in technology will be strongly influenced by conditions of resource supply and product demand.

IMPLICATIONS AND LESSONS

Over the past 50 years, U.S. agriculture has been transformed from a resource-based industry to a science-based industry. It has been transformed from a traditional to a high technology sector. Relatively few sectors in the U.S. economy have been able to maintain their technological leadership—to achieve or maintain world class. Agriculture is one of those sectors. The future growth of the U.S. economy will depend very heavily on those sectors that are able to maintain their technological leadership—that can continue to generate growth dividends resulting from productivity growth. What are some of the lessons that can be drawn from the agricultural research system that may be relevant for research policy in other sectors of the economy?

The first lesson is that the process of technical change in agriculture reflects a much more complex pattern of entrepreneurship than the relatively simple Schumpeterian view. Much of modern biological technology is the product of the insight, skill, and energy of a group of scientific entrepreneurs who have been employed in public sector institutions—primarily the Agricultural Research Service of the U.S. Department of Agriculture and the state agricultural experiment stations. This public sector entrepreneurship has been effective because it has been closely articulated with the interests of both farmer clientele and the private sector suppliers of agricultural technology. Agriculture shares, with the other science-based sectors of the U.S. economy, a complex pattern of articulation between public and private sector entrepreneurship (Nelson, 1982). The opportunities for successful entrepreneurship in both the generation and the use of new agricultural technology are strongly conditioned by changes in resource endowments and in factor and product markets. The opportunities for the advancement of mechanical technologies in societies in which wage rates are low are relatively limited. The opportunities for advancing biological and chemical technologies are weak in an environment characterized by abundant land resources.

A second lesson that should be learned from the agricultural research experience is that both institutional and project support for research have important roles to play in inducing effective research performance. There has been a good deal of criticism of the institutional-support approach that is used to provide core funding at the state agricultural experiment stations, the USDA laboratories, and at a number of other federal laboratories (the national energy laboratories, for example). Some critics have seemed to imply that if research is not funded by competitive grants, it cannot be good research. Experience is somewhat more complex. Institutional funding is clearly necessary to assure the continuity of infrastructure and staff to pursue long-term basic and applied research agendas. It is doubtful that the long-term effort to adapt soybean varieties to more northern environments by the Minnesota Agricultural Experiment Station could have been sustained under a series of competitive grants. But a competitive grant system can be a creative device for the support of high-risk applied research and for supporting the advance of new research frontiers until their potential for technology development becomes more apparent. Much of the work in molecular biology that is now leading to advances in genetic engineering was supported through competitive grants from the National Science Foundation and the National Institutes of Health. It will now take longer-term institutional support, both in the public and private sectors, to translate much of this new knowledge into new biological technology in the fields of human and animal health and in crop production.

A third lesson that we should have learned from the history of agricultural research is that any sector of the economy that is to achieve or maintain "world class"—that is, to remain competitive in the world economy—must be sustained by a carefully articulated program of public and private sector support for and performance of research and development. In framing this appropriate mix of public and private sector research, it is important that we avoid simplistic decision rules. The argument that the public sector should limit its support to basic research and the private sector should assume responsibility for supporting applied research is clearly one of the oversimplifications that should be avoided. The question that should be asked is whether there are sufficient economic incentives to induce an efficient level of private sector research. There are broad areas of what might be termed "generic" applied research in which such incentives do not exist. In some cases the lack of incentive is related to industry structure. In others, it is inherent in the technology itself. There is clearly a need for a more adequate understanding of the forms of institutional design that are conducive to public sector entrepreneurship in those areas in which the gains from private sector research and development are limited.[9] In the case of agriculture, it appears that the decentralized national-state or prefectural research system has been important in guiding the direction of technical change.

A fourth lesson from the history of agricultural research is that rapid growth in demand is not a necessary condition for rapid productivity growth.[10] In the United States and in other developed countries, the rate of growth in demand for agricultural commodities has rarely exceeded 2 percent per year during the last century. Yet relatively modest investments in agricultural research, primarily by the public sector, have been capable of generating growth in output per worker in the 6 percent range and in output per unit of total input in the range of 2 percent per year. It also seems quite clear, given the large share of employment in the agricultural sector at the beginning of the modernization process, that this labor displacement has generated enormous growth dividends. It has generated growth dividends by the release of workers to sectors of the economy that were experiencing rapid growth in demand. And it generated large growth dividends in the form of lower real costs of the commodity component of food and fiber.

It has been possible, through rapid productivity growth, for U.S. agriculture to retain and even enhance its global class status while the share of the total labor force employed in agriculture was declining from approximately 26 percent in 1925 to 3.4 percent in 1984. Employment in the manufacturing sector has declined from 26 percent to 1950 to 20 percent in 1984. But the decline in employment in manufacturing, particularly since the mid-1960s, seems to be due at least as much to loss of capability to compete in world markets as to rapid growth in labor productivity. It is not hard to visualize an American economy in which the manufacturing labor force has declined to little more than 10 percent of the total labor by the year 2000. The challenge to the manufacturing sector is to achieve this transformation while enhancing rather than eroding its competitive position in world markets.

NOTES

1. See, for example, Feder et al. (1985) and Hayami and Ruttan (1985: Ch. 9).
2. The material in this section, "The Contribution of Research to Productivity Growth," is treated in more detail in Evenson et al. (1979) and Ruttan (1980 and 1982a).
3. In this chapter I deliberately avoid restricting the concept of innovation to the narrow Schumpeterian definition. I have argued elsewhere that the Schumpeterian concept of innovation is analytically inconvenient. The term innovation is more appropriately used to refer to the entire range of processes by which "new things" emerge in science, technology, and art. The term innovation can then be defined as that subset of innovations that are patentable (Ruttan, 1959).
4. This section is treated in more detail in Ruttan (1982a and 1982b).
5. The results of the Agricultural Research Institute (ARI) studies are reported in Wilcke and Sprague (1967) and in Wilcke and Williamson (1977). A new survey of private sector agricultural research was initiated by the ARI in 1984.
6. The Hicks theory was criticized by Salter (1960) and others for its lack of a proper microeconomic foundation. After an extensive series of exchanges, the theory of induced innovation had, by the mid-1970s, been placed on a more adequate microeconomic foundation. For a review of the literature, see Binswanger (1974) and Binswanger and Ruttan (1978:13–43).
7. Output per hectare has traditionally been much higher in Japan and output per worker much higher in the United States. Prior to the mid- and late-1960s, it could be argued that, given the differences in land prices and wage rates between the two countries, Japanese agriculture was relatively "efficient." With rapid growth in nonfarm labor demand and rising wage rates, Japanese agriculture has, since the late 1960s, become increasingly "inefficient" in comparative terms. For a discussion of adjustment problems in Japanese agriculture see Hayami (1982).

8. For more rigorous econometric tests of the relationship presented in Figures 2 and 3, see Binswanger and Ruttan (1978) and Hayami and Ruttan (1985).
9. This view is consistent with the conclusions drawn by Nelson (1982) and his associates in a major cross-industry analysis of the role of government in technical progress. The Nelson study suggests that it is difficult to find any global-class U.S. industry that has not benefited significantly from government support or stimulation of R&D.
10. The view that technical change is largely induced by growth in demand has been criticized by Mowery and Rosenberg (1979). Their review of the literature suggests that many of the investigations that purported to demonstrate primacy of growth in demand in the innovation process were seriously flawed.

REFERENCES

Binswanger, Hans P. 1974. A microeconomic approach to induced innovation. *Economic Journal* 84 (December):940–958.

Binswanger, Hans P., and Vernon W. Ruttan, eds. 1978. *Induced Innovation: Technology, Institutions and Development.* Baltimore, Md.: Johns Hopkins University Press.

Brandt, John P., and Ben C. French. 1983. Mechanical harvesting and the California tomato industry: A simulation analysis. *American Journal of Agricultural Economics* 65:265–272.

Brewster, John M. 1950. The machine process in agriculture and industry. *Journal of Farm Economics* 32 (February):69–81.

de Janvry, Alain, Philip LeVeen, and David Runsten. 1980. *Mechanization of California: The Case of Canning Tomatoes.* Department of Agricultural and Resource Economics. Berkeley: University of California.

Evenson, Robert E., Vernon W. Ruttan, and Paul E. Waggoner. 1979. Economic benefits from research: An example from agriculture. *Science* 205:1101–1107.

Feder, Gershan, Richard E. Just, and David Zilberman. 1985. Adoption of agricultural innovations in developing countries: A survey. *Economic Development and Cultural Change* 33 (January):255–298.

Griliches, Zvi. 1957. Hybrid corn: An exploration in the economics of technical change. *Econometrica* 25:501–522.

Hayami, Yujiro. 1985. Adjustment policies for Japanese agriculture in a changing world. Pp. 368–392 in Emory N. Castle and Kenzo Hemmy, with Sally A. Skillings, eds., *U.S.-Japanese Agricultural Trade Relations.* Baltimore, Md.: Johns Hopkins University Press and Resources for the Future.

Hayami, Yujiro, and Vernon W. Ruttan. 1985. *Agricultural Development: An International Perspective.* 2d ed. Baltimore, Md.: Johns Hopkins University Press.

Hicks, John R. 1932. *The Theory of Wages.* London: Macmillan.

Malstead, Illona. 1980. Agriculture: The relationship of R&D to federal goals. Photocopy. Washington, D.C.

Mowery, David C., and Nathan Rosenberg. 1979. The influence of market demand upon innovation: A critical review of some recent empirical studies. *Research Policy* 8 (April):103–153.

Mueller, W. F., J. Culbertson, and B. Peckhorn (with J. Croswell and P. Kaufman). 1980. *Market Structure and Technological Performance in the Food Manufacturing Industries.* College of Agriculture and Applied Sciences. Madison: University of Wisconsin.

Nelson, Richard R. 1982. Government stimulus of technological progress: Lessons from American history. Pp. 451–482 in Richard R. Nelson, ed., *Government and Technical Progress: A Cross-Industry Analysis.* New York: Pergamon.

Office of Technology Assessment. 1984. *Commercial Biotechnology: An International Analysis.* OTA-BA-218. Washington, D.C.: U.S. Government Printing Office.

Peterson, Willis and Yoav Kislev. In press. The cotton harvest in retrospect: Labor displacement or replacement. *Journal of Economic History.*

Ruttan, Vernon W. 1959. Usher and Schumpeter on invention, innovation and technological change. *Quarterly Journal of Economics* 73 (November):596–606.

Ruttan, Vernon W. 1980. Agricultural research and the future of American agriculture. Pp. 117–155 in Sandra S. Batie and Robert G. Healy, eds., *The Future of American Agriculture as a Strategic Resource.* Washington, D.C.: The Conservation Foundation.

Ruttan, Vernon W. 1982a. *Agricultural Research Policy.* Minneapolis: University of Minnesota Press.

Ruttan, Vernon W. 1982b. The changing role of the public and private sectors in agricultural research. *Science* 216:23–29.

Ruttan, Vernon W. 1983. Statement on some lessons from agricultural research. Pp. 415–455 in *Industrial Policy Hearings,* Subcommittee on Economic Stabilization, Committee on Banking, Finance and Urban Affairs, U.S. Congress, House, Serial No. 98-45. Washington, D.C.: U.S. Government Printing Office, 1983.

Salter, W. E. G. 1960. *Productivity and Technical Change.* New York: Cambridge University Press.

Schmitz, Andrew, and David Seckler. 1970. Mechanized agriculture and social welfare: The case of the tomato harvester. *American Journal of Agricultural Economics* 50 (November):469–477.

Schmookler, Jacob. 1962. Changes in industry and in the state of knowledge as determinants of industrial invention. Pp. 195–232 in Richard R. Nelson, ed., *Rate and Direction of Inventive Activity.* Princeton, N.J.: Princeton University Press.

Schmookler, Jacob. 1966. *Invention and Economic Growth.* Cambridge, Mass.: Harvard University Press.

Wilcke, H. L., and H. B. Sprague. 1967. Agricultural research and development by the private sector of the United States. *Agricultural Science Review* 5 (1967):1–8.

Wilcke, H. L., and J. C. Williamson. 1977. *A Survey of U.S. Agricultural Research by Private Industry.* Washington, D.C.: Agricultural Research Institute.

Technology Adoption: The Services Industries

JAMES BRIAN QUINN

In considering the impact of technology on economics, a particular focus is needed in this country on the services industries, in which most new companies are rising. As in earlier eras of development, we do not know today which of these ventures will blossom into entire new industries or giants themselves. But the past predicts that some will do so. A major question is whether they can provide the trading might this nation will need for its future health.

Paul A. David, N. Bruce Hannay, and Daniel I. Okimoto (in this volume) have presented three excellent, thorough, and well-structured discussions of key aspects of industrial competitiveness and how the adoption of new technologies affects competitiveness. This chapter amplifies three themes that I believe are perhaps underemphasized in those chapters, namely, (1) the dominant importance of intellect applied through technology in creating wealth, economic growth, and value added; (2) the extraordinary role that individual fanatics, randomness, and entrepreneurship play in this process; and (3) the importance of technology in the services sector.

TECHNOLOGY, ECONOMICS, AND ENTREPRENEURSHIP

The concepts of economics and technology should be integrated at the most fundamental level. Economics is the study of the creation and distribution of wealth, or value. Technology is the methodology through which wealth is predominantly created. Most prevalent economic models tend to explain the accretion of wealth as a slow, upward climb that is achieved through exploitation of marginally ever-less-productive natural resources (land), marginal productivity gains made by millions of workers (labor), accumulated

357

efficiencies from the deployment of plant and machinery (capital), and improvements in "human capital" through education, training, and health enhancement. Yet within each of these basic factors of production, it can be demonstrated that it is the technology embodied in capital (not the presence of capital), the management and physical technologies that labor uses (not employees working harder), and the resources released by technology (not land itself) are the true growth forces. Technology deserves to be treated as it is in Denison's broad definition—as creating some 70 to 80 percent of U.S. economic growth—and not as a "residual" of unexplained events.

Equally important for policy purposes, however, is the fact that the application of technology and the creation of wealth do not occur through disembodied interactions of capital, markets, profits, or monetary movements. Instead, much of a modern nation's creation of wealth and value results from acts of intellect and energy initially supplied by a few talented and determined (fanatic) individuals and companies whose impact is all out of proportion to the resources they themselves employ. In modern history the four traditional sources of marginal growth have been dwarfed in total by entrepreneurs creating entirely new sources of wealth, launching myriads of new enterprises, hiring people to do things and to provide services not available in the past, and generating whole new industries (often with enormous support infrastructures) never previously envisioned. Often these are based on new scientific concepts or technologies—acts of intellect—never before conceived or exploited.

Many studies have found that entrepreneurial innovators are driven by more than mere economic motives or "profits." They want to be "the first" to accomplish a task, be famous, have "freedom," be their "own bosses," do something "worthwhile," and so on. Watson, Moore, and Swanson (in this volume) recall such comments. Gordon E. Moore (of Intel), for example, says that he and his colleagues broke away from Fairchild to be their own bosses, to control their destinies, to develop the frontiers of their technologies, as well as to make profits. Robert A. Swanson recalls that Herbert Boyer, his cofounder at Genentech, wanted to see the fantastic potentials of biotechnology exploited for human welfare. Abroad, one finds that Mr. Ibuka (founder of Sony Corporation) wanted to help Japan's economic recovery, employ his talented group on worthwhile projects, and invent entirely new electromechanical devices to serve Japan's war-torn economy. Champions in larger companies too (like Alastair Pilkington of Pilkington Bros. Ltd.) are driven "to invent, to revolutionize a staid industry, to do something truly worthwhile." And so on.

Because of such motives, entrepreneurs doggedly persist when mere capital sources would give up. Their high motivation eventually creates a margin of value that would not otherwise exist. Fortunately, our society honors and rewards such actions. Many countries, however, do not appreciate "people who raise their heads above the crowd.'' Because of the driving power of such motivations, maintaining a climate friendly to entrepreneurs should be a central focus of any economic growth policies in the United States.

I was fascinated to note that recently young Japanese were asked what person(s) they would most like to emulate. Their top choices were Akio Morita (chairman of Sony) and Soichiro Honda (founder of Honda Corporation), two of the greatest entrepreneurs in modern Japan. If the Japanese can harness these desires through policy, they may be even more formidable in world markets.

CREATIONS OF THE MIND

Why should policymakers and economists be especially interested in the entrepreneurial component of society? All value is created in the minds of human beings. And technology—systematic application of knowledge to useful purposes—is the most pervasive way of creating economic value. Virtually all modern industries, whether traditional or not, are direct creations of technology, deriving solely from the genius of the human mind. Perkin's analysis of unappealing coal tar derivatives, for example, led to synthetic dyes and to the modern chemicals industry. Carothers created the modern fibers industry and Baekeland the modern plastics industry as their esoteric experiments unraveled the characteristics of very large molecules. Edison's empirical applications of unviewable electron flows and resistances created the electrical equipment industry. Telecommunications is almost entirely an artifact of human intellect with no perceivable analog in nature. Fleming's observations and insights initiated the modern pharmaceuticals industry. Cohen and Boyer started the biotechnology revolution by defining the interactions between restriction enzymes and the genetic structures of plasmids. Observing and manipulating the unwanted Edison effect led to vacuum tubes and to the electronics industry. Intellectual conceptualization of semiconductor phenomena and the abstractions of binary mathematics created the computer industry and its by-products. And so on.

Each of these major industries was created and developed largely by the imagination and intellect of a few fanatic entrepreneurs. In each case marvelous accidents or random events (like the mold blowing onto Dr. Fleming's cultures or Townes's envisioning the laser while looking at the azaleas in Lincoln Park) precipitated major spurts of progress. So probably will the next series of modern industries be created, not by rigorous national planning, but by some unforeseen act of imagination and intellect.

In addition, technology releases the resources to develop these new industries—3 percent of the U.S. population in farming and some 22 percent in manufacturing now produce far more than the 70 percent in agriculture or the 60 percent in manufacturing did in earlier years. Technology and human imagination have opened new energy and mineral resources deep in the earth that were inaccessible a few years ago. And they will doubtless continue to create such unexpected new regimes of wealth in the future. However, to ensure that they do, we must attack economic growth issues with policies and incentives that stimulate the effective development and application of intellect for useful purposes—not primarily as issues relating to monetary policy, investment, market saturation, inflation, and so on.

Technology's force is so great that the absolute and comparative wealth of nations is determined today largely by how well they develop, guide, and utilize their technological capabilities. Japan, Hong Kong, and Singapore— which after World War II had virtually no capital, few natural or raw materials, and minuscule physical space—have proved this point perhaps better than any other carefully controlled experiment could. These nations concentrated on people, technology, motivation, and capital formation. Often forgotten in discussions of the "Japanese miracle" are the country's high investments in technical education and the dramatic lowering of taxes in the early 1960s (brought about principally by Ishibashi and Ikeda) to increase savings rates and redirect Japan's capital flows toward the private sector and industrial investments.

INNOVATION

Other than the exploitation of inexpensive and abundant raw materials, relative national wealth depends primarily on two factors: (1) continuous productivity improvement, predominantly achieved by technology diffusion, and (2) innovation, the first application (or reduction to practice) of a useful concept in a social system. Why the special interest in innovation? Because when the innovator does something better than anyone before, he or she creates a margin of wealth not previously available. Profit margins accessible to innovators, therefore, tend to be temporarily higher than those for more mature enterprises. Verifying this, the major studies of venture capital funds show that average after-tax returns on such investments are greater than 24 percent compounded annually (Figure 1). And, it should be noted, no professionally managed venture capital fund has gone bankrupt to date. This probably means that there has been an undercommitment to this area in the past. However, as Gordon E. Moore notes, this may be changing today.

Various studies have demonstrated the relationship between capital investment and productivity (Figure 2). Venture capital is a special case of investment largely directed specifically at innovation and smaller companies. The classic studies by Birch and the U.S. General Accounting Office (GAO) suggest that from 65 to 80 percent of the new jobs in the United States are created by companies with fewer than 100 employees. Consequently, policies that selectively encourage technological investment, and particularly early

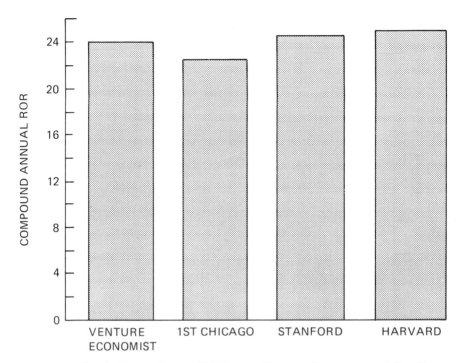

FIGURE 1   Historical rates of return (ROR), according to major venture capital studies. SOURCE: From Centennial Research & Development Company, *Investing in Venture Capital by Pension Funds* (Denver, Colo.: February 1985).

venture investments, should stimulate the greatest long-term economic growth, employment, and widely distributed wealth. The GAO and other studies also indicate that policies stimulating venture capital growth in the United States since 1978 (especially decreasing capital-gains taxes and allowing pension funds to invest in venture capital) have dramatically increased the availability of such capital (Figure 3) and produced an entirely new kind of economic recovery based on many small, highly dispersed high technology and service units.

Besides producing higher margins on their own, these small, innovative firms also stimulate responses by larger companies and leverage their own impact by supplying components for larger companies or by exploiting the "ripple effects" of larger companies' innovations. These interactive relationships help to achieve continuous productivity increases for the entire country. Beyond this, however, most radical innovations come from outside the industries they most seriously affect. And (numerically at least) most seem to come from relatively smaller companies. Why? It is probably inherent in the essentially egocentric, probabilistic, and partially random nature of

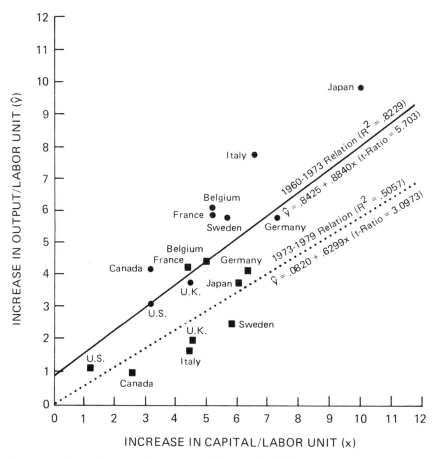

FIGURE 2   Rates of change in output, capital per unit of labor.
SOURCE: From John W. Kendrick, International comparisons of recent productivity
trends, in *Measuring Productivity: Trends and Comparisons*, from the First International
Productivity Symposium, Tokyo, Japan, 1983 (New York: Unipub, 1984).

innovation itself. Whether the innovation occurs in a large or small company,
virtually all technological histories (including Watson's personal classic, *The
Double Helix*) demonstrate that scientific advance and technological innovation are largely unplanned (in a systems sense), highly chaotic and interactive (in organizational terms) and partially irrational (from a financial
viewpoint). From a social as well as corporate perspective, we should begin
to accept these characteristics as fact and learn to manage and stimulate
innovation accordingly.

Unless there are very large amounts of capital involved, the sheer number of trials initiated by small entrepreneurs and their capacity to dedicate themselves single-mindedly to their proposed solutions—combined with their capacity to move rapidly without intervening bureaucratic or power structures hindering progress—undoubtedly increase the probability that some will succeed. If the probability of success is 1 out of 100 and there are 500 to 1,000 dedicated individual entrepreneurs working on a problem, the likelihood that one will succeed is vastly increased. But the small scale and highly dispersed nature of small failures also tend to disguise the true cost of individual entrepreneurial losses to the society. Because we cannot identify the costs of the 499 to 999 who fail, perhaps individual entrepreneurship looks more ''efficient'' than it should.

Entrepreneurship also has another fascinating interaction with economics.

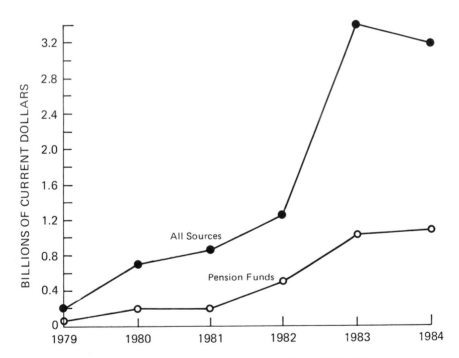

FIGURE 3 Capital commitments to venture firms, 1979 to 1984 (billions of current dollars).
SOURCE: Original data from *Venture Capital Journal*, compiled by Centennial Research & Development Company in *Investing in Venture Capital by Pension Funds* (Denver, Colo., February 1985).

Most industry structures are not so much determined by "competitive analysis" or "industry analysis" as modern strategic texts might indicate. Instead, their basic structures and locations largely derive from the strategic and values choices of the entrepreneurs who created them. The computer industry, for example, is structured the way it is because Watson and Learson decided to concentrate IBM's efforts on a compatible mainframe line for the "center" of the computer market; because Norris and Cray wanted to create the world's fastest and largest computers; and because Olsen and Jobs saw opportunities in much smaller computers when others did not. Regional economies are vastly affected too. For example, the major semiconductor (and, consequently, the later microcomputer) companies (according to Stanford economist Brian Arthur) located on the West Coast and in Silicon Valley basically because William Schockley's mother lived there, and key technologists flocked to join him as the industry formed.

The effectiveness of small-scale entrepreneurial innovation and the need to support this actively through policy seems beyond question. But one of the most often repeated errors of industrial policy (in Europe, the Soviet Union, China, and other industrializing countries) has been to focus on larger enterprises—and government interventions to "rationalize" these units—rather than the much less deterministic processes of stimulating individual entrepreneurs and entirely new enterprises. In the United States, such policies in the last two decades would have led to supporting a group of Fortune 200 enterprises that lost employment and market position, rather than encouraging the new companies (over 600,000 created in 1984 alone, see Figure 4) that produced the most new jobs and wealth for the country. A particular focus is needed in this country on the services industries, where most of these new companies are rising. As in earlier eras of development, we do not know today which of these ventures will blossom into entire new industries or giants themselves. But the past predicts that some will do so. A real question exists, however, whether they can provide the trading might this nation will need for its future health.

THE SERVICES INDUSTRIES

Depending on how it is measured, between 67 and 75 percent of the U.S. economy today is in "services" activities. Our major trading partners are moving in the same direction (Figure 5). Does technology have an impact in the services industries similar to that in manufacturing? What has the adoption of technology been there? How does this affect national competitiveness?

For this short commentary, I have put together only a few measures that suggest the pervasiveness of technology adoption in the services sector. Although productivity in the services industries is notoriously difficult to

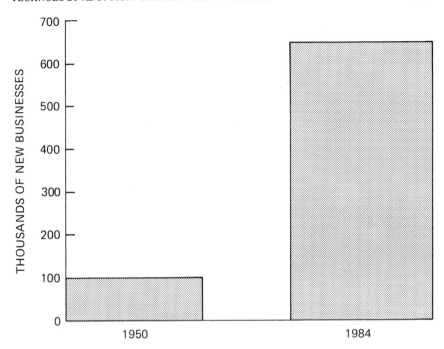

FIGURE 4   New corporate business creation in the United States, 1950 and 1984.
SOURCE: U.S. Department of Commerce, Bureau of the Census, *Statistical Abstract of the United States* (Washington, D.C.: U.S. Government Printing Office, appropriate years), Table 876.

measure, these indicators offer some interesting insights about the macroimpact of technological change in the services sector. Where possible, direct measures of service output were used. When this was not possible, the Bureau of Labor Statistics (BLS) composite productivity measurements, which apply a composite of measurable output factors to approximate "output" in various services sectors, became the preferred source. Some international comparisons between the output of U.S. services industries and those of other countries also are included. However, because of differences in the way data are collected and in the definitions used by various countries, significant international comparisons were not feasible in many cases.

Productivity Versus Manufacturing

U.S. manufacturing productivity improved at an average annual rate of about 2.8 percent between 1960 and 1983. The BLS index of relative output per employee showed that productivity improved in certain important services sectors much more rapidly than in manufacturing. This was most notable in

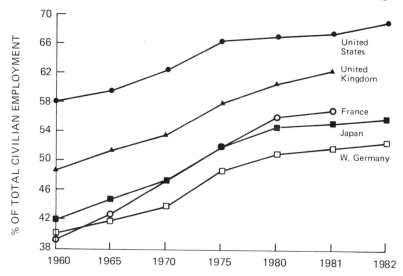

FIGURE 5   Distribution of employment in services industries, selected years, 1960 to 1982.

SOURCES: U.S. Department of Labor, Bureau of Labor Statistics, *Handbook of Labor Statistics*, Bulletin 2175 (December 1983); U.S. Department of Commerce, Bureau of the Census, *Statistical Abstract of the United States* (Washington, D.C.: U.S. Government Printing Office, appropriate years).

telephone/communications, air transportation, railroad, and gas/electric utilities industries during the period 1960–1983 (Table 1). The first three sectors were significantly ahead of the somewhat reduced productivity rate increases in manufacturing during the 1970–1983 period. Some international com-

TABLE 1   BLS Index of Relative Output per Employee

Industry	Average Annual Improvement	
	1960–1983	1970–1983
Telephone/communications	6.1%	6.8%
Air transportation	5.8	4.5
Railroad (rev. traffic)	5.1	4.8
Gas, electric utilities	2.7	1.0[a]
Commercial banking	—	0.9[b]
Hotels/motels	1.6	0.8

[a] 1981 data.
[b] 1982 data.
SOURCE: Bureau of Labor Statistics, Office of Productivity and Technology.

TABLE 2   Labor Productivity Levels (1975 dollars per hour)

Sector	Japan 1970	Japan 1980	U.S. 1970	U.S. 1980	U.S./Japan 1980
Private domestic business	3.59	6.01	9.40	10.06	1.67
Agriculture	1.37	2.38	16.53	18.36	7.71
Selected services					
Transportation and					
communications	3.86	5.66	9.29	13.14	2.32
Electricity, gas, water	14.01	19.74	21.98	25.38	1.29
Trade	2.88	4.53	6.88	7.92	1.75
Financial and insurance	6.69	12.03	8.21	8.20	0.68
Business services	3.39	3.60	7.69	7.59	2.11
Manufacturing	3.91	8.00	7.92	10.17	1.27

SOURCE: *Measuring Productivity: Trends and Comparisons*, from the First International Productivity Symposium, Tokyo, Japan, 1983 (New York: Unipub, 1984).

parisons show the United States outperforming Japan by an important margin in labor productivity levels in selected services sectors (Table 2).

Individual services industries dominated by technological changes (like telephones/communications) had spectacular labor-productivity improvement (Figure 6); others, like hotels, motels, and commercial banking, seemed to have lower increases in labor productivity; and some, like education, are perhaps even negative. In-house studies showed that technology lowered transaction costs significantly for individual banks that automated extensively (Table 3), but, bankers frequently found, as so often happens elsewhere, that—faced with lower costs and greater convenience—customers changed their behavior patterns and increased their number of transactions, thus obscuring overall efficiency changes.

More importantly, many of the services industries on which we rely for employment and convenience simply could not operate without modern communications and computer capabilities. Without these technologies, banking, insurance, financial services, travel, air transportation, hotel, and other industries would operate creakingly at best and chaotically out of control or dangerously at worst.

Support Services Industries

Even though they are no paragons of productivity, the postal services and securities industries provide some sense of labor productivity increases in certain "support" services sectors (Table 4). During the period 1970–1982 both groups' productivity increases exceeded national manufacturing averages by a substantial margin. The postal services, after a long laggard period, began to improve markedly in the 1970s as electronic sorting and new handling systems were developed. Then entrepreneurship and aircraft technol-

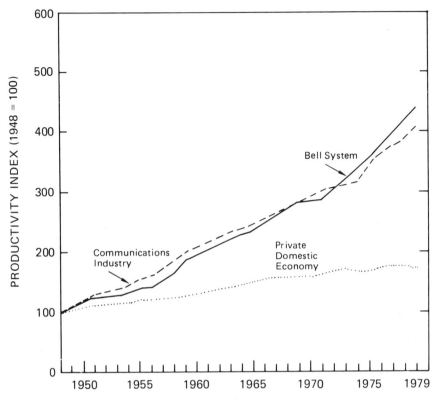

FIGURE 6   Postwar productivity comparisons, 1948 to 1979.
SOURCE: From John W. Kendrick and American Productivity Center, *Improving Company Productivity: Handbook With Case Studies* (Baltimore, Md.: Johns Hopkins University Press, 1983).

TABLE 3   Impact of Technology on Banking Costs

	Transaction Costs		
	Old	New	Saving
Check handling versus electronic teller			
facility	$0.20	$0.09	55%
plus float	—	0.09	100
Automated client payments	0.31	0.06	81
Automated teller costs	0.87	0.40	54

TABLE 4 Average Annual Productivity Increases, Postal
Services and Securities Industries

Years	Postal Services	Securities Industry
1950–1982	2.0	6.4
1960–1982	1.9	10.5
1970–1982	3.4	12.8
1980–1982	3.4	9.7

NOTE: In pieces (shares) handled per employee.
SOURCE: U.S. Department of Commerce, Bureau of the Census, *Statistical Abstract of the United States* (Washington, D.C.: U.S. Government Printing Office, appropriate years).

ogies combined to open the whole "express" mail industry, improving selected services' times and quality by an order of magnitude. Next, dedicated electronics systems lowered costs so much that hard copy could be delivered within minutes to remote points for about one-fifth the cost of a letter. This in turn led to a second-generation express or "zap message" service industry, and so on.

The securities industry's 10 percent productivity improvement per year between 1960 and 1982 suggests how much mail-handling efficiency might perhaps have been improved if its ownership and management structures permitted. Another measure shows loans or deposits handled per employee in banking growing relatively slowly until 1970; then from 1970 to 1982 productivity in these terms grew by an average 5.4 percent per year (Figure 7). Of course, such numbers do not purport to be very accurate measures; they merely suggest the extent of technological change in some services sectors.

Medical Care Services

In other service areas, technology has had even more profound effects. Simple efficiency figures cannot measure the changes technology has wrought in medical care. Whole disease classes—such as diphtheria, smallpox, tuberculosis, poliomyelitis, cholera, whooping cough, and scarlet fever—have ceased to be serious threats in modern societies (Table 5). Orthoscopic and microsurgical techniques have radically altered the cost and pain of joint surgery. Fiber optic techniques allow surgeons to quickly diagnose and remove gall stones, kidney stones, digestive impairments, tumors, and other types of unwanted growths—lowering costs and reducing hospital stays to hours versus days or weeks. Advanced diagnostic techniques can prevent or ameliorate many classes of serious debilitative diseases, including cancers. Survival rates for heart patients have soared since 1970. Pharmacological

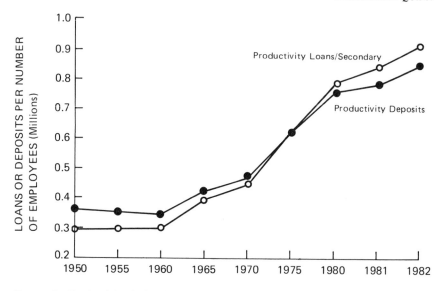

FIGURE 7   Productivity in banking, 1960 to 1982.

treatments have emptied mental hospitals in the last two decades. Much of
this dramatic progress has been technology-driven. And genetic engineering
promises further improvements in diagnostic capabilities and cures for other
specific disease classes in the next decade.

It is interesting to note that prior to the introduction of pharmaceutical
"technology" (in the form of sulfa drugs and antibiotics, there were very
few genuine "cures" that doctors could offer patients. Their primary role
was to ease pain and to allow natural processes to work. As in so many
manufacturing industries, technology radically altered both the capabilities

TABLE 5   Causes of Death per 100,000 U.S. Population, 1900 and 1978

Cause of Death	1900	1978
Influenza/pneumonia	202	27
Tuberculosis	194	1
Gastroenteritis	142	0
Nephritis	81	0
Diphtheria	40	0
Cardiovascular	137	443
Malignancies	64	182

SOURCE: National Center for Health Statistics, *U.S. Vital Statistics* (Washington, D.C.: U.S. Government Printing Office).

of the health care industry and our expectations from it. Technology created a whole "new market" of people living healthily into their mid-80s. And through other "ripple effects," the technologies applied to health services also profoundly altered the economics of insurance, Social Security, retirement housing, special products for the elderly, and so on. So powerful is their effect, even in manufacturing, that health care costs (added as fringe benefits by many large manufacturing companies) now exceed in scale those companies' total profits.

TOTAL IMPACT

There has been much concern that, "since technology could not be readily applied to the services sector," a services economy would be inherently more inflationary than a manufacturing economy. The information just presented suggests this may not necessarily be true. In fact, even within the manufacturing sector, much of technology's impact may be on "services and support" activities, such as automatic R&D assays, CAD/CAE/CAM, quality assurance, planning and control systems, market-information feedback, automatic billing systems, or warehousing and distribution controls.

The more profound impacts of services technology have yet to be measured. Will an 85 to 90 percent services economy in the United States develop an unacceptable dependency on the outside world for the raw materials and manufactures we consume? Or will a lively international trade develop for services as it did in the past for manufactured goods and materials? Can a nation develop a comparative trading advantage (hence a comparative wealth advantage) through services technologies? Will ease of entry and competitiveness force low wage standards in all services industries? Or will technology create new barriers to entry that allow only giants like AT&T or IBM to survive? The near-term effects would appear to be a vast restructuring toward smaller, more localized and entrepreneurial companies, somewhat in the tradition of the "pure competition model." But the long-term effects of technology on the services industries and the total U.S. trade position are considerably less clear. This remains a major subject for study on the application of technology for national competitiveness.

Technology Diffusion, Public Policy, and Industrial Competitiveness

PAUL A. DAVID

The intertwining of the processes of technological innovation and diffusion makes it important to consider how policies intended to promote innovation may affect the rate and the ultimate extent of adoption of new technologies. Yet this is seldom done. By failing to address systematically the issues concerning diffusion in our national policy discussions, we have surrendered the opportunity to see whether it is possible to formulate any consistent set of goals, or to coordinate the actions of the many public agencies that are engaged in de facto setting of policies affecting the development of our technological capabilities. We do not avoid making mistakes by proceeding in this way, however. Rather, we avoid having to acknowledge the mistakes and learning from them.

Technological progress today is widely perceived to be the force propelling the American economy forward, the veritable prime mover of the country's long-run economic growth. Myriad advances in the systematic knowledge of "the useful arts" have been directly and indirectly responsible for the enormous gains achieved in the measured productivity of the nation's labor and capital resources over the course of the past century. They have brought radical improvements in the qualitative attributes of goods and services, transformations that (however difficult they are to measure with precision) contributed palpably to enhancing the competitiveness of our industries abroad and the economic welfare of consumers at home.

Yet the United States does not have a well-articulated set of policy goals with regard to the development and utilization of its technological capabilities, much less a coherent, integrated program directed to the attainment of such goals. This much has been openly acknowledged by the President's Commission on Industrial Competitiveness (see Young, in this volume). The recently published report of the commission, in calling for creation of a cabinet-level Department of Science and Technology, speaks of the need to "transform the current fragmented formulation of policies for science and

373

technology into one that would be far more effective in meeting long-term national goals" (President's Commission on Industrial Competitiveness, 1985, vol. 1:22).

Among the more obvious symptoms of this persistent condition is the comparative lack of attention devoted to economic analysis of public policies impinging on the diffusion of new technologies into actual use. The economic determinants of technology diffusion is a field of research with which I am most concerned, and the one that I will review in this chapter.

My discussion proceeds along the following lines. First, I address the validity of the assessment just offered and suggest some of the reasons why policy issues regarding technology diffusion have come to be neglected in this country, even as the subject now is receiving greater explicit consideration elsewhere in the industrialized world. Next, I contrast this state of affairs with the progress that has been made by theoretical and empirical research on the microeconomics of technology diffusion during the past two decades. The findings have led to many new insights into the demand-side and supply-side aspects of this important class of dynamic processes. But these findings also have given economists a healthy respect for some of the complexities of a subject they have yet to master fully.

This is not the place for a detailed survey of the significant contributions to a voluminous technical literature, so I will only highlight some among many economic factors determining (1) whether and when adoption of specific processes and process innovations is likely to be advantageous for the users and (2) the costs that potential adopters face in order to secure the specific information, equipment, and materials essential to the effective use of the new technologies.

Cursory as such a review must be, it provides a basis for me to comment next on what I believe are important implications of "the new microeconomics of technology diffusion" for the way that the formulation of public policy in the area of technology should be approached. The review should indicate also how we might begin systematically to assess the impact of present and proposed economic policies on private sector decisions affecting the installation of new production methods and the acceptance of new goods and services by consumers. It will be seen that the relevant range of governmental actions is very broad, including the tax treatment of investment, the funding of R&D, the education of scientists and engineers, regulation and standards setting, as well as the monetary and fiscal measures shaping the macroeconomic environment. I shall contrast the tangled mass of economic policy interventions that are being pursued, seemingly without regard for their impact on the diffusion of technological innovations, with the much narrower "domestic technology transfer" programs that have been assigned a formal mission to promote the domestic dissemination of technological information.

The upshot of my review is not some simple, all-purpose policy prescription, but a call for more general recognition of the reality that choices among products and production processes in the private economy are not being left to the unimpeded workings of the market; and that the introduction of additional policies intended to quicken, or perhaps to retard, the adoption of specific new technologies cannot sensibly be justified except by explicit assessments of the extremely varied and changing conditions that obtain in different industries. Where technology diffusion is at stake, therefore, an absolutely indispensable ingredient in the formulation of rational economic policies is detailed assessments on an industry-by-industry basis. A model for such studies exists in the series recently completed by the National Academy of Engineering (1982–1985)—which deals with electronics; steel; machine tools; automobiles; fibers, textiles, and apparel; pharmaceutical products; and civil aviation manufacturing.

One of the central empirical insights guiding the direction of recent economic research is that new technology-diffusion and new technology-development processes often are very closely intertwined. (See David and Olsen, 1984; Ireland and Stoneman, 1984a.) Separation of the two for purposes of analysis may be convenient, but eventually their study must be reintegrated. Moreover, policy actions undertaken in direct reference to the one will more likely than not have significant effects on the other. The importance for intelligent economic and technology policymaking of taking the more integrated approach to the design of innovation and diffusion policy, which the microeconomics of the problem demands, is a point I wish to stress here. To grasp its importance one need only consider the following four, illustrative potential paradoxes of technology policy:

1. Efforts to speed up the rate of innovation in industries supplying capital goods can create expectations of larger capital losses through obsolescence for firms that consider adopting the new technology when it first appears. Hence, the promise of faster innovation rates can delay actual adoption decisions. (See Rosenberg, 1976; Ireland and Stoneman, 1984b.)

2. Tax and other subsidies for R&D can reduce the costs of "imitation" and lead to expected wider diffusion of a new technology throughout an industry. But if it is expected that every one will quickly adopt the technology, the inducements to bear the costs of adopting it early are reduced. So R&D subsidies may slow the initial speed of diffusion even if they do help disseminate information about the new technology more widely and increase the eventual extent of use. (See Stoneman, 1983; David and Stoneman, 1985.)

3. Delaying the imposition of technical standards in order to encourage continuing R&D investment and further innovation can slow effective application of technologies in which compatibility and network integration are vital. It does not, however, prevent the emergence of de facto standards,

which may eventually be discovered to have been suboptimal. (See Arthur, 1983; David, 1985.)

4. Strengthening patent and trade secret protections that convey significant (temporary) monopoly power to suppliers of goods embodying new technologies, while simultaneously providing public funds for the dissemination of information about the benefits to users of those technologies, can have the effect of inducing the supplying firms to set initially higher prices for their wares. Thus, the combination of a policy measure meant to promote innovation and another measure meant to encourage diffusion may perversely work to slow the pace of application. (See David and Stoneman, 1985.)

Rather than elaborating on these particular paradoxical propositions, I shall try in the following to indicate the conceptual framework within which they were derived. From that general perspective it may be seen that a number of policies being advocated to promote greater competitiveness through innovation in the United States today could have unsuspected and costly side effects for technology diffusion. Were they to be as effective in the long run as their adherents claim, they might perversely slow diffusion and the growth of productivity during both the near and medium term.

THE ADOPTION OF NEW TECHNOLOGIES AND THE DOG THAT DID NOT BARK

It would be hard to exaggerate the economic significance of technology diffusion. What determines improvements in productivity and product quality—thereby enhancing the competitiveness of firms and industries—is not the rate at which significant technological innovations are developed, but the speed and extent of their application in commercial operations. However feasible the designs for new products and production processes may be from an engineering standpoint, it is the prospects for their diffusion into use that ultimately impart economic value to this form of new knowledge.

Be that as it may, the plain fact is that adoption of technological innovations has yet to acquire an aura of glamour in contemporary American society. Certainly, both as a field of business endeavor and as a matter for scholarly investigation, it lacks the radiance that currently surrounds the process of designing and commercially introducing new technologies. (See Freeman, 1982; Mansfield et al., 1982; Nelson, 1982, for recent scholarly contributions.)

Many aspects of our history and national character have contributed to forming a climate of opinion more favorably disposed toward governmental support for the generation and commercialization of new products and production techniques than it is toward programs aimed at influencing the timing, and the eventual extent, of the use made of those innovations. As a people we have for a long time displayed an unusual psychological receptivity to novelty and change, on which astute foreign observers—from Alexis de Tocqueville onward—recurringly have remarked: There is an understandable cultural predisposition on the part of Americans to seek a basis for consensus and unity in our shared hopes for the future, rather than in the diversity of our respective experiences of the past.

Success among us as a rule is equated with "leadership"—in this case with pioneering on the *technological* frontiers. To be an assiduous "follower," by comparison, seems somehow to have acquiesced in defeat, abandoning adventure for the haven of routine. Of course, anyone with actual experience of the challenges and opportunities inherent in the transfer and adaptation of modern industrial technologies will be quick to object that nothing could be farther from the truth of the matter. Popular images frequently are distorted, but potent nonetheless. "Mere imitators!" is the epithet that a harried leader is likely to hurl over his shoulder at the ever more closely pursuing pack.

It is perhaps not surprising that in the policy discussions instigated by the worrisome "productivity slowdown" occurring in the United States since the mid-1970s, as well as in the writings of academic economists, interest increasingly has concentrated on understanding the causes of shifts in the rate and direction of technological innovation. But notice that the almost universal fixation on proposals intended to accelerate the pace of advance by influencing the allocation of private sector funds for research and development has had a curious side effect: it contributes to distracting the attention of policymakers from the ultimate goals of application, on which commercial R&D expenditures are predicated.

Innovation has thus become our cherished child, doted upon by all concerned with maintaining competitiveness and renewing failing industries; whereas diffusion has fallen into the woeful role of Cinderella, a drudge-like creature who tends to be overlooked when the summons arrives to attend the Technology Policy Ball. As a case in point, consider that in the report of the President's Commission on Industrial Competitiveness (1985, vol. 1:51–52), the words "diffusion" and "adoption" do not appear anywhere in the summary of recommendations dealing with the nation's technological resources. Here are the "three basic things" the commission has said we need to do in order "to make technology a continuing competitive advantage for the United States": "(1) create a solid foundation of science and technology that is relevant to commercial users; (2) apply advances in knowledge to commercial products and processes; and (3) protect intellectual property by strengthening patent, copyright, trademark and trade secret protections" (vol. 1:18).

At the moment I am not concerned so much with the content of the recommendations as with what is missing from the commission's list. It strikes me as noteworthy that this informed and influential group has recognized "needs" corresponding to the first two but not the third of the elements usually identified in the compound we call technological change. A less innovative document might well have been expected to offer recommendations encouraging activities under every category in the classic tripartite scheme: (1) organized or informal research leading to invention; (2) development of commercial applications leading to the introduction of an innovation, in the form of a new product or process; (3) imitation, or selective adoption of the innovation, resulting in its diffusion into actual use.

Instead, where one looks for specific policies to accelerate the wider diffusion of newly created technologies, there stands something quite different, and possibly antithetical. Concrete measures are recommended for further strengthening economic incentives stimulating innovation—by better delineating and enforcing rights to exclude others from access to the new knowledge thereby created. The closest the Young Commission comes to addressing the issue of the rate of application of new production techniques in U.S. industry is to recommend that private sector, educational, and government organizations "should initiate actions [otherwise unspecified] to improve the development and use of manufacturing technologies to transform R&D results into competitive products and services . . ." (President's Commission on Industrial Competitiveness, 1985, vol. 1:52). In the riddle of the report, entitled *Global Competition*, then, technology diffusion policy has been allotted the part of "the dog which did not bark in the night."

THE NEW MICROECONOMICS OF TECHNOLOGY DIFFUSION— AN OVERVIEW

Despite the drift of the spotlight of public policy interest away from the subject in this country, during the past 20 years there has occurred a quiet revolution in the economists' search for a deeper understanding of the processes involved in the adoption of novel technologies. The "new microeconomics of innovation diffusion" that is emerging from these research efforts is based on both theoretical insights and an accumulating body of empirical evidence.

In this country Edwin Mansfield and his students at the University of Pennsylvania have been responsible for carrying through the most extensive and systematic program of collection and econometric analysis of modern time-series samples, tracing the extent of adoption of many specified production technologies within firms and industries. (See e.g., Mansfield, 1968; Mansfield et al., 1971, 1977; Romeo, 1975, 1977.) This work was directed toward identifying common features and determinants of diffusion processes. Like the earlier, classic studies by Griliches (1957, 1960) of the adoption of hybrid corn, Mansfield's work focused attention on the roles of expected profitability for potential adopters and dissemination of information within the using industry. These were emphasized as of critical importance in overcoming the obstacles placed in the path of rapid diffusion by uncertainties, and the consequent risks for firms contemplating a large investment commitment to the new technology.

In the United Kingdom, parallel econometric studies have been carried out by Nabseth and Ray (1974) at industry, firm, and plant levels. These have confirmed the general role of profitability considerations in adoption decisions, while showing that differences in technical characteristics of production programs, product mixes, and institutional structures of firms are key factors governing the diffusion process. Davies (1979) also has studied the adoption of production innovations in British industry, finding that the speed of diffusion is slower where the scale of production typical of firms is smaller and where there is a longer expected payback period for fixed investments embodying new processes.

New conceptual approaches to the microeconomic analysis of the subject have evolved out of these path-breaking empirical investigations. The point of departure in Mansfield's studies was a model of diffusion involving a new technology having prespecified engineering and economic characteristics, an unchanging population of potential users who had to be persuaded of the profitability of the innovation, and an objective economic environment in which the only consequential change occurring was the gradual dissemination of information. Looked at from this angle, the gradual increase in the extent of an innovation's application across the firms and sectors of the economy takes on the appearance of an adjustment process, which eventually approaches the restoration of equilibrium.

An alternative conception has been developed by considering the historical and contemporary evidence that many new technologies are initially introduced in forms and under market conditions that make them appear profitable in immediate applications only for some firms within the relevant industry; indeed, perhaps only in the operations of some plants and departments within those firms. Subsequently, however, as the new technology and its microeconomic environment coevolve, the extent of profitable application will broaden.

Abundant confirmation of the modern relevance of the major empirical premises on which this approach is grounded has been provided by Gold (1979, 1981, 1983) and his associates at Case Western Reserve University through their detailed case studies of managerial decision processes pertaining to the adoption of innovation. Furthermore, its importance has been confirmed repeatedly through the many individual historical diffusion studies that have absorbed some of the best efforts of a generation of quantitative economic historians.

Analytical work in which I have had a hand (David, 1969, 1975; David and Olsen, 1984) and important contributions by Davies (1979), Stoneman (1983), and others have led to the elaboration of the class of so-called equilibrium diffusion models. These models have emphasized two fundamental points, which can be added to those brought out by Mansfield's contributions. The first is that even if information relevant for rational decision making about the innovation were instantaneously disseminated without cost, there would remain many reasons to expect that states of equilibrium would exist involving less-than-complete diffusion of the new technology within the industry. The second point, following immediately from the first, is that our attention should be directed to the various dynamic forces whose influence gives rise to a "moving equilibrium" in the potential level of fully informed adoption of innovations by rational, profit-seeking agents.

I shall want to carry on from this last point and discuss some of the supply-side forces that have become recognized as crucial in driving technology diffusion forward. (See Rosenberg, 1972; Stoneman, 1976; Metcalf, 1981; Sahal, 1981; Stoneman and Ireland, 1983; David and Olsen, 1984.) But before I can do that, I must briefly address some fundamental aspects of the demand side of the adoption of innovation.

Key Demand Factors in Technology Diffusion

The demand to take up new technologies—whether embodied in intermediate products, such as epoxy resins and ethylene/propylene rubber, or in such equipment as computerized numerical-controlled machine tools, or in complete industrial facilities, such as large-scale ammonia plants—will not be ubiquitous and instantaneous, if only because potential users do not find themselves in identical technical and economic circumstances. They may face different raw material costs, energy prices, and transport charges; they may differ in regard to the makeup of technically related product arrays produced using joint facilities; they may operate in different labor markets and have different implicit or explicit contractual commitments with their employees; they may encounter different terms for borrowing or different opportunity costs of internally financing capital projects. All these may have a bearing on whether a proposed change in production methods to incorporate an innovation will appear worth undertaking when it first becomes available, or at some subsequent point in time.

The preceding catalog does not yet exhaust the list of significant aspects of heterogeneity within the population of "potential adopters"; not even the list of important objective economic differences capable of generating a wide distribution of responses to an innovation about which few technological uncertainties remain. Two further basic aspects of the demand side of microeconomic adoption decisions must be recognized here.

First, in projects characterized by larger fixed costs for state-of-the-art plant and equipment, where offsetting savings in variable costs become significant only at high throughput rates, a critical issue is the scale of output that the enterprise can anticipate maintaining with the production facility in question. Considerations of this kind were as much a factor bearing on the adoption of the early grain harvesting machines, and later of gasoline farm tractors, as it has been in the post-World War II diffusion of new plant designs in the petrochemicals industry, or as it now is in regard to the installation of second-generation industrial robots (see David, 1984, and references).

The second point to note is that the decision to introduce a new industrial process is often bound up with the determination to discontinue operation of existing capital facilities. While an old plant may be technologically obsolescent, prevailing product prices in the industry may permit variable costs to be covered and so make it rational for profit-maximizing firms to defer the date of capital replacement. New technologies are placed at a distinct disadvantage in competition with their predecessors whenever they come embodied in or are technically interrelated with indivisible capital goods that will burden the user with heavy fixed-cost charges (see Frankel, 1955; Salter, 1966).

This is so especially when the old techniques are embedded in extremely durable physical plant with low maintenance requirements. The slow headway made by the Solvay process, in displacing the use of the antiquated Leblanc method for the manufacture of sodium carbonate in Britain during the last quarter of the nineteenth century, has been shown by Lindert and Trace (1972) to be explicable largely on just such grounds. Thus, the legacies of past capital formation decisions, as well as the costs of new investment, may combine to create differences which will determine the timing and pattern of technology diffusion within firms and industries. Durable facilities surviving from earlier epochs may pose barriers to the introduction of best-practice methods that, in pathological cases, cannot be surmounted by the workings of normal competitive market processes (see David, 1975:Ch. 5; and David, 1985).

In light of the foregoing, it should be plain that a decision-process "failure" is not necessarily involved just because we notice that particular innovations are being "neglected," or only haltingly and partially adopted by firms in one place even though they have been applied effectively elsewhere. Such lags are to be expected. For example, in a widely cited study of four important U.S. industries (bituminous coal, iron and steel, brewing, and railroads, spanning the period 1890–1958—when we were not particularly worried about the competitiveness of our staple industries), Mansfield (1968) found that the complete diffusion of new process technologies among just the major firms stretched out over durations of 10 years and longer in 9 out of a sample of 12 process innovations; and for 5 of those same innovations, more than

20 years was required for the complete transition. The causes, and quite possibly also the remedies, may lie at some remove from the immediate locus of decision making within the "laggard" firms. We need not surmise that the managers are poorly informed about the potentialities of emergent technologies, or psychologically wedded to familiar routines, or hesitant to accept risks in search of greater profits; nor must we hasten to implement organizational revolutions that will alter their ways if not their personalities. Human beings—even graduates of schools of business and of engineering—certainly do fall prey to all these weaknesses, which in some instances may prove critical. Yet, there are ample grounds for doubting that sluggish managerial reactions, made more sluggish still by uncertainty, are really what lies behind the long diffusion lags so commonly experienced when process innovations are involved.

Key Supply Factors in Technology Diffusion

Part of the explanation for the length of time it takes for new technologies to supplant old ones is to be found by considering the factors on the supply side that drive forward the diffusion process. I can deal only briefly here with these inherently complicated questions, so it may be excusable for me to report what has been learned in the following, overly simplified way. The terms on which users can acquire effective access to new technologies will reflect one or more of three classes of cost: (1) the costs of securing and evaluating information about them from others who possess it; (2) the costs of obtaining the specialized materials or equipment in which new technologies having particular performance characteristics are physically "embodied" by the supplying firms; and (3) the costs of specialized facilities, ancillary products, or services that are closely tied to the innovation for technical reasons and thus will affect its performance.

The significance of the first two items on this little list seems obvious enough, although it has come as something of a surprise to many economists that the real resource costs of transmitting and absorbing all of the relevant "unembodied" technical knowledge can be very substantial, even under conditions of coordinated technology transfer—such as those effected by multinational firms. A study made by Teece (1976) of 26 technology-transfer projects involving manufacturing ventures in chemicals, petroleum refining, and machinery found that, on average, 19 percent of total project costs was accounted for by these intangibles: pre-engineering information exchanges; engineering costs associated with transferring the necessary designs; R&D personnel utilized during the transfer phase; and pre–start-up training, learning, and debugging.

We should recognize at this point that differences among firms in the costs of absorbing technological information, even information disseminated on a uniform basis by a supplier or an independent agency, may give rise to differences in innovation-adoption behavior. Mowery (1983) suggests that firms that maintain R&D activities are thereby provided with an enhanced capability for monitoring and assessing technologies originating elsewhere, and Teece (1976) also contends that R&D contributes to the ability of transferees to absorb manufacturing technologies at minimum cost. To the extent that this may be confirmed by other studies, especially studies of "domestic technology transfer costs," this effect could turn out to be a substantial if generally unacknowledged source of the privately appropriable benefits derived from expenditures on research and development. It certainly has been overlooked in studies that have sought to assess the private and social returns on R&D solely in terms of the value of the innovations that are generated (see Mansfield et al., 1977).

The existence of R&D capabilities that enable some firms within an industry, or outside it, to "reverse engineer" new products and "invent around" patented processes contributes to reducing the costs of imitation. The "imitation threat capacity" thereby created—even if it is not actually used—may act as a factor limiting the prices that patent holders will charge licensees for access to the technology. Even firms that do not possess such R&D capabilities may benefit from their existence in this way: This is a possible externality (or spillover effect) of company-financed R&D; it may contribute to raising productivity levels in the industry by promoting the diffusion of available technologies, rather than the generation of further innovations.

The third item on my list assumes particular significance for technologies characterized by the presence of network externalities, as they are called in the economists' jargon (see Hanson, 1984; David, 1985; Katz and Shapiro, 1985). Illustrations spring to mind readily in the field of telecommunications, where decisions regarding terminal equipment are affected by the costs of access to other parties over existing transmission networks. In the case of computers, the hardware costs of particular machines are only a part of the story, for, the available range and price of compatible software also matter in determining the use that will be made of the technology. On a more mundane level, conveniently located repair centers staffed with trained technicians and adequately stocked spare-parts depots also constitute a form of "service network" supporting users of specialized equipment—from trucks to vacuum cleaners. As in the preceding cases, service networks may be provided by agents other than the suppliers of the equipment itself.

All three classes of technology-access costs share a common feature that is crucially important for the dynamics of diffusion processes. With the passage of time, and in response to the widening extent of application of the technology in question, each is likely to undergo a decline. The specific details vary among the classes, however:

1. Coordinated technology transfer appears to be a decreasing cost activity, in the sense that its costs decline with each application of a given innovation

or each startup undertaken by the transferor (see Teece, 1976; Stoneman, 1983). In addition, uncoordinated transfers of technical information can and do occur through the accepted mobility of scientific and engineering personnel within and sometimes between industries. The phenomenon was as relevant for the rapid diffusion of production methods within the Japanese cotton textile industry during the late Meiji Era (1890–1912), as it can be seen to be in Silicon Valley today (see Saxonhouse, 1985; Okimoto, 1984; Cohen, 1985). Notice, then, that a given rate of personnel turnover in the industry will have a greater effect in increasing the accessibility of information about a new technology, the larger is the cadre of scientific and engineering workers who are being exposed to it at any one point in time. Consequently, this information-dissemination mechanism will, at least for a time, be positively reinforced by the widening adoption of the innovation as an increasing pro-portion of the relevant skilled manpower pool comes into contact with those who have already had an opportunity to acquire it.

2. Technologies are not static. They undergo instead a gradual, evolu-tionary development that is intimately bound up with the course of their diffusion. This was a point made by Rosenberg (1972), but the rest of us have taken about a decade to catch up with him. The initial versions of a new product or process, even those that reach the market and find purchasers, often suffer from numerous flaws in production or design. Identification and remedy of such defects are, in many instances, dependent on the accumulation of feedback information from users—a process to which Rosenberg (1982) recently has affixed the label "learning by using." By considering that performance improvements in commodities whose costs remain unchanged may be rendered equivalent with reduced costs of products of a constant kind, we can draw a direct analogy with the more familiar and widely documented phenomenon of "learning by doing," or irreversible dynamic scale economies. (See Arrow, 1962; David, 1975:Ch. 2 and citations therein.) Along both kinds of learning curves the accumulation of experience—in production and in utilization—that diffusion itself makes possible is seen to govern and sustain a continuing flow of incremental innovation. And such innovations, by lowering the effective "cost" of successive vintages of the embodied technology, reciprocally extend its penetration into new markets and areas of application.

3. Network technologies exhibit some of the same dynamic features in their development as do "freestanding" product and process innovations. As a network's coverage is extended by linking up additional "subscribers," the cost of providing basic services to each user will decline, and the potential qualitative advantages of being "hooked up" with a widening circle of users tend to increase. The essential economic problem posed by such systems, however, is that integration requires some measure of technical compatibility or standardization and thus imparts to them the characteristics of a public

good (see Kindleberger, 1983): you cannot be linked with me by videotext without my being thus linked with you. This means that the benefits derived (or the effective costs incurred) by any one prospective system user may be dependent on the willingness of others to incur the costs of achieving compatibility with the same network.

Where there are alternative emerging network technologies to choose among, as is currently the case with teletext and videotext (see Tydeman et al., 1982), the public goods problem tends to work to retard the adoption of any one of them; potential subscribers will be inclined to wait in the hope that others will bear the costs of achieving compatibility with them. "Free-riding behavior" of this kind works to prevent the true demand for public goods from being revealed by competitive market processes. Therefore, if de facto standardization does not occur through the market dominance of one among the available alternative systems, there may be a case for public standard setting to foster diffusion of the technology. A difficulty, of course, lies in choosing among technological alternatives at an early stage of their development, while great uncertainty still surrounds both the potential technical capabilities of rival systems and the eventual performance characteristics that users will value most highly. Furthermore, there is the distinct danger that premature imposition of standards will close off opportunities for profitable investment in research, design, and development of still other technological alternatives.

Economics lives up to its reputation as "the dismal science" by telling us again and again that the world is arranged so that one cannot have everything: here we need to recognize the existence of a trade-off between the more certain gains of greater benefits of diffusion today and the chance of having more beneficial innovations tomorrow.

Once we have moved beyond a static conception of technologies, there is another point of great importance to be made about the dynamics of technology choices under conditions of decreasing costs—or system scale economies. It is a point that has emerged clearly in the recent fundamental research on the subject by my Stanford colleague, Brian Arthur (1983). The existence of irreversible, dynamic scale economies—such as those generated in "learning by doing" and "learning by using"—means that small, initial advantages (or disadvantages) can readily cumulate into larger ones. This opens the possibility that a particular product design, process technology, or system can become "locked in," and rival technologies can become "locked out" through the working of competitive market processes. In other words, eventual de facto standardization is the most likely outcome, indeed, under some conditions it is a virtual certainty—as Arthur (1985), based on Arthur et al. (1983, 1985), has shown.

Thus, the lesson borne home to us is that even in the absence of governmental intervention to impose technical standards, even without formal recommendations of industry associations, and in even in markets in which there is no dominant technology supplier (like IBM) or sanctioned monopolist (like the old AT&T), we are quite likely to get technology "standards." They will come to us through the long-run operation of the forces of decreasing cost that I have reviewed in looking at the supply side of the diffusion process. The issue is what kind of technology standards will we get, and what seemingly small "accidents" of industrial history, or temporary public policy twists during the early phases of the diffusion of rival technologies, will leave an unintended but nonetheless indelible mark on the future? If you need a concrete, everyday illustration of the workings of the "lock in" process and the kind of technological outcomes to which we can be led by seemingly small accidents of history, take a look at the awkwardly arranged QWERTY keyboard of your typewriter and your personal computer (see David, 1985).

CONCLUDING PERSPECTIVES ON PUBLIC POLICIES

In light of the ongoing conceptual reorientation whose main aspects I have just reviewed, the terminology of "diffusion" itself now seems less and less helpful as a metaphor for the phenomena it is being used to label—although by now it is inextricably lodged in the economists' jargon. The modern allusions that the word "diffusion" carries to the behavior of gas molecules suggests that new technologies are somehow (randomly) finding their way into application in new locations. But our new explanatory approaches derive from the contrary vision of economic agents purposively acting to acquire and apply innovations.

We are still well short of achieving a full and deep understanding of technology diffusion at a purely theoretical level, and a great deal of painstaking empirical research remains to be undertaken in order to determine the ranges over which various proposed models may be said to apply. What has been achieved is, in a sense, only the first stage of the integration of the subject into the mainstream of modern microeconomic analysis.

But even this much is not without significant implications for our thinking about technology policy. To begin with, it greatly facilitates identification of a wide array of technical, informational, and market factors as impinging on either the supply side or the demand side of technology transfers, and it facilitates investigation of those factors' likely influences on economically rational decisions about when to undertake the application of specific new technologies. In this way, the recognized assortment of effective "policy levers" can be augmented.

Further, the framework being fashioned leads one naturally to think that there is an "optimal" (expected) waiting time before a new technology is adopted for use by a given producer or consumer. It will no longer do to say that something must be amiss with the way private decision processes are working simply because everyone does not decide to adopt technologies as soon as they are commercially introduced. More rigorous economic criteria, showing that there is a divergence between privately and socially optimal "waiting times," must be met in order to justify conclusions that the collective outcome of such individual decisions deferring adoption is unsatisfactory, in the sense of proceeding "too slowly" and therefore leaving the extent of use "too limited."

Both implications constitute bases for initiating a thorough-going re-examination and reformulation of public policies and programs that affect technology diffusion. Here, however, I shall venture no farther than to offer some broad perspectives on the current policy scene.

Formal programs directed toward encouraging wide application of new technologies in the civilian economy are often associated in the public mind and in the mind of legislators with "diffusion policy." For better or for worse, the approach to technology diffusion that those programs represent has not received extensive public funding in this country (see Rhode, 1985).

The Cooperative Extension Service program of the U.S. Department of Agriculture long has remained the major claimant for such federal funding as has been devoted to domestic technology transfer. Although there has never been a thorough economic evaluation of the costs and benefits attributable to this program, it has established for itself a reputation for "field success" that has carried over into academic circles. (See Mosgavero and Shane, 1982; Ruttan, 1982; Rogers, 1983.) This led other federal agencies— such as the National Aeronautics and Space Administration and the Department of Energy—to attempt to imitate its methods on a much smaller scale and in quite different circumstances. Yet, in comparison with federal expenditures for R&D, even with the small outlay for civilian R&D, the Cooperative Extension Service program has remained trivial in its budgetary dimension.

My purpose here is not to lament the small budgetary scale of federally financed technology-transfer efforts, or to bemoan the Reagan administration's evident reluctance to imitate Western European governments, which several years ago began developing industrial policies with greater emphasis on measures aimed at "promoting the diffusion of new technologies" in specified areas (see Stout, 1981; David and Stoneman, 1985).

What I wish to stress instead, is that there is far more to public policies and actions affecting technology diffusion than the information-dissemination programs modeled on the Agricultural Extension Service. Innovation-adoption decisions made by the individual firm are decisions about investment, in essence and usually in substance. As such, they can be critically influenced—by monetary and fiscal policies that affect the costs of borrowing and the after-tax rates of return on new technology-embodying capital goods; by the influence of macroeconomic policies on the prospective rate of utilization of fixed plant and equipment; by the impacts of energy policies on the prices of inputs complementary with capital facilities; by educational policies that may quicken or slow the growth in the supply of workers with specialized skills required by new technologies; by antitrust policies and regulations that shape the market structure in the industries that may take up the innovations; by patent laws and rulings that influence the costs of access to new technologies; by the entire panoply of policies directed ostensibly toward generating future industrial innovations at a faster pace, and the expectations of obsolescence risks that these engender in regard to the innovations already at hand.

We in the United States, therefore, are already in the business of making de facto public policy choices regarding technology diffusion. We have been doing it on a big scale, using a wide array of instruments, without fully facing up to the fact and taking heed of what we are about. In this we resemble the character in Moliere's play *The Misanthrope* who discovered he was a doctor in spite of himself. We have not spared ourselves the effects of the actual policy measures. Rather, for the sake of avoiding the discomfort of addressing systematically the issues concerning diffusion in our national policy discussions, we have surrendered the opportunity to see whether it is possible to formulate any consistent set of goals, or to examine what would be entailed in trying to coordinate the actions of the many different public agencies that are now participating in a de facto technology policy-setting process. We are not avoiding making mistakes by proceeding in this way. One is almost bound to make mistakes in these matters. Instead, we are avoiding having to acknowledge the mistakes we make and limiting our ability to learn from them.

How better should we proceed? Are there some broad implications for public policy discussions that can be drawn from the hurried tour I have conducted of "the new microeconomics of technology diffusion"? Let me close by suggesting these three:

1. The cases for encouraging wider adoption of new technologies must be considered on their respective merits; generalizations in this area are more apt than not to be misleading, and indiscriminate promotion of the maximum possible extent of adoption is not a desirable goal for public policies. The socially optimum extent of diffusion sometimes will exceed that which private markets generate, as when static public goods effects are strong. But this is not always the outcome.

2. Policies designed to quicken the rate of adoption of available new technologies must be framed with due attention to the private and social costs, as well as the benefits associated with establishing a more rapid pace of adoption. In this sphere, "faster" will not invariably be "better."

3. Assessments of the satisfactoriness of the rate of diffusion cannot be undertaken without regard for the many complex and conflicting relationships that obtain between decisions about the adoption of new technologies and the commitment of private resources in pursuit of further technological advances. Innovation policies and diffusion policies have for too long a time been formulated and evaluated separately, as if the two processes were quite independent. It is time to treat them within an integrated approach to enhancing economic welfare by improving the technological and other bases of our industrial competitiveness.

ACKNOWLEDGMENT

The author is indebted to Douglas Puffert, Paul Rhode, and Joshua Rosenbloom for able research assistance on projects supported under a grant to the Technological Innovation Program of the Center for Economic Policy Research at Stanford University, upon which this chapter has drawn.

REFERENCES

Arrow, Kenneth J. 1962. The economic implications of learning by doing. *Review of Economic Studies*, 29 (June):155–173.

Arthur, W. Brian. 1983. On Competing Technologies and Historical Small Events: The Dynamics of Choice Under Increasing Returns. IIASA (Laxenburg, Austria). Paper presented at the Technological Innovation Program Workshop, Stanford University, Department of Economics, November, 1983. Revised version available as *Technological Innovation Program Working Papers*, No. 4 (January 1985). Center for Economic Policy Research. Calif.: Stanford University.

Arthur, W. Brian, Yuri M. Ermoliev, and Yuri M. Kaniovski. 1983. On generalized urn schemes of the polya kind. *Cybernetics* 19:61–71.

Arthur, W. Brian, Yuri M. Ermoliev, and Yuri M. Kaniovski. 1985. Strong laws for a class of path-dependent urn processes. In *Proceedings of the International Conference on Stochastic Optimization, Kiev, 1984*. Munich: Springer-Verlag.

Cohen, David. 1985. Turnover Statistics for Electronics Engineers and Electronics Industry Exempt Personnel in Local U.S. Labor Markets. Silicon Valley Research Project Memorandum, Center for Economic Policy Research, Stanford University, March.

David, Paul A. 1969. A Contribution to the Theory of Diffusion. Center for Research in Economic Growth Research Memorandum, No. 71. Stanford University.

David, Paul A. 1975. *Technical Choice, Innovation, and Economic Growth: Essays on American and British Experience During the Nineteenth Century*. London and New York: Cambridge University Press.

David, Paul A. 1984. The reaper and the robot: The diffusion of microelectronics-based process innovations in historical perspective. *Technological Innovation Program Working Papers*, No. 2. Center for Economic Policy Research. Calif.: Stanford University. Forthcoming in J.-J. Salomon, ed., *Science, Technology, and Society*, Paris, 1985.

David, Paul A. 1985. Clio and the economics of QWERTY. *American Economic Review* 75, 2 (May):332–337.

David, Paul A., and Trond E. Olsen. 1984. Anticipated automation: A rational expectations model of technological diffusion. *Technological Innovation Program Working Papers*, No. 2. Center for Economic Policy Research. Calif.: Stanford University.

David, Paul A., and Paul L. Stoneman. 1985. Adoption-subsidies vs information provision as instruments of technology policy. *Technological Innovation Program Working Papers*, No. 6. Center for Economic Policy Research. Calif.: Stanford University, April. (Forthcoming in *Economic Journal*, 1986.)

Davies, Stephen. 1979. *The Diffusion of Process Innovations*. London: Cambridge University Press.

Frankel, M. 1955. Obsolescence and technological change. *American Economic Review* 45 (June):298–319.

Freeman, Christopher. 1982. *The Economics of Industrial Innovation*. 2d ed. London: Frances Pinter.

Gold, Bela. 1979. *Productivity, Technology and Capital*. Boston: Lexington Books.

Gold, Bela. 1981. Technological diffusion in industry: Research needs and shortcomings. *Journal of Industrial Economics* (March):247–269.

Gold, Bela. 1983. On the adoption of technological innovations in industry: Superficial models and complex decision processes. Ch. 10 in *The Trouble with Technology: Explorations in the Process of Technological Change*, S. MacDonald, D. McL. Lamberton, T. D. Mandeville, eds. London: Frances Pinter.

Griliches, Zvi. 1957. Hybrid corn: An exploration in the economics of technological change. *Econometrica* 25 (October):501–522.

Griliches, Zvi. 1960. Hybrid corn and the economics of innovation. *Science* 132 (July):275–280.

Hanson, Ward A. 1984. Bandwagons and Orphans: Dynamic Pricing of Competing Technological Systems Subject to Decreasing Costs. Paper presented at the Technological Innovation Program Workshop, Stanford University, Department of Economics, January, 1980.

Ireland, Norman, and Paul Stoneman. 1984a. An Integrated Approach to the Economics of Technological Change. Paper presented at Warwick Summer Workshop on the Economics of Technological Change, July, 1980.

Ireland, Norman, and Paul Stoneman. 1984b. Technological Diffusion, Expectations, and Welfare. Paper presented at the Technological Innovation Program Workshop, Stanford University, Department of Economics, February 1984.

Katz, Michael L., and Carl Shapiro. 1985. Network externalities, competition, and compatibility. *American Economic Review* 75(3):424–440.

Kindleberger, Charles P. 1983. Standards as public, collective and private goods. *Kyklos* 36 (Fasc. 3):377–396.

Lindert, Peter D., and Keith Trace. 1972. Yardsticks for Victorian enterpreneurs. Ch. 7 in *Essays in a Mature Economy*, D. N. McCloskey, ed. London: Methuen.

Mansfield, Edwin. 1968. *Industrial Research and Technological Innovation*. New York: W. W. Norton.

Mansfield, Edwin, J. Rapoport, J. Schnee, S. Wagner, and M. Hamburger. 1971. *Research and Innovation in the Modern Corporation*. New York: W. W. Norton.

Mansfield, Edwin, J. Rapoport, A. Romeo, E. Villani, S. Wagner, and R. Husic. 1977. *The Production and Application of New Industrial Technology*. New York: W. W. Norton.

Mansfield, Edwin, A. Romeo, M. Schwartz, D. Teece, S. Wagner, P. Brach. 1982. *Technology Transfer, Productivity, and Economic Policy*. New York: W. W. Norton.

Metcalf, J. S. 1981. Impulse and diffusion in the study of technological change. *Futures* 13(5):347–359.

Mosgavero, Louis N., and Robert S. Shane. 1982. *What Every Engineer Should Know about Technology Transfer and Innovation*. New York: Marcel Dekker.

Mowery, David C. 1983. Economic theory and government technology policy. *Policy Sciences* 16:27–43.

Nabseth, L., and G. F. Ray, eds. 1974. *The Diffusion of New Industrial Processes: An International Study*. London: Cambridge University Press.

National Academy of Engineering. 1982–1985. Committee on Technology and International Economic and Trade Issues. *The Competitive Status of the U.S. Auto Industry* (1982), *The Competitive Status of the U.S. Fibers, Textiles, and Apparel Complex* (1983), *The Competitive Status of the*

U.S. Machine Tool Industry (1983), *The Competitive Status of the U.S. Pharmaceutical Industry* (1983), *The Competitive Status of the U.S. Electronics Industry* (1984), *The Competitive Status of the U.S. Civil Aviation Manufacturing Industry* (1985), *The Competitive Status of the U.S. Steel Industry* (1985), Washington, D.C.: National Academy Press.

Nelson, Richard R., ed. 1982. *Government and Technical Progress: A Cross-Industry Analysis.* New York: Pergamon Press.

Okimoto, Daniel I. 1984. Conclusions. Ch. 6 in *Competitive Edge: The Semiconductor Industry in the U.S. and Japan*, D. I. Okimoto, T. Sugano, and F. B. Weinstein, eds. Calif.: Stanford University Press.

President's Commission on Industrial Competitiveness. 1985. *Global Competition: The New Reality.* Report of the President's Commission on Industrial Competitiveness, John A. Young, chairman. Washington, D.C.: U.S. Government Printing Office.

Rhode, Paul. 1985. Federal Government Policies on Technology Diffusion. Paper presented at Technological Innovation Program Workshop, Stanford University, Department of Economics, January.

Rogers, Everett M. 1983. *Diffusion of Innovations*, 3rd ed. New York: Free Press.

Romeo, Anthony A. 1975. Interindustry and interfirm differences in the rate of diffusion of an innovation. *Review of Economics and Statistics* 57:311–319.

Romeo, Anthony A. 1977. The rate of imitation of a capital-embodied process innovation. *Econometrica* 45 (February):63–69.

Rosenberg, Nathan. 1972. Factors affecting the diffusion of technology. *Explorations in Economic History* 9 (Fall), 2d series.

Rosenberg, Nathan. 1976. On technological expectations. *Economic Journal* 86:523–535.

Rosenberg, Nathan. 1982. Learning by using. Ch. 6 in *Inside the Black Box: Technology and Economics*. New York: Cambridge University Press.

Ruttan, Vernon. 1982. *Agricultural Research Policy*. Minneapolis: University of Minnesota Press.

Sahal, Devendra. 1981. *Patterns of Technological Innovation*. Reading, Mass.: Addison-Wesley.

Salter, W. E. G. 1966. *Productivity and Technical Change*. 2d ed. Cambridge: Cambridge University Press.

Saxonhouse, Gary R. 1985. Mechanisms for Technological Transfer in Japanese Textile History. Paper presented at Social Science History Workshop, Stanford University, Department of Economics, March, 1985.

Stoneman, Paul L. 1976. *Technological Diffusion and the Computer Revolution: The U.K. Experience*. Department of Applied Economics Monographs, No. 25. London: Cambridge University Press.

Stoneman, Paul. 1983. *The Economic Analysis of Technological Change*. Oxford: Oxford University Press.

Stoneman, Paul, and Norman Ireland. 1983. The role of supply factors in the diffusion of new process technology. *Economic Journal*, Supplement (March):65–77.

Stout, D. K. 1981. The case for government support of R&D and innovation. In C. Carter, ed., *Industrial Policy and Innovation*. London: Heinemann.

Teece, David. 1976. *The Multinational Corporation and the Resource Cost of International Technology Transfer*. Cambridge, Mass.: Ballinger.

Tydeman, J., H. Lipinski, R. Adler, M. Nyhan, and L. Zwimpfer. 1982. *Teletext and Videotext in the United States: Market Potential, Technology, Public Policy Issues*. New York: McGraw-Hill.

Determinants of
Innovative Activity

KEITH L. R. PAVITT

Central to policies for promoting the contribution of technical change to economic performance are the relative technological positions of various countries, the determinants of these positions, and the effects of government policy.

In other chapters in this volume, Paul A. David, N. Bruce Hannay, and Daniel I. Okimoto, though different in their style and approach, come to some of the same important conclusions. First, each recognizes the difficulty—indeed the impossibility—of making statements about the sources, determinants, and impact of technical change that are valid for all economic sectors. Second, each stresses the importance of technological activities in national economic performance, even if Hannay and Okimoto concentrate on innovative leads and lags as important determinants of international competitiveness, whereas David emphasizes the contribution of the diffusion of innovations to national productive efficiency. Third, each recognizes that both innovation and diffusion depend on having technological skills firmly embedded within companies.

The three authors also show that further progress should and can be made in beginning to answer three questions central to the development of policies to promote the contribution of technical change to economic performance:

1. What are the relative technological positions of various countries, as reflected in the level and composition of their innovative activities?

2. What are the determinants of the level and composition of those activities?

3. What are the effects of government policy on those innovative activities and the effectiveness of their economic exploitation?

RELATIVE TECHNOLOGICAL POSITIONS OF VARIOUS COUNTRIES

I have been both puzzled and alarmed at the apparent inconsistency of analysis and commentary published in Western Europe, Japan, and the United States on the relative technological levels of the three regions. *The Economist* (1984), for example, published a 10-page analysis, entitled "How Europe Has Failed: Europe's Technological Gap," in which it said that Western Europe was falling behind both the United States and Japan in the development and exploitation of advanced technology. More recently, reports appearing in the Japanese press have pointed to inadequacies in Japanese performance in advancing fundamental technologies (see, for example, *Japan Times,* 1984). To complete a fully inconsistent picture, a cover story appearing in *Business Week* (1985), entitled "America's High-Tech Crisis: Why Silicon Valley Is Losing Its Edge," stressed the increasingly unfavorable U.S. trade balance in all categories of electronics products.

If space were not a constraint, it would be possible to spell out the empirical and methodological weaknesses of these three reports and to suggest how their conclusions might be reconciled. It would also be possible to speculate about the degree to which they either consciously or unconsciously promote special interests. Thus, *The Economist* has a very explicit ideological axe to grind, arguing that Western Europe's technological backwardness reflects too much financial regulation, subsidy, and protection compared with the greater flexibility, entry, and exit of the United States and (apparently) Japan. On the other hand, the two other reports could be seen as special pleadings for more subsidies, but precisely in the United States and Japan, which *The Economist* claims behave otherwise.

I draw somewhat different conclusions from the almost simultaneous appearance and apparent inconsistency of the three reports. First, they reflect an increasing public awareness in all three regions of the importance of technology to industrial competitiveness, living standards, and jobs. Second, they reflect the contemporary fact, shown quantitatively by Harvey Brooks (in this volume), that there are now three regions of the world competing with almost equal per capita technological resources along the world technological frontier. Under such conditions, the picture of relative technological leads and lags across countries is bound to be a complicated one, with considerable variations across sectors and across time.

This is another reason why the analyses of Hannay and Okimoto are so valuable. They have made international comparisons at the sectoral and even subsectoral levels. It is gratifying that they come to broadly similar conclusions.

But we can and should be able to measure more precisely and systematically the sectoral patterns of technological advantage in different countries and regions. The pioneering work of the National Science Board (1983) and

National Science Foundation has laid the foundation for more accurate comparisons in the future. At the Science Policy Research Unit of Sussex University, studies based on statistical data on R&D activities, patenting, the diffusion of major innovation, and scientific publications and citations (Martin et al., 1984; Pavitt, 1984a, 1984b) have led us to conclusions that both reinforce and extend those reached by Hannay and Okimoto:

1. There was significant stability in sectoral patterns of national technological advantage between the mid-1960s and late 1970s, which reflects the cumulative nature of the development of technological skills.

2. In addition to electronics and aerospace, the United States has a relative technological advantage, upstream and downstream of its abundant raw material endowments, in agriculture and oil. (Such U.S. technological strength in and around agriculture is consistent with the analysis by Ruttan, in this volume.)

3. Japan is relatively strong technologically in motor vehicles, in addition to electronics, and there is also evidence of a significantly increasing Japanese share of the world's published scientific papers and citations. On the other hand, chemicals, in addition to aerospace, shows up as a sector of relative technological weakness. We would certainly benefit from an analysis of this sector by Okimoto.

4. Western Europe, on the other hand, is relatively strong in chemicals and in production engineering and related capital goods, including robotics and other aspects of electronics-related production. It is weak in consumer and office electronics and in components. Talk of "Europessimism" or "Eurosclerosis" must be based on this particular, rather than on any general, technological weakness. It therefore reflects, if only implicitly, the expectation that office and consumer electronics and related components will offer greater market opportunities in the future than the sectors in which Western Europe is relatively strong.

DETERMINANTS OF NATIONAL PATTERNS
OF TECHNOLOGICAL ACTIVITY

It is important for both analysis and policy to improve not only our measurement of the level and composition of innovative activities, but also our understanding of the determinants of international differences. In this context, it is interesting to note that in discussing the nature and determinants of Japan's relative technological strengths and weaknesses, Okimoto does not mention the one determinant that would occur immediately to most economists, and the importance of which in inducing patterns of technical change in agriculture has been underlined by Ruttan, namely, the relative price of factor inputs.

Perhaps this is not surprising in a country that was installing and improving state-of-the-art production technology in the 1960s, when wage levels were well below those prevailing in North America and Western Europe. I have argued elsewhere that, in modern manufacturing, technology is localized in firms, differentiated in nature, and cumulative in development (Pavitt, 1984a). As Atkinson and Stiglitz (1969) have pointed out, under such circumstances technological choice in firms reflects not only relative factor costs, but also skills accumulated through past technological activities, together with expectations about future technological and market developments. In comparing U.S. and Japanese strengths and weaknesses in electronics, Okimoto rightly stresses the importance of differences in the nature of both accumulated technological skills and markets. He says less about factors likely to influence the formation of technological expectations and, in particular, the nature and quality of technological skills possessed by management. He also says little about differences in the efficiency with which accumulating and firm-specific skills are transferred into profitable investment opportunities. In this volume, there are two models for such transformation: innovation planning in large firms and the creation of new technology-based firms. I suggest that we also need to learn a great deal, through systematic empirical analysis, about the nature of the organizational and evaluation procedures in established firms that are most conducive to the exploitation of innovative opportunities, in both primary and related-product markets (Pavitt, 1984c).

If we were successful in identifying such procedures, there would be a further challenge to David and other economists studying technology diffusion: how to analyze and explain not just the diffusion of specific innovations but the diffusion of skills, strategies, and structures capable of maintaining a continuing stream of successful innovations and imitations. I would argue that the rates of diffusion of such characteristics are too slow in market economies. Further evidence about them would be valuable for corporate and public policy, as well as for theory.

EFFECTS OF GOVERNMENT POLICIES

Space does not permit me to begin to discuss government policies for technology and innovation. I shall instead restrict myself to some comments on the way in which they are perceived in many analyses of technology and international competitiveness. There is the suggestion—slight in some of the National Academy of Engineering studies summarized by Hannay in his chapter and much stronger in other chapters—that governments in Western Europe and Japan are either cleverer than the U.S. government in promoting technical innovation, or more unscrupulous, or both. This is a natural tendency in a country that, as Hannay points out, has seen a continuous decline in its relative technological position. It happened in my own country, England, when, at the end of the nineteenth century, Germany began to overtake us in industrial technology and competitiveness (see Landes, 1969:328). A related characteristic of such decline is complaints that foreigners are stealing discoveries, inventions, and innovations. This probably reflects an inability or unwillingness to commit large and patient resources beyond (relatively cheap) discoveries, inventions, and innovations in order to maintain a continuous technological lead.

In any event, Okimoto points out gently and firmly that the role and effectiveness of the Japanese government in promoting innovation has not been as great as many Westerners claim. In Western Europe, I would argue similarly, governments are not more intelligent or unscrupulous in promoting innovation than the U.S. government. After all, the percentage of industrial R&D financed by government is higher in the United States than in nearly all other non-Communist countries. Arguing over which country has the mote in its eye, and which has the beam, is not a fruitful activity. Instead of blaming the foreigner, the proper basis for policy should be humility and introspection.

REFERENCES

Atkinson, A., and J. Stiglitz. 1969. A new view of technological change. *Economic Journal* 78:573–578.

Business Week. 1985. America's high-tech crisis: Why silicon valley is losing its edge. March 11:44–50.

Economist. 1984. How Europe has failed: Europe's technology gap. November 24–30:99–110.

Japan Times. 1984. Report pushes basic research in science technology fields, December 19:3.

Landes, D. 1969. *The Unbound Prometheus: Technological Change and Development in Western Europe from 1750 to the Present*. New York: Cambridge University Press.

Martin, B., J. Irvine, and R. Turner. 1984. The writing on the wall for British science. *New Scientist*, 1429 (November):25–29.

National Science Board. 1983. *Science Indicators, 1982*. Washington, D.C.: National Science Foundation.

Pavitt, K. 1984a. International Patterns of Technological Accumulation. To be published in Proceedings of the Prince Bertil Symposium on Strategies in Global Competition.

Pavitt, K. 1984b. Technology in Western Europe. To be published in R. Mayne, *Western Europe*. London: Frederick Müller.

Pavitt, K. 1984c. Technology, Innovation and Strategic Management. Paper prepared for Workshop in Strategic Management Research, Brussels, June 1984 (to be published in workshop proceedings).

Programmed Innovation—
Strategy for Success

H. W. COOVER

In the future, new technologies will require much closer integration of R&D with engineering, manufacturing, and marketing, and thus also with corporate and business-unit strategic planning. In the future, virtually every major industry in the developed world, whether now classified as high-tech or smokestack, must in fact be high-tech to succeed in international competition. Industries will survive and thrive only by integrating advanced information, manufacturing, and computing technologies into their designs, products, and processes, and only through high levels of innovation, quality, and reliability.

This chapter is about the future and how to plan for it. The future is what we make it. Time and circumstance only accidentally shape our experience and our response—they do not set our boundaries; they do not determine the limits of our imagination; they do not define the reach of our vision.

The spirit of science is alive and well today. We have our Lavoisiers, our Pasteurs, our Carotherses, our Salks. They are among us, and they are more compelled than ever. Science and engineering have learned to deal with change. Indeed, that is close to our mission as scientists and engineers.

Creativity and change go hand in hand. How many times has it been said that "We live in a changing world"? Most often it is said in awe, bewilderment, or dejection. And sometimes, as a threat. I hasten to point out that even the rate of change is subject to the same law—it is changing, as well. And it is changing faster by the minute.

To put the pace of change in perspective, let us take a quick look backward, through the eyes of the U.S. chemical industry and its changing place in the environment of the last 30 years.

Will the U.S. chemical industry survive? Can it survive? And why should we talk about this specific industry in a book devoted to the broad subject of economics and technology?

399

The chemical industry is both old and new. Descended from the medieval alchemists, the first industrial chemical company in the United States (Du Pont) is nearly 200 years old. Yet today the industry is both a "smokestack" and a "high-tech" industry, very competitive internationally (where only the British and the Germans are strong, the Japanese are feeble, and there is a possible eventual role for the oil-rich Middle East), and very market oriented, as well. It has enjoyed a favorable balance of trade for the postwar period, peaking at nearly $12 billion in 1981, dropping to $9 billion in 1983 (and probably lower in 1984 as the hard dollar continues to erode competitiveness). It spans an enormous range of products including fertilizers, petrochemicals, drugs, synthetic fibers, plastics, rubbers, petroleum products, detergents, insecticides, and various other highly specialized products used by consumers and industries alike. Its product value is about 7 percent of GNP, with a much less than proportional direct employment.

This industry was automated starting 50 years ago. It spends an average of some 3 percent of sales on R&D and almost three times that much in capital investment. But some of the leaders do much more—Du Pont, excluding Conoco, spends almost 6 percent of its sales on R&D, much of it in electronics, life sciences, and other special areas far from its usual line of business. This company's long history epitomizes the history of change— from black powder to high explosives, to basic chemicals and dyes, to synthetic polymers and fibers, and now to agricultural chemicals, health-care products, and electronics. It is research-intensive and capital-intensive, but not labor-intensive. It is almost entirely private, unlike in countries such as Italy, France, and Holland.

However, structural change is under way in the chemical industry, which was perhaps our first truly high-tech industry in the 1950s and 1960s, and which is now maturing. This is necessitated by new competition, the oil shocks that raised energy costs, deregulation of feedstock prices, the heavy indebtedness of its many customers overseas, the greater international flow of formerly exclusive technology, environmental restrictions, greater product-liability problems arising from the increasingly litigious nature of U.S. society and its increasing desire for a riskless world, the decreasing attractiveness of investing abroad (witness the Bhopal disaster), and the hard dollar, among other factors. Hence, more of the capital spending in the industry in recent years has been for replacement and modernization, rather than new capacity or overseas investment, and a research-led shift to higher value-added specialty and proprietary products. Examples are the moves of Du Pont and Monsanto into biotechnology, the increasing efforts in pharmaceuticals, electronic chemicals, new materials, and so forth and so on, by numerous companies. The companies in these areas that are product-intensive are using R&D to look for new products, perhaps "home runs," to market quickly. Well-known examples of such companies are Lubrizol, Raychem, Great Lakes, Pall, and Millipore.

Thus, clearly, the environment for business and the role of the research organization have changed dramatically over the past several decades. And nowhere is that more true than in the chemical industry, a splendid case history to illustrate what is happening in many other companies and industries.

The chemical industry is in fact representative of a broad cross section of American industry, which now performs about three-quarters of the country's R&D (now approaching the level of $100 billion per year). Industries like aircraft and missiles, electrical equipment, machinery, motor vehicles and other transportation equipment, and instruments are also mainly privately funded in their R&D (over two-thirds on the average) and are research-intensive; some of these industries are also capital-intensive. All technologically based industries together account for 75 percent of total R&D private funding. Aircraft and missiles in this group are exceptional in that over two-thirds of their R&D funding comes from the government. R&D funding has been increasing at 8 percent per year.

Hence, this chapter discusses the chemical industry specifically, looks at its past, but above all considers its future—a future we can guide through programmed innovation—a strategy for success.

Research has progressed from being an affordable luxury to becoming an expensive requirement. But the question today is: Where do we go from here?

Assuming that governmental and societal factors provide a favorable climate for innovation, the future of the chemical industry is in our own hands. Innovation is the sum of invention and implementation, of which the latter is the more difficult part because it deals with risk and capital formation. It will be our responsibility to manage our resources, to manage the innovation process in tomorrow's rapidly changing environment. In that environment, the only constants will be ambiguity, surprise, and change that moves forward at an ever-increasing pace. That environment will require the research director to be part scientist-engineer with an eye on the future, part business person with a firm understanding of corporate goals and objectives, and part manager with an ability to guide.

Following are some ideas on how we can be all that—and more. The discussion is organized around the answers to five questions:

1. How can research be made central to determining a company's future?
2. What is the role of planning in a research organization?
3. How can we manage—and guide—the process of innovation?
4. What are the business aspects of managing an R&D program?
5. How do I see the future of the chemical industry and of industry generally?

To answer these questions, I will draw on my experience with Eastman Kodak's Eastman Chemicals Division, of which, in 1965, I was named director of research.

EASTMAN CHEMICALS: A CASE STUDY
OF THE CHEMICAL INDUSTRY

Making Research Central to a Company's Future

Our approach to research in 1965 was much like that of other companies. Research was somewhat of an island unto itself; there was very little interaction with other company functions. And the director of research was not considered an integral part of the top-level management team. The problem was that the division was successful. Its sales in 1965 were $368 million, up 15.4 percent from the previous year. After-tax earnings were a healthy 16.3 percent of sales. But those of us in the research community have never been interested in what lies behind us—we are always looking forward. And when I looked forward into the late 1960s and early 1970s I began to wonder: How can research be made central to determining the company's future.

That led to a further array of questions, many of which were of a corporate nature. For example: What is our company's culture? What businesses are we really in? And, coincidental with that: What is our approach in our various lines of business? Do we concentrate on commodity products, or products that are differentiated? Are we leaders in a few areas, or competitors across a broad spectrum? And, how important are quality and technical service? Once we were able to define our immediate course of action, we needed to know where we were heading for the future.

We asked ourselves: What businesses should—or could—we be in? What will the future environment be in those lines of business? What will be the best role for our company in those areas? And so on. Today, those questions are obvious. In fact, author John Naisbitt, in the popular book *Megatrends*, writes, "The question for the 1980s is 'What business are you *really* in?' When the business environment changes, a company or organization must reconceptualize its purpose in light of the changing world."*

At Eastman we had the "long haul" in mind, back in 1965, when we directed many of our questions at our own organization. We asked: How should R&D participate in the decision-making process of the corporation? And, how should the strategic thinking of R&D be made a part of the planning of the corporation?

The questions continued: How should we be organized to ensure full coordination of the total corporate R&D program? How can we keep R&D focused on those areas that are most important to the corporation? How do we get our technical people in close touch with the marketplace?

---

*John Naisbitt, *Megatrends* (New York: Warner Books, 1982), p. 85.

What we were really asking was this: What role should research play in the future of our company? And, if we could define that role, could we program—or manage—the innovation process to achieve it?

We needed answers to these questions. But in 1965 we had essentially no mechanism for providing the answers. In fact, few of the questions had even been asked in a formal way. We took on the challenge, nevertheless, and what we really began was a slow but vital evolutionary process in search of excellence in innovation. One critical element in the process was gaining company-wide recognition that research management had a major responsibility for defining the future of the company: that we had responsibility for new products, for new technologies, for new business opportunities to achieve the company goals for growth and profitability—and for providing strategic plans for their achievement.

Research needed to be repositioned from the isolation of the ivory tower to involvement with the corporate offices as part of the top-management team. The total R&D program needed to operate under the direction of a competent scientist and skilled manager. He or she needed to be a member of top corporate management and a high-level officer of the company.

Our research and development mission, we said, was threefold:

1. To generate the new products that are needed to enable our company to achieve its objectives for growth and profitability.

2. To ensure that all company products are based on the most advanced technology consistent with sound economics.

3. To maintain an excellent knowledge base in those areas of science and technology of current or potential interest to our company.

In other words, we defined our responsibility as both applied and basic. But we maintained that all research must be consistent with current and future corporate directions. Because we were a part of the company's business, we, too, had to be a business enterprise and emphasize planning, innovative thinking, and the well-respected principles of sound management.

The Role of Planning in a Research Organization

We were coming out of our ivory tower and getting involved in "the business of our business." That meant a greater reliance on planning. The second of the five questions listed earlier in the chapter phrases that this way: What is the role of planning in a research organization? Research does not usually take place in well-charted territory. No one has clearly defined the new products that need to be invented or the problems that need to be solved. Research management has the responsibility of developing ways of perceiving and conveying to the research scientists those things that the corporation really needs from research.

To tackle the overall planning problem, we found that we had to subdivide the total job into separate business segments or strategic business units. Most of these segments correspond to current lines of business, and a few of them are new areas of potential business interest to our company. These segments are broad enough to be challenging but narrow enough to be manageable.

For each business segment we make a technology and market projection. This is a study to determine the various factors that are likely to affect the product category over the next 15 years. We project the future technological, economic, market, political, and social occurrences that can be expected to have an impact on the products and technology in each business segment; and we try to determine the time frame for each. We identify the new products that will be required to maintain our current market share, and we define new product opportunities that could lead to significant growth for us in the business. We do a critical analysis of current and potential competitors in the business segment and their strengths and weaknesses.

In the technology and market projection, we define what we need to do and when we need to do it to enjoy a timely participation in future opportunities. We also project the financial consequences of pursuing those future opportunities. As a general principle, our target is to achieve a position of leadership in our key business areas, and these studies give us the basis for deciding what we must do to achieve such a position.

Our technology and market projections are developed by teams of five or six people. One member is from the research and development division, and one is from marketing. Each team also has a representative from our manufacturing organization, a market analysis person, a financial analysis person, and a staff person skilled in the techniques of technology forecasting. Consultants and other outside experts are brought in whenever we need to supplement our in-house capabilities. Through this combination, the team is able to take into account all of the influences that are likely to affect the business segment and the interaction of those influences. These studies become the fundamental knowledge base for business planning for the business segment. They are reviewed with top management, and decisions are made about what part of the identified opportunity we want to pursue and to make a part of our corporate plans.

These studies are a form of research. They look into the future and identify technical and market needs and opportunities and give us a world view of science and technology. In our company, R&D management first recognized the need for these studies and took the initiative to develop the needed methodology. Management responsibility for these studies continues to reside with R&D management. R&D managers, by the nature of their work and their responsibilities, are future-oriented thinkers. And R&D is one of the principal users of the information. The technology and market projections work well when we are dealing with an existing line of business or a business area that is rather closely related to some existing product line.

For unfamiliar business areas, we prepare a business area analysis. The objective of this study is to provide the best understanding possible of the target business area. We evaluate the size of the business and the opportunity that might be available to us, the projected growth, and the economic attractiveness. We consider present and projected products; the producers; the customers; the competitors—their capabilities, strengths, weaknesses, and strategies; and the factors necessary for success in serving the target business area.

The results of the study are presented to an opportunities panel comprising our most knowledgeable people from marketing, manufacturing, general management, and R&D. The panel decides which market segments, if any, offer the greatest potential. After additional studies, a new business opportunity may be identified and accepted by top management for further development. Then, the responsibility is assigned to a special venture team operating within an existing venture-management structure. The head of R&D serves as the venture general manager and is given the full responsibility for the program. A venture team comprising representatives of all needed functions is formed and reports to the venture general manager for the duration of the project. The venture team develops and implements a strategic plan for gaining the desired position in the business area. When the new products are commercialized and the new business is established, management responsibility is assigned to existing line organizations or, if appropriate, a new organizational structure is created.

My point in describing our process of analyzing new and existing businesses is this: it underscores our belief that R&D management has a leading role in helping the company define new opportunities for the future. Defining new opportunities for the future requires us in R&D to be involved fully in planning for current businesses. To do that most effectively, Eastman's research and development members participate at three levels of corporate business planning. The first is a line of business. Our company's total business is divided into 35 business segments. A business team, with representation from all the important company functions—including research—has been appointed to develop and implement a strategic plan for each business segment. An R&D manager is assigned the principal responsibility for the R&D program in support of that business segment, and he is responsible for developing and implementing the appropriate R&D strategy.

The next higher level of planning in our company is one that deals with a grouping of business segments which share raw materials and production facilities. We call these product streams. The strategic plan for each stream is based largely on the plans for each business segment but is optimized for the total stream and may necessitate changes at the business segment level.

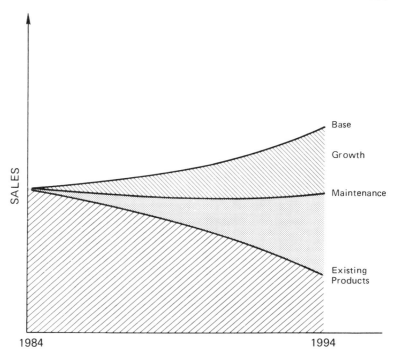

FIGURE 1   Components of base program in R&D planning for a business segment.

There are four such product streams, each of which is headed by one of our manufacturing company presidents. At this level, R&D is represented by one of the top people, either the director of research or the director of development.

Finally, there is a level of planning that covers the total company. At this level, the plans for the four major product streams are optimized from an overall corporate point of view, and plans for developing new businesses are incorporated. At this level, R&D is represented by the company's director of research and development.

These three planning levels—corporate, product stream, and line of business—are all working toward common goals: the company's goals for the future. To help achieve those goals, we in research subdivide each goal into three components and analyze what is needed from R&D for each component.

The first component is a base program for each business segment (see Figure 1). It is made up of things that we as a company know how to do, things that we fully intend to do, and things for which resources have already been provided. It is what we expect to achieve. The base program is made up of three parts. The first is our program for existing products. Left to themselves, these products would decline. The next part is the R&D projects that are necessary for maintaining market share, at satisfactory profitability. The third part of the base program is those R&D projects that will allow us to increase market share, always provided that profitability is maintained or improved. After all, one can always gain market share by giving away the product below cost.

The second component is a "stretch" position—achievable, but challenging (see Figure 2). This position would include growth opportunities that are identified, but for which implementation plans are not yet approved.

The third component is the goal itself—where the company would like to go in the business (see Figure 3). Looking at the elements building up to the goal helps us quantify for each business segment what needs to be done from an R&D point of view toward achieving the company goal.

The gap between the base program and the line represented by the stretch position in Figure 2 represents a challenge to R&D to find ways to make attractive opportunities (which are already identified) into profitable realities. The gap between the stretch position and the corporate goal in Figure 3 represents a challenge to identify new opportunities. Again, it is R&D that must help formulate a response to this challenge, because the solution usually involves new products and new technologies.

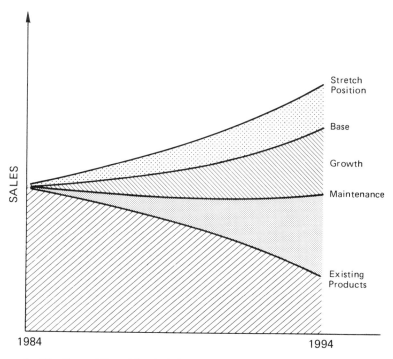

FIGURE 2   The "stretch" position in R&D planning for a business segment.

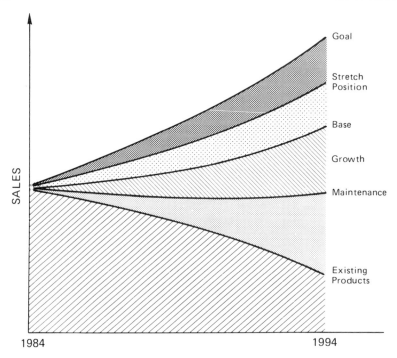

FIGURE 3   The corporate goal for a business segment.

In looking for opportunities, we look to build on the strengths we already have—we seek to become even better at what we already know how to do. We concentrate our attention in areas where our capabilities are strong, and we seek to expand our position from that base of strength. We also follow a principle of seeking breakthrough technologies. This is a more difficult and challenging approach than making incremental improvements, but it is vital if we are to maintain a position of technological leadership.

Managing and Guiding the Process of Innovation

Let us now consider the answer to the third of the five questions listed earlier: How can we manage—and guide—the process of innovation?

Today it is increasingly important to improve our effectiveness by guiding the process of innovation. At Eastman Chemicals, there are three stages in the innovation process:

1. needs
2. projected products and processes
3. innovation projects

Each successive stage represents increased certainty of success for the project and increased commitment of company resources to commercialize the product or process. Following is a description of each stage.

A "need" is simply a description of a valid new product or process for our company. In the case of a new product, the need would profile the properties and performance required for the new product to find utility in the marketplace. For a new process, the need describes the process characteristics that are desired, or the changing economic conditions that necessitate new future techniques. These descriptions then become targets toward which the research and development people can direct their creative efforts.

The identification of needs is critical to the whole process because the usefulness of the subsequent steps is totally dependent on the validity of the original need. People throughout the company, in research and development, in marketing, in manufacturing, and everywhere else, play a role in describing these needs. In this needs-identification stage, we are looking beyond the obvious. We are seeking ideas for value-added products and next-generation products that represent the major opportunities of the future. We use the projected technology changes and the projected market trends as a base for identifying new products and new technologies that will exist in the environment of the future.

To help identify needs, we have a major program to get our research scientists out into the marketplace. We have assigned R&D people to each market segment of major interest. This assignment requires that they become expert in the market. It enables them to find out what our customers expect from our current products and services and to identify future potential needs. These experts participate in the needs-identification research that is part of each technology and market projection. With one foot in the laboratory and one foot in the marketplace, our scientists are in a position to make a major contribution to the innovation process. Clearly, if you cannot define what you need, you cannot innovate it. Half the work of innovation is knowing what to innovate.

Studies of performance show that success in innovation goes up with increased knowledge of real market needs. Through their involvement in the marketplace, our scientists help us to gain that knowledge—to identify real future needs and to stay ahead of our competition, which is also looking for new opportunities.

This process of needs identification results in a needs list, which shows our R&D scientists and engineers the kinds of things that the company requires for continued progress toward its goals. As progress is made toward a solution to the need and we reach the point where the R&D manager judges that there is a better than 50 percent chance that the product or process can be successfully commercialized, the project then becomes a "projected product or process."

When a need becomes a projected product or process, a commercialization target date is established, and specific responsibility is assigned. Before recommending that a product enter this stage, the R&D manager must obtain from our market analysis group the potential market value of the product. He also must obtain from marketing its commitment to add the resulting new product to its market basket of products for commercial sale. Similarly, for a projected process we require an estimate of the economic benefits that will result. The R&D manager must also review the proposal with the engineers who would have to design and build it and with the manufacturing manager in the area where the process would be used to ensure that if it is successful it will be utilized in the manufacturing area. My point is this: by the time a project gets to this stage, it is more than a project solely for R&D. We have involved the appropriate organizations outside of R&D to get broad company commitment to the project.

As additional experimental work is done on one of these projects and the scientist or engineer reaches the point where he has developed a specific concept that will satisfy the need and which he believes the company should push forward to commercialization, the product or process moves into the third stage, the "innovation project" stage. This is a critical and sensitive phase in the life of a project, and we believe that our R&D effectiveness can be greatly influenced by how we handle it.

At the innovation project stage, an innovations committee, with representation from all major areas of the company, reviews the concept and provides the necessary approvals. This group also assigns responsibility and determines priorities needed to commit the R&D organization to translating the concept into commercial reality. A project team is appointed, and the members develop a plan to cover all elements necessary for the project, up to and including commercialization. The project team is composed of representatives from R&D, manufacturing, marketing, and other functions necessary to the success of the project. Team members become fully knowledgeable about the project in the very early stage. They provide input to the direction of the project, and they are committed to its success. This team is responsible for the project from inception to commercialization. The successful conclusion of an innovation project results in the commercialization of a new product or in the commercial practice of a new process or some new technology.

Even after a product has made the long and carefully managed journey through our innovation process, our work is not completed. We learned long ago that marketing is as vital to our company as research or manufacturing. And so, many years ago, we established a New Products Marketing Division to assist in the introduction of new products to the marketplace. Personnel from this division become involved as team members at the innovation project stage. They assume an increasing role for paving the way for market acceptance of the new product as it moves closer to commercial reality.

Thus far, I have talked mostly about management responsibilities on the basis of individual R&D organizational units. Beyond this, we have assigned R&D unit managers to also manage the R&D program in a given business segment. They are responsible for working with the other R&D managers in that product category to develop an R&D strategy and to implement that in a coordinated and effective manner.

Another element in our management system is our project-management concept. For each innovation project, we assign a project team and a project manager to lead that team in carrying out its mission. The project-management concept gives the project managers the principal responsibility for the success of their project. They call on upper management only when obstacles arise that are beyond their ability to handle. The innovation project plan is approved by management, but implementation of the plan is the responsibility of the project manager. This pushes down responsibility to the people who are in the best position to know what is required for their projects.

The project manager is expected to be a champion and advocate of the project. The way he or she performs the job can mean the difference between success and failure.

No R&D management program would be complete without a meaningful way of assessing performance. We evaluate our own performance by comparing the new products and processes that are commercialized each year against the objectives we had set for the year. Each year we obtain a sales forecast for the new products that have been commercialized. These forecasts are prepared by marketing. Using appropriate assumptions, we calculate and compare the net present value of the new products and processes with the cost of the R&D program for that year. This value-to-cost ratio (see Figure 4) is an indicator of the effectiveness of the R&D program. We share this kind of evaluation with our R&D managers and use it in reporting to top

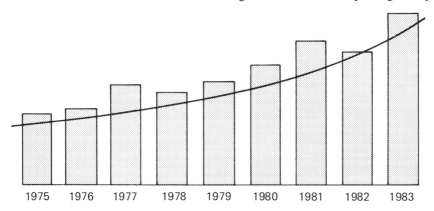

FIGURE 4 Product and process achievement value-to-cost ratio, Eastman Chemicals Division, 1975–1983.

management. We have a goal of improving our effectiveness along the trend line indicated by our past performance, which is about a 20 percent improvement per year.

As we look ahead, we realize we have far to go; but as we look back at the history of our company we are pleased with the results of our emphasis on managing innovation. Figure 5 provides a brief overview of those years.

Period	New Products	Sales
1920s	4	1929—$2 million
1930s	27	1939—$24 million
1940s	67	1949—$100 million
1950s	172	1959—$243 million
1960s	214	1969—$563 million
1970s	425	1979—$1,800 million
1980-1984	320	1984—$2,482 million

FIGURE 5   New products, by decade, Eastman Chemicals Division.

Business Aspects of Managing R&D

Let us turn now to the fourth question: What are the business aspects of managing an R&D program?

I will begin with the matter of budget. In our company, all budgets are based on providing the resources to do the job we need to do; they are not based on a percentage of sales. Each R&D manager is expected to justify 80 percent of his budget request based on approved projects. Twenty percent of the budget request can be for pioneering research. New products and new technology count on the company's bottom line, but we also recognize that the innovation process is centered on creative people, and we must allow and provide for scientific freedom. We do that in part by our provision for pioneering research.

The company's budget also provides for a number of non-mission-oriented research projects aimed at achieving a fuller understanding of the science and technology of our present operations and of new business areas. This work is not directed toward the innovation of new products and processes but toward establishing an improved knowledge base on which innovations of the future might be made. Our non-mission-oriented research program is administered by the director of research as chairman of a science advisory committee. This committee is made up of the key research managers and the senior scientific staff. It gives guidance on the scientific merits of new proposals and evaluates programs already under way.

The overall strategy of the various types of R&D projects for which we budget is well integrated with the company goals for the future and results in a level of support for each business segment that is consistent with its value, mission, and technological potential, plus a balanced commitment to the future by support of new areas of technology.

The Future at Eastman Chemicals

What of the 1980s? In just four years, sales have reached $2.4 billion—and we have already introduced 320 new products to market. Where will we be when the decade ends? No one knows, but we are confident that we will continue to see progress from our efforts based on programmed innovation.

Programmed innovation is not a secret. It is a system. While the system is magical in its effects, there is no magic formula for accomplishing it. It is a slow process to build a comprehensive and integrated system that involves all of the necessary elements. For us, it was an evolution in search of excellence—excellence in innovation. We changed the role of research from passive, to positive, to dominant. We moved research from the ivory tower to a central position in the planning and management of the company. We integrated technology strategy with business planning strategy. We coupled R&D with general management, manufacturing, and marketing. We assigned research management a major responsibility for defining the future of the company as it pertains to new products, new technologies, and new business opportunities. We gave R&D the responsibility for providing a strategic plan to achieve company-wide R&D goals for growth and profitability. We developed the skills and capabilities for programmed innovation.

INTEGRATING TECHNOLOGY WITH CORPORATE STRATEGIC PLANNING

That is the story of Eastman Chemicals. But I believe there is a lesson here for all of us who have responsibility to direct the course of our business and our industry.

Assuming the government adopts a "proindustrial" strategy based on a firm commitment to create conditions under which industry can operate effectively and competitively on the world scene, then the growth and prosperity of the chemical industry, which I have been describing as an exemplar of many others, are in our hands. In the days ahead, the pace of change will be rapid; the choices will be unparalleled; the opportunities will be unlimited.

Our challenge will be to increase our own effectiveness in dealing with change, in making choices, in evaluating opportunities, and in integrating technology into business strategic planning.

The first stage of strategic planning, begun many years ago, was in reality only financial planning. It focused largely on looking at the financial side of the business and cranking out numbers.

The second stage of strategic planning, pioneered by the Boston Consulting Group, occurred mostly during the 1970s and had a very different type of orientation. It focused more on markets and analysis of the market participation of organizations and less on financial measures. This reorientation to markets did not ask a key question of why market shares had been generated. It only gave us labels (dogs, cash cows, and stars) to show how well we had done, not why we had done so well or so poorly.

We are now entering the third stage in the evolution of strategic planning, in which the thinking is based on the recognition that technology has become of primary importance in domestic and international competitiveness, market share, and financial performance and must therefore be reflected in the bases for corporate plans and strategies. This new orientation asks for the causes, not just the results. The successful corporate strategists must better understand the management of technology, its development, its innovation, and its integration into corporate strategic planning.

I have inquired of a number of other leading companies what their current policies are for regularly integrating technological and strategic planning, and they were most cooperative.* After all, there is a relative handful of companies in the R&D-intensive industries I have mentioned previously that conduct the overwhelming amount of private R&D in the United States—companies such as GM, Ford, IBM, AT&T, Du Pont, United Technologies, GE, Eastman, Exxon, Xerox, ITT, Dow, Boeing, Westinghouse, Honeywell, Hewlett-Packard, and the like. Du Pont alone spends about $1 billion per year in R&D. I would like to summarize in this concluding section what I believe exists widely in such companies, recognizing that each company and industry must tailor its approach to its particular circumstances and culture.

It is true that much innovation, perhaps a disproportionate share, arises from smaller, younger companies that basically have no problem in managing this strategic linkage—communication from top to bottom is easy, the market and technology are tightly linked; and if the strategy is inadequate, the company fails! For such technological companies, venture capital is indispensable. Venture capitalists spread their risks over a whole portfolio of companies and sell their interests after a few years, obtaining a large overall return. Large companies must evaluate their internal rate of return over the

---

*I want to thank Ralph Landau for having assisted me in these inquiries and in the evaluation of the replies.

life of an investment. The venture capitalist's return is larger because the second round of investors expect a large future stream of earnings after the initial, great start-up risks have been borne by the venture capitalists. Thus, for the large players, who contribute the wealth and the bulk of the GNP to the U.S. economy, the problems are obviously far more complex.

In general, company and business unit strategic plans do include the relevant program of corporate R&D, and vice versa. Strategic planning currently involves less formal documentation and more identification of issues that could impede or change the direction of technological advances. Basically, planning is now the general line manager's responsibility, is an ongoing process, and is much less bureaucratic than previously. In fact, what is being practiced is strategic management, rather than simply strategic planning.

Industrial R&D must confront the issues of international competitiveness, efficiency, and increased rate of change. Linear or assembly-line innovation is not what actually happens. New ideas and inventions occur at many stages in the process. People are being mixed up and moved around, not separated— from R&D into production, marketing, and general management, and the reverse. R&D is no longer isolated in an ivory tower in progressive companies. Increasingly, business managers whose culture is usually different— a shorter time horizon, more financially oriented, less concerned about peer recognition—must be synchronized with and knowledgeable about innovation to obtain truly novel results and avoid arteriosclerosis of the organization. Thus, it is neither "technology push" nor "demand pull" innovation that emerges, suggesting outside energy for innovation. Much of the energy actually comes from within the innovation organization, from a strong technology-business partnership. It is done by experiment. The longer-range view is more likely to be found at the top levels of companies, so that true, major, long-range research needs close interchange with top management, which must recognize that the very nature of the business itself may be at stake. Progressive multiproduct companies will also plan by taking "technological slices" through the organization, as well as product and business-unit slices, to make sure the interrelationships for planning and strategy integrate technology fully. It helps to have the board of directors engaged, and some companies are already in possession of a board committee on science and technology (such as Alcoa, GE, and Allied) or have science advisory committees of outside technologists (such as GM, Kodak, Arco, Du Pont, Hercules, and many others).

It is true that technology is not always the key, or basis, to specific business strategies. The principal objective of any business strategy is to create and sustain a competitive advantage and thus a better-than-average return on investment. If, however, technology *is* the basis, as in many of the companies and industries cited, it *must* be used strategically, and this necessitates large

R&D expenditures. These generate higher market share and profitability, which in turn justify higher continued R&D spending. R&D is not an end in itself; it must be implemented by successful business strategy and must return better-than-average profits over the long run—a *virtuous circle*. Technology can also create major discontinuities—opportunities and threats.

It is this process that permits increasing competitiveness, productivity, and living standards for the United States. But one cannot forget that economic factors, such as interest rates and tax rates, exert an overwhelming influence on commercial innovation. Education levels are important, too, as are social and political attitudes that favor individual initiative and the entrepreneurial spirit, with less of a ''zero risk'' or ''zero sum'' mentality.

In the future, our leading industrial figures are convinced, new technologies (which are rapidly advancing) will require much closer integration of R&D with engineering, manufacturing, and marketing, and thus also with corporate and business-unit planning. In the future, virtually every major industry in the developed world, whether now classified as high-tech or smokestack, must in fact be high-tech to succeed in international competition. Industries and their employees will survive and thrive only by integrating advanced information, manufacturing, and computing technologies into their designs, products, and processes, and only through high levels of innovation, quality, and reliability.

Not every company is yet aware of the critical need for this by any means. They had better wake up before it is too late.

The Chemical Industry: Challenges, Risks, and Rewards

The chemical industry is strong, branching out in many directions, supported by an effective and growing research establishment and by tried and true manufacturing and marketing organizations. Along with these positives, however, have come a number of negatives, many of which can be ascribed to the public's fear of toxic chemicals.

Technology is the life blood of the chemical industry, and I am pleased to be a representative of the industry in this volume. I would like to touch briefly on some of the challenges, risks, and rewards that are part of chemicals technology today.

The U.S. chemical industry is big, progressive, and very important to the nation. Annual sales total about $200 billion. Its products are critical to just about every other industry and to the population at large, affecting just about every facet of modern life, from cars and airplanes and aerospace to home building and furnishings, from the clothes we wear to the crops we grow and the medicines we take to combat all kinds of illnesses.

The industry employs more than a million Americans and accounts for far more jobs downstream of its own operations. It has been generating a favorable trade balance in excess of $10 billion a year, and in these days of the strong dollar, it is almost unique among U.S. industries in being able to outcompete other countries in international trade.

The chemical industry's past and present successes are due in very large part to the commitment of chemical companies of all sizes to seek competitive advantage through technological advancement. In recent years research expenditures have been increased substantially. For 15 large companies, R&D

expenditures increased from $1.5 billion in 1979 to $2.7 billion in 1984, a 73 percent increase in 5 years. After adjustment for inflation, the increase was approximately 25 percent.

The nature of chemicals research has been changing. Growth rates of major chemical commodity products have slowed as a result of attaining a high-percentage penetration into the economy, and so research is being increasingly focused on new and improved specialty products as opposed to new and improved processes, although process research remains very important. Another effect of the maturity of commodity chemicals is greatly increased emphasis on areas previously outside the normal scope of traditional chemical companies, such as drugs, biosciences, and electronic materials.

The chemical industry, moreover, is the leader in industry-sponsored basic research. Preliminary National Science Foundation figures for 1983 show that, of a total of $2 billion of industry-sponsored basic research, the chemical industry accounted for $510 million, or more than 25 percent, well ahead of the second-place electrical equipment industry.

Also, of obvious importance to the industry is the research being carried out in universities, which account for the bulk of basic research conducted in this country. For 5 years now the academic and industry members of the Council for Chemical Research have been working to increase mutual cooperation and thereby to stimulate innovation.

So here we have a strong industry, branching out in many directions as its traditional commodity products mature, supported by a large, effective, and growing research establishment as well as by tried and true manufacturing and marketing organizations.

Along with the positives, however, have come a number of negatives, many of which can be ascribed to one fundamental factor, the public's fear of toxic chemicals. Although this fear may be exaggerated, it is nonetheless very real. And as long as it persists, it can have very real economic impacts. It can be translated into laws and regulations so punitive and so excessive as to make the industry's operations prohibitively expensive, new products difficult to develop and commercialize, and the industry noncompetitive in the international trade arena.

How did this fear develop? What are the reasons for the enormous gap between what we know about the products and practices of the chemical industry and what the public perceives?

The fear of toxic chemicals developed during the very period that Harvey Brooks describes in his chapter, when technology in general was under attack—roughly the period from the mid-1960s to the late 1970s. In hindsight, the emergence of this fear is very understandable.

How were people supposed to react when, for more than 10 years running, the news media reported in a sensational manner statements of prominent politicians that "up to 90% [of all cancers] are caused by contaminants placed in the environment by man''? Then, in 1978 an authorless National Cancer Institute ''scientific paper'' was released to the press that attributed up to 38 percent of total cancer incidence in the United States to worker exposure to just nine substances! This startling conclusion was immediately communicated by the Secretary of Health, Education, and Welfare, and it frightened not only workers but a good part of the nation as well.[1]

Today many policymakers and scientists have a different view, thanks to the studies of two Oxford epidemiologists, Sir Richard Doll and Richard Peto. Analyzing American cancer mortality rates for the congressional Office of Technology Assessment, they concluded that fully two-thirds of all cancer deaths are due to smoking and dietary habits. Various other causes were given for the remaining one-third. They concluded that carcinogens in the workplace, in the environment, in food additives, and in industrial products all taken together cause less than 8 percent of American cancer deaths. In the few years since their work, according to the *New York Times*, these figures are generally accepted by responsible authorities and experts.[2] Quite a dramatic contrast to that widely publicized 90 percent.

Although the real facts have been emerging, there is a long time lag in the public's perception of those facts. And as long as there is any degree of cancer incidence that is attributable by experts to toxic chemicals, it is incumbent on the industry and the government to identify the chemicals and to minimize exposure to them.

Other major negatives have emerged to bedevil the chemical industry. One is the existence of numerous hazardous waste dump sites scattered across the nation. There has been growing concern that a number of those sites may pose health hazards to nearby residents, primarily by contamination of groundwater. It is clear from examination of Environmental Protection Agency (EPA) lists of potentially responsible parties that thousands of companies representing essentially every manufacturing industry in the country have contributed to this problem through decades of dumping, but the public relates it mainly to the chemical industry.

Now the industry has a major new negative—that involving the danger of catastrophic major releases of substances that might cause numerous injuries and deaths. Of course I am referring to the Bhopal tragedy.

What is the industry doing about these negatives? Individually and through its trade association, the Chemical Manufacturers Association (CMA), it is doing a lot. The CMA has 180 member companies that represent 90 percent of all basic chemical-manufacturing capacity in the United States.

Since a major issue is the toxicity of chemicals, it was immediately obvious that a great amount of toxicity testing would be required. The larger companies built and staffed major laboratories devoted to health-effects testing. In addition, a number of companies joined forces to create the Chemical Industry Institute of Toxicology (CIIT).

Through innovative basic research programs in many aspects of toxicity, through comprehensive testing of suspected problem chemicals, and through a strong commitment to training scientists of the future in the specialized requirements of toxicology, CIIT has earned the reputation of independence and complete objectivity, as well as professional excellence. It recently celebrated its tenth anniversary.

On the subject of hazardous waste sites, the Superfund law obviously should be reauthorized at increased levels of funding, and the chemical industry came out in support of this position early in the debate in 1984. The industry is concerned that the size of the fund should fit with EPA's ability to spend at an effective rate, and it wants the funding system devised fairly and in a manner that does not deal it an excessive economic blow, particularly in the area of international trade.

Fundamentally, the industry wants those sites cleaned up, and the sooner the better. A major deterrent to speedy cleanup of abandoned waste sites has been lengthy litigation between the potentially responsible parties who are the generators (but usually not the dumpers) of the waste and the government. The industry has been urging its member companies to get together at multi-party sites to undertake more cleanups voluntarily, and we have been encouraged by recent EPA policy actions designed to expedite such voluntary cleanups.

Speaking of voluntary actions, a new nonprofit organization, Clean Sites, Inc., became operational recently. Clean Sites is the result of the imaginative cooperation of a group of industry people, environmentalists, and former government officials. I was privileged to serve on the steering committee that conceived this approach. Clean Sites will be able to enlist the vast technical and project management resources of private industry directly to accelerate the cleanup of waste sites. It has the full support of EPA, has already recruited an outstanding corps of talented people, and has a highly respected board of directors, including two former EPA directors and Donald Kennedy, the president of Stanford University. It is currently being funded almost exclusively by the chemical industry, and it is attempting to get other industries to participate.

While pushing to get the sites cleaned up, the industry is also exerting effort to determine the extent of the health effects associated with them. This is important, because there is a strong tendency in the Congress to solve a problem before it is defined. There have already been initiatives in the Congress to establish broad-based, so-called victims compensation funds to compensate alleged victims outside the normal tort system. The needs would have to be major indeed to justify such a radical step.

The Chemical Manufacturers Association determined that despite all the concern, there were no programs in progress to define the scope of the health problems effectively. We joined in a suit filed by an environmental organization to force the government to implement a 1980 Superfund provision that mandated studies to determine the health effects of dump sites. As a result, an appropriate agency was identified and studies are under way.

Not satisfied with this minimal effort, the CMA contracted with the pathology departments of 15 leading universities to undertake a million-dollar study to compile and evaluate scientific information on the effect of waste sites on nearby residents. Several other organizations, including the World Health Organization, also sponsored this work. The conclusions recently became public.[3]

The study indicated there is little evidence to support the claim that there have been detectable health effects on people living near waste sites. It indicated that there is a large gap between public perception and demonstrated incidence of health effects. However, the study team recognized that we need to learn much more about potential hazards, and it recommended much additional research on the subject.

The latest preoccupation of CMA is to determine what initiatives should be taken as a result of Bhopal. We know that we should not sit back and merely say that it can't happen here. We know that we cannot take refuge in the statistical evidence of the National Safety Council, which shows that workers in the chemical industry have the best safety record of all 42 principal U.S. industries. In fact, the chemical industry rated 0.53 cases of lost-time injury per 100 full-time employees. Compared with the average incidence rate of 2.2 for all 42 industries, chemical workers have more than four times fewer accidents than the average industrial employee.[4]

Notwithstanding this fine record, in the wake of Bhopal, essentially every one of our member companies directed that all of their worldwide plant locations conduct immediate reviews of their safety and emergency-response procedures to be sure they are well understood and thoroughly up to date.

On an industrywide level, the CMA recently announced further initiatives that the industry will take. These include improved emergency-response procedures and more effective involvement of community leaders and response organizations.

In summary, the chemical industry is a great, technologically driven industry whose products have been critically important throughout the economy. So pervasive are chemicals in our lives that we could not reverse this condition even if we wanted to. While this growth and propagation of products through technology has its negative as well as its positive sides, I am optimistic that our powerful science and technology base, combined with enlightened management, will cope with the negatives effectively. We are taking many steps to define the problems carefully and to take positive initiatives, in some cases quite bold, to solve them. We intend to restore public confidence in the chemical industry by results, not by rhetoric.

NOTES

1. Edith Efron, *The Apocalyptics* (New York: Simon & Schuster, 1984), pp. 68–70, 438–440, 449–452.
2. *New York Times*, March 2, 1981, pp. C1, C12–C13.
3. Universities Associated for Research and Education in Pathology, *Health Aspects of the Disposal of Waste Chemicals* (New York: Pergamon Press, 1985).
4. National Safety Council, Chicago, 1984 data.

Entrepreneurship and Innovation: The Electronics Industry

GORDON E. MOORE

What does it take to make a successful entrepreneurial environment? First, it takes sources of ideas and people, particularly technical people. Second, it requires a rapidly changing technology, preferably with many varied applications. Third, it requires large and diverse markets. Fourth, it takes risk capital. And fifth, it takes a society that recognizes the entrepreneur when he or she is successful.

This discussion of entrepreneurship and innovation in electronics focuses on the semiconductor industry. It is not based on any scholarly study, but on a close personal association with this industry and on personal observation of the process from a variety of perspectives.

Although I have never really thought of myself as an entrepreneur, I participated in starting two companies, and before that had been the eighteenth employee of another start-up company. That was Shockley Semiconductor, William Shockley's pioneering venture, which put the silicon in Silicon Valley initially.

My first start-up, to give an example of how some of these things come about, was completely for negative reasons. A group of us had burned our bridges at Shockley Semiconductor and decided that we had to look elsewhere for jobs. We liked working together. When some of us by chance met an employee of an investment banking company, we asked him if he knew of a company that might like to hire the group of us. He sent two people out from the East Coast to talk to our group of eight young scientists and engineers.

The two emissaries told us, "You don't want to work for someone, you want to start your own company." This was a completely new concept for us, but we decided at least that way we wouldn't have to move. They took on the job of tracking down some capital for us and soon ran into Sherman Fairchild. That was the beginning of Fairchild Semiconductor. We were very naive about the whole process, but we did have a product vision that we wanted to pursue.

Eleven years later I started Intel, also for mostly negative reasons. There were problems in the first company that I was not in a position to control very well. It seemed easier to start over again than to fix them.

With each company, however, there was a product-market opportunity that seemed viable and a new technological direction that seemed appropriate for approaching that opportunity. In the case of Fairchild, it was the silicon transistor, which then became the Planar silicon transistor, and fortunately that was the technology appropriate for the practical integrated circuit, which was so important in Fairchild's early history. At Intel, it was the idea of semiconductor memory, which a few years later led to the invention of the microprocessor, which in turn became the principal area that Intel has pursued ever since.

Looking at my involvement in the entrepreneurial process from another viewpoint, my companies have spawned several start-ups. In fact, sometimes it seems that half of Silicon Valley found its origin in either Fairchild or Intel, to say nothing of the "Silicon Forest" in Oregon, and so on. There are really many reasons for this. In electronics, an important force has been the diverse opportunities available. Any company active in the forefront of semiconductor technology uncovers far more opportunities than it is in a position to pursue. When people become enthusiastic about a particular new opportunity but are not allowed to pursue it, they become potential entrepreneurs. As we have seen over the past few years, when these potential entrepreneurs are backed by a plentiful source of venture capital, there is a burst of new enterprise.

Successful new enterprises, especially those started by people considered less capable or less deserving of success than the people with a new idea, accelerate the process. When people see their peers setting up successful companies (and success in this business is generally measured by economic success, since we do not have the usual ways of measuring success typical in the academic community), it creates an environment in which more people want to try.

A certain amount of this entrepreneurship is very healthy. Otherwise, important products and ideas would never see the light of day. Anyone who has been in management positions at large, technology-oriented companies has had the experience of refusing to support an idea for a variety of good reasons, often only to have a start-up develop a major business based on that idea. I personally turned down the opportunity to do home computers in the early 1970s. I could not imagine my wife putting her recipes on a computer.

That was about the only example the people proposing the idea could come up with at that particular time, but they had a very strong feeling that the idea of the personal computer was a valid business opportunity.

Why is there so much exploitation of innovation, if not the innovation itself, by start-ups? I think there are a variety of reasons, including, first of all, focus. This is really the advantage of the start-up company. You can focus all your energy on realizing whatever product the company sees as important. There is no existing product line to worry about. Any established company has many other things to maintain. It can only devote a small portion of total available energy to a new enterprise. This lack of focus, however, does not exist in the start-ups. Often the start-up companies have a much more powerful team focused in an area than a big company can put together. This happens because the big company has many other alternative positions in which it wants to employ its better people.

The start-up environment is also a more efficient way to get some things done. For example, in the early days of Intel when we were purchasing our first capital equipment, we gave each of the engineers a purchase-order book, not requisitions, but purchase orders. The engineer would talk to the equipment supplier and when he found the piece of equipment he wanted, he would write out a purchase order and hand it to the salesman. This is a very efficient way of getting started compared with the bureaucratic ways that usually develop in a larger company, again for a variety of good reasons.

The United States went through a period when there was probably too little venturing. In the 1970s in particular, as venture capital dried up, largely because of the changes in the capital gains tax provision in the 1969 tax law, it was hard for anyone with a new idea to get financial support for it. Since the 1979 tax law changes, we may have swung too far in the opposite direction. There is too much venture capital chasing too few different opportunities. The slogan of the venture capitalists appears to be, "Anything worth doing is worth doing in excess."

An article in *Time* magazine last year said that there were some 180 different personal computers available for the consumer to choose among, although the number reported elsewhere is closer to 300. There are now 71 manufacturers of floppy disks and 84 manufacturers of hard disks, to say nothing of the innumerable new semiconductor start-ups. The semiconductor industry has become a capital-intensive business in which a minimum economic manufacturing module is probably a $100 million investment. It seems an unlikely place for venture capital. While I am not an expert in biotechnology, when I hear of some 200 companies in that area, I cannot help thinking that some excess exists there also. To correct this excess, there will be a lot of consolidations, associated market disruptions, and disrupted lives.

An excess of venture capital is also often disruptive to the company the entrepreneurs leave when they start their venture. For example, at Intel we have one area in which every person familiar with a particular technical operating system was taken by a start-up, leaving us with a void where we had developed significant expertise. Another example is a major project, important for our international competitive position, that was delayed for a year or more because of the people leaving for a start-up. More than 30 engineers left from an advanced microprocessor project, which was delayed significantly as a result.

Too many start-ups also dissipate energy through duplication and overlap. Well-qualified people, particularly with the specific technical training required in these areas, represent a finite resource. When this is dissipated, it can hurt our global competitiveness. Too many start-ups diffuse technology. Foreign companies have learned that little companies running out of money can transfer a lot of U.S.-developed technology. It has happened over and over again in electronics, and I suspect that we are going to see a rash of it occurring again. You can look at situations like Fujitsu's early investment in Amdahl when Amdahl could not find any other support. Certainly it helped Fujitsu's position in the worldwide computer competition. Several Japanese companies have acquired small U.S. semiconductor companies, and the Koreans are now proceeding to do exactly the same thing as a way to extract our technology and establish it in other parts of the world.

My last point is about a special problem in the semiconductor industry, where patent protection has not been an important factor, for several reasons. First, the very rapid rate of technological change and second, the very complex, serial nature of the processing involved result in the patents being very widely dispersed. In order to make a semiconductor device, you probably use the patents owned by 20 or 30 companies. Each company tries to get enough of a patent position that it can trade with everybody, usually at zero or trivial royalty rates so no other company can put it out of business. The net result is that patenting has not had a strong impact on what goes on in the industry. As mentioned elsewhere in this volume, an industry that changes monthly has a real problem when it has a legal system that is 25 years behind.

Although many people are inclined to point to high-tech and the electronics industry specifically as our economic salvation, we ought to recognize that there is significant cause for concern. In electronics, the U.S. balance of trade with Japan last year was $-\$15$ billion. Our electronics trade deficit with Japan is larger than our automotive trade deficit with Japan. It is projected to grow to some $20 billion this year. Even in leading-edge semiconductor technology, MOS LSI (metal oxide silicon large scale integration), the balance of trade crossed over in 1980 and was $-\$800$ million last year. And it is increasing rapidly in that direction.

If we lose the manufacturing battle to our overseas competitors, the research and development that creates the opportunities is in real danger of losing the revenue stream that is required to support it. Manufacturing in the electronics industry is being moved offshore at an extremely rapid pace, not only by our foreign competitors but also by U.S. companies pursuing lower labor rates and cheaper component sources. As manufacturing goes overseas, the technology leadership is very likely to follow. It is a problem that requires considerable attention if we expect to make high technology a major portion of future U.S. economic growth.

What does it take to make a successful entrepreneurial environment? First, it takes sources of ideas and people, particularly technical people. These sources are typically the large companies with extensive R&D capabilities, and sometimes universities, as in the case of the biotechnologies. Second, it requires a rapidly changing technology, preferably with many varied applications. Third, it requires large and diverse markets to provide many opportunities for market niches to be developed by the companies getting started. Fourth, it requires risk capital—which dried up in the 1970s and seemed overly prevalent in the first few years of the 1980s. Successful examples are valuable in motivating people to overcome the inertia to start a company. And, finally, it takes a society that recognizes the entrepreneur when he or she is successful. Certainly these are the things that we have in abundance in Silicon Valley.

Entrepreneurship and Innovation: Biotechnology

ROBERT A. SWANSON

The United States is at the point of risking significant export of jobs and technology to Japan and Europe if the regulatory costs and delays associated with marketing biotechnology in the United States become prohibitive. This potentiality reflects a pattern. The United States develops, finances, and builds a new technology only to have the profits skimmed off by foreign competitors who spend their money on manufacturing development and marketing.

The history of biotechnology, or genetic engineering, is short, because it was only 1973 when Herbert Boyer (my cofounder at Genentech) and his colleague Stanley Cohen of Stanford University inserted DNA into a host bacteria that reproduced the foreign DNA.

It was in 1976 that Dr. Boyer and I formed Genentech. In the following year, 1977, Genentech scientists expressed in bacteria the brain hormone somatostatin, which was the first useful protein to be produced by recombinant DNA technology. The president of the National Academy of Sciences described the production of somatostatin as a "scientific triumph of the first order."[1] It then took one more year to produce human insulin and another five to move it to the market. Today, human insulin is the only recombinant DNA product available at the pharmacy.

The industry's gestation period took a bit longer, because the basic research on which recombinant DNA technology is founded had gone back a number of years. For example, the federal government had been partially funding

---

[1] Statement by Philip Handler, President, National Academy of Sciences, at hearings on Recombinant DNA before the Subcommittee on Science, Technology, and Space of the U.S. Senate Committee on Commerce, Science, and Transportation, November 2, 1977.

Dr. Boyer's research in microbiology at the University of California at San Francisco for 15 years. Or as he likes to put it, "Who would have dreamed that my work on how bacteria have sex could combine with other pieces of basic research to help form a new industry?" With enough basic research to choose from, American business can continue to spawn new industries.

OPPORTUNITIES AND RISKS

The United States is the world's leader in both the basic science and the commercial development of biotechnology because of enormous sums invested by the government dating back to World War II. For example, in 1983 expenditures by the U.S. government on basic research in biotechnology were the largest in the world—over $500 million. This basic research has provided industry with a smorgasbord of knowledge from which to choose in order to produce solutions to major world problems such as disease and malnutrition. Basic research funding has also provided the training ground for the scientists who are staffing today's companies.

In the United States, there are now more than 200 biotechnology companies. These are divided into two distinct categories: small entrepreneurial firms, like Genentech, and large established companies, such as Eli Lilly, Monsanto, and Du Pont. Most small firms have been founded since 1976. These ventures were started specifically to commercialize the applications of biotechnology. Many were formed around a nucleus of university-based research scientists.

During the industry's early development period, the competition among biotechnology firms was in the areas of cloning and expressing desired products. The focus is now shifting. The cutting edge of the technology is now in scaleup and downstream processing. And the emphasis is on getting products to market.

Bringing a product (especially a human health care product) from the laboratory to the marketplace demands an enormous front-end investment in human and capital resources. It has been largely for this reason that a major pharmaceutical firm has not been formed in this country since Syntex in 1957. While the biotechnology industry has already spent hundreds of millions of dollars on research and development, it is just entering the stage of product manufacturing and sales. This is exactly the stage at which fledgling industries are most vulnerable and in need of a positive environment—the stage at which government needs to provide positive incentives. However, historically, our government has not offered its support at this development stage, and this has allowed foreign competition to close the gaps.

Federal funding of generic applied research, which focuses on process development and bioprocess engineering, is small—less than 10 percent of the funding for basic research. There is little focus on international manufacturing competitiveness. International comparisons show that several competitor countries, such as Japan, Germany, and the United Kingdom, are already spending a significant amount on generic applied science in biotechnology. In Japan, the biggest share of every research dollar is funneled into bioprocess engineering rather than into basic research. The Japanese have relied on the United States and other countries to provide the breakthroughs. Then, by rapidly applying considerable expertise in process development and scaleup, they can jump well ahead and capture a large share of the world market for biotechnology products.

Highly skilled personnel for this stage of development is another area in which our competitive position is in jeopardy. Only a few programs are available in the United States for training personnel in the applied aspects of biotechnology, and there are few government programs, such as training grants, to support education in this field. Part of this lack can be made up by industry itself—with the proper government incentives. For the larger companies, one alternative is tax credits. The 25 percent tax credit, which is due to expire on January 1, 1986, gives companies a reasonable incentive to increase spending on R&D. It also allows industry needs to determine how R&D money is spent.

Especially important to the smaller biotechnology companies is the availability of capital. Without the equity funding to develop innovative ideas, most young high technology companies would not exist today. This is especially true for biotechnology. The availability of venture capital has been instrumental in the founding of new biotechnology firms in the United States.

The treatment of capital gains is particularly critical to the formation of venture capital. Fortunately, in 1978 Congress cut the capital gains tax rate from 40 percent to 28 percent. The results of reducing the tax rate were dramatic. Within 18 months, more than $1 billion of new venture capital flowed into funds for investment in new and growing companies. In 1983, aided by further cuts in the capital gains tax rate, to 20 percent, $4.1 billion of new venture capital was made available for investment. This is in stark contrast to the $50 million that was added annually, on average, to the venture capital pool during 1971–1977, when the tax rate was high.

Although the Treasury Department had warned that the 1978 capital gains tax cut would reduce federal tax revenues, those losses never materialized. In fact, capital gains tax receipts increased markedly with the lower rates. It will be important to ensure that new tax legislation does not reverse this trend and thereby reduce the availability of capital needed by new innovative companies.

Should all this sound a little self-serving, I would like to point out that it is the smaller companies that have in fact been the technology leaders and innovators. In 1967 a Commerce Department study found that more than half of all U.S. inventions and innovations were accounted for by small businesses and individual inventors. In 1976 an MIT study found that young technology companies far exceeded their larger, more established competitors in rates of sales growth, taxes paid, and, especially, number of jobs created. In the past 10 years, small innovative businesses have created 3 million jobs, while net employment in the 1,000 largest U.S. corporations has remained more or less level.

The case of my own company, Genentech, Inc., illustrates many of the points I have been making. Our company is just 9 years old, but we have already created 700 new jobs and spent close to $146 million in research and development. We have also invested over $112 million in facilities for research, manufacturing, and administration, facilities that now exceed 350,000 square feet. And, most importantly, since Genentech's founding, our research has led to a number of important products for human and animal health care. These include t-PA, a blood-clot-dissolving substance used during heart attacks; gamma interferon, an anticancer and anti-infective agent; tumor necrosis factor, another exciting new anticancer drug; human insulin for the treatment of diabetes; Factor VIII, an essential blood-clotting factor for the treatment of hemophilia; and human and animal growth hormones. This list of products illustrates the contribution that an entrepreneurial firm like Genentech can make in advancing the frontiers of biotechnology through ongoing technological innovation.

It takes a long time, however, to bring a product to market, particularly in the pharmaceutical sector, where all products are subject to extensive clinical testing and regulatory review. For example, human insulin was developed by Genentech and licensed for manufacturing and worldwide marketing to Eli Lilly. To bring this product to market required nearly five years of effort by Lilly and our company after the time the microorganisms had been engineered. Costs to build a production facility exceeded $80 million, and development expenses were well into the tens of millions of dollars. It required more than 1,000 man-years to bring the product through the various stages of development—beginning with fermentation scaleup and purification, through animal and human testing, and finally obtaining approval for marketing from the Food and Drug Administration (FDA).

As my discussion has illustrated, the early risks and investment are great for biotechnology companies. Most small firms still have few or no products generating revenues, yet they are now faced with financing production scale-up. Consequently, many new firms have already had to obtain second- and third-round financing, relying heavily on public stock issues, private placements, and R&D limited partnerships for additional funds.

R&D partnerships are an ideal funding vehicle for small biotechnology companies having to raise money to complete the development of their products—particularly to fund clinical research, which is the most expensive phase of a development program. The risks of product development are shared with private investors and the government. R&D partnerships provide tax advantages to the investor, who looks to a percentage of product sales for his return. Such partnerships can be critical for a new company in the pharmaceutical industry, where product-development cycles of 5 to 7 years and front-end expenses of $50 million to $70 million are the norm.

Patent Protection

Opportunities in biotechnology also depend to a great degree on the protection given research and innovation by patents. Without the means to prevent competitors from unfairly capitalizing on one's investment, most pioneering research projects would never be undertaken. Risk to investors would be prohibitive if the products of invention were likely to become freely accessible early on to others who had not incurred the same R&D costs.

Not surprisingly, the number of biotechnology-related patent applications received by the U.S. Patent and Trademark Office has increased dramatically each year for the past several years, putting this agency to a severe test. Currently there is a backlog of 1,000 applications related to genetic engineering and a total of 2,600 related to biotechology in general. The critical issue is timing of issuance, and the average pendency has reached 28 months. Part of the bottleneck is due to lack of staff—there are only 26 examiners in the biotechnology area. To ease the situation, the Patent Office is planning to streamline the review process and increase the staff (to 40 biotechnology examiners by the fall of 1985). This should help alleviate the problem.

A final point pertains to patents and international competition. A large share of biotechnology-related patents issued by the U.S. Patent Office goes to foreign parties. This certainly is a good indication of the intent of overseas firms to stake a claim in the U.S. market. It is important that Americans get the same fair treatment when they file for patent protection in other countries.

REGULATIONS

So far, the United States has avoided the regulation of biotechnology. Guidelines sponsored by the National Institutes of Health and adhered to by academia and industry have provided a flexible and safe environment for the development of this technology. This is one reason why the United States is still ahead of Japan. Japanese research has been hindered by strict regulatory controls. However, Japan's restrictions have recently been relaxed, and biotechnology efforts are now progressing rapidly.

FDA Regulations

Pharmaceuticals are the prime commercial products of biotechnology, and they are subject to FDA approval. The FDA has taken a constructive attitude in making the first products of biotechnology quickly available to the public without lowering the agency's high standards for proof of safety and efficacy. However, the time it takes for a drug to go through the approval process is lengthy—an average of 40 months for drugs approved in 1984. And the FDA now faces a flood of applications for approval of biotechnology products.

European countries have a distinct advantage over the United States because they are often not subject to the strict product-approval regulations deemed appropriate in this country. I have to agree with the Office of Technology Assessment's statement that "the regulatory environment favors the European companies, over those of Japan and the United States reaching their own domestic markets sooner for pharmaceuticals and animal drugs."[2] If this happens, the European companies, fueled by profits from product sales in secure home markets, will be able to invest in further research and cost reduction with a view to exporting their products to the United States.

The FDA's timing of approvals can have significant economic implications. For example, in the last 20 years, more than 1,100 new pharmaceutical products have been approved for use in the United States, but only a little more than 100 of those will be approved first in the United States. While we do not want to change our high standards, it is clear that there needs to be better understanding of how regulatory delays can affect our country's international competitiveness.

Export Policy

One final regulatory consideration that I would like to address is the impact of U.S. pharmaceutical export regulations on biotechnology products. Export controls in this country are the most restrictive of any nation competing in the field, and they negatively affect our competitive position.

U.S. export regulations state that new drugs not yet approved for sale in the United States cannot be exported for sale outside the United States— even if the regulatory agency in the recipient country has already approved the product for marketing. The United States is the only country in the world with such a law.

This policy has several implications. Most large U.S. pharmaceutical companies have built manufacturing facilities in foreign countries. This results in the transfer of technology outside the United States, lost jobs for the U.S. labor force, and lost opportunity to help the U.S. balance of payments. It also provides these large companies with an advantage over small U.S. biotechnology firms that cannot afford to establish manufacturing plants

---

[2]Office of Technology Assessment, *Commercial Biotechnology: An International Analysis* (Washington, D.C.: U.S. Government Printing Office, 1984), p. 21.

overseas. The biotechnology industry is working hard to change this law before the United States gives foreign competitors too much of a helping hand in biotechnology.

SUMMARY

The American biotechnology industry is at a critical stage in its development. Enormous R&D investments have been made, but the industry has not yet reached the manufacturing and marketing levels at which it can be self-sustaining. Many small biotechnology companies will fail altogether if they do not bring products to market in the near future. The larger companies will survive, but they may lose to overseas competition if they are forced to delay market entry.

The United States is at the point of risking significant export of jobs and technology to Japan and Western Europe if the regulatory costs and delays associated with marketing products in the United States become prohibitive. The transfer of technology out of the United States is particularly worrisome given the enormous public funding that was largely responsible for the development of the basic biological sciences on which this technology is based. This has become a pattern. The United States develops, finances, and builds a new technology only to have the profits skimmed off by foreign competitors who spend their money on manufacturing development and marketing.

The U.S. government has been a major contributor in establishing the leadership position of the United States in biotechnology. However, if we are to maintain our lead, we must act quickly to address a number of critical issues—continued tax incentives for research and capital formation, timely review of patent and new drug applications, well-informed export policies, and increased funding for process technology and generic applied research. With concerted, cooperative, and timely efforts on the part of government, industry, and academia to address these critical issues, I am confident that the United States can maintain its lead in biotechnology.

Impact of Entrepreneurship and Innovation on the Distribution of Personal Computers

DAVID A. NORMAN

Two trends will have a major effect on the U.S. electronic business equipment industry. First, by the end of the 1980s distribution power will have shifted from independent retail outlets to company- or manufacturer-owned chains, and this will limit the number of new ventures and opportunities in this market. Second, standardization of products will mean slower growth for new high technology companies that have failed to recognize that there is indeed a standard in the industry today.

Changes in the method of product distribution are having and will have a major effect on the computer and electronics high technology industries, particularly in the United States. The U.S. market is huge, and the market for electronic business equipment, which my company, Businessland, addresses, is very large. There are 53 million white-collar workers today, for example, only about 10 percent of whom have personal computers or electronic workstations. (I describe electronic workstations as the telephone and computer coming together.) My former company, Dataquest, the high technology market research firm, estimates that the market will be $25 billion in 1988, in comparison with about $9 billion in 1984. Interesting products will be introduced in 1985, and there will be high growth in 1986, 1987, and 1988. We are looking at a very, very large market opportunity, indeed. Many people forget, however, that we really need to look at the markets for which we are developing products and not just develop products for their own sake.

In the past, U.S. electronics manufacturers had direct sales forces calling on the business community. That makes a lot of sense when you are selling a $50,000 or a $100,000 piece of equipment. But now the prices of electronic products have come down dramatically and, at the same time, the cost of making a direct sales call has continued to increase. I contend that to be competitive in the world's marketplace any product that has a selling price under $10,000 must now be sold through retail distribution outlets and the manufacturer must have the volume of production necessary to be a low-cost producer.

Businessland, for example, buys in large volumes from manufacturers and sells to all segments of the business marketplace. It competes with the manufacturer's direct sales force, but it tends to offer more service, training, and support to the end user than the manufacturer's direct sales force does. Businessland is a viable competitor at the high end of the market, selling to the Fortune 1,000 companies, but at the same time it has covered all segments of the business marketplace as well.

There are a huge number of computer manufacturers, companies that make peripherals (e.g., printers, hard disk drives, floppy disk drives), and software companies. They are all trying to get marketing distributors because they cannot afford to call on all of the U.S. companies directly. They need to go through retail distribution channels, such as Businessland, in order to reach the marketplace. The problem today, however, is that many of these companies are not able to get shelf space and thus are having a very difficult time marketing their products. The point of distribution is where the profit and the power are in the marketplace today.

Unfortunately, distribution channels are going to change dramatically over the rest of the decade. Just reflect on what has happened to distribution in other industries in the United States. In the 1950s, for example, chains of grocery stores came in and displaced the independent grocers. The same thing is going to happen in this new, infant industry, which is now made up of numerous independent computer stores and franchises—currently run by independent businesspeople. Independent stores make up about two-thirds of the outlets today; the other one-third are company-owned or manufacturer-owned chains. I believe that by the end of the 1980s there will have been a major shift in distribution power from the independents to company- or manufacturer-owned chains. If that happens, and if 8 or 10 major chains have 50 percent of the market, then the variety of products reaching the market through retail distribution will be very limited. Businessland, for example, can carry personal computer product lines from only, perhaps, three manufacturers and a limited number of software and peripheral products. Many entrepreneurial, high technology companies are going to lack shelf space in the future. This will greatly limit the number of new ventures and the opportunities in this marketplace. Unfortunately, the growth of new technological products will slow dramatically as this change in the channels of distribution to the marketplace proceeds.

Another trend that will slow technological growth in electronic business equipment is the standardization that is taking place in the industry. Today the IBM personal computer, the MS DOS operating system, is clearly a standard in corporate America. It is less so in the home office and in small businesses. But standardization is having a major effect, even though many people are not aware of the changes that have taken place in a short period of time. Today, IBM personal computers account for 60 percent of the units sold, and 70 percent of the volume in the business market. There has been a major shift in the last year to their dominance in the marketplace. This means there will be slower growth for new high technology companies, particularly companies that have not realized or do not believe that there is a standard in the industry today. Major computer manufacturers in the United States have given up billion-dollar markets because they did not recognize early enough that there was a standard and did not build products to meet that standard. They were building products for engineers and designing products with features for a very small segment of the market, while the major part of the market was not being listened to. Products were being designed that did not meet the needs of the end user, who wanted standardization. We are now seeing standardization in hardware and software, and we are seeing the need for it in the networking and telecommunications areas. The key is to listen to the marketplace, analyze that market, and develop products that the market really wants and needs. And when you do, you will see explosive growth.

Businessland is a good example of that explosive growth. In just 24 months, from November 1982 to December 1984, the company went from start-up to $25 million a month in sales. Its annual sales are now at $300 million. That is the kind of growth that is possible.

The markets are large, the opportunity is great, but companies must clearly address the marketplace. They must understand that there is a standard out there, they must build within that standard, and they must develop compatible products that have price and performance advantages for end users. Large, qualified distribution channels are now developing in all segments of the business marketplace. But clearly they must have products to sell that meet the customers' needs.

Making the Transition From Entrepreneur to Large Company

Three major problems must be overcome in order for a small, technically innovative company to survive the transitional stage of growth that separates small from large companies. They involve (1) management, (2) financing of growth, and (3) product-line depth. These are all problems of economics, some knowledge of which is essential to directing the program of a modern corporation.

There is something almost ironic about my being a contributor to this volume. Somewhere above, there must be someone quietly chuckling to himself over the fact that I am involved in this book that deals with engineering and economics. When I was at Stanford, I took a course in engineering economics from the then authority on that subject, Eugene Grant. It was the only course I failed in college.

As I study other chapters on entrepreneurship in this volume (e.g., those by Gordon E. Moore and Robert A. Swanson) and consider Ruben F. Mettler's discussion of technological innovation in major corporations, I sense that there is a serious transitional stage that must be successfully negotiated in order for grass-roots-level firms in technical innovation to continue to grow. How does a company move from the level of the individual entrepreneur to that of a very large technically innovative company?

First, let me note that no two companies are necessarily the same in their approach to this transitional problem, so it is very difficult to generalize. For example, Genentech may have a very different set of problems from those of Intel. Let us go back about 25 years to a time when this transitional process can be seen in simpler form. At that time, a number of people observing the process referred to the "$10-million syndrome," reflecting their observation that many technically oriented companies reaching about that size ran into serious problems. The problems were severe enough that management could not handle them, and those companies either went out of business or were acquired by larger organizations.

I believe that there were at least three problems that, occurring simultaneously, tended to cause this crisis. The first had to do with management itself. Small, technically innovative firms were typically started by engineers or scientists whose primary skills were in technical fields. Their attitude was that management functions would take care of themselves. Unfortunately they do not, and the entrepreneurs would suddenly realize that the organization they had created was not capable of meeting the challenges of the future. The effect of management weakness is cumulative.

The second problem was that of financing growth. The financial problems of a small company are very different from those of a large one. Initial capital is often available from the individuals themselves, from associates or friends, and (certainly in small amounts) from banks. However, these funds are quickly swallowed up by the basic working-capital needs of a growing company. It is therefore essential that stress be put on the principle of financing growth from earnings, and if that is not done, the company will not survive.

The third problem involves product-line depth. A new, innovative product has a logical life. Having demonstrated the viability of such a new concept, a company soon meets competition from other companies attempting to exploit its ideas, or, as it often happens, newer technologies invalidate earlier inventions. It is essential, then, that if a company is to survive, its product line be expanded and strengthened. This speaks to continuing research and development efforts, which again need to be financed.

In 25 years, there has been a major change in one aspect of the transitional problems faced by small innovative firms. That change is one of degree: we have gone from a $10-million critical level to somewhere around a $100-million to $200-million critical level, with the associated increase in risks. Other than that, the three problems discussed above come into play today just as they did 25 years ago. We still have the same problems with management and management development. Modern financing, such as venture capital, has taken some of the importance away from a company's financing its own growth, but venture capital "is not free," and unless it is carefully controlled, it may pose more problems than it solves. And, finally, with far more competition existing in technically innovative fields, the question of product-line obsolescence is of increasing importance.

Viewed from another angle, these are all problems of economics, because technically innovative companies, large and small, are equally affected by the economic environment in which they exist. Some knowledge of economics is essential to directing the program of a modern corporation.

Cultivating Technological Innovation

WILLIAM J. PERRY

Four significant factors will contribute to continued U.S. leadership in cultivating technological innovation: (1) our accelerating ability to foster technological discontinuities, (2) cooperative university-industry ties, (3) a large pool of risk capital for innovative start-up companies, and (4) strong cultural underpinnings for innovation.

In the first 150 years of the Republic, the United States experienced unprecedented growth and prosperity. In that era, our economy could be viewed as a non-zero-sum game: wealth was being injected into our economy from the new land that was being opened up, the new minerals that were being discovered, and the new people who were coming into the country. Today we live in an era of limits: we are not opening new land, we face a declining mineral production, and we are experiencing relatively small population increases. Nevertheless, the country is still experiencing growth and prosperity, and our economy can still be viewed as a non-zero-sum game. The new wealth today, rather than coming from mines and farms, is coming from innovative technology. Indeed, we might say that in the nineteenth century the wealth in California came from the gold in our mountains; today it comes from the silicon in our valleys. Silicon Valley is the wonder and the envy of the world. Countless study groups and panels from such technological superpowers as Great Britain, France, West Germany, Sweden, and Japan are trying to learn what our "secret" is—what has caused this unprecedented explosion of innovation.

In attempting to explain the explosion of innovation, I will start by quoting

G. W. Dummer, the British engineer who *almost* invented the integrated circuit. At a technical conference in 1952, Dummer said:

With the advent of the transistor and the work in semiconductors generally, it seems now possible to envisage electronic equipment in a solid block with no layers of insulating, conducting, rectifying, and amplifying materials, the electrical functions being connected directly by cutting out areas of the various layers.

That was 6 years before the integrated circuit was invented. One does not have to be an electronics engineer to understand that he was anticipating the development of the integrated circuit, and indeed he later spent many years working on that development (supported by the Royal Radar Establishment in England). But it was not G. W. Dummer who invented the integrated circuit, nor was it England that had the opportunity to exploit it. The integrated circuit was developed by Kilby at Texas Instruments and Noyce at Fairchild, and the explosion in technology that followed occurred in the United States. Years later, looking back wistfully on this lost opportunity, Dummer said:

It is worth remembering that the giant American electronics companies were formed since the war by a relatively few enterprising electronics engineers, setting up with either their own capital or risk capital from a bank. Often a government contract would start them off. Hard work was necessary, and the large home market was a great asset, but the climate of innovation was such that any advanced technical product could be sold. . . . The American system of encouraging employees to hold shares in the company is one which should be emulated, as a part share in the firm's prosperity gives a sense of increased responsibility. . . . Successful businesses are almost always dependent on a few people who are innovative and enthusiastic.

That is Dummer's assessment of why the integrated circuit revolution took place in the United States and not in England.

UNDERPINNINGS OF TECHNOLOGICAL GROWTH

I would like to generalize on Dummer's points. First, a dramatic change in technology—a technological discontinuity—can create an opportunity to form a new industry, and certainly the development of the integrated circuit was such a discontinuity. Since that development, there has been a stream of discontinuities that are best characterized by observing that, for the past two decades, the computer industry has experienced a 20 percent annual improvement in price and performance, largely as a result of technological changes in semiconductors. There is no other industry in which anything even remotely like that has happened, and that sustained improvement in price and performance has led to new products, new companies, and the creation of entire industries that did not exist a decade or two ago. Since technological discontinuities are the key to this growth, one might question whether we are at the tapering-off point in the introduction of technological discontinuities in the semiconductor and computer fields. I believe not. In fact, I expect that in the next decade we will see a much greater improvement in price and performance than occurred in either of the past two decades. In particular, I anticipate that in the next decade we will see aggregate price and performance improvements of more than a hundredfold in the field of semiconductors and computers. A hundredfold improvement is not an extravagant estimate; in fact, it may very well be conservative.

The second critical feature in this creation of new wealth through innovative technology is cultural, and that is primarily the point Dummer was making in the second quotation. In Europe or Japan if the chief engineer of a major company resigned his job in order to start up a new company, his friends and his neighbors would think there was something wrong with him. In the United States, particularly in Silicon Valley, if the chief engineer of a major company did *not* leave his job to form a new company, his friends and neighbors would think there was something wrong with him. And that summarizes the cultural differences between the United States and Europe or Japan.

A point that might be added to Dummer's statement is the importance of having great research universities intimately tied to industry. There is no better example of that than the industry-university cooperation taking place at Stanford, which is being emulated at a number of other universities in the country, including MIT and Berkeley.

The final point, one that was alluded to briefly by Dummer, is the availability of risk capital. If new technological enterprises are financed, risk capital must be available—for they *are* risky enterprises. In Europe, if a person wants to start a company, he or she probably gets the money, if it comes at all, from commercial banks. In the United States, banks are an unlikely source of risk capital for an enterprise. In my experience in working with start-up companies, commercial banks play a very limited role indeed, namely the role of providing loans that are secured by equipment, receivables, or the founder's personal guarantees.

A second alternative source for financing technological innovation is the public. There was a brisk market in the early 1980s in what was called "penny stock." The penny stock market operated primarily out of Denver, and it provided public financing for high-risk enterprises. That market is now out of favor. Although it may be premature to proclaim its demise, the penny stock market is certainly in very weak condition today. The problem with the public as a source of financing for high-risk, high technology companies is that once a company receives public financing, there exists very great pressure for early financial performance, which is not well suited to the kind of ventures that involve the development of complex, new technological products. Also, while a high-risk venture can have a high reward, that high reward comes with a low probability, and too often the investors forget that a low probability of success means a high probability of failure. Enough of these failures in fact happen that eventually this market gets a bad name. In my view, the public markets are not an appropriate way to finance high-risk start-up companies; the proper role they play is in the financing of emerging technology companies with products already being marketed. The existence of a vigorous public market for such emerging high technology companies is critical to the existence of a vigorous venture capital market. So, the role of the public market in risk capital is indirect in that it provides a means of liquidity for the venture capitalists.

A third way of financing high-risk, high technology companies is through R&D partnerships, the basic idea of which is sharing the risk—the company, the public, and indeed the government all share the risk of failure. Moreover, the partnership is structured so that it operates on a suitable timetable; many partnerships are structured so that the payback on them is not scheduled to occur for 5 or more years in the future. Nevertheless, R&D partnerships have fallen out of favor lately because of several spectacular failures, of which Trilogy and Storage Tech Computer are two prominent examples. One of these companies has gone out of business, and the other has fallen on hard times, each after raising more than $60 million of partnership funding. Such spectacular and highly visible failures have given R&D partnerships a bad name. Despite this, they will probably make a comeback because they have fundamental appeal; that is, they are an appropriate vehicle for financing high-risk ventures because of their risk sharing and long time horizon. They will likely come back, however, in a particular way, namely, in the form of partnership-pooled funds that allow the investor to get many of the benefits of an R&D partnership, but with the further benefit of spreading the risk over many enterprises.

Another important way of financing venture operations is through private means, that is, through the founders themselves or their friends and relatives. How much financing of this sort is actually done is not known, but it is used in a significant number of start-up companies. Indeed, I started my own company, ESL, in 1964 entirely that way; that company, which today has a quarter of a billion dollars in annual revenues, never at any time in its history received a dollar of venture financing. It was financed entirely with funds from the founders and grew on retained earnings. That mode of financing puts obvious constraints on the growth rate of the company, but those constraints may be a blessing in disguise in that they do not allow the entrepreneur to get into the kind of problems that go with unconstrained growth. (Another company a little better known than ESL—Hewlett-Packard—financed itself the same way.) Today most founders seem to prefer to get venture capital and only go to private funding if they fail to get venture funding. Private financing has much to recommend it, however, and it should be considered as a first resort, rather than a last resort, for founders.

Of course, the most popular means of financing start-ups today is with venture capital. We have seen in the past few years a dramatic increase in the funds available to venture capital. We have all been bombarded with statistics and other information on this point. To summarize just the principal numbers: during most of the 1970s about $100 million to $200 million a year of new money came into the venture capital community, but in the past few years that figure has risen to between $2 billion and $4 billion a year. Why has this dramatic growth occurred? One very obvious reason is the change in the tax laws that occurred in 1978 and again in 1981, which reduced the effective capital gains tax rate to 20 percent. There is no need to repeat the arguments about the critical importance of tax policy in technological innovation, except to note that while tax policy plays an important role, it is not the only reason for this dramatic increase in venture funds. Probably the primary reason that we have gone from a hundred million to a few billion dollars a year is the record of performance of venture funds during the 1970s. Hambrecht & Quist venture funds, which were started in the early 1970s, showed an average rate of return in excess of 40 percent for that decade. A number of other venture firms that were started in the late 1960s and the early 1970s showed comparable rates of return. Not surprisingly, this caught the attention of the managers of pension funds and other institutions. When they compared the 40 percent growth rates of venture funds with the relatively low rates they were getting from their investments in blue-chip stocks, major fund managers began to invest in venture capital funds.

How was this venture-fund performance achieved? One fundamental factor leading to this performance has been the underlying improvements in technology—the 20 percent per year price and performance improvement resulting from technological advances allowed the successful companies in this field to sustain very impressive secular growth in earnings year after year. The second fundamental factor has been the related growth in the over-the-counter (OTC) market for high technology companies, which allowed the venture funds to achieve liquidity at attractive multiples. Public market prices depend on cyclical as well as secular factors, as illustrated by the Hambrecht & Quist Technology Index of about 150 stocks (Figure 1), which serves as a surrogate for the price increase of emerging technological companies in the past decade. Two things are apparent in looking at Figure 1. The first is that high-tech stocks, compared with the Standard & Poor's 400, are highly volatile. They have been characterized as having a beta* of two; actually in the past year or so, it has been much greater than that. The second is that, notwithstanding this volatility, there is a pronounced secular growth. While the market volatility is exceedingly important, as the past two years have demonstrated all too clearly, it is dominated in the long term by the secular

---

*A factor describing the relative volatility of a stock's price with cyclical market variations.

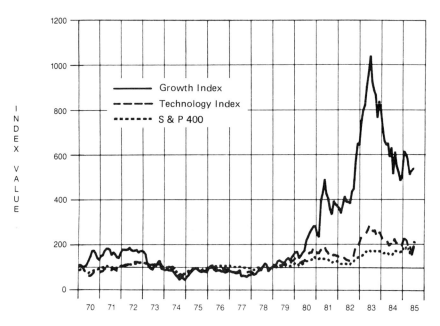

FIGURE 1   Hambrecht & Quist growth and technology indexes, Standard & Poor's 400 index, 1970–1985.

NOTE: For the purpose of comparison, all indexes have been set at 100 at December 31, 1978. Chart reflects month-end values. Latest values are for June 28, 1985.

SOURCE: Hambrecht & Quist, Inc. Reprinted with permission.

growth, which is being driven by the sustained improvement in price and performance resulting from technological improvements.

A CLOSER LOOK AT VENTURE FUNDS

The public markets are key to understanding the performance of venture funds because the growth in venture funds is driven by the increase in the price of the venture stock when it becomes public. Thus, the capital gains tax rate affects the availability of venture funds in two ways: first, by increasing the attraction of venture capital for private investors (they are attracted by the potential of retaining more of their earnings in capital gains); and second, by increasing the attraction of high-growth public stocks for investors. This latter effect tends to increase the growth rate of venture funds, which increases the attractiveness of venture investments, even to tax-free institutional funds.

There has been a lot of publicity in the past year or two suggesting that venture capital is drying up. That is a misunderstanding of what in fact is happening. The performance of venture funds in 1984 was lackluster largely because of the lackluster performance of the public market for high-tech stocks. But this is the cyclical aspect of venture-fund valuation. Venture investments will continue to have appeal because of the secular growth in technology. Even in 1984, which was a dismal year for technology stocks in the market, a number of venture funds were formed at levels of $50 million to $100 million each. So, money continues to flow into venture capital—not as much as in 1983, but certainly as much as in any other year in the history of venture capital. There will be a cyclical interest in venture capital as a result of the cyclicality of the public market in high technology stocks. But what will override that will be the continuing sustained improvements in technology, which will lead to secular growth in stock earnings, which will—in time—lead to secular growth of stock prices, which in turn will bring up the average rate of return of the venture funds.

Where do we stand today in venture capital? Can a start-up company get venture money if it wants it? There are literally billions of dollars available in venture funds, but if you talk to someone trying to start a company today, he has a different perspective. He sees a very tight market. The reason it is tight does not have to do with the lack of money, but with the fact that venture funds, having made major investments in 1981 and 1982, now are holding companies needing second- and third-round financing, which may not be available from public markets as it was in 1982 and 1983. For that reason the venture funds are tending to reserve their money for these later-stage financings. Thus, while the money is there, it is not being made available to start-up companies to the same extent that it was in 1982 and 1983.

LARGE COMPANIES AND TECHNOLOGICAL INNOVATION

Thus far, I have talked about innovation through start-up companies. But the amount of money that IBM alone spent on research and development last year was about equal to the total amount spent by venture funds on start-ups. So, why do we not look to the large companies for technological innovation? The research laboratories of large companies are very efficient at developing products that evolve from their predecessor products. However, to the extent that a new product depends on technological discontinuities, the large companies are not nearly as effective. Their size and bureaucratic organization tend to work against the timely development of products that are a dramatic departure from earlier products. But there is another factor that may be even more important. Large companies suffer from what I call "the liability of leadership." The following is a case in point.

At the time the transistor was being commercialized, Sylvania Electric

Products was one of the three largest manufacturers of vacuum tubes in the world. Sylvania fully understood the potential of the transistor for making the vacuum tube business obsolete, so it established a research center to develop transistor technology. The company brought together the same kind of physicists, the same kind of engineers and technicians, and the same kind of equipment that existed at Shockley Semiconductor and later at Fairchild Industries. They then took this activity and assigned it to the manager of the vacuum tube division—the rest is history.

There is a psychological as well as a technological problem in this liability of leadership. A major company that is a leader in a given field has a very difficult time embracing a discontinuous technology that can lead to a product that has the potential of killing off the product that is yielding most of its earnings. IBM had exactly the same problem with the minicomputer as Sylvania had with the transistor. It wasn't that it did not know how to build minicomputers, but it hung back and let a then unknown company—Digital Equipment—define and create that market rather than develop a minicomputer that would have cannibalized the low end of its mainframe product line. Later, when IBM decided that the personal computer market was real, it entered that market in a vigorous, entrepreneurial manner because the personal computer was not competing so directly with other of its major products.

More and more of the larger companies are saying: What can we do to participate in these venture activities, recognizing the limitations we have because of our size and our leadership in related markets? Some of them have gone into the venture business themselves; that is, they have formed and managed venture capital funds. Good information on the results of these ventures is not available, but, in general, they have not worked well. Whether or not the investments were successful, corporate-managed venture funds have not generally achieved the primary thing they wanted—the transfer of technology and the creation of new products.

In the past few years, a number of companies have tried a different approach. Known as corporate partnering, this approach is an alternative both to corporate venture funds and to corporate acquisition of smaller companies. An example is the strategic relationship that General Motors (GM) has formed with a small company called Teknowledge. In this relationship, Teknowledge remains an independent company but works with General Motors to develop applications of artificial intelligence to the automobile industry. GM provides funding and market-wise guidance for the R&D projects that are involved. Teknowledge gets a ready market for the product, and GM gets a head start on its competitors with the new products. In addition, GM has made a minority investment in Teknowledge. Thus, corporate partnering has become an alternative way for small companies to raise equity financing. General Motors is perhaps the most experienced practitioner of corporate partnering today. This in itself is remarkable, since a decade ago the company deservedly had the reputation of believing that all wisdom in the automotive field stemmed from General Motors—looking outside for ideas was the last thing that would have occurred to the GM management. General Motors has made dramatic changes in its point of view, and a number of other large corporations are following its lead.

This new trend has been noted by William Miller, the president of SRI, International, and a professor at Stanford (where he teaches a course on innovation and technology). He observed that in the past few centuries, the periods of greatest innovation and prosperity occurred when industry was practicing eclecticism. Eclecticism is reaching out for ideas—it is the opposite of the NIH (not-invented-here) complex that plagued General Motors during the 1970s. Miller observes that this trend for companies like General Motors to reach out to other companies for ideas is a very favorable indicator for the future.

SUMMARY

I believe four significant factors will contribute to continued U.S. leadership in cultivating innovation across a broad spectrum of technologies. First, I anticipate that our ability to foster technological discontinuities will continue and accelerate, resulting in such developments as a hundredfold improvement in the price and performance of computers during the next decade. Second, I expect our research universities to further strengthen their ties to high technology industry, thereby advancing our nation's competitive advantage in world markets. Third, a large pool of risk capital will continue to be available for innovative start-up companies. And, finally, our culture will continue to provide strong underpinnings for innovation. Especially in recent years, the cultural values that promote innovation have spread from entrepreneurial start-up firms to major corporations, which are now reaching out to find ideas for new technology and new products wherever those ideas exist.

The Role of Large Banks in Financing Innovation

JOHN S. REED and GLEN R. MORENO

The role of major financial institutions in stimulating technological innovation is not limited to the simple lending of funds. In the broadest sense, it lies in creating new financial techniques, or in innovation of financial technology. It is as innovators themselves that large financial institutions play their most decisive role in supporting innovation among their client companies.

There is growing recognition that technological innovation is a key determinant of continuing economic growth and prosperity. International attention has focused on the United States, where the emergence of a service economy, the rapid growth of high technology companies, and the apparent linkage between the growth of small companies and job creation offer promise of maintaining growth in the postindustrial economy. The increasing importance of high technology industries in Japan, where economic growth, though slower, continues, seems to offer further hope of a reasonably ordered transition from an economic system based on heavy industry to one centered on the emerging technologies of our times.

These trends have been closely observed in Europe. There, policy initiatives to maintain economic growth and employment over the past decade are generally recognized to have failed. Policies based on maintaining employment through increasing public sector intervention—rigid labor practices, industry protection, and subsidies—have arguably hastened, rather than delayed, the competitive demise of the industries concerned. Thus, throughout the developed economies, there is an emerging consensus that innovation brings growth, and policymakers are increasingly seeking ways to stimulate technological innovation and new company formation.

As a subset of these broad economic policy considerations, there is a growing perception of the importance of national and international financial systems to the process of technological innovation and economic growth. This is most evident in the keen international interest in the venture capital phenomenon in the United States, and in the various public and private sector initiatives to emulate its successes abroad. The venture capital system, however, represents only a tiny portion of the capital-formation process. It is, therefore, important to enhance the overall effectiveness of the financial system in supporting technological innovation.

Our purpose in this chapter is to describe briefly the role of large banks in financing technological innovation in industry. Since there is little published material on the subject, we have of necessity relied on the collective experience of our own organization (Citibank Corporation) and our interpretation of general trends in the global financial system. The theme that emerges quite consistently from our observations is that the role of major financial institutions in stimulating technological innovation is not limited to the simple lending of funds. In the broadest sense, it lies in creating new financial techniques, or in innovation of financial technology. It is as innovators themselves that large financial institutions play their most decisive role in supporting innovation among their client companies. Financial innovation supports technological innovation. Thus, the public interest is best served by a financial system that provides maximum scope for competition and innovation in financial services.

BANKS AND TECHNOLOGICAL INNOVATION

It is worth noting that banks' involvement in the innovative process is not limited to their role as financial intermediaries. Technology has significantly influenced the historical development of the banking system and is a major factor for change in the financial services industry today.

The historical evolution of America's large financial institutions is closely intertwined with the process of technological innovation in the nineteenth century. In transportation technology, the opening of the Erie Canal in 1825 and advent of the railroad in the 1830s strengthened New York's position as the country's manufacturing and trading center. This, in turn, led to New York's emergence as the dominant financial center in the country. Country banks kept balances with New York banks as liquid reserves for clearing the variety of commercial transactions that passed through the city, and the New York banks soon held a major part of the total banking resources in the country. Thus, technological innovation was instrumental in creating the forerunners of the "money center" banks 150 years ago.

Citibank offers an interesting example of the historical linkage between technology and banking, for its fortunes during the nineteenth century were closely linked to technological innovation. The basis of the bank's wealth and influence and that of its dominant shareholders progressed from trading coal to dominating the New York lighting utilities, whose technology was based on gas manufactured from coal. This activity led to heavy investment in the railroads that brought the coal to New York City and investment in iron manufacturing, another heavy user of coal. The bank was involved in the progress of the metallurgy industry in the United States and financed the introduction of the Bessemer steel process at the Lackawanna Iron Company. Citibank was also active in the development of communications technology; it financed the laying of the first transatlantic cable from 1858 to 1866 and at one point dominated the Western Union Telegraph Company, then the largest enterprise in the world.

Today, the tables have been turned and it is the financial services industry that finds itself dominated by the new information technologies. A recent study for Congress by the Office of Technology Assessment described the scope of this influence: "The applications of advanced information and tele-communications technologies in systems for delivering financial services change the way those services are created, delivered, priced, received, accepted and used."[1]

It is therefore not surprising that possibly the most direct way in which financial institutions fund innovation is as purchasers and users of information technology. U.S. depository institutions spent well over $8 billion in 1984 on data processing equipment and services, excluding office automation. Commercial banks alone spent just under $5 billion on purchases of data processing equipment and services from outside vendors. Almost half of those purchases were made by the country's 240 largest banks. Citicorp itself is, of course, a major user of technology-related services and equipment. Our estimated expenditures in these areas are approaching half a billion dollars a year.

As users, large financial institutions are actively exploring and developing commercial applications for new technologies as they are introduced. Rapid advances in voice, facsimile, image, and graphics processing, as well as communications technologies, give rise to new commercial opportunities for accessing, manipulating, and using information in financial businesses. Automated teller machines, point-of-sale terminals, and home-banking networks are spreading across the United States. Many banks, including Citicorp, are building worldwide computing networks linking common databases around the globe. Electronic trading systems and international fund-transfer networks are part of this growing international financial network. Some large financial institutions, again including Citicorp, have invested in or operate their own technology affiliates, working with other companies to develop specific hardware and software for application within their financial services businesses.

These aggregate activities represent a significant source of concentrated orders and revenue to the technology companies whose products and services are involved. In addition, they provide a screening process in the selection of commercially viable technological innovations. At least in the field of information technology, innovation in financial services quite demonstrably supports technological innovation.

THE ROLE OF LARGE BANKS IN THE FINANCIAL SYSTEM

The direct role of banks as users of technological innovation is relatively simple to describe and quantify. When viewing the broader role of banks as financial intermediaries, however, it is much more difficult to establish direct links between bank finance and technological innovation. Part of this difficulty lies in the nature of bank lending itself, which is designed to avoid or mitigate risks predicated on the success of a particular innovation. Bank lending by its very nature tends to finance innovation indirectly. Thus, to better understand the role of banks in financing innovation, it is useful to understand the role that banks and other financial institutions play in financing the total economy.

Domestic financial institutions held total assets of over $6 trillion in 1983. Banks and savings and loan institutions accounted for almost half of those assets, and life insurance companies and pension funds made up another quarter. Large banks held a concentrated share of those assets. Out of the nation's 14,500 banks, the roughly 240 banks with balance sheets of more than $1 billion held about 60 percent of total domestic banking assets. Clearly large banks play a very significant role in the U.S. financial system.

This does not mean that large banks or the banking system as a whole are dominant providers of funds to American industry. In fact, bank debt is used to fund less than 10 percent of the total assets of American manufacturing companies. This reflects the importance of public bond issues, equity, internal cash generation, and trade credit in financing American enterprise.

The U.S. system is quite different from some other major financial systems in this respect. In Japan banks play a much more dominant role in the supply of finance to industry. Japanese companies are much more leveraged than their U.S. counterparts, and the vast majority of Japanese borrowings is represented by bank debt, which accounts for as much as 75 to 80 percent of total external borrowings of Japanese companies. This high level of bank borrowing, combined with the system of "main bank" relationships, leads to a much more dominant role of Japanese banks in the affairs of Japanese companies.

The situation in West Germany is not as pronounced as that in Japan, but German banks do play a more important role in financing enterprise than is the case in the United States. This is due to the relatively high leverage of German companies, the German universal banking system (in which banks provide most sources of funding), and the house bank system (wherein one bank normally enjoys board representation and traditionally plays a leading role in the arranging of a company's finance).

The British banking system provides the closest parallel to the limited role of banks in the United States. Since the Industrial Revolution, British companies have sought to maintain a measure of independence from the banking system by covering the bulk of their finance from internal sources. Over the last several years retained earnings accounted for 68 percent of the sources of funds of British companies, compared to only 17 percent for individual bank borrowings and less than 5 percent for United Kingdom capital market issues.

In sum, large banks are a very important factor in the U.S. financial system. But even allowing for public debt underwritten by investment banks, borrowings through U.S. financial institutions play a somewhat limited role in financing American business, both as a percentage of total funding sources and in comparison with other major financial systems. Moreover, our experience indicates that the role of large banks in financing technological innovation appears to increase in importance with company size. This may be demonstrated by examining the role of large banks in financing innovation in companies at three phases of maturity: the start-up company; the emerging growth company; and the large, established company.

LARGE BANKS AND THE START-UP COMPANY

Banks rarely finance start-up operations directly. This prudence is essential to the effective functioning of the banking system.

True start-up ventures are risky. They involve plans, hopes, and uncertainty. If successful, the rewards are significant. Failure can mean losing all, and failure rates are statistically high. It is thus clear that the appropriate funding for start-up ventures is equity capital. Equity investors tie their fortunes to the risk of failure of the enterprise they back. They take high risk for high reward and understand that the failure of the enterprise means the probable loss of their equity.

This is clearly an inappropriate role for bank lending. One of the primary functions of the banking system is to provide a safe home for depositors' savings. This means that the quality of its assets must be excellent. Banks are leveraged 20 to 1, spreads to cover loan losses are small, and, to quote one Citibanker: "Banks need to bat around .990 to survive." It is therefore standard credit doctrine in American commercial banks that loans to start-ups cannot be solely dependent on the success of a single innovation or product. Good commercial lending practice dictates two or even three sources of repayment in any lending situation. Adherence to this doctrine is an essential ingredient of the health and solidity of the banking system.

Banks may play an indirect role in the early stages of business start-ups, however. Peter Drucker has posed the question: "But who nurtures the true start up enterprise? And how? We really do not know, yet the money clearly is there. . . ."[2] It seems probable that at least part of the answer lies in the retail financial services industry. Personal savings through a growing variety of investment instruments, as well as home equity loans and other forms of secured personal borrowing, may be a large source of funding to America's infant businesses.

There is certainly no similar obscurity about the significant role of venture capital finance in developing the new enterprise. While small in absolute terms, venture capital finance clearly has played a very important role in the development of new companies, and particularly in those involved in innovative technology.

Large banks and other financial institutions play an important role in venture finance. The venture capital affiliates of banks appear to have provided roughly $1.5 billion, or more than 10 percent of total resources, to the venture capital business by the end of 1983. In that year banks provided $130 million of the $1.8 billion incremental investment. Large banks are dominant in this process; fewer than 100 banks are active, and a handful provide between one-third and one-half of total bank venture capital funding.

Citicorp's venture capital portfolio at the end of 1984 had 122 investments, with a market value of over $300 million. Our investments span a broad range of industries, including information technology, health care, energy, and transportation. We also maintain a $200 million leveraged budget fund to enable managers to purchase and run their companies. This is often an important further source of innovation in the companies concerned.

Banks and insurance companies tend to specialize in the later stages of venture capital financings. Increasingly, these institutions provide important liquidity in the expansion of venture companies. This makes the venture capital business less dependent on the fluctuating outlook for public sector securities offerings and provides additional staying power in troubled times.

Large banks have played an important role in the development of the innovative financing techniques of venture capital. They have provided many talented people for the venture capital industry and have been instrumental in establishing the industry outside the United States and in transferring professional skills and knowledge. Citicorp, for example, has been an important factor in the relatively young venture capital market in the United Kingdom since 1980 and has over £20 million invested in almost 30 companies. We have also recently established new venture capital businesses in West Germany, France, and Italy. We are generally viewed as an important source of financial innovation in those markets.

Venture capital affiliates offer an interesting example of how a bank's holding companies can respond to the different needs and opportunities of new ventures without compromising the lending practices of their commercial banking arms. They function with specially trained staff using quite different investment criteria. Thus, banks can play an active role in one of the most innovative sectors of finance while maintaining the prudential standards required of depository institutions.

BANKS AND THE EMERGING GROWTH COMPANY

One of our colleagues describes the very different roles of bank lending and seed capital in this way: "The venture capitalist finances ideas—the banker finances sales." Once a company has begun to translate its products and services into sales revenue, banks can begin the process of evaluating the ongoing commercial viability of the enterprise. That analysis is not limited to the new product itself, but to the overall capabilities of the company: management, marketing, and finance.

In this sense, financial intermediaries play an important role in screening the commercial usefulness of technological innovation. The banker who extends credit, or the investment banker who takes a new company to the public markets, is performing a financial "gatekeeper" role analogous to that ascribed by Nathan Rosenberg to the technical gatekeeper in user industries. In a broader context, the aggregate of these screening decisions probably represents a valuable economic benefit. The financial gateway function helps to ensure that scarce resources are allocated to those innovative opportunities most likely to bring maximum economic return.

Initial banking contacts for the emerging company tend to be established with local or regional banks, due to the strong local networks and knowledge of the local marketplace that these banks enjoy, and because local banks can provide checking accounts, payroll services, and other depository and transactional services to new companies. These noncredit services are an important link to subsequent bank credit, since bankers have much better insight into the financial affairs of a young company when they are involved in its trade payments and have a reasonable overview of its flow of funds.

It is worth noting that regulatory constraints on interstate banking prohibit all institutions from providing local depository and payment services. This, in turn, limits or delays their ability to begin providing credit at an early stage in the development of new companies. It is thus probable that regulation has limited the flow of funds from large financial institutions to smaller companies. Logic dictates that this restriction limits competitive choice and increases the cost of financing in these firms.

Large banks begin to play a significant role in the emerging company's affairs when its financing needs become large in comparison with the normal lending capabilities of local banks. This relationship generally begins with the desire of the company to establish contact with a major institution that will have the capacity to meet significant financing requirements in future years.

As a company grows, large banks tend to satisfy its increasingly complex financial needs. The introduction of financial management systems to control and optimize cash flows offers one example. Large banks also offer a growing array of risk-management techniques: financial futures, floor- and ceiling-rate products, currency options, and many other instruments designed to cushion the company against volatile financial markets. Most of these financial innovations have been developed in major commercial and investment banks. They play an important role in transferring this financial technology to the emerging company.

Most technology companies are involved in international markets at a relatively early stage. This occurs through export sales and component or assembly relationships abroad. Meeting the international financial needs of these companies is very much the province of large banks, which represent a very high percentage of U.S. overseas bank branches.

The banks' knowledge of overseas markets and how to do business there is very important to younger companies. They also provide local-currency financing for new entrants into overseas markets where capital markets are not as deep as in the United States, and it is the bank's introduction and assessment of the company that may well establish its credit standing in those markets.

All of this highlights the important role that large banks play in assisting the emerging company to develop financial skills and capabilities to help it manage its growth in the United States and world markets. Through the development of increasingly complex financial problems in a competitive world, banks provide support to the growing company well beyond the simple provision of finance.

FINANCING INNOVATION IN THE ESTABLISHED COMPANY

The most important role of large financial institutions probably lies in financing technological innovation in the large and established companies that represent such a significant portion of the total U.S. and global economy. Within the "safe confines" of these established enterprises, the evidence is that technological innovation imposes an increasingly heavy burden. Nathan Rosenberg has noted that: "A central feature of high-technology industries that is likely to become increasingly significant is an apparently inexorable rise in the development costs of new products."[3]

There is a popular tendency to equate invention and innovation with small companies. Indeed, the list of significant technological innovations generated by small enterprises is impressive. But it would be wrong to ignore the tremendous importance of research, development, and innovation activity that occurs in the world's large corporations. To our knowledge there is no significant relationship between innovation and the size of a firm. R&D expenditures and patent activity tend to show roughly the same proportion to sales in both small and large companies. While these are not the only proxies for technical innovation, the implication is clear that innovation is not predominantly a small-company phenomenon. Finally, of course, small companies that consistently introduce successful innovative products tend to become large companies very quickly, and some, like IBM, become giants in the global economy within a generation or so.

Financing development costs through increasingly innovative financial techniques is probably the key challenge faced by large financial institutions in supporting technological innovation. Indeed, it is arguable that innovative financial techniques have been instrumental in clearing the way for commercial development of some key technological applications.

Following are some important examples, starting with the commercial aircraft industry regarding which Rosenberg has highlighted "the extreme impact of rising development costs in the commercial aircraft industry especially since the advent of the jet engine in the 1950s. . . ."[3]

Banks played an important role in the introduction of jet aircraft to the commercial airline industry beginning with the Boeing 707 and the Douglas DC-8. In the late 1950s and early 1960s, the commercial airlines faced the need to finance aircraft costing up to $5 million as opposed to the $1 million or less typically paid for non-jet aircraft up to that time. The money center banks developed new forms of revolving credit and brought in long-term money from the insurance industry to finance these purchases, thus helping to create an adequate market for the production of the 707 and the DC-8.

Later, when the 727 was being considered for production, there was concern that one major carrier's inability to finance new aircraft would jeopardize the entire program. Citibank, Chase Manhattan, Boeing, and Eastern Airlines executives worked out a financing program that made development of this commercially successful aircraft possible.

Aircraft leasing was a financial innovation directly attributable to a small group of bankers and lawyers who introduced the investor tax lease. This financial innovation became a critical factor in financing future commercial aircraft sales on a large scale. Another was the development of export finance programs in conjunction with the Export-Import Bank.

The Boeing 747, the first commercial wide-bodied jet, was originally financed by a $1 billion syndicated credit led by Citibank—a huge amount for a single credit in the late 1960s. Nor was that loan without its moments of drama; difficulties with the jet engines for the "jumbo" delayed sales and put the entire program at risk. The banking syndicate involved, which included all major U.S. banks in those days, was held together and provided additional finance through a very difficult and trying period for the company and the banks involved.

The point to be stressed is that in several crucial phases of the development and introduction of commercial aircraft over the past 30 years, innovative financial solutions have been instrumental in assisting the development process. The link between financial innovation and technological innovation is direct and demonstrable.

The same process appears to have been at work in the energy field. The commercial exploitation of oil resources in Alaska and the North Sea was aided by very large scale bank finance based on extremely complicated and innovative project-finance and syndication techniques. A variety of financing packages were devised to enable producers to fund developments requiring capital expenditure many times their normal annual levels, while spreading the financial risks among a very wide base of lending institutions.

Rosenberg has also noted that "the exploitation of new fossil-fuel energy sources, involving liquefaction and gasification, is almost certain to encounter spectacular development costs, as is already clear at the pilot-plant stage."[3] The world's banking system is responding to similar challenges with innovative financial techniques to raise the sums involved. Citicorp, for example, led the financing of New Zealand's synfuel project, a plan for converting natural gases for the Maui offshore fields into gasoline using a process developed by Mobil and so far only tried in a very small scale pilot plant. The project is designed to produce 35 percent of New Zealand's total gasoline needs. Using a variety of new financing techniques devised to divide the project risk into separate management pieces, Citicorp was able to raise $1.7 billion, spread among a very large syndicate of international banks.

Similar financial techniques that rely heavily on off-take agreements from major users have been employed recently to assist the exploitation of gas resources in Australia's Northwest Shelf. These agreements have permitted the phased financing of various stages of that development.

In all these projects the institutions involved have used innovative techniques to disaggregate the huge technological, financial, insurance, political, and other risks involved and then have spread each of the risk elements among as many participants as possible. These techniques enable technology projects whose risks exceed the capacity of any one entity to assume, to be broken down into digestible pieces for the projects' sponsors, suppliers, operators, customers, insurers, and lenders.

Today, similar techniques are being adapted to deal with satellite systems and other extraterrestrial projects. Citicorp has a department that specializes in developing financing techniques for these projects. We have so far arranged or participated in total financings of almost $1 billion in this field.

These cases provide examples of direct financing of technological innovation. Most large companies' innovation expenditures are financed, of course, through general corporate funding programs. Here, financial institutions play an increasingly important role as innovators in the international capital markets.

LARGE FINANCIAL INSTITUTIONS AS GLOBAL INTERMEDIARIES

The rapid development of global, integrated capital markets may provide the long-term solution to large-scale funding needs of the new technologies. That integration is being driven by the world's leading commercial and investment banks.

The growth of the international capital markets has, of course, been dramatic over the past two decades. Total international bank lending, for example, has been estimated by the BIS at roughly $1.2 trillion at the end of 1983. This large Eurocredit market has been supplemented in recent years by market developments, which clearly suggests the emergence of a single, global, integrated capital market. Eurobond borrowing, for example, was until recently a relatively small portion of the world's capital markets reserved for public sector borrowers and the very best known international companies. It has now become an important source of finance for many corporate borrowers, including U.S. companies. International bond issues by U.S. companies tripled in 1984 to U.S. $24 billion out of total Eurobond issues of over U.S. $100 billion. The introduction of note-issuance facilities over the past year suggests the beginning of an international commercial paper market. A key development is the emergence of a variety of innovative arbitrage and hedging techniques (interest rate and currency swaps, financial futures, and currency options, to name just a few). These provide growing linkages between the world's major capital markets and enable technology companies to search for capital across the globe.

Examples of this trend abound:

- Wang Laboratories has raised funds in the Swiss franc convertible bond market.
- Sperry has borrowed in the Swiss franc straight bond market with a novel repayment feature in dollars.
- United Technologies and Intel have borrowed in the Euro-yen market, swapping the proceeds back into dollars.

The significance of these developments is that savings are moving among the world's various capital markets, stimulating the flow of capital from where it is produced to where it can be most gainfully employed. This is particularly evident in the case of Japan, a traditional high-savings country, which is exporting savings to the United States at a rate that substantially offsets its hefty trade surplus with us. Indeed, the flow of foreign capital into the United States over the past few years is ready evidence of the importance of the world's capital markets to U.S. investment and the attractiveness of U.S. investment opportunities to the international investor. The world's leading banks and investment banks play a crucial role in this process through the underwriting and distribution of international securities and the provision of arbitrage mechanisms between the various markets.

This phenomenon is not limited to the debt markets alone. In the past 2 years, some major equity issues have crossed national boundaries. It is not surprising that they have been concentrated in the information and telecommunications industries, where innovation and investment rates are particularly high.

The Reuters, Telerate, and Telecom public equity offerings, all very large by historical standards, show the ability of the U.S. and British markets to respond, even simultaneously, to major demands for risk capital. These transactions are probably indicative of future trends. Spain's private telecommunications company, Telefonica, has already announced plans for initial public equity issues in the world's major stock markets.

U.S. bank holding companies play a significant role in these capital markets through their investment-banking affiliates. Traditionally strong in the Eurocredit and Eurosecurities market, these affiliates are increasingly active in the world's stock markets. Unfortunately, banking regulation in the United States prevents the banks from providing in this country fund-raising services that are routinely provided abroad.

These developments in the international capital markets probably provide the most striking example of the impact of financial innovation by large institutions on the funding alternatives available to companies around the world. The pace of change has been hectic, but the results are quite consistent: companies today have far wider access to a variety of sources and forms of finance than at any time in the past.

CONCLUSIONS

This chapter has outlined key aspects of the role of large financial institutions in supporting technological innovation. It is clear that these institutions support technological innovation in many ways: as users of technology, venture capitalists, equity underwriters, lenders, advisers and consultants, project financiers, and conduits to the international capital markets.

It is equally clear that financial institutions play their most valuable role as innovators developing new and creative financial techniques to meet the increasingly large and complex needs of corporate enterprises. As the demand for funds for technological innovation has increased, new financial mechanisms have been developed to satisfy them, and risk has been to a great extent actuarially dispersed.

It is fair to conclude that "financial innovation *does* support technological innovation." A sensible goal of public policy is, therefore, to encourage the development of a responsive and innovative financial system.

There is much evidence that policymakers around the world are moving toward this conclusion. In the United Kingdom, the development of a deregulated and freely competitive financial system is seen as a critical ingredient in London's continuing preeminence as an international service center and in the ability of British industry to access funds in globally competitive terms. In West Germany, where the banking system has always been relatively free and competitive, there is a growing focus on the need to enhance competition and depth in the equity markets—indeed, half of all new West German equity issues since the war have been introduced in the past 2 years. France has declared its support for the development of a private venture capital industry, and Italy is using privatization of public sector industries to help stimulate a more active equities market. Even in Japan traditional market structures are changing, and the potential effects on that nation's and the world's borrowing and investment patterns are significant.

All of these policy initiatives reflect a growing awareness that responsive, innovative capital markets are key ingredients to economic growth. This trend in public policy dovetails with much more fundamental forces at work in the world's financial markets. Information technologies have broken through the traditional market barriers of geographic distance, special cartels, and exclusive market trading "floors." These technologies are bypassing cartel and regulatory segmentation of the financial markets and leading to integrated, competitive financial institutions. And, as we have seen, we are moving quite rapidly toward an integrated global capital market. This convergence of policy and market trends is encouraging, but we cannot take the pace of deregulation for granted.

In the United States, the remaining panoply of financial regulation impedes innovation by maintaining artificial competitive barriers. Anachronisms like the various prohibitions on interstate banking and the artificial division between commercial and investment banking stand in stark contrast to the rapidly evolving global financial markets that this chapter describes. Indeed, most of these regulations predate the very existence of the technologies and industries that drive our economy today. Continuing critical review and reform of financial regulation in this country remain a key priority if we are to succeed in creating a truly innovative financial system capable of meeting the challenges of funding technological innovation in the last 15 years of this century.

NOTES

1. Office of Technology Assessment. 1984. *Information Technology on Financial Services Systems*. Washington, D.C.: U.S. Government Printing Office.
2. Peter F. Drucker. 1984. Our entrepreneurial economy. *Harvard Business Review* 62(1): 58–64.
3. Nathan Rosenberg. 1982. *Inside the Black Box: Technology and Economics*. New York: Cambridge University Press.

A View From Wall Street

ROBERT H. B. BALDWIN

It can be expected that volatility will persist in high-tech stocks and that there will be very quick reactions to disappointments in earnings. More high-growth companies will look to large corporations as a source of capital. However, if the Treasury Department's proposal to increase the capital gains tax passes, the future of small-growth companies looks very uncertain.

In contrast to more formal presentations in this volume, the following discussion flows from personal experience—in this case, forty years of experience on Wall Street at Morgan Stanley. I joined the firm in 1946, and will highlight here some pertinent points in the history of growth stocks as I observed them and then will comment on some present problems and prospects in this area.

My experience with public offerings of high-growth stocks began early in my career. I started working on the Texas Instruments (TI) account in 1954, when the company had approximately $16 million in sales and approximately $1.6 million of net income. It took me a long while to even begin to understand the product TI was making. Morgan Stanley underwrote a common-stock offering of IBM in 1957, when the stock was selling at 40 times earnings and at less than a 1 percent yield basis. Our major job was to convince people that they should buy a stock that was selling at such a high earnings multiple and such a low yield. That was the beginning of the growth cult in stocks that lasted until 1973.

In 1958 we did an issue for Upjohn, and that issue was so much in demand that it was hard to believe. In fact, it was quoted in the market at 80 times earnings before the prospectus was even out. We finally sold the issue at 30 times earnings when all the other drug stocks were selling at about 20 times earnings. The result in the marketplace was that all the other drug stocks went up and Upjohn did not come down. Then in spring of 1962, there was a sharp drop-off in the market. We had filed a registration statement for a then-little-known company called Schlumberger. We could not proceed with the issue in such an unsettled market until after we had done a General Motors issue that had a good dividend with a resultant high yield. With confidence reestablished in the market, we were finally able to offer Schlumberger successfully, and it subsequently became one of the great growth stocks of the next 20 years. In 1972 the market reached the peak of the growth cult when we sold four issues—Avon, Kresge, Johnson & Johnson, and Lilly—all between 35 and 50 times earnings, and they were all snapped up. I might remind readers that the pension funds at that time were investing in the area of 125 percent of their cash flow in equities.

The advent of high interest rates in 1973 and 1974 and the impact of the 49 percent capital gains tax rate brought the end of the initial public offering (IPO) market for some time. William Perry (in this volume) started tracing what happened with the high-growth stocks in 1973, so his index markedly outperformed the Standard & Poor's 500 average. If he had started with the year 1969, the high-growth stocks' performance relative to the Standard & Poor's 500 average would have been substantially lower but would still have outperformed the market.

Ed Zschau (in this volume) describes what went on when the capital gains tax was reduced in 1978. He and I appeared before the House Ways and Means Committee in early March 1978, when he was representing the American Electronics Association and I was chairman of the Securities Industry Association. In that one day, we explained from two different points of view, he, from the empirical point of view and I, using a very complicated mathematical formula developed by Data Resources, Inc., what we thought would happen to the economy and several economic factors if the capital gains tax was reduced. The late Congressman Bill Steiger was instantly persuaded by our arguments and took up the crusade. He was followed by Jim Jones and, fortunately, by Russell Long, and Congress cut the capital gains tax from 49 percent to 28 percent.

The Treasury Department calculated the potential loss of tax revenues by taking the 21 percent difference between the 49 percent rate and the proposed 28 percent rate and dividing it by the 49 percent rate. Then they multiplied the resulting percentage by the total dollar amount of capital gains paid in the previous year and said that was what the Treasury would lose. The Treasury Department continues to make these static assumptions even now— the assumption that people do not change their investment behavior if tax rates are changed. While some Treasury officials insisted for as many as

2 years after the capital gains tax was reduced that no positive impact had resulted, even they finally admitted that the reduction produced worthwhile results.

Many of the figures mentioned above are noted in other chapters, but it is important to realize that once we got through the period of high interest rates brought on by tight money, which we had to do to bring inflation down, the record number of IPOs and the money for venture capital went hand in hand with the capital gains tax reduction. In 1983 the market had $12.6 billion worth of IPOs; in 1984, $3.8 billion; in January-February 1985, $0.8 billion. This last surge of issues was really the result of the jump in the market in January 1985. During the period 1983–1984 money was thrown at start-ups, which were overvalued both initially and when they went public. Barton Biggs, who was in charge of investment strategy at Morgan Stanley, warned in his investment strategy letters of May and June 1983 that market valuations were being overdone, but it took until late 1983 to slow the flood of new issues and reduce the valuations.

The role of the institutions in the IPO market is of interest here. According to Morgan Stanley's syndicate department, 40 to 50 percent of the issues Morgan Stanley sold in the 1960s and early 1970s went to individuals. In the 1983–1984 period, the figure was more like 20 percent. Only when there was a very difficult job to do and someone added a big selling commission to the sales effort did the figure get up to the 40 or 50 percent range. When the market for those high-flying stocks broke in late 1983 and early 1984, the performance record of many of the institutional buyers who overstayed the market was dismal. Of course, this was one of the reasons why 82 percent of the investment managers underperformed the Standard & Poor's averages in 1984.

As a member of the board of the Geraldine Rockefeller Dodge Foundation, I have heard the presentations of a number of investment managers who came before the board for periodic reviews. Two of the investment managers were leading buyers of the smaller companies' common stocks and had done very well in the several years before mid-1984. However, their comments to the board in mid-1984 were that they had had a wonderful time in the market but were going on to other things. Neither of them has done much investing in small stocks since then.

Many institutions came back into the high-tech market in early 1985, but some did not, which has caused quite a difference in the performance of the two groups. If an investing institution was not in high-tech stocks in the first few months of 1985, it underperformed the market. However, if an institution was in high-tech stocks and stayed too long, it lost a good bit of its January gains in early March. The big question after the early rise in the market was whether an institution wrapped up its profit then and hoped that a conservative policy for the rest of the year would enable it to outperform the Standard & Poor's index. That is a very important point when talking about who the buyers in the stock market are going to be.

Turning to the venture capital firms, I believe these companies are faced with a crisis that has several dimensions. First, there is a crisis of management in the high-tech companies; as a result, the management in venture capital firms is stretched very thin. Second, it is estimated that there are 2,500 high-tech companies that are going to need an estimated $6 billion to $8 billion in capital over the next 3 to 5 years—a time when capital sources will be drying up. My associates tell me that "mezzanine" financing (those subordinated securities which are junior to debt but senior to equity in a company's capitalization) has tended to dry up; it is interesting to note that a great deal of this type of capital was coming from Europe. This means that the venture capital firms must put up more of their own money in third- and fourth-round financings and spend their time on companies that they had previously financed which need help. Thus, I suspect there will not be as much money available for start-up companies. I recently talked with members of three of the oldest venture capital firms who said that they are spending the majority of their time working with old clients in need of help. At the same time, they see a positive side to this, that is, the opportunity to get good positions at reasonable prices in what they consider to be sound companies.

As I consider the future, I recall the words of the head of Morgan Stanley's research division, Dennis Sherva, the acknowledged expert in the investment world on small-growth stocks: "The trouble with investing in small-growth companies is that every week they take one of those stocks out and shoot it." There have been a number of excellent examples recently. As a result of unexpectedly poor earnings, some highly regarded highfliers have been shot, if not in the head, in the foot. Wang set a high in 1984 of 37⅝, and then in 1985 a high of 29¼, after which it dropped on poor earnings estimates to 20⅛. Data General hit a high in 1984 of 59¾, went to 76 in early 1985, and then fell to 48⅝. Computervision was selling at 33; it dropped 10 points in one day. Apollo, which has really done quite well, has been extremely volatile. It had a range in 1984 of 29¼ to 15¾. In early 1985, it dropped from the 29-to-30 range to 20½, and then came back to 23¼ in one day. That kind of volatility is worrisome to investors, particularly individuals. They see a stock lose one-third of its value in one day and think that an insider has taken advantage of them. In early March of 1985, *Barrons* carried a list of 25 issues brought public in 1984 that gained anywhere from 116 percent to 36 percent and a list of issues that had declined between 37 and 95 percent. I am happy to say that Morgan Stanley was the underwriter of 3 of the top 6 performers and sponsored none of the 25 underperformers. But as James D. Marver (in this volume) says, very few of the top performers were high-tech companies and a substantial number of poor performers would be classified as high-tech. It is not a surprise that it has been the quality companies that have done well. They will be able to obtain financing, but it will take very good quality companies to accomplish this feat.

In conclusion, it can be expected that volatility will persist in high-tech stocks and that there will be very quick reactions to disappointments in earnings; the IPO market will return, as it has in the past, but only slowly; valuations for both public offerings and private placements will be much lower. I also believe that more high-growth companies will look to large corporations as a source of capital, the way Intel and Rolm went to IBM. Finally, and of great importance, if the Treasury Department's proposal to increase the capital gains tax by 75 percent passes—which I consider to be extremely ill-advised—the future of the small-growth companies looks very uncertain.

Trends in Financing Innovation

JAMES D. MARVER

A general assessment of financing innovation through the public equity markets indicates that there is much less creativity in the financing of quality emerging growth companies than in the financing of other types of corporations in the United States.

While I have written more broadly elsewhere on the subject of financing innovation,* my purpose here is to comment on two other chapters—those by William J. Perry and by John S. Reed and Glen R. Moreno—in this volume.

In discussing the role of venture capital in financing innovation, Perry says that the initial public offering (IPO) market for emerging growth companies is highly cyclical. He also alludes to its recent revival—but probably only for the more seasoned companies—after a particularly depressed market in 1984. It is my belief that we can no longer attribute cyclicality simply to the economic cycle. In 1983, venture capitalists, company managements, institutional investors, and investment bankers contributed to a frenzied IPO market environment. Fear and greed have always ruled the stock market, and collectively we were inordinately greedy in 1983. We fueled an already hot stock market with many qualitatively uneven offerings. The stock prices of 20 companies went up 50 percent or more by the day after the companies

---

* See James D. Marver, Planning the business for a future initial public offering, ch. 21 in Richard D. Harroch, ed., *Start-up Companies: Planning, Financing, and Operating the Successful Business* (New York: Law Journal Seminars-Press, 1985).

went public. Beginning in the fall of 1983, the stock prices of most of these companies came tumbling down—in many cases to well below their IPO prices. Some were worthy companies, some were not, and the fate of many of those companies still remains to be seen. The backlash in 1984 was a fierce skepticism shown by institutional investors toward new issues—a skittishness that transcended the economy and the Dow Jones Industrial Average generally. There were only 136 IPOs of at least $5 million for industrial companies in 1984, versus 361 in 1983, and their stock prices increased an average of 2.6 percent as of the first day after the offering in 1984, versus 9.2 percent in 1983.

The now-increased cyclicality of the IPO market is especially problematic for companies in an early stage, that is, companies that have a product in a "beta site" (i.e., product test site), or even for those that are beyond that stage—perhaps those with significant revenues but with no consistent or predictable profits. However, even in generally unreceptive markets, there will be public market access for quality companies with proprietary technology, differentiated products, or dominant market share.

In late 1984, for example, I was involved in taking public two companies— Wyse Technology and AST Research—whose valuations were one-half to one-third what they would have been if they had gone public approximately 15 months earlier. The offerings were completed successfully, but the effort was arduous. Stock was sold in one-on-one meetings with institutional investors in contrast to the modus operandi in 1983 when salesmen simply sat by their phones and took orders on the day a registration statement was filed. Investors did not blindly bid up the prices of these two stocks. (Wyse was up 1.8 percent and 0.9 percent after one day and one week, respectively; and AST climbed 6.3 percent and 15.2 percent, respectively.) Instead, after-market price movements reflected fundamental performance achievements by the companies—for example, meeting or surpassing investors' expectations for earnings, or for introducing exciting new products. Accordingly, the prices of Wyse's and AST's stocks were up 57.1 percent and 135.7 percent, respectively, as of March 15, 1985.

Moderate price appreciation of this nature is much better for the capital markets generally and for these firms specifically than are frenetic bidding wars. This renewed rationality provides investors greater confidence in markets and results in the continued access that quality companies have enjoyed in 1985.

Even in very down cycles the IPO market nearly always offers a company a better valuation than an institutionally placed private offering, since the latter vehicle is simply priced at discount—typically 30 percent to 40 percent—to the public market at that time no matter how depressed that market happens to be. Moreover, once a company is public, there is stock for acquisitions; there is access to the public market for additional capital subsequent to the initial public offering; there is liquidity for the stock holdings of the entrepreneur and other shareholders; and there are certain image advantages (e.g., in marketing to large customers who will want the assurance that they are dealing with a public entity—that being, rightly or wrongly, a proxy for business and financial stability). Being public also provides a currency (through options, warrants, and the like) to attract key employees, who increasingly are demanding substantial equity positions (and liquidity for the same) over time.

One by-product of down cycles is that considerable venture funding is being directed to more seasoned companies (relative to start-ups). One way in which this is demonstrated is through the recent proliferation of bridge, or mezzanine, funds. This results not just from the greater selectivity of the public market but, I believe, also from changing appetites for risk, as well as from the excellent values that some mature private companies offer today. In addition, several factors—a skeptical, value-conscious public market; limited access to private capital from institutional investors; limited partic-ipation by substantial corporations in the less attractive deals; and the fact that many companies were premised on imitative business concepts that could not, as Jane Morris, editor of the *Venture Capital Journal*, put it, "achieve marketing differentiation or, in some cases, timely product delivery"—all contributed to the 1984 result that "most venture capital firms, especially those with established portfolios, concentrated more of their efforts in 1984 on working with existing portfolio companies rather than new investments" (*Venture Capital Journal*, February 1985).

Moreover, much venture money in 1984 was invested in public companies. More than one prominent venture capitalist has mentioned to me that if he had liked or invested in a company privately at, say, $20 per share, then he had to love it at $10 per share a year later—especially if the company had enjoyed a year of solid progress and steadily increasing revenues and profitability.

Perry (in this volume) noted what I view as one of the fastest-growing trends in financing innovation: corporate partnering. I worry, though, that in too many cases it is being accomplished more or less willy-nilly and that we will experience a backlash in a year or two as corporations realize (1) that they overpaid for their minority interests, or (2) that they do not know how to integrate their partners' achievements.

Another form of partnering is the spinning off of an R&D idea or work group with the original corporation holding perhaps an initial 50 percent of the equity. (The corporate partner's ownership interest may be diluted as the start-up raises additional capital, or it will remain the same if the corporate partner makes subsequent pro rata investments.) Tektronix, in Oregon, was the first major corporation to pursue this strategy consistently. Its initial spinoff was Planar Corporation, a manufacturer of electroluminescent flat panel displays.

One additional mechanism, utilized recently by International Business

Machines Corporation (IBM) and Convergent Technologies, Inc., is the organizing of a separate, quasi-independent business unit to develop and produce a new product. The IBM Personal Computer (PC) emerged in this way: in 1981 Philip D. Estridge was provided a 12-person task force in Boca Raton, Florida. This independent business unit had the responsibility for developing what *Electronics News* recently called "small microprocessor based systems for tiny business and personal use." That unit is now the Entry Systems Division of IBM and has 10,000 employees. It shipped 2 million units in 1984, and it is considered a $5-billion business for IBM today.

The R&D limited partnership is another financing mechanism that is growing rapidly in popularity. Despite some highly visible failures, the concept's popularity is demonstrated by the fact that large new funds are announced every month or so. My own belief is that this is a relatively costly means of financing growth, particularly if the young company has no mechanism for buying out the royalty stream or for repurchasing any equity that may have been offered. There are three negative consequences of this type of financing. First, there is a direct negative effect on a company's valuation due to the reduced net income. (Valuation is typically a multiple of net income.) Second, there is an indirect negative effect on the valuation because of the fact that, except in the biomedical field, the R&D partnership is typically seen as a second-class mechanism for raising funds; it is often used by companies that would be unsuccessful in selling straight equity. Third, the problem of control often arises, since what is beneficial for the limited partners and what is beneficial for the company are not always coincident. I experienced this firsthand recently when a designer, manufacturer, and seller of turnkey office automation products decided that it could expand its market significantly by making available to larger potential customers its software component only, rather than software bundled into a computer of its own design. The company's co-general-partner in its R&D limited partnership, which had provided $2 million in funds for the development of this product, insisted that the company not offer stand-alone software because the partnership receives a percentage of gross revenues, which obviously are much higher for a turnkey product that incorporates a computer. The computer portion of the product, however, has far lower margins than the software, and its inclusion would restrict the company's customer base to small offices that are not already automated. As a result, the co-general-partner has inhibited the company's ability to provide the type of product it believes will be most acceptable to its market. This is the kind of help that young companies do not need.

I wish to make one comment on John Reed and Glen Moreno's interesting and provocative chapter. It is quite clear from their discussion that commercial banks are in an excellent position to help start-ups in a variety of ways.

Although their participation has been limited to date in most of the following areas (interest-rate swaps excepted), commercial banks are not precluded by law from raising equity and debt capital for corporations privately, from providing a variety of merger and acquisition services, or from assisting clients with their corporate partnering. In addition, certain commercial banks have performed advisory functions for start-ups. They have offered venture advisory work by determining capital needs, assisting in the preparation of business plans, and helping refer companies to venture capitalists and other entrepreneurs. One of California's largest banks has even established a formal IPO advisory service to educate young companies about the process and even to select and to negotiate with investment bankers themselves. This service is one that investment bankers typically want to provide. We offer the education process gratis, and obviously we wish to be involved in this informal process partly because it is a means of initiating, developing, and nurturing what we hope will be a long-term relationship. The commercial bank's ultimate benefit is presumably a long-term commercial banking relationship, which typically is probably much less lucrative than the investment banker's relationship and thus probably justifies the fee that the commercial bank charges for this service.

In closing, my general assessment of innovation financing through the public equity markets leads me to posit that there is much less creativity in the financing of quality growth companies than there is creativity in the financing of other types of corporations in the United States. Entrepreneurial companies, and especially their investment bankers, appear to focus less on the lowest cost of funds and much more on the future availability of funds. As investment bankers for high technology companies, we are very concerned with accomplishing a "successful offering." One cannot price new issues precisely. Our intent is to be roughly right rather than precisely wrong. Lesser companies must resort to warrants, indices, and the like, but for quality high technology companies we essentially want to do straight equity financing when a company makes its initial public offering, and we are striving for an after-market price that climbs consistently over time and in concert with the company's results, which we hope are also improving consistently. Basically, we want to be able to return to the public markets repeatedly, largely since the quality high technology company typically requires considerable capital as it grows. Consequently, it is very important for investors to have made money the last time the particular company raised funds.

If as investment bankers we limit ourselves to quality companies with solid track records, and if we price these issues realistically, we are much more likely to achieve the desired results. For example, my firm, L.F. Rothschild, Unterberg, Towbin, took Intel Corporation public in 1971 through an $8.25-million equity offering. Subsequently we raised $150 million in convertible debt (1980), $40 million through Puerto Rican Industrial Revenue Bonds

(1982), $50 million in Euro-Yen bonds (1985), and $93.6 million through the issue of $215 million in zero coupon notes with attached warrants (1985). Another example is Tandem Computer Corporation, which we took public in an $8-million offering in 1977 and for which we subsequently raised $14.1 million in equity (1978), $23.4 million in equity (1979), $93.1 million in equity (1980), and $3.1 million through a sale-leaseback of a warehouse facility (1983).

I am pleased to report that this advocated behavior is already occurring. In 1984 there were many fewer IPOs, and they were generally of greater quality than those in the previous year. I believe that partially as a result of our industry's more conservative posture, the after-market performance of these new issues has been more consistently positive. As of March 15, 1985, the 1984 IPOs had appreciated an average of 19.5 percent in contrast with the 1983 IPOs which had declined 0.6 percent (though general market changes are not taken into account in these figures). Because of this implicit self-regulation, there remains a very reasonable IPO market in 1985. (The 17 IPOs of over $5 million by industrial companies had appreciated an average of 18.3 percent by mid-March 1985.) It is not a frenzied market; indeed, it is a skeptical market, but it is highly receptive to high-quality high technology companies.

Technology and Trade:
A Study of U.S. Competitiveness
in Seven Industries

N. BRUCE HANNAY

In the aggregate, the U.S. economy is less dependent on foreign trade than many other nations, but more and more U.S. industries are finding that they must compete internationally to survive. Despite the emerging competitive situation, international trade and relationships with other economies simply are not yet accorded the same importance in the United States as in Japan and Western Europe. It is essential that public policy take into account the international implications of any new initiatives, not only in policy formulation but also in administrative practice.

For some years after World War II, the leadership of the United States in the development and application of technology, and in world trade that stemmed from it, was unchallenged. At least in part, this resulted from the circumstances that left us as the only major industrialized country with a manufacturing capability that was intact at the end of the war. But, as other countries rebuilt their economies over the next two decades, they employed the best available technology in modern, efficient production facilities. With active participation by their governments, their industries developed along lines that not only took care of national needs, but also gave them an advantage in world trade competition in selected market areas. The United States actively encouraged and supported this rebuilding with both financial and technical assistance.

By the early 1970s, doubts about our competitiveness began to emerge, and they have been expressed with increasing urgency since then. Our productivity growth rate was significantly lower than that of other countries, and it was declining. Our industrial plant was aging. Our historically favor-

This chapter is adapted from *The Competitive Status of U.S. Industry—An Overview* (Washington, D.C.: National Academy Press, 1985) by Lowell W. Steele and N. Bruce Hannay.

479

able trade balance first diminished, then turned negative. Our trade in tech-nology-intensive products began to reflect a shrinking share of world markets. It was evident that we were not using technology as effectively as we might, or perhaps as well as some other countries were using it. Our innovative capacity was, for the first time, in doubt. A large part of our R&D was for defense and space, and without commercial objectives. Key industries, like steel, autos, and consumer electronics, were in deep trouble. Countries we had been assisting were becoming, to an ever greater extent, successful competitors in world trade.

The unanswered question then, and to a certain degree today also, was whether this trend reflected only an inevitable closing of the gap, as the war-damaged economies of Europe and Japan recovered, or whether it was a sign of inherent weakness in our own system, weakness that would eventually undermine our preeminent world position and even bring a loss of leadership. There were those who thought they saw such weakness in our educational system, or in industry's management practices, or in government policy and the relationship between the public and private sectors. Compounding the difficulty in understanding the implication of trade shifts has been the per-sistent imbalance in exchange rates.

When these concerns first emerged, the National Academy of Engineering (NAE) undertook what turned out to be a series of studies that examined central issues relating to technical and international economic and trade is-sues.[1-4] The studies were conducted by a committee, established in coop-eration with the National Research Council, of experts from industry, academia, labor and government—scientists, engineers, economists, business and fi-nancial experts, labor representatives, and government specialists.

The first major study of the committee was a broad examination of the relationship among technology, trade, and U.S. competitiveness.[2] The pur-pose of the study was to reach an understanding of the issues and to determine priorities for the committee's future work. The main conclusion was that our national performance with respect to technological innovation, productivity improvement, and competitiveness in world trade was primarily determined by the health of the domestic economy and the constraints put on it, rather than by events outside the United States. Based on this examination the committee subsequently studied the effects of federal tax policy, regulation, and antitrust policy on technological innovation and recommended modifi-cation of those policies in ways that would be likely to increase our rate of technological change.[3] In certain areas, policies have since moved in ways consistent with those recommendations, to some extent at least.

The conclusions reached in these studies tended to be generalizations. Even though federal policies have a unique impact on each industrial sector, very little research had been done to disaggregate industry in the analysis of governmental policies in the areas of technology and trade. This led the committee to embark on industry-by-industry sectoral studies, choosing seven industries that represented a broad spectrum of characteristics. Each of the sectors contributes significantly to employment and to the GNP; the industries range from high to low technology, from rapidly growing to mature, from capital-intensive to those that are not, from industrial to consumer products, and from industries dominated by large firms to those with many small companies. The industries selected were automobiles, electronics, pharmaceuticals, machine tools, fibers and textiles, steel, and commercial aircraft.[4]

The committee's belief in undertaking these studies was that by understanding specific industrial sectors better, public policies could be more effectively formulated. The study program was designed to identify global shifts in production and in trade, to relate shifts in international comparative industrial advantage to technological and other factors, and to assess the probable impact of public policy options on the rate and nature of technological change and on the international competitiveness of the U.S. industry.

There follows a very brief review of some of the results of these sectoral studies. First, specific findings are presented, by sector, then some similarities and differences among the sectors are noted, and finally some general conclusions are drawn.

FINDINGS OF INDUSTRY STUDIES

Automobiles

At the time of the study, the automobile industry had recently undergone major changes, and there was great uncertainty as to the outcome of those changes. The U.S. automobile companies faced severe foreign competition at a time when they had to deal with restructuring their products in the face of great market uncertainty. Huge amounts of capital were required at a time when future profits were in doubt. It was unclear whether the prevailing situation was temporary, whether maturation of the industry was forcing a long-term shift to lower-cost foreign manufacture, or whether new technology and production practices would fundamentally alter the industry.

For some years prior to the mid-1970s, technological change had been incremental in the industry. Key competitive factors in the mass market were cost, styling, and a strong dealer network. Over the course of the last several years, however, the industry had once again introduced new technological concepts, including, for example, downsizing, new materials, electronic controls, and engine design.

The imposition of government regulations regarding safety, pollution, and energy efficiency also had a major impact on the industry. These mandates claimed both resources and management attention at a time of competitive upheaval, high interest rates, inflation, and a sluggish economic growth.

The study also analyzed foreign competition in detail. In the early 1980s the Japanese automobile firms had an estimated landed cost advantage of $750 to $1,500 per small vehicle. This advantage reflected differences in labor rates, materials costs, and productivity, as well as the effect of exchange rates. Despite the popular image of Japanese superiority in advanced technology, the Japanese advantage was found to lie rather in management—management of technology, of operations, and of the work force—and in culture—attitudes toward work and both individual and corporate responsibility. Other major factors that contributed to the Japanese advantage were the reliability of parts suppliers' delivery schedules, elimination of downtime, drastic reduction of setup and rework time, and a job structure and workplace environment that placed responsibility for quality and output on the workers.

The Japanese situation contrasts starkly with the adversarial labor-management relationship in the U.S. industry. Planning and control of work have been performed by staff groups organizationally remote from the workplace, and supervision has emphasized the meeting of demanding production goals. This system does not inspire loyalty or commitment, and it fails to take advantage of the knowledge and experience of the work force.

The efficacy of available policy options in the automobile industry is strongly influenced by the scenario selected for future events. If, for example, the industry is mature, production is likely to continue to diffuse around the world; the U.S. industry is likely to be much smaller and to emphasize specialty manufacture, with less value added. Without permanent trade barriers, cost disadvantages on standard models would be unlikely to be reversible. If the difficulties are seen as transient, while the industry restructures its product line and manufacturing capacity, then temporary protective measures help. If a new period of technological innovation and performance-oriented competition is emerging, then U.S. management has an opportunity to re-establish leadership. Even so, the U.S. share of value added is likely to decline, especially on standard models.

Electronics

The United States was the unchallenged leader in the electronics industry for some years after World War II and has maintained its leadership in much, but not all, of the industry for four decades. A conspicuous loss of leadership to Japan has occurred in consumer electronics, and the United States now faces a major challenge from Japan in other areas of electronics.

The development of the industry in the United States differs from that in the rest of the world. Except for defense and space electronics, the government has had little involvement (although the Defense Department's VHSIC program is expected to have significant commercial fallout in semiconductors). The industry has been characterized by a few dominant, innovative, giant firms in telecommunications and in computers, and by many entrepreneurial firms that have excelled at innovating new products and developing new markets in semiconductors, components, subsystems and systems, and, more recently, in telecommunications and computers. In these smaller firms, the level of vertical integration is low. The consumer electronics industry, before it lost its markets to Japan, was dominated by old-line radio manufacturers.

In contrast to the U.S. situation, the involvement of foreign governments in supporting and guiding the industry is common. Electronics is regarded as vital to future economic growth, national security, and even a self-image of leadership or equality in the industrialized world. Most of the manufacture comes from large, broadly based, highly integrated companies.

Japan has advanced dramatically in electronics. Government support is extensive—for very large scale integration (VLSI), pattern recognition, artificial intelligence, and fifth-generation computers and supercomputers. The financial structure of Japanese companies and the financial environment in which they operate are very different from those of U.S. companies—in recent years the cost of capital has been little more than half the U.S. rate.

In the United States, R&D and capital costs in electronics are very high, because the technology is changing extremely rapidly. Volume must be sufficient to generate the needed resources for investing in technology, added capacity, and new equipment. Another industry problem is the serious shortage of the electronic engineers, computer scientists and engineers, software programmers, and technicians needed to maintain a strong competitive position.

The U.S. position in four key industry segments—semiconductors, computers, telecommunications, and consumer electronics—is summarized below:

1. In semiconductors, the United States retains a lead but is under serious challenge by the Japanese. Japanese trade and investment barriers severely restrict imports, but U.S. firms supply more than half of Europe's total needs. The U.S. industry is changing. New entrants are inhibited by high start-up costs. Systems manufacturers are integrating forward. Major foreign investments are being made in U.S. firms to acquire technology and market share. U.S. strength results from aggressive technology development and a strong equipment industry. Japanese focus on narrow, high-volume markets, such as 16K and 64K RAMs, has enabled heavy penetration in those markets, but the United States is ahead in microprocessors and custom circuits. In the future its lead will depend on its success in resolving capital and human resource problems, in maintaining its present leadership in basic research and innovation, and in removing trade and investment barriers.

2. In computers, the United States retains a powerful position in mainframes, minicomputers, and microcomputers, in software, and in distribution and service. In hardware and standardized high-volume manufacture, it faces a severe challenge from Japan.

3. In telecommunications, government intervention plays a crucial role.

The United States has a strong position in switching and transmission. The Japanese are challenging in optical transmission. Competition in digital technology is severe. The structure of the U.S. industry is undergoing profound change, the consequences of which are not yet clear. The ability of the restructured industry to continue to lead the world in basic advances in telecommunications science and in new telecommunications technology remains to be seen. Interestingly, both Japan and the United Kingdom are privatizing their telephone monopolies.

4. In consumer electronics, since the mid-1950s the United States has fallen from a position of dominance in market share and in pioneer technology and all but ceded position to Japan. Japanese firms have been aggressive in adopting integrated circuitry and in developing manufacturing techniques that cost and improve quality. A combination of long-term commitment to consumer markets and aggressive application of technology, aided by long-term availability of capital, a well-trained work force, a protected home market, favorable exchange rates, and willingness to use discriminatory pricing, have propelled Japan to a position of world dominance.

Any consideration of possible steps to strengthen the competitive position of the U.S. electronics industry should address four issues: long-range research, capital formation, human resources, and international trade policies. The management of this industry has a record of innovative, flexible approaches to problems. It should be encouraged to continue its experimentation in cooperative programs, joint ventures, and the like. Antitrust policy must recognize the imperative of evolving to meet world competition. Tax and depreciation policies that recognize the large and rapid obsolescence of equipment are of critical importance.

Strengthening the academic base that produces needed skills, from technician to Ph.D. scientist and engineer, warrants high priority. Government support of basic research and increased cooperative industry-university programs should both be strengthened.

The high leverage associated with electronics leadership has led virtually all developed countries to undertake programs to foster a domestic industry. Aggressive pursuit of multilateral trade liberalization must receive persistent, high-priority attention.

Steel

The study of the steel industry concentrated on the integrated producers, who constitute 80 percent of capacity and face the greatest competitive difficulties.

The importance of the steel industry to the economy and national security is universally accepted, but it is far from clear what part of our needs should be supplied internally. The industry is no longer technologically progressive. Of 28 process advances currently under development, only 2—direct reduction and continuous casting, both well established technologically—are expected to achieve significant adoption in 5 years, and only 5 others are projected to be adopted in 20 years. It appears that capital limitations and the projected rate of return on the investment, rather than the proprietary nature of the technology, are the problems. In recent years some of the principal changes in process technology have been the result of investment in plant that utilizes technology developed many years earlier but not adopted previously. New alloys are introduced more rapidly than new production processes because the plant investment is much lower. For this reason, the specialty steel industry has fared better than the large producers.

Leadership in technology does not assure economic success, and technology by itself cannot solve the steel problem. In addition to the pricing and capacity policies of foreign competitors, such factors as labor productivity, the cost of raw materials, energy, and labor, and plant location in relation to markets play a powerful role.

In terms of delivered cost, which is the important criterion, the study estimated that most of the scrap-based producers and many current-practice integrated steel plants in the interior of the United States should be able to meet the full-cost delivered price of Japanese competitors. Ten percent or more of domestic capacity is estimated to be nonviable and a candidate for shutdown.

Long-term estimates of capacity and consumption suggest an overcapacity problem for many years. Developing and Eastern bloc countries account for most of the additions to capacity. Thus, the domestic industry can expect to face increased pressure from imports and worldwide potential for overproduction that will lead to lower prices. The problem of chronic overcapacity results from a number of reinforcing circumstances: (1) foreign government investment in capacity, irrespective of demand; (2) foreign subsidies that increase output and reduce the rate of plant closures; (3) protectionism in domestic markets; and (4) growth in the use of steel that lags the growth in GNP.

Any attempt to revitalize the industry must balance a number of complex and often contradictory factors: determining the minimum domestic capacity needed for national security, achieving the inevitable restructuring while protecting the interests of affected workers and communities, providing U.S. consumers with access to the lowest-cost steel available worldwide, ensuring free and fair global trade in steel, and recognizing the aspirations of developing countries. Irrespective of the policy changes implemented, the industry will encounter some permanent shrinkage and represent a declining fraction of world capacity, and no measures will make all of those involved—steel producers, steel workers, and consumers—better off.

Fibers, Textiles, and Apparel

Developing countries regard manufacture of fabrics and apparel as an important source of employment and export earnings. They have extensive government programs to encourage investment and growth, to establish favorable terms for exports, and to restrict imports. Conversely, U.S. policies have been designed to slow the decrease in employment resulting from import competition.

Each of the three segments of this textile complex—fibers and yarn, textiles, and apparel—stands in a somewhat different competitive position. Fibers and yarn are produced primarily by large, powerful concerns that are able to finance investment in technology development and new equipment. The United States enjoys a favorable position in both the technology and trade of these products. The industry is capital-intensive, and its technology diffuses rapidly. The technology for this industry is developed by the fiber producers, who emphasize new fibers first and then reductions in cost. Economies of scale and aggressive R&D have enabled the U.S. firms to maintain competitive leadership, and this leadership can be sustained.

Technological advance in textiles is concentrated in the equipment manufacturers; little R&D is conducted by the fabric and apparel producers. Advances in textile equipment diffuse rapidly around the world and enable the developing countries to upgrade their operations. The U.S. position in textile machinery has weakened dramatically. Imports represented 9 percent of shipments in 1963 and 50 percent in 1980, with West Germany and Switzerland accounting for over 60 percent. Many key technical advances are now being made overseas.

Technological advances in fabrics have emphasized improved productivity. Many of the major advances have been made abroad, but U.S. firms have adopted them, along with other international competitors. The United States now has a clear technological lead in nonwovens, but that lead is expected to narrow. In general, the United States has a strong favorable balance of trade, but the picture is highly variable.

Computer technology has had a substantial impact on apparel manufacture, but the industry is still labor-intensive; economies of scale are not an important driving force. Smaller firms have been particularly hard hit by changes in technology and competition. Most have lacked the expertise, capital, and vision to take advantage of foreign market opportunities and to establish lower-cost foreign manufacturing facilities. As a consequence, these firms have been under severe competitive and financial pressure, and many have disappeared.

Japanese firms have responded to changing international competition by following the shifting of comparative advantage to developing countries. By a combination of establishing local facilities and partnerships, licensing, loans, and intricate purchasing and selling arrangements, the Japanese have played an active role in the emerging textile complex in the Asian-Pacific area.

The textile complex in the United States faces a shortage of technical workers and managers at all levels in comparison with what is needed to sustain a strong competitive position. The levels of compensation and limited attractiveness of careers in the industry contribute to the problem. Aggressive pursuit of technological developments and improved competence in international business are critical to success.

The need for developing countries to increase their exports and the high future growth in developing-country markets create political and diplomatic dilemmas that complicate any attempts to change the international framework of trade.

Trade in textiles is subject to destabilizing surges. Mechanisms and resources for more rapid response to sudden changes could be helpful. Even though tariff barriers are substantial, nontariff barriers, such as customs clearance, inspection, and local-content requirements are often greater deterrents and more difficult to identify. Present restrictions on offshore processing of some stages of manufacture reduce the flexibility of producers to achieve lowest cost and thus diminish the U.S. international competitiveness.

Machine Tools

The very competitive machine tool industry is highly fragmented with many small, independent, family-owned firms. The industry is relatively small. Nevertheless, it is of key strategic importance both to national security and to international economic competitiveness. Continued improvements in productivity are critically dependent on a healthy, technologically advanced machine tool industry. The availability of sophisticated but inexpensive new electronic devices, especially microprocessors and sensors, is opening up major opportunities for automation of production equipment.

A number of indications of the declining health of the U.S. industry have emerged. The U.S. share of world exports dropped from 23 percent in 1964 to 7 percent in 1980, while imports increased from 4 percent to 24 percent of domestic consumption. The United States now has a negative balance of trade in machine tools, and it is worsening. The major problem facing the industry is the traditional one of extreme cyclicality. The severe swings in volume reduce the investment attractiveness of the industry and lead to undercapitalization. This, in turn, severely impedes the upgrading of facilities and introduction of new technology. The same conditions have led to a persistent inability of the industry to attract skilled manpower at all levels— tool and die makers, industrial engineers, software programmers, and general management. Employment uncertainty has deterred entry. College courses pertaining to manufacturing technology generally have not been highly regarded by students, and careers have had a low appeal. There has been little government funding of manufacturing research. Only very recently has attention in the United States been given to these circumstances, which are in sharp contrast to the situation in both Europe and Japan.

The reduction in exports takes on added significance because export sales can help alleviate the extreme swings of the domestic market. Export sales also provide additional revenue to help defray the cost of developing and introducing new products and new manufacturing technology.

In general, the technology of American machine tools as products is roughly comparable to that of other nations, although American products are regarded as behind competition in the use of electronic controls and the associated software. Also, U.S. manufacturing technology employing machine tools is behind in moving to flexible, computer-integrated manufacture and in applying numerical controls, both of which were first introduced in the United States. Given the decline in market share and unattractive financial performance, the prospects are uncertain that the industry will exploit technology to the extent necessary to attain a competitive edge.

Small, family-owned U.S. firms are poorly equipped to pursue international sales. Moreover, the loan criteria of the Export-Import Bank focus on transactions that are much larger than typical machine tool sales.

The long-term viability of the U.S. industry will be strongly influenced by the growth and vitality of the U.S. economy, the level and stability of interest rates, and the development of a coherent export policy. Measures aimed more directly at supporting exports by small business would be especially useful to the industry, as would increased attention to development of applicable human resource skills and of advanced manufacturing technology. Changes in management with respect to pursuit of exports, investment in new technology, human resource development, and closer ties with customers are also called for.

Pharmaceuticals

The profitability, excellent growth, and dramatic technical advances of the U.S. pharmaceutical industry have tended to obscure the pronounced deterioration in relative performance of U.S. pharmaceutical firms vis-à-vis their foreign counterparts. In part, this unnoticed deterioration results from the long time lag—as much as 20 years—between decisions to invest in discovery of new drugs and a perceptible impact of any drugs discovered on the sales and profitability of the firm. In addition, the general and very rapid advance in the basic sciences of human health is generating sales growth worldwide, and this makes the U.S. industry appear to be growing, innovative, and profitable. Thus, the relative performance of pharmaceutical firms vis-à-vis other sections of the U.S. economy looks favorable despite the relative decline internationally.

As evidence of our deteriorating relative position, in roughly the past two decades the U.S. share of world pharmaceutical R&D expenditures has fallen by one-half, as have the number of new U.S.-owned drugs entering clinical trial, the U.S. share of world production, and the U.S. share of world exports. Foreign firms now market their innovations directly in the United States. For their part, U.S. firms have invested widely in other countries and this is affecting the planning and conduct of their R&D.

The principal determinant of competitive success is the ability to introduce a continuing stream of commercially successful new products through technological innovation. However, the regulatory costs and delays imposed on U.S.-based R&D are significantly higher than elsewhere. The costs associated with the development and introduction of new drugs have become so large that access to the sales volume available from worldwide markets has become a critical consideration in determining competitive viability. Thus, the deterioration of the U.S. share of world markets is cause for concern. Small firms are in an especially precarious position because they lack the financial resources to develop new drugs and clear them through the regulatory agency.

Changes in government regulations and in the regulatory climate with respect to R&D, introduction of new therapeutic agents, export of experimental drugs, and acceptance of foreign data could have high leverage on competitive position. The process is at present subject to intense political pressure, requires massive amounts of documentation, and tends to delay clinical trial, even under carefully controlled conditions. Reforms that clarify and expedite the Food and Drug Administration's (FDA's) new drug-approval process, by providing a more significant role for experts from outside the FDA and by encouraging a more productive dialogue with industry, could significantly reduce the cost and time required to introduce new drugs. Also, the U.S. effort to deter economic concentration can limit the merging of firms that are not large enough themselves to be viable in global competition.

The lengthy time required to obtain FDA approval eliminates nearly half of the intended 17-year protection granted by a patent. This led the NAE committee to recommend restoring patent life consumed by regulatory review to increase the incentive for innovation. Very recently, the government has taken a step of this kind.

Civil Aviation Manufacturing

The civil aviation industry, including both manufacturers and the commercial airlines, is in the midst of profound change. Some features of the change result from domestic actions and circumstances, for example, economic deregulation of air transport, while others result from external trends and events, such as the emerging foreign competition in commercial transports, civil helicopters, and business aircraft.

No other industry plays as crucial a role as aviation in national security, national economic health, and foreign trade. Civil aircraft manufacture provides both the base load for key design and production teams and a huge (15,000 firms) production infrastructure in a high state of readiness for national defense. Export of aircraft continues to be the largest single source of revenue from trade in manufactured goods (and second only to agriculture overall). After dominating world markets since the end of World War II, the U.S. aircraft industry now faces a significantly more challenging competitive environment. Among the factors worthy of special notice are the following:

1. Due to a combination of deep recession and economic deregulation, the financial performance of domestic airlines has deteriorated drastically, and continuation of the airlines' traditional role in launching new aircraft is uncertain.

2. Aircraft manufacture is recognized as an attractive industry worldwide. After decades of persistence the Europeans, through Airbus Industries, have demonstrated commercial success. The Japanese have targeted aircraft as a growth industry of the future. Many smaller countries are mounting programs in helicopters and small aircraft. These foreign competitors enjoy a special supportive relationship with their governments that gives them access to sources of financing for developing, production, and sale of aircraft that are not available to a private firm in the United States.

3. Air travel in the United States is projected to grow less rapidly than in foreign markets. Thus, export sales and product planning for export markets will become increasingly important.

4. Countries are demanding a participative role in manufacture as the price of entry into their markets. The manufacturers seek to spread risks and to develop additional capital. Thus, aircraft manufacture is becoming increasingly internationalized.

5. Because of the industry's close connection with national security, the U.S. government plays a determining role in controlling aircraft exports. The task of balancing national security and commercial interests is becoming increasingly complex and controversial.

6. The technology underlying the design and manufacture of aircraft and engines offers major opportunities for improved performance, economy, and reliability. The United States has leadership or parity in all the key technologies. However, the margin of leadership has narrowed, and competitors have the capability to equal or even surpass us if U.S. effort loses momentum either in R&D or in its application to new aircraft. Since trade in aircraft is dominated by foreign governmental actions that apply economic and social

criteria not possible for a privately owned company, trade negotiations become central to competitive success. In the competitive environment that is emerging, the traditional U.S. approach of seeking to create discipline in the rules of international trade faces serious handicaps, unless it is pursued more vigorously with respect to (a) negotiation of agreements that prohibit trade-distorting practices, (b) inclusion in the agreements of all countries competing in aircraft markets for all classes of planes, and (c) provision of adequate response mechanisms and deterrents to violators.

In considering policy initiatives for the future, the following areas warrant special attention:

• Ensuring pursuit of U.S. interests in trade agreements and in mechanisms for timely, effective response to predatory practices.
• Modifying lending practices of the Export-Import Bank to ensure that its terms and conditions are adequate to meet the behavior of competitors.
• Preserving momentum in research and technology development.
• Examining more broadly the trade-offs between technology transfer and the impact of export restrictions on the U.S. competitive position.
• Ensuring maximum synergy between national defense and commercial interests in the development, design, and production of aircraft.

SECTORAL SIMILARITIES AND DIFFERENCES

What similarities and differences appear among these various industries? What lessons can be drawn with respect to public policy, management practices, and academic programs and priorities?

Need for a Global Perspective

The most dramatic common theme that emerges is that, despite the disparate nature of these various industries, all must now be termed world-scale industries. They must be managed in that context, and public policy must reflect the reality of growing and more pervasive international competition. For some industries, escalating costs of R&D, combined with burgeoning demands for large quantities of capital to obtain modern facilities, necessitate tapping global markets in order to generate the needed sales volume. For others, decisions regarding capacity expansion and future demand must be made in a global context; otherwise, serious errors—either in creating overcapacity or in lacking capacity to serve growth—are almost inevitable. Thus, even though, in the aggregate, the U.S. economy is less dependent on foreign trade than many other nations, more and more U.S. industries are finding that they must compete internationally in order to survive. Moreover, in most of the industries studied, foreign markets will be growing more rapidly than domestic ones.

Despite the emerging competitive situation, international trade and relationships with other economies simply are not yet accorded the same importance in the United States as in Japan and Western Europe. The sheer size and vitality of the U.S. market, combined with the size and richness of the land mass of the United States, make foreign trade and relations with other countries seem remote and relatively unimportant.

The low level of proficiency in foreign languages and the limited knowledge of foreign cultures and customs provided by our educational system are an unmistakable indicator of the limited importance attached to international trade. Government policies—antitrust, regulatory, tax, trade, and many others—mostly reflect concern with domestic issues, and there is little regard for their effect on U.S. competitiveness in international markets.

This same situation is mirrored in U.S. executive development programs, which usually put little weight on international experience, and in the U.S. approach to product planning. Most U.S. firms develop products for the American market and then offer them, more or less as an afterthought, for export. Consumer products reflect American tastes and standards of living. Industrial products are built to U.S. standards and reflect U.S. trade-offs among the costs of labor, capital, and energy. In contrast, the Japanese work diligently and remarkably effectively to achieve congruence between the requirements of domestic and export markets.

The recurring hostility between government and industry on market matters, and the bureaucratic tangles that ensnarl licensing, certification, approvals, and so on, also reflect the low importance attached to trade, as do the limited resources made available to support trade negotiations, to administer customs regulations, and to collect and analyze trade and economic data and information on foreign technology.

Control of technology transfer, while legitimate for national security, has not been consistent and imposes delays that call into question the reliability of U.S. shippers. In addition, the control is sometimes imposed without sufficient perspective on the availability to foreign customers of alternatives that could negate the results the United States seeks and without adequate consideration of the potential negative impact on the competitive status of U.S. firms.

The value-added tax (VAT) widely used in Europe has a built-in bias that supports exports as compared with our corporate income tax. In the United States continual and extensive education and persuasion are required to preserve critical financial supports, such as DISC and Export-Import Bank loans, while, in contrast, foreign government representatives are frequently virtual partners in the negotiations for large transactions and provide visible evidence of their government's support for the transaction.

Inconsistency of Policies, Institutions, and Priorities

A second major common theme was the lack of coherence and mutual reinforcement among policies and institutions and the lack of consistency in setting priorities that one generally finds in the United States. This contrasts with the situation in Japan and, to some extent, in West Germany. In those countries monetary, fiscal, export, and tax policies, the educational system, capital markets, and industrial management and labor relations have a consistency and coherence of purpose that we lack. This is not to suggest that we should adopt their ways, as the pluralism of our society and our institutions and a government based on checks and balances have both served us well. Nevertheless, it is imperative for us to scrutinize our own strengths and weaknesses with a realistic eye in the light of both the growing importance of international trade and the strengthened competition we face.

Small Firms Handicapped

Another sectoral similarity is the handicap of small firms in pursuing international sales. Some important industries, such as machine tools and textiles, are characterized by small firms, and in electronics small firms are prominent. The foreign-language deficiency noted above is one impediment. Inadequate knowledge of foreign markets and foreign business and legal practices is another. Many banks, especially those outside the major coastal cities, have no experience in international finance to aid local businessmen. The NAE studies pointed out that appropriate help for small business is thought to be lacking at government agencies. The priorities and lending practices of the Export-Import Bank in the past have been directed very heavily toward large transactions, which virtually exclude smaller firms; fortunately, that situation is now changing.

High Cost of Capital

The cost and availability of capital for U.S. companies (particularly in electronics and steel), as compared with foreign competitors, and the projected rate of return on investments increasingly threaten the ability of important U.S. industries to invest the capital necessary to remain competitive in international markets. In part, the difference in the cost of capital reflects special foreign government tax programs, as well as direct subsidies, to foster exports. In part, it also includes general economic considerations, such as the rate of saving, interest rates, taxes, rate of inflation, and monetary policy. But the problem of projected rates of return goes farther. It involves problems of highly cyclical industries (such as steel and machine tools), inadequate rate of return in critical industries, short time frames for evaluating investment by U.S. managers and U.S. investors, and volatility in flows of capital. This last subject is particularly important because of its impact on the time horizon for planning investment—the pursuit of higher return on investment, in principle, leads to greater efficiency in the allocation of resources, but it may lead to shortened time horizons and risk-aversion in investment decisions.

Role of Developing Countries

The developing countries are becoming increasingly important in the competitive equation. In some industries—steel, and fibers and textiles—their impact is evident through increases in capacity. In other industries—autos, pharmaceuticals, and aircraft—their impact is a combination of the growing importance of their markets, due to the more rapid growth of these less mature economies, and their insistence on domestic content as the price of market access.

Shortage of Trained Personnel

In several sectors—electronics, machine tools, and textiles—there is a widespread shortage of trained people at various levels, from shop floor to management. The shortage applies to specific technical skills in electronics, computers, software, and machine design. Two other broad personnel categories of special importance are people trained in international business, with direct experience in foreign commerce, and people trained in sophisticated manufacturing. The latter reflects the low status of manufacturing in the United States, in education and as a career, a situation that is in striking contrast to that in Japan, West Germany, and elsewhere.

The shortage of specific technical skills is particularly acute in electronics. Our production of electronic and other engineers is relatively much lower than that of our major international competitors, especially Japan and West Germany. Moreover, the shortage of faculty in electronic engineering and computer science, resulting from the competition with industry for these specialists, is serious. The escalating cost of modern equipment and the high proportion of foreign students are also important elements in our inability to provide sufficient numbers of well-educated professionals in these fields.

This problem appears not to be severe in the automobile and steel industries, because they have been undergoing major retrenchment, or in pharmaceuticals, because of the massive government support of university research in the life sciences. On the other hand, both machine tools and textiles suffer because they are not viewed as glamorous, high-growth industries. In aircraft the principal concerns involve ameliorating the effects of extreme cyclicality and holding skilled design and production teams together during troughs in volume.

Role of New Technology

The prospects for the development of new technology are very bright in most of the industries studied. This is particularly true of electronics, aircraft, pharmaceuticals, and machine tools, and the opportunity is there in autos and in fibers and textiles. Only in steel was there any real doubt about the possibility that new technology could produce a comparative advantage for U.S. industry. These observations point to the importance of strengthening our national capability in the development of new technology through measures ranging from the reinforcement of our science and engineering base in the universities to tax incentives to industry for R&D and for investment in new plants.

Some additional common themes were noted with respect to conditions needed for maintenance of technological leadership. The close tie between technological leadership and financial performance, including the ability to obtain capital, was noted particularly in electronics, pharmaceuticals, machine tools, and textiles. Similarly, the requirement for large, well-funded R&D programs for maintenance of the technological leadership needed to achieve and sustain a strong competitive advantage was evident in the industries—electronics, pharmaceuticals, and aircraft—that are experiencing the most rapid technological progress. The competitive leverage obtainable from technology is also very important in machine tools, but in steel, autos, and textiles it is diluted by such factors as labor and energy costs, the cost of raw materials, and government trade policies. In no case was technological leadership, by itself, an adequate basis for competitive success. Adequate technology is a necessary but not a sufficient basis for success.

Other Common Themes

Several other common themes were apparent. Managerial skills and practices were highlighted as critical factors in automobiles, machine tools, and textiles. Deficiencies were noted in the U.S. capability to pursue international business and to achieve high productivity and high quality in mass-production industries. In machine tools the tradition of independence in pursuing technological development and relatively limited interactions with customers were noted as special management problems.

Three industries, automobiles, textiles, and steel, are projected to experience permanent decline from earlier levels of output, irrespective of public policy. In these cases, policy initiatives should include consideration of needed restructuring and ameliorating the disruption caused by the transition to a new, sustainable level of operations.

POLICY IMPLICATIONS AND CONCLUSIONS

The original premise on which the study of the seven industries was based was borne out by the studies themselves; namely, no two industries are alike in their patterns of technological development, in the problems they must solve in order to remain healthy and competitive in international markets, and in the public policies that would be most helpful to them in achieving their ends. Despite the differences among the industries, however, it is generally the case that important concerns go beyond the bounds of a single industry. Thus, there is ample opportunity for policy actions that would have broad, if not universal, effects on industry. Several conclusions with respect to policy actions of this kind follow.

The first general conclusion drawn from the studies is that government policy must be based on a substantially more informed view of the characteristics, needs, and prospects of individual industries than it has been to date. This is not to say that government policy should amount to nothing more than an accumulation of responses to perceived or claimed needs of every industry, but rather that it should be an enlightened policy in the sense that it recognizes that no single action can meet all needs, no simple "fixes" exist, and not all sectors can be equally satisfied by any policy. The studies do demonstrate that there are abundant opportunities for policy changes that would benefit important segments of industry, the U.S. economy, and the U.S. position in international technology competition. Some examples of such policy actions are changes in regulation in pharmaceuticals, support for exports from small machine-tool manufacturing firms, and steps to lower the cost of capital for the steel and electronics industries. In any efforts to strengthen government policies and actions, three overriding requirements must remain paramount: (1) the need for consistency over time in our approach to issues, (2) the need for persistent, visibly high-priority attention to international trade negotiations and the monitoring of the behavior of foreign competitors, including foreign governments (a particularly troublesome problem in aircraft), and (3) the need to establish a mutually reinforcing set of policies and actions relating to trade negotiations, monetary and fiscal policy, encouragement of capital formation, export support instruments, education, restructuring of industry, and so on.

Clearly, this implies a need for a continuing, coordinated review and awareness of technology and trade issues at a high enough level in the government that effective action can be taken. It is essential that public policy increasingly take into account the international implications, as well as the domestic effects, of any new initiatives, not only in policy formulation but also in administrative practice. While our system of government and the limits of our understanding of the dynamics of the economy certainly do not permit us to adopt a fully articulated "industrial policy" in the foreseeable future, a higher degree of coordination among the many separate policies and policymakers of our government is clearly called for. This same high degree of coordination is needed to provide the knowledge and information base to support policy formulation and administration.

A closely related general conclusion is that there must be continuing attention at the highest levels of government to the basic contributors to the country's economic health—education, science and technology, and a climate that is conducive to the industrial application of new technology being conspicuous among them. Thus, we must address such shortages as those in manufacturing engineering and in the supply of electronics engineers and computer scientists. We must give greater attention to the basic health of science and engineering in our universities. And, we must adopt policies that encourage capital formation and investment in new technology in the private sector.

Another general conclusion from the studies is that there is a challenge to U.S. management and labor. We have no monopoly on managerial competence, foresight, or competitive drive. Exogenous factors, such as a giant dynamic market, plentiful national resources, an educated, industrious work force, political stability, and private enterprise, have contributed historically to managerial success. They may also have delayed recognition of managerial weaknesses. These exogenous strengths are no longer the dominant force they once were. Increased attention on the part of both large and small companies to world markets, to foreign competition, to foreign policies on trade and on technology, and to foreign managerial innovation is becoming critical to survival. As a corollary, increased public support for education in foreign languages and foreign cultures, as well as more rigorous standards for public literacy in science and technology, are other dimensions of the change that is needed. Unless the public comes to recognize the vital role that international trade plays in the nation's economic health and in the competitive viability of our own industries, the sustained support that is required for progress in other areas is unlikely to emerge.

The challenge to labor is to show that American labor can make contributions to productivity and to product quality that match those of our principal foreign competitors, especially the Japanese. On the positive side, U.S. labor has generally been more flexible in the acceptance of technological advances than have its counterparts in many European countries. As the pace of technological change increases, labor and management will need to work together creatively to develop mechanisms for ameliorating the disruptions brought about by technological change. Both management and labor will have to accept job retraining as a way of life.

A fourth general conclusion is that the government needs to give more sustained attention to the problems faced by small companies. Tax policy has alternately favored and discouraged venture companies—at present, it mostly favors them, but it is far from clear that this will last. Small companies often need special help from the government in competing in foreign markets, and for the most part this help has not been forthcoming. Small companies, individually, generally lack the expertise and experience to deal successfully with foreign regulations, procedures, and market systems and could benefit greatly from government assistance in those areas. Until recently the financial assistance available from the Export-Import Bank has been unavailable to smaller companies or for smaller transactions in all companies.

Finally, what would the committee now say about the concern that started it on its studies nearly a decade ago? Was it inevitable that U.S. preeminence in technology and trade would erode as Japan and Europe rebuilt their economies, or were there basic weaknesses in the U.S. system that were primarily responsible for our apparent loss of momentum?

As is usually the case, there are elements of truth in the opposite viewpoints. Certainly Europe and Japan found it possible to take advantage of existing technology and to use that as an important lever for the rapid economic growth they experienced and the gains they made relative to us after World War II. The readjustment process seems to have about run its course, and as far as Europe is concerned we may now be in balance. But Japan has gone beyond this and has emerged as our real economic competitor, and the outcome is not at all clear.

At the same time, we are no longer complacent. The very fact that we have recognized our previous inattention to our economic vitality has led us to at least some remedial policies and actions, although probably not enough. There are ample signs that we have not lost our ability to innovate, our productivity has turned up, and we are becoming more competitive. However, we have not yet fully met the Japanese challenge, and we will not until we give more serious national attention to issues of international trade and to its dependence on technology. Not only in the so-called high technology industries, but in the others as well, we need a continuing flow of new technology if we are to remain the world's economic leader. Technologists and economists are in essential agreement on the issues and on the directions in which the United States must move—the challenge to them is to make their voices heard.

NOTES

1. The studies were funded primarily by the National Science Foundation; portions were also sponsored by the U.S. Department of Commerce and the National Aeronautics and Space Administration. See notes 2, 3, and 4 for titles of specific studies.
2. National Research Council and National Academy of Engineering, Committee on Technology

and International Economic and Trade Issues, *Technology, Trade, and the U.S. Economy* (Washington, D.C.: National Academy of Sciences, 1978).

3. National Research Council and National Academy of Engineering, Committee on Technology and International Economic and Trade Issues, *The Impact of Regulation on Industrial Innovation* (1979); *The Impact of Tax and Financial Regulatory Policies on Industrial Innovation* (1980); *Antitrust, Uncertainty, and Technological Innovation* (1980) (Washington, D.C.: National Academy of Sciences).

4. National Academy of Engineering, Committee on Technology and International Economic and Trade Issues, *The Competitive Status of the U.S. Auto Industry* (1982); *The Competitive Status of the U.S. Machine Tool Industry* (1983); *The Competitive Status of the U.S. Pharmaceutical Industry* (1983); *The Competitive Status of the U.S. Fibers, Textiles, and Apparel Complex* (1983); *The Competitive Status of the U.S. Electronics Industry* (1984); *The Competitive Status of the U.S. Civil Aviation Manufacturing Industry* (1985); *The Competitive Status of the U.S. Steel Industry* (1985). (Washington, D.C.: National Academy Press, 1982–1985).

Global Competition—The New Reality:

Results of the President's Commission on Industrial Competitiveness

JOHN A. YOUNG

Our ability to compete in world markets depends on decisions made by both public servants and private citizens in pursuit of four key goals: (1) to create, apply, and protect technology—our greatest competitive advantage; (2) to increase the supply of capital available for investment and reduce its cost to American business; (3) to develop a more skilled, flexible, and motivated work force; and (4) to make trade a national priority at home and to strengthen the world trading system in which we operate.

Those of you who were around some 25 years ago can remember what we felt at that very visible image of a Russian rocket blasting its way into space. That first sputnik wounded our pride, strengthened our resolve, and set off a national effort to be the first on the moon. And, of course, we were. What this country needs today is to have the Japanese launch a Toyota into space. Or perhaps a Sony Walkman.

The competitive challenge we face today has consequences just as serious as the threat we felt a quarter of a century ago. This one is just subtler, and a whole lot quieter. Perhaps that is why this nation has not yet responded wholeheartedly or effectively to the challenge of competition from abroad. Emphasizing the urgency of competitive renewal in this country is not an easy task in the middle of the strongest economic expansion of recent history.

For the past 18 months I have been the chairman of the President's Commission on Industrial Competitiveness. The commission comprised leaders from industry and labor, from the high-tech and basic industry sectors, from large and small businesses, and from government and academia. Both Democrats and Republicans participated—even in the middle of an election year.

Yet the final report that the commission submitted to the President[1] was unanimous in its key findings, which were these:

1. There is compelling evidence that this nation's ability to compete has declined over the past 20 years. We see its effects both in our domestic markets and in our ability to sell abroad.

2. We must be able to compete if we are going to meet our national goals of a rising standard of living and strong national security for our people.

3. Decision makers in both the public and private sectors must make improved competitiveness a priority on their agendas. As a nation, we can no longer afford to ignore the competitive consequences of our actions—or our inaction.

Before I go any farther in outlining the dimensions of our nation's competitiveness problem, let me try to explain its significance.

Competitiveness can be defined as the degree to which a nation can, under free and fair market conditions, produce goods and services that meet the test of international markets *while at the same time maintaining or expanding the real incomes of its citizens.* That definition was a matter of choice for this nation, and it demonstrates what is at stake in being competitive. As a nation, we are not going to lower our wages in order to compete. At least no one I have met has ever offered to cut his or her paycheck in honor of this worthy cause.

The challenge, then, is to earn our wages in an interdependent and highly competitive global economy. One-fourth of the goods produced in the world cross national borders, and fully 70 percent of the goods produced here in the United States compete against products made abroad. These facts lead to this simple conclusion: the wages we get paid—the high standard of living we enjoy—must be earned in the world market. No one bestows them on us as a right. In a world in which only guest speakers receive a free meal, competitiveness is what pays for whatever we have placed on our personal and public menus.

INDICATORS OF DECLINING U.S. COMPETITIVE PERFORMANCE

No single indicator gives an adequate representation of our nation's competitive performance. The commission identified five trends, and they all point to a declining ability to compete. First, growth in American productivity has been surpassed by that of all our major trading partners. The Japanese productivity growth rate is five times greater than our own. In absolute terms, Japan is more productive than American industry in autos, steel, and electrical

---

[1]President's Commission on Industrial Competitiveness, *Global Competition: The New Reality*, John A. Young, chairman (Washington, D.C.: U.S. Government Printing Office, 1985).

and precision machinery. It is no coincidence that these are the industries in which the United States has seen the greatest effects of foreign competition.

Second, real hourly wages in the business sector have remained virtually stagnant since 1973, and they have actually declined in the past five years. Recall that competitiveness was defined above as our ability to succeed in world markets *while maintaining our standard of living*. Our failure to earn increasing real incomes means we are not meeting that test.

Third, our manufacturing sector is not generating the kinds of real returns on assets that encourage investments. Twenty years ago the average real pretax return on manufacturing assets was almost 12 percent. In 1983, it averaged about 4 percent. Investors can do a lot better by putting their money in financial assets. The members of the commission were firm in their conviction that we cannot rationalize the poor performance of manufacturing by arguing that we are becoming a service economy, anyway. Our manufacturing sector is the *foundation* on which many services rest.

The fourth trend that concerned the commission is even more dramatic: U.S. trade deficits are at all-time highs—more than $125 billion in 1984. For this entire century—until 1971—we ran a positive balance of trade. Since then there has been a steady—and alarming—trend to the negative. Much of our current deficit can be blamed on the strength of the dollar, but that does not explain it all. Our trade deficits started in the 1970s when most people thought the dollar was 20 to 30 percent undervalued.

The fifth and final warning signal I would cite hits close to home. Since 1965, 7 out of 10 U.S. high technology industries have lost world market share. In 1984 this country had a trade deficit in electronics. Our bilateral deficit with Japan in electronics was $15 billion. That is more than our bilateral deficit in autos. Silicon Valley is *not* so far removed from Detroit.

In assessing our ability to compete, we should not take comfort from the fact that our economy is outperforming the European economies. That is like congratulating ourselves for finishing a race second to last. Instead, we should look to Japan and its neighbors—the newly industrializing nations of the Pacific Rim. The United States now does more trade with the countries of this area than with all of Europe combined. And our new Pacific Rim competitors have set a challenging standard by which to judge our own performance.

What can we do to reverse the competitive erosion of the past two decades? It would be nice if we could say, ''Do just this, and everything will improve.'' But our ability to compete depends on many factors—all of which are interrelated.

FACTORS THAT AFFECT COMPETITION

The commission grouped the factors that affect our ability to compete into four subject areas that served as the basis for its working committees: technology, capital, human resources, and international trade. Let me highlight the key findings and recommendations in each area.

Technology

Technology is our strongest advantage in world competition. Yet we do not capitalize on our preeminent position, and other countries are rapidly closing the gap. Our first cause for concern should be about the kinds of technologies we investigate. As a nation, we spend a smaller percentage of GNP on civilian R&D than either West Germany or Japan. In other words, we invest relatively less than our trading partners in those basic areas of inquiry that could lead to commercial competitive advantage. Roughly half of all the R&D performed in this country is funded by the federal government. But most of that spending is for defense and space research. And, in the commission's view, any spillover of those R&D efforts to commercial applications is incidental at best. That is why the commission called for the creation of a cabinet-level Department of Science and Technology. Federal R&D funding that is *not* earmarked for defense represents an annual investment by taxpayers of more than $18 billion. But it is an investment from which we do not reap enough reward. Federal efforts are scattered throughout several organizations and some 700 federal laboratories. Several recent studies, David Packard's[2] among them, point to major administrative inefficiencies.

By one count, there are some 2,700 distinct federal R&D program elements that receive line-by-line budget scrutiny from 54 congressional committees and subcommittees. That is a managerial maze that few scientists are equipped to navigate.

As part of the effort to create technology, the commission called for permanent tax credits to stimulate more industry research and development. Tax credits are preferable to direct government project oversight, because they allow the market to determine which technologies have commercial potential.

Encouraging private sector research and development is an appropriate goal of government. Technological advances create a rippling of benefits throughout the economy. Those who pay for the research cannot capture all the benefits. Take the microprocessor as an example. It is now used in cars, microwave ovens, stereo equipment, medical diagnostics, and a whole range of other applications. It has provided a competitive advantage for many American industries that did not in any way contribute to its development.

---

[2]White House Science Council Federal Laboratory Review Panel, *Report of the White House Science Council Federal Laboratory Review Panel*, David Packard, chairman, May 1983. PB 83255620. Springfield, Va.: National Technical Information Service.

Turning now from *creating* technology to *applying* it, perhaps this nation's most glaring weakness in technology is the failure to devote enough attention to manufacturing applications. It does little good to design state-of-the-art products if someone abroad can rapidly copy and produce them at a lower price. Robotics and statistical quality controls were both first developed here in the United States. But it was the Japanese who applied them—and brilliantly—to the manufacturing function.

But manufacturing simply has not been stylish with us. Within industry, manufacturing managers have been paid less than people in marketing or in R&D. Within our universities, there has been little interest in process technologies and manufacturing management. You can count on one hand the number of universities doing research in this area.

Creating and then applying technology are just the first two steps in a competitive strategy. The results of innovation must also be protected from counterfeiting and other forms of misappropriation. In this regard, we need to review and reform our patent laws, better protect the scientific information that American business provides to government, and insist that our trading partners—especially the newly industrializing countries—provide better protection, too. According to the International Trade Commission, counterfeiting alone cost American business $8 billion in sales and 131,000 jobs in 1984.

Capital Resources

Let us assume that, as a nation, we do a magnificent job in technology. We have a wealth of research that has commercial potential. We quickly and broadly apply technological innovation to create market advantages, and we protect our intellectual property. All these advantages could be to no effect if we have created for ourselves a major disadvantage in another area— capital resources. This is where economics and technology really merge.

If you rank our six major trading partners on capital formation, that listing will almost exactly mirror their ranking in productivity growth. Moreover, Japan would be at the top of both rankings and the United States at the bottom.

The commission investigated the reasons for the low level of U.S. investment by asking for testimony from a wide range of economists. To our great surprise, they were in agreement. The consensus of their opinion was that high capital costs are a competitive disadvantage for American firms. In fact, compared with Japanese costs, American capital costs are at least twice as high. This disparity in costs hurts the ability of U.S. firms to compete. In fact, studies have concluded that lower capital costs—not technological supremacy—were the prime factor behind the Japanese incursion into the U.S. semiconductor industry.

If we are going to reduce the cost of capital to American industry, however, we will have to deal with some major "macroeconomic" issues. First, we will have to cut the deficit. Government must reduce competition with industry for scarce capital resources. Federal borrowing pushes up interest rates and makes the dollar strong. Since 1980, the value of the dollar has almost doubled compared with the value of major European currencies. For companies trying to sell in international markets, that means higher prices for our exports and fewer sales abroad.

Second, our tax system must be restructured. It is currently a de facto industrial policy, and a poor one. It discourages savings and encourages borrowing. It also results in the highest effective tax rate for that sector of our economy most affected by international competition—manufacturing.

The commission did not evaluate the likely consequences of the many tax reform proposals currently under discussion, but it did propose several criteria that can be used to judge the consequences of each proposal for U.S. competitiveness. Among the criteria are the goals of more neutral tax treatment for different industries and kinds of assets and encouraging investment, such as by indexing inflation for calculations of capital gains and allowing fuller deductions for capital losses on individual income tax returns.

A third way to lower the cost of capital to American firms is to pursue a more stable monetary policy. The commission's final report has a graph that plots the variation in the consumer price index and prime interest rates since 1971. It looks like a roller coaster, but one with jagged peaks. Unstable monetary policy adds to high capital costs, because it forces lenders to add risk premiums to their loans.

And to those who blame American business for its short-term investment perspectives, I say that there is a reasonable excuse. It is difficult to do long-term planning and investment in a wildly changing business environment. Besides, no lender would put out a 20-year note anyway. High capital costs force a short-term outlook.

Human Resources

So far I have talked about only two of the four areas the commission explored—technology and capital resources. But it is more complicated than that. Our ability to compete in world markets—and to maintain the technological preeminence that is our strongest advantage—also depends on other factors.

The most insightful business strategy in the world is doomed to failure if it lacks a dedicated team of players to carry it out. The commission's third area of inquiry was human resources, and the members concluded that the United States faces a number of unmet challenges in this area. First, as Donald Kennedy (in this volume) explains so well, we must strengthen the capacity of our nation's research universities to explore promising areas of innovation and to train the scientists and engineers we need.

Second, we must create better ways of helping our mature work force adapt to change—whether that be retraining for displaced steelworkers or on-going education to keep electrical engineers abreast of developments in their field.

Third, both American management and labor need to recognize their shared stake in the competitive challenge and find ways of forming a consensus on goals within their business organizations. That is why the commission advocated broader use of such incentives as profit sharing and employee stock-purchase programs.

International Trade

The subject of international trade—both the way we approach it here in the United States and the global trading environment that American business operates in—raises tough issues.

The commission's first conclusion was that international trade has simply not been a national priority. Responsibility for trade policy is splintered. A diagram of who makes and implements policies affecting trade would have to include the two major actors—the Commerce Department on one side, and the U.S. trade representative on the other. Then there would have to be lines representing the various pieces of the action owned by the Departments of Defense, Treasury, Agriculture, State, and a host of other executive agencies and congressional committees.

The resulting picture of the process by which our trade policy is formulated would be more complicated than a design schematic for the most advanced integrated circuit. The complexity and lack of accountability make it impossible for us to deal with the growing importance, and the number, of issues we must resolve.

That is why the commission recommended the creation of a cabinet-level Department of Trade: to provide a single, strong voice for trade issues. We have been told that we cannot expect such a major reorganization to happen in the near future, that it is not politically feasible. But we have some opportunities for greater focus with the formation of the new Cabinet Council on Economic Affairs headed by Treasury Secretary James Baker.

There are a number of other things we should do to get our own house in order when it comes to trade. First, we need a new omnibus trade bill that provides ways to help U.S. industry adjust to international competition before the damage is irreparable. Second, we must search for a more uniform approach to export controls. We often prohibit the export of technology that our allies consider allowable. The commission heard testimony that put the cost of our stricter rules at more than $12 billion in lost U.S. sales each year. For technology that we do allow for export, we need to streamline the licensing process. It takes American exporters far longer to obtain licenses than their competitors abroad. Third, we should be looking for ways to encourage U.S. exports. These include more competitive export financing, better information about foreign markets, and the active support of U.S. embassies abroad.

As it looked at the international trade environment in which American business operates, the commission saw two trends going on simultaneously—and pointing in opposite directions. On the one hand, the total volume of world trade has grown enormously—a sevenfold increase since 1970. On the other, the *portion* of that trade covered by agreed rules has shrunk dramatically. There is no coverage in those rules for trade in services or investments. There is little provision for agriculture or state-owned industries. And while tariffs have come down, the use of nontariff barriers has increased significantly.

Like American trade law, international rules have not yet responded to foreign governments' targeting policies and nontariff barriers. And the newly industrializing nations have only the weakest commitment to the rules, at best.

We must strengthen the international trading system by increasing the amount of trade and the kinds of practices it covers. And we should get our trading partners—especially the newly industrializing countries—to commit to its rules.

SUMMARY

I began by saying that our ability to compete in world markets depends on decisions made by both public servants and private citizens in four basic areas, and I have sketched some actions we can take to attain key goals in each of them. Those goals are as follows:

1. to create, apply, and protect technology—it is our greatest competitive advantage;
2. to increase the supply of capital available for investment and reduce its cost to American business;
3. to develop a more skilled, flexible, and motivated work force; and
4. to make trade a national priority at home and to strengthen the world trading system in which we operate.

Let me share with you my personal reactions to the response our final report has received so far. I am sometimes asked to choose *the* major recommendation that the commission made. This I refuse to do, because I do not want anyone to think that improving our competitiveness can be done with just one act. That would be like saying that a business can succeed by just managing its inventory better—while at the same time ignoring its R&D activity, accounts receivable, employee development, and the rest of its activities.

Some have expressed disappointment that the commission did not come up with "anything really new." To those who are attracted to "newness," I say that there is simply no substitute for excellence in executing the basics.

The commission did not identify any new roles for government. Rather, what it tried to make clear is the fact that government has not yet effectively performed the legitimate roles it already has. Government is responsible for creating an environment within which American business can effectively compete. That basic goal has not been achieved.

The commission's call for renewed attention to the fundamentals also applies to those of us in the private sector. The ultimate responsibility for being competitive rests with us. The foresight of our strategies, our responsiveness to customers, the cost and quality of our products, the commitment to developing our work force—these affect our performance far more than anything government can do for us. These challenges are not new, but we must address them with new vigor.

What do I think will be the result of the commission's efforts? President Reagan and the Cabinet Council were very interested in the commission's findings, and we have received many requests for copies from members of the administration and other Washington leaders.

It is still too early to judge the final effect of the commission's efforts. History moves a bit more slowly than that. Of this I am certain, however: our nation's policymakers are beginning to pose the question that most needs to be asked: "How does that decision affect our ability to compete?"

What gives me even greater hope is the fact that American industry has not been waiting for a commission report. I see a renewed aspiration to excellence—an unleashing of competitive potential—in industries across the country. If it accomplishes just that—makes improved competitiveness *the standard* by which public and private leaders weigh the decisions they make daily—then the Commission on Industrial Competitiveness will have accomplished its goal.

All of us face a new reality—global competition. It requires from us a new vision and a new resolve. If we can forge these, we can—and will—meet the challenge we face.

The Need for National Consensus to Improve Competitiveness

ALBERT BOWERS

Many Americans do not recognize the full significance and seriousness of the decline in this country's international economic competitiveness. Therefore, we do not as yet have sufficient national resolve to take the steps necessary to regain and sustain our international technological and industrial leadership.

In January 1985 I was cochairman, with Admiral Bob Inman, of a session on the transition from basic research to commercial application at a meeting of the Business-Higher Education Forum. (The Forum is a group of university presidents and business leaders who get together to discuss critical common issues.) The discussion in this chapter represents the collective wisdom of the participants of that meeting and, in particular, the contribution by Denis Prager of the MacArthur Foundation. The ideas expressed at that meeting are relevant to the goals of this volume, in which many of the concerns voiced at the Forum meeting are raised.

America's competitive decline in international markets can readily be seen by the increasing share of world markets being captured by our competitors. We see it in our traditional industries, such as automobiles and steel. We also see it in a wide range of high technology, entrepreneurial industries, such as semiconductors, computers, machine tools, consumer electronics, and many others. As Robert A. Swanson (in this volume) points out, pharmaceuticals and biotechnology are areas that have been targeted by our competitors, particularly Japan.

In attempting to identify some of the major factors responsible for this country's relative competitive decline, it is instructive to compare our nation's environment with that of one of our principal competitors, Japan. The Japanese approach to international economic competition is marked by national commitment and dedication, cooperation, strong government leadership and involvement, and targeted strategies. How did Japan, with virtually no indigenous natural resources, rise from the ashes of a devastating defeat at the end of World War II to become, in less than 40 years, the country to be reckoned with in international technology markets? They did it by

• Resolving to become the strongest nation economically.

• Placing that goal above all others and making the sacrifices and compromises necessary to make that goal a reality.

• Establishing legal, regulatory, financial, and social environments that strongly support the efficient development and commercialization of technology.

• Organizing government, industry, labor, banking, and higher education into an effective and efficient team to achieve that goal.

• Targeting specific markets, establishing market-share goals, and adhering to stringent timetables for achieving those goals.

• Sticking tenaciously to a long-term strategy, even though it meant forgoing immediate profits.

• Concentrating resources on the development of superior manufacturing technologies rather than on research.

• Establishing a first-rate intelligence system to identify foreign scientific discoveries and technological innovations for appropriation and commercialization by Japanese industry.

• Acquiring the needed technologies through joint ventures and other arrangements. For example, between 1950 and 1978, Japanese companies entered into 32,000 such arrangements at a total cost of $9 billion—a very small fraction of their actual worth. Japanese companies, helped by their government, bought technology at bargain prices.

• Infusing selected industries with plentiful, low-cost capital, which allowed them to offer to the world's markets products priced at levels well below those of their competitors.

• Inhibiting access to Japanese domestic markets by foreign competition.

The American approach to international economic competition stands in marked contrast to that of the Japanese and reflects, to a large degree, the difference in the two cultures. In Japan, a very tiny, highly homogeneous country, a national consensus is relatively easily established and implemented. In the United States, a large, highly diverse country of independent-minded people, a national consensus on a complex issue is extremely difficult to achieve and even more difficult to implement. In the Japanese culture, the line dividing the public and private sectors is very fine. This allows strong government leadership and involvement in innovation. On the other hand, our free enterprise system requires a strict division between the public and private sectors. There is little or no government involvement in industrial technology development or industrial competitiveness. These broad cultural characteristics of the United States explain why our large, resource-rich country, with its excellent scientific research, often finds itself increasingly less effective than its competitors in converting the results of its research into commercially competitive products.

Many Americans do not recognize the full significance and seriousness of the decline in this country's international economic competitiveness. There remains a strong tendency among many people in the United States to believe that the situation is still much like it was after World War II—a time when our potential competitors were worn down and our scientific and technological leadership was unchallenged. Therefore, we do not as yet have sufficient national resolve to take the steps necessary to regain and sustain our international technological and industrial leadership. Daniel Yankelovich, president of the Public Agenda Foundation, refers to this lack of resolve as this country's "commitment gap."

One reason for the decline in our international competitiveness is that the United States does not maintain an environment conducive to the efficient commercialization of technology. In fact, the process is often impeded. There are many legal, regulatory, and financial barriers to the efficient translation of new concepts and technologies into commercially competitive products. It will be extremely difficult to organize and mobilize the resources required to regain and sustain our international competitiveness. The development of specific national strategies, such as targeting specific market sectors, is viewed as antithetical to the free enterprise system.

We also suffer from the "not invented here" syndrome. Because of our intense chauvinism, many of those responsible for the development and commercialization of technology are oblivious to the scientific discoveries and technological innovations from other countries. As a nation, we fail to provide training in the languages, cultures, and practices of other countries; and we clearly do not have a good commercial foreign intelligence system capable of identifying foreign innovations for possible use by our industries.

Another reason for our declining competitiveness is that American industry tends to manage by the bottom line—making decisions on the basis of how they will affect next quarter's profits. Such decisions are often made at the expense of long-term benefits.

Those cited above are only some of the reasons why there is a growing gap between the industrial competitiveness of this country and one of its principal economic rivals. However, looking at generalities such as these tends to mask underlying differences and gradations among various industries and technologies. Each industry has strengths and weaknesses that determine the degree to which it succeeds or fails in international markets. Some industries translate research results into commercial application very efficiently, collaborate closely with university scientists, manage with a long-term view, and develop effective means of penetrating foreign markets. Others do not. Some universities facilitate the translation process by developing innovative research and training programs and actively pursue partnerships with industries and governments. Others do not. Some government policies and practices facilitate efforts by industry to compete internationally. Others put up real roadblocks.

Although international competitiveness is a complex issue, it appears that two elements are critical to improving our ability to compete. First, we must have an adequate pool of talented scientists and engineers. There is widespread agreement that both the quality and quantity of this country's future talent pool are in jeopardy. We need a concerted effort by academia, industry, and state and federal governments to change the situation. Much can and must be done if we are to solve this problem. Second, we have to recognize that the corporate, academic, legal, regulatory, and financial environments within which technological innovation takes place in this country often impede rather than stimulate the translation of new concepts and technologies into commercially competitive products.

A number of suggestions have been made about how to improve our international competitiveness:

- We have to change our corporate culture into one that takes a long-term view of profitability.
- Industries must recognize the need for higher investment levels in corporate research.
- Capital improvements in both research and production facilities must become a priority.
- Corporations must place greater emphasis on innovation in manufacturing technology.
- We must drive harder bargains in licensing technology to foreign competitors.
- We should establish intelligence networks that are capable of identifying foreign technologies which are appropriate for licensing and commercialization by U.S. companies.
- Corporations and universities must create innovative relationships to facilitate technology transfer.
- Industry must work with the legislative and executive branches of both the federal and state governments, as partners rather than adversaries, to try to develop policies that will increase our ability to compete.

The role of the federal government in efforts to improve our international competitiveness will be critical. Major aspects of that role should include the following:

• The federal government must continue to assume the primary responsibility for the support of basic science, and it must increase that level of support.

• The government should work on establishing access to foreign markets for U.S. companies rather than artificially protecting our markets against foreign competitors.

• The government should provide and sustain tax incentives and other ways to stimulate the establishment of small companies—companies that play an important role in the commercialization of emerging technologies.

• The government should adopt antitrust laws and policies that reflect the realities of an internationally competitive marketplace.

• Perhaps most important, as government wrestles with assessments of the costs and benefits of environmental health and safety regulations, it must assess the impact of the various degrees of regulation on the international competitiveness of the affected industries.

• In general, the federal government should be a partner, not an adversary.

The discussions that took place at the meeting of the Business-Higher Education Forum were characterized by a certain sense of frustration and impatience. One participant said, "We know what to do. Why don't we get on with it?"

The answer to that question seems to lie in our inability to reach a national consensus on the importance of restoring our competitiveness and then to make a commitment to do so. This volume represents a step toward developing a national consensus and a public policy that might make it possible for this country to regain its leadership in high technology and the international marketplace.

Innovation, Job Creation,
and Competitiveness

RUBEN F. METTLER

The difference between economic winners and losers in world markets lies essentially in making a clear national commitment to growth and competitiveness—a commitment the United States has yet to make. The winners are those whose national policies emphasize savings, investment, technology, competitiveness, and work, to support growth. The losers are those who emphasize current consumption over investment or turn to government intervention and control as substitutes for market forces. Slowly but surely in recent decades the economic policies of the United States have been moving to the side that is losing.

My purpose in this chapter is to bridge the discussions (in this volume) of innovation and entrepreneurship and the discussions that focus on industrial competitiveness and the related issue of creating new jobs and expanding employment. In so doing, I look at several issues: how innovative activities differ among major industries, what role large companies have in job creation, and what major changes in public policy could improve the growth and competitiveness of the U.S. economy. And, I do so from the perspective of a large company.

I must confess that I am somewhat ambivalent about being a spokesman for large companies, since I deliberately left a good job in a large company in the early 1950s to cast my lot with a small venture company, called Ramo-Wooldridge, not anticipating that a few years later the company would be acquired and would then grow to be a large company. A modest investment in 1953, in the newly formed Ramo-Wooldridge (RW) company, by Cleveland-based Thompson Products, now the "T" of TRW, led to the acquisition of RW by Thompson in 1958 and the establishment of "a company called TRW." In 1984 about $3.5 billion of TRW's $6.0 billion of sales came directly from the growth of that initial small venture investment. Not too shabby, even by Silicon Valley standards!

517

INNOVATIVE ACTIVITY IN DIFFERENT INDUSTRIES

Let me begin by commenting on how innovative activity differs among industries, and in large companies as compared with small. We start with much confusion about the nature of different industries because of a tendency to talk and to write about simplifications that do not exist. For example, putting whole industries into neat compartments like "smokestack," "high-tech," "manufacturing," or "service" does not help our understanding. The statistics and projections of growth and decline of these supposedly separate categories can be highly misleading.

A few examples may highlight the point. Automotive plants use advanced sensors, microprocessors, computer controls, and robotics to produce vehicles that are designed by advanced computer simulation and that literally teem with electronic controls and sophisticated metallurgy. After the automobiles are sold, one of the world's most sophisticated distribution networks supplies and services the aftermarket using on-line computers and worldwide communication networks. The automotive industry may safely be described as "high-tech."

In another dimension, "manufacturing" and "service" are inseparably interwoven and are not two separate sets of industries, as often portrayed. We are not becoming a "service economy." We are instead a "salami economy" with alternating slices of "manufacturing" and "services," from product conception to final use. We must be competitive in both manufacturing and services if we are to grow and prosper. Manufacturing is a core capability—the root, trunk, and branches that bear the leaves and fruit of service industries and new technologies.

Global competition compels all industries to improve their performance. The margin that makes for success is very thin. Even a small competitive edge can make a big difference, but large and aggressive steps may be necessary to achieve even a small competitive edge. Improvements that only equal those of competitors yield no net gain.

The challenge is to integrate into all of our industries, in innovative ways, the most advanced technologies in communications, metallurgy and new materials, microelectronics and process control, computer-aided design and manufacturing, expert systems, and more, in a market-driven and cost-effective way. And of course, that includes using advanced technology in managing an enterprise—large or small.

The challenge for managers of large and small companies is to learn how to develop (or buy) technology that is best for their specific purposes, how to control the cost of using it, and how to finance it, all while earning enough profit to continue to invest and compete and grow in world markets on a sustained basis. In short, the challenge is to be an entrepreneur.

Large, established companies became so because they were entrepreneurial. And if they lose their innovative, risk-taking spirit, they will eventually decline, and surely will not make a full contribution to their nation's prosperity and growth. Indeed, I believe a close and necessary relationship exists between large and small companies if both are to develop and maintain an entrepreneurial thrust.

In sum, what is common to all industries and companies of all sizes, new and old, is the need for entrepreneurship and innovation. As the chief executive officer of a large, diversified company in electronics, space, automotive, industrial, and energy markets, I see little difference in the fundamentals of innovative activity across industries. Small companies must be entrepreneurial and innovative to establish an initial market niche; then they must begin to think about diversification and sustainable growth, and that will require more innovation, but in different dimensions and increasingly on a larger scale. When they get to be large and diversified, they will still need the same fundamental entrepreneurial drive to maintain the capacity and willingness to change their business mix and adapt to new competitive conditions.

JOB CREATION

Let us move now to the second issue. Since the number and quality of jobs can serve as one proxy for a healthy economy, how are jobs created and employment expanded, and what role do large companies play in that process?

In 1980 David L. Birch of MIT published a study that concluded that about 70 percent of new jobs in the United States are created by businesses employing fewer than 100 people.[1] Several related studies have also been made by the Brookings Institution and other organizations.

Birch's study was highly influential. Many policies and programs were affected by it. In my view, his study was interpreted much too narrowly. Not enough attention was given to the linkage that exists between large companies and small or to the effect of this linkage on the job creation process.

Let me take my company as an example. We currently employ about 95,000 people, only about 5,000 more than a decade ago, despite large increases in assets, sales, and profits. Does this mean that we have made little contribution to the creation of new jobs? By no means. During the same period our outside purchases more than quadrupled, increasing from under $500 million to well over $2 billion a year. We have played an active part in helping a number of smaller companies get started, and thus in providing

---

[1]David L. Birch, *The Role of High Technology Firms in Job Creation*, Working Paper of the MIT Program on Neighborhood and Regional Change (Cambridge: Massachusetts Institute of Technology, 1984).

some new jobs. We have helped them grow and develop and find their first niche in the market—sometimes by an equity investment or by providing direct funding for research and development, sometimes by being one of their first major customers. Often our purchases have helped to ensure their growth beyond the start-up phases, creating more new jobs.

Our best estimate is that the growth in our outside purchasing has created from 25,000 to 30,000 jobs during the past decade, beyond our own direct employment. A similar contribution by hundreds of other large companies adds up to millions of jobs.

Even the role of corporate pension funds in job formation should not be overlooked. In our company, for example, pension funds have also increased more than fourfold during the last decade, from under $300 million to over $1.3 billion. These funds serve as vehicles for capital formation and, thus, as sources of job formation.

So there is a symbiotic relationship between large business and small. It is necessary to look at an entire system, not at isolated components, to understand the dynamics of job creation.

With respect to public policies aimed at creating new jobs and increasing employment, we should be cautious about intervention that distorts market relationships and that introduces rigidities affecting large *or* small companies. To the greatest extent possible, job creation should be left to market forces, because in the end that will mean healthier economies, more entrepreneurs— large and small—and more and better jobs.

Also, in thinking about economic growth and job creation, it is important to keep in mind the mass and aggregate scale of large companies taken as a group. For example, although comprehensive statistics organized by company size are difficult to find, reasonable estimates suggest that our 500 largest companies (out of a total of millions of companies) account for almost 30 percent of our gross national product, perform about 90 percent of privately financed research and development, perform over 90 percent of the government-sponsored research and development that is not done in government laboratories, employ about 80 percent of the scientists and engineers who work in industry, and spend about $20 billion annually in private skill-training programs. Two additional points: the 1,000 largest U.S. manufacturers boosted their capital appropriations in 1984 by about one-third, about double the national average, and about 18 percent of U.S. exports are made by a mere 50 companies.

Thus, large companies taken as a group have a dominant role in the creation of our national wealth and in our technological competitiveness. They provide a stability and strength that are essential to companies of all sizes, especially in the context of intense competition in world markets, often against very large foreign companies, both private companies and those that are state supported.

MAJOR CHANGES IN PUBLIC POLICY

What major changes in public policy are needed to improve the growth and competitiveness of our economy? First, we should recognize the fact that many leading spokesmen and policymakers and many of the general public believe our economy is doing rather well and do not see competitiveness as a burning issue. They are thus not highly motivated to take steps that might rock the boat. They say: "Aren't we winning again, now, at long last? Isn't our economy recovering? Aren't industry profits up, inflation down, and our productivity improving? Isn't unemployment down, and employment up? Hasn't the American economy done a tremendous job of expanding job opportunities—enabling us to absorb a vast, unexpected influx of women into the work force?" Yes, all these things are true. And they show significant economic progress.

Yet, when we look beyond the rising corporate profits and economic indicators, there is a sense of concern about the long-term future of our economy and society. There is concern that unless strong new steps are taken, we may be facing a slow decline in our real living standards. In broad terms, we see huge trade deficits, grossly unbalanced federal budgets, and rapidly rising domestic and international debt, and perhaps not surprisingly, an anxious financial community and a nervous stock market.

Our alarming twin deficits—fiscal and trade—suggest that we can no longer pay the combined costs of our social welfare commitments, military defense, foreign aid, and environmental protection, let alone maintain the vast private and public infrastructure on which our economy depends. Either we have overcommitted our resources or our economy is failing to perform as it should. Which is it? In my view, it is both. That means we must both restrain the demands on our economy and improve its performance.

A major cause of the concern about the long-range performance of our economy comes down to a not very electrifying phrase: *competitive decline*. If the phrase is abstract, its consequences are not. The erosion of our competitive position in world markets has been well documented, and is discussed by other contributors to this volume, including John A. Young, who discusses the report of the President's Commission on Industrial Competitiveness, on which he served as chairman.

We are presented with a clear choice. We can do what is necessary to restore our competitive primacy and build our economy to meet our society's multiple objectives, or we can settle for a less ambitious future, and cut our cloth to fit it. American jobs, economic security, and living standards, American social goals and dreams, America's place in the world—all are at stake in the decision we make. If we want to maintain an open, benevolent, and humanly productive society; improve the quality of education; restore our private and public capital resources; pay our debts; defend our national interests; and continue to be a leader in world affairs, then we must also want a competitive economy.

In order to achieve these goals, we must grow. And in order to grow, we must compete. And today, as never before, we must act in a worldwide context. The world's problems are partly our problems. We cannot turn our backs on them. We cannot hide from them. We cannot wish them away. We must deal with them because our domestic economic health and vigor have become dependent on world markets. Our economy is only a part—a big and important part, but only a part—of something bigger—an integrated world economy. We have to understand it. And we have to deal with it. The question is, How?

We can begin by asking, *Why is* our society falling behind in worldwide competition? We are the world's strongest industrial nation, so what is our problem?

The answer is, in part, that our historical focus on our domestic market led to inefficiencies and to a kind of competitive myopia. We failed to recognize that others, particularly the countries of the Far East, were gaining on us, by building their own comparative advantages.

In part, the problem is a matter of unfocused U.S. economic policies that fail to grasp and meet the needs of competitiveness in a global market. We simply have not put high priority on the need and the means to be competitive. We have not made competitiveness a central criterion by which to judge our private actions and our public policies.

We can learn much by looking around the world at other economies. The difference between economic winners and losers in world markets lies essentially in making a clear national commitment to growth and competitiveness—a commitment the United States has yet to make. The winners are those whose national policies emphasize savings, investment, technology, competitiveness, and work, to support growth. The losers are those who emphasize current consumption over investment or turn to government intervention and control as substitutes for market forces. Slowly but surely in recent decades the economic policies of the United States have been moving to the side that is losing.

Staying competitive is a total package. It is not fixing just one deficiency. It is not just employment costs, or trade negotiations, or technology, or productivity, or currency exchange rates, or the cost of capital, or marketing, or any one of many very important factors. It is a commitment by all companies and all groups and institutions tied to them to develop strategies and programs as needed to stay ahead of specific competitors for specific products in specific markets. And it is government policies that put high priority on building and maintaining our competitive strength.

IS THERE A WINNING GAME PLAN?

Turning now to government policies, the changes that are needed to bring about a competitive society can be conveniently put into three groups:

1. Macroeconomic policies—fiscal and monetary—that encourage growth, competitiveness, savings, investment, and international trade, without trying to mastermind the process through government intervention in particular industries;

2. Generic policies applicable to all industries, covering such national competitiveness issues as stimulating research and development, upgrading general and scientific and technological education, upgrading work skills in the population, reducing hard-core unemployment, encouraging labor mobility, and prudently managing the public infrastructure;[2] and

3. Communication policies between managers and employees that gradually shift emphasis from the traditional adversary relationships to cooperation and commitment to the task of improving productivity, quality, and competitiveness, with all parties committing to longer-range outlooks and a new concept of mutual interest.

Of these three groups of policies, I will say a few words about only the first, competitive macroeconomic policies.

Competitive Macroeconomic Policies

In order to have competitive macroeconomic policies, we must first understand that many of our existing policies seriously erode our competitiveness, and then we must make competitiveness a central standard against which to judge our policies and programs—both old and new. To begin, we need to spread the burden of maintaining a sound economy more evenhandedly between fiscal and monetary constraints. At present, our fiscal policies and monetary policies are at loggerheads, and we see heavy strains on the economy, including high real interest rates, an overvalued dollar, enormous budget and trade deficits, and a much higher cost of capital for U.S. companies than for their most important foreign competitors. We need to set the objective of a competitive cost of capital, an essential requirement for competitiveness, and then develop the steps needed to achieve it.

We need a mighty effort, above and beyond the administration's current proposals and those being discussed in the Congress, to gain control of

---

[2]The new Decade III program of the National Academy of Engineering is a good example of an institutional program to help build a technologically competitive economy.

government spending and to wipe out our enormous deficits and the rapid growth in national debt and debt-service costs. This year, 1985, is a truly critical time for action. If it turns out that the large cuts needed in spending can only be achieved in a compromise that includes new revenues, it will be very important that competitiveness be a high-priority criterion in deciding how to raise revenue.

We need to eliminate disincentives and develop new incentives for individuals and companies to work and save and invest. Despite all the talk of supply-side economics, we still have economic policies that are heavily biased toward current consumption and dividing up what we produce now. We *have* an "industrial policy" and its name is "consumer spending."

We need to reconcile our domestic antitrust enforcement with the reality of worldwide markets, not with the purpose of reducing competition, but to encourage it on a fair and effective basis. This recognition should allow, under appropriate circumstances, the pooling of resources and information among those in a single industry and among our industry groups, particularly in competing overseas.

We need an aggressive trade policy that demands and enforces fair and equal competition in world markets, including access to the markets of other countries equal to the access they are granted by us, and a related policy that encourages those industries that by their nature must compete in world markets. Currently, our fiscal policies often do the opposite; they favor those industries that are largely inherently domestic and not significantly exposed to foreign competition.

We should understand that financial and trade matters (both domestic and international) are inextricably tied together. Policies and negotiations on both must be tightly coordinated.

CONCLUSION

To take all the steps referred to above will require a change in our outlook and in our political economy as sweeping as those that brought about the New Deal legislation in the 1930s, though in quite a different direction.

I am not talking revolution. But I am talking about basic changes that will tilt the balance of governmental incentives away from consumption-first, distribution-oriented policies—the kind the world's losers are following— to pro-work, pro-savings, pro-investment, pro-growth, pro-competition policies: the kind the winners are following.

It is a big order, and a big change for Americans. Yet this is the policy America really needs—not a solution related to just one part of the problem, or one interest group, but a good, strong "competitiveness policy." That is what it will take to restore the kind of America we all want: a strong leader in the world; a strong competitor at home and in global markets; a strong and compassionate helper for those who can't provide for themselves; a country once again, of rising hopes and rising living standards for all our people. That is what being competitive means! Let's remember that history is written by winners!

Dangers in U.S. Efforts to Promote International Competitiveness

The realization that the United States has lost international competitiveness in a number of important industries indeed provides an opportunity for us to rethink our policies toward innovation. But in carrying out this assessment, we must understand that what we are really questioning is the ability of our system of government to deal with a totally different set of issues, issues that it may not be equipped to handle.

In his chapter in this volume, Harvey Brooks divides postwar U.S. science policy into three phases. The first, covering the period 1945 to 1965, was driven by cold war fears and marked a steady increase in financial support for research and development. The second, from 1965 to 1977, was characterized by a rise to prominence of social priorities, suspicion of technological change, and leveling off and even decline in support for innovation. The third and current period, which dates from 1977, marks a new resurgence, this time driven by concerns about industrial competitiveness.

The chapter by Milton Katz describes a shift in legal thought that roughly paralleled the shift in financial support noted by Brooks. Katz argues that, certainly during the immediate post–World War II period and possibly even up to the mid-1960s, the relative emphasis in the legal system was on creating conditions favorable to growth and innovation. After that, the emphasis shifted to equity and the protection of rights. But at the end of his chapter, Katz indicates that he sees the first signs of a shift in relative emphasis back toward the promotion of growth and innovation, and he applauds that shift.

Both authors thus characterize this country as being in the early stages of an important new transition—a transition leading to a renewal of our ability to compete internationally. While I would like to think that this is true, I am

more pessimistic. In explaining the reasons for my pessimism, I will draw
on the discussions in this volume by Paul A. David, Daniel I. Okimoto, and
N. Bruce Hannay—especially Hannay.

BACKGROUND OF U.S. COMPETITIVE DECLINE

I find a statement by Milton Katz particularly interesting: it is his assertion
that what set us up for the initial shift in legal thinking that he describes—
the shift from an emphasis on promotion of growth and innovation to an
emphasis on equity and rights—was the overwhelmingly dominant position
of the United States as it emerged from World War II. We were the technological leader, the model that other nations seeking to rebuild their economies sought to emulate. Our system produced unparalleled increases in
living standards for our population. The economic pie from which our individual slices were all cut grew enormously. And one of the principal factors
fueling this growth was innovation.

However, the very success of this period laid the groundwork for its
undoing. The *fact* of sustained economic growth fueled by innovation created
the *belief* that this system was somehow self-sustaining. And the increased
level of wealth it generated created the perception that we had "enough"
and could turn our attention to other matters—specifically, to seeing to it
that this "enough" was distributed more equitably.

What the new emphasis on innovation and competitiveness reflects is the
realization that the postwar engine of American economic growth was not
self-sustaining and that our failure, especially during the 1960s and 1970s,
to pay attention to its foundations has gotten us into real trouble. While we
put our primary emphasis on equity and fairness, other nations—Japan is
the best-known example—have been stressing growth. In the process, some
of our most important industries have become hopelessly uncompetitive.
Others, though still strong, show signs of following in their footsteps.

In order to understand how American industry became uncompetitive, we
must be willing to study the evolution of individual industries. Such studies
also provide important clues as to how industries react as the signs mount
that they are becoming uncompetitive. Both sorts of understanding are vital
to the design of intelligent policies to reverse our decline.

It is in this context that the series of studies by the National Academy of
Engineering (NAE)—the studies summarized by Hannay in his chapter—
are so important.[1] To be sure, the individual studies add importantly to our
knowledge of the problems of the specific industries they cover. But as a

---

[1] See note 4 in "Technology and Trade: A Study of U.S. Competitiveness in Seven Industries,"
by N. Bruce Hannay (in this volume) for list of the individual studies.

group these studies provide important clues to how industries become un-competitive and how they react, both positively and negatively, to this development.

Hannay's chapter, in providing brief accounts of the individual industries and what was found concerning them, constitutes a good guide book to the NAE effort. But because of space limitations, it inevitably oversimplifies both the individual studies and the nature of any cross-cutting conclusions, and so I recommend examination in some depth of the individual studies themselves.

Upon such examination (see also Okimoto's discussion of the Japanese challenge), it becomes clear that it has been the challenge from Japan that has focused attention on the competitiveness problem of most, if not all, of the industries covered by these studies. Okimoto's chapter provides a useful antidote to some of the more extreme claims that I have heard about what the Japanese really have done and how they have done it.

The individual NAE studies also reflect the need stated by David for giving increased attention to the process of diffusion in the study of technological change and its impact on productivity, though Hannay does not capture this element fully in his brief summary and synthesis. In reading various reports on the recent performance of major U.S. industries, especially their accounts of the sources of the remarkable Japanese productivity improvements, one quickly sees that the productivity improvements derive primarily *not* from an emphasis on major innovations and big breakthroughs but from patient, across-the-board efforts to improve production processes and to develop moderately innovative products that meet genuine consumer needs. That is to say, the Japanese practiced good engineering in its most basic sense.

Indeed, the most interesting question in regard to Japan—one that Okimoto does not claim to be able to answer—is whether Japan, having excelled at moderate innovation and diffusion, is now equipped to play a leading role in the process of invention and radical innovation. For if a rediscovery of the importance of patient, moderate innovation and steady diffusion will represent for U.S. industry not a new departure but merely a return to earlier successfully applied principles, the need to take an important role in the generation of fundamental scientific knowledge will represent a major change for Japan.

I have advocated that people who want to understand how U.S. industry got into its current sorry shape closely examine available studies. But I must provide a warning to all who might be tempted to heed my advice—such reports, which document in detail the decline of competitiveness of major U.S. industries, make depressing reading. For they demonstrate, as Paul David no doubt would forecast, that there are likely to be no quick, easy, or painless solutions—if solutions can in fact be found—to the problems facing some of our industries. The various studies describing the erosion of competitiveness in the U.S. steel industry[2] show that it took our industry 20 years of hard work to turn an overwhelming competitive advantage—one that allowed us to compete successfully in the face of a 10-to-1 wage differential favoring the Japanese—into massive uncompetitiveness—uncompetitiveness that prevents us from competing successfully against a 2-to-1 Japanese advantage in labor costs. Our competitive decline in automobiles may have taken even longer; it took the shift in demand caused by the second oil shock to bring it into sharp focus.

IMPLICATIONS OF LIKELY U.S. RESPONSES

What do the NAE studies tell us about this country's likely response to the realization that many of its industries have become uncompetitive? Brooks's vision is an optimistic one—a vision of renewed innovation and productivity. But as I have already indicated, my reading of these various studies suggests a very different possible outcome. For the reaction I see in industry after industry—most clearly in steel, machine tools, and textiles and apparel, but also in automobiles and, most regrettably, even in electronics—is for industries to resort to political strategies both to deny the need to change and to undercut the pressures stimulating it.

Why this response? Here I must return again to Katz's discussion. If we were propelled into our shift in legal emphasis from promotion of growth and innovation to the promotion of equity and fairness by our perception of overwhelming strength and success in the immediate postwar period, we seem to be propelled into our current reassessment of that position by a perception of overwhelming weakness, failure, and unfairness in having to make the sort of changes that we now face. Moreover, the legal environment that Katz describes, an environment that stresses equity and fairness, still predominates and, as I will argue below, is likely to continue. Such a legal environment, coupled with our sense of weakness, failure, and unfairness, lays the groundwork not for the sort of quiet determination to bring about the sort of industrial renewal that I hear Brooks describing, but a xenophobic response in which we focus our energies on halting what we perceive to be the source of the unfairness.

Consider the seemingly reasonable claim that our antitrust laws should be modified to "recognize the realities of international competition." I am not certain of precisely what that means. But most businessmen I talk to translate the phrase as requiring that actual and potential foreign competitors be treated

---

[2] I recommend Donald F. Barnett and Louis Schorsch, *Steel: Upheaval in a Basic Industry* (Cambridge, Mass.: Ballinger, 1983), as the most complete and thorough.

as domestic competitors when determining the lawfulness of proposed domestic mergers.

In a world in which U.S. firms increasingly compete on an international basis, the clearing away of an anachronism—for that is what many consider our domestically oriented antitrust enforcement to represent—would seem to be just the sort of shift in legal structures that one favoring an increased emphasis on innovation and competitiveness would advocate. Indeed, Katz refers approvingly to such a change. But it is not that simple, especially when one considers how such a change might interact with other of our laws—in particular, with our statutes governing the regulation of trade.

There was a time during America's Great Depression when the antitrust laws attempted to limit the ability of domestic firms to reduce prices. A firm's cutting its prices to a level above its costs but below a competitor's costs was considered to constitute "price discrimination" and to represent "predatory pricing." The antitrust laws were also invoked to slow the spread of merchandising innovations, such as chain stores. Why was this? Because during that period, competition—competition from almost any source—was considered "unfair" and even dangerous to our weakened economic system. Fortunately, such concepts went out of favor in antitrust enforcement decades ago. Anyone seeking to bring such a case today would be laughed out of court.

Why the change in antitrust doctrine? Better understanding of the underlying economic concepts may have had something to do with it. But I believe that the greater cause was realization that competition—even competition that eliminated some competitors—was a vital, positive force in our economy. We began to focus more on preserving the necessary conditions for the workings of competition than on preserving each and every individual competitor.

But while these highly desirable developments in antitrust were occurring, developments in trade law and its administration were moving in the opposite direction. Largely due to the growing perception of competitive weakness on the part of many U.S. industries and their determination to fight what they believe are its unjust causes, definitions of "dumping" and "predation" have been made stronger, so that the test for them resembles the tests applied by the domestic antitrust laws to "price discrimination" and "predation" 30 years ago. Indeed, it is no longer even necessary for a domestic industry to prove that a foreign industry is doing anything "unfair" (other than merely exporting goods to the United States) in order to obtain relief. Under various "escape clause" procedures, all that must be shown is that imports are entering the country in a volume sufficient to depress domestic profits and displace domestic workers. Were such a standard to be carried over to domestic antitrust policy, a firm like Hewlett-Packard could be successfully sued by Texas Instruments merely for cutting its price sufficiently to win sales away from the latter, even though Hewlett-Packard's prices remained at all times above its costs.

Given the opposing trends in antitrust and trade law I have described, the following scenario is entirely plausible. Two or more domestic firms in an industry that is highly concentrated nationally but much less concentrated worldwide merge. (In the extreme case, all domestic firms in an industry might be permitted to combine.) Assume then that the resulting combination attempts to take advantage of any resulting increase in market power by raising its prices sharply. Given the worldwide nature of competition in this industry, one would expect imports to increase sharply, undercutting this price increase. So far so good. However, this domestic combination would have the option of invoking the trade laws to prevent the exercise of the very competitive influence that had been used to justify the merger in the first place. Indeed, under some proposals being discussed, the domestic industry's case against the foreign competition could even be filed preemptively. That is, the demonstration that foreign imports might enter in response to higher domestic prices would be sufficient to establish the case for erecting barriers to those imports.

This is hardly the way to encourage the renewal of domestic competitiveness! However, those who advocate modifying the antitrust laws to "reflect the realities of international competition" seldom, if ever, also advocate harmonizing concepts of what is "fair competition" in a manner that would treat imports and domestic goods similarly. Yet we need to see that, just as our protectionist version of antitrust could be safely discarded—indeed, it absolutely needed to be eliminated to enable the American economy to grow and prosper—so our increasingly protectionist attitudes toward trade need to be discarded. But given our current perceptions about our industrial weakness and the sources of it—perceptions that are as out of tune with reality as were our fears of "excessive competition" during the Depression—I am afraid that this will not happen.

Katz claims to be able to see a shift in our legal system away from an emphasis on equity and fairness and toward an emphasis on promoting growth and innovation. But he was careful to label that shift a relative one. He seemed to believe—and I certainly believe—that our political and legal system will always be slanted quite sharply in the direction of promoting equity and fairness. (And that can mean equity—protection—for import-impacted industry and fairness—again, protection—for its workers.)

Indeed, we need to understand that such a bias is deliberately built into our system of government. Katz refers to this fact when he observes that the flood of litigation we all bemoan is the price we pay for our unwillingness as a nation to turn the solution of complex issues of government over to a professional bureaucracy. In a recent book, Harvard Business School Professor Joseph Bower has reflected a similar sentiment in a chapter titled provocatively "The United States Isn't a Company, It's Not Even Japan."[3] Bower usefully reminds us of the deep historic roots of our "amateur government," which is staffed primarily by lawyers. In breaking free from England, we were in large part breaking free from a highly professional government bureaucracy whose task was seen to be promoting industrial competitiveness—the competitiveness of British industry at the colonies' expense. We set up a government specifically designed *not* to promote efficiency but to prevent the arbitrary exercise of power by government officials, elected and unelected. Our primary mechanism for doing this was to erect a system of checks and balances, based largely on a powerful system of courts.

Thus, even if the relative emphasis of our legal system shifts, we need to keep in mind that our political process has embedded in it a strong bias against the encouragement of economic growth and in favor of the promotion of equity and fairness. Business may complain about this bias when it favors environmentalists and those who fight technological progress, but business is quick to take advantage of it when it can be used to protect them against foreign competition.

Indeed, the most difficult dilemma posed by our growing realization of the consequences of our loss of international competitiveness is how we forge a set of policies to make the situation better without running grave risks of actually making it worse. Those like Paul David or John Young (in this volume) who call for a rationalization of our current patchwork of policies affecting industry through governmental reorganization and the creation of some sort of industrial oversight function fail to understand the likely consequences of their proposals. In my view, they are either calling for a greater emphasis on fairness and equity at the expense of competitiveness—for that is what our current system of government is almost certain to deliver—or they are calling for a fundamental overhaul of this system, one that would go well beyond the sort of minor organizational tinkering they appear to be advocating.

Our realization that we have lost competitiveness in a number of important industries provides an opportunity to rethink our policies toward innovation. For we will not reverse this trend if we do not find ways of promoting innovation and technical progress. But in carrying out this reassessment, we must understand that what we are really questioning is the ability of the system of government that has served us well for 200 years to deal with a totally different set of issues—issues that it may not be well equipped to handle.

---

[3]Joseph L. Bower, *The Two Faces of Management* (Boston: Houghton Mifflin, 1983).

Government Policies for
Innovation and Growth

ED ZSCHAU

The proper role of government in technological advancement and economic growth is not to target specific companies, industries, or technologies, but to target the process by which those industries, technologies, and companies are fostered—the process of innovation. That is, government's proper role is to establish a set of policies that create an environment in the United States in which new ideas and new enterprises are likely to flourish.

When I arrived in Washington, D.C., in 1983 I found that there was intense interest in the area that I represent as a congressman—Silicon Valley, California. Everyone wanted to be associated with high technology. There was a group called the "Atari Democrats" (although they are frantically searching for a new name since Atari has fallen on harder times), and when I was asked to chair the Republican Task Force on High Technology Initiatives, 138 of the 167 lonely House Republicans joined the task force, which indicates the level of interest in technological issues.

Unfortunately, any hot political topic spawns a lot of bad ideas about how government can help out. High-tech was no exception. Many people thought that to stimulate science and technology in this country we needed a "high-tech planning board"—bureaucrats who would look into the future and determine where the opportunities are, where scientific advances should come from, and what the industries of choice might be. They would dip into an $8.5 billion fund that Congress would have voted for their disposal and invest in the technologies and companies they had identified. But it is pure folly to suppose that government can identify in advance where the opportunities and technological advances will come from. Technology, science, and entrepreneurship are not driven by government decision making.

535

Why were these ideas proposed? Well, Japan has a Ministry of International Trade and Industry (MITI), and since the Japanese do pretty well when it comes to technology, some have assumed that MITI is the reason for that country's success. However, even the Japanese are beginning to question this kind of approach. The dean of the Namura School of Advanced Management in Tokyo recently observed that the Japanese structure is too inflexible to meet the challenges of a changing world. He recommended that in the future the Japanese look, for their model, to "entrepreneurs like those in Silicon Valley." It seems to me the height of irony, although not unusual, that Washington politicians are talking about copying something the Japanese are doing while the Japanese are trying to emulate something in our own backyard!

It cannot be denied that government plays a role in technological advancement and economic growth, but we must determine government's proper role. It seems to me that rather than targeting specific companies, specific industries, or specific technologies, the proper role of government is to *target the process* by which those industries, those technologies, and those companies are fostered—the process of innovation. That is, government's proper role is to create in this country an environment in which new ideas and new enterprises are likely to flourish.

The Republican Task Force, which I chair, has identified four prerequisites for an environment in which innovation will flourish. We suggest that *all* policies of the federal government—for example, those related to research, taxes, fiscal and monetary matters, education, trade, antitrust matters, and procurement—be evaluated in terms of whether they strengthen these prerequisites for an environment for innovation or whether they are detrimental to it. Policies that are detrimental or that are not as stimulative as they might be should be modified accordingly.

The prerequisites for innovation identified by the task force are well known. First is *a commitment to basic research.* Year in and year out, in good years and bad, we should conduct basic research of the kind done in colleges and universities. This fundamental research is not product-driven. It is a search for knowledge, a quest to find out how the world works. From basic research comes the foundation for future technologies, future products, and future companies.

A commitment to basic research means adequate federal funding. It means incentives for industry to fund research in research institutes. It means evaluating the role of the federal laboratories and determining whether that role could be improved or whether federal laboratory research ought to be redirected. It means changing the antitrust laws, as was done in 1984, to permit R&D joint ventures to be formed by corporations so that more fundamental research programs—those that would not normally be undertaken because of their great expense or high risks—can be pursued by the corporations. A commitment to basic research applies not just to science, but also to research in basic engineering and technology practices, specifically, manufacturing technology.

The second prerequisite for a healthy environment for innovation is *incentives for risk taking*. There are many failures for every great success, which suggests that we need incentives for risk taking in this country. Regulatory and tax policies are the primary means of encouraging risk taking. If the regulations that must be complied with are too extensive, people will not experiment with new ideas. The R&D tax credit that encourages companies to invest in more research and development and stock options that enable young companies to attract key people to set entrepreneurial activity in motion are government mechanisms to encourage risk taking. The capital gains tax reduction in 1978 was very important for stimulating risk-capital investments. And, finally, other incentives for investing in long-term R&D projects include patent policies that protect the inventions that require so much risk to develop. All of these incentives for risk taking by investors, by entrepreneurs, by innovators, engineers, and corporations are important to an environment for innovation.

Let me voice my concern here that in seeking "simplicity" and "fairness" in our tax system we might unwittingly destroy some of the incentives for capital formation, research, and risk taking in this country. The Treasury Department's tax reform proposal aimed at what I consider to be the elusive objectives of simplicity and fairness would reduce the distinction between ordinary income taxation and capital gains taxation. It would also make it less attractive to invest in new plant and equipment. Without capital-formation incentives, the United States will lack the productivity growth and economic growth it needs.

The third prerequisite, in addition to commitment to basic research and incentives for risk taking, is *an adequate supply of trained technical people*. Since Joseph Pettit (in this volume) discusses engineering education issues, I will simply mention that I think the federal government has a role here, too, at least a limited role. Through proper tax credits, the federal government can encourage corporations to contribute equipment and funds to colleges and universities for educational purposes as well as for research.

The last of the four prerequisites is *ample market opportunities*. Since people will not take the risks associated with new-product development unless they can sell those products in sufficient volume, we need an aggressive trade policy that breaks down trade barriers in other countries and enables us to participate in world markets. We also need a domestic economic policy that reduces our enormous federal deficits. Also, we need balanced export-control policies. Sometimes in our zealousness to control the export of sensitive technologies to prevent their getting to the Eastern bloc, we make it unnecessarily more difficult for our exporters to compete in Western markets.

Let me elaborate briefly on the deficit issue. All of the policies of the federal government and all of the changes that we might make in them to improve the environment for innovation in this country will be squandered if we in the federal government continue to spend far more than the tax revenue we collect. If we do not cut spending significantly now, deficits in the future will increase dramatically, growing rather than decreasing in a time of rapid economic growth.

My experience with my own company, System Industries, provides an analogy. The company was "growing like gangbusters" at one time, but it was losing money. I said, "This is as good as it gets. If we can't make money when things are going good, we're going to be in real trouble when things slow down!" So I sold off a couple of divisions, eliminated some product lines, cut back on overhead, and got the company to the point where it could make money at a lower level of sales. I later realized that I should have made those decisions much sooner—it was just good business to do so. Our country is now in exactly the same position that my company was in during those times. The United States has accumulated a set of spending activities that are driving up the deficit even as the economy is growing. If we cannot reduce the deficit in good economic times, we will have no chance to do so when the economic growth subsides.

How did we get here? Let me illustrate. You may not know who I am. Many people don't. So I "carry an American Express card." However, I also have another card, a better one—the voting card of the House of Representatives. When the bells ring in the House to call members for a vote, I have 15 minutes to run up, pull out my card, and stick it in the voting machine. If I push the green button to vote yes, I can spend $5 billion just like that. Or $350 million, if it's a slow day. Or, as we did in October 1984, on the last day of the session, $500 billion in one vote. After voting, I put this card—I call it my "American Distress" card—back in my wallet and go back to the office. Then the phones start ringing and the mail comes in. My constituents say, "Thanks, Ed, for supporting my program." And I say, "It was nothing!" Which is true. It didn't cost me a dime. You see, the American Distress card is much better than the American Express card because I get the credit but you get the bill.

That is why we have budget deficits—the constant and unbalanced pressure to spend more money. I hope that the American people understand that continued deficit spending is a clear and present danger. Congress must act and act now. All spending, every program in the federal budget, must be scrutinized for savings. We must freeze spending across the board, but we must do more than that. We must eliminate programs that have outlived their usefulness or, despite laudable objectives, cannot be justified when deficit spending is putting our economic future at risk. Moreover for those programs that are retained, we must make them more effective and efficient, just as we would if we were a business.

In conclusion, let me reiterate that the proper role of government in advancing technology and economic growth in this country is not to target specific industries, technologies, or companies. Rather, it is to have a set of policies that stimulate the environment for innovation so that the private sector can operate as it is supposed to. This concept was implicit in the recommendations of the President's Commission on Industrial Competitiveness, chaired by John Young (for discussion of recommendations, see "Global Competition—The New Reality," in this volume).

Finally, we should recognize that this debate on the role of government in fostering technological advancement can be reduced to some fundamental questions: Who is responsible for creating jobs in this country? Who is responsible for advancing technology? Who is responsible for creating economic growth, exports, and new ideas? Some people believe that those are the government's job and that is why we have jobs programs and industrial policy advocates. But I say that those in academia and industry are responsible for creating jobs and for technological advances. And it is our job—those of us in government—to create an environment in which people in academia and industry can do their jobs in the future as well as they have done them in the past.

The Japanese Challenge
in High Technology

DANIEL I. OKIMOTO

Japan may have to embark on a crash program to expand and upgrade its infrastructure in science and technology so that it can innovate. It can no longer exploit the advantages of latecomer status. It may not be able to follow a low-cost, low-risk strategy of second-to-market by capitalizing on low production costs. As comparative advantage shifts to the newly industrializing states, Japan will have to compete head to head with the United States in what has been the traditional U.S. stronghold, high technology.

BACKGROUND

Since the end of World War II, the United States has dominated the area of high technology. Virtually all the major high technology industries, from nuclear energy to microelectronics, were started in the United States, most emerging out of the structure of the so-called military-industrial complex and reaching maturity in the commercial marketplace. Even today, U.S. producers hold the lion's share of world markets in most high technology products. Indeed, individual American companies like IBM (computers), AT&T (telecommunications), and Boeing (commercial jet airliners) set the pace of competition, define standards for their industries, and demonstrate a capacity to dominate product markets even when competitors enter first.

Less than 25 years ago, however, the same could be said of American manufacturers in heavy industries. U.S. producers had a corner on the largest share of world markets, stood at the cutting edge of technology, and dictated the pace of commercial competition. Twenty-five years ago (1960), U.S. companies accounted for more than a quarter of world steel production, over half of total auto assembly, and (in the early- to mid-1960s) nearly 90 percent of all color television sets produced. Famous American brand names—U.S. Steel, General Motors, and Zenith—were synonymous with leadership in these industries.

It took less than two decades, however, for Japanese manufacturers to overtake U.S. front-runners. By 1980, America's share of world production in steel had fallen from 26 percent to 14 percent, from over 50 percent to 21 percent in automobiles, and from 90 percent to less than 30 percent in color televisions. Japan's share of world production rose from 6.4 percent to 15.5 percent in steel, from less than 5 percent to 30 percent in automobiles, and from almost zero to over 50 percent in color televisions. The speed with which the Japanese overtook American pacesetters surprised everyone, including the Japanese themselves.

Against the background of this experience in the "smokestack" sectors, the question arises: Is America's current leadership in high technology safe from the Japanese challenge? The Ministry of International Trade and Industry (MITI) has "targeted" virtually all areas of high technology as national priorities. Does this mean that the Japanese will be able to replicate their smokestack successes? The Japanese may already be ahead in certain areas of high technology, such as robotics; as of 1982, Japan had installed more than three times the number of robots as the United States (President's Commission on Industrial Competitiveness, 1985, vol. 1:22). In other areas in which Americans still hold a lead, such as semiconductors and optoelectronics, U.S. companies are hearing the footsteps of the Japanese, who are moving speedily to close the gap. In the most lucrative commercial markets, such as computers, telecommunications, home and office automation, and medical instrumentation, Japanese manufacturers have already emerged as America's most formidable competitors, combining some state-of-the-art technology with traditional strengths in manufacturing, pricing, and marketing. Although the Europeans possess strengths in certain market niches, none of the European states appears to be mounting a serious challenge across all areas. The race in high technology is shaping up as largely a bilateral competition between Japan and America, with Europe straining not to fall too far behind.

There are not many fields in which the Japanese can be counted out. Even in areas in which American preeminence once appeared relatively unassailable—such as software, CAD/CAM (computer-aided design and computer-aided manufacturing), and laser technology—the Japanese appear to be making substantial headway. Convinced that these technologies are of crucial importance for their capacity to compete effectively over the long run, the Japanese are mobilizing human and capital resources to close the gap. Only in areas in which Japan is at a decisive disadvantage—as in military-related endeavors or in products for which the costs of energy or raw material inputs are prohibitively high—can the Japanese be judged completely out of the running. Falling into this category are avionics, military hardware (due in part to Japan's self-imposed ban on weapons exports), commercial jet aircraft, space and satellites, and petrochemicals. In most other areas, the high technology sweepstakes appear to be wide open.

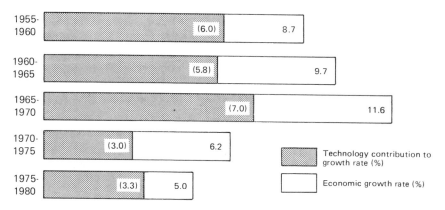

FIGURE 1   Technology's contribution to Japan's economic growth, according to analysis by Dr. Hisao Kanamon, president of Japan Economic Research Center. (Figures for 1975–1980 include estimates.)

Japan's swift emergence in high technology is unsettling, because Americans used to take comfort in the belief that, for whatever reason, the Japanese were inferior when it came to technological innovation. Of 500 seminal breakthroughs in technology identified between 1953 and 1973, only 34, roughly 5 percent, were achieved in Japan, compared with 63 percent in the United States (Moritani, 1982:159–173). Indeed, Japan's relative backwardness in technology has been reflected in its heavy dependence on foreign technology. It has run chronic deficits in its technological balance of trade throughout the postwar period (Ozawa, 1974:80). According to one estimate, Japan's "economic miracle" can be ascribed largely to the contributions made by technology, much of which was imported from the United States and adapted or incrementally improved (see Figure 1).

Importing the most advanced foreign technology had the effect of setting in motion a virtuous cycle, fostering heavy investments in new plant facilities (which embodied new production technology), stimulating economic growth, and generating greater demand for products manufactured under foreign license. In addition to its import-substitution effects, the assimilation of foreign technology also had the effect of making Japanese manufactured goods in such industries as electrical machinery, chemicals, and iron and steel more competitive in foreign markets. The mutually reinforcing nature of import substitution and export expansion, made possible by the assimilation of foreign technology, thus undergirds Japan's record-setting economic growth (Ozawa, 1974:46–51).

In a very real sense, therefore, Japan's so-called economic miracle owed at least as much to the availability of foreign know-how as it did to indigenous technology. The importance of imported know-how is underscored by MITI's survey of Japanese business leaders in 1978 concerning the relative contributions made by domestic and foreign technologies to product quality and production processes. According to MITI's survey, purely indigenous technology accounted for only 5 percent of the improvements in Japanese product quality and 17 percent of the advances made in production processes (Ministry of International Trade and Industry, 1982:36). Although such survey data should not be taken too literally, they tend to confirm what appears to be a fairly widespread impression: namely, that Japan has not been a seedbed of scientific ferment or technological originality. This image of Japan as a technological follower and the contrasting image of Japan as a technological innovator are elaborated below.

Image I: Technological Follower

The impression that Japan is a technological follower gains credence by looking at a variety of indirect indicators. Despite its large population base, for example, Japan has won fewer Nobel Prizes in the basic sciences than much smaller countries, for example, Sweden, the Netherlands, Switzerland, and Belgium. In 1964 Japan spent only 1.4 percent of GNP on R&D, compared with America's 3.4 percent and the United Kingdom's 2.3 percent. In 1971 the number of researchers per 10,000 population base was only 18 in Japan, compared with 25 in the United States (Ministry of International Trade and Industry, 1982:42, 44). Against this background, it is not hard to understand how the stigma of imitator and technological free rider came to be attached to Japan.

A variety of reasons have been cited for Japan's relative lack of technological originality. They range from historical circumstances (especially Japan's status as an industrial latecomer) to sociocultural impediments (e.g., the tendency toward group conformity), inadequacies of Japan's educational system (e.g., deficiencies in university-based research), and institutional factors (e.g., the lack of a venture capital market). Other obstacles to innovation sometimes cited include the practice of seniority-based, lifetime employment (said to limit the diffusion of innovation) and conservative, risk-averse attitudes on the part of highly levered Japanese corporations (alleged to inhibit bold R&D investments).

Whether the Japanese are simply incapable of technological innovation, however, is far from clear. Those refusing to believe so can point out that the same kind of doubts used to be expressed about Japan's alleged inability to ensure high standards of quality control. Look at what the Japanese have done to shatter that myth! Even those who believe that Japan is a follower tend to view the problem as essentially correctable, provided certain institutions, practices, and policies can be overhauled. Unless one assumes that the problem is genetic, therefore, Japan's undistinguished technological record can be traced back to structural impediments in Japan's catch-up R&D system.

Very much aware of these impediments, the Japanese are trying hard to overcome them through structural change. Some of these changes are being explicitly engineered for the purpose of building an environment more conducive to innovation; others are the by-product of evolutionary development. The essential point is that most of the impediments are not insurmountable. From the standpoint of short-term results, probably the only obstacle that may not be immediately changeable is the deeply ingrained, sociocultural values and patterns of socialization. To the extent that Japan's problems are entangled with sociocultural impediments, the prospects for rapid correction do not appear bright.

On the other hand, since culture consists of a "collage" of diverse, inconsistent, and incompatible ingredients—not a single, coherent blend—its impact on something as complex as innovation is exceedingly hard to measure. Out of this collage the specific elements that emerge to affect human behavior usually depend on the structure of institutions and the set of policies and practices that give culture its concrete shape within a given, time-bound context. One indirect way of altering what are otherwise deeply embedded cultural parameters, therefore, is to restructure the institutional framework within which they exist.

Japan appears to be doing just that. It is trying to upgrade the quality of research at leading Japanese universities. The embryo of a venture capital market seems to be taking shape. Japanese labor markets are adapting to the functional requirements of high technology. The government is doing all it can to push Japan beyond the frontiers of technology by organizing a variety of ambitious national research projects in such seminal areas as new materials and optoelectronics. And with the deregulation and internationalization of financial markets, many Japanese corporations have reduced their levels of dependence on debt financing in order to cope with the loss of insulation against wide interest rate fluctuations. All these changes could significantly affect Japan's capacity to innovate.

Public policies are also undergoing change. Having graduated from being a latecomer, Japan finally finds itself in a position to take on the challenge of trying to innovate at the frontiers of technology. Prior to this time, Japan had been wholly absorbed in the task of industrial catch-up. In this sense, the question of technological originality is only meaningful now that the era of playing catch-up is over. Because frontier innovation has become more important than ever, Japan seems bent on mobilizing to upgrade its technological capabilities. It is now spending 2.4 percent of an ever-expanding GNP on R&D, and the projections are that allocations will eventually reach 3 percent in the 1990s. The number of researchers per 10,000 population has risen from 18 to 27. This growing investment of capital and manpower in R&D is beginning to pay dividends. Although Japan still runs an overall deficit in its balance of technological trade, the ratio of Japanese technological exports to imports is climbing. What used to be a 1:47 ratio has become a 2:3 ratio; in 1980, exports of Japanese technology amounted to $638 million and imports of foreign technology came to $958 million (Ministry of International Trade and Industry, 1982:173). Areas in which Japanese technology is so advanced that it can be sold overseas include agricultural chemicals, construction equipment, transportation machinery, electrical machinery, iron and steel, and ceramics—areas in which Japan also happens to be successful at exporting finished goods.

Image II: Technological Leader

Notwithstanding its imitator stereotype, Japan has managed to achieve state-of-the-art technology in certain fields of telecommunications (e.g., fiber optics), microelectronic components (e.g., gallium arsenide memory chips), robotics (e.g., numerically controlled devices), office automation (e.g., computer peripherals), nuclear energy (e.g., fast breeder reactors), and biotechnology (e.g., fermentation). It is even making big strides in technologies in which America's lead once seemed insurmountable, such as in artificial intelligence (e.g., expert systems).

Japan's rapid technological progress and its long-term commitment to compete across the board suggest an image that stands in sharp contrast to that of technological imitator and free rider: namely, that of a technological leader or possibly even a pacesetter. Indeed, against the background of Japan's astounding accomplishments in heavy manufacturing and the unexpected speed of its advance in high technology, a new image has emerged outside of Japan: that of an almost invincible Goliath, capable of vanquishing any rival, whatever the field of endeavor. Yesterday, it won in the smokestack sectors; tomorrow, it might be high technology; and thereafter, the service sectors. Japan is thought to possess superior strength in such areas as political stability, economic policies, government-business cooperation, labor-management relations, corporate financing, business-banking ties, and so on. It is almost as if "victory" is assured when the government "targets" an industry as central to its economic future and proceeds to mobilize massive resources to ensure eventual domination.

Which Is the "Real" Japan?

Is Japan a technological imitator and industrial overachiever? Or an astute learner and unbeatable colossus? Is America up against a David or a Goliath? Will Japan dislodge the United States from its current position of dominance in high technology as convincingly as it did in the smokestack sectors? Or has Japan reached the limits of its phenomenal postwar growth? The answer to these questions is bound to have a crucial bearing on America's industrial future, not to mention the fundamental shape of the world system. In order to provide an adequate answer, one must evaluate Japan's strengths and weaknesses, review where it has advanced and where it has not, understand some of the underlying reasons, identify where significant changes seem to be taking place, and assess what it all means. Of course, no analysis—no matter how detailed—can offer a definitive assessment on which accurate predictions can be based. The variables are much too complex. The most that can be realistically achieved is to provide a crude overview of some of the major factors at work in Japan's transition from a war-ravaged economy to one based increasingly on high technology.

JAPAN'S TECHNOLOGICAL STRENGTHS AND WEAKNESSES

Perhaps the best way of approaching the questions just raised is to examine in what fields of high technology the Japanese have fared comparatively well and in what fields they have been less successful. Such a review should help sort out the characteristics that underlie the patterns of successes and short-comings. Consumer electronics and semiconductors stand out as perhaps the best-known success stories. CAD/CAM technology, avionics, and space and commercial aircraft represent technologies in which Japan's progress to date has been notably less impressive. The review begins with the common features of Japan's successful forays into high technology.

Successful Industries

Consumer Electronics Despite the fact that transistors and integrated circuits were invented in the United States and despite America's pioneering work in solid-state physics, Japan was the first country to succeed in commercializing transistor technology for radios and televisions; miniaturization revolutionized the entire consumer electronics industry. Japan's commercial successes, especially in the early stages, can be attributed largely to several factors: the availability of basic patents from the United States, the ability of Japanese companies to modify imported technology and bring it to very high levels of refinement, sustained and growing levels of capital investments in R&D, low production costs, aggressive pricing, and mass marketing at home and abroad. A typical example of Japanese product improvement based on foreign patents is the video tape recorder, one of Japan's biggest export items (accounting for nearly $6 billion in export revenues), which happened to be invented in the United States but was adapted and commercially exploited by the Japanese.

The Japanese have also excelled in consumer electronics because of heavy and sustained investments in both R&D and in new plant facilities. To survive in Japan's fiercely competitive environment, Japanese corporations must allocate a significant portion of revenues for investment in ongoing R&D and manufacturing facilities. Indeed, low-cost, highly reliable manufacturing is a hallmark of the country's industrial success. Part of Japan's manufacturing prowess can be attributed to the quality of its labor force, techniques of quality control, and extensive subcontracting networks; but part of the explanation can also be traced back to the high priority placed on investing in world-class process and production technology, which are thought in Japan to constitute the keys to commercial success.

The emphasis placed on process and production technology is accentuated by such distinctive characteristics of Japanese industrial organization as the practice of permanent employment. Company secrets on process and production technology can be safeguarded in Japan, a task far more difficult in the United States where labor is more mobile. Investing in process and production technology thus makes sense because it can give companies the competitive edge they seek. In sum, Japan's experience in consumer electronics demonstrates that if latecomers cannot compete at the cutting edges of new-product design, they can still compete effectively as second-to-market entrants by concentrating on manufacturing and process know-how, incremental product improvements, and mass marketing.

Japan's success at mass marketing has grown out of a large and rapidly expanding domestic market (protected from the 1960s to the mid-1970s by "infant-industry" measures), access to big overseas markets, and aggressive pricing (leading in some instances to charges of dumping abroad). Gaining large shares of the world consumer electronics market has provided a springboard on which diversified Japanese electronics giants have been able to expand into technologically related industries—such as semiconductors, computers, and telecommunications. Hand-held and desk calculators, for example, created brisk demand for mass-memory chips and generated momentum for the development of Japan's semiconductor industry (Okimoto et al., 1984:179).

One noteworthy aspect of the consumer electronics experience is that Japan's development in this field took place outside the scope of industrial policy "targeting." Consumer electronics did *not* grow out of a long-term MITI blueprint or plan. It was not weaned on preferential credit allocations, ambitious national research projects (except for related industries like semiconductors and information processing), research subsidies, extensive administrative guidance, or government intervention. Only in such areas as export facilitation and protection of infant industries did MITI extend a visible hand. In most other fundamental respects, market competition supplied the kinetic energy behind the development of the consumer electronics industry.

This illustrates that technological innovation in Japan—contrary to popular misperception—does not depend necessarily on industrial policy targeting (Okimoto, 1983).

The government's power to foster innovation is not nearly as great as is sometimes assumed (Semiconductor Industry Association, 1983). It can identify the high-priority technologies, to be sure, but it cannot guarantee that private corporations will succeed in commercializing them. It can throw up a cordon of infant-industry protection around domestic markets in order to keep foreign competitors out, but that often has the perverse effect of dulling incentives to innovate. It can channel subsidies into "targeted" R&D, but that can lead to distortions and waste in aggregate R&D investments. What lies within the government's effective power is largely limited to the creation of a healthy environment for business growth. MITI officials believe that a favorable overall environment is best achieved through sound macroeconomic policies, generous tax provisions, and compensation for deficiencies in the market mechanism. It is no accident that in high technology, the two most dynamic countries—the United States and Japan—are also the ones where market competition is keenest.

Semiconductors Most of the factors cited as an explanation of Japan's success in consumer electronics—the importation of basic foreign patents, high and sustained investments in R&D and state-of-the-art manufacturing facilities, superior process and production technology, economies of scale (achieved in part through aggressive export efforts), severe price competition, and so on—also account for its progress in semiconductors. Japan's fast-paced development in semiconductor technology since the early 1970s is reflected in the fact that it has come from nowhere to capture more than a 20 percent share of world production of integrated circuits. Japanese manufacturers are especially adept at producing very large scale integrated (VLSI) circuits, most notably random access memory (RAM) chips, which are based on straightforward, fairly predictable technologies. Japan is also advancing rapidly in the production of semiconductor equipment, an area that used to be dominated by U.S. merchant houses but which is now witnessing notable market inroads by specialized Japanese companies owned by the Japanese electronics giants. These companies produce the gamut of production equipment, including mask aligners, ion implanters, die-sorting machines, processing treatment machines, and testing equipment.

As with consumer electronics and heavy manufacturing, Japanese manufacturers of semiconductors place tremendous importance on process technology, an emphasis that seeks to take full advantage of Japan's outstanding strengths in process innovation. Examples of state-of-the-art Japanese semiconductor process technology include very fast automated bonding machines, uniform film epitaxial processes, highly pressurized oxidation, low-temperature passivation, anodization processes, and sophisticated ion-beam machines (Okimoto et al., 1984:51). Here again, nearly all the basic breakthroughs in semiconductor process innovation, including electron beam lithography, ion implantation, and plasma etching, first occurred in the United States. Making use of these breakthroughs, the Japanese adapted and incrementally improved on them in ways that eventually enabled Japanese equipment manufacturers to compete in their own market against American imports.

Looking at the area of seminal new-product design, however, Japan's contributions have not been very impressive relative to its share of world semiconductor production. Except for Esaki's discovery of the tunnel diode, practically all seminal breakthroughs have been made outside Japan. Until the 1980s, Japan gave very little indication of being able to compete in complex, state-of-the-art semiconductor technology. Indeed, owing to their limitations, Japanese companies felt compelled to enter into licensing or second-sourcing agreements with leading American designers of microprocessors, logic devices, and semicustomized and customized chips.

The government has played a larger role in the development of the semiconductor industry than it did in consumer electronics. As a "targeted" technology, semiconductors received industrial policy supports never extended to consumer electronics—early tariff protection, national R&D projects, R&D subsidies, and the like. However, precisely how much of a difference industrial targeting made is hard to measure. It was probably not decisive. National research projects, like the VLSI, helped to mobilize resources and to close the technological gap with the United States, but in all likelihood, Japanese companies would have narrowed the gap anyway, albeit at a slower pace. The amount of government funding for R&D in high technology (not just electronics) is surprisingly modest. From 1980 to 1990, a conservative estimate places it at roughly $2.3 billion, or about $230 million per year, an amount substantially smaller than that of the U.S. or French government (Okimoto, forthcoming, Ch. 2). If government funding as a percentage of total R&D expenditures for all sectors is compared for Japan and other leading countries, Japan comes out with the lowest share, even controlling for defense-related expenditures (Table 1).

What about government funding across sectors as a percentage of R&D and R&D as percentage of total sales (research intensity)? The comparative data in Table 2 show a significantly higher level of research intensity in the United States, but note how much higher the percentage of government funding is in most categories. Since the categories are broad, the data should be interpreted with care. Nevertheless, the contrast in government funding for the category of electrical machinery (into which semiconductors fall) is striking. As Tables 1 and 2 reveal, the notion that technological progress in Japan is the by-product of heavy state subsidization simply fails to accord with the facts. The private sector in Japan carries a heavier share of the

TABLE 1   Government Funding As a Percentage of Total R&D Expenditures, Selected Countries

Country	Government Funding	
	Total	Non-defense-related
Japan (1980)	25.8%	25.4%
United States (1980)	47.9	33.2
England (1978)	48.1	31.6
West Germany (1979)	46.8	43.6
France (1979)	51.1	37.9

SOURCE: Kagaku Gijutsu-cho, *Kagaku Gijutsu Hakusho* (Science and Technology White Paper) (Japanese Government Printing Office, 1982).

national R&D burden than in other major non-Communist countries. The Japanese government's role in semiconductors, as in most "targeted" technologies, should be understood in this context. While government assistance should not be underestimated, particularly with respect to coordination and consensus building, the main driving force behind the semiconductor industry's development has been the energy, manpower, and capital resources invested by the private sector.

Of all possible government actions having an impact on the growth of high technology industries, the most important has not been industrial policy targeting; rather, it has been effective macroeconomic management. Mon-

TABLE 2   Government Funding and Research Intensity, 1981 (percentages)

Category	Japan		United States	
	Gov't Funding	Research Intensity	Gov't Funding	Research Intensity
Chemicals	0.82	3.05	7.19	3.83
Petroleum refining and extraction	4.48	0.18	7.29	0.72
Rubber products	—	2.32	23.8	2.56
Ferrous materials	4.49	1.44	25.0	0.81
Nonferrous metals	2.82	1.37	37.6	1.21
Machinery	1.63	2.18	10.9	2.57
Electrical machinery	1.69	4.52	37.9	6.82
Telecommunications	1.63	4.72	33.9	8.90
Transportation equipment	3.88	2.69	59.8	8.37
Precision instruments	0.46	3.73	17.3	8.38

SOURCES: Sorifu, *Kagaku Gijutsu Kenkyu Chosa Koku, 1982* (Survey Report on Science and Technology, 1982) (Japanese Government Printing Office, 1982); National Science Foundation, *Research and Development in Industry, 1981* (Washington, D.C., 1982); Gary R. Saxonhouse and Daniel I. Okimoto, Technology and the Future of the Japanese Economy. Paper prepared for Japanese Political Economy Research Conference, Honolulu, Hawaii, January 1985.

etary and fiscal policies cannot help but be important because they affect interest rates, inflation, and growth rates, the basic determinants of economic vigor or stagnancy. At the early stage of its industrial life cycle, the semiconductor industry was especially responsive to macroeconomic conditions, owing to the high elasticity of demand for semiconductor products. The higher the growth rate, the faster its development. Its rapid growth since the mid-1970s, in fact, can be attributed in significant measure to the soundness of macroeconomic policies (far more than industrial policy). Simply put, Japan's macroeconomic performance during the period provided the semiconductor industry with a healthier climate for vigorous growth than did that of the United States and the European countries. This, in turn, made the implementation of industrial policy easier and more effective.

Looked at in comparative perspective, the pace of Japan's development in microelectronics has been remarkable. Japan may already have passed the United States in complicated, superconductivity technologies, like gallium arsenide and Josephson junction. Unlike IBM, which abandoned its work on Josephson junction after many years of experimentation, Japanese companies appear bent on carrying their R&D through to commercial fruition; Japanese executives obviously believe that IBM's decision may have been premature. If their forecast proves accurate, the Japanese might find themselves in a position to make their first major contribution to microelectronics through the technology of superconductivity, a technology that could alter the whole field of silicon-based engineering.

Regardless of whether they do, the point is that the Japanese are demonstrating that they can innovate at the frontiers of technology, not just in the areas of incremental product improvement and process adaptations. They have done very well in fields other than semiconductors and consumer electronics—in optoelectronics, telecommunications (e.g., power transmission cables), pharmaceuticals, fine ceramics, and new composite materials. The evidence is sufficiently plentiful, indeed, that the myth of Japan's technological inferiority can be put to rest.

Innovation in Non-Export-Dependent Industries   As pointed out earlier, Japan tends to excel at technologies that are closely tied to commodities with huge export markets—continuous casting in steel, emission-control technology for automobiles, and so forth. The powerful pull of overseas demand has helped Japanese companies move down the learning curve and advance technologically. What is not as well known, however, is that Japan has also done well in some industries that are not dependent on exports for a significant share of production, like pharmaceuticals (e.g., Interleukin-II), biotechnology (e.g., fermentation, gamma interferon from synthetic genes), and telecommunications (e.g., digital switching equipment, power transmission cables). This suggests that, even without the boost of overseas demand, the Japanese are capable of innovating on a par with front-running foreign competitors. Of course, the availability of foreign know-how and the size of Japan's domestic market have helped make innovation in non-export-oriented sectors possible. The smaller size of markets in individual European countries certainly makes it harder for local manufacturers there to compete. From this standpoint, Japan and America hold a major advantage over European entrants in the high technology sweepstakes.

It is also worth noting that some of these domestically preoccupied but technologically vital industries used to be shielded (and still are to a significant extent) from the full force of international competition. Usually, protectionism diminishes incentives to innovate, since profits can be made—with survival assured—without having to face up to the threat of foreign competition. Normally, this is a formula for commercial complacency and technological stagnation. That the state of technology has not stagnated is a reflection of the fact that, even behind closed doors, Japanese producers have had to operate in a domestic crucible of fierce interfirm competition. (This unusual, seemingly incongruous combination of domestic protectionism and technological dynamism helps to explain why key Japanese industries have been able to graduate from infant-industry status to world-class competitors while protected industries in other countries fail.)

Characteristics of Technological Achievements By way of concluding this portion of the analysis, the following list summarizes some of the common characteristics of Japan's best-known technological achievements:

Technological Features
- Predictable technological trajectories (RAMs)
- Known theoretical parameters (solid-state physics)
- Emphasis on process and production technologies (ion-beam etching)
- Steep learning curves
- Concentration on applied research and development
- Importation and modification of foreign know-how

Industrial Organization
- Dominance of large corporations
- Fierce interfirm competition
- Close, cooperative relations with networks of small subcontractors
- Lifetime employment: relatively limited labor mobility between firms
- Reduction and diffusion of risk through organizational mechanisms

Commercial Factors
- High and sustained R&D investments
- Large and growing domestic demand
- Usually, a powerful export thrust
- Difficulties of penetration by foreign competitors
- Success even in sectors not "targeted" by government (consumer electronics)

Government Policy
- Overwhelming concentration on commercially valuable technology
- Targeting of "strategic" sectors and technologies
- Consensus building across public and private sectors
- Cooperative national research projects in areas of high risk and heavy cost but of potentially great commercial benefit
- Modest R&D subsidies
- Use of positive incentives (taxes, pragmatic antitrust enforcement)
- Creation of favorable macroeconomic environment

"Targeted" Technologies: Slower Progress

Turning now to areas in which the pace of technological progress in Japan has lagged that of the United States, space, commercial jet aircraft, software and CAD/CAM, and lasers represent "targeted" technologies in which the Japanese have progressed more slowly than expected. The characteristics that have made progress in these technologies difficult for Japan can be summarized as follows:

Technological Features
- Heavy dependence on basic scientific research (space, lasers)
- Complex parameters for problem solution (aircraft design)
- Technological trajectories not clearly predictable (CAD/CAM)
- Complicated systems integration of a multitude of components (aerospace, aircraft)
- Large-scale, multidisciplinary R&D of long gestation (aircraft, space)
- Commercial uncertainties or the prospect of limited spillovers for commercial markets
- Unavailability of classified technology from the United States

Industrial Organization
- Limited experience in organizing international consortiums for subcontracting of R&D and production (aircraft)
- Exceedingly high barriers to new entry (aircraft, space)
- Lack of a venture capital market
- Labor and capital market constraints on the exploitation of new technological opportunities by independent, small-scale companies
- Inhibitions on the diffusion of technology by limited labor mobility

Commercial Factors
- Exceedingly high costs of R&D and manufacturing (aircraft, space)
- Comparatively small volumes for commercial sales (aircraft, space)
- Very high per unit prices (aircraft, space)
- Limited domestic demand (space, aircraft)
- Dim prospects for large-volume exports (except for lasers)

Government Policy
- Need to tie large budgetary outlays to national defense or security justifications
- Difficulties of building very costly support infrastructure for testing, flight simulation, and so on (aircraft, space)
- Limited powers of procurement

As indicated above, the Japanese have had difficulty dealing with technologies that are highly complex, not very predictable, and heavily dependent on basic research. Japan's strength and overwhelming emphasis have been applied research, dealing with known parameters and predictable technological trajectories (as in the geometric progression of density in integrated circuits). The Japanese are superb at problem solving, particularly when it comes to applied engineering problems. Neither their college nor on-the-job training has prepared them to excel at less straightforward problems involving, say, systems software or CAD/CAM technology.

Problems in the Educational System   Japan's educational system, though good at turning out students whose performance on standardized mathematics and science tests places them at or near the top of all national groups, does not appear to bring out creativity in the most gifted students. It stresses rote memorization over creative synthesis or critical analysis. Japanese students, even at the doctoral level, shy away from tackling research topics that require building new theories (Interview with a professor of computer science at the University of Tokyo, May 10, 1984). They prefer problems with known parameters and for which solutions can be found using extant theories. Such training suggests strengths at solving discrete problems but weaknesses at research tasks that call for creative conceptualization, like the design of advanced systems software and large jet aircraft.

In certain technologies that are closely tied to the basic sciences, like space, aircraft, or biotechnology, Japan may also be at a disadvantage because of the lower level of scientific research at Japanese universities compared with leading universities in the United States, England, and other of the European countries. Moreover, researchers at Japanese corporations do not interact as synergistically with university faculty as their counterparts in the United States. As civil servants, faculty members at leading national universities cannot spend substantial portions of their time consulting for private industry. The value of close university-industry ties can be seen in the history of interactions between Stanford University and Silicon Valley firms. It is no accident that industrial centers of high technology in the United States have sprung up around major research universities.

So long as Japan's R&D needs could be met without reliance on basic research, the inadequacies of its universities did not hamper its industrial progress. However, as Japan has moved into high technology, the shortcomings are becoming more serious. Indeed, Japan's whole R&D system—oriented overwhelmingly toward applied research and its rapid commercialization, with scant attention paid to basic research—may require extensive revamping. How far and fast Japan is able to progress in, say, pharmaceuticals and biotechnology may come to hinge increasingly on the quality of its university-based research in biology, biochemistry, chemistry, and other natural science fields.

Japan's laser industry has failed to keep pace with its U.S. counterpart largely because university-based research in applied physics has lagged. University-based research in lasers has not received anywhere near the level of support that it has in the United States. Moreover, effective allocation of research funds in Japan is seriously hampered by the fact that the country's leading universities are public, not private, and therefore dependent on budgetary allocations from the conservative, bureaucratically rigid Ministry of Education. There is no system of competitive peer review, comparable to that used in the United States, by which research support is allocated to the most deserving scientists and projects at whatever university they happen to be. Funds tend to be funneled through the same hierarchy of universities, almost as if inertially following the grooves of past channels. Although the system is not devoid of meritocratic considerations, it is not nearly as meritocratic, flexible, or cost-effective as America's competitive peer review system. In a system like Japan's, exciting new fields of scientific inquiry can be neglected.

The bureaucratic rigidities built into Japan's educational system also make it difficult for the country's leading public universities to adjust graduate enrollments in specific fields to changing student interests and needs. At the University of Tokyo, for example, the number of graduate students in computer science is very small—despite considerable student interest and the obvious commercial importance of the field. Why are enrollments so small? The main reason is administrative inflexibility. To expand the number of graduate students in, say, applied physics or computer science, the university must reduce the number in other fields, such as agriculture; the aggregate number of students must stay the same. This means that the departments of applied physics or computer science must persuade the agriculture department to give up part of its enrollment allocation, something any department is unlikely to do. Hence, Japan's capacity to adapt to the changing needs of university-based research and manpower training is circumscribed by the rigidities of its educational bureaucracy.

National Security-related R&D and Government Procurements Besides the deficiencies in higher education and basic research, Japan's R&D system is also not geared to underwrite very expensive but militarily important projects, such as aerospace and aircraft. These industries obviously suffer from the government's inability to sponsor very costly programs involving multidisciplinary research projects of high risk, great uncertainty, and long gestation. Comparing government R&D expenditures by broad categories (Table 3) reveals a striking contrast between Japan and the United States and France with respect to three categories—defense and aerospace, agriculture,

TABLE 3 Government R&D Expenditures, by Fields, 1980 (percentages)

Field	United States	Japan	France
Defense and aerospace	47.3	16.3	49.3
Industry	0.3	12.2	7.9
Agriculture	2.7	25.4	4.3
Energy and infrastructure	14.2	34.4	16.0
Health and welfare	15.2	11.2	7.5

SOURCE: Adapted from Gary R. Saxonhouse and Daniel I. Okimoto, Technology and the Future of the Japanese Economy. Paper prepared for Japanese Political Economy Research Conference, Honolulu, Hawaii, January 1985.

and industry. Within the context of these spending priorities, it is hardly surprising that Japan's space and aircraft industries have lagged far behind American and French front-runners, or that Japan is advanced in technologies related to agriculture (e.g., agricultural chemicals), industrial applications (e.g., numerically controlled robots), and energy utilization (e.g., superconductive toroidal magnets for nuclear fusion reactors).

A feature of Japan's R&D system that stands in stark contrast to the American system is the Japanese government's relative lack of procurement powers for high technology products. No ministry possesses anything like the vast sums of money at the disposal of the U.S. Department of Defense or the National Aeronautics and Space Administration (NASA). Only 25 percent of the Japanese Defense Agency's small budget, which is only 1 percent of GNP, is earmarked for hardware acquisition. MITI has almost no budget for procurements. Only Nippon Telegraph and Telephone (NTT), a public corporation (but privatized in April 1985) had the budgetary means to purchase large quantities of high technology products.

This situation, quite unusual among advanced industrial states, has had a number of important implications for Japan's R&D process: (1) macroeconomic policies aimed at expanding aggregate demand have played a greater role than targeted industrial policy in promoting the growth of high technology products; (2) MITI has had to rely predominantly on supply-related incentives, not demand-pull measures; (3) inefficient resource allocation, waste, and politicization have been kept under comparative control; (4) Japanese producers have had to recoup up-front R&D investments quickly through profits earned from consumer markets, and this has prompted Japanese management to stress applied research and development instead of basic or prototype-development research; (5) with no assurances of government demand for new products, Japanese companies have followed a fairly conservative approach to R&D, emphasizing reasonably high prospects of commercial feasibility—this may be one reason the Japanese have not been noted for creating whole new industries or major new product designs; and (6) Japanese engineers and scientists have not been diverted from commercially oriented

R&D to carry on highly specialized research for military and space applications. Like practically all other characteristics of Japan's R&D system, the implications have been neither all positive nor all negative, but a mixture of the two.

Aerospace Space research in Japan was begun much later than in the United States or the Soviet Union, the two world leaders, which account for more than 95 percent of the 2,800 artificial satellites launched to date. Japan's motivation for entering into space research had less to do with national security or international prestige than with long-range commercial opportunities in communications and broadcasting, scientific observation, and, more recently, the construction of space factories for bioengineering and new materials. Although Japan takes pride in the fact that it became the fourth country in the world to launch an artificial satellite (after the Soviet Union, the United States, and France), and although it produces about one-third of the earth station equipment for INTELSAT (the international telecommunications consortium), its technology in rockets and artificial satellites is inferior to that of the United States.

In the early phases of its space research, Japan had no choice but to borrow rocket technology from the United States; however, with technological independence an explicit goal, it did manage to develop its own small N-I and N-II rockets. In 1981 it began development for the H-I rocket, using domestically developed technology for second- and third-stage propulsion and for the induction control system. Once tested, the H-I rocket will be capable of launching an artificial satellite of around 550 kg into geostationary orbit.

In artificial satellite technology, Japan has followed a familiar pattern of development, moving from overwhelming dependence on foreign licensing to increasing technological independence. To build its CS Sakura satellite (1977), Japan was forced to rely heavily on U.S. technology and U.S. satellite components. However, in building the CS-2 communications satellite (1983), Japan was able to draw on more domestically developed technology; over 60 percent of the components installed were manufactured, assembled, and tested in Japan (Ministry of International Trade and Industry, 1982:64–77).

While Japan is making headway, it is still a long way from complete self-sufficiency in aerospace technology, and an even longer distance behind the United States. The National Space Development Agency (NASDA) continues to depend on American technology. Several American satellite manufacturers are involved in NASDA projects (e.g., Hughes Aircraft-NEC, General Electric-Toshiba, RCA-NEC), and TRW Inc. has helped with down-range tracking, software, satellite parts, and systems integration (Davis, 1985:21–28). U.S. manufacturers (e.g., Hughes Aircraft and Ford Aerospace) would like to sell satellites directly to the Japanese market, which would make sense from the standpoint of cost-effectiveness and technological criteria, but so far at least, U.S. companies have been unable to do so, owing in part to Japan's long-term goal of achieving self-sufficiency.

Although some of the R&D work in consumer electronics conducted by such big, diversified firms as NEC, Toshiba, and other diversified electronics firms can be applied to space technology, the spillovers from consumer electronics to aerospace are not that large. Moreover, it would be unrealistic to think that such limited spillovers could overcome the serious shortcomings in Japan's overall space effort—small government expenditures, a short history of experience (and early position on the learning curve), an inadequate base of highly skilled R&D manpower in aerospace, bureaucratic conflicts, deficiencies in basic scientific research, and weaknesses in software and systems integration. Here is a field, in short, in which the United States can expect to maintain its dominant position into the foreseeable future.

Commercial Jet Aircraft For some of the same reasons as stated above, the same conclusion can be reached with respect to the commercial jet aircraft industry. As Mowery and Rosenberg (1985) point out in their excellent study, Japan's commercial jet aircraft industry seems to be mired in a puzzling predicament: neither advancing along a fast track toward technological self-sufficiency as a world-class manufacturer of jet aircraft nor taking the route of establishing specialized niches in world markets. It is following policies that combine contradictory elements of both.

The Japanese government has "targeted" aircraft as a national priority, critical as an end-user industry bringing together many other high technology endeavors—microelectronics, new materials, CAD/CAM, and so forth. Yet, MITI has not sunk sufficient resources into aircraft or followed a sufficiently consistent strategy to turn it into a world-class industry. Moreover, the aircraft industry is not especially well suited for Japan. Airspace over the Japanese archipelago is narrow, mass transportation by land (especially railways) is extensive, sales volumes are very small, the soaring costs of R&D make the organization of international consortiums for R&D and production increasingly attractive but Japan has had limited experience at organizing such consortiums, Japan maintains a comparatively modest military aircraft capability, and the government has not installed costly testing equipment for manufacturers. Japan also seems ill-prepared to meet the demanding technological requirements, including highly complex designs, CAD/CAM, avionics, and systems integration. For all these reasons, the barriers to new entry have to be considered prohibitively high. Here, in short, is another area in which—despite government "targeting"—Japan is not likely to mount a serious challenge to American dominance. Indeed, if ever there was an illustration of fallibility in Japanese industrial policy targeting, the commercial jet aircraft industry would be the clear-cut example. Regardless of the criticisms that can be leveled at America's so-called military-industrial complex—such as cost-effectiveness, limited civilian spillover effects, costly trade-offs in terms of commercial opportunities—the system has succeeded in creating dominant aerospace and aircraft industries.

Strictly Commercial Orientation   It can be argued, on the other hand, that the aerospace and commercial aircraft industries are atypical and that the dominance of military considerations in America's R&D system is, on balance, more of a liability than an asset. In industries in which highly skilled research manpower is finite and in which the technological and commercial spillovers from military-oriented R&D are almost nonexistent, as in lasers, the opportunity costs of diverting manpower and resources can be substantial. There is already some concern being expressed in the U.S. laser industry that the "Star Wars" space defense concept could divert such large resources from commercially promising endeavors that Japanese companies could slip past the United States unnoticed, concentrating solely on commercial applications and benefiting from MITI's organization of national research projects in industrial lasers (Conversation with Professor Robert L. Byer, Department of Applied Physics, Stanford University, and executives from a leading laser manufacturing company, February 28, 1985).

In having the leeway to pursue purely commercial objectives, Japan may possess an advantage over the United States. It is not easy for the U.S. government to underwrite R&D programs designed to accelerate the development of key commercial technologies of high cost and uncertainty and of long gestation, no matter how essential they might be deemed for the future competitiveness of American industry. To secure substantial government funding, key technologies, such as artificial intelligence, usually have to fulfill some kind of military or national security need. The Defense Advanced Research Projects Agency's (DARPA's) project on artificial intelligence is a recent example; compare the fits and starts of DARPA's project with MITI's Fifth Generation Computer project, a cooperative undertaking that seems to be moving Japan's capabilities in artificial intelligence ahead at impressive speeds (Conversation with Professor Edward A. Feigenbaum, Department of Computer Science, Stanford University, January 18, 1985; see also Feigenbaum and McCorduck (1983)).

From the standpoint of R&D cost-effectiveness and Japanese competition, what may be as much of a problem for the United States as the domination of military priorities is the "public goods" nature of basic research conducted in the United States. The outflow of basic knowledge cannot be regulated, even if Japan pays for none of its costs. This suggests that Japan's low rate of investment in basic research and the government's relatively modest R&D funding may not really hamper the country's technological advance (though it obviously hurts some industries, like aerospace and aircraft, more than others).

Japanese National Research Projects To what extent, if at all, do government-sponsored R&D projects give Japan a competitive advantage over the United States? No doubt projects like the VLSI have facilitated technological catch-up. But the value of national research projects—like that of industrial "targeting"—is often exaggerated. The historical record to date is mixed; there have been some notable successes and several equally noteworthy failures. In the latter category can be counted the 3.75 Computer project (1972–1976), which failed to come up with the operating system it sought, and the Software Development project (1976–1981), which produced only a small number of computer-written, applications software packages suitable for commercial sale.

Even the heralded VLSI project (1976–1980), hailed as an unprecedented model of cooperative research, failed to push Japanese semiconductor technology beyond the frontiers of knowledge (except perhaps for liquid crystal displays). While the VLSI project did advance the state of Japanese semiconductor knowledge, especially in the area of production technology (e.g., silicon crystal growth and processing), Japanese companies probably would have made such advances eventually anyway. If so, the project's main accomplishment may have been to hasten the timetable of development, a nontrivial but hardly revolutionary accomplishment.

Organizing national research projects is no easy task. Even if all the organizational wrinkles can be ironed out, success is by no means automatic. To obtain useful results, the technological capabilities of participating firms must be relatively even. One or two firms cannot be too far ahead of the others, or they will not be willing to divulge proprietary information or cooperate in ways that help their competitors close the gap. Other things being equal, the smaller the number of firms, and the higher the market concentration, the greater the leeway for effective organization. The large number of firms and wide technological disparities between them help to explain why Japan has had trouble organizing major cooperative projects in biotechnology, pharmaceuticals, and applications software—symbolically and substantively important areas of high technology.

If government-sponsored, cooperative research is not as easily organized, nor as uniformly effective, as Americans assume, why has Japan continued relying on it? Indeed, why have national research projects expanded in number and scope? One intriguing answer is that they serve to compensate for structural shortcomings in Japan's capital and labor markets. Structural imperfections, such as the underdevelopment of Japan's equities market, Saxonhouse (1982) argues, have prompted the government to encourage capital investments through the christening of seminal technologies and industries. At the company level, high debt-to-equity financing has perhaps caused Japanese management to be more risk-averse and conservative with respect to R&D decisions (both in terms of money amounts and the uncertainty factor) than is optimal from the aggregate standpoint of national R&D investments. Similarly, because the high walls of lifetime employment impede the diffusion of technology across firms, the Japanese government is forced to step in and facilitate diffusion through interfirm participation in national research projects. Instead of viewing Japanese national research projects as decisive advantages, therefore, Saxonhouse sees them as necessary instruments of compensation for market imperfections in Japan.

If Saxonhouse's assessment is valid, one can infer that America's decentralized, market-driven system is clearly more efficient (in terms of capital allocation) and arguably more effective (in terms of stimulating technological innovation) than Japan's centralized, state "targeted" system. Indeed, one may question the effectiveness and suitability of Japan's system of industrial targeting for the swiftly changing requirements of high technology. Is public policy better suited to keep pace with the rapidity of commercial and technological change than the invisible hand of the free market? Is the state better at picking winners and losers than the decentralized marketplace? Can the state channel capital as neutrally? Japan's system of industrial targeting may have been appropriate for the needs of an earlier era of latecomer catch-up, but is it as effective, now that Japan has reached the frontiers of technology?

Lack of a Venture Capital Market   A striking difference in Japanese and American patterns of capital allocation for high technology is the lack of a venture capital market in Japan. In the United States, the cumulative total of venture investments, as of 1983, exceeded $7.5 billion; in Japan, by contrast, the total fell short of $90 million. The availability of venture funds in the United States has had a profound impact not only on the pace of technological progress but also on the evolving structure of high technology industries. It has created enticing incentives for energetic entrepreneurs to convert technological know-how into small start-up companies that offer new or differentiated products on the market.

Looking at the positive effects from an aggregate perspective, the steady stream of new start-ups serves to keep competition brisk, fosters technological ferment, and promotes efficiency in capital allocation for the high-growth sectors. From the perspective of established firms, however, venture capital can also lead to such dysfunctional side effects as unpredictable personnel turnovers, costly disruptions in R&D plans, escalating salaries for research personnel, difficulties in protecting proprietary information, and deepening entanglements in litigation concerning intellectual property rights. The actual effects—whether positive or negative—depend on the stage of an industry's life-cycle (the earlier the stage, the more positive the effect) and the type of companies involved.

It can be argued that the lack of a venture capital market, in combination with the characteristics of Japanese financial and labor markets, has hindered the creation of independent new start-ups. Even without a venture capital tradition, however, the small business sector has made important contributions to innovation in Japan, particularly in process and production technology. As Ken'ichi Imai (1984) points out, the flow of information, degree of R&D cooperation, and synergistic interaction between large parent firms and their many small subcontractors and subsidiaries constitute one of the great strengths of Japan's industrial organization. A number of innovations—mostly in process and production technology but also in some new-product designs—have emerged out of the structure of such vertical relationships.

Compared with the dynamism of independent, small firms in, say, Silicon Valley, however, Japan's small enterprise sector has not functioned as a fertile seedbed for technological innovation. A National Science Foundation (1976) study found that the number of innovations made by small and medium-sized firms in five countries was lowest in Japan. Research activity in small companies tends, on the whole, to be very limited. In 1981, only 8 percent of the small firms reported that they even engaged in R&D, compared with 56 percent for large companies (Organisation for Economic Cooperation and Development, 1982:199). Small firms in Japan labor under some significant handicaps, including a systemic bias in favor of big business, higher costs of capital, weaker drawing power for recruitment of top-notch researchers, lower prestige, and higher bankruptcy rates. It is no wonder they have not contributed as much to innovation as their counterparts in other countries.

The lack of a venture capital market is attributable to a variety of factors. There appears to be more than enough money for the creation of a large venture capital market; Hambrecht and Quist, for example, recently created a venture fund in Japan with Sanwa Bank and Oriental Leasing. But the problem is that Japan's stock market is not designed to handle small start-up companies. Without an entry vehicle into the stock market, venture investments cannot be liquidated, and venture capitalists cannot cash in on early-round financing. More importantly, the preference of the top college graduates for permanent employment at established corporations and the near impossibility of lateral reentry once an employee has left make it difficult for new start-ups to attract the best R&D talent from big corporations; most appear to prefer job security to the allure of making personal fortunes. Unless labor patterns change, therefore, the availability of venture capital will not have the same far-reaching impact in Japan that it has had in America. Small, independent firms in Japan will not have the luxury of operating in an environment as conducive to innovative dynamism as small companies in the United States.

CONCLUSIONS: MUST JAPAN INNOVATE?

Whatever one's view of Japan's technological future, there seems to be general agreement about the type of technologies in which the Japanese have excelled to date. These are listed below, along with the contrasting U.S. strengths:

Japanese Strengths	U.S. Strengths
Applied research and development	Basic research
Incremental improvements	Breakthroughs and inventions
Commercial applications	Military applications
Process and production technology	New-product design
Components	Systems integration
Hardware	Software
Predictable technologies	Less predictable trajectories
Quality control	New functionalities
Miniaturization	New architectural designs
Standardized, mass volumes	Customization and semicustomization

Lest the mistaken notion be conveyed that these technological characteristics emerge out of immutable national attributes, it should be pointed out that the areas of comparative strength are continually evolving, as high technology industries in the two countries mature. Japan is making progress in such areas as software, while America seems to be paying more attention to process and production technology. One should not regard current strengths and weaknesses, therefore, as either fixed or accurate indicators of where the two countries seem headed. Technology is moving too rapidly for time-bound generalizations to be valid for very long.

Even Japan's institutional structure is being transformed. As this happens, the country's capacity to innovate cannot help but be altered. For example, educational reform ranks near the top of the list of Prime Minister Nakasone's agenda of policy priorities. Despite bureaucratic inertia, infighting, and rigidities, Japan's educational system is undergoing change. More resources are being funneled into basic research, links between universities and industry are being expanded, rules governing personnel are becoming more flexible, and the curriculum is being revised. Japanese leaders realize that the educational system is badly in need of reform.

The financial sector, another critical area, is also changing rapidly, with far-reaching implications for Japanese industrial organization. As pointed out earlier, the deregulation of what used to be one of the most tightly regulated and insulated financial systems in the world is bound to alter the segmented banking structure, the "banking-industrial complex," patterns of corporate financing, *keiretsu* or bank-centered industrial groupings, and the willingness to take greater R&D risks. Financial deregulation may thus loosen the grip of nonmarket organizations on Japan's economy, freeing market forces to play a greater role.

Other changes under way include: (1) trends toward the "spinning off" of more R&D activities from large parent firms to small subcontractors and subsidiaries; (2) the creation of small subsidiaries designed to serve as the functional equivalent of small venture start-ups; (3) the appearance of the rudiments of a venture capital market; (4) signs of at least some shift toward greater labor mobility; (5) some erosion in the government's power to intervene in the market; (6) changes in the substance and role of Japanese industrial policy for high technology; and (7) greater attention to basic and precommercial, prototype research. As with financial deregulation, these changes could have the effect of freeing up market forces. They might also create a research environment that is more conducive to the kind of bold, new-product designs and state-of-the-art breakthroughs for which Japan has not heretofore been known.

In short, some of the rigidities of Japan's old R&D system—one geared to latecomer catch-up in the heavy manufacturing sectors—may be giving way to an adaptable R&D system that is more suitable to meeting the functional needs of high technology. Whether this heralds the onset of a new era of technological originality is still too early to tell. The evidence is too mixed to make simple projections possible.

To this point, this discussion has assumed that in order to compete in high technology, Japan will have to find ways of being more innovative. But is this assumption valid? Must Japan innovate? Why would it not be possible for Japan to continue doing exactly what it has done so successfully in the past: namely, follow a conservative, second-to-market strategy, letting America pay the high costs and take the risks of developing new industries and markets? Why not simply continue concentrating on the less glamorous but commercially more decisive areas of process and production technology and mass marketing? Is not the history of technology replete with examples of inventors being soundly thrashed in the commercial marketplace by technological second-comers?

There is no doubt that a distinction needs to be drawn between technological innovation and commercial success. The two are not necessarily linked. The first is no guarantee of the second. Nevertheless, because high technology sectors have steep learning curves and comparatively short product life cycles, the advantages of being first-to-market can be worth far more than the costs and risks of early investment. First-comers can secure dominant market share, win brand name recognition, move down the learning curve, raise the barriers to entry and, in some cases, push second-comers right out of existence.

Relying on foreign technology, as an alternative to domestic innovation, can leave companies at the mercy of foreign firms, which may or may not be willing to grant licenses in return for royalty payments. If patent holders believe they can gain more than they lose by withholding basic patents, Japanese second-to-market firms could find themselves closed out of burgeoning markets. Moreover, Japanese companies must also accept the reality of attempts by the U.S. government to impose restrictions on the international transfer of militarily sensitive, dual-purpose technologies. What would Japanese firms do if there was a groundswell of technological nationalism that restricted their access to foreign know-how?

Of course, for the latter, worst-case scenario to materialize, the international situation would probably have to deteriorate. Even then, it would be hard to shut off the flow of knowledge completely. In this era of high technology, the United States and Japan have common interests in keeping the transfer of technology open. The volume of technology transfer across the Pacific, including licensing, second-sourcing, original equipment manufacturer (OEM) agreements, and cross-licensing, is greater today than ever before. Nevertheless, even under an open international regime, Japanese companies would have to have their own technology in order to cross-license foreign know-how. In international technology transfers, more bartering seems to be taking place, a manifestation perhaps of the mounting costs and value of innovation. To obtain foreign technology, therefore, the Japanese believe they must develop their own in order to obtain something of comparable value from abroad. If their perception is correct, it means that they must be able to innovate.

Perhaps the most compelling reason why Japan needs to innovate is because the rapidly developing countries in Asia are moving quickly up the ladder of manufacturing value-added—into, for example, the low end of consumer electronics. As South Korea, Taiwan, and Singapore develop the infrastructure to mass-produce consumer electronics products, Japanese producers will have no choice (short of protectionist recourse) but to scramble up the ladder of value-added. They will have to move, for example, from consumer to industrial electronics, from hardware to software, from components to integrated systems. As "mini-Japans" spring up all around it, the only way of staying ahead will be to accelerate the pace of R&D.

For all these reasons, therefore, Japan may have to embark on a crash program to expand and upgrade its infrastructure in science and technology so that it can innovate. Japan can no longer exploit the advantages of latecomer status. It may not be able to follow a low-cost, low-risk strategy of second-to-market by capitalizing on low production costs. As comparative advantage shifts to the newly industrializing states, Japan will have to compete head to head with the United States in what has been the traditional U.S. stronghold, high technology.

The challenge facing Japan will almost certainly be harder than the past challenge of industrial catch-up in the smokestack sectors. Known for their adaptability, however, the Japanese are trying hard to overcome some of the old institutional constraints that have impeded innovation in the past. Whether they succeed remains to be seen. Notwithstanding the image of infallibility, success is by no means assured. But Japan's formidable storehouse of strengths, combined with the changes that are now taking place in its old R&D system, suggest that it certainly would be foolhardy to count Japan out.

REFERENCES

Davis, Neil W. 1985. Japanese space activities: Taking off in a big way. *The ACCJ Journal* 22(3): 21–28.

Feigenbaum, Edward A., and Pamela McCorduck. 1983. *The Fifth Generation: Artificial Intelligence and Japan's Computer Challenge to the World*. Menlo Park, Calif.: Addison-Wesley.

Imai, Ken'ichi. 1984. Japanese Industrial Policy for High Technology. Unpublished paper, prepared for Northeast Asia–United States Forum on International Policy, Stanford University.

Ministry of International Trade and Industry. 1982. *Japan Science and Technology Outlook*. Tokyo: Fuji Corporation.

Moritani, Masanori. 1982. *Japanese Technology*. Tokyo: The Simul Press.

Mowery, David C., and Nathan Rosenberg. 1985. *The Japanese Commercial Aircraft Industry Since 1945: Government Policy, Technical Development, and Industrial Structure*. Stanford: Northeast Asia–United States Forum on International Policy, Stanford University.

National Science Foundation. 1976. *Indicators of International Trends in Technological Innovation*. Washington, D.C.

Okimoto, Daniel I. 1983. *Pioneer and Pursuer: The Role of the State in the Evolution of the Japanese and American Semiconductor Industries*. Occasional Paper of the Northeast Asia–United States Forum on International Policy. Calif.: Stanford University.

Okimoto, Daniel I. Forthcoming. *Between MITI and the Market: Japanese Industrial Policy for High Technology*. Calif.: Stanford University Press.

Okimoto, Daniel I., Takuo Sugano, and Franklin B. Weinstein. 1984. *Competitive Edge: The Semiconductor Industry in the U.S. and Japan*. Calif.: Stanford University Press.

Organisation for Economic Cooperation and Development. 1982. *Innovation in Small and Medium Firms*. Paris.

Ozawa, Terutomo. 1974. *Japan's Technological Challenge to the West, 1950–1974*. Cambridge, Mass.: MIT Press.

President's Commission on Industrial Competitiveness. 1985. *Global Competition: The New Reality*, vol. 1. Washington, D.C.: U.S. Government Printing Office.

Saxonhouse, Gary R. 1982. Japanese High Technology, Government Policy, and Evolving Comparative Advantage in Goods and Services. Unpublished paper, prepared for Japanese Political Economy Research Conference, Honolulu, Hawaii.

Semiconductor Industry Association. 1983. *The Effect of Government Targeting on World Semiconductor Competition*. Cupertino, Calif.

The Macroeconomic Background for High-Tech Industrialization in Japan

MASAHIKO AOKI

The stringent macroeconomic management rule and high household savings that prevail in Japan are likely to keep generating surplus savings in that country. Because of the relatively abundant supply of capital, coupled with organizational innovations of large established firms (such as ever-increasing hiving off of semiautonomous subsidiaries and reliance on long-run relational contracting with suppliers), the lack of a venture capital market and start-ups does not seen to be particularly disadvantageous to successful high-tech industrialization in Japan. A substantial portion of surplus savings will possibly be directed to the United States if the domestic savings-investment gap in this country continues. Increasing direct investment by Japanese companies may pose a hitherto unknown political-economic problem.

This discussion of the macroeconomic background for high-tech industrialization in Japan focuses on the following questions: Will not the fiscal stringency currently exercised by the Japanese government reduce the effectiveness and feasibility of industrial policy and thus make the future of high-tech industrialization rather dismal? Despite the diminishing role of the government, as well as the lack of a significant development of the venture capital market, can the excess of savings over investment in the household sector be channeled into high-tech industry? For a better understanding of these problems, it is important first to recognize that a significant change in the characteristics of the macroeconomy as well as in the role of government has taken place since the last decade. Let me begin, therefore, with a very brief review of the 1970s, during which a new set of macromanagement rules was gradually shaped.

THE 1970s—A TRANSITION INTO THE NEW
MACROMANAGEMENT RULES

In the 1970s the Japanese economy was preoccupied with an ad hoc adaptation to a series of unanticipated events. The set of macromanagement rules that was so effective in the period of regular cyclical growth during the 1950s and 1960s (referred to here as the period of high growth) was abandoned in the 1970s for a new set of emerging rules. In order to understand the nature of the macroeconomic background for high-tech industrialization in the 1980s and 1990s, it is necessary to understand the significance of this irreversible transition.

Macroeconomic management during the high-growth period was based mainly on the following four rules: (1) Maintain a fixed exchange rate of 360 yen per U.S. dollar. (2) Supply money as far as the balance of international payment position permits. (3) Balance the central government budgets. (4) Maintain a constant tax burden of around 20 percent of the national income. The ground for these rules was laid in the stabilization policy of 1948–1949. Many observers consider these rules to be of a classical nature based on fiscal and monetary orthodoxy rather than of an expansionary Keynesian nature.* However they may be characterized, it is under these rules that high growth was realized for two decades. But the aftermath of high growth, as well as the rapidly changing external environment, made these rules increasingly difficult to maintain toward the 1970s. Yet the transition to the new rules was neither smooth nor well planned.

The 1970s opened with alarming irritation among city dwellers over the adverse effects of industrial growth, e.g., pollution, congestion, and the lack of sufficient housing stocks. This discontent culminated in the successive defeats of conservative candidates in gubernatorial elections in such major metropolitan areas as Tokyo, Osaka, Kyoto, and Kanagawa. Alarmed by this political unrest, the conservative central government and bureaucrats moved swiftly to accommodate the welfare-oriented policies of the opposition parties and ''progressive local autonomy groups (*chiho jichitai*).'' Generous social security provisions began to be introduced around 1973 without precautionary calculations of their impact on the future fiscal burden. The Tanaka cabinet elected in 1972 tried to solve the deficiencies of social infrastructures and private housing stocks by the now-notorious ''National Land Reform Plan.''

The publicity that attended the plan came at a time when the increased international competitiveness of the Japanese economy made it almost im-

---

*See Yukio Noguchi, Public Finance, and Yutaka Kosai, Macroeconomic Management, submitted for Japanese Political Economy Research Committee Conference, Hawaii, January 1985 (forthcoming in conference volume).

possible and irrational to maintain the exchange ratio of the Japanese yen that was fixed in 1949. Yet, fearing the loss of competitiveness, the Japanese government tried in vain to adhere to rule (1) by converting insurmountable surplus dollars at the out-of-date ratio and then at the revised rate of 308 yen per dollar beginning in December 1971. The outflow of excessive liquidity only inflamed the land speculation aroused by Tanaka's land reform policy. The fixed exchange rate system was finally replaced by the floating rate system in February 1973.

But subsequent to the abandonment of the old rule (1), the first oil shock hit Japan. About 55 percent dependent on OPEC oil as an energy source at that time, Japan experienced a 25 percent increase in electricity costs for industries from 1973 to 1974. The inflation ignited demands for higher wages, and, anticipating continued inflation, management and government yielded to those demands. Wage rates were increased by about 33 percent during wage negotiations in the spring of 1974. The high wage costs, as well as high interest costs incurred by excessive borrowing in the period of land speculation and excess liquidity, weakened the financial positions of major corporations.

The semidefeat of the ruling party in the Upper House election of 1974 made price stability the public goal. Learning from mistakes committed in the early 1970s and encouraged by the growing influence of the monetarism doctrine, the monetary authority began to shift to the money-quantity targeting policy. In reaction to this anti-inflationary policy, the so-called "on diet" management, which sought to reduce redundant employment as well as excessive borrowing from banks, became the catchword among the business community. Despite the somewhat mystified practice of lifetime employment, a substantial amount of employment adjustment occurred even in major corporations. In addition, after industrial pollution had become a big social issue and business ethics had been questioned in connection with corporate speculation on land, it became increasingly difficult for large corporations in smokestack industries to build large, pollution-prone factories. The Ministry of International Trade and Industry's (MITI's) well-publicized targeting of knowledge-intensive industries was a modicum of an ad hoc reaction to this changing business environment, although the foresightedness of concerned bureaucrats cannot be neglected. In my assessment, the morale of MITI in this transitional period was not particularly high. However, in this difficult period, most business corporations shifted their emphasis from the exploitation of economies of scale to flexible adaptability to an increasingly uncertain environment. They restrained uneconomical growth by hiving off ever increasing numbers of subsidiaries and by making more extensive and systematic use of long-run subcontracting relations. This organizational shift turned out to have, as we shall see later, an interesting implication for subsequent commercialization of innovation.

Although the shift to the new monetary rule was swift, the reestablishment of a new fiscal rule was not smooth. Beginning in the mid-1970s, the central government started to rely more and more on national bond issues to finance its expenditures. The impact of the earlier reform of the welfare system began to be felt. In addition, under the pressure brought about by an agreement at the Bonn summit meeting in 1978 to make the United States, West Germany, and Japan a triad of "engines" for the recovery from the worldwide depression, as well as in the hope of mitigating the expected adverse effect of yen appreciation, the government, led by Fukuda (long known as a believer in fiscal austerity), reluctantly adopted an expansionary fiscal policy. This expansionary policy aggravated the fiscal deficit without bringing about the expected effects.

The ratio of bond issues to total revenue in the general account of the central government exceeded 30 percent in 1977, an upper limit that the Ministry of Finance (MOF) insisted be kept. A tax reform, including the introduction of a general-consumption tax, seemed to be inevitable, and the MOF began to maneuver for its early introduction. But a tactical mistake committed by Prime Minister Ohira in the election campaign of 1979 and the near-defeat of the ruling party made tax reform politically impossible.

Problem solving became more systematic and coherent toward the 1980s, however, as learning accumulated. The second oil shock, which started in 1978, was absorbed by the restraint of wage increases. In 1979 wage bargaining, influential steel-union leaders called for a "macroconsistent wage demand" that would not cause cost-push inflation. The monetary authority was by then confident in the management of monetary-quantity targeting and the flexible exchange system. In the fiscal sphere, zero ceilings on budgetary increases in public expenditures, except for defense expenditures, were introduced in the early 1980s by the MOF as a means of keeping the fiscal deficit at a manageable level. The increased national deficit also produced an interesting side effect. The secondary markets of national bonds, such as the *gensaki* market (repurchase agreement market), spontaneously grew and provided the means for deregulated financial transactions. Increasing international criticism of Japanese trade barriers led to ad hoc, but significant, steps toward successive liberalizations of trade and capital flows in the late 1970s.

In order to solve the deficit problem from a longer-run point of view, a temporary council headed by a widely respected businessman, Toshio Doko, was set up in 1981 and empowered by the government to recommend wide-ranging, extraordinary measures for simplifying administrative structures to save on government costs. The government made restoring the fiscal balance, albeit somewhat vaguely, a target by 1990. Although there is some controversy as to the necessity of reducing national deficits by such a substantial proportion, fiscal stringency seems to have become another new rule for macromanagement, at least for a while. Fearing increased tax burdens in the form of corporate tax, the business community as a whole is supportive of this stance, although some business leaders directly affected by expenditure reductions do complain.

Thus, the new set of macromanagement rules that will operate for some years to come can be summarized, in a somewhat simplistic way, as follows: (1) adherence to the flexible exchange rate system with a minimum of interference by the monetary authority; (2) anti-inflationary quantity targeting of the money supply; (3) general restraint on public expenditures, with the possible exception of defense expenditures; and (4) implicit social agreement between management and labor that annual wage revisions should be made as consistent as possible with the security of the job and control of inflation.

SETTING NEW NATIONAL GOALS—THE MID-1980s

As we have seen, the 1970s was not, in retrospect, a decade in which the Japanese economy was directed by a well-designed policy based on a well-defined set of rules for macroeconomic management. It was, rather, a decade characterized by a series of ad hoc reactions to evolving events as well as the disturbing aftereffects of previous policies. The public mood of the period was not that optimistic. One of the best-selling books of that decade was a science fiction novel entitled *Sinking of the Japan Archipelago*. Many people drew an analogy between the state of the economy and the title of the book.

In retrospect, however, the Japanese economy showed remarkable adaptability to a series of external and internal challenges throughout the 1970s. Accordingly, the public mood began to change around 1980. One of the noteworthy cultural events marking the transition was the enthusiastic reception of Ezra Vogel's *Japan As No. 1*. Parallel to this publication, problems of American industrial relations in unionized industries were publicized by the mass media in rather exaggerated ways. The Japanese came to realize for the first time since the end of World War II that the economy can be, and should be, directed neither in terms of a catching-up strategy nor an ad hoc, passive adaptation to the external environment. A more positive attitude was needed.

Through animated public discourse, three important objectives emerged that were widely agreed to be in the public interest. They are as follows:

1. *A shift to a high-tech-oriented industrial structure.* It is warned, at times, that this shift may cause disturbing effects comparable to the pollution and congestion caused by the industrialization of conventional technology. Among the possible effects often cited are the rapid obsolescence of human skills and the resulting difficulty of maintaining conventional labor practices (such as lifetime employment), the breaking up of traditional human bonds, and invasion of privacy. But there seems to exist a broadly based belief that, despite such possible costs, high-tech industrialization is inevitable and de-

sirable if the international competitiveness of the Japanese economy is to be maintained. The Japanese perception in regard to the competitiveness of the American economy has achieved a balance and the United States is now regarded rightly as a formidable international competitor in successful high-tech industrialization.

2. *Overhauling institutional frameworks of the economy to increase its competitiveness and efficiency.* Specifically, important agenda items include deregulation of the financial market, the reduction of government intervention through administrative reform, pension reform, and privatization of some of the giant public enterprises, such as Nippon Telegraph and Telephone (NTT) and, possibly, National Rail Lines (NRL). Although there are always conflicts between general public interests and specific interests in this sphere, the trend toward more competitive and deregulated economic institutions seems to be clear.

3. *Reforming the educational system toward more diverse educational opportunities.* Although the educational system in Japan has been praised internationally as effective for accumulation of human resources, an educational reform is now overdue domestically because of various internal problems as well as the need for accommodation to the age of technology. Prime Minister Nakasone appointed a temporary Council for Educational Reform in September 1984, and a heated debate on educational reform is now under way in and out of the council. Although the conservatism of Ministry of Education bureaucrats may be a significant obstacle to reform, and it is extremely difficult to forge a consensus among the public on this subject, I would conjecture that a rather important reform might come out of this public debate. (Who predicted 10 years ago that the dissolution of NTT and NRL would become serious public agendas in the near future?)

Are the three objectives consistent and compatible? Are they achievable under a new set of macromanagement rules? Below I will discuss some issues relevant to these problems. (Although the educational issue is important and highly relevant, I do not address the subject because of space limitations.) Since the external and internal environments have changed substantially since the period of high growth, the future of high-tech industrialization may not be predicted on linear extrapolations of past experience.

IS TARGETING OF HIGH-TECH INDUSTRIALIZATION COMPATIBLE WITH MACROMANAGEMENT RULES?

Sectoral economic management, such as that administered by industry-based bureaus of the Ministry of International Trade and Industry, is often regarded as more important than macroeconomic management in explaining Japanese economic performance. But even in the period of high growth, sectoral policies were feasible and effective as long as they were compatible with overall macromanagement. This may be inferred from the preeminent position enjoyed by MOF bureaucrats (particularly budgetary bureaucrats) in the bureaucratic power structure over the entire postwar period.

The availability of sectoral assistance in the form of tax incentives and subsidies was basically constrained by fiscal feasibility as determined under old rules (2), (3), and (4) during the high-growth period. This assistance was distributed to various ministries and then to those bureaus and sections that were in charge of particular sectors of the economy. Of course, there was a priority ranking of various policy needs, but increments were distributed among ministries and their bureaus rather evenly (the so-called budget incrementalism). The growing industries got a fair share of assistance, but so did declining sectors, such as agriculture in the form of distributional compensations (e.g., rice-price support). Possible intersectoral conflicts were skillfully resolved through quasi-bargaining among ministries, which was mediated by the Budgetary Bureau of the MOF. Effective in this process was compartmentalized administrative territorialization, through which pluralistic group interests were channeled and guarded through relevant and specific bureaucratic organs. But the effectiveness of this "administered pluralism" seems to have begun to erode to some extent.

First, the new macromanagement rule (3) has made it increasingly difficult for the MOF not only to distribute incremental assistance evenly to various sectors, but even to single out a favored target sector into which generous fiscal and tax backing can be directed. Second, partly because of this need for fiscal stringency and partly because of the increasing complexity and intertwining of sectoral interests, compartmentalized administrative territorialization and mediation of conflicting interests are becoming somewhat ineffectual. A corollary to this is that the leadership of party politicians in interest mediation is gaining in relative importance vis-à-vis that of bureaucrats.

This fundamental picture seems to be applicable to the area of high technology as well. Despite rather exaggerated publicity in the United States regarding the co-op labs for VLSI (very large scale integration) administered by MITI, government assistance of research and development in the computer industry in Japan is, as Daniel Okimoto (in this volume) correctly points out, not so important from an international standpoint. In addition, potential high-tech development is so diverse and intertwined that jurisdictional disputes among such concerned ministries as MITI, Ministry of Posts and Telecommunications (MPT), Ministry of Agriculture (biotechnology), Ministry of Welfare (medicine), Ministry of Education (copyright administration), the Agency for Science and Technology, and so on, may potentially hinder the effectiveness and efficiency of sectoral management in the field of high technology. These two problems can be well illustrated by a recent decision concerning the privatization of NTT.

NTT, which had monopolized telecommunication and telephone services in Japan and had been fully owned by the government, was privatized on April 1, 1985. The book value of net assets of the new private corporation was about three-quarter trillion yen (about $3 billion); one-third of the stock is to be owned by the government, and the other two-thirds is scheduled to be marketed over a 5-year period. The capital gains due to stock sales to the public is estimated in the range of 3 trillion to 5 trillion yen. MITI wanted the proceeds of stock sales allocated for the establishment of a new Industrial Technology Center, which would finance private corporations engaged in research and development of high technology, especially electrocommunication. The MPT wanted the proceeds to be used for the establishment of the Organization for Promotion of Electric-communication, under its control.

The MOF disappointed both by deciding that the stock to be liquidated publicly will first be allocated to the National Bonds Redemption Special Account; the proceeds from stock sales and dividend receipts therefrom will be used exclusively for the redemption of national bonds. The estimated amount of net redemption of national bonds in 1986 is 1.6 trillion yen. A small public corporation will be established from the dividend revenues from government holdings of the new NTT stock and possibly by financing from the Development Bank. This new corporation will be engaged in financing private technological development under the joint administration of MITI and MPT. In this settlement of jurisdictional disputes among the three rival ministries, party politicians played a decisive role.

The high-tech industrialization under the new macromanagement rules will thus be likely to take shape in a politico-economic environment different from the one that prevailed under effective sectoral management in the high-growth period. But does it mean that the future of Japanese high-tech industrialization is dismal?

EXCESS SUPPLY OF PERSONAL SAVINGS

Despite the stringency of the fiscal assistance to be expected from the government for high-tech industrialization, the future of fiscal assistance must be assessed from a broader, macroscopic perspective. In this and the next section, I will discuss the implications of the macro investment-savings balance for financial aspects of high-tech industrialization.

As is well known, one of the important characteristics of the Japanese economy is its high personal savings rate. In the period of high growth, some tried to explain this phenomenon as being the result of the lag in the adjustment of the consumption level by households to the unexpectedly continuous increase in income levels (the permanent-income hypothesis). Others attributed the high personal savings ratio to the fact that the population was composed of relatively younger generations who needed to save for their life-cycle planning (the life-cycle hypothesis). Still others considered the inadequate social security provisions responsible for the phenomenon. These explanations may have been partially valid, but not entirely, because the personal savings rate went up throughout the first half of the 1970s, a time when the growth rate started to slow, the population became relatively aged, and the social security system became as generous as in Western countries. The personal savings rate has become somewhat lower since then, but in the early 1980s the ratio of households' excess saving over investment to GNP still remains as high as around 10 percent. So, the target level of wealth relative to income for households is considered still high.

One of the incentives for the household to accumulate wealth was to finance an investment in housing stock. Throughout the 1970s, about 15 million housing units were built, which was equal to about 40 percent of the total number of households in 1980. Because of this accumulation of housing stocks, there is some indication of a sluggishness on the demand side of the housing market in the 1980s. Instead, the households, specifically relatively high-income households, began to show a preference for the relatively lagged accumulation of financial assets. A midterm forecast by the Economic Planning Agency predicts that a substantial amount of savings will continue to be supplied by the household sector of the economy until the end of this century despite the slowdown of housing demand, aging of population, and so on. Which sector of the economy will absorb this excess saving? According to a basic macroeconomic accounting identity, excess savings of the household sector must be equal to the sum of the excess of investment over saving of the corporate sector, government deficit, and current external surplus.

Until the mid-1970s, the excess savings of the household sector was mostly absorbed by excess investment of the corporate sector, but since then corporate investment has started to fall and, instead, the government has assumed the major role as savings absorber. In the early 1980s the government absorbed about one-third of the excess savings of households. Also, current external surplus started to rise in the 1980s after the effect of the second oil shock was subdued. Japan's export of long-term capital began to rise accordingly, and its total amount between 1981 and 1984 is estimated at $90 billion. In the last year alone Japan exported as much as $50 billion, out of which $6 billion was invested in common stocks, as well as in factories, largely in the United States. Japan became the largest capital exporter in the world economy.

Today there is some controversy in Japan about the domestic capability to absorb the excess savings of the household sector. Some argue that an innovative expansionary policy can be, and should be, employed domestically to avoid a further worsening of trade frictions abroad. Others, represented by MOF bureaucrats, alarmed by accumulating national debt and in an effort to legitimize macromanagement rule (3), are reluctant to move in that direction, arguing that a substantial proportion of the increasing capital export is an inevitable consequence of the maturity of the Japanese economy. The controversy is not settled, but the prospect is that, given macromanagement rule (3), a substantial amount of funds is likely to be available to the corporate sector as well as to the external sector for some years to come.

FINANCING HIGH-TECH INDUSTRIALIZATION

It has been argued that the lack of a venture capital market, as well as the stigma against takeover, is the Achilles' heel of Japanese high-tech development. Others have argued, based on a somewhat stereotypical perception of the role of government in the period of high growth, that government assistance will provide a substitute for risk-bearing private capital. But I would submit that both of these views should be examined critically in light of the macroeconomic characteristics summarized above, specifically the significant excess savings of the household sector. I have already noted that the availability of direct financial assistance by the government will be limited under the new macromanagement rule (3). What about the venture capital market? Will it grow as a means of channeling the excess savings of the household sector to high-tech industries? Or will some other means of financing high-tech industrialization develop with the background of a relatively ample supply of savings?

A comparison of the financial mechanisms of the United States and Japan leads me to conjecture that the main supply-side causes of the relatively advanced development of the venture capital market in this country are attributable to the combination of the following three factors: the relative scarcity of capital supply to the business sector, the relatively risk-taking attitudes of investors, and the current tax structure, which treats capital gains relatively favorably. The first two factors encourage investments in assets whose expected returns are relatively high, albeit risk may be relatively high, too. The tax reform of the Reagan administration also makes equity investment more advantageous to investors in relatively higher income-tax brackets and they are major capital suppliers. Further, it motivates entrepreneurial individuals to start up their own corporations rather than to remain as high-salary earners.

In Japan, in contrast, households of all tax brackets more or less contribute to savings, and until recently, they have equally revealed solid preferences for investments in safe assets, such as bank deposits and postal savings, despite the fact that after-tax returns from stockholdings far exceeded, on average, that from deposit holdings in the past. (The average annual rate of after-tax returns from stockholdings of listed corporations was around 17 percent in the period between 1964 and 1984, whereas the average annual deposit rate was around 5 percent.) This indicates that Japanese investors are, on average, very risk-averse. But there are growing signs that relatively higher-income households tend to diversify their financial portfolios more. They are active participants in the stock market despite an apparent decline in the relative ratio of individual stockholdings of listed corporations. (Individuals do not disclose their stockholdings fully in order to evade tax. But a recent official *Survey on Household Savings*, conducted by the Prime Minister's office, clearly shows the increasing shift of portfolios by relatively high-income households toward stockholdings.) Whether this trend will lead to a significant development of the venture capital market in Japan is yet to be seen. However, the relatively higher level of savings in Japan tends to reduce the supply price of capital. Also, pooling and diversification of relatively ample funds by conventional financial institutions (such as banks) and growing investment funds (the Japanese equivalent of mutual funds) would make the reduction of aggregate-risk costs possible. Therefore, from the supply-side point of view, one cannot conclude decisively, despite the relatively infant development of the venture capital market, that financing of the risky high-tech industry is disfavored in Japan.

One has to look at the demand side as well. One of the demand-side factors responsible for the development of the venture capital market in the United States is, needless to say, that commercialization of new technology very often takes the form of start-ups of new venture firms. In my opinion, one of the reasons for this is, in turn, the conflict between the individualistic and independent tendency of highly capable engineers and entrepreneurs and the near perfection of technocratic control in large, highly integrated firms. In this respect, too, Japan stands somewhat in contrast to the United States. While Japanese engineers and managers are not entirely conformists lacking any inclination toward independence, as often caricatured in the West, Japanese corporations have developed a moderate organizational innovation that will reduce the technocratic stifling of individual initiatives and the poor communication that are often observed in highly integrated corporate firms.

Since the mid-1970s, there has been an increasing tendency among large corporate firms to hive off fully or partially owned subsidiaries, to invest in joint ventures with other corporate firms (the so-called corporate partnership), and to rely on outside suppliers under long-run relationships. This is very much in contrast to the tendency for major American corporations to integrate through acquisition as well as internal diversification. For instance, in 1970 major corporations in the electric machinery and electronics industry, as listed on the Tokyo Exchange, reinvested 20.0 percent of their paid-in capital in majority-owned subsidiaries, but this ratio climbed to 72.6 percent in 1984. Investment in partly owned (20 to

49 percent), so-called related, corporations has increased similarly. This
hiving-off tendency is certainly different from the spinning off of venture
business firms from established firms by the aid of venture capital markets
as observed in this country. However, it should be noted that the relative
merits of small-scale firms in high-tech industrialization, such as the more
direct exposure to market incentive, the creation of an atmosphere favorable to individual initiative, the savings on the cost of informational exchanges by reducing hierarchical layers, the flexible and ad hoc adjustments
of labor conditions, and so on, also apply, at least potentially, in those
subsidiary corporations. Also "partial" ownership of major corporations
is one way of attracting external funds that would be unavailable in the
case of corporate venturing. Further, partial ownership of large corporations provides a certain degree of insurance for minority investors in
potentially risky investments. Still further, joint venturing (corporate partnership) may facilitate quickly combining and amalgamating hitherto unrelated technological know-how and realizing discontinuous technological
progress, which would be impossible under in-house research and development, yet without spoiling existing corporate cultures, as happens in
acquisitions.

I would submit that this tendency toward hiving off and joint venturing
(between major corporations, between foreign and domestic corporations,
between larger and smaller corporations, between corporations and other
investors including individuals, and so on) is one important way of commercializing and financing risky high technology in Japan. And these may
be realized without great, if any, help from the venture capital market, but
with the use of more conventional banks, securities markets, and internal
funding.

Finally, it should be noted that Japan is likely to become the largest
capital exporter in the rest of the 1980s, as the household sector is likely
to keep generating more savings than the business and government sectors
can absorb. A substantial proportion of capital exports will possibly be
directed to the United States if the domestic savings-investment gap in
this country continues. Japanese corporations will set up subsidiaries and
joint ventures here as in their home country. In the Los Angeles area, it
is estimated that there are already 1,600 subsidiaries and branch offices
of Japanese firms, but the number is increasing at the rate of one per day.
Joint ventures between American and Japanese corporations, if economically profitable, may also contribute to the establishment of a new business
paradigm suitable for the age of high technology by amalgamating two
important corporate cultures of the modern world. But, on the other hand,
some of the investments by Japanese corporations in this country may
possibly take the form of acquisition since the stigma against it is not as
strong here as in Japan. This will provide a quick way for Japanese cor-

porations to acquire know-how. Will, however, the overpresence of foreign ownership in strategic high-tech industries not cause resentment among the American public? The asymmetry of investment-savings gaps between the two countries, if it persists, may pose a hitherto unknown, potentially serious problem for Japan.

Capital Formation in the United States and Japan

RALPH LANDAU and GEORGE N. HATSOPOULOS

It is important to sharpen our understanding of how economics and technology come together to affect the competitiveness of capital formation processes and the financing of innovation and technological contribution to economic growth. In this critical area can be found one of the major reasons why the Japanese growth rate in GNP is outstripping that of the United States. This is hardly the time for business and politics as usual. The United States has many inherent advantages if its economic policies can be harnessed in a benign way for innovation and investment, leading to a higher sustained growth rate. Americans are good at this, too, as their history proves.

Several chapters in this volume* stress that the industrialized countries now do business in truly global markets. The United States, which dominated these world markets after World War II, has seen its market share eroded in product after product as other countries recovered from the war, invested in new and modern facilities, and employed the latest technology. The countries of the Common Market and those of the Pacific Rim, led by Japan, now compete vigorously and often very successfully inside the United States and in world markets generally. Thus, maintaining and increasing its competitiveness is the foremost contemporary challenge to the United States as it seeks to raise the standard of living of its population, reduce unemployment, alleviate social concerns, and provide for the necessary defense.

Many factors contribute to a nation's competitiveness, but in the long run, productivity of the human being is the fundamental determinant of international competitiveness. Productivity is the *efficiency* with which an economy utilizes the economic resources available to it. With a given quantity of resources, productivity increase means obtaining greater and better-quality

---

*See, for example, chapters by John A. Young, N. Bruce Hannay, Stephen D. Bechtel, Jr., Ruben F. Mettler, Daniel I. Okimoto, Robert Malpas, and Albert Bowers.

output per hour worked or per unit of capital input (*factor productivity* is the designation for this broad definition). A country not only seeks to provide greater total output of goods and services from its available resources for its population, but also tries to do so with greater economy and skill by raising productivity, getting more "bang for the buck." The greater the rate of growth in efficiency or productivity, the greater will be the rate of increase of the economy's output, and hence the greater will be the economy's growth rate, even if the resources available are constant. With more labor and capital resources, the economy will grow even faster. *Thus, the basic determinants of the growth rate of the economy as a whole are growth in productivity plus the growth in capital and labor inputs (the resources).* Of course, if a society chooses to work less or invest less, but consumes more, it will grow less. In addition, its productivity will also be adversely affected, as described below.

As Vernon W. Ruttan (in this volume) describes it, the process of increasing productivity in agriculture (where land is also an important resource) means an increase in output per man-hour. As a result, the percentage of the population engaged in agriculture has dropped over the years from a majority to barely over 3 percent. The increased labor thus made available, plus the new additions to the work force, was absorbed into a growing manufacturing sector and subsequently into a diversified services sector.

The rate of productivity increase in the United States over the period since the Civil War has been a little under 2 percent per year. So great is the power of compounding that this enabled the United States to develop from a largely rural economy into the world's greatest industrial power and increase the real per capita income at about 2 percent per year while absorbing a huge increase in population. In the process, this nation overtook the United Kingdom, the greatest power of 1850, which is now not even one of the richer members of the Common Market. But since World War II, other countries, especially Japan, have had greater rates of economic growth and productivity (as Dale W. Jorgenson details in this volume) and are catching up rapidly with the United States. At present, Japan is already the second greatest industrial power in the world, and if its relatively higher rate of growth vis-à-vis the United States were to continue for not much more than another generation, it would overtake the United States in total gross national product. As Jorgenson also indicates, the United States has suffered an alarming decline in its own productivity growth since the late 1960s. It seems clear, therefore, that the *challenge to the United States in meeting the vigorous global competition it now encounters is to raise its rate of investment in human and physical capital and to raise its rate of productivity growth,* i.e., to improve the efficiency of its economic engine systematically and purposefully. Economic growth at an increased rate of efficiency is the prerequisite for a rising standard of living and for the more humane society that can result from such increasing wealth.

Classical economics identified land, labor, and capital as the basic resources available to the economy to provide for economic growth. Of these resources, capital is the most complex and least understood factor of production. In another chapter in this volume, Nathan Rosenberg explains the origin of the fairly recent discovery by economists of a fourth component— namely, the "residual," which has been attributed to technological change and which now appears to be the fundamental determinant of productivity growth. The rate of growth in productivity is at least as important as capital input is to economic growth in historical perspective, as Jorgenson details. Daniel I. Okimoto (in this volume) provides a table of technology's contribution to Japan's economic growth since 1955; in most periods technology accounted for over 50 percent of the economic growth rate. The conclusions for the United States are similar in principle.

Michael J. Boskin (in this volume) further examines the key role of technological progress in economic growth and, more significantly for future policy, its role in *increasing the economic growth rate (i.e., raising the rate of productivity growth)*. He states that the only way to raise the long-run growth rate *permanently* is to increase the rate of technical change (e.g., by R&D expenditures) or to increase the rate of improvement in the quality of the labor force by education and training (human capital). He makes a further point that experience ("learning by doing"), if positively fed back on the rate of technical change through embodiment in higher investment rates, could *permanently* increase the long-run rate of growth in productivity. Considering the historical evidence, this seems plausible (see, for example, Figure 2 in James Brian Quinn's chapter in this volume). Such an increase would be in addition to the more straightforward effect of investment in "old" technology. The latter *temporarily* increases the productivity growth of the economy by increasing the capital:labor ratio (e.g., by providing economies of scale, by reducing transportation costs, by supplying more tools per worker, or by similar means), and yields a *temporarily* higher growth rate and a *permanently* higher level of income.

In other words, real per capita income grows at the rate of technical change, and labor quality improvement at a given capital:labor ratio. If, somehow, more investment in "old" technology alone takes place, there is a spurt in the short-run growth rate until the same long-term growth rate at the new ratio of capital to labor is achieved; this long-term rate must still reflect the underlying rate of technical change and change in human capital quality. Every technologist knows that the latest technology is frequently embodied in new investment and is a spur to it. Hence, Boskin emphasizes that "the rate at which new technology really does augment the productivity of labor and machinery will depend on the rate at which new capital is generated, i.e., our investment rate." Paul A. David (in this volume) makes the same point. *Thus, technological change and the capital investment embodying it, employed by properly trained people, are seen as the keys to productivity growth and rising standards of living in the face of increasing international competitiveness.*

As noted above, the countries in the Common Market (e.g., Germany, France, the United Kingdom) or on the Pacific Rim (e.g., Korea, Taiwan, Singapore, Hong Kong) are not unimportant competitors either to the United States or to Japan. In many areas they already excel. And mainland China, with its cheap and abundant labor, looms on the horizon. This is not the time for complacency. Nevertheless, the principal international competitor of the United States is Japan, and the principal disparity between the United States and Japan is in the rate of capital formation. This chapter, therefore, deals more specifically with capital formation in the United States and in Japan.

Macroeconomic and "second-tier" policies (as Boskin terms tax, regulatory, spending priority, and trade policies) have a profound effect on both capital formation and its cost. They also affect currency exchange rates, which are highly significant for competitiveness and trade. Table 1 shows the recent change in American manufacturers' competitiveness as a result of productivity changes, labor wage rates (another important determinant of competitiveness), and currency adjustments.[1] The left-hand section of the table shows the effect of man-hour productivity and wage rates on labor costs in several major countries between 1980 and 1984. It also shows a correction for the relative inflation rates, which thereby indicates how much the purchasing power of the work force has changed. Despite the lower Japanese inflation, the yen:dollar ratio has hardly changed (as it should). The Japanese work force, therefore, has achieved greater purchasing power in real terms while retaining its export competitiveness. The yen should have strengthened, but it did not. The right-hand section of Table 1 shows the currency effect for the same countries in the same period. The column at the far right combines the three effects.

While the United States has made significant gains in productivity, it has fallen sharply behind Japan—which signals a challenge to management. Management's role is to invest in labor-saving and technologically advanced equipment to the degree, as explained below, that it finds the economic climate favorable. Likewise, management and labor have a role to play in wage-rate restraint. The column in Table 1 entitled "Unit Labor Costs," which combines data in local currencies with rates of inflation relative to that of the United States, shows that the United States still lags West Germany and Japan somewhat. However, when these data are corrected for currency values, the picture changes drastically, and the hard dollar, which neither management nor labor can control, becomes the overriding factor in relative competitiveness.

Relative to trends in other countries, the United States has lagged significantly in competitiveness in unit labor costs; the principal European powers are the leaders. However, in view of the overall balance-of-payments figures, the fundamental problem for American competitiveness is still Japan, against which the United States seems not to be able to compete either inside Japan, inside the United States, or in third-country markets in a whole range of products, because the yen:dollar relation changes little even as the dollar weakens against European currencies. There are few compensating areas in which the United States is unequivocally strong, as in agriculture. Comparable data are not available for the Pacific Rim countries, although Korea is in the Japanese class in productivity and investment and has lower wage rates.

Competitiveness not only involves productivity growth, which is strongly related to the pace of technological change and investment rates, but also requires labor wage rates and overhead costs that are competitive. As shown above, the United States is a high-wage country, and Japan, which has actually been increasing its wage rates faster than the United States over the postwar era, is no longer low cost relative to *its* Asian competitors. This is true even in recent years when adjustment is made for relative inflation. Most raw material and energy costs have started to equalize among countries, although there are still local advantages. R&D is intensive in all the industrial countries that compete with the United States, particularly civilian R&D. However, because of the rapid diffusion of technology in the age of telecommunications and personal mobility, any advantage gained by any firm or country will be short-lived unless embodied in physical capital. Capital is involved in the R&D phase as well as in development, design, plant-improvement modifications, automation, and so on, without any new inventions necessarily being required per se—mainly the incorporation of the "learning by doing" process described by Boskin. Stephen S. Roach (in this volume) also elucidates how capital-intensive the internationally competitive service industries have become, where little invention occurs and only a small part of the economy's total R&D is performed.

The innovation process in its complete form consists of two stages: invention and implementation. The former is usually a function of R&D and experience; the latter is primarily a function of capital investment (which includes the development and design stages) and is the much riskier part of the innovation process. Thus, in examining capital formation and costs in the United States and Japan, this chapter focuses on capital formation in the business sector, which, however, consists of a very wide diversity of companies in various stages of development. Most of the chapter deals with the manufacturing sector, since this sector is the primary component of international trade flows (very few domestic service companies, except those in banking, insurance, and the like, contribute much to imports). Also, as

TABLE 1   Comparison of Unit Labor Cost: United States
Versus Key Industrial Countries

	Unit Labor Cost Effects Indices (1977 = 100)				
	In Home Currencies			Corrected for Relative Inflation	Unit Labor Costs
	1980	1984	% Change 1980–1984	% Change 1980–1984	1984 as % of 1980
France					118.0
Productivity	112.4	135.2	20.3	2.1	
Wage rates	148.1	247.5	67.1	41.8	
Unit labor costs	131.7	183.1	39.0	18.0	
Germany					117.7
Productivity	108.4	122.3	12.8	23.2	
Wage rates	125.0	152.1	21.7	32.9	
Unit labor costs	115.3	124.3	7.8	17.7	
Italy					117.0
Productivity	116.9	134.4	15.0	− 19.1	
Wage rates	160.2	306.0	91.0	34.5	
Unit labor costs	137.0	227.7	66.2	17.0	
United Kingdom					111.0
Productivity	99.9	123.0	23.1	17.4	
Wage rates	162.8	233.4	43.4	36.7	
Unit labor costs	163.0	189.8	16.4	11.0	
Japan					109.6
Productivity	128.6	167.4	30.2	54.1	
Wage rates	121.2	146.0	20.5	42.6	
Unit labor costs	94.2	87.2	−7.4	9.6	
United States					112.3
Productivity	101.7	115.6	13.7	13.7	
Wage rates	132.7	169.4	27.7	27.7	
Unit labor costs	130.5	146.5	12.3	12.3	

SOURCE: See note 1 in this chapter.

	Currency Effects			Corrected for Relative Inflation	Unit Cost Based on Currency	Combined Effects
						Unit Labor Cost at Actual Exchange Rates
	Actual Exchange Rates					
	1980	1984	% Change 1980–1984	% Change 1980–1984	% Change 1980–1984	1984 as % of 1980
France	0.237	0.114	−51.9	−43.3	56.7	66.9
Germany	0.550	0.351	−36.2	−41.6	58.4	68.8
Italy	0.00117	0.00060	−48.7	−27.1	72.9	85.2
United Kingdom	2.326	1.336	−42.6	−39.8	60.2	66.9
Japan	0.0044	0.0042	−4.5	−19.4	80.6	88.4
United States	1.000	1.000	0.0	0.0	100.0	112.3

NOTE: Based on exchange-rate movements through Fall 1985, the unit-labor-cost differentials between the United States and other countries shown in the last column would still be significant although somewhat smaller.

H. W. Coover (in this volume) shows, the manufacturing sector performs the bulk of the R&D undertaken by U.S. companies, hence investment in knowledge and technology.

THE MANUFACTURING SECTOR

The vital role of manufacturing in the U.S. economy can br, seen from the fact that manufacturing accounts for the following:

- About 20 percent of total employment (in Japan it runs close to 25 percent);
- About 23 percent of total output;
- 50 percent of goods output for the economy as a whole; and
- About 60 percent of exports and 75 percent of imports.

Moreover, the goods-producing sector has a much greater rate of productivity increase than other sectors of the economy. Total factor productivity in the goods-producing sector, for example, increased 175 percent between 1960 and 1984, whereas the rate in the service-producing sector was only about 135 percent.

The average rate of productivity growth over the postwar period in manufacturing has been 2.8 percent; in services, 2 percent; and in the overall economy, about 2.5 percent. In constant 1972 dollars, the GNP:worker ratio in manufacturing is about $20,000, and in all services about $11,000 (some services, such as banking, are more efficient than the average). Because of the recent cyclical recovery, manufacturing productivity increased by 4.5 percent, and services by about 3 percent, over the last 2½ years. Thus, the manufacturing sector is a vital part of the productivity growth of the entire economy and is the most robust.[2]

The Japanese have done much better in their manufacturing sector than has the United States, due to factors beyond the favorable dollar:yen ratio and the government restrictions placed by the Japanese on imports or manufacture in Japan by foreigners. They have been investing in their manufacturing sector at rates that are between 2 and 2½ times the U.S. rate of investment in capital per worker (Figure 1).[3] It would seem clear, therefore, that the stock of capital is growing more rapidly in Japan than in the United States. Between 1970 and 1981 the rate of growth in constant-dollar gross capital per worker in manufacturing in Japan was 7.1 percent per year, more than twice the 3.5 percent annual rate of gain in the United States. No data are available for gross capital after 1981 for Japan, and none for net capital on a replacement basis. The only data available are for net capital on a historical basis. It is estimated that the net tangible capital per worker among principal manufacturers, on a historical basis, is $48,000 for Japan in 1982, and $32,000 in the United States.

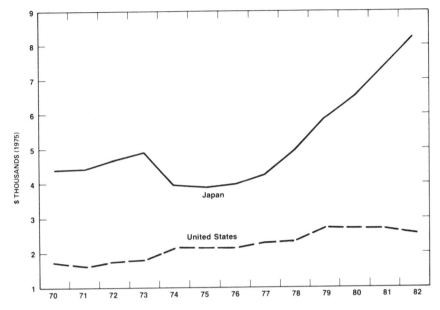

FIGURE 1   Manufacturing fixed investment per year per employee (thousands of 1975 dollars).
SOURCE: Hatsopoulos and Brooks (note 3 in this chapter).

As noted above, it is well supported in the literature that productivity is closely linked to capital:labor ratios. The higher rate of growth of capital per worker in Japan, therefore, has resulted in a higher rate of productivity growth in Japan as compared to the United States (Figure 2).[4] Whatever the reasons for changes in the rate of productivity growth, as discussed for the United States in Jorgenson's chapter, Japan's advantage in capital investment must be a major factor in its ability to do better than the United States. It becomes important, therefore, to learn more about the quantity and cost of capital in the two countries.

CAPITAL AVAILABILITY

A striking difference between the United States and Japan is the sheer availability of capital. This is due in part to the much higher savings rate in Japan. In the United States, personal savings have averaged about 5 to 8 percent of disposable income over a long period of time, whereas Japan's personal savings rate is in the 17 to 18 percent range (having been above 22 percent before 1975)—almost three times as great. In the United States,

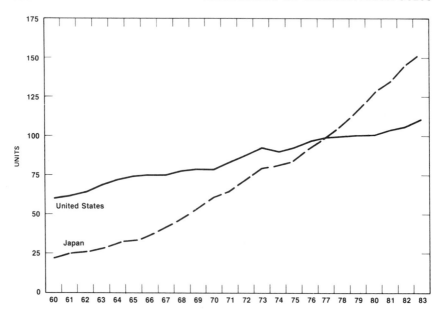

FIGURE 2   Output per hour in manufacturing (1977 = 100).
SOURCE: Hatsopoulos and Brooks (see note 3 in this chapter).

overall gross fixed-capital formation, as a percentage of GNP, is in the range of 15 percent, whereas in Japan it is over 30 percent, or nearly twice as much. While savings in the corporate and household sectors vary from one country to the other, the overall effect is clearly that the greater Japanese savings rate contributes to the greater availability of capital for private investment (both governments run roughly comparable deficits as a percentage of GNP).

What causes this greater Japanese savings rate is not easy to determine, even for Japanese economists. There seem to be at least two fundamental factors (before the war the Japanese did *not* have as high a savings rate, so cultural factors are not likely to be the cause):

1. A conscious government policy to increase savings by means of favorable tax policies, control over financial markets, and investment options available to the private saver; and

2. Limitations on social security provisions combined with early retirement (at 55) for employees of large corporations.

John Shoven of Stanford University and Toshiaki Tachibanaki of the Kyoto Institute of Economic Research have made an extensive survey of the tax policies in Japan.[5] Among many favorable features should be listed the absence of a capital-gains tax and the existence of a tax-free savings plan that permits an individual to save up to $56,000 in nontaxable form (considerably higher than the average monetary assets per capita). When all the members of a household are included and the widespread evidence of evasion is taken into account, it is clear that households can save large sums tax free. Dividends are taxed at a lower rate than is salary income (the opposite was true in the United States until 1981 when the Economic Recovery Tax Act was adopted, which made the tax on the two forms of income the same, although some states still maintain a differential in favor of earnings as against investment income from interest and dividends). On the other hand, mortgage interest and the like are not deductible from income in Japan, unlike in the United States. Thus, the Japanese tax system, Shoven and Tachibanaki say, "is responsible for lowering the overall effective tax on income from capital." Hence, they continue, "the Japanese example . . . does seem to imply that tax policy can be valuable in promoting a transition to a more capital intensive economy." (Masahiko Aoki, in this volume, deals with the economic policies of Japan and its enduring high savings rate in some detail.)

The fundamental difference between the two economies that arises from this sheer abundance of capital in Japan is that the United States currently imports perhaps $100 billion of capital annually to finance its investments and government deficits, while Japan exports more than $40 billion of capital annually, including, of course, exports to the United States. This performance demonstrates how economic policy is of critical importance in competitiveness. It also demonstrates that the financing of innovation is crucial to economic growth—it is the area in which economics and technology truly intersect.

TYPES OF COMPANIES AND FINANCING REQUIREMENT

Not every manufacturing company is of the same size or maturity or has the same financing needs. In the United States, three types of companies are generally recognized: (1) start-up or fledgling, (2) rapidly growing, and (3) mature.

The financial needs and financing methods are different for each type of company. William J. Perry and James D. Marver (each in this volume) describe the usual techniques employed by start-up and, therefore, very risky companies. For these companies, private capital and venture capital funds provide the necessary finances. Borrowing is generally too risky for both borrower and lender, so the investments are usually in the form of equity purchases. Currently, most young companies, after the infusion of venture capital has run its course, cannot generate enough internal cash flow to fuel the necessary or desired growth. In the event that they remain independent, this means they must go to the equities markets, which leads to an initial public offering (IPO) and subsequent equity issues (as Marver describes).

Eventually, borrowing becomes feasible, and the banks and insurance companies are the normal sources of funds. However, because younger and rapidly growing companies are still deemed to be high-risk enterprises by both management and the investors or lenders, these companies retain a high ratio of equity to total capitalization.

In recent years, when venture capital has been abundant and the new public-issues markets strong, many young companies have gone public even before establishing a proven record of profitability. Often they refinance in this way several times. Much depends on the company and the economic climate prevailing at a given time. It was not as hectic a pace in 1985 (Marver).

However, as William Hewlett (in this volume) says, at about the level of $100 million to $200 million per year in sales, these start-up companies face critical problems. In addition to new management and product-line problems, they must either grow by finding major new sources of capital (as venture capital and the equities markets become unsuited, too expensive, and unavailable) or they must disappear either by failure or absorption (in whole, or in part, by establishing partnerships or joint ventures) into a large company. Of course, it is possible to do neither of these and instead to restrain the growth rate so that the necessary capital can be found in retained earnings alone (Hewlett-Packard followed this practice, as William J. Perry states in this volume).

The large, mature companies usually have all the borrowing capacity they require, as described by John S. Reed and Glen R. Moreno (in this volume). There is a wide range of permissible debt:equity ratios among companies of various types; recently, the spate of mergers and leveraged buyouts has tended to raise the proportion of debt. Nevertheless, manufacturing companies in the United States, on the whole, have between 60 and 70 percent equity in their total capitalization, as compared with about 30 to 40 percent in Japan (based on inflation-adjusted figures for assets).

In Japan there are few start-up companies and essentially no venture capital (Perry). Large companies often form joint ventures with other large companies, or they form wholly or partially owned subsidiaries designed to undertake special missions or product lines. The many small companies in Japan are basically "mom-and-pop" enterprises incorporated to take advantage of the very favorable tax policies afforded small corporations; they contribute very little to overall growth, productivity, or technology. Probably 1 percent of Japanese companies pay the bulk of the taxes and, since corporate tax is a larger proportion of total revenue in Japan than in the United States (about 28 percent versus 8 percent), this demonstrates the concentration of economic power in the hands of a relatively small number of large Japanese corporations.

As a consequence of the specific Japanese industrial structure, large Japanese corporations that dominate the economy and exports are basically the only ones that need to be studied with regard to their financing needs. As noted above, they are much heavier borrowers than are their American counterparts. This has significance for their capital costs, of course, but it also suggests that Japan, more than the United States, manages to spread the risks at the firm level over society as a whole, and even internationally.

How the Japanese do this is a subject of much study; Aoki (in this volume) and papers by Hodder,[6] Shoven and Tachibanaki,[5] and Hatsopoulos and Brooks[3] describe many of the salient features, such as:

1. Ownership by banks in companies to which they lend (a practice forbidden in the United States by the Glass-Steagall Act).

2. The role of the "main bank" in advising and monitoring company management, with short-term borrowing and rollovers (the fundamental instruments employed) as the means to assure close cooperation and to control the company in the event of business reverses.

3. Stability of government economic policies, which has also led to a high, sustained growth rate.

4. Absence of fear of unfriendly takeovers as a result of ownership of shares by many companies in each other (the *keiretsu*, or affiliate groups, which have taken the place of the old *zaibatsus*).

5. Subcontracting to a much larger extent than American firms do.

6. Conscious diversification into a full line of products, which reduces the risk that downturns in a few products or markets will seriously injure the company. The domination of large companies, compared with the spectrum of sizes in the United States, contributes to the stability of firms and their ability to borrow. (Hannay, in this volume, discusses the problem smaller American companies have in export markets.)

7. Japanese management's view of shareholders as impersonal providers of funds (which are amply available), rather than demanding owners of a company that should consider itself fortunate to receive their resources, as in the United States. Nevertheless, because of their lower costs, the companies' returns are very attractive, and price:earnings multiples are much higher than in the United States (somewhere around 26–28:1 versus 10–12:1).

8. Close collaboration between government and private companies, with many senior government employees moving to industry after their official careers.

9. Single-party (liberal Democrat) domination since the war and the absence of a credible alternative, leading to freedom from political interference in the private sector.

10. Internationalization of domestic markets and risks by determined export drives coupled with manufacture abroad as circumstances require. Jap-

anese managers recognize the greater political instability in the world today, and always manage foreign operations from Japan so that local and national aspirations do not interfere with the overall Japanese strategy (many American firms are still limited by geographic priorities).

These and other features make the provision of risk premiums in investment decisions much less significant in Japan than in the United States. While there is employment constraint to some degree as a result of the "lifetime" system of employment in large firms, capital constraints are much less severe and the employment limitations are overcome by retraining, subcontracting, "hiving off" of subsidiaries and joint ventures, and incessant expansion and growth.

This recitation of Japan's capital advantages is indeed a sobering one. The one area in which the United States has a substantial advantage is in the entrepreneurial start-up world and the venture capital and IPO systems that sustain it. This kind of risk taking suits the American culture very well, and derives from its pioneering history. Entrepreneurs start their businesses completely confident of ultimate success, indifferent to the short-term financial picture but determined to make and keep a fortune (based on favorable tax rates) and prepared to work infinitely long hours. They are not true gamblers, since they calculate that the odds are all in their favor—is the entrepreneur not smarter, quicker, harder working, and possessed of superior knowledge than the big companies (as Gordon E. Moore, in this volume, suggests)? Entrepreneurs strike the best deals they can with venture capitalists (usually giving up 40 to 60 percent of their company), but they do not figure that the money costs them anything, since they cannot get it any other way.[7] However, why does the venture capitalist finance the entrepreneur when the risks of success must be seen objectively as very great?

The secret lies in the portfolio method employed by experienced venture capitalists, much like the product-diversification strategy of a large company. Perhaps only a few of the dozens of companies in any portfolio will hit big and most will be failures, but those few successful ones provide (at low capital-gains tax rates) a fine rate of return for the overall venture capital pool, the rewards thus justifying all the risks taken. The venture capitalists can realize these high returns because they sell their interest in the successful business after a few years through an IPO or to a large company. The large company, on the other hand, in undertaking a project of similar character, must evaluate the potential rate of return over the life of the investment. The venture capitalist earns a substantial multiplier on his investment because the second round of investors (sometimes the third round), anticipating a large future earnings stream after the initial risks have been borne, is now willing to invest in the new business.

The pool of venture capital has risen sharply and is now abundant, led by the 1978 and 1981 reductions in the capital-gains tax and the subsequent flow of pension funds into this area. The general surge in the equities markets resulting from these tax actions and the lower inflation rate brought about by monetary policy have sustained the IPO and equities markets.

In this entrepreneurial venture capital area, the United States by far leads the world. It is a tremendous advantage in innovation and technological change. Likewise, as Reed and Moreno describe, the large American banks have a major role in the financing of large American and foreign enterprises. The intermediate, growing firms have the greatest problems in financing themselves and in competing with the Japanese, for the reasons cited in this section.

THE COST OF CAPITAL

The abundance of capital or lack of it has been described above for the United States and Japan in terms of the different types of organizations and stages in their evolution. Equally important in assessing the competitive situation is the cost of that capital. This is a much more complex subject, and the material in this section is based largely on the work of George Hatsopoulos, as exemplified in his paper with Brooks (see note 3 in this chapter).

Cost of Funds (Cost of Capital)

The AAA corporate bond yield is a measure of the cost of low-risk, long-term debt at fixed interest rate. In recent times, because of the steep yield curves, U.S. corporations have switched to a greater proportion of short-term debt at lower rates; this is the result of the Federal Reserve Board's easing of the monetary policy. However, the recent decline in long-term bond yields is leading corporate treasurers to a renewed interest in such fixed-yield instruments. Hence, even the cost of debt in the United States is now more difficult to track than it used to be.

Debt cost is deductible from gross income by corporations. Moreover, it is the nominal interest cost that is deductible, not the real cost (as the Treasury I tax proposal of November 1984 would have provided). Hence, in times of inflation the tax structure favors debt. As an example, consider interest at 12 percent and corporate tax at 50 percent with expected inflation of 5 percent. The net nominal cost to the corporation of the interest is $12 \times 0.5 = 6\%$. Subtracting the expected inflation yields a net real interest cost of just 1 percent. In the recent past, that cost has been strongly negative because the rate of inflation was higher. If the short-term interest rate is 9 percent, then the real interest cost becomes negative again with 5 percent inflation, as the lender and the government subsidize the borrower. Since corporations have incurred different debt obligations over past years, the average cost of debt requires a historical analysis for each company. However, in computing the marginal cost of debt for a new investment, the calculation will be based on the proposed method of financing.

The cost of equity is a considerably more elusive number. It is not, however, to be equated with the reciprocal of the price:earnings ratio (P/E), i.e., the E/P ratio as found on the stock markets. The underlying worth of a corporate share is the discounted present value of the stream of cash flows into the future that is anticipated by the owner. Dividends, capital distributions, and so forth have historically served as proxies for investors' expectations about the future cash flows of the firm. In an efficient stock market, the quoted stock prices will reflect such an underlying value. Each stockholder has his or her own calculation of what such a future cash flow might be and what the appropriate discount rate should be. The net effect of the perceptions of all stockholders results in the market value of the stock. If the stock is unlisted, or private, management would use comparisons with listed stocks of similar companies or would apply discount rates prevailing in the economic climate of the day. Often, management's perceptions of future dividends differ from those of the public, in which case the P/E ratio of the stock market may be low although dividend expectations of management may be high.

Conditions in the stock markets change with general economic conditions, interest rates, supply and demand of equities, and many other factors. Thus, a rise in the market, or in a particular equity, will raise a company's P/E ratio and hence lower the cost of its equity. These changes in market values may occur almost independently of the expected dividends; what changes is the appropriate discount rate. In addition, management's expectations of future dividends may change rather abruptly if new technology becomes available to competitors, or simply new market entrants appear. If this is not realized by the market for some time, the cost of equity of the company is temporarily reduced. Also, the stock market valuation is based on the overall effective tax rate of the corporation, not the marginal rate for a new investment. Hence, past performance and the tax laws affect the marginal cost of equity in an investment. These are examples of the complexity of calculating the cost of equity. Nevertheless, it is possible to study groups of companies in Japan and the United States and to derive reasonable estimates of their cost of equity.

Dividends, of course, are not deductible by American corporations; they are in effect partly deductible in Japan since profits paid out as dividends are taxed at a *lower* rate than retained earnings. In any case, the corporation in each country must earn pretax dollars of sufficient amount to pay the taxes and the dividend: this represents the pretax cost of equity. It will be appreciably higher than the pretax cost of debt (with prevailing corporate tax rates, more than twice for new investments) because it includes, in addition to taxes, a substantial risk premium inherent in equities that are subordinate to debt as to distribution of earnings and security of the assets. On an after-tax basis, therefore, equity is much more expensive in real cost than debt because of the deductibility of the nominal interest cost (shown above). Despite this, well-managed mature organizations use debt within prudent limits only, because of the risk of insolvency or business reverses. In the United States this generally runs about 1:2. The Japanese, however, because of their unique financial and corporate structure, as described above, have traditionally used much higher leverage; although it is somewhat less so today than in the past, the debt to equity ratio is more like 2:1.

These relationships also help explain why leveraged buyouts, restructuring, takeovers, and acquisitions in the United States often feature a substantial valuation for a company's equity in excess of market. This is not necessarily because the markets are inefficient but because these maneuvers substitute cheaper debt for more expensive equity. It is the tax system that makes corporate takeover specialists like Boone Pickens and Carl Icahn viable, because debt is tax deductible. Of course, the company's risk becomes much greater, too.

Real interest rates in Japan have also been lower than in the United States because of controls on financial markets. Tax rates on corporations in Japan are slightly higher than in the United States, but the effect of this difference is not as great as that of the leveraging and of interest rates.

When a corporation's costs of debt and equity are calculated, the overall cost of funds is obtained by weighting them in the actual pattern. It is, of course, most meaningful if corrected for projected (not current) inflation, to arrive at real costs after taxes.

The nominal after-tax cost of funds is used as a basis in calculating "hurdle" rates by corporations planning a new investment. They would typically add a risk premium, which could be just as much. The resultant sum, which may then be twice the nominal after-tax cost of funds, is the "hurdle" rate, below which a project would not be justified. Then the cash flow after taxes for the new project to the end of its expected useful life is computed, and discounted back to the present using the "hurdle" rate as the discount rate. If the net present value so obtained is equal to or greater than the original total investment, the project is likely to be approved.

Tables 2 and 3 show calculations of the cost of funds for the United States and Japan, respectively, in the three years 1975, 1981, and 1984. Notable conclusions from these data and the facts underlying them are highlighted below:

- Japanese real costs have been and are much below American costs.
- During the period 1975 to 1981, when Japan was engaged in a massive

TABLE 2 U.S. Cost of Funds: 1975, 1981, 1984 (percent)

	1975	1981	1984
Marginal tax rate (annual)	52.0	50.3	50.3
Expected inflation	6.5	9.0	4.7
Interest-bearing debt			
Coupon rate (nominal pretax cost)	8.5	13.3	12.0
Real coupon rate	2.0	4.3	7.3
Nominal cost after taxes	4.1	6.6	5.9
Real cost after taxes	− 2.4	− 2.4	1.2
Equity			
Nominal cost before taxes	33.7	38.8	25.4
Nominal cost after taxes	15.0	17.6	11.9
Real cost after taxes	8.5	8.6	7.1
Funds[a]			
Nominal cost after taxes	11.0	13.1	9.1
Real cost after taxes	4.5	4.1	4.3

NOTE: All rates are instantaneous, except as noted.
[a]Mix of funds: Interest-bearing debt   14.1%
                    Interest-free debt   16.7%
                    Equity   69.3%
SOURCE: Calculated from methodology of Hatsopoulos and Brooks (note 3 in this chapter).

TABLE 3 Japanese Cost of Funds: 1975, 1981, 1984 (percent)

	1975	1981	1984
Marginal tax rate (annual)	52.6	54.7	54.7
Expected inflation	10.1	5.4	3.7
Interest-bearing debt			
Coupon rate (nominal pretax cost)	9.2	8.0	7.6
Real coupon rate	− 0.9	2.6	3.9
Nominal cost after taxes	4.3	3.6	3.4
Real cost after taxes	− 5.7	− 1.8	− 0.2
Equity			
Nominal cost before taxes	36.6	24.9	20.4
Nominal cost after taxes	16.0	10.7	8.8
Real cost after taxes	5.9	5.3	5.2
Funds[a]			
Nominal cost after taxes	7.0	4.9	4.2
Real cost after taxes	− 3.0	− 0.4	0.6

NOTE: All rates are instantaneous, except as noted.
[a]Mix of funds: Interest-bearing debt   32.9%
                    Interest-free debt   31.9%
                    Equity   35.1%
SOURCE: Calculated from methodology of Hatsopoulos and Brooks (note 3 in this chapter).

investment program, the actual real cost of funds was negative. Control of interest rates by the government and high leveraging, together with a high corporate statutory rate, produced this remarkable result. Only recently has the real cost of funds become slightly positive.

• Equity costs are lower in Japan, partly because of favorable taxation of income from equities. Not only does a corporation pay less tax on distributed dividends, the shareholder gets a lower tax rate than on earned income, plus valuable exemptions. In addition, corporations are allowed to accumulate substantial tax-free reserves. The Japanese tax structure, as Shoven and Tachibanaki show (see above), makes equity investments very attractive, particularly in view of the fact that the Japanese have no capital gains tax. They calculate that, from the individual Japanese shareholder's perspective, the effective marginal tax rate in 1980 for all classes of industry and assets (on a weighted basis) was −1.5 percent versus 37.2 percent in the United States. Even if somewhat different indices of inflation are used, this effective rate lies only in the 7 to 17 percent range. In essence, the marginal investor is slightly subsidized rather than taxed, under the former assumption, or there is nearly an effective expenditure tax in the latter case at the corporate level. The high leveraging of Japanese companies, the special depreciation rules, and the low rate of taxation of interest and dividends at the personal level yield this startling result.

• Under the Japanese system, the low cost of funds is available at the margin only if the company is expanding. If a successful company does not increase its total capital, i.e., for expansion, the debt:equity ratio starts to shrink, because the corporation pays off debt (this is cheaper overall than paying dividends beyond those required by the stock market yields, because of the double taxation). As it does so, its reduced leveraging raises its average cost of funds. This is what is now occurring with some successful Japanese companies, such as Toyota, which is faced with export quotas and hence has become cash rich for want of expansion. They, therefore, pay more taxes and help offset the lost tax revenues from rapidly growing companies, which borrow heavily for expansion and obtain all the benefits therefrom at the expense of the tax collector. The successful basic industries keep the cost of capital low for the expanding high-tech companies.

This tax-financial system works differently for companies in the United States, where lower leveraging, lower corporate taxes, and higher equity costs favor companies that are not expanding rapidly. Only incentives such as accelerated depreciation and investment tax credits tend to offset this fact. Lowering the corporate statutory rate further would reduce the cost of equity somewhat for all corporations and reward capital investment already made, but it would also decrease the double taxation of corporate income and therefore tend to reduce expansion in favor of paying out dividends to investors who will be clamoring for them as their marginal rate goes down (a feature of the Treasury tax proposals of May 1985). It is the interplay of a high statutory corporate tax rate (higher for retained profits than for dividends paid out), lower dividend taxation, no capital-gains tax, high leveraging, and a financial-social system that spreads corporate risk that makes the Japanese climate so unique for growth.

• The lower cost of funds in Japan means that Japanese companies can sell products at cost, while their American competitors are losing money. Over a long enough period of time, a determined well-financed Japanese company can drive its competitors out of business. This seems currently to be happening in memory chips. Thus, this study of the cost of capital demonstrates an enormous Japanese advantage. The hard dollar adds insult to injury, and so an American company is crippled when it tries to retaliate in Japan or in other overseas markets.

Cost of Capital Services

Raising money leads to the cost described above. However, the real overall cost of capital depends on how it is used, and here there are different adjustments for inflation, taxation, depreciation, and investment allowances. Thus, for equipment and similar fixed assets, the cost of capital is the cost of funds, plus the cost of depreciation, less the tax benefits from various investment allowances, and less the benefit from inflation (the replacement cost of the assets is appreciating because of inflation).

Land is not depreciated, but appreciates with inflation, and so on. The overall real cost of capital is higher than the real cost of raising the money (cost of funds) because depreciation raises the cost of fixed assets, and the cost of receivables is high because there is no offset for inflation or tax.

All these factors are taken into account when the cost of capital services is computed. This concept was first introduced by Hall and Jorgenson,[8] and developed further by Hatsopoulos and Brooks (note 3) to include inflation, to reflect the timing of tax payments and tax credits, and to include intangible assets, such as the technology resulting from an investment in R&D. Hatsopoulos and Brooks set forth the details of the calculations for the two countries. A simple way of expressing it is to see it as equivalent to the fee for which a leasing company would lease a piece of equipment (or a whole plant), over the life of the item involved, including no profit in the fee (i.e., at the scrapping of the unit there is nothing left, but the full cost has been retrieved after provision for all the elements described above, including all applicable taxes). This figure, then, is the minimum pretax earning on a new investment that a company could afford to make, assuming no risk involved.

Table 4 is a summary of the calculation for the United States in 1984. It uses the cost of funds shown in Table 2 for that year. These costs of capital services include all the costs associated with the use of an asset: the real cost

TABLE 4   Summary Cost of Capital Calculations for the United States in
1984 (percent)

Concept		Equipment	Structures	10-year R&D Ventures
ρ	After-tax cost of funds	0.091	0.091	0.091
π	Expected inflation	0.047	0.047	0.047
ITC	Investment tax credit	0.10	0	0.125[a]
τ	Marginal corporate tax rate	0.503	0.503	0.503
β	Portion of the ITC that reduces the basis of equipment for tax depreciation	0.5	0	0
Z	Present value of depreciation allowance (under ACRS)	0.83	0.63	1.0
δ	Rate of economic decay	0.123	0.066	0.05
d	Utilization delay (years)	0	0	10.0
C	Gross cost of capital	0.169	0.151	0.106

NOTE: A simplified version of the cost of capital equation is shown below. It ignores the timing
of taxes and assumes that magnitudes of the key parameters are relatively small:

$$C = (1 + \rho - \pi)^d \frac{(1 - ITC - \tau(1 - \beta)Z)(\rho + \delta - \pi)}{1 - \tau}$$

[a]Investment tax credit of 0.125 on R&D assumes that only direct costs that constitute one-half of
R&D expenditures are allowed under the 25 percent R&D tax credit.

of debt and equity, costs associated with taxes and credits, and the cost
associated with the economic depreciation of the asset. The same calculations
can be made for land and inventories, and when weighted appropriately yield
the gross cost of capital services for a company, an industry, or a whole
sector, as desired. Hatsopoulos and Brooks's methodology (note 3) shows
that for the years given in Tables 2 and 3 the comparative weighted results
are:

Gross Real Cost of Capital Services
(cents per year per dollar of capital)

	U.S.	Japan
1975	15.5	3.0
1981	13.6	6.8
1984	13.0	8.2

This again illustrates how the Japanese policymakers kept capital costs low
in order to spur the investments they deemed necessary to compete in world
markets. They did this despite the sharp increase in inflation in the later
1970s, by controlling interest costs.

Table 4 also gives a calculation for the cost of capital of an R&D project
that lasts 10 years before it can be commercialized; although it can be ex-
pensed in the year incurred under tax law, it is still a capital investment and

has a cost. In the case shown, that cost is 10.6 percent. As mentioned above, since company balance sheets do not reflect intangible investments in technology, such investments may even be larger than tangible investments, as for example, at IBM.

These basic differences between Japan and the United States are what have permitted the Japanese to invest approximately 2½ times as much in fixed assets per worker as their U.S. competitors, and they lie behind the manufacturing productivity increase in Japan of 6.8 percent per year between 1973 and 1983, compared with the 1.8 percent in the United States disclosed by Jorgenson (in this volume). The Japanese thus can compete very effectively in world markets for manufactured goods; the United States is fast losing its competitive position, as the chapters by Young and Hannay demonstrate. It is true that the United States has created many jobs in the service sectors, especially in smaller companies, but except perhaps for a few large financial institutions, the productivity and the competitiveness of the service sectors are far below those of the manufacturing sector.

A further conclusion from the data given above is that the cost of capital differential in Japan's favor would permit a Japanese company to invest in longer-term R&D projects, or to invest much more than its American counterpart. Then, when the fruits of that R&D are to be implemented by physical investment as a completed innovation, the Japanese again enjoy an advantage. This double advantage in the more technologically based manufacturing industries of the future bodes ill for the United States and suggests imminent moves for protectionism and its consequences, such as inflation and loss of markets elsewhere (e.g., in agriculture).

One of the important questions raised by these studies is how the costs of capital compare with actual returns. Returns on investments, of course, are not necessarily the "hurdle" rates; they can be higher or lower, depending on the competitive situation, the economic climate, the state of the technology, and other factors. Management seeks the highest return that conditions permit, not just to retrieve the cost of capital. However, good data on actual returns are difficult to obtain, as they must be based on cash flows after tax and not on reported profits. Furthermore, accounting practices do not permit ready calculation of the cash flows of many corporations. It would appear that in recent years many U.S. corporations had a cost of capital above their returns and the stock market reflected this fact, which explains why market prices may be and often are below book value.[9] This may be due to incompetent management, powerful competition, excessive regulations, obsolete technology, poor labor contracts, or a whole host of possible problems. As mentioned above, this is what attracts leveraged buyouts and acquisitions at seemingly much higher than such market prices. The rise in the market in the last several years suggests that increased corporate cash flow aided by the tax advantages of the 1981 act (Accelerated Cost Recovery System and

Investment Tax Credit) and reduced inflation is bringing earnings on new investments into an acceptable range. However, the Japanese are still well ahead, as indicated.

There have been a few other studies of the subject of this chapter, e.g., by the Chase Manhattan Bank,[10] the Department of Commerce,[11] and Richard R. Ellsworth. While methodologies differ, the general conclusions do not.

SOME RECOMMENDATIONS ON CAPITAL FORMATION AND COMPETITIVENESS

This is not the place for an extended discussion of tax and other policies required to put American companies into a more competitive position. Both authors of this chapter have written separately on these matters.[13] But a consideration of the studies described herein suggests several very basic conclusions:

1. Interest rates need to be reduced. In view of the low American savings rate in the private sector, dissaving by the government (through its deficit) should be reduced. Permanent reductions will come only by cutting expenditures. This is because the level of spending, to a first approximation, ultimately determines the level of taxation, whether current or future. If inflation is employed by government monetary policy to conceal this effect, it merely substitutes a hidden tax for an overt one. A reduction in the deficit would permit monetary policy to ease and become less volatile.

2. Stability of government policies is essential if America is to remain competitive. Japan has had a long period of relative stability; the United States has had widely varying monetary policies and three major tax bills in four years. To enact another major tax bill incorporating many controversial provisions would be an experiment with unforeseeable results affecting the entire U.S. economy. It is far better to make changes slowly and incrementally.

3. The savings rate in the United States is not likely to increase significantly until the tax system moves toward a consumption tax and away from an income tax. This can be accomplished incrementally, for example, by easing the constraints on Individual Retirement Accounts, by allowing expensing for all capital investments (tangible or intangible) in the year in which they are incurred, and by permitting the issuance of qualified new preferred issues—deductible to the issuing corporation—that are limited to expansion. While an income tax system remains, the incentives for new investment like the Accelerated Cost Recovery System and the Investment Tax Credit are important. Elimination or reduction of capital-gains taxes on financial assets, especially on rollovers into other investments, would yield greater market liquidity and risk taking, and would help compensate for the double taxation of corporate investment.

   This chapter, then, is an attempt to sharpen understanding of how economics and technology come together in studying the competitiveness of capital formation processes, the financing of innovation, and the technological contribution to economic growth in the United States and Japan. In this critical area can be found one of the major reasons why the Japanese growth rate in GNP is outstripping that of the United States. This is hardly the time for business and politics as usual. The United States has many inherent advantages if its economic policies can be harnessed in a benign way for innovation and investment, leading to a higher sustained growth rate. Americans are good at this, too, as their history proves.

NOTES

1. Table 1 is based on data supplied by Charles B. Reeder of the Du Pont Economics Division, updated with recent information from the Department of Labor and modified to include the effects of inflation. (See also Reeder's chapter in this volume.)
2. Stephen S. Roach, Manufacturing, Cyclical Vulnerability and Growth Recession, Morgan Stanley & Co., June 12, 1985.
3. From G. N. Hatsopoulos and S. H. Brooks, The gap in the cost of capital: Causes, effects and remedies, in *Technology and Economic Policy*, R. Landau and D. W. Jorgenson, eds. (Cambridge, Mass.: Ballinger, forthcoming).
4. Ibid.
5. John B. Shoven and Toshiaki Tachibanaki, The Taxation of Income from Capital in Japan, paper presented at Stanford Center for Economic Policy Research Conference on Government Policy Towards Industry in the United States and Japan, May 1985.
6. James L. Hodder, Investment and Financial Decision Making in Japanese Firms: A Comparison with U.S. Practices, paper presented at a Stanford University-Northeast Asia Forum Conference, Honolulu, January 1985.
7. In strict financial terms it does have a cost. This cost would be measured by the value of the intangible capital the entrepreneur brings to the enterprise. Unfortunately, accounting practices of companies everywhere make no provision for showing intangible capital assets in balance sheets and profit and loss statements, so that using only financial-asset reporting frequently understates a firm's true strengths.
8. R. E. Hall and D. W. Jorgenson, Tax policy and investment behavior, *American Economic Review* 57(June 1967):391–414.
9. *Bank Credit Analyst*, May 1985:23ff; C. G. Callard and D. C. Kleinman, *Financial Analysts Journal*, May–June 1985:51.
10. *U.S. and Japanese Semiconductor Industries: A Financial Comparison*. Report prepared by the Chase Manhattan Bank N.A. for the Semiconductor Industry Association, June 9, 1980.
11. U.S. Department of Commerce, International Trade Administration, *A Historical Comparison of the Cost of Financial Capital in France, the Federal Republic of Germany, Japan, and the United States*, April 1983.
12. Richard R. Ellsworth, Capital markets and competitive decline, *Harvard Business Review*, September–October 1985:171.
13. See *Technology and Economic Policy* (note 3 above).

Contributors

MASAHIKO AOKI is Takahashi Professor of Japanese Studies and Economics at Stanford University and professor of economics, University of Kyoto. Dr. Aoki has held faculty positions in economics at Harvard University. He is a fellow of the Econometric Society and an associate editor of the *International Journal of Industrial Organizations*; he serves on various government committees in Japan.

Dr. Aoki received his B.A. and M.A. degrees in economics from the University of Tokyo and his Ph.D. in economics from the University of Minnesota.

WILLIAM O. BAKER retired in 1980 as chairman of the board of Bell Telephone Laboratories, Inc., following service since 1973 as president. He joined Bell Laboratories in 1939, becoming head of polymer research and development in 1948; from 1951 to 1954 he was assistant director of chemical and metallurgical research, and during the next year was director of physical sciences research. He became vice-president of research in 1955 and had overall responsibility for Bell Laboratories research programs for the next 25 years.

Vice-chairman of the New Jersey Board of Higher Education and co-author of *A Nation at Risk: The Imperative for Educational Reform* (1983), he is a trustee of Carnegie-Mellon, Princeton, and Rockefeller (chairman) universities. On the Board of Overseers of the College of Engineering and Applied Science at the University of Pennsylvania, he serves also as a trustee of the Harry Frank Guggenheim Foundation, the Fund for New Jersey, General Motors Cancer Research Foundation, the Charles Babbage Institute, and the Andrew W. Mellon Foundation (chairman). He presently serves as director of the Summit Bancorporation, Johnson & Johnson, Annual Reviews, and the Health Effects Institute.

Dr. Baker received a Ph.D. degree from Princeton University, holding Harvard and Proctor fellowships, after receiving a B.S. in physical chemistry from Washington College.

ROBERT HAYES BURNS BALDWIN is chairman of the Morgan Stanley Advisory Board, a select group of business and financial leaders who offer advice and counsel on key issues of importance to both Morgan Stanley and its clients throughout the world. He retired as chairman of Morgan Stanley, Inc., on January 1, 1984, after serving in that post since January 1983. He had served as president and managing director of Morgan Stanley from 1973 to December 1982.

Mr. Baldwin joined Morgan Stanley in April 1946 and became a general partner in 1958. On June 30, 1965, he retired as a general partner and became a limited partner of the firm. The following day he was sworn in as Under Secretary of the Navy and remained in that position until July 31, 1967. He resumed a general partnership in Morgan Stanley & Co. on September 1, 1967.

He is a member of the Council on Foreign Relations; a member of the Advisory Council of Stanford University's Graduate School of Business; a senior member of the Conference Board; chairman of Cities In Schools (Washington, D.C.); a director of Arthur J. Gallagher & Co. (Chicago) and of Organization Resources Counselors (New York); a trustee of the Presbyterian Hospital in the City of New York and chairman of the current fund drive for the Columbia-Presbyterian Medical Center; and a trustee of the Geraldine Rockefeller Dodge Foundation (Morristown, New Jersey) and of the Committee for Economic Development.

Mr. Baldwin recently served as a member of President Reagan's Commission on Industrial Competitiveness. He is past-chairman of the Securities Industry Association and a past member of the Business Roundtable and its Policy Committee.

STEPHEN D. BECHTEL, JR., is chairman of Bechtel Group, Inc., a leading world-wide engineering/construction firm.

First employed by one of the Bechtel companies in 1941, Mr. Bechtel held many jobs and responsibilities, both in the field and in the San Francisco home office, before being elected president in 1960. In 1973 he was elected chairman, a position that had been vacant since the retirement of his father, S. D. Bechtel, in 1965.

Mr. Bechtel is chairman of the National Academy of Engineering; a member of the Business Council; a life-term councillor of the Conference Board; a member of the Board of Trustees of the California Institute of Technology; a member of Caltech's Building and Grounds Committee; a member of the President's Council, Purdue University; a director of the National Action Council on Minorities in Engineering; an honorary trustee of the California Academy of Sciences; an officer of the French Legion of Honor; a member of the Policy Committee of the Business Roundtable; and a member of the Labor-Management Group.

Mr. Bechtel's other business affiliations include board directorship of International Business Machines Corporation.

Mr. Bechtel holds a B.S. degree in civil engineering from Purdue University and an M.B.A. from Stanford University School of Business.

MICHAEL J. BOSKIN is professor of economics, chairman of the Center for Economic Policy Research at Stanford University, and research associate, National Bureau of Economic Research.

He is the author of approximately 50 articles and editor of six volumes of essays on taxation, fiscal policy, capital formation, labor markets, social security, and related subjects. The recipient of numerous honors and awards, Dr. Boskin received his B.A., M.A., and Ph.D. degrees (the latter in 1971) from the University of California, Berkeley.

He has been a consultant and frequent witness to the committees of Congress dealing with economic policy and to the Treasury Department. He was a member of several of President Reagan's economic policy task forces during the 1980 presidential campaign.

Dr. Boskin's current research is focused on more comprehensive and conceptually proper government budgets, analysis of postwar U.S. consumption and saving, tax theory and policy, and social security and the economic status of the elderly.

ALBERT BOWERS is chairman of the board and chief executive officer of Syntex Corporation.

Dr. Bowers joined Syntex in 1956 as a group leader in research and subsequently held a number of research and management positions in the international pharmaceutical and life sciences company. Among his major scientific accomplishments is his pioneering work in developing methods for the selective fluorination of steroids, leading to the synthesis of new topical corticoids for the treatment of skin diseases.

He is a former chairman of the board and currently a director of the Pharmaceutical Manufacturers Association. He is also a member of the Board of Directors of U.S. Leasing, Inc.; the Business-Higher Education Forum; and the Rockefeller University Council. He is a founding member of the Board of Trustees of the University of California San Francisco Foundation.

Dr. Bowers was born in Manchester, England. He graduated from London University with a B.Sc. degree in chemistry, earned a Ph.D. degree in organic chemistry at the University of Manchester, and did postdoctoral studies in the United States under a Fulbright Fellowship.

HARVEY BROOKS is Benjamin Peirce Professor of Technology and Public Policy and Gordon McKay Professor of Applied Physics at Harvard University. He came to Harvard from General Electric in 1950 as professor of applied physics. He became dean of engineering and applied physics in 1957 and served in that capacity until 1975, when he was appointed professor of technology and public policy and transferred most of his teaching and research to the Kennedy School of Government, where he heads the Science, Technology, and Public Policy Program.

Dr. Brooks has served in many government and quasi-government advisory positions, including those with the Advisory Committee on Reactor Safeguards of the Atomic Energy Commission, the President's Science Advisory Committee, the National Science Board, the Naval Research Advisory Committee, and various project advisory committees to the Office of Technology Assessment. He was also chairman of the National Academy of Sciences Committee on Science and Public Policy and of its Commission on Socio-technical Systems, and was cochairman with E. L. Ginzton of its Committee on Nuclear and Alternative Energy Systems, whose report, *Energy in Transition, 1985–2010*, was published in 1979.

In 1982 Dr. Brooks was a member of the National Academy of Sciences Panel on Advanced Technology Competition and the Industrialized Allies. In 1983 he contributed an essay, "Technology As a Factor in American Competitiveness," to the volume *U.S. Competitiveness in the World Economy*, edited by George Lodge and Bruce Scott and published by Harvard Business School Press as one in a series of colloquia in honor of the seventy-fifth anniversary of the Harvard Business School.

He is a graduate of Yale University (A.B., 1937) and holds a Ph.D. in physics from Harvard (1940).

H. W. COOVER retired as vice-president of Eastman Kodak Company in 1984. After joining the Eastman Kodak Company in 1944, he held positions of leadership in the research and development functions of the Tennessee Eastman Company and the Eastman Chemicals Division, including vice-president and director of research. From 1973 to 1981 he was executive vice-president and in 1981 was named vice-president of Eastman Kodak Company. After 1973 he had overall responsibility for the R&D program for the seven companies comprising the Eastman Chemicals Division of Eastman Kodak Company and had direct responsibility for the leadership of some 1,300 R&D scientists and engineers.

Dr. Coover has devoted much time and energy to achieving increased awareness among industrial research managers of their responsibility to be innovative and progressive in their approaches to the management of research. His creative leadership has inspired a number of commercially significant technological advances. During the time of his leadership of its R&D effort, the Eastman Chemicals Division grew from $319 million in sales to $2.3 billion in 1983. Dr. Coover's management and leadership capabilities have been recognized by his peers through his participation in a number of research management organizations, including the Industrial Research Institute (IRI), for which he served as president in 1981–1982. Under his leadership, a Strategic Plan for the 1980s was developed to provide long-range direction in IRI.

Dr. Coover is a graduate of Hobart College and received his master's and doctorate degrees in chemistry from Cornell University. He is the author of more than 60 papers and more than 400 patents. He is a member of numerous professional societies and a member of the National Academy of Engineering.

PAUL A. DAVID, professor of economics and professor of history by courtesy at Stanford University, was named the William Robertson Coe Professor of American Economic History in 1977. A former Fulbright Scholar, Guggenheim Fellow, Visiting Fellow of All Souls College, Oxford, and the Pitt Professor of American History and Institutions at the University of Cambridge, Professor David is an elected fellow of the International Econometric Society and a fellow of the American Academy of Arts and Sciences. He received his A.B. degree in economics, summa cum laude, and his Ph.D. in economics from Harvard University.

Professor David is internationally known for his contributions to the development of a new approach to economic history in which the methods of modern economics are used in reconstructing and analyzing the economic life of past eras. His research has focused on technological, institutional, and demographic factors in long-term economic change. He is the author of *Technical Choice, Innovation and Economic Growth: Essays on American and British Experience in the Nineteenth Century* and *Reckoning With Slavery: A Critical Essay in the History of American Negro Slavery;* editor of *Nations and Households in Economic Growth;* and a frequent contributor to professional journals.

Professor David has served recently as a consultant to the Committee on Science and Technology Policy of the Organisation for Economic Cooperation and Development and currently codirects the Technological Innovation Program under the auspices of the Center for Economic Policy Research at Stanford University.

GEORGE C. EADS is dean of the School of Public Affairs at the University of Maryland, College Park. He joined the school as a professor in December 1981.

Between June 1979 and January 1981, Professor Eads served as a member of President Carter's Council of Economic Advisers (CEA) where he supervised the council's participation in policy areas such as energy, agriculture, industry, and international trade. He was especially active in regulatory reform issues and, on behalf of CEA, chaired the Regulatory Analysis Review Group. He was the U.S. delegate to the High-Level Group on Positive Adjustment Policies of the Organisation for Economic Cooperation and Development and chaired the subgroup on Policy Transparency. He cochaired the interagency review of industrial policy undertaken by the Carter administration during the spring and summer of 1980.

Prior to joining CEA, Professor Eads headed the Rand Corporation's Research Program in Regulatory Policies and Institutions, a program that he founded. He has also served as executive director of the National Commission on Supplies and Shortages, as assistant director for governmental operations and research of the Council on Wage and Price Stability, and as special assistant to the Assistant U.S. Attorney General, Antitrust Division. He has taught at Harvard, Princeton, and the George Washington University.

Professor Eads received his B.A. degree in economics from the University of Colorado and his graduate degrees in economics from Yale.

ANN F. FRIEDLAENDER is a professor of economics and civil engineering and dean of the School of Humanities and Social Science at the Massachusetts Institute of Technology (MIT). She came to MIT in 1974 as professor of economics and civil engineering and served as head of the Department of Economics in 1983 and 1984. Prior to that she taught at Boston College from 1965 to 1974.

Professor Friedlaender has served on a number of directorships, panels, and committees including the following: Board of Directors, National Bureau of Economic Research, 1983 to the present; Board of Directors, Consolidated Rail Corporation, 1978 to 1981; and Executive Committee, American Economic Association, 1981 to 1984. In addition, she has served on the Board of Editors of the following journals: *Transportation Science*, since 1979; *Public Finance Quarterly*, since 1972; *Quarterly Journal of Economics*, 1972 to 1978; and *American Economic Review*, 1973 to 1974.

Professor Friedlaender received a B.A. degree from Radcliffe College in 1960 and a Ph.D. from MIT in 1964.

N. BRUCE HANNAY was vice-president for research, Bell Laboratories, Murray Hill, New Jersey, until 1982. Dr. Hannay joined Bell Laboratories in 1944. He is the author of approximately 80 technical articles, primarily in the areas of mass spectroscopy, molecular structure, semiconductors, and solid-state chemistry.

He has served on many National Academy of Engineering, National Academy of Sciences, and National Research Council committees and as an adviser to many universities, government agencies, and international organizations.

Dr. Hannay is a member of the National Academy of Engineering, a member of the

National Academy of Sciences, a corresponding member of the Mexican National Academy of Engineering, and a fellow of the American Academy of Arts and Sciences. He is past-president of the Electrochemical Society and of the Industrial Research Institute and past-chairman of Directors of Industrial Research. He is chairman of science advisory councils at Atlantic Richfield and Gulf Applied Technologies and a member of advisory councils at Cortexa International Fund (Parisbas), SCI/TECH Holdings, Chrysler, Comsat, and United Technologies; he has also served on the Merck Institute Board of Scientific Advisors. He is on the Board of Directors of the General Signal Corporation, Plenum Publishing Corporation, Rohm and Haas Company, Alex. Brown Cash Reserve Fund and Tax-free Fund, and Flag Investors Fund.

Dr. Hannay graduated from Swarthmore College in 1942 (B.A. in chemistry) and received M.A. and Ph.D. degrees in physical chemistry from Princeton University in 1943 and 1944, respectively.

GEORGE N. HATSOPOULOS is the founder, chairman of the board, and president of Thermo Electron Corporation, a company whose principal business is the development and manufacture of process equipment and instruments for energy-intensive industries. Since its founding in 1956, Thermo Electron has grown to an international company with sales of over $250 million.

Dr. Hatsopoulos received his education at the National Technical University of Athens and the Massachusetts Institute of Technology (MIT) where he received his B.S. degree in 1949, M.S. degree in 1950, M.E. degree in 1954, and his Sc.D. degree in 1956.

Dr. Hatsopoulos served on the faculty of MIT from 1956 to 1962 and has continued his association with the Institute, currently serving as senior lecturer.

He is a member of the board of the Federal Reserve Bank of Boston and a member of the board of the National Bureau of Economic Research. He has testified at numerous Senate and congressional hearings on national energy policy and capital formation and has served on many national committees on energy conservation, environmental protection, and international exchange.

Dr. Hatsopoulos is a member of the National Academy of Engineering and received the Pi Tau Sigma Gold Medal Award for Outstanding Achievement in the Field of Engineering for the years 1950 to 1960.

He is the principal author of three books, including *Principles of General Thermodynamics* (1965), and has published more than 60 articles in professional journals.

WILLIAM R. HEWLETT is vice-chairman of the board of the Hewlett-Packard Company. With David Packard, he founded Hewlett-Packard in 1939.

Mr. Hewlett is a member of the National Academy of Engineering and of the National Academy of Sciences and a fellow of the American Academy of Arts and Sciences. He has been a trustee of the Carnegie Institution of Washington since 1971 and became chairman of the Board of Trustees in 1980. Mr. Hewlett previously served as a trustee of Stanford University and of the Rand Corporation and as a director of the Chase Manhattan Bank, Chrysler Corporation, and Utah International.

Mr. Hewlett holds B.A. and E.E. degrees from Stanford University and an M.S. from the Massachusetts Institute of Technology. In 1985 he received the National Medal of Science from President Ronald Reagan.

EDWIN C. HOLMER is president of Exxon Chemical Company in Darien, Connecticut, and is also a vice-president of Exxon Corporation. Exxon Chemical is responsible for Exxon's worldwide chemicals business.

Mr. Holmer joined the Exxon organization in 1942 as a process engineer at the Bayway Refinery in Linden, New Jersey, after receiving a bachelor's degree in chemical engineering from Rensselaer Polytechnic Institute. Following a series of engineering assignments with Exxon Research and Engineering Company, he was appointed assistant director of the Chemicals Research Division in 1956. In 1959 Mr. Holmer transferred to the Jersey Production Research Company in Oklahoma and was named president three years later. In 1964 Exxon's exploration and production research organizations were combined into Exxon Production Research Company in Houston, and Mr. Holmer became its first president.

He moved to Exxon Chemical in 1966 as senior vice-president and director, was appointed executive vice-president in 1968, was named executive vice-president of Esso Middle East in 1974, and assumed the presidency of Exxon Chemical in May 1976.

Mr. Holmer is immediate-past-chairman of the Board of Directors of the Chemical Manufacturers Association; immediate-past-chairman and a member of the Executive Committee of the Society of Chemical Industry, American Section; a member of the Advisory Board of the Center for History of Chemistry; a member of the Board of Directors of the International Executive Service Corps; and a member of the Board of Directors of National Starch and Chemical Corporation.

PETER W. HUBER, an associate of Science Concepts, Inc., in Washington, D.C., is a lawyer and an engineer. He has a doctorate in mechanical engineering from the Massachusetts Institute of Technology (MIT) and served as an assistant and later associate professor at MIT for six years. His law degree is from Harvard Law School. He clerked on the D.C. Circuit Court of Appeals for Judge Ruth Bader Ginsburg and then on the U.S. Supreme Court for Justice Sandra Day O'Connor.

Mr. Huber's professional expertise is health, safety, and environmental regulation in federal administrative agencies and in the courts. He is the author of numerous papers and law review articles in this area, the latest of which is "Safety and the Second Best: The Hazards of Public Risk Management in the Courts," published in the March 1985 issue of the *Columbia Law Review*.

DALE W. JORGENSON is currently Frederic Eaton Abbe Professor of Economics at Harvard University, where he has been professor of economics since 1969. Before arriving at Harvard, Dr. Jorgenson taught at the University of California, Berkeley, from 1959 to 1969. He has been visiting professor of economics at Stanford University and the Hebrew University of Jerusalem and visiting professor of statistics at Oxford University. He has also served as Ford Foundation Research Professor of Economics at the University of Chicago.

Dr. Jorgenson was elected to membership in the National Academy of Sciences in 1978 and the American Academy of Arts and Sciences in 1969. He was elected to fellowship in the American Association for the Advancement of Science in 1982, the American Statistical Association in 1965, and the Econometric Society in 1964. He received the John Bates Clark Medal of the American Economic Association in 1971.

He holds a B.A. degree from Reed College and A.M. and Ph.D. degrees from Harvard University.

MILTON KATZ is Henry L. Stimson Professor of Law and director of international legal studies, Harvard Law School, emeritus. He is currently Distinguished Professor of Law at Suffolk University Law School and is a past-president of the American Academy of Arts and Sciences.

Mr. Katz has served in many academic, professional, and governmental capacities, including U.S. executive officer, combined Production and Resources Board (U.S.-U.K.-Canada); lieutenant commander, USNR, and deputy chief of secret intelligence, OSS; chief of the Marshall Plan in Europe (with rank of ambassador) and chairman of the Financial and Economic Committee of NATO; chairman, National Research Council's Committee on the Life Sciences and Social Policy; and member of the National Academy of Engineering's Committee on Technology and International Trade and Economic Issues.

Mr. Katz is the author of numerous articles and books, including *Foreign Economic Policy for the Twentieth Century* (with others), (1958); (with Kingman Brewster) *Law of International Transactions and Relations* (1960); *The Things That Are Caesar's* (1966); *The Relevance of International Adjudication* (1968); *Man's Impact on the Global Environment* (with others), (1970); *Assessing Biomedical Technologies* (with others), (1975); *Technology, Trade, and the U.S. Economy* (with others), (1978); and *Strengthening Conventional Deterrence in Europe—A Proposal for the 1980's* (with others).

DONALD KENNEDY received his A.B., A.M., and Ph.D. degrees in biology from Harvard University. A Stanford faculty member since 1960, he received the Dinkelspiel Award, the university's highest honor for outstanding service to undergraduate education, in 1976. He was chairman of the Department of Biological Sciences from 1965 to 1972 and chairman of the Program in Human Biology from 1974 to 1977. From 1976 to 1977 Dr. Kennedy served as senior consultant to the then-new Office of Science and Technology Policy, Executive Office of the President, and in 1977 took a two-year leave to become commissioner of the Food and Drug Administration. In August of 1979 Dr. Kennedy returned to Stanford to become vice-president and provost, and on August 1, 1980, he became Stanford's eighth president.

BURTON H. KLEIN is professor of economics, emeritus, of the California Institute of Technology. Prior to becoming a professor of economics at Caltech, he conducted numerous studies of research and development at the RAND Corporation.

At Caltech, Dr. Klein has profited from lessons learned from other disciplines when bringing dynamic considerations into play. In his book *Dynamic Economics* (1977), he contrasted a static concept of stability (microstability) with a dynamic concept (macro-stability). He argued that unpredictable behavior at the microlevel leads to smooth progress at the macrolevel. In *Prices, Wages, and Business Cycles* (1984), Dr. Klein provided a statistical demonstration of how the quest for microstability, especially if aided by government, can lead to increasingly large economic downturns. His current interests are to explain the particular behaviors necessary to assure the longer-run survival of firms, and a new book, near completion, that will show that the arms race can be regarded as a positive-sum cooperative game between the various bureaucratic participants.

Dr. Klein holds B.A. and Ph.D. degrees from Harvard University.

STEPHEN J. KLINE is professor of mechanical engineering and professor of values, technology, science and society at Stanford University. Since joining Stanford in 1952, Professor Kline has served as director of the Thermosciences Division and is currently supervisor of the Internal Flow Program. Professor Kline has served as a consultant to various private corporations including General Motors Research, General Electric, E. I. du Pont de Nemours & Co., and Proctor and Gamble.

Professor Kline holds B.S. and M.S. degrees from Stanford, and he earned his Sc.D. from the Massachusetts Institute of Technology. He was elected to the National Academy of Engineering in 1981.

RALPH LANDAU, former chairman of the board of The Halcon SD Group, Inc., New York City, is now with Listowel Incorporated. From 1941 to 1945 he was a process development engineer for M. W. Kellogg and head of the chemical department of Kellex Corporation, a subsidiary. In 1946 Dr. Landau became executive vice-president of Scientific Design Company, Inc., of which he was cofounder and co-owner. In 1963 Scientific Design became Halcon International, Inc., with Dr. Landau as president. From 1975 he was chairman of this high technology company in the chemicals field; it was succeeded in 1981 by The Halcon SD Group, Inc. In 1966 he cofounded the Oxirane Company with Atlantic Richfield Corporation. Oxirane has become a major petrochemical company entirely based on new technology, with seven plants producing about 5 billion pounds of products per year. In 1980 Halcon sold its half-interest in Oxirane to ARCO.

His numerous affiliations with universities and industry include the following: Dr. Landau is a life member of the Massachusetts Institute of Technology Corporation and vice-president of the National Academy of Engineering; a life trustee of the University of Pennsylvania, a trustee of the California Institute of Technology, a trustee of the Cold Spring Harbor Laboratory, and a director of the Aluminum Company of America. He is an adjunct professor of management, technology, and society of the University of Pennsylvania. He is consulting professor of economics at Stanford University and a fellow of the faculty of the Kennedy School of Government at Harvard University.

He graduated from the University of Pennsylvania in 1937 with a bachelor of science degree and in 1941 from Massachusetts Institute of Technology as a doctor of science; both degrees are in chemical engineering. In 1985 he was among the first recipients of the National Medal of Technology from President Ronald Reagan.

ROBERT MALPAS, C.B.E., is a managing director of the British Petroleum Company. He is chairman of BP Chemicals, BP Ventures, and Scicon International. He is responsible for the Group's Research and Development and for its Engineering and Technical Centre.

Mr. Malpas was born in England in 1927. He has a first class degree in mechanical engineering from Durham University. In 1948 Mr. Malpas joined Imperial Chemical Industries (ICI). Having become head of engineering in the Petrochemical Division, he was appointed a general manager of a joint venture in Spain in 1963, work for which he was awarded the Spanish Order of Civil Merit. From 1966 to 1975 he worked in ICI Europa, of which he was made chief executive in 1973, before becoming a main board director of ICI in 1975. In 1975 he was made a Commander of the Order of the British Empire (C.B.E.). In 1978 Mr. Malpas resigned from ICI to become president of Halcon International, Inc., a New York-based chemicals process research company, which was in 1982 acquired by Texas Eastern Corporation. He joined BP in 1983.

EDWIN MANSFIELD is director of the Center for Economics and Technology and professor of economics at the University of Pennsylvania. Before joining the University of Pennsylvania faculty, he taught at Carnegie-Mellon, Yale, Harvard, and the California Institute of Technology.

Professor Mansfield has been elected a fellow of the American Academy of Arts and Sciences, the Econometric Society, and the Center for Advanced Study in the Behavioral Sciences, and he has held Fulbright and Ford Foundation fellowships. He received the 1982 Publication Award of the Patent Law Association and has served as U.S. chairman of the U.S.-U.S.S.R. Working Party on the Economics of Science and Technology. In 1984 he was appointed to the National Technology Medal Committee. He has been an editor of six journals, including the *Journal of the American Statistical Association*, and is general editor of a series of books on technological change published by the Univeristy of Wisconsin Press. He is the author of 150 articles and 20 books, including leading texts in introductory economics, microeconomics, and statistics.

JAMES D. MARVER is special partner/principal in the San Francisco Corporate Finance Department at L.F. Rothschild, Unterberg, Towbin, where he divides his time between venture capital, private placements, and public offerings. Previously he was with Goldman, Sachs & Co. and SRI International (formerly Stanford Research Institute).

The holder of a Ph.D. degree from the University of California, Berkeley, and a B.A. from Williams College, Mr. Marver has published a book, several chapters, and numerous articles and book reviews in such diverse fields as corporate finance, government regulatory policy, social policy, and consulting. He has also been a consultant to many private and public organizations, including the National Academy of Sciences/National Research Council, and has been a lecturer at California State University, San Jose.

RUBEN F. METTLER is chairman of the board and chief executive officer of TRW Inc. He was elected to his present position in December 1977, after serving as president and chief operating officer since 1969. He has been a director of the company since 1965.

Dr. Mettler serves on the boards of BankAmerica Corporation and Merck & Company. He is chairman of the Board of Trustees of the California Institute of Technology, chairman of the Business Council, and a former chairman of the Business Roundtable.

Dr. Mettler received the Eta Kappa Nu award for the Nation's Most Outstanding Young Electrical Engineer in 1954. The U.S. Junior Chamber of Commerce named him one of the Ten Outstanding Young Men in America in 1955. In 1965 he was elected to the National Academy of Engineering. In 1966 he received one of the first Alumni Distinguished Service Awards given by the California Institute of Technology.

Born in Shafter, California, in 1924, Dr. Mettler attended Stanford and then the California Institute of Technology, where he received a B.S. degree in electrical engineering in 1944. In 1946, after completing Navy service, he entered graduate school at

Caltech and received an M.S. degree in 1947 and a doctorate in electrical and aeronautical engineering two years later.

GORDON E. MOORE is chairman of the board and chief executive officer of Intel Corporation, a company that he cofounded in 1968. Prior to that time he was director of research and development for the Semiconductor Division of Fairchild Camera and Instrument Corporation. He was one of the eight founders of Fairchild Semiconductor Corporation in 1957; the organization evolved into the Semiconductor Division.

Dr. Moore received a B.S. in chemistry from the University of California, Berkeley, in 1950 and a Ph.D. in chemistry and physics from the California Institute of Technology in 1954.

In 1976 he was elected to membership in the National Academy of Engineering.

GLEN R. MORENO was born in California in 1943. He was educated at Stanford University (A.B. with Distinction, 1965) and Harvard Law School (J.D., 1969). He spent a year at the University of Delhi as a Rotary Foundation Fellow (1965–1966).

He joined Citibank in 1969 and is now group executive of Citicorp's Investment Bank for Europe/Middle East/Africa. He is a member of Citicorp/Citibank Policy Committee, chairman of Citicorp Investment Bank Limited, and a director of several Citicorp affiliates.

Mr. Moreno is a director of the Academy of St. Martin-in-the-Fields and a governor of the Ditchley Foundation.

DAVID A. NORMAN is president and chief executive officer of Businessland, Inc., which he founded in 1982. Businessland computer centers sell and service microcomputers and related office automation equipment to business and professional people, in addition to providing customer training at each center. Before founding Businessland, Mr. Norman was president, chief executive officer, and director of DATAQUEST Incorporated, which he founded in 1971. He was responsible for all phases of management, consulting, research, and marketing. In 1978, DATAQUEST Incorporated became a wholly owned subsidiary of the A. C. Nielsen Company. He was also a founder and vice-president of Creative Strategies, a privately held research consulting firm.

Mr. Norman received a B.S. degree in mechanical engineering from the University of Minnesota and an M.S. degree in industrial engineering from Stanford University.

DANIEL I. OKIMOTO is associate professor of political science and co-director, Northeast Asia–United States Forum on International Policy at Stanford University. Professor Okimoto was a coeditor of and contributor to *Competitive Edge: The Semiconductor Industry in Japan* and the author of *Between MITI and the Market: Japanese Industrial Policy for High Technology* (forthcoming from Stanford University Press).

Professor Okimoto holds a B.A. degree from Princeton University, an M.A. from Harvard University, and a Ph.D. in political science from the University of Michigan.

KEITH L. R. PAVITT is deputy director of the Science Policy Research Unit (SPRU) at the University of Sussex. SPRU is a research group of natural and social scientists working on problems of policy for R&D and technical innovation, both in the industrialized and developing countries. From 1961 to 1970 Professor Pavitt worked at the Organisation for Economic Cooperation and Development (OECD) in the Directorate for Scientific Affairs on a variety of science and technology policy problems. He was a visiting lecturer at Princeton University in 1971, and from 1971 to 1984 he was a senior fellow at the Science Policy Research Unit, leading SPRU work on science and technology policy in industrial countries. Professor Pavitt is also director of studies for postgraduate research. His current research is on the sources, directions, and determinants of innovative activities and their implications for theory and for policy.

Professor Pavitt read engineering and industrial management at Cambridge and economics and public policy at Harvard.

WILLIAM J. PERRY is the managing partner of H&Q Technology Partners. Prior to forming H&Q Technology Partners, he was an executive vice-president of Hambrecht & Quist Incorporated, an investment banking firm in San Francisco specializing in high technology companies. Before joining Hambrecht & Quist he was Under Secretary of Defense for Research and Engineering. As the Under Secretary, he was responsible for all weapon systems procurement and all research and development; he was the principal adviser to the Secretary of Defense on technology, communications, intelligence, and atomic energy.

Dr. Perry was one of the founders of ESL, Inc., in 1964 and served as its president until 1977 when he entered government. Before that, he had been with Sylvania/General Telephone and was the director of the company's Electronic Defense Laboratories.

He is currently a senior fellow at Stanford University and was elected to the National Academy of Engineering in 1970.

Dr. Perry is a director of ARGOSystems, Avantek, Par Technology, Inc., Stanford Telecommunications, Inc., and a number of private companies. He is a trustee of Rockefeller University, MITRE Corporation, and the Carnegie Endowment for International Peace and serves on a number of U.S. government advisory boards, including the President's Commission on Strategic Forces and the Defense Science Board.

Dr. Perry received his B.S. and M.S. degrees from Stanford University and his Ph.D. from Pennsylvania State University, all in mathematics.

JOSEPH M. PETTIT is the eighth president of the Georgia Institute of Technology; he was appointed in October 1971. Prior to that time he was at Stanford University where he served as professor of electrical engineering and dean of the School of Engineering.

Before joining the Stanford faculty in 1947, Dr. Pettit spent five years in research and development at Harvard University and at the Airborne Instruments Laboratory, Inc., in New York. He was awarded the Presidential Certificate of Merit for his contributions in radar countermeasures during World War II.

He served as a member of the National Science Board and is currently one of eight university presidents on the DOD/University Forum. Dr. Pettit is a member of the National Academy of Engineering and is currently chairman of its Education Advisory Board.

He is a fellow of the Institute of Electrical and Electronics Engineers and the 1983 recipient of its Founders Medal. He is a fellow and past-president of the American Society for Engineering Education.

JAMES BRIAN QUINN is William and Josephine Buchanan Professor of Management at the Amos Tuck School of Business Administration, Dartmouth College. Professor

Quinn is an authority in the fields of strategic planning, the management of technological change, and entrepreneurial innovation. He joined the Tuck School faculty in 1957 as assistant professor and assistant dean, having taught marketing for three years previously at the University of Connecticut. From 1951 to 1954 he was a new-product analyst in the research division of the Allen B. Dumont Laboratories, Inc.

Professor Quinn has been the recipient of fellowships from the Alfred P. Sloan Foundation, the Ford Foundation, and the Fulbright Exchange Program. He has been a member of the Board on Science and Technology for International Development for the National Academy of Sciences and the Agency for International Development, and of the Technical Advisory Board of the U.S. Department of Commerce. He was chairman of the Academic Committee for the President's Domestic Policy Review on Innovation and Productivity, coordinated by the Department of Commerce. He has served on National Research Council teams on science and technology planning, technology transfer, and education for science and technology in Colombia, Peru, Nepal, and the People's Republic of China.

Professor Quinn is a consultant to leading U.S. and foreign companies, the United States and foreign governments, and a number of small enterprises. He has published extensively on both corporate and national policy issues involving strategic planning, research and development management, and the management of entrepreneurial concerns.

He holds a B.S. degree from Yale University, an M.B.A. from Harvard University, and a Ph.D. from Columbia University.

JOHN S. REED became chairman and chief executive officer of Citicorp and its principal subsidiary, Citibank, N.A., on September 1, 1984. Before assuming the chairmanship, Mr. Reed had served as a vice-chairman with responsibilities for directing the worldwide consumer business and coordination of Citicorp's personnel planning and technological development.

Mr. Reed is a trustee of the Russell Sage Foundation, a director of Philip Morris Inc., a director of Monsanto Company, and a trustee of the Memorial Sloan-Kettering Cancer Center (New York). Other boards on which he serves include those of the Massachusetts Institute of Technology (MIT), the Center for Advanced Study in Behavioral Sciences (Palo Alto, California), the New York Blood Center, and United Technologies Corporation.

Mr. Reed received his B.A. degree from Washington and Jefferson College and his B.S. degree from MIT under a joint degree program in 1961. He returned to the Sloan School of MIT to earn his M.S. in 1965.

CHARLES B. REEDER is chief economist for E. I. du Pont de Nemours & Co. in Wilmington, Delaware. He joined the Du Pont Company in 1955 as an associate economist and was appointed chief economist in 1970.

Dr. Reeder is a member of several professional societies and was president of the National Association of Business Economists in 1966. He serves on the boards of the Bank of Delaware, the Delaware Council on Economic Education, the First Federal Savings Bank (of Delaware), and the Sigma mutual funds. He currently is chairman of the Delaware Economic and Financial Advisory Council. He was the 1982 winner of the Annual Silbert Economic Forecasting Award sponsored by the Sterling National Bank & Trust Company of New York for accuracy in economic forecasting.

He received his Ph.D. in economics from the Ohio State University in 1951, his master's degree in business administration from the Harvard Business School in 1947, and his bachelor's degree in business administration from the Ohio State University in 1945.

STEPHEN S. ROACH is senior economist and a vice-president of Morgan Stanley & Company, Inc., and is responsible for the firm's forecasting and analysis of U.S. economic activity.

Before joining Morgan Stanley in 1982 he was vice-president of economic analysis for the Morgan Guaranty Trust Company. Prior to that he served for six years on the research staff of the Federal Reserve Board in Washington, D.C., where he supervised the production of official staff forecasts of the U.S. economy. He has also been a research fellow at the Brookings Institution in Washington, D.C.

Dr. Roach holds a Ph.D. degree from New York University and a bachelor's degree from the University of Wisconsin.

NATHAN ROSENBERG is chairman of the Department of Economics and professor of economics at Stanford University. Before assuming his current position, Dr. Rosenberg served as the chairman of the Stanford Program on Values, Technology and Society and as director of the Stanford Program on Public Policy. Dr. Rosenberg is the author of numerous articles and several books focusing mostly on the history of technological change in industry.

Before moving to Stanford in 1974, Dr. Rosenberg served on the faculty of the University of Wisconsin, Harvard University, Purdue University, and the University of Pennsylvania. He was a Fulbright Scholar at Queen's College, Oxford University, between 1952 and 1954 and a Visiting Rockefeller Professor at the University of the Philippines in 1970–1971. He served as editor of the *Journal of Economic History* between 1972 and 1974, and in 1981 Dr. Rosenberg became a fellow of the American Academy of Arts and Sciences. His most recent book, *Inside the Black Box*, was published by Cambridge University Press in 1982.

Dr. Rosenberg earned his B.A. degree from Rutgers University and his M.A. and Ph.D. degrees from the University of Wisconsin.

VERNON W. RUTTAN is professor in the Department of Agricultural and Applied Economics and in the Department of Economics at the University of Minnesota. He has held academic appointments at Purdue University, and at the University of Minnesota where he served as professor and head of the Department of Agricultural and Applied Economics from 1965 to 1970 and as director of the Economic Development Center from 1970 to 1973.

Dr. Ruttan has also had substantial nonacademic experience. In 1961 and 1962 he served on the staff of the President's Council of Economic Advisers. Between 1963 and 1965 he was agricultural economist with the Rockefeller Foundation at the International Rice Research Institute in the Philippines. He was president of the American Agricultural Economics Association in 1971–1972, and from 1973 to 1978 he was president of the Agricultural Development Council.

His book (with Yujiro Hayami) *Agricultural Development: An International Perspec-*

tive (Johns Hopkins University Press, 1971 and 1985) has become a standard reference in the field of agricultural development. He is also the author of *Agricultural Research Policy*, published by the University of Minnesota Press in 1982.

He received his B.A. degree from Yale University in 1948 and his M.A. and Ph.D. degrees from the University of Chicago in 1952 and 1954, respectively.

ROBERT A. SWANSON is a founder of Genentech, Inc., and served as the president from the time he and Dr. Herbert Boyer founded the company in 1976 until 1985 when he became chief executive officer. He continues as a director. Before founding Genentech, Mr. Swanson was a partner with Kleiner & Perkins venture capital partnership. From 1970 to 1974, he was an investment officer with Citicorp Venture Capital Ltd. Mr. Swanson has a B.S. degree in chemistry from the Massachusetts Institute of Technology (MIT) and an M.S. degree from the Alfred P. Sloan School of Management at MIT.

JAMES D. WATSON is director of the Cold Spring Harbor Laboratory. Dr. Watson, a molecular biologist, shared the Nobel Prize for Medicine and Physiology in 1962 with two British biophysicists, Dr. Maurice H. F. Wilkins and Dr. Francis H. C. Crick. Drs. Watson, Wilkins, and Crick were honored for their contribution to the understanding of the basic life process through their discovery of the molecular structure of deoxyribonucleic acid, the substance of heredity.

As a National Research Fellow, Dr. Watson did research in 1950–1951 in Copenhagen and 1951–1952 as a National Foundation of Infantile Paralysis Fellow in the Cavendish Laboratory at the University of Cambridge, England. From 1953 to 1955 he was a senior research fellow in biology at the California Institute of Technology. He joined the Harvard faculty in 1955 and became associate professor of biology in 1958 and professor in 1961.

Beginning in 1965 he served on the Board of Trustees for the Cold Spring Harbor Laboratory in Cold Spring Harbor, Long Island, New York, becoming director of the laboratory in 1968 while continuing as a professor at Harvard. In June 1976 he resigned from Harvard in order to serve full time as director.

JOHN A. YOUNG is president and chief executive officer of Hewlett-Packard Company. He has served as Hewlett-Packard's chief executive officer since May 1978 and as chairman of the Executive Committee of the company's Board of Directors since March 1983. He had served as the company's chief operating officer and president since September 1977.

Mr. Young joined Hewlett-Packard's marketing planning staff in 1958 after receiving an M.B.A. from Stanford University. He subsequently served as a regional sales manager, a member of the corporate finance staff, and marketing manager of the former Microwave Division. In 1963 he was appointed Microwave Division general manager.

In 1968 Mr. Young was named vice-president of the company and assumed responsibility for the newly formed Electronic Products Group, which included the instruments, components, and measuring systems produced by Hewlett-Packard. He was appointed executive vice-president and elected to the company's Board of Directors in September 1974. At the same time, he was named to the Executive Committee, established to coordinate all phases of the company's operations. As executive vice-president, Mr. Young was responsible for Hewlett-Packard's Instrument, Computer Systems and Component Groups.

Mr. Young is a director of the Wells Fargo Bank, Wells Fargo & Company, and SRI International. He is cochairman of the Western Technical Manpower Council, a member of the Business Council, the Business Roundtable, and the Executive Committee of Machinery and Allied Products Institute. He also serves on the Board of Governors for the San Francisco Symphony Association and is a member of the Board of Directors of the Bay Area Council. His professional affiliations include membership in the American Electronics Association.

On June 28, 1983, Mr. Young was appointed by President Ronald Reagan to be chairman of the President's Commission on Industrial Competitiveness.

ED ZSCHAU came to Congress from Silicon Valley in California, where he had founded an electronics company, System Industries, in 1968. He served as president of System Industries for 13 years, until he resigned to run for Congress in 1982. Today, the company has annual sales of more than $100 million and employs about 800 people.

Prior to founding System Industries, Dr. Zschau was an assistant professor at the Stanford Graduate School of Business and the Harvard Business School for five years. He received an A.B. in philosophy (cum laude) from Princeton University in 1961 and attended Stanford University where he received an M.B.A. in 1963, an M.S. in statistics in 1964, and a Ph.D. in business administration in 1967.

Dr. Zschau's interest in politics grew from his industry leadership activities. In 1978, as a private citizen, he chaired the Capital Formation Task Force of the American Electronics Association, which proposed and lobbied for a significant reduction of capital gains tax rates that year. Since then he has served as a spokesman on the issues of high technology, innovation, small business, and economic growth.

*   *   *   *   *

Funds for the National Academy of Engineering Symposium Series on Technology and Social Priorities, which supported the Symposium on Economics and Technology, were provided by the Andrew W. Mellon Foundation, the Carnegie Corporation of New York, and the Academy Industry Program.

Center for Economic Policy Research (CEPR) sponsorship of the Symposium on Economics and Technology was supported by the Koret Conference Series, which is operated by CEPR with funds provided by the Koret Foundation.

The Symposium on Economics and Technology was also supported by the Industrial Affiliates Program of the Stanford University Departments of Chemistry and Chemical Engineering.

The views expressed in this volume are those of the authors and are not presented as the views of the Mellon Foundation, the Carnegie Corporation, the Academy Industry Program, the Koret Foundation, or the Industrial Affiliates Program.

Index

Abernathy, William J., 160
Abramovitz, Moses, 4, 21
Accounting practices, research treatment in, 112
Accrediting Board for Engineering and Technology, 256
Adjustment mechanisms in market forces, 19, 20, 21
Agent Orange, and damage awards, 193, 209
Agricultural Research Institute, 337, 339, 352
Agricultural Research Service, 119
Agriculture
  adoption of new technologies in, 8, 319, 334
  entrepreneurship in, 352
  labor force in, 354
    productivity of, 359
  land available for, 345, 348
  productivity in various countries, 346
    and growth in U.S., 353–354
  research and development in, 333–354
    in biological and chemical technology, 344–345
    expenditures by public and private sectors, 337–343, 353
    funding of, 154, 352–353
    for mechanization, 340–341, 344
    for plant varieties, 341–343
    and productivity growth, 334–336
    rate of return from, 308, 310, 334–335
    by state experiment stations, 339
  technical changes in U.S. and Japan, 345–352
  technological strength in U.S., 395
Airbus Industries, 299, 490
Aircraft industry

competitiveness of, 489–491
and Concorde as commercial failure, 147, 277, 299
economic benefits of jet engines in, 25
financing by banks, 461
innovations in, 280–281, 299
in Japan, 557, 559–560
new technology affecting, 495
origins of turbojet engine, 285
shortage of trained personnel in, 494–495
Altshuler, Alan, 134
Amdahl, Japanese investment in, 426
American Association for the Advancement of Science, 128
American Electronics Association, 468
American National Standards Institute, 160
American Society for Testing Materials, 160
Ames test for mutagenic chemicals, 198
Antitrust policies
  modifications in, 132, 161, 188, 524, 530–532
  restrictive effects of, 259
Aoki, Masahiko, 3, 7, 11, 12, 14, 15, 16, 569–581, 593, 595, 607
Apollo, performance in stock market, 470
Apparel industry
  competitiveness of, 486–487
  innovations in, 280
  productivity growth in, 331
Arab oil embargo, 19, 72–73
Arber, Werner, 220
Argentina, agricultural productivity of, 346
Arrow, Kenneth J., 312, 384
Arthur, Brian, 364, 376, 385

Asbestos use, litigation concerned with, 181, 193
Aspin, Les, 134
AST Research, 474
Atkinson, A., 396
Atomic Energy Commission, 125, 130
Australia
    agricultural productivity of, 346
    exploitation of gas resources in, 462
Austria, agricultural productivity of, 346
Automobile industry
    competitiveness of, 481–482
    decline in, 542
    development costs in, 300
    and improved carburetion-induction system, 291, 292
    indirect subsidies for, 120
    investments in research and development, 134
    in Japan, 85–87, 328, 395, 482, 542
    management problems in, 495
    new technology affecting, 495
    patents affecting innovations in, 316
    productivity in, 328, 331
        in Japan and U.S., 85–87
    regulations for, and technological innovations, 159–160
    supplier industries for, 281
Avon, stock issues in, 468
Ayres, Robert U., 146

Baker, James, 507
Baker, William O., 9, 227–254, 607
Baldwin, Robert H. B., 14, 467–471, 608
Bangladesh, agricultural productivity of, 346
Banks
    aid to emerging companies, 459–460
    costs affected by technology, 367
    financing of innovations, 11, 453–465, 476–477
        in large established companies, 460–462
    as global intermediaries, 463–464
    lending to start-up companies, 457–459
    regulations in U.S., 459, 464
    role in financial system, 456–457
    technological innovations in, 454–456
Barrow, Robert, 45, 46
Baruch, Jordan J., 132
Bauer, Raymond A., 130
Baxter, William F., 132, 188
Bechtel, Stephen D., Jr., 4, 14, 115–118, 608
Belgium
    agricultural productivity of, 346
    defense expenditures in, 108
    government expenditures in, 111
Bell Laboratories, 230, 250, 254
Berg, Paul, 220–221
Bergström, Sune, 264
Bhopal tragedy in India, 208, 400, 419, 421
Biotechnology, 429–435
    development costs in, 299
    and development of plant varieties, 341–343
    export policy for, 434–435
    funding for research in, 154, 353, 430–431
    government-sponsored programs for, 122
    opportunities and risks in, 430–433
    patent protection in, 433

products produced by, 429, 432
regulations in, 433–435
    for recombinant DNA, 223–224
    and time needed to bring products to market, 429, 432
    training of personnel in, 431
    venture capital in, 431
Birch, David L., 519
Biros, G., 309
Black box of technology, viii, 4, 5–6, 278–279, 280
Blackwelder Company, 341
Boeing, 87, 277, 299, 461
    as partner with Mitsubishi, 86
Bohr's complementarity principle, 246
Bok, Derek, 270
Boskin, Michael J., 2, 3, 5, 6, 7, 8, 15, 33–55, 585, 586, 587, 608–609
Boston Consulting Group, 414
Bower, Joseph L., 156, 532–533
Bowers, Albert, 9, 11, 13, 14, 16, 511–515, 609
Boyer, Herbert, 358, 429
Bracero program, ending of, and mechanization in agriculture, 341
Bragg, Lawrence, 215
Brandt, John P., 341
Brazil, agricultural productivity of, 346
Brenner, Sidney, 213
British Petroleum, 105, 112
Brookhaven National Laboratory, 139
Brooks, Harvey, 2, 4, 6, 109, 119–162, 227, 229, 394, 418, 527, 530, 609–610
Brooks, S., 595, 602, 603
Bruce, Sharon Schur, 329
Budget projections to 1989, 48
Bureaucracies, compared to legal system, 13, 15, 187
Bush, Vannevar, 123, 124–126
Businessland, Inc., 437, 438, 439
Byer, Robert L., 560

Caltech University, 215, 216, 220
Canada
    agricultural productivity of, 346
    economic growth in, 62
    energy price increases in, 73
Cancer
    deaths from, causes of, 418–419
    research in, support for, 126–127, 130, 219, 267
Capital
    allocation schemes by government, 43
    costs of, 505–506
        and competition in foreign markets, 493
        in Japan and U.S., 597–605
    deficit affecting formation of, 48–52
    exports from Japan, 463, 580
    formation in U.S. and Japan, 583–606
    in global markets, 463–464
    incentives for formation of, 537
    input of. See Investment
    internationalization of flow, 47–48
    ratio to labor, 585, 591
        and growth rate, 36
        in information sector, 98–99

in mechanized agricultural system, 344
  and productivity change, 100
resources in U.S., 11
Capitalism, and views of Karl Marx, 20
Carnot, Sadi, 84
Carothers, [W. H.], 230, 359, 399
Carter administration, 43, 132
Cash flow techniques, discounted, effects of, 112
Center for Integrated Systems, at Stanford, 265, 273
Chayes, Abram, 204
Chemical industry, 417–421
  basic research in, 418
  case study of Eastman Kodak's Chemical Division, 402–413
  changes in, 400–401
  expenditures for research and development, 400, 417–418
  in agriculture, 339
  rate of return from, 308
  patents in
    affecting imitation costs, 314
    affecting innovation, 316
  and public's fear of toxic chemicals, 418–420
  safety record of, 421
  technological strength in Europe, 395
Chemical Industry Institute of Toxicology, 419–420
Chemical Manufacturers Association, 419–421
Chevron v. *Ferebee*, 205
Chiang, Wang, 329
Chile, agricultural productivity of, 346
Christensen, Laurits R., 57
Chrysler, 107
Citibank Corporation, 454–455
Class action suits, 193–194
Clean Sites, Inc., 420
Clean Water Act of 1977, 159
Clinch River Breeder Reactor, 133
Clothing industry. *See* Apparel industry
Cohen, David, 384
Cohen, Stanley, 429
Colombia, agricultural productivity of, 346
Commercial applications of technology, and role of government intervention, 146–162
Commercial incentives in basic research, 271–273
Communication, and diffusion of innovations, 319
Communications industry. *See* Telecommunications industry
Competition
  and availability of substitutes, 83
  challenges in, 13–16
  domestic, increase in, 84
  economic results of, 5–6
  and risk taking, 78–81
Competitiveness in foreign trade, 77–88, 479–498
  in aircraft industry, 489–491
  in automobile industry, 481–482
  and challenge to industry, 7
  decline in U.S., 131, 132–135, 502–503, 511, 521
    background of, 528–530
    indices of, 145–146
    likely responses to, 530–533
  in electronics industry, 482–484

government policies affecting, 113, 132–135, 491–498, 513, 515, 521–525
and impact of developing countries, 494
and increase in foreign competition, 85, 90
and innovative activity, 518–519
Japanese strategies in, 2, 146, 512
and job creation, 519–520
in machine tool industry, 487–488
management problems affecting, 495
and need for improved manufacturing technology, 112
and need for national resolve, 511–515, 522
in pharmaceutical industry, 488–489
President's Commission on Industrial Competitiveness, 9, 115, 117, 373, 377–378, 501–509, 521, 539, 542
productivity affecting, 583–584
and role of private sector, 133
and shortage of trained personnel, 494–495, 506
and spending for research and development, 133, 135
in steel industry, 484–485
steps for improvement in, 514–515, 523–525
targeting in, 12
technology affecting, 495, 504–505
and technology gap in U.S., 131
in textile industry, 486–487
and trade policies, 507–508
Comroe-Dripps study, in evaluation of basic research, 270–271
Computer industry
  and CAD/CAM, 29, 94, 293
  in Japan, 559
  competitiveness of, 483
  development costs in, 299
  improvements in price and performance, 444–445
  personal computers in, 437–439, 450
  software availability affecting, 383
Computer use
  applications of, 30
  and changes in industries, 280, 281
  in telecommunications industry, 282
Computervision, performance in stock market, 470
Concorde, as commercial failure, 147, 277, 299
Congressional Budget Office
  projections to year 1989, 48
  views on economic growth, 57, 74
Conoco, 400
Constant, Edward W., 285
Consumer Products Safety Act, 205
Consumer spending
  as economic policy, 524
  Keynesian analysis of, 44–45
  and low savings rates, 15
Contract, related to market, 170
Convergent Technologies, Inc., 476
Coover, H. W., 9, 12, 14, 105, 113, 289, 295, 399–416, 587, 610
Corn varieties, development of, 342
Corporate partnering, 14, 450–451, 475, 579–580
Corporate planning for innovation, 399–416
Corson, Dale R., 161
Costs
  of capital, 505–506

and competition in foreign markets, 493
in Japan and U.S., 597–605
of development, affecting innovation, 298–300, 304
of diffusion of technology, 382–383
external, 170–171
of imitation of innovations, 312–315
of labor. *See* Labor, costs of
of marketing, and problems in financing, 109–110
and prices. *See* Prices
of production, need for control of, 90
and productivity gains, 79
of research in universities, 264
Council for Chemical Research, 418
Crick, Francis, 213–214, 215
Crystals and glasses, studies of, 231–234
Cucumber harvester, development of, 341
Cultural factors in entrepreneurship, 445

Daddario, Emilio, 172
Data General, performance in stock market, 470
Data Resources, Inc., 468
Dataquest, 437
David, Paul A., 14, 15, 322, 357, 373–389, 393, 396, 528, 529, 533, 585, 610–611
Davies, Stephen, 379, 380
Davis, Neil W., 558
Deadweight drag, problems with, 83, 85
Dean, John, 254
Debt
ratio to equity, affecting companies, 11
ratio to GNP, 48, 50, 51
Defense Advanced Research Projects Agency, 125
Defense spending
for high technology products, 557
impact on civilian economy, 134–135
reduction of, 15, 16
for research and development, 128, 131, 270
in various countries, 108
Deficits
and capital formation, 48–54
dangers in, 538
and decline in net exports, 47, 52
financing by foreign capital, 52
increase in, 90
inflationary effects of, 50
and interest rates, 47–48, 49, 85
and saving and investment figures, 53
Delbruck, Max, 215
Demand
elasticity of
affecting prices, 79
and availability of substitutes, 83
policies for stimulation of, 45
and technology diffusion, 380–382
Denison, Edward, 4
Denmark
agricultural productivity of, 346
defense expenditures in, 108
Department of Agriculture, 338, 339, 352, 387
Cooperative Extension Service, 387
Department of Defense, 557. *See also* Defense spending
Department of Energy, 128, 130, 132, 133, 153

Department of Science and Technology, 504
Department of Trade, 507
Developing countries, competitiveness of, 494
Development costs, affecting innovation, 298–300, 304
Diffusion of technology, 14, 318–320, 373–389, 529
and concern with innovation, 376–378
costs of, 382–383
related to output, 381
research and development affecting, 383
demand factors in, 380–382
federal funding of, 387
and feedback information from users, 15, 277, 286–287, 289, 293, 384
and heterogeneity of adopters, 380
and implications for public policies, 386–389
microeconomics of, 378–386
and nature of accumulated skills and markets, 396
performance improvements affecting, 384
and personnel turnover as information-dissemination mechanism, 384
policy interventions affecting, 373–376
and protection of property, 14
and replacement of existing facilities, 381
and states of equilibrium, 380
supply factors in, 382–386
and survival of durable facilities, 381
time factors in, 381–382, 386–387
Digital Equipment, 450
DiLorenzo, J., 254
Dingle, R., 249, 254
Discipline, related to technology, 259
Discontinuities, technological, as key to growth, 444–445
Distribution of products, changes in, 437–439
DNA research, 213–225
central dogma in, 215–216
double helix in, 214–215
funding for, 225
and genetic code, 216–217
recombinant procedures in, 220–222, 429
regulation of, 223–224
replication in, 217–218
restriction enzymes in, 219–220
and rules for gene expression, 218
in tumor viruses, 219
Doko, Toshio, 572
Doll, Richard, 419
Dollar valuation
economic effects of, 8
increase in 1984, 90
and international trade, 506
Donohue, Jerry, 214
Drucker, Peter, 458
Dummer, G. W., 444, 445
Du Pont Company, 400, 414, 430
Dupree, A. Hunter, 120, 122, 123

Eads, George C., 13, 15, 16, 322, 527–533, 611
Eastman Kodak's Chemical Division, approach to research in, 402–413
Eckstein, Otto L., 134, 160
Economic policies

in Japan, 569–573
recent trends in, vi–ix, 48–54
schools of thought on, 44–48
second-tier policies in, 54
Economic Recovery Tax Act of 1981, 52, 593
Economists
analysis of technological change, viii–ix, 18–23
classical, 19–20, 21
neoclassical, 20, 21, 45–46
views on production function, 327–328
Edison, Thomas, 24–25, 30, 116, 278, 287, 359
Education
in foreign languages and cultures, 492, 497, 513
in Japan, 544, 545, 555–556, 564, 574
and quality of labor force, 36
for technical manpower, 134, 138, 255–262, 537
in biotechnology, 431
federal support for, 13, 129
future directions for, 260–262
in Japan, 258–259
in U.S., 256–258
Efficiency
and growth at aggregate level, 63
and growth at sectoral level, 64
in information economy, 100–101
Egypt, agricultural productivity of, 346
Einstein, Albert, 228
Eisenhower administration, 59
Electric power generation, improvements in, 282–283. See also Energy programs
Electron capture, 246
Electronics industry, 423–427
in Asian countries, 566
competitiveness of, 482–484
development costs in, 299
in Japan, 547–552
new technology affecting, 495
patents in
affecting imitation costs, 314
affecting innovations, 316
product distribution in, 437–439
shortage of trained personnel in, 494
standardization in, 438–439
and technological skills in various countries, 395
trade deficit in, 426, 503
Eli Lilly, 430, 432, 468
Elkana, Yehuda, 135
Ellsworth, Richard R., 605
Embodiment hypothesis, and rate of technical change, 40
Employment, and factors in job creation, 519–520
Energy prices
and inflation, 42
and oil crisis. See Oil prices
and productivity growth, 69, 72–73
and reallocation of output, 64–65
Energy programs
development costs in, 299
for solar energy, 277
federal investments in, 132
financing by banks, 462
and improvements in electric power generation, 282–283

international fusion energy program, 157–158
nuclear power in. See Nuclear power
public subsidies for, 154
and tax credits for household investments, 158–159
technology in, 22
Engineering Research Centers, 13
Engineers
education for, 255–262
as manufacturing technologists, 113, 134
number in U.S. and other countries, 137–138
publications by, 139–141
specialists in high-tech industries, 260, 262
views of production function, 328
England, J. Merton, 124, 129
Enos, John, 283
Entrepreneurs
in agriculture, 352
in biotechnology, 429–435
cultural factors affecting, 445
development and application of, 359–360
economic climate for, 9–10
and economic effects of innovations, 360–364. See also Innovations
in electronics industry, 423–427
federal encouragement of, 132–133
financing of. See Financing
innovations of. See Innovations
market served by, 14
motivation of, 358–359
needs for, 7
probability of success, 363
transition to large company, 441–442
Environmental damage
allocation of costs of, 171
and tort doctrine of nuisance, 175–178
Environmental Protection Agency, 130, 149, 195, 224, 419, 420
Equilibrium diffusion models, and decision making about innovations, 380
Equipment and facilities, in university and research laboratories, 138–139
ESL Company, 446
Estridge, Philip D., 476
Euratom at Ispra, 158
Eurobond borrowing, 463
Eurocredit market, 463
Europe. See also under individual countries
economic growth in, 62
government policies affecting innovation in, 397
technological position of, 105–113, 394–395
European Airbus, 299, 490
Evenson, R., 308
Expectations
affecting economy, 46
for problem solving by science, 130
for return on capital, 111
Export
of capital from Japan, 463, 580
deficit affecting, 47, 52
of high technology products, U.S. share of, 144
regulations on biotechnology products, 434–435
Export-Import Bank, 11, 488, 491, 492, 493, 498

Fairchild, Sherman, 424

Fairchild Industries, 450
Farm machinery industry, expenditures for research in agriculture, 338, 339
Federal Reserve Board, 43, 89, 597
Feedback process in innovations, 15, 277, 286–287, 289, 293, 384
Feigenbaum, Edward A., 560
Feldstein, Martin, 42, 46
Fertilizer industry, expenditures for research, 339
Fertilizer use in Japan and U.S., prices affecting, 350
Fiber optics, applications of, 28
Films and surfaces, technology of, 244–248
Financial climate and innovation, 10–12
Financial institutions. See Banks; Stock markets
Financing
  by banks, 453–465, 476–477
  by business units of corporations, 476
  corporate partnering in, 14, 450–451, 475, 579–580
  and costs of marketing, 109–110
  initial public offering market, 468, 469, 471, 473–475, 478, 593
  mezzanine funds in, 470, 475
  private funding in, 446
  problems in small companies, 442
  public market in, 445–446
  R&D partnerships in, 10, 111, 161, 432–433, 446, 476
  for research in universities, 264
  risks in, 299, 300–301
  sources of risk capital in, 445
  trends in, 473–478
  venture funds in. See Venture capital
Finland, agricultural productivity of, 346
Fischer, Stanley, 42
Fletcher v. Bealey, 194, 196
Flexibility, dynamic, and productivity, 85–86
Fluctuations in economy
  control of, 34, 36–37
  and tax policies, 38
Food and Drug Administration, 148–149, 199, 432
  drug approval, process of, 489
  regulations for biotechnology, 433–434
Food industry, expenditures for research in agriculture, 338, 339
Ford, Henry, 29
Ford administration, 266
Ford Motor Company, expenditures for research and development, 300
Foreign capital
  and financing of deficit, 52
  and information economy, 101
  from Japan, 463, 580
    and acquisition of U.S. semiconductor companies, 426
Foreign trade, 77–88, 479–498. See also Competitiveness in foreign trade
Foster Associates, 310
France
  agricultural productivity of, 346
  defense expenditures in, 108
  economic growth in, 62
    slowdown in, 63

  expenditures for research and development in, 136, 557
  government expenditures in, 111
  labor costs in, 588
  productivity related to investment rate, 144
Frankel, M., 381
Freeman, Christopher, 376
French, Ben C., 341
Friedlaender, Ann F., 5, 6, 327–332, 611
Friedman, Milton, 44, 45
Fujitsu, investment in Amdahl, 426
Fusion energy program, international, 157–158

Gas utilities, productivity growth in, 331
Gene expression, rules for, 218
Genentech, Inc., 358, 429, 430, 432, 441
General Electric, 24
General Motors
  corporate partnering by, 450–451
  expenditures for research and development, 300
  performance in stock market, 468
Generic applied research, 156–157
Genetic code, solving of, 216–217
Genetic engineering, 222. See also Biotechnology
Geological Survey, 119
Geraldine Rockefeller Dodge Foundation, 469
Germany
  agricultural productivity of, 346
  economic growth in, 62
    slowdown in, 63
  energy price increases in, 73
  government expenditures in, 111
    for biotechnology, 431
    for defense, 108
    for research and development, 136, 137
  labor costs in, 588
  number of scientists and engineers in, 137–138
  patents granted in U.S., 142
  productivity related to investment rate, 144
  role of banks in, 456–457, 465
  textile machinery from, 486
Glasses and crystals, studies of, 231–234
Global capital markets, 463–464
Global competition. See Competitiveness in foreign trade
Godwin, William, 32
Gola, Bela, 379
Goldberg, L., 317
Goodson, R. Eugene, 160
Gossard, A. C., 249, 254
Government expenditures in various countries, 111
Government policies in U.S.
  affecting competitiveness, 113, 132–135, 491–498, 513, 515, 521–525
  affecting growth rate, 4
  antitrust measures in, 132, 161, 188, 259, 524, 530–532
  for basic science, 122–123, 148
  capital allocation schemes in, 43
  components of spending in, 38
    changes in, 42
  contracting of research to private organizations, 124–126
  controversies in, 12, 152–158

expenditures as percentage of GDP, 111
expenditures for R&D. *See* Research and development, government expenditures for
expenditures for technology transfer, 387
for fragmented industries, 154
for generic applied research, 156–157
for innovation and technology, 6–9, 110, 121–122, 132–133, 146–162, 396–397, 535–539
  inappropriateness of, 151–152
  social returns in, 153–154
and intellectual property rights, 160–161
in international programs, 157–158
and intervention in markets, 15, 147
  in narrow markets, 154–155
  and political processes, 161–162
  risks in, 152–153
investment in instrumentation in university and research laboratories, 138–139
for key industries, 155–156
national industrial policy, 44
national science policy, 119–162
for public goods, 147–148, 155
regulatory issues in. *See* Regulatory actions
for research on externalities, 148–151
subsidies for industries in, 119–120
taxation in. *See* Taxes
wage and price controls in, 43
Grabowski, Henry G., 122
Great Society programs, 130, 184
Greece, agricultural productivity of, 346
Gregory, Gene, 143
Gregory, William H., 133, 155
Griliches, Z., 135, 152, 308, 310, 322, 345, 378
Growth
  at aggregate level, analysis of, 59–63
  capital input affecting, 3, 59, 63, 64
  divergent views on prospects for, 57–58, 74
  energy prices affecting, 72–73
  factors affecting, 35–36
  government policies for, 4, 535–539
  and interest on national debt, 51
  labor input affecting, 59, 63, 64
  limits to, 4, 19
  long-term prospects for, 3, 19, 21, 35–36
  obstacles to, 12–13
  and per capita income, 35, 36
  and productivity, 59–65
  quality of labor force affecting, 3
  rates in U.S., 2, 62
  rates in various countries, 62
  reallocations affecting, 63, 64
  at sectoral level, analysis of, 63–65
  and short-term concerns, 3, 21
  slowdown in, 41, 62, 73
    in various countries, 63
    and supply-side economics, 47, 58, 74
  technical changes affecting, vi–ix, 3, 4–5
  and unexplained residual, 63, 73

Hagstrom, Homer, 252–253
Hall, R. E., 46, 602
Hambrecht & Quist Incorporated, 447, 563, 618
Handler, Philip, 122

Hannay, N. Bruce, 5, 8, 11, 12, 14, 16, 357, 393, 394, 395, 396, 479–498, 528, 529, 595, 604, 611–612
Hanson, Ward A., 383
Harger, Alan E., 129
Harvey Aluminum, 177
Hatsopoulos, George N., 2, 5, 6, 11, 12, 13, 14, 583–606, 612
Hayami, Yujiro, 340
Health care
  basic research in, 270–271
  and development of "orphan drugs," 154–155, 202
  and investments in technologies, 155
  research issues in, 265–267
  support for research in, 154
  technology affecting, 369–371
Health Research Facilities Act of 1968, 264
Hewlett, William R., 10, 11, 441–442, 594, 612
Hewlett-Packard Company, 446, 594
Hicks, John, 3
High Penn Oil Company, 176
Himsworth, Harold, 215
Historical aspects
  of economic events in 1970s, 41–44
  of impact of technological changes, 17–32
Hodder, James L., 595
Hollomon, J. Herbert, 129
Holmer, Edwin C., 4, 13, 14, 15, 417–421, 613
Honda, Soichiro, 359
Honda Corporation, 359
  motorcycle plant in Columbus, 86, 87
Hoover, Herbert, 123
Housing, support for research in, 154
Huber, Peter W., 4, 13, 191–210, 613
Hufbauer, G., 320
Husen, Torsten, 138
Hydrocarbons, 242–244

Icahn, Carl, 599
Imai, K., 134, 146, 563
Imitations of innovations, costs of, 312–315, 375
  and industry concentration, 315
  and market entry, 314
  patents affecting, 313–314
  ratio to innovation cost, 313
  research and development affecting, 383
Impact of technological change, 17–32
Imports
  of high-tech equipment, 101, 102
  increase in 1984, 90
Income, per capita, and growth rate, 35, 36
India, agricultural productivity of, 346
Indiana University, 215, 220
Indonesia, government expenditures in, 111
Industrial firms
  analysis of price performance in, 81–84
  attitudes on waste disposal management, 149–150
  classification by biases of productivity growth, 66–69
  regulation of, and technological innovations, 159–160
  relationship with universities, 264–265, 445, 555

research laboratories in, 27, 28
spending on research and development, 133–134
  rates of return from, 310
  ratio to GNP, 137
subsidized by government, 119–120
voluntary standard setting in, 160
Industrial policy, national, 44
Inflation
  decrease in 1984, 90
  and effects of deficits, 50
  energy prices affecting, 42
  and natural rate of unemployment, 45
  and slowdown in economic growth, 41–42
  and unemployment, 42, 45
  and wage and price controls, 43
Information sector, 93–103
  capital:labor ratio in, 98–99
  corporate profits in, 94–95
  foreign capital in, 101
  growth of, 8
  high-tech equipment in, 98
  introduction of efficiencies in, 100–101
  investment in, 96–97
  as key industry, 156
  labor force in, 96
  and law of intellectual property, 188
  output compared to goods sector, 94, 95
  productivity of, 100
  and technology use by financial institutions, 455
Initial public offering market, 468, 469, 471, 473–475, 478, 593
Inman, Bobby R., 511
Innovation, 9, 275–304
  in agriculture, 333–354
  and available alternatives, 284
  as black box system, viii, 4, 5–6, 278–279, 280
  characterization of, 279–285
  corporate planning for, 399–416
  coupling of activities in, 301–302
  cultivation of, 443–451
  design process in, 286, 292–293, 302
  determinants of, 393–397
  development costs in, 298–300, 304
  and differing views of production function, 327–328
  diffusion of, 14, 318–320, 373–389, 529
  economics of, 277, 298–302
  employment-expanding, 30
  and enlargement of resource base, 21–22
  and entrepreneurial climate, 9–10
  factors affecting, 36
  feedback signals in, 15, 277, 286–287, 289, 293
  financial climate affecting, 10–12
  financing of. *See* Financing
  and gap between private enterprise and government policy, 109
  and global competition, 518–519
  government policies affecting, 132–133, 146–162, 396–397, 535–539
  imitations of, 312–315
  impact of, 17–32
    and potential significance, 25–26, 30–31
    and transitions in industry, 23–25

  underestimation of, 25
  inconspicuous changes in, 282
  and interaction of entrepreneurship and economics, 360–364
  interaction with science, 286–288, 290–291, 302–303
  international differences in, 395–396
  labor-saving, 29
  and lack of predictive science, 296–297, 304
  in large companies, 449–451
  lead times affecting, 296, 301
  limits to achievement of, 23–28, 276
  and macroeconomic climate, 6–9, 89–91
  market forces in, 275, 276, 278, 289–290
  microeconomics of, 307–323
  models of, 285–294
    chain-linked, 289–294, 303
    linear, 285–288, 303
  patent system affecting, 315–316
  and persistence of old technologies, 284–285
  planning for, 297–298
  and productivity growth, 21, 69
  rates of return on, 280, 309–311
  resistance to, 278, 292, 300
  and risk taking, 78–79. *See also* Risk taking
  and service employment, 31
  and stages of product cycle, 295
  state of knowledge affecting, 295–296, 304
  technical needs in, 275, 276
  technological environment affecting, 327–332
  and technological levels of various countries, 394–395
  timing of, 277, 301
  uncertainty in, 275–276, 294–298, 303
  and unemployment, 4, 20, 28–31
Instruments industry
  patents affecting innovation in, 316
  productivity growth in, 331
Instrumentation, in university and research laboratories, investment in, 138–139
Insurance industry, productivity growth in, 331
Intel Corporation, 424, 425, 441, 463, 477
Intellectual property
  and expansion of information industry, 188
  and flow of research information, 160–161
  international trade in, 142–143
  protection of, 151
Intelligence, artificial, development in Japan, 560
Interest rates
  and cost of capital, 506
  and deficit financing, 47, 48, 49, 85
  and initial public offering market, 468
  and investment activity, 14
  in Japan, 599
  levels in 1984, 90
  and ratio of national debt to GNP, 51
International Business Machines Corporation (IBM)
  business units of, 476
  expenditures for research and development, 299
  outlook in 1950s, 30
  personal computers of, 439, 450
  stock offering in 1957, 467
  work on Josephson junction, 552
International capital markets, 463–464

International cooperative programs, 157–158, 299
International differences in technological activity, 395–396
International Harvester, 84
International technology transfer, 320–321
International trade, 77–88, 479–498
International Trade Commission, 505
Interstate Highway System, 120
Investment
    available funds in Britain, 108
    and costs of marketing, 109–110
    decline in rates of, 42
    federal deficit affecting, 53
    and financing of innovations. *See* Financing
    and growth patterns, 3, 59, 63, 64
    in information sector, 96–97
    in instrumentation in university and research laboratories, 138–139
    interest rates affecting, 14
    outlays in, 1984, 90
    price of, affecting productivity growth, 68–69
    and productivity rates, 5, 143–144
    return on, expectations for, 111
    tax policies affecting, 13, 14, 38, 52–53, 70
Ireland, agricultural productivity of, 346
Ireland, Norman, 375, 380
Iron ore supplies, expansion by technology, 22
Isotopes, radioactive, 248–249
Israel, agricultural productivity of, 346
Italy
    agricultural productivity of, 346
    defense expenditures in, 108
    economic growth in, 62
    energy price increases in, 73
    government expenditures in, 111
    labor costs in, 589
    productivity related to investment rate, 144

Jacoby, Hank, 112
Japan, 541–567
    acquisition of U.S. semiconductor companies, 426
    agricultural productivity of, 334, 335, 346
        technical changes affecting, 345–352
    aircraft industry in, 490, 557, 559–560
    auto industry in, 85–87, 328, 395, 482, 542
    bond issues in, 572
    capabilities in artificial intelligence, 560
    capital exports of, 463, 580
    capital formation in, 583–606
        cost of, 11
    changing market structures in, 465
    characteristics of technological achievements in, 553–554
    competitive strategies of, 1–2, 146, 512
    cooperation among firms in, 161
    deficit problem in, 572
    economic growth in, 62
        slowdown in, 63
    economic policies in, 12, 569–573
        new goals for, 573–574
    educational system in, 258–259, 544, 545, 555–556, 564, 574
    electronics industry in, 483, 484, 547–552

    energy price increases in, 73
    exchange rate system in, 570–571
    exports of high technology products, 144
        ratio to imports, 546
    generic research in, 157
    government expenditures in, 111
        for biotechnology, 431
        for defense, 108
        for research and development, 136, 137, 544, 545–546, 548, 550, 557
    government policies affecting innovation in, 397
    imports of foreign technology, 543–544
        ratio to exports, 546
    interest rates in, 599
    investment in manufacturing, 548
    labor costs in, 530, 571, 572, 589
    labor force in, 544, 545, 548
        productivity of, 366
    land reform policy in, 570, 571
    manufacturing technology in, 112
    marketing development in, 548
    materials technology in, 146
    Ministry of International Trade and Industry, 536, 542, 544, 571
    monetary policies in, 571
    national goals in, 16
    national research projects in, 561–562
    number of scientists and engineers in, 113, 137–138
    patents granted in U.S., 142
    product design in, and market penetration, 146
    productivity in, 502, 529
        related to investment rate, 143, 144
    protectionism in, 107, 300
        domestic, 553
    role of banks in, 456
    savings in, 576–578, 591–592
    semiconductor industry in, 133–134, 549–552
    space industry in, 557, 558–559
    strengths and weaknesses in, 547–563
    structural changes in, 564–567
    successful industries in, 547–554
    targeted technologies in, 554–564, 574–576
    tax policies in, 572, 592–593
    technological position of, 394–395
        as follower, 544–546
        as leader, 546
    textile industry in, 384, 486–487
    venture capital in, 544, 545, 562–563, 578–580, 594
    very large scale integrated circuit project in, 549, 550, 561, 575
    welfare system in, 570, 572
Job creation, factors in, 519–520
John Deere & Company, 84, 87
Johns-Manville Products Corporation, 181
Johnson administration, 43, 59, 126, 184
Johnson & Johnson, stock issues in, 468
Jones, Jim, 468
Jorgenson, Dale W., 2, 4, 5, 46, 57–74, 322, 330–331, 584, 602, 613–614
Josephson junction, work on, 552

Kamien, M., 324

Karlesky, Joseph J., 138
Katz, Michael L., 383
Katz, Milton, 2, 9, 13, 14, 169–189, 227, 527, 528, 530, 532
Keeton, Robert E., 179
Keizai Koho Center, 143
Kendrew, John, 215
Kendrick, John, 4
Kennedy administration, 43, 59, 130, 132
Kennedy, Donald, 13, 263–273, 420, 506, 614
Kennedy, Ted, 266
Key industries, support for, 155–156
Keynes, J. M., 3, 40–41, 44–45
Kindleberger, Charles P., 385
Kislev, Yoav, 340
Klein, Burton H., 5, 6, 77–87, 322, 614–615
Kline, Stephen J., 9, 15, 275–304
Korea
    acquisition of U.S. semiconductor companies, 426
    economic growth in, 62
    electronics industry in, 566
    government expenditures in, 111
Kornberg, Arthur, 217
Kresge, stock issues in, 468
Kuhn, Thomas, 286

Labor force
    in agriculture, 8, 354
        costs of, 350
        productivity of, 348, 359
    challenges to, 497, 507
    costs of
        in Japan, 350, 530
        and productivity growth, 69
        in various countries, 588–589
        for wages. See Wages
    education for technical manpower, 13, 129, 134
        in biotechnology field, 431
    employment in small businesses, 432
    engineering manpower in U.S., 258, 260, 261
    increase in, 43
    in information sector, 96
    input of, and growth patterns, 59, 63, 64
    in Japan, 544, 545, 548
    in manufacturing, 8, 354
        productivity of, 359
    number of scientists and engineers in U.S. and other countries, 137–138
    personnel turnover as information-dissemination mechanism, 384
    quality of
        and growth rate, 3, 36
        and productivity, 143
    ratio to capital, 585, 591
        in information sector, 98–99
        in mechanized agricultural system, 344
        and productivity change, 100
    reallocation of, 64
    shortage of trained personnel in, 494–495, 506, 537
Labor-saving innovations, effects of, 29
Landau, Ralph, v–x, 1–16, 117, 583–606, 615
Landes, D., 397

Large companies
    entrepreneurial spirit in, 518–519
    financing by banks, 460–462
    innovations introduced by, 318, 449–451
    interaction with small companies, 14, 361, 519, 520
    risk taking in investments, 113
    transition from entrepreneurs, 441–442
Laser technology
    applications of, 28
    discovery of, 250
    in Japan, 556
    manpower and resources in, 560
    pulsed beams on crystal surfaces, 246
Lawrence, Robert Z., 143
Layton, Edwin T., 123
Learning-by-doing hypothesis, and rate of technical change, 40
Leather industry, productivity growth in, 331
Legal Services Corporation, 187
Legal system, 169–189
    compared to bureaucracies, 13, 15, 187
    constraining aspects of, 174–183
    as facilitator of enterprise and innovation, 170–171
    federal structure of, 187
    and judicial fact finding, 182–183
    and liability issues, 13
    and litigation increase in U.S., 187
    and right to counsel, 187
    shift in emphasis of, 527, 528, 530, 532
    shifting judicial trends in, 184–186
    technological development affecting, 172–174
    tort law in, 174–182
        and availability of information about hazards, 197–198
        bipolar disputes in, 192–193, 201
        compensation in, 181–182, 200–201, 206–209
        and competence of courts and agencies, 203–204
        doctrine of negligence in, 174–175
        doctrine of nuisance in, 175–178, 192–193
        doctrine of strict products liability in, 178–182, 186
        expansion in reach of, 197
        expert opinions in, 204–206
        and focus on public risk, 191–210
        immunities and liability limits in, 201–203
        multiparty disputes in, 193–194
        and political legitimacy, 209–210
        regressive incentives in, 199–200
        and rule of proportional causation, 194
        as social engineering, 201
        timing of actions in, 194–197
Levin, Richard, 322
Lewis, Jordan D., 132
Liability of manufacturers
    affecting growth, 13
    and limits on tort recoveries, 202–203
    market share of, 193–194
    tort doctrine of, 178–182, 186
Libya, agricultural productivity of, 346
Life sciences research, support for, 126, 154

Lindert, Peter D., 381
Litigation, excessive, affecting growth, 13
Long, Russell, 468
Lucas, Robert, 45, 46
Luck, and productivity gains, 78, 79, 81
Lull Engineering Co., 179
Lumber industry, productivity growth in, 331
Luria, Salva, 215, 220

MacArthur Foundation, 511
Machine tool industry
  competitiveness of, 487–488
  decline in U.S., 145
  innovations in, 280
  management problems in, 495
  new technology affecting, 495
  shortage of trained personnel in, 494
Machinery production, patents affecting, 314, 316
Macroeconomics
  in Japan, 569–573
  in United States, 6–9, 33–35, 89–91, 93–103
    and components in government spending, 38.
      See also Government policies in U.S.
    and composition of aggregate output, 38–40
    and fluctuations in economy, 34, 37
    issues related to technology, 34–40
    and long-run growth performance, 35–36
    tax policies in, 38. *See also* Taxes
Malaysia, government expenditures in, 111
Malpas, Robert, 5, 7, 9, 10, 11, 14, 15, 16, 105–
  113, 615–616
Malstead, Illona, 337
Malthus, Thomas Robert, 18, 19, 21, 22
Management
  challenges to, 497, 507, 518
  problems with, and competitiveness of U.S. in-
    dustries, 495
Mansfield, Edwin, 4, 6, 14, 152, 153, 159, 307–
  323, 332, 376, 378, 381, 616
Manufacturing
  investments in
    in Japan, 548
    in U.S., 503
  labor force in, 354
    productivity of, 359
  lack of interest in, 505
  productivity in
    in Japan, 590–591
    in U.S., 365, 590–591
  rate of return from research and development
    spending, 308
  shortage of trained personnel in, 494
Marconi, [Guglielmo], 25, 26
Market
  adjustment mechanisms in, 19, 20, 21
  development costs for narrow markets, 154–155
  distribution channels in, 437–439
  entry affected by imitation costs, 314
  government intervention in, 15, 147
  identification of needs in, 409
  and innovations, 275, 276, 278, 289–290
  penetration strategies of Japanese, 146
  policies affecting participation in, 537
  and political decision making, 161–162

  and role of property and contract, 170
  and service by entrepreneurs, 14
  targeting of, 12
  analysis of business areas in, 405
Market pull and technology push, 142, 147, 289–
  290
Marschak, Thomas, 297
Marshall, Alfred, 170
Martin, B., 395
Marver, James D., 10, 11, 14, 470, 473–478, 593,
  594, 616
Marx, Karl, 4, 20, 28
Materials
  price of, and productivity growth, 69
  technology in Japan, 146
Mauritius, agricultural productivity of, 346
Mechanical technology in Japan and U.S., prices
  affecting, 350
Mechanization research in agriculture, 340–341,
  344
Medical care. *See* Health care
Medicare system, 49–50
Merrifield, D. Bruce, 161
Metals industry
  and innovations in metallurgy, 280, 281
  patents affecting innovations in, 316
  productivity growth in, 331
Metcalf, J. S., 380
Mettler, Ruben F., 7, 8, 9, 10, 11, 12, 13, 14,
  15, 16, 441, 517–525, 616–617
Mexico, agricultural productivity of, 346
Mezzanine funds, 470, 475
Microeconomics of innovations, 307–323
  and productivity, 57–76, 330–331
Military activities
  and defense spending. *See* Defense spending
  and research contracts with scientists, 123–124
  as source of technological innovation, 120–121
Miller, William, 451
Minasian, J., 308
Minnesota Crop Improvement Association, 342
Mission-oriented research, 156–157
Mitsubishi, as partner with Boeing, 87
Modigliani, Franco, 42, 44
Monetary policies
  in Japan, 571
  in U.S., 45, 506
Monsanto, 400, 430
Moore, Gordon E., 7, 8, 9, 10, 14, 358, 360,
  423–427, 441, 596, 617
Moore, William, 295
Moreno, Glen R., 8, 11, 12, 453–465, 473, 476,
  594, 597, 617
Morgan Stanley & Company, Inc., 93, 94, 467,
  469, 470
Morison, Elting, 120
Morita, Akio, 359
Moritani, Masanori, 543
Morris, Jane, 475
Mosgavero, Louis N., 387
Motor vehicle industry. *See* Automobile industry
Mowery, David C., 120, 130, 157, 383, 559
Multinational firms, technology transfer in, 320,
  321

Musgrave, Richard A., 154
Muth, John, 45

Nadiri, M., 309
Naisbitt, John, 402
Namura School of Advanced Management, 536
Nasbeth, L., 379
Nathan Associates, 310
National Academy of Engineering, 5, 117–118, 157, 172, 375, 480, 528
National Academy of Sciences, 117, 118, 150, 161, 172, 429
National Advisory Committee for Aeronautics, 119, 125, 157
National Aeronautics and Space Administration, 125, 133, 157, 557
National Bureau of Standards, 119, 131–132
National Cancer Institute, 219, 419
National Cooperative Research Act of 1984, 188
National Institutes of Health, 125, 126, 216, 225
National Radioastronomy Observatory, 139
National Research Council, 132, 162, 480
National Research Foundation, 125
National Science Board, 131, 135, 137, 138, 139, 140, 141, 142, 143, 144, 394
National Science Foundation, 125, 126, 131, 134, 135, 139, 148, 216, 307, 310, 311, 317, 395, 563
National science policy, 119–162
  historic aspects of, 119–124
  in postwar era, 124–128
  in cold war period, 129
  in period of industrial competitiveness, 132– 135
  in social priorities period, 129–132
National security
  and aircraft industry, 490
  and flow of research information, 161
  and maintenance of key industries, 155–156
  and steel industry, 484
Natural resources
  depletion of, 18–19
  and diminishing returns, 21
  and limits to growth, 4
  optimal allocation of, 21
  technological changes affecting, 21–22
Negligence, tort law relating to, 174–175
Nelson, Richard R., 120, 129, 130, 147, 157, 284, 322, 352, 376
Netherlands, the
  agricultural productivity of, 346
  defense expenditures in, 108
Network technologies
  compatibility or standardization in, 384–385
  in telecommunications industry, 329, 383
New Zealand
  agricultural productivity of, 346
  synfuel project in, 462
Nippon Telegraph and Telephone, 557, 574, 576
Nixon administration, 42, 127, 131, 132
Nobel prize awards, 140, 264, 544
Norman, Colin, 139
Norman, David A., 437–439, 617
Norway

agricultural productivity of, 346
defense expenditures in, 108
Nuclear power
  development costs for, 299
  lag in standardizing designs for, 160
  and Rasmussen report on reactor safety, 196, 198
  shared liability of plant operators, 194
  and tort immunity of organizations, 202
  and waste disposal management, 150
Nuclear Regulatory Commission, 149, 198, 206
Nuclear science and radioisotopes, 248–249
Nuisance, tort law relating to, 175–178, 192–193

Occupational Safety and Health Administration, 195–196
Oettinger, Anthony, 188
Off-budget spending, 48
Office equipment, patents affecting innovations in, 316
Office of Management and Budget
  Regulatory Review group in, 132
  views on economic growth, 58, 74
Office of Science and Technology Policy, 132, 133
Office of Scientific Research and Development, 123, 124
Office of Technology Assessment, 150, 340, 419, 455
Oil prices. See also Energy prices
  and creation of Department of Energy, 153
  effects in Japan, 571, 572
  impact on economic growth, 63
  increase in, 19
Okimoto, Daniel I., 7, 11, 12, 14, 15, 107, 357, 384, 393, 394, 395, 396, 397, 528, 529, 541–567, 575, 585, 617
Olsen, Trond E., 375, 380
Organisation for Economic Cooperation and Development, 63, 73
Organization of Petroleum Exporting Countries, 19
Over-the-counter market, 447
Ozawa, Terutomo, 543

Packard, David, 504
Pakistan, agricultural productivity of, 346
Panish, M., 250, 251
Paraguay, agricultural productivity of, 346
Parsons, C., 146
Particles and waves, dualism of, 246
Partnering, corporate, 14, 450–451, 475, 579– 580
Partnerships, R&D, 10, 111, 161, 432–433, 446, 476
Patents
  affecting application of technology, 376
  antitrust implications of, 188
  in biotechnology, 433
  commercial basis for, 276
  granted to U.S. and foreign inventors, 141–142
  and imitation costs, 313–314
  and incentives for risk taking, 537
  and innovation rate, 315–316
  and intellectual property rights, 151

Plant Patent Act of 1930, 342
policy modifications for, 132
and prices for access to technology, 383
rights for university faculty members, 271–272
in semiconductor industry, 426
Pauling, Linus, 214
Pavitt, Keith L. R., 9, 15, 141, 322, 393–397, 617
Pear, Robert, 134
Peer review to evaluate research, 269
Penner, Rudolph, 58
Penny stock market, 445
Pension funds, and job formation, 520
Perry, William J., 9, 10, 11, 14, 443–451, 473, 475, 593, 594, 618
Peru, agricultural productivity of, 346
Perutz, Max, 215
Pesticide industry, expenditures for research, 339
Peterson, Willis, 308, 310, 340
Peto, Richard, 419
Petroleum industry
expansion of, 281
innovations in, 283
patents affecting, 316
as key industry, 156
oil prices in. *See* Oil prices
rate of return from research and development spending, 308
Pettit, Joseph M., 13, 14, 255–262, 537, 618
Pfann, W. G., 231
Pharmaceutical industry
competitiveness of, 488–489
development of "orphan drugs," 154–155, 202
expenditures for research, 489
for animal drugs, 339
international technology transfer in, 319–320
and legal problems of vaccine industry, 197, 199, 202
market share liability of, 193
new technology affecting, 495
patents in
affecting imitation costs, 314
affecting innovation, 315, 316
problems of, 11
regulation by FDA, 148–149, 433–434
Phelps, Edmund, 45
Philippines, agricultural productivity of, 346
Phillips, Julia, 254
Phillips Curve, 40, 42, 45
Photonics, 231, 251
Physical science studies, 227–254
chronology of, 228–230
in crystals and glasses, 231–234
in hydrocarbons, 242–244
and innovations in electronics and photonics, 249–254
in nuclear science and radioisotopes, 248–249
and phase rule applications, 234–242
in surface technology, 244–248
Pickens, Boone, 599
Pigou, A. C., 170
Pilkington, Alastair, 358
Piper Aircraft Corporation, 180
Planar Corporation, 475

Planning for innovation, in corporations, 399–416
Plant varieties, research in development of, 341–343
Poate, J. M., 250
Policy analysis, schools of thought in, 44–48
Portugal, agricultural productivity of, 346
Postal services, technology in, 367–368
Postwar science policy, 128–135
Prager, Denis, 511
Prandtl, L., 287
President's Commission on Industrial Competitiveness, 9, 115, 117, 373, 377–378, 501–509, 521, 539, 542
Price, Derek de Solla, 293
Price-Anderson Act, 194, 207, 208, 209
Prices
and agricultural technology in U.S. and Japan, 348–350
and availability of substitutes, 83, 84
and cost differences, 69. *See also* Costs
and indexes for research and development inputs, 316–318
of inputs and outputs, affecting productivity growth, 65–69
performance analysis in industries, 81–84
schemes for control of, 43
Printing and publishing, productivity growth in, 331
Private sector
and development of American science, 123
government contracts for research in, 124–126
role in research and development, 123, 133, 401
trends in, 126–128
as source of risk capital, 446
Product distribution, changes in, 437–439
Production function, differing views of, 327–328
Productivity, 57–74
in agriculture
research affecting, 334–336
in U.S. and Japan, 348
and analysis of growth, 59–65
at aggregate level, 59–63
at sectoral level, 63–65
and basic research, 311–312
and capital:labor ratios, 100
and competitiveness, 77–88, 583–584
and dynamic flexibility, 85–86
endogenous growth of, 65–69
of information workers, 100
investment rate affecting, 143–144
luck as factor in, 78, 79, 81
macroeconomic policies affecting, 89–91
in manufacturing, 365
and microeconomics, 330–331
and prices of inputs and outputs, 65–69
prospects for growth in, 69–73
relation to research and development, 308–309, 322
in service industry, 365–367
tax rates affecting, 5
technology affecting, 9, 21
and utilization of capacity, 8
Profitability, and diffusion of innovations, 318, 379

Property, related to market, 170
Protectionism, 107–108
  of automobile market in Japan, 300
  domestic, in Japan, 553
Public Agenda Foundation, 513
Public goods, universal access to, 147–148, 155
Public market, role in risk capital, 445–446
Public opinion on technology, 4, 116
  and expectations for scientific achievements, 130–131
  and fears of toxic chemicals, 418–420
  and sensitivity to potential hazards, 13, 15
Publications, by scientists and engineers, 139–141
  and citation counts, 140
Publishing, productivity growth in, 331

Quantum mechanics, 229–230
Quinn, James Brian, 4, 8, 9, 10, 14, 15, 16, 357–371, 618–619

Radioisotopes, 248–249
Ramo, Simon, 150–151
Ramo-Wooldridge, 517
Rasmussen Report on nuclear reactor safety, 196, 198
Rates of return
  private, 309
  from research and development, 308–311
    in agriculture, 308, 310, 334–335
  social, 309
Ray, G. F., 379
Reagan administration, 89, 115, 118, 128, 132–133, 387, 509, 578
Real estate industry, productivity growth in, 331
Reallocations, and productivity growth, 63, 64
Reed, John S., 8, 11, 12, 476, 594, 597, 619
Reeder, Charles B., 8, 12, 14, 89–91, 619–620
Regulatory actions
  affecting growth, 12–13, 15, 41, 43
  for banking in U.S., 459, 464
  in biotechnology, 433–435
  and comparative risk assessment, 204, 206
  and government responsibility for research programs, 148–151
  and incentives for risk taking, 537
  modifications in, 132
  and stimulation of technology, 159–160
Research, basic
  and accounting practices, 112
  in chemical industry, 418
  commitment to, 536–537
  government support for, 122–123, 148
  in industrial laboratories, 27, 28
  mission-oriented, 27
  and productivity, 311–312
  in universities, 13, 27–28, 263–273, 418. See also Universities, basic research in
Research and development (R&D)
  in agriculture, 333–354. See also Agriculture, research and development in
  in automobile industry, 134
  in biotechnology, 430
  in chemical industry, 400, 417–418

  comparative expenditures in various countries, 135–137
  corporate planning for, 402–416
    assessment of, 411–412
    base program in, 406–407
    business area analysis in, 405
    business aspects of, 412–413
    commercialization target date in, 410
    company goal in, 407
    defining of responsibilities in, 402–403
    identification of needs in, 409
    innovation project stage in, 410
    integration of information in, 413–416
    levels of planning in, 403–408
    marketing in, 410
    project managers in, 411
    projections in, 404
    stretch position in, 407
  and costs of marketing, 109–110
  expenditures in France, 557
  expenditures in Japan, 544, 545–546, 548, 550, 557
  expenditures in United Kingdom, 544
  and government contracts with private organizations, 124–126
  government expenditures in U.S., 4, 6, 38, 116, 263, 401, 504, 544, 557
    affecting growth rate, 3, 4–5
    in agriculture, 337–344, 353
    in biotechnology, 430
    controversial areas in, 152–158
    distribution of, 128, 131
    estimation with GNP deflator, 317
    in postwar era, 128–135
    and rate of technical change, 36
    risk taking in, 152–153
    and role of private sector, 133
    trends in, 126–128
  and imitation costs, 383
  impact on competitiveness in international trade, 133, 135
  industrial spending for, 133–134, 299–300
    ratio to GNP, 137
  and international technology transfer, 320
  military, and contracts with scientists, 123–124
  partnerships in, 10, 111, 161, 432–433, 446, 476
  in pharmaceutical industry, 339, 489
  price indexes for inputs in, 316–318
  private funding of, 123, 133, 401
    trends in, 126–128
  rate of return from, 308–311
    in agriculture, 308, 310, 334–335
  relation to productivity growth, 308–309, 332
  subsidies for, and diffusion of technology, 375
  tax credits for, 159, 537
  and technology transfer costs, 383
  for waste disposal management, 149–150
Resources
  allocation to less productive uses, 64
  optimization of, 3
Retraining of labor force, need for, 13
Rhode, Paul, 387
Ricardian equivalence theorem, 46, 47

Ricardo, David, 18, 19, 20, 28
Risk capital, sources of, 445. *See also* Financing
Risk taking
  aversion to, 16
  and costs of marketing, 109–110
  and federal support of research and development, 152–153
  incentives for, 537
  in innovations, 299, 300–301, 310
  by large companies, 113
  and motivated competition, 78–81
  propensity to engage in (PERK), 78, 80–81
RNA research, 215–216, 217
Roach, Stephen S., 7, 8, 93–103, 587, 620
Roberts, Paul Craig, 58
Robotics
  application of, 505
  in Japan, 542
  technological strength in Europe, 395
  use in manufacturing, 146
Rockefeller Foundation, 215, 216
Rogers, Everett M., 319, 387
Romeo, Anthony A., 378
Roosevelt, Franklin D., 124
Rose, Mark H., 120
Rosenberg, David, 204
Rosenberg, Nathan, v–x, 1–16, 17–31, 120, 121, 130, 157, 275–304, 375, 380, 384, 459, 460, 461, 462, 559, 620
Rubber industry
  and development of synthetic rubber, 284
  patents affecting innovation in, 316
  productivity growth in, 331
Ruttan, Vernon, 8, 13, 322, 333–354, 387, 395, 584, 620–621

Sahal, Devendra, 380
Sakuma, A., 134, 146
Salter, W. E. G., 381
Samuelson, Paul, 3
Sargent, Thomas, 45
Satellite industry
  financing by banks, 462
  in Japan, 558
  for monitoring of environment, 155
Savings rate
  and consumer spending, 15
  decline in, 42
  federal deficit affecting, 52, 53
  increase in 1984, 90
  in Japan, 16, 576–578, 591–592
  taxes affecting, 605
Saxonhouse, Gary R., 384, 561–562
Schankerman, M., 317
Scherer, F. M., 322
Schlesinger, Arthur M., Jr., 130
Schmitz, Andrew, 310, 341
Schmookler, Jacob, 345
Schumpeter, Joseph, 307, 352
Schwartz, M., 320
Science
  affecting innovation, 287–288, 290–291, 302–303

policy of U.S. government, 119–162. *See also* National science policy
Seckler, David, 310, 341
Sectoral productivity growth, 72–73
  econometric model of, 66
Securities industry. *See also* Stock market
  technology affecting, 369
Securities Industry Association, 468
Seed companies, development of plant varieties in, 341–343
Semiconductor industry
  competitiveness of, 483
  entrepreneurship in, 423–424
  foreign acquisition of U.S. companies, 426
  improvements in price and performance, 444–445
  in Japan, 133–134, 549–552
  market penetration by, 122
  patent protection in, 426
  and study of crystal composition, 231
  and surface technology, 246
Service industries, 357–371
  expansion of, 31
  investment in, 8
  medical care in, 369–371
  productivity in, 365–367
  support services in, 367–369
  for users of specialized equipment, 383
Shane, Robert S., 387
Shapiro, Carl, 383
Sherva, Dennis, 470
Shipbuilding, as key industry, 155–156
Shockley, William, 27, 364, 423
Shockley Semiconductor, 450
Shoven, John, 592–593, 595, 601
Showalter, M. R., 291, 292
Silbertson, Z., 314
Silkwood, Karen, 205
Singapore
  electronics industry in, 566
  government expenditures in, 111
Skinner, Wickham, 138
Small companies
  economic impact of, 360–361
  entrepreneurial spirit in, 519
  financial problems in, 442
  importance of, 8, 9
  jobs created by, 432
  management weakness in, 442
  problems with international sales, 493, 498
  product line expansion in, 442
  relations with large companies, 14, 361, 519, 520
  transition to large companies, 441–442
Smith, Adam, 1, 3, 23, 87
Smith, Bruce L. R., 138
Smith, Hamilton, 219, 220
Smith, John, 220
Smithsonian Institution, 122
Social benefits from innovations, 309–311
Social programs, and expectations for scientific achievements, 130–131
Social Security system, 49–50
Socony Vacuum Corporation, 175–176

Solar energy, costs of, 277
Solid-state physics, 27–28
Solow, Robert, 4, 21
Sony Corporation, 358, 359
    television plant in San Diego, 86
South Africa, agricultural productivity of, 346
Soviet Union, technological rivalry with U.S., 124,
    129
Soybean varieties, development of, 342, 353
Space industry
    in Japan, 557, 558–559
    and spending for research and development, 128,
        131
    technological strength in U.S., 395
Spain
    agricultural productivity of, 346
    defense expenditures in, 108
    telecommunications company in, 464
Specialization
    effects of, 87
    and limitations of expertise, 23–28
Spectroscopy, optical, 249
Sperry Corporation, 463
SRI International, 451
Sri Lanka, agricultural productivity in, 346
Standardization
    in electronic industry, 438–439
    in network technologies, 384–386
Standards setting in industry
    imposition of, 375–376
    voluntary, 160
Stanford Center for Integrated Systems, 265, 273
Start-up companies
    advantages of, 425
    critical size for, 11
    excess of, 425–426
    financing of. *See* Financing
    innovation in, 9
Steam engine, applications of, 26–27
Steel industry
    competitiveness of, 484–485, 530
    decline in, 542
    indirect subsidies for, 120
    in Japan, 542
    production in 1960, 541
    protection of, 83
Steiger, Bill, 468
Stiglitz, J., 396
Stock market
    initial public offering market, 468, 469, 471,
        473–475, 478, 593
    in Japan, 563
    over-the-counter, 447
    penny stocks in, 445
    performance of investment managers in, 469
    Unlisted Securities Market in United Kingdom,
        11, 111
    and view from Wall Street, 467–471
    volatility of high-tech stocks in, 471
Stockman, David, 58, 133
Stoneman, Paul, 375, 376, 380, 384, 387
Storage Tech Computer, 446
Stout, D. K., 387
Stürmer, H., 254

Superfund law, 420
Super-Phénix reactor program, 158
Supersonic aircraft transport
    and British-French Concorde project, 147, 277,
        299
    cancelled by U.S. Senate, 130, 131, 147
Supply factors, in diffusion of technology, 382–
    386
Supply-side economics, 47, 58, 74
Surface technology, 244–248
Surinam, agricultural productivity in, 346
Swanson, Robert A., 10, 11, 13, 14, 15, 110,
    358, 429–435, 441, 511, 621
Sweden
    agricultural productivity in, 346
    government expenditures in, 111
Switzerland
    agricultural productivity in, 346
    government expenditures in, 111
    textile machinery from, 486
Sylvania Electric Products, 449–450
Syntex Corporation, 11, 430
Syria, agricultural productivity in, 346
System Industries, 538

Tachibanaki, Toshiaki, 592–593, 595, 601
Taiwan
    agricultural productivity in, 346
    electronics industry in, 566
Tandem Computer Corporation, 478
Targeting policies, 12
    and analysis of business areas, 405
    in Japan, 554–564, 574–576
Tax Equity and Fiscal Responsibility Act of 1982,
    52
Taxes
    on capital gains
        proposal for increase in, 471
        reduction in, 468–469
    and competitiveness in foreign trade, 506
    credit for household alternative investments, 159
    credit for investments, 52–53, 70
        ratio to statutory rate, 70
    credit for research and development spending,
        159, 537
    high marginal rates in, 42
    and incentives for innovations, 14, 537
    and investment projects, 13, 38
    policies in Japan, 572, 592–593
    and productivity growth, 5, 69–72
    and savings rate, 605
    and slowdown in economic growth, 41
    on Social Security benefits, 50
    and spending decisions, 44–45, 46
    and supply-side economics, 47
    value-added tax, 492
    and venture capital availability, 431, 447, 448
Taylor, C., 314
Technological change. *See* Innovation
Technology
    black box of, 4, 5–6, 278–279, 280
    creation and application of, 504–505
    diffusion of, 373–389. *See also* Diffusion of
        technology

and economic growth, 358
issues in commercialization of, 110–113
levels in various countries, 394–395
as positive sum game, 9
and production function as black box, 327
and productivity growth, 9
public attitudes on. *See* Public opinions on technology
transfer of
  export policy affecting, 434
  by foreign acquisition of U.S. companies, 426
  international, 320–321
  by multinational firms, 320, 321
  from research universities, 265
  and variation in industry concentration levels, 315
Teece, David, 382, 383, 384
Teknowledge, 450
Tektronix, 475
Telecommunications industry
  applications in financial institutions, 455
  competitiveness of, 483–484
  computers in, 282
  development costs in, 299
  network technologies in, 329, 383
Telefonica, 464
Telephones, voice transducers in, 246
Television set production
  decline in U.S., 542
  in Japan, 542
Terleckyj, N., 308
Texas Instruments, 467
Textile industry
  competitiveness of, 486–487
  in Japan, 384
  management problems in, 495
  new technology affecting, 495
  patents affecting innovation in, 316
  productivity growth in, 331
  shortage of trained personnel in, 494
Thailand, government expenditures in, 111
Thermodynamics, Second Law of, 84, 229–230
Thomassen, K. I., 158
Thompson Products, 517
Three Mile Island, 209
Tilton, J., 320
Time factors
  affecting economy, 46
  in biotechnology, and bringing products to market, 429, 432
  in diffusion of innovations, 318
  in expenditures by imitators of innovations, 313
  and success of innovations, 277, 301
  and transition to new technologies, 381–382, 386–387
Tobacco industry, productivity growth in, 331
Tomato harvesting, mechanization of, 340–341
Tort law. *See* Legal system
Toxic chemicals, feared by public, 13, 15, 418–420
Toyota, 601
Trace, Keith, 381
Trade
  deficit in U.S., 503

in electronics, 426
internationalization of, 47, 479–498
  competition in. *See* Competitiveness in foreign trade
  and technology transfer, 320–321
Trade law in U.S., development in, 531–532
Trade secrets protection
  affecting application of technology, 376
  compared to patent protection, 316
Transitions in industry, and applications of technical skills, 23–28
Transistors, discovery of, 27, 250, 252
Transportation industry
  production processes in, 329
  productivity growth in, 331
Traynor, Roger, 178–179
Treasury Department, 468–469, 471, 537, 597
Trilogy, 446
Trucking industry, productivity growth in, 329–330
Tsang, W., 252
Turkey, agricultural productivity in, 346
Tushman, Michael, 295

Unemployment
  and inflation, 42
  natural rate of, 45
  technological change as cause of, 4, 20, 28–31
United Kingdom
  adoption of innovations in, 379
  agricultural productivity of, 346
  centralized finance system in, 111–113
  dialogue between economists and technologists in, 108–109
  economic growth in, 62
  energy price increases in, 73
  engineers in, 113
  government expenditures in, 111
    for biotechnology, 431
    for defense, 108
    for research and development, 136, 544
  labor costs in, 589
  patents granted in U.S., 142
  productivity related to investment rate in, 144
  role of banks in, 457, 465
  Unlisted Securities Market in, 11, 111
United States
  agricultural productivity in, 346. *See also* Agriculture
  capital formation in, 583–606
  defense expenditures in, 108. *See also* Defense spending
  government policies of. *See* Government policies in U.S.
  investments for research and development compared to other countries, 136–137
  labor costs in, 589. *See also* Labor force
  Naval Observatory, creation of, 120
  productivity related to investment rate in, 144
  technological education in, 256–258. *See also* Education for technical manpower
  technological position of, 394–395
  technological rivalry with Soviet Union, 124, 129

United Technologies, 463
Universities
 basic research in, 13, 27–28, 263–273, 418
  commercial incentives in, 271–273
  formulation of policies in, 267–273
  growth rate of, 268
  and patent rights for faculty members, 271–272
  peer review in, 269
  quality-utility issue in, 265–267
  social utility of, 269–271
  and technology transfer, 265
  ties to industry, 264–265, 445, 555
Unlisted Securities Market, in United Kingdom, 11, 111
Upjohn, 467–468

Vaccine use, legal problems with, 197, 199, 202
Variations among sectors and companies, competition as factor in, 5–6
Venezuela, agricultural productivity of, 346
Venture capital, 10–11, 447–449, 593–594, 596–597
 in biotechnology, 431
 bank financing for, 457–459
 corporate-managed, 450
 and economic growth, 360–361
 excess of, 425–426
 importance of, 111, 414–415
 in Japan, 544, 545, 562–563, 578–580, 594
 and returns on investments, 360
 taxes affecting, 431, 447, 448
 third-round financing by, 449, 470
Vernon, John M., 122
Vernon, Raymond, 142, 143, 145
Victim compensation, in industrial accidents, 181–182, 200–201, 206–209
Vietnam War, 126, 129, 130, 218
Vincenti, Walter G., 281
Vogel, Ezra, 573

Wages. See also Labor, costs of

and competition in world market, 502
 increased rates in Japan, 571
 and productivity growth, 69
 schemes for control of, 43
Waldrop, M. Mitchell, 133, 155
Wallerstein, Mitchel B., 161
Wang Laboratories, 463, 470
Waste management
 and hazardous dump sites, 419, 420
 and health effects of dump sites, 421
 and investments in research and development, 149–150
 and multiparty legal disputes, 193
 and tort immunity of companies, 202
Water pollution regulations, and technological innovations, 159
Water power, use of, 285
Watson, James D., 6, 9, 13, 15, 213–225, 227, 362, 621
Watson, Thomas J., 30, 364
Waves and particles, dualism of, 246
Weather services, as public goods, 155
Weaver, Warren, 215
Weigle, Jean, 220
Western Union, 24
White, Kerr, 266
Wiegmann, W., 249
Winter, S., 322
Wood industry, productivity growth in, 331
Worker's compensation systems, 207
World War II, and development of American science policy, 121, 123–124
Wright brothers, 25
Wyse Technology, 474

Yellin, Joel, 204
Young, John A., 7, 9, 11, 12, 13, 501–509, 521, 533, 539, 604, 621–622
Yuba Power Products, 178
Yugoslavia, agricultural productivity of, 346

Zschau, Ed, 6, 7, 15, 110, 468, 535–539, 622